# EXPERIMENTS
# IN BEHAVIOUR THERAPY

'Psychology as the behaviorist views it is
a purely objective experimental branch of
natural science. Its theoretical goal is
the prediction and control of behavior.'

JOHN B. WATSON

# EXPERIMENTS IN BEHAVIOUR THERAPY

*Readings in Modern Methods of Treatment*
*of Mental Disorders derived from*
*Learning Theory*

EDITED BY

## H. J. EYSENCK

PROFESSOR OF PSYCHOLOGY, UNIVERSITY OF LONDON
DIRECTOR, PSYCHOLOGICAL LABORATORIES,
INSTITUTE OF PSYCHIATRY
PSYCHOLOGIST,
MAUDSLEY AND BETHLEM ROYAL HOSPITALS

THE QUEEN'S AWARD
TO INDUSTRY 1966

## PERGAMON PRESS

OXFORD · LONDON · EDINBURGH · NEW YORK
TORONTO · SYDNEY · PARIS · BRAUNSCHWEIG

Pergamon Press Ltd., Headington Hill Hall, Oxford
4 & 5 Fitzroy Square, London W.1
Pergamon Press (Scotland) Ltd., 2 & 3 Teviot Place, Edinburgh 1
Pergamon Press Inc., 44–01 21st Street, Long Island City, New York 11101
Pergamon of Canada, Ltd., 6 Adelaide Street East, Toronto, Ontario
Pergamon Press (Aust.) Pty. Ltd., Rushcutters Bay, Sydney, N.S.W.
Pergamon Press S.A.R.L., 24 rue des Écoles, Paris 5e
Vieweg & Sohn GmbH, Burgplatz 1, Braunschweig

First published 1964
Second impression 1967

Library of Congress Catalog Card No. 63–19263

Printed in Great Britain by
Compton Printing Ltd., Aylesbury, Bucks.

08 001176 4

*To J. Wolpe*

# CONTENTS

## PART III

## OTHER METHODS

## PART IV

## BEHAVIOUR THERAPY WITH CHILDREN

# FOREWORD

THIS book contains a series of reports on experiments involving the application of modern theories of learning and conditioning to behaviour disorders. Most of these disorders would be called "neuroses" by psychiatrists, but as there is so little agreement on the definition or meaning of this term, it might be better to use noncommittal words not carrying the implications of "disease" or nervous dysfunctioning. Some of these behaviour disorders are extremely serious, debilitating, and indeed tragic; others are quite trivial, unimportant, and may even be amusing. In principle, however, they all illustrate the same general laws of learning, and the modification in behaviour effected through sensitization, deconditioning, negative practice or counterconditioning is equally dependent on knowledge of these laws; the falling apple and the precession of the equinoxes are both explained in terms of the same underlying theories. The psychiatrist concerned with the application of psychological principles to his problems will probably be more interested in the accounts of treatment applied to the more severe cases, but it should be recognized that a paper reporting the change in behaviour of a child with undesirable eating habits, or some other slight behavioural deviation, may be just as significant in suggesting methods or illustrating principles. The possibility held out by modern psychology of altering human behaviour in a lawful manner, and in accordance with lawful principles, is the inspiration behind behaviour therapy, and it is the hope of the editor that some at least of his readers will come to appreciate the tremendous possibilities held out by these new developments — possibilities of changing personality and behaviour in the direction of greater sanity, greater happiness, and greater social usefulness.

It is another hope of the editor's that behaviour therapy will in time replace the current orthodoxies in psychiatric treatment and theorizing, orthodoxies which owe little to experimental research, patient verification, or consistent system building. It is surely time that we abandoned the curiously schizophrenic situation where behaviour disorders, which by common consent are acquired through some form of learning or conditioning, are treated in terms of methods and theories which take no cognizance of the accumulated scientific information on the topics of learning and conditioning of the last fifty years! If the contribution of modern learning theory had been rejected on the basis of thorough knowledge, extended trial and proved uselessness, no complaint would be justified, but, like Christianity, behaviour therapy has not been tried and shown to fail; it has never been tried. Its rejection on the basis of *a priori* considerations by those not intimately acquainted with its theories, experiments and applications cannot be taken as being based on rational grounds; as the contributions to this volume will show, behaviour therapy, in spite of its youth, has already been astonishingly successful in practice, and current improvements in theoretical comprehension and in practical application bid fair to make it even more so.

Important as these practical implications are, even more important is the insistence of behaviour therapists on experimental demonstration, theoretical rigour, and empirical validation. This substitution of scientific methodology for the thaumaturgical hagiolatry which pervades so much of present-day psychiatry seems long overdue; by their fruits shall ye know them! Treatment of mental disorders has for too long been frozen in antiquated postures; a thaw is much needed.

Some of the more rational criticisms of behaviour therapy have been dealt with in the Introduction; others have been answered in *Behaviour Therapy and the Neuroses,* the companion volume of this book, and the first set of readings in the application of learning theory to the treatment of these behaviour disorders. Future work on these lines will be reported in the pages of *Behaviour Research and Therapy,* a new international journal founded especially to bring together studies of the theory and practice of behaviour therapy. In concluding this foreword, the editor would like to pay homage to the men whose outstanding pioneering work has determined the modern conception of neurotic disorder and its treatment; J. B. Watson, H. O. Mowrer, N. E. Miller, J. Wolpe, and B. F. Skinner. He would also like to thank the numerous authors who consented to have their work represented on these pages, and who often made important alterations and additions to earlier versions of their reports.

*Institute of Psychiatry*
*(Maudsley Hospital)*                                      H. J. EYSENCK
*University of London*


NOTICE TO READERS

The text in the articles in this volume has been set either with English or American spelling, according to the location of the author. However, in order to observe conformity in the layout of the book as a whole, the page headlines have been set consistently in English.

# The Nature of Behaviour Therapy

H. J. EYSENCK

BEHAVIOUR therapy may be defined as the *attempt to alter human behaviour and emotion in a beneficial manner according to the laws of modern learning theory*. The use of the term "beneficial" distinguishes it from certain types of manipulation, such as brain-washing, which also seek to alter behaviour, but in the interest of the manipulator rather than the sufferer. Specious arguments may of course be brought forward to show that really the sufferer is mistaken, and that he will be better off after brain-washing; the Inquisition was as adept as certain modern political parties in using such excuses. We shall assume here that the term "therapy" does not easily fit such cases, and that it should be reserved for instances where the patient voluntarily seeks treatment. The use of the term "modern learning theory" implies a clear distinction between the methods here advocated and those of psychoanalytic psychotherapy; we are concerned with the application of laboratory-based, scientific findings in the fields of learning and conditioning, rather than with the use of Freudian principles. Lastly, the use of the term "behaviour and emotion" implies clearly that the changes made should be capable of being observed and studied objectively by the outside observer, rather than being accessible, if at all, only through introspection and interpretation. Strictly speaking "emotion" should probably be conceived of as a subclass of "behaviour", but a distinction between skeletal and hormonal activity, or between Central Nervous System and Autonomic Nervous System, is too useful to be sacrificed easily (Mowrer, 1950).

The actual term "behaviour therapy" is only a few years old, but of course the methods subsumed under that name have been in use for a much longer period. Recent summaries by Eysenck (1960a), Bandura (1961) and Metzner (1961) may help readers not acquainted with the history of these techniques to obtain an overall view, and to appreciate the enormous difference between what is being attempted here, and orthodox types of treatment. The present book has been put together to enable readers to see for themselves some of the most important and interesting publications in this field, and thus receive at first-hand a glimpse of the successes and failures, the theories and experiments, the methods and the concepts, which are at the moment agitating behaviour therapists. The book is a successor to *Behaviour Therapy and the Neuroses* (Eysenck, 1960a), but it can be read and understood on its own; acquaintance with the earlier volume will of course be an advantage. It is hoped that by thus bringing together publications from a wide range of journals unlikely to be read in their entirety even by the most enthusiastic psychiatrist or psychologist, the book will open new doors and vistas to many of its readers, and will encourage them to experiment with some at least of these new methods.

There are certain objections and criticisms which experience has shown to arise quite frequently in connexion with discussions of behaviour therapy, and it may be useful to try and answer these as far as possible in this introduction. The first objection arises from the fact that reports such as those reprinted in *Behaviour Therapy and the Neuroses*, or in this book, seldom include control groups; how, it is asked, can one evaluate the claims made for a given type of therapy when there is no clearly demarcated base-line? How can we demonstrate the alleged beneficial effects of behaviour therapy when no attempt is made to exclude the effects of spontaneous remission? Is not this reliance on single case reports a throw-back to the often criticized clinical methods of psychoanalysis? The point is well taken, but there are several considerations which must be borne in mind.

In the first place, attempts have in fact been made by Wolpe (1959), Cooper (1961), Lazarus (1962), Ellis (1957), Anker and Walsh (1961), Gwynne Jones (1960), Lovibond (1961), Lang and Lazovik (1962), and others to provide the type of evidence requested; rudimentary as these attempts have sometimes been, and inconclusive as they undoubtedly are when looked upon from the point of view of pure science, they should be compared with the complete failure of psychoanalysts even to attempt any such comparative studies. This difference becomes even more obvious when it is realized that psychoanalysis has many thousands of trained practitioners, has been flourishing for half a century, has at its disposal vast sums for research, and makes exceptionally far-reaching claims. By contrast there are probably not more than a few dozen trained practicioners of behaviour therapy in the whole world, having little or no access to research funds. In addition, behaviour therapy is a very young discipline; admittedly there are a few isolated examples of treatment along these lines in the literature of the twenties and thirties, but these methods were not seriously taken up until the appearance of Wolpe's book on *Psychotherapy by Reciprocal Inhibition* in 1959. The critics are of course right in demanding more and better studies of this type, but this can hardly be interpreted as a criticism of behaviour therapy; it requires time to perfect methods of treatment, and it requires even more time to mount and carry out an experiment comparing the effects of different types of treatment. If behaviour therapists allow as much time to elapse without producing any evidence of this type as did the psychoanalysts, then such criticisms would indeed be only too justified; considering the limited time they have had to work out their methods and test them, their performance would seem to call for praise rather than blame.

Individual case studies are of course published quite frequently, but it would not seem reasonable to condemn this practice. Not every publication is intended to establish unequivocally an important and general scientific truth; there is ample room for papers demonstrating techniques, illustrating theoretical discussions, or introducing newcomers to points of detail in treatment. Even from the most severe scientific point of view, a single case *may* suffice to establish an important theoretical point—if only to disprove a universal negative! Studies of single cases, or even of groups of such cases, should be judged in relation to what the author claims to have established; neither universal condemnation nor universal approbation seems appropriate.

This point may be carried a little farther. There are other ways of demonstrating that one has achieved experimental control over a given phenomenon than the use of control groups (Sidman, 1960); one such way is the clear-cut demonstration that one can at will produce changes in the dependent variable (which may of course be a neurotic symptom) by changing the independent variable. Katsch (1955) has demonstrated in the treatment of a case of asthma, where severe attacks regularly occurred when the patient retired to bed with his wife, that these attacks ceased immediately and completely when a large picture of the mother-in-law was removed from its place on the wall; she had played an important role in producing the conflict hypothetically underlying the asthmatic attacks. It is difficult to see how control groups would provide better and more impressive evidence of the correctness of the hypothesis than does the experimental control exercised by Katsch in this case. Shapiro (1961) has discussed this point at length.

Altogether it is possible that there is here a conflict of aim between the critics and the behaviour therapists. To the scientist, the first and most essential aim must be to bring the phenomenon he is concerned with under experimental control; other things, such as the improvement of a neurotic symptom, are confidently expected to follow later once this over-riding need has been met. An experiment such as that of Yates (1958), in which he showed that severe tics could be manipulated at will by means of variations in a conditioning schedule, should be interpreted as a demonstration of experimental control; it would be quite wrong to regard its main purpose as the alleviation of the patient's suffering. Criticism based on such a misunderstanding is clearly erroneous; the author did not try to demonstrate on the basis of a single case that the method of negative practice was an infallible one for the cure of tics, and should not therefore be criticized as if he had in fact had this intention. The preoccupation of many psychiatrists with curing patients (not an unworthy one, of course) tends to blind them to the fact that the development of rational techniques of treatment has to pass through several stages, not all of which are directly concerned, in an immediate way, with cures. Altogether, the actuarial counting up of "cures" is not necessarily the best method of demonstrating the correctness of a given psychological hypothesis, and in many instances it may in fact be most inappropriate. Such "counts" have their place, but other methods of proof should not be neglected.

Among the most important considerations in this connexion is the observation of certain consequences which follow from the theory under investigation, but which may have no, or only a tangential relation to the patient's improvement. If, as has often been contended, neurotic symptoms are essentially conditioned autonomic responses, together with associated skeletal ones, then such effects as stimulus generalization and extinction should be observed; similarly, if treatment implies some form of counter-conditioning or reciprocal inhibition, then the development of the new responses should follow a course in line with prediction from learning theory. Many instances will be found in the pages that follow of close agreement between prediction and fact; such agreement lends considerable support to the theory, without requiring a control group, and may indeed be demonstrated to advantage even in a single case. The psychiatrist, rightly or wrongly, concentrates entirely on the recovery of the patient; the experimentally minded psychologist considers many other behavioural effects of his experimental manipulation of the independent variables. If we already possessed sure and certain methods of cure, experimentation of this kind might be considered unethical; but this is not the position. As Appel *et al.* (1953) have pointed out, "none of the treatments studied—including psychotherapy—gave recovery rates significantly greater than that reported for groups receiving only routine hospital care". And in a similar vein, Hastings (1958), in discussing follow-up results in psychiatric illness, says that "one is reluctantly forced to admit that we simply do not possess the factual knowledge . . . which permits us to say that we have any treatment procedure in psychiatry which promises a better outlook for a particular illness than does nature left to her own devices". This being so, experimentation is mandatory, and singleminded attention to the "recovery" of the patient, with complete disregard of the importance of other variables, is not likely to lead to the scientific break-through which is so essential if we are ever to come to grips with the problem of neurosis.

An altogether different type of criticism is sometimes heard, to the effect that learning theory is not sufficiently advanced to provide a safe and satisfactory stepping-stone to such important fields as the treatment of neurotic disorders. Are there not conflicting views about quite fundamental points; are there not continuous disputes, sometimes quite acrimonious, between different schools? How can safe predictions be made when so much is in doubt? Such objections may have some superficial appeal, but they are not likely to trouble anyone unduly who is experienced in the ways of scientists with theories. Consider what Sir George Thomson, F.R.S. and Nobel-Laureate in physics, has to say on the topic: "If differences of opinion . . . are still possible about space, time, and gravitation, this is an example of something common in physics. Very different points of view may lead to identical or nearly identical conclusions when translated into what can be observed. It is the observations that are closest to reality. The more one abstracts from them the more exciting indeed are the conclusions one draws and the more suggestive for further advances, but the less can one be certain that some widely different viewpoint would not do as well." (Thomson, 1961.)

The same is true of psychology. Take a practical problem, such as how to produce conditioned response of a certain type in a dog, or how to "shape" the behaviour of a pigeon, or how to extinguish without relapse the enuretic behaviour of a child, and you will find considerable agreement, or even unanimity, among behavioural scientists. Ask for theoretical justifications for the methods advocated by them, and you will receive many alternative hypotheses between which no rational choice may be possible at the moment. But this great variety is no weakness, and it does not detract from the practical value of the methods suggested for solving a given problem. To the academic teacher and to the research worker, these different theories are important, and much of his work is concerned with deducing consequences which follow from one but not from the other theory, and then testing these consequences in the laboratory. This is right and proper, even though scientists so occupied may easily be accused of "ivory tower" attitudes, and of concentrating on trivial and unimportant problems. Disagreement on the theoretical plane, and on the borderline of knowledge, does not imply disagreement with respect to established facts in well-explored areas. It is on these facts that we must build our system of behaviour therapy, and here there is far less disagreement, and indeed much commonality of knowledge.

Take as an example Humphrey's paradox, i.e. the well-known fact that extinction after conditioning is prolonged after partial reinforcement, but accelerated after 100 per cent reinforcement. There are many theories about the reasons underlying this phenomenon, but no one doubts the accuracy of the facts themselves. Consequently, when Lovibond (1961) tried to reduce the relapse-rate of enuretic children treated by means of the bell-and-blanket method, he was able to do so by changing the conditioning method from 100 per cent reinforcement to partial reinforcement. Thus we can make use of ascertained facts, without necessarily being in agreement about the more far-reaching theoretical reasons behind the facts. The position is exactly the same here as it is in physics; if we had to wait for universal theoretical agreement between physicists before we could make use of the discoveries of physics for practical ends, we would still live in a pre-Renaissance world. In saying this I have no wish to deny the obvious vast disproportion between the amount of factual knowledge in physics and in psychology, or the equally obvious superiority of the existing theoretical systems in physics compared with those we have to work with in psychology; I merely wish to draw attention to an essential similarity running through all the sciences, from the most developed to the least advanced.

One important consequence follows from what I have just said. We should, in approaching the problems of treatment in the neuroses, try to take as unbiased a view of modern psychology as possible. Hullians and Skinnerians may have their internecine quarrels within the academic stamping ground, but when it comes to practical work they should leave their tomahawks, and use whatever useful methods may come to hand in relation to any particular problem. The most successful behaviour therapists are likely to be those who have a wide grasp of the whole literature, and owe no allegiance to any particular school; the weapons in our armamentarium are not so numerous that we can afford to neglect any that may be there, on the ground that we do not like their colour or shape! In *Behaviour Therapy and the Neuroses*, the Hullian viewpoint was perhaps stressed a little too much; I have tried to redress the balance by incorporating much material relating to operant conditioning in the present volume.

A third objection, which is frequently heard, asserts that behaviour therapy has been tried but has been found wanting. This is particularly often said of aversion therapy as applied to alcoholism, but other types of behaviour therapy also are sometimes criticized along these lines. Now it must be admitted that aversion therapy raises certain special problems; these are discussed in some detail elsewhere (Eysenck, 1962). But in essence this criticism should be looked at from the most general point of view, because it raises a number of interesting problems. It will be obvious that it must be at least as difficult to disprove the usefulness of a method as to prove it; I know of no experimental studies along these lines that have been carried out and given results unfavourable to behaviour therapy. What is meant is usually that the speaker (or more rarely the writer) has either tried out some of these methods on a few patients, or has been in touch with someone else who has done so, and that the results were poor and unsatisfactory. Now the evidential value of such assertions clearly depends on certain questions which require to be put. Has the person concerned been properly trained for doing this type of work? If not, then his results may have been botched for reasons which have nothing to do with the adequacy or otherwise of the theory in question. Were the cases selected suitable for the treatment given? An inappropriate choice—as in the case of psychotic involvement, for instance—would invalidate the test. Was the treatment properly administered? The literature is full of reports of aversion therapy unsuccessfully applied where it is quite clear that the planning and administration of the treatment were not in line with current knowledge, or even contravened quite elementary rules. Was the follow-up sufficiently lengthy and detailed to enable anything useful to be said about the case? And were controls available to compare the effects of the treatment with? These and many other questions arise, and unless they are answered satisfactorily it must be doubted if much attention should be paid to the results reported. Psychoanalysts rightly lay much stress on the adequate training of those who carry out treatment along Freudian lines; a similar stress must be laid on training, both theoretical and practical, of behaviour therapists. We shall return to this point.

Consider now an actual case history illustrating this third type of criticism. At a meeting at which a paper had been read advocating the bell-and-blanket method for the treatment of enuresis, a psychiatrist got up to say that he had had wide experience of this type of treatment, and that the success rate was very small indeed, probably no greater than could be accounted for in terms of spontaneous recovery. Investigation disclosed that this psychiatrist only prescribed the blanket as a last resort, when every other method had failed; we are therefore not dealing with a random sample, but with a very selected one. He had not been trained in the use of this instrument, and consequently made numerous errors in applying it. He failed to instruct the parents properly in the use of the blanket, leaving them essentially to their own devices. He failed to check the adequacy of the blanket and the buzzer, so that broken contacts interfered with its working efficiency. He discontinued treatment far too soon, not giving the method time to work. He openly disparaged the instrument in front of the parents, thus lowering their motivation to undergo the considerable trouble involved for them. He finally managed to add up his cases of recovery wrongly, transforming what was still a respectable total into a minute one! Yet because of his prestige, his judgement of the method obviously impressed other psychiatrists present more than had the detailed experimental and statistical account given during the lecture, demonstrating the clear-cut superiority of the blanket over other methods. Such cases are unfortunately not isolated ones; their occurrence suggests caution in accepting adverse comments not backed by detailed evidence.

A fourth type of comment is sometimes made, to the effect that psychoanalytic treatment goes far beyond symptom removal, and that behaviour therapy fails to "rebuild" the character of the patient, even though it may succeed in eliminating the symptom. Psychoanalysis, as Wolpe (1961) points out, "is credited with a unique capacity to bring about changes characterized by such terms as 'maturation' or 'balanced integration'. When these terms are adequately defined, it will become possible to examine whether or not psychoanalysis is a superior method of bringing about the changes specified. In any event, such changes should surely be sought after only in those who desire them: they should not be represented as prerequisites to lasting recovery from neurotic symptoms." Nor, one might add, should they be represented as alternatives to such recovery; analysts often seem to be more concerned with these nebulous, ill-understood and poorly defined changes than with relief from those symptoms which originally caused the patient to seek help. It is indeed curious that those who cannot *even* cure the patient of his symptoms criticize others for *only* curing him of his symptoms!

Given, then, that these various criticisms of behaviour therapy do not carry much weight, what is the present state of the art, and what are the main problems facing us? The main problems, in my view, relate to *training* and *research*; this is of course not unusual in new and interdisciplinary developments, but in this case the difficulties are aggravated to a considerable extent by the intrusion of certain medical aspects. Psychiatrists are apt to state that responsibility for treatment is exclusively medical, and that consequently training in behaviour therapy should only be given to medically and psychiatrically qualified persons. Szasz (1959) has given a good critical discussion of this view. Rigid observance of this rule would lead to the rather comic spectacle of non-medical psychologists, who had developed these methods of treatment and done a considerable amount of research on them, being allowed to train psychiatrists in their use, but not being allowed to practise them themselves! The fact that a situation is absurd does not of course make it unlikely to occur; until quite recently it was illegal in England for a psychologist (who might have developed and standardized a mental test, and taught its use to psychiatric students) to test the intelligence of a mental defective for purposes of certification, while any of his medical students, however ill-equipped for the purpose, might freely do so! Apart from this absurdity, the situation is complicated by the fact that the application of behaviour therapy demands an adequate knowledge of learning theory and intimate acquaintance with the methodology of conditioning; a minimum of three years of concentrated study would have to be added to the curriculum of the budding psychiatrist to make him capable of carrying out the work of behaviour therapy properly. In view of the many complaints already voiced by students about the inordinate length of training, this does not seem a feasible suggestion.

This point of adequate background knowledge, which I have touched upon before in this Introduction, is so important that I want to discuss it in some more detail. Psychiatrists (and clinical psychologists without special training in learning theory and conditioning) often feel that a short introductory course, possibly augmented by the reading of one or two books, is quite sufficient to enable them to carry on behaviour therapy. It cannot be too strongly stated that this is not so. It is indeed frequently possible, particularly in relatively easy and obvious cases, to be surprisingly successful without going any more deeply into the subject; I have often been surprised by the quick and lasting cures effected by newcomers to this field who had read nothing but one or two articles, and perhaps *Behaviour Therapy and the Neuroses*. Nevertheless, the proper application of these methods must be based on knowledge and training if disappointments are to be avoided, and if standards are to be maintained, and as I have pointed out before in this article, so-called "failures" of behaviour therapy in unskilled hands are usually due, not to faults in the theory, but rather to ignorance in the practitioner. To avoid a situation in which many untrained people dabble in behaviour therapy, accepting or rejecting it on equally irrelevant grounds, proper facilities for training are obviously required.

Should responsibility for treatment then be placed upon the shoulders of psychologists? Again there are powerful arguments against such a course. In the first place, many psychologists (particularly clinical psychologists in the United States) know little more than psychiatrists about learning theory and conditioning; their training is likely to have emphasized psychotherapy, projective techniques, interviewing and interpretation, rather than objective techniques of behaviour manipulation. In the second place, medical responsibility for treatment is firmly anchored in our legal and academic rules; considerable difficulties would arise in trying to alter this situation. In the third place, behaviour therapy often calls for medical knowledge and qualifications, such as in the administration of drugs to facilitate conditioning or extinction, or to weaken certain autonomic reaction to conditioned stimuli. Diagnostic problems, too, are relevant; would many psychologists be able to discriminate between hysteria and porphyria? These and many other considerations make it undesirable for the psychologist to "go it alone".

The answer to this problem, then, would surely lie in a compromise solution which recognizes the special contribution which both sides can make to the treatment of neurotic disorders. Team-work in this field is often praised but seldom realized, and it is of course recognized that such team-work would raise problems as well as solve them. Several possibilities could with advantage be explored under this heading. Psychologists might carry out the therapy on patients specially referred to them by the psychiatrist, who would retain overall medical responsibility. Psychiatrists might carry out a scheme of therapy suggested by the psychologist. Both might co-operate in the therapeutic process, with responsibility for planning and carrying out divided according to knowledge and experience. Other permutations and combinations will suggest themselves, and many such have in fact been tried out with success in the past. The difficulty would not seem to be insuperable, given good will on both sides, and agreement that there is no question of inequality, other than in terms of knowledge and experience; psychology is not an ancillary discipline to psychiatry, but a fundamental science basic to it. On questions involving the application of psychological principles, therefore, the psychologist would obviously occupy the senior position; on medical questions relating to the patient, the roles would equally obviously be reversed.

Such co-operation, based on the principle of equality, can alone provide the proper ground for a system of training, requiring, as this does, both academic learning and practical experience. It also provides the best foundation for further research into the best methods of treatment for specific types of symptom; research too is best carried out in co-operation rather than in isolation. Unlikely as reason is to prevail in matters so shot through with feeling and emotion, I submit that the interests of the patient, of further advance in psychiatry, and of greater understanding in psychology are most likely to be advanced by a system of close integration, such as that suggested here. Successful training is unlikely to prosper in an atmosphere of hostility and strife.

The question of *research* poses another fundamental problem at the moment. It is of course well known that in physics theoretical advances usually precede practical application by a period of fifty years or so, and that much devoted and complex research is required before theory is translated into practice. Even if the theories underlying behaviour therapy are on the whole along the right lines, yet the precise methods of application still pose a tremendous problem for research, and it must be said that this research has hardly begun as yet. Many people seem to feel that the statement of a general rule, such as the principle of reciprocal inhibition, is all that is required, but this notion is clearly erroneous. It becomes necessary in each type of symptom to discover the precise nature of the CS, the UCS and the response in question; the way in which these variables have become associated, and the host of other variables in turn associated with each; and the best method of achieving the "reciprocal inhibition" called for by the theory. It is likely that different types of personality will react differently to any proposed scheme of treatment, and diagnostic methods will have to be worked out precisely geared to the problem in hand. Such variables as age, sex and social class will have to be considered, as well as intelligence, extraversion, and emotionality; detailed information will be required from each patient regarding his responsiveness to conditioning and extinction, his autonomic lability, and his susceptibility to hypnosis, drugs, and other agents (Eysenck, 1960b). Readers familiar with the application of behaviour therapy to the treatment of phobias may like to consider for a moment the difficulties presented, say, by anorexia nervosa; clearly a beginning has been made in the one case but not in the other, and even the most elementary theoretical formulation of the problem is still missing. No doubt the next fifty years will see a great deal of work along these lines, and it is to be hoped that this work will be characterized by greater rigour, better experimental design and more careful statistical treatment of data than is found at present. But at the moment the important thing to stress, I think, is the enormity of the task, and the low level of theorizing and applied work currently possible. Considering the difficulties of the problem, and the hostility of many present-day experts in the field, behaviour therapists have come a long way surprisingly quickly, but this relative success should not blind them to the gigantic size of the task still to be done.

We may perhaps contrast work done in relation to two different disorders to illustrate the kind of research needed, and all too often not done. Consider first of all the conditioning treatment of alcoholism. Pre-eminent here is the work of Voegtlin, Lemere and their associates, who published results of treatment and follow-up of over 4000 cases (Voegtlin, 1940; Lemere and Voegtlin, 1942; Shadel, 1944; Voegtlin, 1947; Lemere and Voegtlin, 1950).

Using emetine rather than the more popular apomorphine, these workers employed a rather sophisticated technique, in which the patient is given a hypodermic injection of a mixture of emetine, ephedrine and pilocarpine. At the same time they give the patient an oral dose of emetine, so as to bring him to the verge of nausea and vomiting, with both gastric mucosa and CNS in a hypersensitive state; the additional gastric irritation of a small drink of spirits then produces nausea after 30 sec to a minute. Vomiting is usually delayed another 2 min or so, and may not take place at all. These time relations suggest that nausea rather than vomiting is the un-conditioned response and that in any case we are probably dealing with delayed conditioning in some form. (The main purpose of the vomiting in this procedure is probably the elimination of the oral emetine and the alcohol, so as to avoid toxic action on the heart and the depression of the conditioning process. Cf. also Kant, 1944.) There are other parts of the procedure which are stressed by Voegtlin: the treatment room is quiet, bare and darkened, with a spotlight on the row of bottles in front of the patient, thus ensuring predominance of the desired stimuli as CS. Soft drinks are given freely between sessions, so as to extinguish undesired conditioning to inappropriate CS. Under these conditions, over 4000 patients were followed up for a year or more, of whom the following percentages succeeded in reaching the criterion of complete abstinence:

Abstinent for 1–2 years after treatment:    60%
Abstinent for 2–5 years after treatment:    51%
Abstinent for 5–10 years after treatment:   38%
Abstinent for 10–13 years after treatment: 23%

Twenty per cent of the original patients relapsed and were treated a second time; of these 39 per cent remained abstinent subsequently. At the time of writing, Lemere and Voegtlin (1950) quote an overall abstinence rate of 51 per cent of all their patients. Considering the points raised by Eysenck (1962) about aversion therapy and relapse, this is an astonishingly encouraging figure, particularly as the procedure leaves much to be desired. There was no effort, for instance, to take account of differential conditioning rates of extraverted and introverted patients (Vogel, 1962); more extraverted patients could with advantage have been given stimulant drugs to increase the rate of conditioning. The timing is far from perfect, CS and UCS being separated by a very sub-optimal interval, which in addition seems to have been very variable. No attempt was made to decrease the occurrence of relapses by using partial reinforcement; 100 per cent reinforcement was used throughout. In spite of these critisms, it must be said that the work of Voegtlin and his associates does present a genuine, scientific effort to make use of the principles of conditioning in treatment, and that on the whole success has been quite remarkable. Here we would seem to have a secure base from which future research could have started, with the aim of improving upon the success rate achieved.

Unfortunately nothing of the kind happened. There are several studies in the literature purporting to test Voegtlin's claims, but usually these studies contain variations from his procedure so serious, and so counter to the laws of learning theory, that positive results would have been a miracle; Edlin's (1945) study is one example, and Wallerstein's another (Wallerstein *et al.*, 1957). Many other studies claimed to use "conditioning" treatment of one kind or another, but again scant attention was paid to quite elementary principles of learning theory (cf. comments by Franks, 1958). The reader may like to contemplate the glorious mix-up of conditioned stimuli, unconditioned stimuli, conditioned and unconditioned reactions, together with their attendant trains of generalization gradients, adventitious conditioning, pseudo-conditioning, inhibition of reinforcement, sensitization, sensory preconditioning and what-not offered by Oswald (1962) as a serious suggestion for work in this field, to realize that for all the attention that is being paid to them by practitioners in the field, the theoretical and experimental advances of learning and conditioning methodology might just as well not have taken place. Instead of serious research advancing treatment beyond the position reached by Voegtlin and his associates, there has instead been a severe deterioration, leading to quite unacceptable procedures being used under the heading of "behaviour therapy", and offered in disproof of the very principles of learning theory so obviously flouted in the design of the treatment.

In contrast, consider the treatment of enuresis nocturna by means of the bell-and-blanket method. Pfaundler in 1904 demonstrated the efficacy of this type of treatment, discovered accidentally when an apparatus of this kind was constructed to inform nurses of the fact that the bed had been soiled; the apparatus was found to have curative properties not at first suspected. Mowrer and Mowrer (1938) independently rediscovered the method on the basis of theoretical considerations derived from learning theory, and reported considerable success with its use. Many small advances were then made in the construction of the blanket, so as to speed up the occurrence of the signal once urination had taken place, but the main theoretical improvements had to await the work of Lovibond (1961). He argued against the theoretical model used by the Mowrers, according to which the bell is the UCS, the stimulation arising from the bladder distention the CS, and the awakening and sphincter contraction on the part of the patient the response. He argued that if the CS elicits inhibition of urination a number of times without the occurrence of the UCS, its tendency to elicit that response would be weakened, and extinction should take place. He suggested as an alternative hypothesis that the bell was an aversive stimulus which provided the basis for the development of a conditioned avoidance response of awakening and sphincter contraction. According to this theory, the contraction of the detrusor and relaxation of the sphincter when micturition occurs are followed by the noxious stimulus. After a number of such conjunctions, the stimulus arising from detrusor contraction and sphincter relaxation and the passage of urine becomes the CS for the antagonistic response of sphincter contraction and destrusor relaxation which avoids the aversive stimulus. According to this theory, awakening is irrelevant, but the response termination of the CS becomes important; accordingly Lovibond has constructed a "twin-signal" apparatus which gives a brief, self-terminating loud signal when urination occurs; this is the aversive stimulus which causes urination to cease reflexly, but may not wake the patient up. If the patient does not wake up and switch off the apparatus, then a second, more prolonged signal occurs a little later. By carrying out well controlled studies with different groups of patient, Lovibond has demonstrated the superiority of his method and apparatus over the Mowrer type. He was also able to demonstrate that partial reinforcement was superior to 100 per cent reinforcement in cutting out relapses, as would have been predicted from learning theory. In these ways Lovibond showed that the rigorous application of scientific principles to this problem can indeed improve significantly the efficacy of a method already superior to any other method available (Gwynne Jones, 1960). It is this type of advance and experimentation that I am advocating, and which is so sadly missing in the work on alcoholism mentioned above, and in most other fields as well.

Drawing together some of the matters discussed in this short Introduction, I would say that one's hopes for, and belief in behaviour therapy rest in part on its achievements to date, and in greater part in expectancy of things to come. The fact that quite large numbers of cases have been treated successfully and have remained well over lengthy periods of follow up is satisfying and may even be impressive to those primarily concerned with the immediate "pay-off" associated with new suggestions and procedures. The fact that the treatment was usually short and concentrated on a small number of sessions only, so that the alternative hypothesis of spontaneous remission was ruled out more sharply than would be the case if treatment had been continued for several years, is reassuring, as is the further fact that some relatively well-controlled clinical trials have shown behaviour therapy to be superior, or at least not inferior, to any alternative method of treatment. More impressive from the scientific point of view has been the fact that behaviour under treatment has been found to be *lawful* and *predictable;* it is on this fact, rather than the others mentioned, that I would like to rest any claims for behaviour therapy. The kind of development indicated by Lovibond's work on enuresis could only have come about by strict adherence to the principles of learning theory, and the striking success of this work in turn supports these principles, and augurs well for their application to other related types of disorder. Even the fact that unskilled applications of behaviour therapy have so often been unsuccessful should give us cause for satisfaction; it provides in a manner of speaking the negative instance which is required by any scientific argument. Clearly the argument that the application of method A is essential for producing effect alpha is strengthened by the demonstration that the application of method B does not produce alpha, particularly if A and B are similar except in relation to some component theoretically believed to be essential for producing the effect. This point will be too obvious for detailed documentation; it is surprising that its relevance has so often been overlooked. Altogether, the fact that the first few tentative applications of the principles of learning theory to the treatment of neurotic disorders have had such positive results must suggest that further ventures along these lines may be well worth the while. Only such further work can tell us the answers to the many questions which will occur immediately to the reader. Is behaviour therapy particularly useful in certain types of neurotic disorder, or is its application universally indicated? Are all patients equally likely to benefit from behaviour therapy, or is it more appropriate for introverts, say, than for extraverts? What is the relative importance of the method and the therapist? Can we lay down more precise rules for the course of treatment, at least in certain disorders, so as to make the treatment less subject to individual biases and judgements? What is the precise role of psychotherapy, conceived of as an adjunct of behaviour therapy, and itself an application of the principles of behaviour therapy? The fact that the answers to these questions are not known indicates that behaviour therapy is still in its extreme infancy; it would be a bad mistake to claim more for it than it can at the moment perform. Nevertheless, the future for this lusty infant does not look altogether bleak.

## REFERENCES

ANKER, J. H. and WALSH, R. P. (1961) Group psychotherapy, a special activity program, and group structure in the treatment of chronic schizophrenia, *J. Consult. Psychol.* **25**, 476–481.
APPEL, K. G., AMPER, J. M. and SCHEFLER, G. G. (1953) Prognosis in Psychiatry, *A.M.A. Arch. Neurol. Psychiat.* **70**, 459–468.
BANDURA, A. (1961) Psychotherapy as a learning process. *Psychol. Bull.* **58**, 143–159.
COOPER, J. E. (1961) Some aspects of the use of behaviour therapy in psychiatry. D.P.M. Dissertation, Institute of Psychiatry, London.
EDLIN, J. V., JOHNSON, R. H., HLETKO, P. and HEILBRUNN, G. (1945) The conditioned aversion treatment in chronic alcoholism, *Amer. J. Psychiat.* **101**, 806–809.
ELLIS, A. (1957) Outcome of employing three techniques of psychotherapy, *J. Clin. Psychol.* **13**, 344–350.
EYSENCK, H. J. (1960a) *Behaviour Therapy and the Neuroses*, Pergamon Press, Oxford.
EYSENCK, H. J. (1960b) A rational system of diagnosis and therapy in mental illness. In ABT, L. E. and RIM, B. F. (Eds.) *Progressive clinical psychology*, IV, Grune and Stratton, New York.
EYSENCK, H. J. (1963) *Behaviour therapy, extinction, and relapse in neurosis*. Reprinted in this volume.

FRANKS, C. M. (1958) Alcohol, alcoholism and conditioning: A review of the literature and some theoretical considerations, *J. Ment Sci.* **104**, 14–33. (Reprinted in *Behaviour Therapy and the Neuroses.*)

HASTINGS, D. W. (1958) Follow-up results in psychiatric illness. *Amer. J. Psychiat.* **114**, 1055–1066.

GWYNNE JONES, H. (1960) The behavioural treatment of enuresis nocturna. In H. J. EYSENCK (Ed.) *Behaviour Therapy and the Neuroses.* Pergamon Press, Oxford, 377–403.

KANT, F. (1944) The conditioned reflex treatment in the light of our knowledge of alcohol addiction. *Quart. J. Stud. Alc.* **5**, 371–377.

KATSCH, G. (1955) *Dtsch. Med. Wschr.* quoted by D. MÜLLER-HEGEMANN: *Über bedingt-reflektorische Therapie, Psychiatrie, Neurologie und medizinische Psychologie,* **14**, 8–12 (1962).

LANG, P. S. and LASOVIK, A. V. (1962) The experimental desensitization of a phobic. *J. Alc. Soc. Psychol.* (In press.).

LAZARUS, A. A. (1963) Group therapy of phobic disorders by systematic desensitization. Reprinted in this volume.

LEMERE, L. F. and VOEGTLIN, W. L. (1950) An evaluation of the aversion treatment of alcoholism, *Quart. J. Stud. Alc.* **2**, 199–204.

LEMERE, F., VOEGTLIN, W. L., BROZ, W. R., O'HOLLAREN, P. and TUPPER, W. E. (1942) The conditioned reflex treatment of chronic alcoholism VII. Technic., *Dis. Nerv. System,* **3**, 243–247.

LOVIBOND, S. H. (1961) The theory and method of conditioning in relation to enuresis and its treatment. Unpublished Ph.D. Thesis, Adelaide.

METZNER, R. (1961) Learning theory and the therapy of neuroses, *Brit. J. Psychol.* Mon. Supplement, No. 33, London.

MOWRER, O. H. (1950) *Learning theory and personality dynamics,* Donald Press, New York.

MOWRER, O. H. and MOWRER, W. M. C. Enuresis—A method for its study and treatment. Reprinted in Mowrer, 1950.

OSWALD, I. (1962) Induction of illusory and hallucinatory vices with consideration of behaviour therapy. *J. Med. Sci.* **108**, 196–212.

PFAUNDLER, M. (1904) Demonstration eines Apparatus für selbstspätige Signalisierung stattgehabter Bettnässung, *Verb. Ges. Kinderheilkunde,* Wiesbaden, **21**, 219–220.

SHADEL, C. A. (1944) Aversion treatment of alcoholic addiction. *Quart. J. Stud. Alc.* **5**, 216–228.

SHAPIRO, M. B. (1961) The single case in fundamental clinical psychological research. *Brit. J. Med. Psychol.* **34**, 255–262.

SIDMAN, M. (1960) *Tactics of scientific research.* Basic Books, New York.

SZASZ, T. S. (1959) Psychiatry, Psychotherapy, and psychology. *A.M.A. Arch. Gen. Psychiat.* **1**, 455–463.

THOMSON, G. (1961) *The inspiration of science,* Oxford University Press.

VOEGTLIN, W. L. (1947) The conditioned reflex therapy of chronic alcoholics: ten years' experience with the method. *Rocky Mountain Med. J.* **44**, 807–812.

VOEGTLIN, W. L., LEMERE, F. and BROZ, W. R. (1940) The treatment of alcoholism by establishing conditioned reflex. III. An evaluation of present results in the light of previous experiences with this method. *Quart. J. Stud. Alc.* **1**, 501–516.

VOGEL, M. D. (1961) G.S.R. conditioning and personality factors in alcoholics and normals. *J. Abnormal Soc. Psychol.* **63**, 417–421.

WALLERSTEIN, R. S. and associates (1957) *Hospital treatment of alcoholism.* Imago Press, London. Menniger Clinic Monograph. Series No. 11.

WOLPE, J. (1959) *Psychotherapy by reciprocal inhibition.* Stamford University Press.

WOLPE, J. (1961) The prognosis in unpsychoanalysed recovery from neurosis. *Amer. J. Psychiat.* **117**, 35–39.

YATES, A. J. (1958) The application of learning theory to the treatment of tics. *J. Abnormal Soc. Psychol.* **56**, 175–182. Reprinted in *Behaviour Therapy and the Neuroses.*

# PART I

# RECIPROCAL INHIBITION

THE papers in this section all deal with a type of therapy which has come into popular use mainly through the theories and experiments of Professor J. Wolpe. He has coined the term "reciprocal inhibition" to serve as a shorthand notation for the various therapies subsumed under this title, and although some of these are perhaps better known under the heading of "aversion therapies" it is nevertheless not unreasonable to regard these as being merely a distinct sub-group within the major classification. A detailed exposition of his theoretical position is given by Wolpe in the first paper in this section, and there would be little point in attempting to duplicate it here.

It should nevertheless be pointed out that the usefulness of the therapy developed by him, and its relative success as compared with other method does not depend on the truth or acceptance of the theoretical position taken up by Wolpe. It is possible to argue that reciprocal inhibition has not in fact been unambiguously demonstrated to occur, and that alternative theories may account equally well for the facts. Thus extinction through failure to reinforce the conditioned fear response may account for a good many of the cures that have been reported, and the editor has argued in a paper reprinted in this section that the "spontaneous remission" of neurotic illnesses so frequently reported to occur can be explained along these lines. It does not seem impossible that the same theory may serve to explain many cures achieved through the use of Wolpe's technique. Adaptation is another technical concept within learning theory which could with advantage be studied a little more closely in this connexion; it is by no means certain that the remission of neurotic symptoms may not be brought about through the facilitation of adaptation.

These suggestions are not made in any way in order to denigrate the achievements of the "reciprocal inhibition" type of therapy. From the point of view of the practising psychiatrist, the undoubted success of the method developed by Wolpe is the main concern; he will find much support for Wolpe's claims in these pages. But from the point of view of the experimental psychologist, the practical success of a method of treatment is of secondary interest; his main concern is with the rigour of the theoretical derivation, and the completeness of the experimental proof. Much time and effort will have to be devoted to specially planned investigations before we can be sure that the brilliant conceptions which supply the theoretical basis of this edifice are in fact in line with reality; Wolpe's system is distinguished sharply from almost all other psychiatric systems by being susceptible to disproof along experimental lines, and undoubtedly many clinical psychologists and experimentally-minded psychiatrists will take up the challenge which it presents. It is unlikely to survive exactly in its present form—indeed, it would be a miracle if any of the theoretical systems proposed in the infancy of our science should outlive their creators. No doubt the practical success of the treatment will supply much of the drive necessary to investigate its theoretical basis. At the moment, however, the position is simply this—we have a method of treatment which appears to be extremely successful in its application to many diverse types of neurotic symptoms, and we have a theoretical account, closely linked with modern learning theory and with specific experimental researches, which supplies this method with a rationale. To have provided both of these closely imbricated contributions constitutes a major advance in psychiatry; the existence of possible alternative explanations does not detract in any way from this achievement.

# The Systematic Desensitization Treatment
# of Neuroses*

## JOSEPH WOLPE, M.D.

SOME years ago, studies on the induction and elimination of experimental neuroses in animals[23] showed that these conditions were persistent habits of unadaptive behavior acquired by learning (conditioning); and that their therapy was a matter of unlearning. The central constituent of the neurotic behavior was anxiety, and the most effective way of procuring unlearning was repeatedly to feed the animal while it was responding with a weak degree of anxiety to a "weak" conditioned stimulus. The effect of this was to diminish progressively the strength of the anxiety response to the particular stimulus so that it eventually declined to zero. Increasingly "strong" stimulus situations were successively dealt with in the same way; and finally, the animal showed no anxiety to any of the situations to which anxiety had been conditioned. The basis of the gradual elimination of the anxiety response habit appeared to be an example, at a more complex level, of the phenomenon of *reciprocal inhibition* described originally by Sherrington.[17] Each time the animal fed, the anxiety response was to some extent inhibited; and each occasion of inhibition weakened somewhat the strength of the anxiety habit. The experiments suggested the general proposition that *if a response inhibitory to anxiety can be made to occur in the presence of anxiety-evoking stimuli so that it is accompanied by a complete or partial suppression of the anxiety response, the bond between these stimuli and the anxiety response will be weakened.*

I have argued elsewhere[24, 27, 28] that human neuroses are quite parallel to experimental neuroses. On this premise and during the past twelve years, the writer has applied the reciprocal inhibition principle to the treatment of a large number of clinical cases of neurosis, employing a variety of other responses to inhibit anxiety or other neurotic responses. In a recent book[27] an analysis has been given of the results in 210 patients, of whom 89 per cent either recovered or were much improved, apparently lastingly, after a mean of about 30 interviews.

In the case of neurotic responses conditioned to situations involving direct interpersonal relations, the essence of reciprocal inhibition therapy has

* This article is reprinted with the permission of the author and the editor from the *Journal of Nervous and Mental Disease*, **132**, 189–203 (1961).

been to instigate in the situations concerned new patterns of behavior of an anxiety-inhibiting kind whose repeated exercise gradually weakens the anxiety response habit.[16, 19, 20, 25, 27, 28] Neurotic responses conditioned to stimuli other than those arising from direct interpersonal relations do not lend themselves, as a rule, to behavioral treatment in the life situation of the patient; and consulting-room applications of the reciprocal inhibition principle have been necessary. The most straightforward examples of neurotic responses requiring such measures have been the phobias. Relatively "simple" though they are, they have hitherto constituted a difficult therapeutic problem. For example, Curran and Partridge[2] state, "Phobic symptoms are notoriously resistant to treatment and their complete removal is rarely achieved". A very different picture is in prospect with the use of conditioning methods,[1, 4, 10–12, 14, 15] which are no less effective when used for much more subtle neurotic constellations. Examples will be found below.

In the office treatment of neuroses by reciprocal inhibition, any response inhibitory of anxiety may in theory be used. The almost forgotten earliest example of therapy of this kind[7] involved inhibiting the anxiety of phobic children by feeding (just as in the animal experiments mentioned above). Conditioned motor responses have occasionally served the same end;[27] and Meyer[14] and Freeman and Kendrick[4] have made use of ordinary "pleasant" emotions of daily life.[27] But the behavioral response that has had the widest application is deep muscle relaxation, whose anxiety-inhibiting effects were first pointed out by Jacobson.[5, 6] It has been the basis of the technique known as *systematic desensitization* which, because of its convenience, has been most widely adopted.[1, 9, 11, 12]

Though several descriptions of the technique of systematic desensitization have been published[26, 27] it is now clear that more details are needed to enable practitioners to apply it without assistance. It is the aim of this paper to present a more adequate account, and also for the first time to give a separate statistical analysis of results obtained with this treatment.

## THE TECHNIQUE OF SYSTEMATIC DESENSITIZATION

It is necessary to emphasize that the desensitization technique is carried out *only after a careful assessment of the therapeutic requirements of the patient*. A detailed history is taken of every symptom and of every aspect of life in which the patient experiences undue difficulty. A systematic account is then obtained of his life history with special attention to intrafamilial relationships. His attitudes to people in educational institutions and to learning and play are investigated. A history of his work life is taken, noting both his experiences with people and those related to work itself. He is questioned about his sexual experiences from first awareness of sexual feelings up to the present. Careful scrutiny is made of his current major personal relationships.

Finally, he is asked to describe all kinds of "nervousness" that may have afflicted him at any time and to narrate any distressing experiences he can remember.

The problems posed by the case are now carefully considered; and if there are neurotic reactions in connection with direct interpersonal relations, appropriate new behavior based on the reciprocal inhibition principle is instigated in the patient's life situation.[19, 20, 25, 27, 28] Most commonly, it is assertive behavior that is instigated. When systematic desensitization is also indicated, it is conducted as soon as possible, and may be in parallel with measures aimed at other sources of neurotic anxiety.

Systematic desensitization is used not only for the treatment of classical phobias involving anxiety responses to nonpersonal stimulus constellations (like enclosed spaces or harmless animals), but also for numerous less obvious and often complex sources of neurotic disturbance. These may involve ideas, bodily sensations, or extrinsic situations. Examples of each are to be found in Table 1. The most common extrinsic sources of anxiety relate to people in contexts that make irrelevant the use of direct action, such as assertion, on the part of the patient. As examples, one patient reacts with anxiety to the mere presence of particular persons, another to definable categories of people, a third to being the center of attention, a fourth to people in groups, a fifth to inferred criticism or rejection, and so forth. In all instances, *anxiety has been conditioned to situations in which, objectively, there is no danger.*

In brief, the desensitization method consists of presenting to the imagination of the deeply relaxed patient the feeblest item in a list of anxiety-evoking stimuli—repeatedly, until no more anxiety is evoked. The next item of the list is then presented, and so on, until eventually, even the strongest of the anxiety-evoking stimuli fails to evoke any stir of anxiety in the patient. It has consistently been found that at every stage a stimulus that evokes no anxiety when imagined in a state of relaxation will also evoke no anxiety when encountered in reality.

The method involves three separate sets of operations: 1) training in deep muscle relaxation; 2) the construction of anxiety hierarchies; and 3) counterposing relaxation and anxiety-evoking stimuli from the hierarchies.

*Training in Relaxation*

The method of relaxation taught is essentially that of Jacobson[5] but the training takes up only about half of each of about six interviews—far less time than Jacobson devotes. The patient is also asked to practice at home for a half-hour each day.

The first lesson begins with the therapist telling the patient that he is to learn relaxation because of its beneficial emotional effects. He is then directed to grip the arm of his chair with one hand to see whether he can distinguish any qualitative difference between the sensations produced in his forearm and those in his hand. Usually he can, and he is asked to take note of the forearm sensation as being characteristic of muscle tension. He is also enjoined to remember the location of the flexors and extensors of the forearm. Next, the therapist grips the patient's wrist and asks him to pull, making him aware of the tension in his biceps; and then, instructing him to push in the opposite direction, draws his attention to the extensor muscles of the arm.

The therapist now again grips the patient's wrist and makes him tense the biceps and then relax it as much as possible, letting go gradually as the patient's hand comes down. The patient is then told to "keep trying to go further and further in the negative direction" and to "try to go beyond what seems to you to be the furthest point". He may report sensations like tingling and numbness which often accompany relaxation. When it appears that the patient has understood how to go about relaxing he is made to relax simultaneously all the muscles of both arms and forearms.

At the second lesson in relaxation, the patient is told that from the emotional point of view the most important muscles in the body are situated in and around the head, and that we shall therefore go on to these next. The muscles of the face are the first to be dealt with, beginning with the forehead. This location lends itself to demonstrating to the patient the step-like manner in which tension is decreased; and I do this by contracting the eyebrow-raising and the frowning groups of muscles in my own forehead very intensely simultaneously, and then relaxing by degrees. The patient is then made aware of his own forehead muscles and given about ten minutes to relax them as far as possible. Patients frequently report spontaneously the occurrence of unusual sensations in their foreheads, such as numbness, tingling, or "a feeling of thickness, as though my skin were made of leather". These sensations are characteristic of the attainment of a degree of relaxation beyond the normal level of muscle tone. At this session attention is drawn also to the muscles in the region of the nose (by asking the patient to wrinkle his nose) and to the muscles around the mouth (by making him purse his lips and then smile). After a few minutes he is asked to bite on his teeth, thus tensing his masseters and temporales. The position of the lips is an important indicator of successful relaxation of the muscles of mastication. When these are relaxed, the lips are parted by a few millimeters. The masseters cannot be relaxed in the mouth is kept resolutely closed.

At the third lesson, attention is drawn to the muscles of the tongue, which may be felt contracting in the floor of the mouth when the patient presses the tip of his tongue firmly against the back of his bottom incisor teeth. Thereafter, with active jaw-opening, infra-hyoid tensions are pointed out. All these muscles are then relaxed. At the same session, the tensions produced in the eye muscles and those of the neck are noted and time given for their relaxation.

The fourth lesson deals with the muscles of the shoulder girdle, the fifth with those of the back, thorax and abdomen, and the sixth with those of the thighs and legs. A procedure that many patients find helpful is to co-ordinate relaxation of various other muscles with the automatic relaxation of the respiratory muscles that takes place with normal exhalation.

## Construction of Anxiety Hierarchies

This is the most difficult and taxing procedure in the desensitization technique. Investigation of any case of anxiety neurosis reveals that the stimuli to anxiety fall into definable groups or *themes*. The themes may be obvious ones, like fear of heights, or less apparent ones, like fear of rejection.

Hierarchy construction usually begins at about the same time as relaxation training, but alterations or additions can be made at any time. It is important to note that the gathering of data and its subsequent organizing are done in an ordinary conversational way and *not under relaxation*, since the patient's *ordinary* responses to stimuli are under scrutiny.

The raw data from which the hierarchies are constructed have three main sources: 1) the patient's history; 2) responses to the Willoughby Questionnaire;[22] and 3) special probings about situations in which the patient feels anxiety though there is no objective threat. Abundant material is often obtained by setting the patient the homework task of listing all situations that he finds disturbing, fearful, embarrassing, or in any way distressing.

When all identified sources of neurotic disturbance have been listed, the therapist classifies them into groups if there is more than one theme. The items of each thematic group are then rewritten to make separate lists and the patient is asked to rank the items of each list, placing the item he imagines would be most disturbing at the top and the least disturbing at the bottom of the list.

In many instances, the construction of a hierarchy is a very straightforward matter. This is true of most cases of such fears, as of heights (where the greater the height the greater the fear), or enclosed spaces, or, to take a somewhat more complex instance, fears aroused by the sight of illness in others. In such instances as the last, exemplified in Case 1 below, although the items have only a general thematic linkage and do not belong to a stimulus continuum (as do, for example, the items of a height hierarchy), all that has to be done is to obtain a list of situations embodying illnesses in others and then to ask the patient to rank the items according to the amount of anxiety each one arouses.

In other cases, hierarchy construction is more difficult because the sources of anxiety are not immediately revealed by the patient's listing of what he avoids. For example, it may become clear that he reacts to social occasions with anxiety, and that different kinds of social occasions (e.g. weddings, parties, and musical evenings) are associated with decreasing degrees of anxiety. There may then be a temptation to arrange a hierarchy based on these types of social occasions, with weddings at the top of the list and musical evenings at the bottom. Usually, little effective therapy would follow an attempt at desensitization based on such a hierarchy, and more careful probing would almost certainly reveal some facet of social occasions that is the real source of anxiety. Frequently, fear and avoidance of social occasions turns out to be based on fear of criticism or of rejection; or the fear may be a function of the mere physical presence of people, varying with the number of them to whom the patient is exposed. The writer once had a patient whose fear of social situations was really a conditioned anxiety response to the smell of food in public places. A good example of the importance of correct identification of relevant sources of anxiety is to be found in a previously reported case[27] where a man's impotence was found to be due to anxiety related not to aspects of the sexual situation as such, but to the idea of trauma, which in certain contexts, especially defloration, enters into the sexual act.

It is not necessary for the patient actually to have experienced each situation that is to be included in a hierarchy. The question before him is of the order that, "If you were today confronted by such and such a situation, *would you expect* to be anxious?" To answer this question he must *imagine* the situation concerned, and it is usually not much more difficult to imagine a merely possible event than one that has at some time occurred. The temporal setting of an imagined stimulus configuration scarcely affects the responses to it. A man with a phobia for dogs has about as much anxiety to the idea of meeting a bulldog on the way home this evening as to recalling an encounter with this breed of dog a year previously.

A small minority of patients do not experience anxiety when they imagine situations that in reality are disturbing. In some of these, anxiety is evoked when they *describe* (verbalize) the scene they have been asked to imagine. As in other patients, the various scenes can then be ranked according to the degree of anxiety they evoke.

To a therapist inexperienced in the construction of anxiety hierarchies, the most common difficulty to be encountered is to find that even the weakest item in a hierarchy produces more anxiety than can be counteracted by the patient's relaxation. In many cases, it is obvious where weaker items may be sought. For example, in a patient who had an anxiety hierarchy on the theme of loneliness, the weakest item in the original hierarchy—being at home accompanied only by her daughter—was found to evoke more anxiety than was manageable. To obtain a weaker starting point all that was needed was to add items in which she had two or more companions. But it is not always so easy, and the therapist may be hard put to find manipulable dimensions. For example, following an accident three years previously, a patient had developed serious anxiety reactions to the sight of approaching automobiles.

At first it seemed that anxiety was just noticeable when an automobile was two blocks away, gradually increasing until a distance of half a block and then much more steeply increasing as the distance grew less. This, of course, promised plain sailing, but at the first desensitization session even at two blocks the imaginary car aroused anxiety much too great to be mastered: and it was revealed that the patient experienced anxiety at the very prospect of even the shortest journey by car, since the whole range of possibilities was already present the moment a journey became imminent. To obtain manageable levels of anxiety, an imaginary enclosed field two blocks square was postulated. The patient's car was "placed" in one corner of the field and the early items of the hierarchy involved a trusted person driving his car up to a stated point towards the patient's car, and of bringing this point ever closer as the patient progressed. Another case in whom weak anxiety stimuli were not easily found was a patient with a death phobia, whose items ranged in descending order from human corpses through such scenes as funeral processions to dead dogs. But even the last produced marked anxiety, when they were imagined even at distances of two or three hundred yards. A solution was found in retreating along a temporal instead of a spatial dimension, beginning with the (historically inaccurate) sentence, "William the Conqueror was killed at the Battle of Hastings in 1066".

## DESENSITIZATION PROCEDURE

When the hierarchies have been constructed and relaxation training has proceeded to a degree judged sufficient, desensitization can then begin. First "weak" and later progressively "strong" anxiety-arousing stimulus situations will be presented to the imagination of the deeply relaxed patient, as described below.

When relaxation is poor, it may be enhanced by the use of meprobamate, chlorpromazine, or codeine given an hour before the interview. Which drug to use is decided by trial. When pervasive ("free-floating") anxiety impedes relaxation, the use of carbon dioxide–oxygen mixtures by La Verne's[8] single inhalation technique has been found to be of the greatest value[27] and with some patients this method comes to be used before every desensitization session. In a few patients who cannot relax but who are not anxious either, attempts at desensitization sometimes succeed, presumably because interview-induced emotional responses inhibit the anxiety aroused by the imagined stimuli.[27]

It is the usual practice for sessions to be conducted under hypnosis with the patient sitting on a comfortable armchair. He may or may not have been hypnotized in an exploratory way on one or more occasions during earlier nterviews. With patients who cannot be hypnotized, and in those who for a ny reason object to it, hypnosis is omitted and instructions are given merely to close the eyes and relax according to instructions. (There is a general impression that these patients make slower progress.)

The patient having been hypnotized, the therapist proceeds to bring about as deep as possible a state of calm by verbal suggestions to the patient to give individual attention to relaxing each group of muscles in the way he has learned.

The presentation of scenes at the first session is to some extent exploratory. The first scene presented is always a neutral one—to which a patient is not expected to have any anxiety reaction whatsoever. This is followed by a small number of presentations of the mildest items from one or two of the patient's hierarchies. To illustrate this, we shall make use of a verbatim account of the first session of Case 2, whose hierarchies are given below. After hypnotizing and relaxing the patient, the therapist went on as follows.

> You will now imagine a number of scenes very clearly and calmly. The scenes may not at all disturb your state of relaxation. If by any chance, however, you feel disturbed, you will be able to indicate this to me by raising your left index finger an inch or so. (*Pause of about 10 sec.*) First, I want you to imagine that you are standing at a busy street corner. You notice the traffic passing—cars, trucks, bicycles, and people. You see them all very clearly and you notice the sounds that accompany them. (*Pause of about 15 sec.*) Now, stop imagining that scene and again turn your attention to your muscles. (*Pause of about 20 sec.*) Now, imagine that it is a work day. It is 11 a.m. and you are lying in bed with an attack of influenza and a temperature of 103°. (*Pause of about 10 sec.*) Stop imagining the scene and again relax. (*Pause of 15 sec.*) Now, imagine exactly the same situation again. (*Pause of 10 sec.*) Stop imagining the scene and relax. (*Pause of about 20 sec.*) Now, I want you to imagine that you are at the post office and you have just sent off a manuscript to a journal. (*Pause of 15 sec.*) Stop imagining the scene and only relax. (*Pause of about 5 sec.*) In a few moments, I will be counting up to five and you will wake up feeling very calm and refreshed. (*Pause of about 5 sec.*) One, two, three, four, five. (*The patient opened his eyes looking somewhat dazed*).

On being brought out of the trance, the patient is asked how he feels and how he felt during the trance, since it is important to know if a calm basal emotional state was achieved by the relaxation. He is then asked to indicate whether the scenes were clear or not. (It is essential for visualizing to be at least moderately clear.) Finally, the therapist inquires whether or not any of the scenes produced any disturbance in the patient, and if they did, how much. It is not common for a patient to report a reaction to the neutral control scene. It is worth remarking that even though the patient has a signal at his disposal with which to indicate disturbance, the fact that he has not done so during a scene by no means proves that it has not disturbed him at all, for it is a rare patient who makes use of the signal if only mildly disturbed. But the provision of a signal must never be omitted, for the patient will use it if he has a strong emotional reaction, which may not be otherwise manifest. *Exposure, and prolonged exposure in particular, to a very disturbing scene can greatly increase sensitivity.* With less marked disturbance there may be perseveration of anxiety, which makes continuance of the session futile.

At subsequent sessions, the same basic procedure is followed. If at the previous session there was a scene whose repeated presentations evoked anxiety that diminished but was not entirely extinguished, that scene is usually the first to be presented. If at the previous session the final scenes from a hierarchy ceased to arouse any anxiety, the scene next higher is now presented, except in a few patients who, despite having had no anxiety at all to a final scene at a previous session, again show a small measure of anxiety to this scene at a subsequent session. It must again be presented several times until all anxiety is eliminated before going on to the next scene.

In order to gauge progress, the following procedure is adopted after two to four presentations of a particular scene. The therapist says, "If you had even the slightest disturbance to the last presentation of this scene, raise your left index finger now. If you had no disturbance, do nothing." If the finger is not raised, the therapist goes on to the next higher scene in the hierarchy. If the finger is raised, the therapist says, "If the amount of anxiety has been decreasing from one presentation to the next, do nothing. If it has not been decreasing, raise your finger again." If the finger is now not raised, this is an indication for further presentations of the scene, since further decrements in anxiety evocation may be confidently expected; but if it is raised, it is clear that the scene is producing more anxiety than the patient's relaxation can overcome, and it is therefore necessary to devise and interpose a scene midway in "strength" between this scene and the last one successfully mastered.

There is great variation in how many themes, how many scenes from each, and how many presentations are given at a session. Generally, up to four hierarchies are drawn upon in an individual session, and not many patients have more than four. Three or four presentations of a scene are usual, but ten or more may be needed. The total number of scenes presented is limited mainly by availability of time and by the endurance of the patient. On the whole, both of these quantities increase as therapy goes on, and eventually almost the whole interview may be devoted to desensitization, so that whereas at an early stage eight or ten presentations are the total given at a session, at an advanced stage the number may rise to 30 or even 50.

The *duration* of a scene is usually of the order of five seconds, but it may be varied according to several circumstances. It is quickly terminated if the patient signals anxiety by spontaneously raising his finger or if he shows any sharp reaction. Whenever the therapist has a special reason to suspect that a scene may evoke a strong reaction he presents it with cautious brevity—for one or two seconds. By and large, early presentations of scenes are briefer, later ones longer. A certain number of patients require fifteen or more seconds to arrive at a clear image of a scene.

The *interval* between scenes is usually between ten and twenty seconds, but if the patient has been more than slightly disturbed by the preceding scene, it may be extended to a minute or more, and during that time the patient may be given repeated suggestions to be calm.

The *number* of desensitizing sessions required varies according to the number and the intensity of the anxiety areas, and the degree of generalization (involvement of related stimuli) in the case of each area. One patient may recover in as few as a half-dozen sessions; another may require a hundred or more. The patient with a death phobia, mentioned above, on whom a temporal dimension had to be used, also had two other phobias and required a total of about a hundred sessions. To remove the death phobia alone, a total of about 2000 scene presentations were needed.

The *spacing* of sessions does not seem to be of great importance. Two or three sessions a week are characteristic, but the meetings may be separated by many weeks or take place daily. Occasional patients, visiting from afar, have had two sessions in a single day. Whether sessions are massed or widely dispersed, there is almost always a close relation between the extent to which desensitization has been accomplished and the degree of diminution of anxiety responses to real stimuli. Except when therapy is nearly finished, and only a few loose ends of neurotic reactions are left (that may be overcome through emotions arising spontaneously in the ordinary course of living[27]), very little change occurs, as a rule between sessions. This was strikingly demonstrated by Case 1 (below) in whom the marked improvement of a severe claustrophobia achieved by a first series of sessions remained almost stationary during a three and one-half year interval, after which further sessions overcame the phobia apparently completely.


EXAMPLES OF HIERARCHIES FROM ACTUAL CASES

Single or multiple anxiety hierarchies occur with about equal frequency. Each of the following two cases had multiple hierarchies. (*The most disturbing item, as always, is at the top of each list with the others ranked below it.*)

CASE 1—Mrs. A. was a 50-year-old housewife, whose main complaint was of very disabling fears on the general theme of claustrophobia. The fears had begun about 25 years previously, following a terrifying experience with general anesthesia, and had subsequently spread in a series of steps, each associated with a particular experience, to a wide range of situations. The patient also had other phobias and death, the most important of which, concerning illness and death, had its origin during childhood. In 46 desensitization sessions between March and July, 1956, all phobias were overcome except the most severe of the claustrophobic possibilities indicated in the first three items of the hierarchy given below, and with item 4 still incompletely conquered therapy was terminated when the writer went overseas for a year. The patient returned to treatment in October, 1959, having maintained her recovery in all areas, but having made very little additional progress. During the next two months, 16 additional sessions were devoted to desensitizing to numerous scenes relevant to the "top" of the claustrophobia hierarchy. She was eventually able to accept, in the session, being confined for two hours in an imagined room four feet square, and reported complete freedom from fear in tunnels and only slight anxiety in "extreme" elevator situations.

## HIERARCHIES

A. *Claustrophobic Series*

1. Being stuck in an elevator. (The longer the time, the more disturbing.)
2. Being locked in a room. (The smaller the room and the longer the time, the more disturbing.)
3. Passing through a tunnel in a railway train. (The longer the tunnel, the more disturbing.)
4. Traveling in an elevator alone. (The greater the distance, the more disturbing.)
5. Traveling in an elevator with an operator. (The longer the distance, the more disturbing.)
6. On a journey by train. (The longer the journey, the more disturbing.)
7. Stuck in a dress with a stuck zipper.
8. Having a tight ring on her finger.
9. Visiting and unable to leave at will (for example, if engaged in a card game).
10. Being told of somebody in jail.
11. Having polish on her fingernails and no access to remover.
12. Reading of miners trapped underground.

B. *Death Series*

1. Being at a burial.
2. Being at a house of mourning.
3. The word *death*.
4. Seeing a funeral procession. (The nearer, the more disturbing.)
5. The sight of a dead animal, e.g. cat.
6. Driving past a cemetery. (The nearer, the more disturbing.)

C. *Illness Series*

1. Hearing that an acquaintance has cancer.
2. The word *cancer*.
3. Witnessing a convulsive seizure.
4. Discussions of operations. (The more prolonged the discussion, the more disturbing.)
5. Seeing a person receive an injection.
6. Seeing someone faint.
7. The word *operation*.
8. Considerable bleeding from another person.
9. A friend points to a stranger, saying, "This man has tuberculosis".
10. The sight of a blood-stained bandage.
11. The smell of ether.
12. The sight of a friend sick in bed. (The more sick looking, the more disturbing.)
13. The smell of methylated spirits.
14. Driving past a hospital.

CASE 2—Dr. B. was a 41-year-old gynecological resident who had felt anxious and insecure for as long as he could remember. Five years earlier, when anxieties were intensified by divorce proceedings, he had consulted a follower of Harry Stack Sullivan, who had tided him over the immediate situation but left him with attitudes of "acceptance" which had resulted in his becoming more anxious than before. After a few weeks' assertive training, he felt considerably better, but was left with the anxious sensitivities ranked in the hierarchies below. After six desensitization sessions he was completely free from anxiety responses to any actual situations similar to those contained in the hierarchies.

## HIERARCHIES

A. *Guilt Series*

1. "Jackson (Dean of the Medical School) wants to see you".
2. Thinks "I only did ten minutes work today".
3. Thinks "I only did an hour's work today".
4. Thinks "I only did six hours' work today."
5. Sitting at the movies.
6. Reading an enjoyable novel.
7. Going on a casual stroll.
8. Staying in bed during the day (even though ill).

B. *Devaluation Series*

1. A woman doesn't respond to his advances.
2. An acquaintance says, "I saw you in Jefferson Street with a woman". (This kind of activity had locally acquired a disreputable flavor.)
3. Having a piece of writing rejected.
4. Awareness that his skill at a particular surgical operation left something to be desired. (Anxiety in terms of "Will I ever be able to do it?")
5. Overhearing adverse remarks about a lecture he delivered that he knows was not good.
6. Overhearing, "Dr. B. fancies himself as a surgeon".
7. Hearing anyone praised, e.g., "Dr. K. is a fine surgeon".
8. Having submitted a piece of writing for publication.

## RESULTS

Table 1 presents basic datails of 39 cases treated by desensitization. These patients, comprising about one-third of the total number so treated up to December, 1959, were randomly selected (by a casual visitor) from the alphabetical files of all patients treated. They are considered to be a representative sample of the total treated patient population. Rather than to summarize results from nearly 150 cases, it was felt desirable to present some details about a more limited series.

Many of the patients had other neurotic response habits as well, that were treated by methods appropriate to them. Interspersed among the 39 cases reported were six others eligible for desensitization who had between two and six sessions, but who are excluded from the series because they terminated treatment for various reasons (even though usually showing some evidence of progress). It is felt proper to exclude these, as in evaluating the therapeutic efficacy of an antibiotic it would be proper to omit cases that had received only one or two doses. Also excluded are two cases that turned out to be schizophrenic. Psychotic patients do not respond to this treatment and of course receive it only if misdiagnosed as neurotic. On the other hand, every presenting neurotic case is accepted for treatment.

TABLE 1

*Basic case data*

| Patient, sex, age | No. of sessions | Hierarchy theme | Outcome | Comments |
|---|---|---|---|---|
| 1. F, 50 | 62 | a) Claustrophobia | ++++ | See case data above. |
| | | b) Illness and hospitals | ++++ | |
| | | c) Death and its trappings | ++++ | |
| | | d) Storms | +++ | |
| | | e) Quarrels | ++++ | |
| 2. M, 40 | 6 | a) Guilt | ++++ | See case data above. |
| | | b) Devaluation | ++++ | |
| 3. F, 24 | 17 | a) Examinations | ++++ | |
| | | b) Being scrutinized | ++++ | |
| | | c) Devaluation | ++++ | |
| | | d) Discord between others | ++++ | |
| 4. M, 24 | 5 | Snakelike shapes | ++++ | |
| 5. M, 21 | 24 | a) Being watched | ++++ | |
| | | b) Suffering of others | ++++ | |
| | | c) "Jealousy" reaction | ++++ | |
| | | d) Disapproval | ++++ | |
| 6. M, 28 | 5 | Crowds | +++ | |
| 7. F, 21 | 5 | Criticism | ++++ | |
| 8. F, 52 | 21 | a) Being center of attention | 0 | No disturbance during scenes. Was in fact not imagining self in situation. |
| | | b) Superstitions | 0 | |
| 9. F, 25 | 9 | Suffering and death of others | +++ | |
| 10. M, 22 | 17 | Tissue damage in others | ++++ | |
| 11. M, 37 | 13 | Actual or implied criticism | ++++ | |
| 12. F, 31 | 15 | Being watched working | +++ | |
| 13. F, 40 | 16 | a) "Suffering" and eeriness | ++++ | This case has been reported in detail.[26] |
| | | b) Being devalued | ++++ | |
| | | c) Failing to come up to expectations | ++++ | |
| 14. M, 36 | 10 | a) Bright light | ++++ | |
| | | b) Palpitations | ++++ | |
| 15. M, 43 | 9 | Wounds and corpses | +++ | |
| 16. M, 27 | 51 | a) Being watched, especially at work | +++ | No anxiety while being watched at work. Anxious at times while watched playing cards. |
| | | b) Being criticized | +++ | |
| 17. M, 33 | 8 | Being watched at golf | +++ | |
| 18. M, 13 | 8 | Talking before audience (Stutterer) | 0 | No imagined scene was ever disturbing. |
| 19. M, 40 | 7 | Authority figures | ++++ | |
| 20. M, 23 | 4 | Claustrophobia | ++++ | |

TABLE 1–*concluded*

| Patient, sex, age | No. of sessions | Hierarchy theme | Outcome | Comments |
|---|---|---|---|---|
| 21. F, 23 | 6 | a) Agoraphobia | 0 | Later successfully trea- |
| | | b) Fear of falling | 0 | ted by conditioned mo-tor response method.[27] |
| 22. M, 46 | 19 | a) Being in limelight | +++ | |
| | | b) Blood and death | ++++ | |
| 23. F, 40 | 20 | Social embarrassment | ++++ | |
| 24. F, 28 | 9 | Agoraphobia | 0 | |
| 25. F, 48 | 7 | Rejection | +++ | |
| 26. M, 28 | 13 | a) Disapproval | +++ | |
| | | b) Rejection | ++++ | |
| 27. M, 11 | 6 | Authority figures | ++++ | |
| 28. M, 26 | 217 | a) Claustrophobia | ++++ | |
| | | b) Criticism (numerous aspects) | +++ | Finally overcome com-pletely by use of Malleson's method.[13] |
| | | c) Trappings of death | +++ | |
| 29. F, 20 | 5 | Agoraphobia | ++++ | |
| 30. M, 68 | 23 | a) Agoraphobia | ++++ | |
| | | b) Masturbation | ++++ | |
| 31. F, 36 | 5 | Being in limelight | ++++ | |
| 32. M, 26 | 17 | a) Illness and death | +++ | |
| | | b) Own symptoms | +++ | |
| 33. F, 44 | 9 | a) Being watched | ++++ | |
| | | b) Elevators | ++++ | |
| 34. F, 47 | 17 | Intromission into vagina | +++ | After 15th session gra-dual *in vivo* operation with objects became possible, and subse-quently, coitus with husband. |
| 35. M, 37 | 5 | a) Disapproval | ++++ | |
| | | b) Rejection | ++++ | |
| 36. F, 32 | 25 | Sexual stimuli | ++++ | |
| 37. M, 36 | 21 | a) Agoraphobia | ++++ | |
| | | b) Disapproval | ++++ | |
| | | c) Being watched | ++++ | |
| 38. M, 18 | 6 | a) Disapproval | +++ | |
| | | b) Sexual stimuli | ++++ | Instrumental in over-coming impotence |
| 39. F, 48 | 20 | a) Rejection | ++++ | Stutter markedly impro-ved as anxiety dimi-nished, partly as re-sult of desensitization, and partly due to assertive behavior in relevant situations. |
| | | b) Crudeness of others | ++++ | |

Outcome of treatment is judged on the basis of several sources of information. In addition to the patient's report of his reactions to stimuli from the hierarchies during sessions, there frequently is observable evidence of diminished anxious responding, inasmuch as many patients display, when disturbed, characteristic muscle tensions (such as grimaces of finger movements). The greatest importance is attached to the patient's reports of changed responses, in real life, to previously fearful situations. I have not regularly checked these reports by direct observation, but in several cases in whom I have made such checks the patient's account of his improved reaction has invariably been confirmed. In general, there is reason to accept the credibility of patients who report *gradual* improvement. A patient who wished to use an allegation of recovery in order to get out of an unsuccessful course of treatment, would be likely to report recovery rather suddenly, rather than to continue in treatment to substantiate a claim of gradual recovery.

Degree of change is rated on a 5-point scale ranging from 4-plus to zero. A 4-plus rating indicates complete, or almost complete, freedom from phobic reactions to all situations on the theme of the phobia; 3-plus means an improvement of response such that the phobia is judged by the patient to retain not more than 20 per cent of its original strenth, 2-plus means 30–70 per cent, and 1-plus indicates that more than 70 per cent of the original strength of the phobia is judged retained. A zero rating indicates that there is no discernible change. (It will be noted that only 4-plus, 3-plus and zero ratings have been applicable to the patients in this series.)

Table 2 summarizes the data given in Table 1. There were 68 phobias and neurotic anxiety response habits related to more complex situations among the 39 patients, of whom 19 had multiple hierarchies. The treatment was judged effective in 35 of the patients. Forty-five of the phobic and other

TABLE 2

*Summary of data of Table 1*

| | |
|---|---|
| Patients ......................... | 39 |
| Number of patients responding to desensitization treatment ........ | 35 |
| Number of hierachies ............. | 69 |
| Hierarchies overcome ............. | 45 ⎫ 91% |
| Hierarchies markedly improved ...... | 17 ⎭ |
| Hierarchies unimproved ........... | 6   9% |
| Total number of desensitizations sessions ......................... | 762 |
| Mean session expenditure per hierarchy ......................... | 11·2 |
| Mean session expenditure per successfully treated hierarchy ........ | 12·3 |
| Median number of sessions per patient ......................... | 10·0 |

anxiety habits were apparently eliminated (4-plus rating) and 17 more were markedly ameliorated (3-plus rating). (It is entirely possible that most of the latter would have reached a 4-plus level if additional sessions could have been given; in cases 16 and 29, progress had become very slow when sessions were discontinued, but this was not so in the other cases.)

Among the failures, cases 8 and 18 were unable to imagine themselves within situations; case 22 could not confine her imagining to the stated scene and therefore had excessive anxiety, but was later treated with-complete success by means of another conditioning method;[27] case 25 had interpersonal anxiety reactions that led to erratic responses and, having experienced no benefit, sought therapy elsewhere.

The 39 patients had a total of 762 desensitization sessions, including in each case the first exploratory session although in many instances scenes from the hierarchies were not presented at that session. The mean number of sessions per hierarchy was 11·2; the median number of sessions given to patients 10·0. It should be noted that a desensitization session usually takes up only part of a three-quarter hour interview period, and in cases that also have neurotic problems requiring direct action in the life situation there may be many interviews in which a session is not included.

At times varying between six months and four years after the end of treatment, follow-up reports were obtained from 20 of the 35 patients who responded to desensitization. There was no reported instance of relapse or the appearance of new phobias or other neurotic symptoms. I have never observed resurgence of neurotic anxiety when desensitization has been complete or virtually so.

## DISCUSSION

The general idea of overcoming phobias or other neurotic habits by means of systematic "gradual approaches" is not new. It has long been known that increasing measures of exposure to a feared object may lead to a gradual disappearance of the fear. This knowledge has sometimes,[21] but unfortunately not very often, contributed to the armamentarium of psychiatrists in dealing with phobias. What is new in the present contribution is 1) the provision of a theoretical explanation for the success of such gradual approaches and 2) the description of a method in which the therapist has complete control of the degree of approach that the patient makes to the feared object at any particular time. The situations, being imaginary, are constructed and varied at will in the consulting room.

The excellent results obtained by this method of treatment are naturally viewed with skepticism by those who in the psychoanalytic tradition regard phobias and other neurotic anxiety response habits as merely the superfical manifestations of deeper unconscious conflicts. Some attempt to clarify the issue must be made. In the majority of cases a phobia is found to have begun at a particular time and in relation to a particular traumatic event. Before that time, presumably the patient already had his assumed un-conscious conflicts, but did not feel any need for treatment. At the very least, then, it must surely be admitted that if through desensitization the patient is restored to the state in which he was before the traumatic event, something important has been gained from the point of view of his suffering. The reply could, of course, be made that unless the unconscious conflicts are brought to light and resolved, the patient will relapse or develop other symptoms; but in keeping with follow-up studies on the results of non-analytic psychotherapy in neurotic cases in general my experience has been that relapse or the appearance of new reactions is rare, unless a major group of stimuli in a desensitized area has been neglected.

At the same time, it is indisputable that only a minority of individuals exposed to a given traumatic event develop a phobia; some predisposing condition or conditions must determine which individuals do. The psycho-analysts are undoubtedly right in insisting on this point. But we are not therefore compelled to accept their version of the nature of the predisposing conditions, especially as the factual foundations of that version are far from satisfactory.[30] Objective behavior theory can also point to factors that may predispose an individual to particularly severe conditioning of anxiety. First, some people are apparently endowed with much more active auto-nomic nervous systems that others.[18] Second, previous experience with similar stimulus constellations may have induced low degress of anxiety conditioning which would sensitize a person to the traumatic experience. Third, there may be circumstances in the moment of trauma that may bring about an unusually high degree of focusing upon certain stimulus constellations. The second of these suggested factors is probably the most important, for patients do frequently tell of minor sensitivity having pre-existed the precipitating event. In the course of desensitization, these original sensitivities also come to be removed, along with whatever has been more recently conditioned.

Critics of the conditioned response approach to therapy of the neuroses frequently assert that when the desensitization method leads to recovery, it is not the method as such that is responsible, but the "transference" established between patient and therapist. If these critics were right—if desensitization were incidental to rather than causal of recovery—it would be expected that improvement would affect all areas more or less uniformly, and not be confined to those to which desensitization had been applied. The facts are directly contrary to this expectation, for practically invariably it is found that *unless different hierarchies have unmistakable common features desensitization to one hierarchy does not in the least diminish the reactivity to another (untreated) hierarchy.* For example, a recent patient had both a widespread agoraphobic constellation, and a fear of airplanes, extending to the sight and sound of them. Having constructed hierarchies to both series, the writer proceeded to desensitize the patient to the agora-phobia, but ignored the airplane phobia until the agoraphobia had been almost completely overcome. At this stage, re-assessment of the airplane phobia revealed not the slightest evidence of diminution. This is in accord with observations made in connection with experimental neuroses, in which eliminating anxiety conditioned to visual stimuli does not affect the anxiety-evoking potential of auditory stimuli that were conditioned at the same time as the visual stimuli.[23, 27]

From the point of view of the scientific investigator the desensitization method has a number of advantages that are unusual in the field of psycho-therapy: 1) the aim of therapy can be clearly stated in every case; 2) sources of neurotic anxiety can be defined and delimited; 3) change of reaction to a scene is determined during sessions (and accordingly could be measured by psychophysiological means); 4) there is no objection to conducting therapy before an unconcealed audience (for this has been done without apparent effect on the course of therapy); and 5) therapists can be inter-changed if desired.

## SUMMARY

The desensitization method of therapy is a particular application of the reciprocal inhibition principle to the elimination of neurotic habits. The experimental background and some theoretical implications of this principle are discussed.

A detailed account is given of the technique of desensitization and an analysis of its effects when applied to 68 phobias and allied neurotic anxiety response habits in 39 patients. In a mean of 11·2 sessions, 45 of the neurotic habits were overcome and 17 more very markedly improved. Six month to four year follow-up reports from 20 of the 35 successfully treated patients did not reveal an instance of relapse or the emergence of new symptoms.

## REFERENCES

1. BOND, I. K. and HUTCHISON, H. C. (1960) Application of reciprocal inhibition therapy to exhibitionism, *Canad. Med. Ass. J.*, **83**, 23–25.
2. CURRAN, D. and PARTRIDGE, M. (1955) *Psychological Medicine*, Livingstone, Edin-burgh.
3. EYSENCK, H. J. (1960) *Behavior Therapy and the Neuroses*, Pergamon Press, New York.
4. FREEMAN, H. L. and KENDRICK, D. C. (1960) A case of cat phobia, *Brit. Med. J.*, **2**, 497–502.
5. JACOBSON, E. (1938) *Progressive Relaxation*, Univ. of Chicago Press, Chicago.
6. JACOBSON, E. (1940) Variation of blood pressure with skeletal muscle tension and relaxation, *Ann. Int. Med.*, **13**, 1619–1625.
7. JONES, M. C. (1924) The elimination of children's fears, *J. Exp. Psychol.*, **7**, 382–390.
8. LaVERNE, A. A. (1953) Rapid coma technique of carbon dioxide inhalation therapy, *Dis. Nerv. Syst.*, **14**, 141–144, 1953.

9. LAZARUS, A. A. (1959) The elimination of children's phobias by deconditioning, *Med. Proc.*, **5**, 261.
10. LAZARUS, A. A. (1957) New group techniques in the treatment of phobic conditions. Ph.D. dissertation, Univ. of the Witwatersrand.
11. LAZARUS, A. A. and RACHMAN, S. (1957) The use of systematic desensitization in psychotherapy, *S. Afr. Med. J.*, **31**, 934–937.
12. LAZOVIK, A. D. and LANG, P. J. (1960) A laboratory demonstration of systematic desensitization psychotherapy, *J. Psychol. Stud.*, **11**, 238.
13. MALLESON, N. (1959) Panic and phobia, *Lancet*, **1**, 225–227.
14. MEYER, V. (1957) The treatment of two phobic patients on the basis of learning principles, *J. Abnorm. Soc. Psychol.*, **55**, 261–266.
15. RACHMAN, S. (1959) The treatment of anxiety and phobic reactions by systematic desensitization psychotherapy. *J. Abnorm. Soc. Psychol.* **58**, 259–263, 1959.
16. SALTER, A. (1950) *Conditioned Reflex Therapy*, Creative Age Press, New York.
17. SHERRINGTON, C. S. (1906) *Integrative Action of the Nervous System*, Yale Univ. Press, New Haven.
18. SHIRLEY, M. (1933) *The First Two Years*, Univ. of Minnesota Press, Minneapolis.
19. STEVENSON, I. (1959) Direct instigation of behavioral changes in psychotherapy, *A. M. A. Arch. Gen. Psychiat.*, **1**, 99–107.
20. STEVENSON, I. and WOLPE, J. (1960) J. Recovery from sexual deviations through overcoming nonsexual neurotic responses, *Amer. J. Psychiat.*, **116**, 737–742.
21. TERHUNE, W. S. (1949) The phobic syndrome, *Arch. Neurol. Psychiat.*, **62**, 162–172.
22. WILLOUGHBY, R. R. (1932) Some properties of the Thurstone Personality Schedule and a suggested revision, *J. Soc. Psychol.*, **3**, 401–424.
23. WOLPE, J. (1952) Experimental neuroses as learned behavior, *Brit. J. Psychol.*, **43**, 243–268.
24. WOLPE, J. (1956) Learning versus lesions as the basis of neurotic behavior, *Amer. J. Psychiat.*, **112**, 923–927.
25. WOLPE, J. (1952) Objective psychotherapy of the neuroses, *S. Afr. Med. J.*, **26**, 825–829, 1952.
26. WOLPE, J. (1959) Psychotherapy based on the principles of reciprocal inhibition. In BURTON, A., ed. *Case Studies in Counseling and Psychotherapy*, Prentice-Hall, Englewood Cliffs, N. J., pp. 353–381.
27. WOLPE, J. (1958) *Psychotherapy by Reciprocal Inhibition*, Stanford Univ. Press, Stanford, pp. 152, 166, 173, 198.
28. WOLPE, J. (1954) Reciprocal inhibition as the main basis of psychotherapeutic effects, *A. M, A. Arch. Neurol. Psychiat.*, **72**, 205–226.
29. WOLPE, J. Recoveries from neuroses without psychoanalysis: Their prognosis and its implications, *Amer. J. Psychiat.* In press.
30. WOLPE, J. and RACHMANN, S. (1960) Psychoanalytic "evidence": A critique based on Freud's case of Little Hans. *J. Nerv. Ment. Dis.*, **131**, 135–148.

# The Experimental Desensitization of a Phobia*†

PETER J. LANG and A. DAVID LAZOVIK

*University of Pittsburgh*

IN RECENT years there has been increasing interest in the development of psychotherapeutic techniques based on learning theory models. These efforts are not limited to the translation of accepted psychotherapeutic practice into a laboratory language, in the manner of Shoben (1949) and Dollard and Miller (1950), but are attempts to extrapolate from laboratory findings to new methods of treatment. The most promising of these techniques with respect to clinical findings, is Wolpe's systematic desensitization therapy of phobic reactions (1958). In a recent article (1961) he reported that desensitization was effective in the treatment of 35 of 39 phobic patients. Similar results have been reported by Lazarus (1961), utilizing group desensitization.

In a pilot project (1960) the present authors demonstrated that desensitization could be successfully carried out under controlled laboratory conditions. This result opens the way not only to a more precise evaluation of treatment outcomes, but also makes it possible to test conflicting theories of the treatment process.

According to Wolpe (1958), desensitization is effective to the extent that Ss learn to make responses to phobic objects which reciprocally inhibit (are incompatible with) fear. Specifically, the treatment is designed to substitute muscular relaxation for anxiety. It is assumed that this process—not suggestion, "hello–goodbye" effects, or transference—is the agent of behavior change. It is further assumed that explorations with the patient of the genesis of the fear are not necessary to the elimination of a phobia. Wolpe proposes that the unlearning of a phobia follows the rules of what is generally called association-learning theory. He therefore expects that therapy will be more difficult, the more generalized the anxiety response, but that "symptom substitution" is not a consequence of successful behavior therapy.

* This article is reprinted with the permission of the author and editor from the *J. Abnorm. Soc. Psychol*, 66, 519–525 (1963).

† This research is supported by NIMH Grant M–3880. The main content of this paper was presented by A. David Lazovik at the meeting of the American Psychological Association in New York, September, 1961.

A very different set of predictions would be made by psychoanalytic therapists. This frame of reference expects little positive result unless the background of the phobia and its symbolic meaning is elucidated and worked through with the S. If this approach is not employed, only a temporarary "transference cure" may be anticipated. It is further assumed that the difficulty of the case is related to the importance of the symptom in the individual's "psychic economy", and that its temporary removal can only lead to the substitution of some new symptom.

The current experiment is designed to evaluate these two interpretations of desensitization therapy. The procedure developed previously (Lazovik and Lang, 1960), while it submits to the rigid control of the laboratory is nevertheless sufficiently flexible that it can be employed in the treatment of actual phobic behavior. In this experiment, snake phobic individuals served as Ss. This fear was chosen because it is frequent in a college population (approximately 3 in 100 students are to some degree snake phobic), and also because of the symbolic, sexual significance attributed to this fear by psycho-analytic theory (Fenichel, 1945, p. 49). The fact that snake phobias are held to reflect conflict in more fundamental systems of the personality, suggests that this is good ground for a stringent test of behavior therapy.

Specifically, the study is designed to: (a) evaluate the changes in snake phobic behavior that occur over time, particularly the effects of repeated exposure to the phobic object; (b) compare these changes with those that follow systematic desensitization therapy; (c) determine the changes in behavior that are a direct function of the desensitization process, as opposed to those that may be attributed to a complex of factors including hypnosis, training in deep muscle relaxation, and the establishment of a good patient-therapist relationship. In addition, an attempt is made to isolate factors which determine the success or failure of this method with individual subjects.

## METHOD

### Systematic Desensitization

The experimental treatment consists of two sequential parts, training and desensitization proper. The training procedure requires five sessions of about 45 min each, during which an *anxiety* hierarchy is constructed (a series of 20 situations involving the phobic object, graded from most to least frightening). S is then trained in deep muscle relaxation, following the method presented by Jacobson (1938). Finally, S is introduced to hypnosis, and an effort is made to teach S to visualize vividly hypnotic scenes.

Following training, there are 11 sessions of systematic desensitization in which S is hypnotized and instructed to relax deeply. Items from the anxiety hierarchy are then presented as scenes, which S is told to visualize clearly.

The less frightening scenes are presented first. When $S$ can experience these without anxiety, items farther along in the hierarchy are administered, until $S$ reports no distress while experiencing the maximum "dose" of phobic stimulation.

### Subjects

A total of 24 $S$s participated in this research. They were all college student volunteers, attending undergraduate psychology courses. The experimental groups included a total of four males and nine females. The control groups consisted of three males and eight females. None of these $S$s presented evidence of a severe emotional disturbance on the basis of MMPI and interview data.

$S$s were selected on the basis of a classroom questionnaire which asked students to list their fears and rate them as mild, moderate or intense. All $S$s who participated in this experiment were afraid of non-poisonous snakes, and rated this fear as "intense". Furthermore, the two authors interviewed all $S$s who met this criterion. If despite the high self-rating on the screening questionnaire $S$'s fear was judged to be weak, he was not asked to participate in the project. $S$s who formed the final experimental sample were characterized by most of the following behaviors: the reported somatic disturbance associated with the fear—"I feel sick to my stomach when I see one". "My palms get sweaty. I'm tense." They habitually avoided going anywhere near a live snake. They would not enter the reptile section of the zoo or walk through an open field. They became upset at seeing snakes at the motion pictures or on the television screen, and would leave, close their eyes or turn off the set. Even pictures in magazines or artifacts such as a snake skin belt were capable of evoking discomfort in many of these $S$s.

### Measures of Phobic Behavior

All $S$s filled out a Fear Survey Schedule (FSS) at the beginning and end of the experiment, and again at a six-month follow-up evaluation. The FSS is a list of fifty phobias each of which is rated by $S$ on a seven-point scale. An estimate was thus obtained not only of $S$'s snake phobia, but of other related and unrelated fears.

A direct estimate of $S$'s avoidance behavior was obtained by confronting him with the phobic object. $S$ was informed that a non-poisonous snake was confined in a glass case in a nearby laboratory. He was persuaded to enter the room and describe his reactions. The snake was confined at a point fifteen feet from the entrance to the room. On entering the room with $S$, $E$ walked to the case and removed a wire grill that covered the top. $S$ was assured that the snake was harmless. $E$ then requested that $S$ come over and look down at the snake as he was doing. If $S$ refused, he was asked to come as close as he felt he could and the distance was recorded.

If S was able to come all the way to the case, he was asked to touch the animal (a five-foot black snake) after he had seen the experimenter do this. If S succeeded in this, the experimenter picked up the snake and invited S to hold it. After the avoidance test, S was asked to rate his anxiety on a 10-point "fear thermometer" (Walk, 1956). S's degree of anxiety was also rated on a three-point scale by the E.

In addition to the subjective scales and the avoidance test, all Ss were extensively interviewed concerning their fear. These interviews were tape-recorded. The E who conducted the interview and administered the avoidance test participated in no other phase of the project.*

## Procedure

Following a initial interview and the administration of Form A of the Stanford Hypnotic Scale (SHS), (Weitzenhoffer and Hilgard, 1959), Ss were placed in the experimental or control groups. Assignment was essentially random, although an effort was made to balance roughly these groups in terms of intensity of fear and motivation to participate in the experiment. All Ss were administered Form B of the SHS when the experimental Ss completed the training period, and before desensitization began.

TABLE 1

*The design of the experiment, showing the times at which Ss were evaluated (the snake avoidance test, experimenter's rating, fear thermometer, and taped interview)*

| Group | Experimental procedures | | | | |
|-------|--------|----------|--------|-----------------|--------|
| E-1 | Test 1 | training | Test 2 | desensitization | Test 3 |
| E-2 | | training | Test 2 | desensitization | Test 3 |
| C-1 | Test 1 | — | Test 2 | — | Test 3 |
| C-2 | — | — | Test 2 | — | Test 3 |

The basic plan of the study is described in Table 1. It consisted of two experimental and two control groups. The sub-groups were created so that the effects of repeating the avoidance test, pre-therapy training, and desensitization itself could be separately evaluated. Thus, the experimental groups E-1 and E-2 both experienced the laboratory analogue of desensitization therapy already described. However, Ss assigned to E-1 were administered the avoidance test before the training period, prior to desensitization, and again at the end of the experiment. E-2 Ss, on the other hand, were tested before desensitization and after, but did not participate in the initial evaluation. The control Ss did not participate in desensitization, but the C-1 and

* The authors would like to thank David Reynolds, who acted as interviewer and conducted the snake avoidance test.

C-2 groups were evaluated at the same time as their opposite numbers in the experimental series. All available $S$s were seen and evaluated six months after the termination of therapy.

Four replications of this experiment are reported here. They varied only in the therapists who were assigned to the experimental groups. Four experimental $S$s and five controls participated in the first replication. The authors each saw two of the experimental $S$s. In the second, third and fourth replications (which included 3, 4, and 2 experimental $S$s and 2, 3, and 1 control $S$, respectively) three other therapists participated.* While two of these individuals are engaged in full-time private practice, they had never before attempted desensitization therapy. The third therapist was an advanced clinical graduate student, who also had his initial experience with the desensitization method in this project.

## RESULTS

### The Avoidance Test

The results of this test were evaluated in two ways: (a) an absolute criterion in which touching or holding the snake constituted a test pass; (b) scale scores based on $S$'s distance in feet from the snake. Table 2 presents the number of $S$s from the separate experimental and control groups who met the former criterion.

TABLE 2

*The number of Ss who held or touched the snake during the avoidance test*

| Group | N | Test 1 | Test 2 | Test 3 |
|---|---|---|---|---|
| E-1 | 8 | 1 | 1 | 5 |
| E-2 | 5 | — | 1 | 2 |
| C-1 | 5 | 0 | 0 | 0 |
| C-2 | 6 | — | 1 | 2 |
| E-1 and E-2 | 13 | | 2 | 7 |
| C-1 and C-2 | 11 | | 1 | 2 |

Note that the reliability of this test is high. The control $S$s show no appreciable change, even with three exposures to the snake. Furthermore, the pre-therapy training period does not effect the performance of the experimental $S$s: no more E-1 $S$s pass at test 2 than at test 1. However,

* The authors would like to thank Drs. Robert Romano and Richard Miller, and Mr. James Geer, who participated as therapists in this project.

following therapy, the incidence of test passes goes up significantly in the experimental group. The percent increase from test 2 to 3 yielded a $t$ of 2·30, $p < 0.05$. A similar test of the control $S$s was not significant.*

The above analysis does not, of course, measure subtle changes in behavior. In an attempt to increase the sensitivity of the avoidance test, $S$s were assigned scores on a 19-point scale which roughly corresponded to their closest approach in feet to the phobic object. Holding the animal was equal to a scale score of 1, touching 2, the one-foot mark 3, two feet 4, and so on up to a score of 19 for $S$s who refused to go to the testing room.

TABLE 3

*Mean snake avoidance scale score at test 2 and 3, mean change scores, and the Mann–Whitney test of significance*

|  | Test 2 | Test 3 | Change scores | $U$ |
|---|---|---|---|---|
| Experimental Groups | 5·35 | 4·42 | 0·34 | 34·5* |
| Control Groups | 6·51 | 7·73 | −0·19 | |

\* $p$ 0·05

The correlation between the first two presentations of the avoidance test ($N = 19$) yielded an $r$ of $+0.63$.† Although this statistic suggests some degree of reliability, nothing is known about the relative distance between values at different places on the scale. The control sample employed in the experiment is too small to make an adequate analysis. Nevertheless, it is logical that the probability of a positive increase in approach lessens the closer $S$ is to the phobic object, i.e. movement from a score of 15 to 12 is more likely or easier than movement from a scale score of 4 (2 ft away) to a score of 1 (holding a live snake). Thus, a simple difference score does not appear to be the best estimate of change.

The change score used in the following analysis was the difference between pre-and post-therapy scale scores divided by the pre-therapy score. For example, an $S$ who achieved a scale score of 12 on test 2 and a score of 5 on test 3 was assigned a change score of 0·58 — the solution to the

* A live snake varies to some extent in activity, and this appears to be related to its effectiveness as a stimulus. In order to determine whether this factor influenced our results, the experimental assistant's ratings of the snakes activity during tests of the control and experimental $S$s were subjected to a $t$ test. No significant difference in snake activity for the two groups was found.

† The sample ($N = 19$) used in estimating the reliability of the avoidance scale and the other fear measures includes the members of the control sample plus the 8 $S$s of the E-1 group. Although the training period does intervene between the first and second presentations of the fear measures for the E-1 group, it appears to have no appreciable effect on the phobia. The E-2 $S$s could not, of course, be included in a reliability estimate, as actual therapy intervenes between their first and second fear evaluation.

equation: change score $= \dfrac{12 - 5}{12}$. The mean change score for the first two avoidance tests $(N = 19)$ was only $+0.03$. This suggests that the score has considerable stability, and tends to minimize change fluctuations. The mean change scores for the experimental and control $S$s from test 2 to test 3 may be found in Table 3. Note that the Mann–Whitney test of the difference between groups is significant.

### The Fear Thermometer and the FFS Snake Item

The correlation between the first two tests for the reliability sample $(N = 19)$ was $r = +0.75$. The average difference score (obtained by subtracting the second fear thermometer score from the first) was only $+0.63$. As in the case of the avoidance test, no significant change was associated with the pre-therapy training period. The mean difference score for the E-1 group from test 1 to test 2 was $+0.38$, less than the group mean cited above.

TABLE 4

*Mean rating scale measures of phobic behavior before (test 2) and after (test 3) desensitization therapy*

|  | Fear thermometer | | |
|  | Test 2 | Test 3 | Difference |
|---|---|---|---|
| Experimental groups | 7·62 | 5·15 | 2·47 |
| Control groups | 6·45 | 5·45 | 1·00 |

|  | FSS-*S*'s rating of snake fear | | |
|  | Test 1* | Test 3 | Difference |
|---|---|---|---|
| Experimental groups | 6·69 | 5·31 | 1·38 |
| Control groups | 6·27 | 5·73 | 0·54 |

\* The FSS was not administered at test 2. The difference score is between test 1 and test 3.

The difference between test 2 and test 3 scores for the experimental and control groups are presented at the top of Table 4. While the therapy groups show greater mean change than the control $S$s, this difference did not attain statistical significance on the Mann–Whitney test. The same trend and statistical findings were obtained for the snake item of the FS. The experimenter's rating of $S$'s level of anxiety during the avoidance test, did not differentiate between experimental and control groups. In this case the failure to discriminate may be attributed to the selection, prior to the experiment, of a three-point rating scale. $E$ reported that this measure was too gross for the behavior under observation.

*Follow up Study*

All Ss who were still available (N = 20) were re-evaluated approximately six months after the experiment was completed. This included eleven members of the original experimental group, six of whom, touched or held the snake at the final avoidance test. Two of these Ss no longer met this criterion six months later. However, neither S indicated an increase in self-rating fear and one actually showed improvement on this dimension. Furthermore, because of gains by others, the mean avoidance test change score for the entire experimental group indicates a slight reduction in phobic behavior from test 3 to the six-month follow up.

The therapy group showed even greater gains on the fear thermometer. The increase was sufficient that the difference between experimental and control Ss from test 2 to the follow up was statistically significant ($U = 16.5, p < 0.05$). Ss who had experienced therapy also showed a significant reduction in their overall estimate of the intensity of their phobia as measured by the snake item of the FSS. The change in this score from pre-therapy to the six month follow up was significantly greater for experimental than control Ss ($U = 8.5, p < 0.02$).

*Therapy Terminated and Unterminated*

The design of the current experiment arbitrarily limited therapy to eleven sessions. This resulted in Ss being tested for change at varying points in the therapeutic process. Fortunately, in desensitization therapy

TABLE 5

*Avoidance test behavior change from test 2 to test 3 for therapy Ss who completed more than 15 hierarchy items, for those who completed less than 15, and Mann–Whitney tests of significance*

| Number of hierarchy items successfully completed | Snake avoidance scale | | | |
|---|---|---|---|---|
| | Test 2 | Test 3 | Change score | U |
| More than 15 (N = 7) | 6.71 | 3.93 | 0.49 | 5.0* |
| Less than 15 (N = 6) | 4.17 | 5.00 | − 0.07 | |
| | Fear thermometer | | | |
| | Test 2 | Test 3 | Difference | U |
| More than 15 (N = 7) | 7.57 | 4.00 | 3.57 | 8.0† |
| Less than 15 (N = 6) | 7.67 | 6.50 | 1.17 | |

Note—All scores are mean values.

\* $p < 0.03$
† $p < 0.08$

it is possible to define a subject's degree of progress by referring to the number of hierarchy items successfully completed. It will be recalled that all $S$s started with a 20-item hierarchy. This represented the combined efforts of the therapist and the $S$ to build an equal-interval scale, extending from a remote point where $S$ felt little or no fear to a maximum fear involving close contact with the offending object. Normally, therapy would be terminated when the twentieth item had been passed. In the present experiment four $S$s achieved this goal. Seven $S$s completed 16 or more items and six $S$s completed 14 or less items.

TABLE 6

*Changes in the fear survey schedule (FSS) following desensitization therapy for Ss who completed more than 15 hierarchy items, for those who completed less than 15, and Mann–Whitney tests of significance*

| Number of hierarchy items successfully completed | Fear survey schedule | | | |
|---|---|---|---|---|
| | Pre-therapy | Post-therapy | Difference | $U$ |
| More than 15 (N = 7) | 2·34 | 1·85 | 0·49 | 4·5* |
| Less than 15 (N = 6) | 3·21 | 3·20 | 0·01 | |
| | FSS-$S$'s rating of snake fear | | | |
| | Pre-therapy | Post-therapy | Difference | $U$ |
| More than 15 (N = 7) | 6·71 | 4·14 | 2·57 | 3·0† |
| Less than 15 (N = 6) | 6·67 | 6·67 | 0·00 | |

Note—All scores are mean ranks or mean rank differences.
* $p < 0.02$
† $p < 0.01$

All $S$s who completed their hierarchies touched or held the snake at the final avoidance test. Furthermore, $S$s who completed over 15 items (N = 7) showed significant improvement on nearly all measures employed in this experiment: $S$s who completed under 15 items differed little from controls. Table 5 presents the difference between the two therapy groups on the snake avoidance scale and the fear thermometer. Note that the improvement of the over 15 items group is significantly greater than that of $S$s completing less than 15 items. Similar results were obtained for the FSS snake item and they are presented in Table 6. Note in this same table that the mean rank of the FSS also shows a significantly greater reduction in the over 15 items group, than in the group completing fewer items. This finding suggests that the elimination of snake phobic behavior does not initiate an increase in other fears, but in fact leads to a significant reduction in overall anxiety.

## DISCUSSION

The results of the present experiment demonstrate that the experimental analogue of desensitization therapy effectively reduces phobic behavior. Both subjective rating of fear and overt avoidance behavior were modified, and gains were maintained or increased at the six-month follow up. The results of objective measures were in turn supported by extensive interview material. Close questioning could not persuade any of the experimental $S$s that a desire to please the $E$ had been a significant factor in their change. Furthermore, in none of these interviews was there any evidence that other symptoms appeared to replace the phobic behavior.

The fact that no significant change was associated with the pre-therapy training argues that hypnosis and general muscle relaxation were not in themselves vehicles of change. Similarly, the basic suggestibility of the subject must be excluded. The difference between the SHS Form A scores of the experimental and control groups did not approach statistical significance ($U = 58$). Clearly, the responsibility for the reduction in phobic behavior must be assigned to the desensitization process itself. This is evidenced not only by the difference between experimental and control $S$s but also by the relationship within the experimental groups between degree of change and the number of hierarchy items successfully completed.

One must still raise the questions, however, why desensitization therapy could be accomplished in eleven sessions with some subjects and barely gotten underway with others. The intensity of the phobia is obviously not a relevant factor. The mean avoidance test 2 score is actually higher for the experimental $S$s who completed more than 15 items than for those who completed less (see Table 5). The base FSS snake item rank and the fear thermometer scores are almost exactly the same in both groups. On the other hand, a negative relationship ($r = -0.58$) exists between the total FSS score at the first testing and the number of hierarchy items completed by individual members of the experimental group. The FSS is in turn positively related to the Taylor (1953) anxiety scale ($r = +0.80$ for the experimental group). Thus, the degree of progress attained in therapy in a constant period of time (11 sessions) appears to be a function of generalized anxiety, as measured by both the MAS and FSS. These data suggest that desensitization therapy is more difficult, or at least slower, when many stimuli in the $S$'s environment are capable of eliciting anxiety responses. This is of course consistent with the clinical findings of Wolpe (1958) and the prediction of a learning theory model.

The present experiment also reveals an interesting connection between changes in overt avoidance behavior and the $S$'s verbal report. The relationship between these two dimensions is generally positive. However, even when precisely the same event is being evaluated, it is sometimes surprisingly low (Test 3 avoidance scale and fear thermometer $r = +0.40$). Furthermore, initial changes in phobic behavior seem to occur in either one dimension or the other, rather than in both simultaneously. Most frequently subjective report lags behind overt behavior. Thus avoidance test scores differentiated between experimental and control Ss immediately following the experiment, but it was not until the follow-up interview that the subjective scales yielded the same finding. It will be interesting to observe in future studies if this pattern continues, and to what extent it is characteristic of any reduction in phobic behavior, or simply a function of the desensitization technique.

But of greatest interest are the implications of the present research for traditional theories of clinical practice. The findings suggest the following important conclusions: (a) It is not necessary to explore with a subject the factors contributing to the learning of a phobia or its "unconscious meaning" in order to eliminate the fear behavior; (b) The form of treatment employed here does not lead to symptom substitution or create new disturbances of behavior; (c) In reducing phobic behavior it is not necessary to change basic attitudes, values, or attempt to modify the "personality as a whole". The unlearning of phobic behavior appears to be analogous to the elimination of other responses from a subject's behavior repertoire.

## SUMMARY

Twenty-four snake phobic Ss participated in an experimental investigation of systematic desensitization therapy. Ss who experienced desensitization showed a greater reduction in phobic behavior than did non-participating controls. The findings suggest that this change is directly attributable to desensitization, and may not be attributed to rapport, or the general effects of hypnosis or muscle relaxation.

## REFERENCES

DOLLARD, J. and MILLER, N. E. (1950) Personality and psychotherapy: an analysis in terms of learning, thinking and culture, McGraw, New York.
FENICHEL, O. (1945) The psychoanalytic theory of neurosis, (Norton) New York.
JACOBSON, E. (1938) Progressive relaxation, Univ. of Chicago Press, Chicago.
LAZARUS, A. A. (1961) Group therapy of phobic disorders by systematic desensitization, J. Abnorm. Soc. Psychol., 63, 504–510.
LAZOVIK, A. D. and LANG, P. J. (1960) A laboratory demonstration of systematic desensitization psychotherapy, J. Psychol. Stud., 11, 238–247.
SHOBEN, E. J. (1949) Psychotherapy as a problem in learning theory. Psychol. Bull., 46, 366–392.
TAYLOR, JANET, A. (1953) A personality test for manifest anxiety, J. Abnorm. Soc. Psychol., 41, 285–290.
WALK, R. D. (1956) Self ratings of fear in a fear-invoking situation, J. abnorm. soc. Psychol., 52, 171–178.
WEITZENHOFFER, A. M. and HILGARD, E. R. (1959) Stanford hypnotic susceptibility scale, Consulting Psychol. Press, Palo Alto, Calif.
WOLPE, J. (1958) Psychotherapy by reciprocal-inhibition, Stanford Univ. Press, Stanford.
WOLPE, J. (1961) The systematic desensitization treatment of neuroses, J. Nerv. Ment. Dis., 132, 189–203.

# A Case of Cat Phobia*†

## Treatment by a Method derived from Experimental Psychology

H. L. FREEMAN,†† M.A., B.M., B.CH., D.P.M.

*Formerly Registrar, Bethlem Royal and Maudsley Hospital, London*

and

D. C. KENDRICK, B.A., PH.D., DIP.PSYCHOL.

*Lecturer in Psychology, Institute of Psychiatry, University of London*

IN RECENT years a new therapeutic technique—reciprocal inhibition (Wolpe, 1958)—derived from the field of experimental psychology has become available in psychiatry. The concept was originally introduced by Sherrington, and refers to situations in which the elicitation of one response causes a reduction in the strength of evocation of another, simultaneous response. When stimuli producing incompatible responses are present at the same time, the response that is stronger will cause the reciprocal inhibition of the other.

The aim of the technique is to make a response antagonistic to anxiety to occur in the presence of anxiety-evoking stimuli. These is a superimposition of non-anxiety responses to these stimuli, which tends to weaken the bonds between them and the anxiety responses, through lack of reinforcement.

## BACKGROUND

Research over the past thirty years into psychodynamically orientated therapy has generally been disappointing. Most of the findings have either been unreliable, in the sense that they have not been or could not be repeated, or have failed to provide any evidence of positive benefit. Glover (1955) has disavowed any claims for the therapeutic usefulness of psychoanalytic methods. However, there is an increasing quantity of material concerned

* This article is reprinted with the permission of the author and editor from the *Brit. Med. J.*, **11**, 497–502 (1960). Dr. Kendrick has added a brief follow-up note to the published report.

† Based on a paper read at the Annual Conference of the British Psychological Society, Hull, April, 1960.

†† At present, Senior Registrar, Littlemore Hospital, Oxford.

with therapeutic techniques which have been derived from conditioning and learning theory, and claiming some success. Unfortunately, as yet, no controlled study has been attempted to compare the efficacy for any psycho-therapeutic techniques against those of behaviour therapy. The techniques derived from learning theory have two main advantages over those derived from psychoanalytic theory: (a) they can be tested experimentally, and (b) under certain circumstances the behaviour disorders can be experimentally manipulated in a predictable manner (Yates, 1958).

The modern learning theorist considers that neurotic symptoms are learned patterns of behaviour (Eysenck, 1959) which are unadaptive in the social sense but designed to relieve anxiety in the individual. A phobic symptom probably represents a surplus conditioned response which in its original setting may have been relevant but is now unadaptive. In general, the strength of a habit depends upon the magnitude and the number of reinforcements of the response. However, traumatic single-trial learning is an instance of super-reinforcing conditions, and there is considerable experimental evidence to support the notion of one-trial learning (Hudson, 1950). On the other hand, subtraumatic pain and fear responses can also build up conditioned reactions more slowly (Solomon, Kamin and Wynne, 1953). These unadaptive patterns of behaviour fail to extinguish themselves because the performance of the habits leads to their own reinforcement. This reinforcement can occur either by avoiding the situation—for example, a phobia—or by reducing anxiety in the situation—for example, a tic or obsessional ritual. Because neurotic symptoms are considered to be mal-adaptive behaviour patterns, the aim of behaviour-therapy technique is to retrain habits so that they again become adaptive patterns of behaviour. Treatment of the "unconscious" causes is disregarded in this type of therapy, which therefore rests on a different basis from the psychodynamic theories.

Behaviour therapy represents an alternative approach to the treatment of certain abnormal behaviour symptoms, but at this point in its development claims for its efficacy must not be overstated.

A person who developed neurotic symptoms once would almost certainly be predisposed to develop them again if the necessary environmental situation occurred. This is not symptom-substitution, but the reconditioning of old symptoms or the conditioning of new ones, in a situation in which anxiety is first produced and then reduced by the symptom.

The present case can be regarded as a model for illustrating a particular form of behaviour therapy.

## CASE REPORT

The patient, a married woman aged 37, was referred from an out-patient department to Dayholme, Bethlem Royal Hospital, because of a phobia for cats associated with tension, anxiety, and occasional depression. She had never previously seen a psychiatrist or had any treatment for the phobia, but was advised to seek help by a neighbour, who had been a mental nurse.

## Family History

Her father died of coronary thrombosis in 1950, at the age of 53. He was a cable and wireless engineer—very rigid and meticulous; lacking in humour and overt affection. He was very strict with the children, dominated his wife, and made the family conform to his ideas. However, he never ill-used them physically. The patient says that he disapproved of all her friends and would steam open her letters. She was afraid of him as a child and felt that she never had any love for him. However, she never openly quarrelled with him or even answered him back.

Her mother is alive, aged 61. She is a simple, rather garrulous woman who is subject to "nerve rashes". She was prone to threaten her children in their earlier years with action by their father. After her husband's death she is said to have come into her own, having previously been dominated by him completely. She lives at present with her own mother, aged 92, and the patient's younger sister. The two latter get on badly, so that the home is not very happy. The patient and her mother have never been on terms of real confidence.

The patient is the eldest of three children.

Her brother, aged 36, is an insurance clerk, married with two children. He is said to be silent, morose, and henpecked. The patient has always been jealous of him, and considered that he was favoured by the parents in comparison with herself.

Her sister, aged 31, is partly deaf and was backward, but attended an ordinary school and was not abnormal in behaviour or appearance until the age of 14, when she developed epileptic fits. These continued until the age of 20, since when she has had no further fits, but has continued to take anticonvulsants. During adolescence she also developed a deformity of the back. She went out to do domestic work until six years ago, when she was knocked down by a car and has since remained at home, helping in the house. In recent years her behaviour has been very abnormal; she talks to herself loudly and has episodes in which she shakes and weeps, but is calmed down with hot milk. The patient was told by her mother that she attempted to abort this child and has therefore felt under an obligation to her ever since. The sister has apparently never had any specialist or hospital attention.

There is no other family history of nervous or mental illness.

## Personal History

The patient was born in Lewisham in 1922. Birth and milestones were normal. She was considered to be a very handsome child, but was rather nervous and bit her nails, having a good deal of trouble with her father over this.

*School.*—She attended primary schools from the age of 5 to 11, being an average pupil and quite happy, but rather timid of the teachers. She then attempted the grammar school scholarship and failed. Her father, however, was very ambitious for her and she went as a fee-payer, after passing the entrance examination. After a short time she felt quite out of her depth and came consistently bottom of the class, so that she eventually gave up trying. There were terrible scenes at home at the end of every term when her reports arrived, and her father would shout at her. She preferred the practical subjects and left at the age of 15.

*Work.*—On leaving school she became a clerk and remained in this work for the next four and a half years, having two different jobs. Then, largely to get away from home, she joined the W.R.N.S., in which she served for two years. She failed a course in gunnery control, which had a good deal of theory, but then became a control operator at a gunnery training school and did well in this work. She married during her service and was discharged when she became pregnant. In the last few years she has had part-time jobs as a cook in a café, a clerk for football pools, and, more recently, as a church verger.

The menstrual history shows nothing abnormal, except for some premenstrual tension.

*Sexual.*—She first had sexual relations with a boy friend at the age of 18, and this continued until their friendship was broken off. She had no premarital relations with her husband, but told him of her previous experience. Their sexual relations are said to be quite satisfactory and at present occur about fortnightly.

*Marital.*—The patient was married at the age of 22, having known her husband for four years. He was then in the Navy and has been a schoolteacher since the end of the war. He is about the same age as the patient, and is a placid, easy-going, good-natured man. He has always been very concerned about the patient's symptoms and has done his best to protect her from cats. His personality is almost exactly the opposite of her father's. The engagement was bitterly opposed by the patient's family, and she states that she was "sent to Coventry" by them for several months. Her family had received an anonymous letter stating that her fiancé's father and four other members of his family had died of tuberculosis. The patient's father told her that if she married her fiancé, both of them, as well as any children they had, would die of tuberculosis also. He even went to the length of getting a copy of the death certificate of her fiancé's father from Somerset House, to try to convince her. However, he eventually realized that she was adamant about her engagement and then completely reversed his attitude, making her fiancé very welcome.

*Friends.*—The patient had several boy friends before her engagement, and forms social relationships easily.

*Children.*—The patient has two children—a daughter aged 14 and a son aged 12. They are both healthy and get on well together. Like her husband, they have done a good deal to protect her from cats.

## Medical History

The patient had scarlet fever at the age of 16, after a sinus operation at Gray's Inn Road Hospital. Her father told her, when she applied to join the W.R.N.S., that she would not be accepted, because she probably had a bad heart as a result of this.

The only other condition of note is paraesthesiae in the hands. This first occured 12 years ago and again three years ago, clearing up on both occasions with tablets from her doctor. It recurred in July, 1958, and she was seen in October by a physician at St. Helier Hospital. He diagnosed carpal-tunnel compression, and during the next few months she had hydrocortisone injections into both wrists, followed by cortisone tablets. Her symptoms resolved completely during the past summer, but are now present again mimimally.

*Personality.*—The patient's personality is sociable and outgoing. She has many friends and likes to be active, both in the home and at evening classes. She is rather houseproud, and this had been excessive in the last year or so. She is sensitive, easily irritable, and readily shows her feelings. She is fond of all animals except cats; her children have guinea-pigs, a tortoise, and a bird, none of which upsets her. For some years she has had occasional episodes of depression, lasting for a day, which would sometimes follow fright from seeing a cat. However, these have been very infrequent.

## Present Illness

The patient states that her fear of cats has existed for as long as she can remember. The earliest incident she can recall is at the age of 4, when her father drowned a kitten in a bucket in front of her. Her mother has no recollection of this incident, and the patient says that her parents did not take this fear very seriously. She remembers sitting at the table with her legs held straight out in front of her if the cat was prowling about the floor, and screaming outside the front door of the house if there was a cat on the step.

When she was 14 her parents, for some reason which is not clear, put a fur inside her bed on one occasion. She states that she became quite hysterical in finding it. Her mother states that at the age of 18 the patient had another fright when a cat got into her bedroom, but the patient has forgotten this.

During her time in the W.R.N.S. she was often frightened by cats, and always insisted on sleeping in a top bunk, though she did not tell anyone of her fear.

Her mother says that her fear became worse after the age of 22, when she was married and went to live in a rather dark and depressing house. However, it does not seem to have been affected by the move to her present house, a few years later. There then seems to have been a period of almost 10 years, including the time of her father's death, in which the phobia remained unchanged.

However, during the last year or two, and particularly in the six months before coming to Dayholme, the fear became steadily worse. In this last period the house next door had been empty; the grass in the garden grew very long and it became a rendezvous for all the local cats. The patient said that she was terrified by the thought that cats would spring on her and attack her. She knew that this was very unlikely in fact, but could not rid herself of the fear. At the sight of a cat she would panic and sometimes be completely overwhelmed with terror. She always walked on the roadside edge of the pavement, to avoid cats on the walls, and would never go out alone at night.

She would not, if she could possibly help it, go into any room where there was a cat. On visiting friends or relatives who had a cat, her husband or children would usually enter ahead of her, to see that the cat was turned out. She was afraid to go into her garden alone, and washdays were a torment to her. She could not bear to touch any cat-like fur or wear fur gloves, and felt uneasy sitting next to anyone wearing a fur coat on public transport. Pictures of cats in books, or on television or the cinema made her feel uneasy. In recent months her life was filled with fear of cats, and she could think of nothing else. She interpreted any unexpected movement, shadow, or noise as due to a cat. She would be upset by her daughter's toy koala bear if she saw it or touched it unexpectedly.

On waking in the morning her first thought was how many cats she would meet during the day. It was as a result of this, she felt, that she would work up a fury of activity in the house and never sit still. From time to time she had terrifying nightmares, concerned with cats.

The details of her illness were confirmed by her husband.

## Mental State

On admission to Dayholme she was found to be a woman of rather immature manner who was readily emotional. She spoke freely and gave a detailed account of herself. She was rather tense, and wept when describing her experiences with cats. There were no other features of depression or of a compulsive nature, and she had a very strong motivation towards cure.

She settled at Dayholme and established good relations with staff and patients. She was rather anxious, however, about cats in the grounds. Physical examination was normal, except for a slightly elevated blood-pressure and some cyanosis of the extremities, which the patient said was usual for her.

Special investigations were all normal. Her I.Q. was 112 on Raven's progressive matrices. The Maudsley personality inventory showed a mild degree of extraversion.

## Method

The patient was referred to the psychologist as possibly being suitable for behaviour therapy. She was interviewed by him to determine which stimuli produced the fear reaction; this revealed a number of them which showed a clearly defined stimulus-generalization gradient. This refers to the fact that an animal or person conditioned to one stimulus also responds, though less and less strongly, to stimuli further and further removed from the original one. The stimuli producing the fear reaction, in descending order of significance, were as follows: (1) the sight of a cat in reality; (2) the thought that a cat might be about to spring out on her while she was walking along the pavement; (3) the thought of going out by herself at night in case she should meet a cat in the dark; (4) pictures of cats, and cats on television; (5) cat-like toys; (6) cat-like fur. She was *not afraid* of cat's mewing.

These stimuli produced the following behaviour disorders, of which the patient complained: (1) panic at the sight of a cat; (2) she walked along the roadside edge of the pavement; (3) she could not go out alone at night; (4) she could not go into a room where a cat was, even though it was under control; (5) she was uneasy when she had to go into her garden alone, and hanging out the washing was a torment to her; (6) she would be startled by a toy koala bear, belonging to her daughter, if she came upon it unexpectedly; (7) she could not wear fur gloves; (8) she felt uneasy when somebody sat beside her in a fur coat on public transport; (9) she could not bear to touch cat-like fur, though she could quite easily touch the hair of a dog or other similar animal.

The case report has referred to the situations in which she was frightened by the sight of her father drowning a kitten at the age of 4, and by discovering a fur in her bed at the age of 14.

Thus, not only did the patient's fear reactions show a stimulus generalization, but also she had undergone two traumatic experiences, concerned with cats and fur, which could have been the conditioning situations for the phobic symptoms. The system of disabilities, therefore, is accountable in learning-theory terms—that is, two super-reinforcing conditions—and the stimulus-generalization gradient.

The form of behaviour therapy considered by the psychologist to be relevant to this case was reciprocal inhibition.

A strong sympathetic reaction has to be overcome by a stronger parasympathetic one. To do this, use is made of the concept of stimulus generalization—that is, attempting to establish a new response at the end of the gradient, where the fear reaction is weakest and where there are competing responses. If the fear response at this point can be overcome, then stimulus generalization works in our favour. A generalization occurs to other stimuli nearer the main stimulus, and so it becomes easier for us to establish the new response to the stimuli producing the stronger anxiety reactions.

## Plan of Treatment

The patient was strongly motivated to get better, and therefore any improvement she experienced was highly rewarding to her, with relief of anxiety.

It was considered that the weakest point of the stimulus gradient would be material that had some of the texture of fur without looking like it—for example, velvet. A series of pieces of material would have to be prepared, graded in texture and appearance from most unlike cat fur to very like cat fur (rabbit). The patient would then have to handle these materials (in order of similarity to cat fur), and before she proceeded with the next piece in the series she would have to be quite sure that she felt no uneasiness whatsoever in handling it. After overcoming the fear reactions to handling cat-like fur, she was to be presented with a toy kitten, and with pictures of cats, which she was to become accustomed to, until they caused no anxiety. Once this state was achieved she was to be shown a live kitten, and gradually to approach and touch it. When she was quite prepared she was to take it home and keep it. As it grew, so the generalization to large cats would occur and, finally, she would be free from her phobia for cats.

The use of a kitten is similar to the method reported by Jersild and Holmes (1935) for treating a child's fear of dogs through a puppy. The puppy is sufficiently unlike a grown dog to elicit the fear to only a small degree, while its antics create pleasurable responses. As it grows, these responses spread to all dogs.

## Treatment

At his interview with the patient the psychologist outlined the programme he had formulated and gave the eventual aim as being that she should be able to touch a fully grown cat without distress. The patient felt that the method seemed reasonable to her, but was very sceptical about the outcome; she could not conceive of herself as ever being able to touch even a kitten.

The psychiatrist then began the presentation of stimuli at the day hospital, and told the patient to handle each material in turn, until it caused her no uneasiness. When a glove made of rabbit fur was eventually offered the patient was so upset by it that she wrapped it up in a newspaper. However, another patient encouraged her by putting the glove on himself and persuading her to stroke it. Within a few days it had ceased to cause her any unpleasant feelings.

The patient's intelligent co-operation in the procedure was illustrated by her experience with pictures of cats. When this point was reached she was advised to obtain some large pictures and put them up at home. She was a little overenthusiastic, and arranged nine in different parts of the house, particularly in corners where they would surprise her. This proved rather distressing for her and she had to take down some of the more frightening ones, but in the course of the next week or so she became used to all of them.

At the end of three weeks, fur, toys, and pictures had all been fully assimilated and a significant lessening in anxiety had already occurred. She was much less preoccupied with cats in general and her family had noticed, that she was altogether more cheerful. She could walk within about 10 yards of a cat without flinching, and when opening the curtains in the mornings her first reaction was no longer to look round the garden for cats.

The rapidity of response so far seemed remarkable, and the patient now felt ready to deal with a live kitten. One of a suitably placid disposition was obtained and the patient was brought into the room, where she saw it resting on the lap of one of the nurses. She sat down next to the nurse, stroked the kitten herself, and then took it on to her own lap. During this process she became very emotional, both laughing and crying, but this passed off in a few minutes, and she explained afterwards that it was not from distress, but from relief at having done something of which she imagined herself incapable. She later described this as "one of the greatest days of my life".

In the next two days she looked after the kitten at the day hospital and then took it home, where it has remained since. This occured one month after her first attendance, and during the next two months she continued to attend twice weekly, but mainly for the art classes, in which she was very intersted. During this time she was assessed weekly by the psychiatrist, and her improvement was seen to be continuing. She said that she felt as though a cloud had been lifted from her, and she had stopped biting her nails for the first time in her life.

One month after taking the kitten home she had her second interview with the psychologist. She stated that she no longer walked along the edge of the pavement, and could wear fur gloves and sit next to people in fur coats without feeling uneasy. She was no longer upset by pictures or films of cats and could consider some of them as beautiful creatures. She could pass near to a full-grown cat without panicking, and felt she would be able to go out alone at night, but her family had not let her try so far. She had stopped having cat nightmares; however, she dreamed without distress of kittens and later of full-grown cats.

On two successive nights the following week she had aggressive dreams concerned with her father and was very miserable in the intervening day. In one dream she was murdering her father with a poker. In recounting these she stated that she had often had feelings of this sort when her father was alive, but had not allowed herself to express any hostility against him.

Ten weeks after beginning treatment she touched a fullgrown cat for the first time. She was so thrilled by this that she felt like running down the street and telling everyone and then was reluctant to wash her hands afterwards. She then touched her mother's black cat, though cats of this colour had been the ones which previously frightened her most. Whereas previously all cats had an almost uniformly sinister aspect, she could now see individual differences.

After three months she discontinued attendance at the day hospital, but came to report progress to the psychiatrist at intervals of three weeks, lengthening to one month. She states that her life has been completely transformed, and that she no longer goes round in a state of fear. Nor does she feel the need any longer to occupy herself in constant activity inside the house to relieve her anxiety. The kitten has grown considerably, and she has no difficulty in dealing with it. At the end of the fifth month from beginning treatment she had been out by herself at night, even in dimly lit streets. The only episode which caused her any distress was going into the back garden at night on her own. At the end of the eighth month (and two months after the previous interview) she remained well, except for a brief relapse, which followed her cat being involved in a fight with another one. She then realized that she was afraid of only one particular cat, and there was no generalization in this episode.

Throughout the treatment both direct suggestion and reassurance have been avoided. Interviews, both by the psychologist and by the psychiatrist, have been confined to explaining the procedure, administering the stimuli, and assessing the position reached.


## PSYCHOLOGICAL DISCUSSION

Considering the case from the viewpoint of learning theory, several behavioural changes deserve comment. The reduction of the stimulus-generalization gradient of the fear responses is clearly shown by the progressive remission of symptoms, which never required direct treatment. The most striking example is that of the patient's reversion to walking in the middle of the pavement rather than on the roadside edge, while another example is that of her becoming able to discriminate between cats aesthetically.

A dramatic feature of the case was the dream sequence; this also could be explained by the mechanism of the reduction of the stimulus-generalization gradient. She was able to accept larger and larger cats in her dreams with severe anxiety (nightmares), until finally, when her conscious fear of cats had almost disappeared, the original unconditioned stimulus for the fear responses (her father) appeared, and then disappeared. This event almost coincided with the termination of the treatment. This is not to quarrel with psychodynamic interpretations of the dream sequence, but only to point out that it followed a pattern which would be consistent with a learning-theory mechanism. Why the dream sequence occurred is another matter.

So far, the discussion has been concerned with the remission of the maladaptive habits, but another feature of the case was the patient's diminished irritability and general anxiety. Having started to break through the vicious circle of the phobic reactions, we not only get a remission of the behavioural symptoms, but also a reduction in the general anxiety level. The phobic response can be regarded as functionally autonomous—that is, self-stimulating and self-rewarding. The sight of a cat produces fear;

this leads to an avoidance response, and the avoidance response to a reduction of fear, which rewards the avoidance response. At the same time general anxiety is produced in the patient by her knowledge of how her behaviour is distorted because of her fear, and how disrupting to normal behaviour these avoidance responses are. Having broken part of this chain of events, it is not surprising that we get a lowering of general anxiety. This was clearly shown in the patient by the reduction in her anxiety-avoidance activity in the home, and by the cessation of nail-biting, two symptoms which were never treated or even discussed by the therapist with the patient.

Finally, the patient was extremely eager to get well and was very co-operative, so that the slightest reduction in her symptoms was highly rewarding to her. Had the patient not been so co-operative, the treatment would probably have not proceeded so smoothly and rapidly. Instead of getting positive reinforcement, which quickly developed positive habits, antagonistic to the ones we wished to remit, we might then have had to proceed by massing practice of the maladaptive habits in the first instance. This would have produced a negative habit, antagonistic to the maladaptive ones (Kendrick, 1958; Yates, 1958).

## CLINICAL

It is appreciated that this report is likely to be criticized as describing a single case, followed up over a very short period. Nevertheless, we felt it merits attention in view of the extremely rapid resolution of symptoms which had been present to some extent for about 30 years, and which did not seem likely to respond to the conventional methods of treatment. It is also appreciated that the treatment situation and subsequent course of events can be interpreted in terms other than those of learning theory. During the crucial stage of the treatment the patient was attending the day hospital and benefiting from its activities and social support. While we would not wish to underestimate these factors, our experience does not suggest that phobic symptoms in general are likely to resolve in the day-hospital situation without other specific treatment. Nor can it be maintained that the phobia was replaced by a dependence on the day hospital, since there was no return of symptoms when the patient ceased attending.

In the era of the National Health Service it may be considered surprising that a disturbance of this severity should remain for so many years without any reference for treatment. However, neurotic conditions which do not include definite somatic symptoms tend not to be regarded as "illness" meriting the attention of doctors, but rather as personal peculiarities. The difference in many cases may be one of degree—for example, in this country a fear of snakes is unlikely to assume the importance of a phobia. However, fear of cats appears to be relatively common and was the subject of a recent discussion on the B.B.C.'s programme, Woman's Hour. In the end it was the intervention of a friend which resulted in this patient seeking medical help.

It may also be objected that a patient who had endured symptoms for so many years without help would have responded to any therapeutic measure—particularly to any one involving personal attention and a specially designed programme, such as the treatment given. This assumes that the relief of symptoms is to be attributed entirely to suggestion. We would not deny that suggestion played some part in the cure, in spite of the efforts made to avoid direct suggestion during interviews. However, we believe that methods involving suggestion alone would not be expected to produce such a dramatic resolution of long-standing symptoms.

So far as the patient's relationship to the two therapists is concerned, general observation suggested that she had strongly positive feelings towards both, but discussion of this aspect was avoided during interviews. It is possible to offer a number of psychodynamic explanations, in terms of transference, to account for relief of symptoms—for example, that the therapists benefited from positive feelings which had been inhibited from expression towards the father. In this connexion it would have been very interesting to observe the result if the patient had been treated by female therapists. However, we do not feel that such concepts necessarily invalidate the learning-theory aspect of this case, and Jones (1960) has pointed out that the concept of transference might well fit into its conceptual framework. The therapist would presumably lie along the stimulus-generalization continuum, derived from other significant males.

## SUMMARY

The successful remission of symptoms connected with a cat phobia, by a technique derived from experimental psychology, is described. An argument is developed for using learning theory and behaviour therapy as an alternative approach to psychotherapy in the treatment of certain psychiatric symptoms.

This case was admitted under Dr. E. H. Hare, to whom we are grateful for permission to publish.

## REFERENCES

EYSENCK, H. J. (1959) *J. Ment. Sci.*, **105**, 61.
GLOVER, E. (1955) *The Technique of Psycho-analysis*, Baillière, Tindall and Cox, London.
HUDSON, B. B. (1950) *Genet. Psychol. Monogr.*, **41**, 99.
JERSILD, A, T. and HOLMES, F. B. (1935) *J. Psychol.*, **1**, 75.
JONES, H. G (1960) In *Handbook of Abnormal Psychology*, edited by H. J. Eysenck, chapter 20, in press. Pitman, London.
KENDRICK, D. C. (1958) *J. Exp. Psychol.*, **56**, 313.
SOLOMON, R. L., KAMIN, L. J. and WYNNE, L. C. (1953) *J. Abnorm. Soc. Psychol.*, **48**, 291.
WOLPE, J. (1958) *Psychotherapy by Reciprocal Inhibition*, Stanford Univ. Press. Stanford, Calif.
YATES, A. J. (1958) *J. Abnorm. Soc. Psychol.*, **56**, 175.

## 3-YEAR FOLLOW-UP ON CAT PHOBIA

The patient is still very well. She herself says it seems as though she has been "two persons, the one with all the fear and the one now".

The patient still has her own cat and frequently looks after another one. Only one cat disturbs her and that is a black mangy one, which used to fight with her own cat, but it does not produce terror. All other symptoms such as being afraid of going out at night, walking along the edge of the pavement and dreaming of cats have disappeared completely. There has been no symptom substitution.

# The Treatment of Anxiety and Phobic Reactions by Systematic Desensitization Psychotherapy*

STANLEY RACHMAN

*University of the Witwatersrand, Johannesburg*
*(Now at the Maudsley Hospital)*

THE AIM of this paper is to present a detailed account of systematic desensitization psychotherapy in action. The present case was chosen for description because it clearly illustrates the principle and practice of this type of therapy and because of its intrinsic clinical interest.

The patient, Miss A. G., was a 24-year-old female teacher who complained of an inability to undergo injections of any kind. On those few occasions where she had been unable to avoid them, she had always fainted during or immediately after the injection. She requested therapy at the time she did because of an impending trip for which she would be required to have a yellow fever injection and smallpox vaccination. Her fear of injections was of long standing, dating back to either six or seven years of age. She experienced a moderate reaction (slight trembling and "butterflies in the stomach") when asked to imagine a person receiving an injection and ordinarily preferred not to talk about injections or related topics, e.g. visits to the dentist. She also complained of "a sexual problem" and a fear of using internal sanitary pads.

In addition to a symptom history, the patient was given the Willoughby Neurotic Tendency Inventory (Willoughby, 1934) and a form of the Incomplete Sentence Test during the first interview. Her Willoughby score was moderately high (44) and the I-S Test, which was only partially answered, revealed a slightly disturbed childhood, an exaggerated need for company and acceptance by other people, and vague fears about the future. Her relationships with her parents, with whom she lived, appeared to be unsatisfactory, but no serious difficulties seemed to be present. The general picture was one of mild insecurity.

In view of the nature and history of the chief symptom, it was decided to employ systematic desensitization psychotherapy and to attempt at the same time to relieve the feelings of insecurity by discussion and reassurance.

* This article is reprinted with the permission of the author and the editor from the *J. Abnorm. Soc. Psyehol.* **58**, 259–263 (1959).

The systematic densitization procedure was first described by Wolpe (1952b, 1954) in his attempt to develop techniques for the treatment of neuroses on the basis of reciprocal inhibition. The experimental basis (1948) for this type of therapy and the mechanisms and theory (1950, 1952a) underlying its formulation have been described elsewhere. The present paper is restricted to an account of systematic desensitization in practice.

## TREATMENT

*General Procedure*

An inquiry is first conducted in desensitization therapy in order to ascertain which stimulus situations provoke anxiety in the patient. The patient is told that he can add to or modify this list at any time. The stimuli are then categorized by the therapist, and the patient is asked to rank the categories of stimuli in order from the most to the least disturbing. This ranked list of anxiety producing conditions is referred to as the hierarchy. In the present case, for example, one would refer to the "injection hierarchy" and the "sanitary pad hierarchy". Hierarchies typically contain from 5 to 25 items. The construction of the relevant hierarchies generally takes from one to three interviews, and the patient is concurrently given practice in hypnotic and relaxation procedures. Hypnosis is not an essential requirement, and, in those cases where the patient refuses to be hypnotized or requires prolonged practice, the procedure can be omitted and deep nonhypnotic relaxation employed instead.

When the hierarchies have been worked out, the subject is told which stimuli are to be presented in the individual session and is advised to signal with his hand if a stimulus presentation disturbs him unduly. This is an important instruction and is on no account omitted, because the arousing of anxiety during the session is sometimes extremely antitherapeutic. With most patients, it seems possible by observing facial expressions, bodily tension, respiration, and so forth, to perceive such disturbances before the patient actually signals. When such disturbances occur, the therapist immediately withdraws the stimulus and calms the patient. No session is concluded when a disturbance occurs, but before rousing the patient, the therapist presents an "easy" stimulus which has already been successfully overcome.

When the preliminary instructions have been given, the patient is relaxed (hypnotically or otherwise) and then told to visualize the various stimuli, e.g. "Picture a hospital in the distance. ... Now stop picturing that and go on relaxing." Each visualization of this kind is referred to as a "presentation". Each stimulus is visualized for five to ten seconds, and from two to four different items are presented each session. Each item is generally presented twice. When the requisite number of stimuli have been presented, the patient is slowly roused and then asked for a report on his reactions. If the items were visualized vividly and without undue disturbance, the therapist then proceeds to the next stimuli in the following session. The items lowest in the hierarchy (i.e. the least disturbing ones) are introduced first, and the therapist proceeds slowly up the list, depending on the progress achieved and the patient's reactions. In this way it is possible for the patient eventually to imagine formerly noxious stimuli without any anxiety whatever. This ability to imagine the noxious stimulus with tranquillity then transfers to the real-life situation.

*Interview No. 2.* A discussion of A. G.'s responses to the Incomplete Sentence Test revealed that some 18 months earlier, she had unsuccessfully attempted to use an internal sanitary pad. On the first attempt she fainted after the pad had been inserted. She left it in when she had regained consciousness, but it felt uncomfortable, and she was anxious lest she would not be able to extract it. The second attempt, a day later, was unsuccessful. She only managed to place the pad half way in after much effort. Her hand seemed to be stiff and almost paralysed, and she was perspiring and trembling. This failure left her very upset. A third attempt on the following day was also unsuccessful, and the emotional upset was repeated. Since that time she had used external pads exclusively. The patient also reported that she experienced pain during intercourse. This sexual difficulty had been present from her first experience of sex and was consistent. Her menstrual periods were regular, and she rarely experienced pain or other difficulties.

During this second interview the patient was given her first lesson in relaxation to which she responded very well and achieved a calm state within 15 min. She was instructed to practice relaxation for 15 min every day.

*Interview No. 3.* As the reaction to internal sanitary pads was judged to be less disturbing than that of injections, it was decided to commence with this problem. The following hierarchy was constructed for the patient progressively to imagine: box of Tampax, an opened pad, holding a pad, holding a pad next to the vagina, seeing someone else using a Tampax, placing a pad at the vaginal entrance, sliding it in slowly, completely inserted. The patient was given a second lesson in relaxation and again responded well.

*Interview No. 4.* After a discussion about her ambitions and future plans, the patient was relaxed and asked to visualize each of the first three items in the hierarchy twice (i.e. box of pads, opened box of pads, holding a pad). She reported afterwards that the images had been slightly disturbing but not very vivid.

*Interview No. 5.* In the fifth session, A. G. revealed the history of the protracted relationship with the man she was in love with. She expressed doubts about the wisdom of marrying him and also about his attitude to wards her. After some discussion, her feelings and motives became more lucid and she experienced some relief. Items 3, 4, and 5 in the anxiety hierarchy were successfully presented but again were not very vividly perceived.

*Interview No. 6* The patient reported that she "felt better" since the last interview and had been practicing relaxation regularly. In view of her inability to visualize the hierarchy items vividly, she was given some instruction and practice to remedy this. She was then relaxed and Items 5 and 6 were presented three times each. The images were reported as slightly disturbing and a bit more clear.

*Interview No. 7.* A. G. said that she had been feeling tense for the past two days, but no incident or other cause for this upset could be located. She had seen a bullfight film after the development of this tension and reported that the bullfighting and darting of the bulls, previously upsetting to her, had left her unaffected. Desensitization of Items 6 and 7 (placing a pad at vaginal entrance, sliding it in slowly) was proceeded with. Each item was presented three times, and A. G. reported vivid images and a slight disturbance.

*Interview No. 8.* The patient's menstrual flow had started the previous afternoon, and she decided to try an internal sanitary pad. She reported, "I had a bath, felt a bit nervous, and then tried to insert a Tampax in the bathroom. I started perspiring, felt very hot, and got terribly upset. I tried to relax myself, then managed to put the tip of the pad in. Just then I had a 'thing' (near panic, almost fainted). I should have stopped but could not. I pushed and pushed and got terribly upset. I felt scared and started crying. Then C. (a friend) came in and tried to help me. I could not do it and eventually gave up. I felt dizzy and weak and was extremely upset."

The patient was given deep relaxation for 15 min and then the last two items were presented twice each (sliding pad in, pad fully inserted). The last item was more than usually disturbing. She was then given another five minutes of relaxation and told to attempt an actual insertion in an adjoining room in the presence of a friend. This she managed to do with some difficulty after three minutes. When she had succeeded, however, she felt extremely pleased and had no dizzy spells or feelings of weakness.

She was instructed to insert a pad by herself that night after relaxing for 10 min and also to relax for a further 10 min after insertion.

*Interview No. 9.* A. G. reported that she had successfully inserted the sanitary pads on four occasions and had experienced two failures, neither of which had upset her very much. She said that she was now able to insert them more quickly and with little or no pain.

During this interview, an injection hierarchy was constructed. The items were (in ascending order) seeing a hypodermic syringe, holding a syringe, filling a syringe, seeing a cinema slide of a person receiving an injection, seeing a bull receive an injection, seeing a dog receive an injection, another person being injected, being injected at home, being injected at the district surgeon's rooms. The first three items in this hierarchy were then presented twice each. They were visualized vividly and were not disturbing.

*Interviews 10 and 11.* These sessions were mainly devoted to systematic desensitization. By this time, all the items up to and including No. 8 (seeing another person being injected) had been successfully presented.

*Interview No. 12.* The patient having received a jolt in her love relationship, this session was restricted to a sort of nondirective, cathartic discussion. No desensitizing was undertaken because of A. G.'s depressed mood and obvious desire to "just talk".

*Interview No. 13.* The cathartic process of the last interview was continued, and the patient was subsequently relaxed. Item 7 (dog being injected) was given once, Item 8 (person being injected) three times, and Item 9 (A. G. being injected at home) presented once very briefly. This last item caused some disturbance and was therefore not repeated in this session.

*Interview No. 14.* In anticipation of the patient's menstrual period, the sanitary pad image was reinforced under deep relaxation three times. Item 8 of the irjection hierarchy (person being injected) was also visualized three times.

In the meantime, various difficulties regarding A. G.'s projected trip had arisen and were fully discussed.

*Interview No. 15.* Since the onset of her menstrual flow two days earlier, A. G. had successfully inserted sanitary pads on three out of four attempts. She was put under deep relaxation and then instructed to insert a pad while alone in the relaxation room. She managed perfectly in very rapid time with no disturbance whatsoever.

She reported that she had attempted sexual intercourse a week earlier but had been forced to give up because of the pain and anxious feelings engendered. She added hesitatingly that she was worried lest she had some physical defect which would always prevent her from experiencing anything but pain in sexual activities. Analysis of the unsuccessful sexual attempts indicated that a contributing factor was inadequate foreplay. The patient was given information and advice about loveplay and told to relax fully before lovemaking. It was also suggested to her that there would probably be a spontaneous transfer of relaxation effect, and, therefore, success in sex was likely once the other two anxiety areas had been desensitized.

*Interview No. 16.* The menstrual flow had ceased and the "score" for the month was that six out of seven attempts at insertion of sanitary pads were successful. A. G.'s realization of this success had a marked beneficial effect, and she was quite elated about a long behaviour difficulty which had at last been remedied.

The patient was then desensitized to Items 8 (person being injected) and 9 (self being injected at home). Each item was presented three times, and the patient reported no disturbance but inadequate visualization of the images.

*Interview No. 17.* A. G. stated that her trip was almost certainly cancelled and expressed considerable disappointment. She was also experiencing further uneasiness about her love relationship as a result of some action on the part of her partner which had given her cause to doubt his positive, affectionate feelings towards her.

Desensitization of the last two items in the hierarchy was carried out successfully. Each image (self being injected at home, being injected at district surgeon's rooms) was presented three times. They were vividly pictured and caused little disturbance, the patient being very deeply relaxed and extremely calm.

*Interview No. 18.* A. G. reported that she had experienced sexual intercourse two days previously. For the first time in her life, it had been completely free of even the slightest pain. She had felt slightly anxious but had managed to control this reaction and to indulge in pre- and post-coital loveplay unhindered. The fear of some physical defect had disappeared entirely, and she felt reassured about her sexual adequacy.

The last two items on the injection list were presented again, three times each. They were vividly imagined and caused no disturbance.

*Interview No. 19.* In reply to A. G.'s queries, information regarding the etiology of neurotic behaviour was supplied, and her own case was then discussed in some detail. She was told that phobias such as hers develop out of painful experiences and that despite their apparent senselessness they nevertheless persist. The usual reason for the persistence of the phobia, she was informed, is that it produces an avoidance of the painful situation. Because of her fear of injections, she had successfully managed to avoid having any form of injection for many years. Both the fear and avoidance reactions were reinforced over the years because they were never followed by pain and were in this way satisfying patterns of behaviour.

The patient was desensitized to injections at the district surgeon's (three times) and to the sanitary pad situation (three times) in anticipation of the menstrual period again. Both items were seen vividly and without disturbance.

*Interview No. 20.* The patient reported that sexual intercourse had again been successful. She had experienced minimal anxiety and no pain. She also felt a change in her attitude to injections: "They no longer seem to bother me when I think about them."

After a final three presentations of the district surgeon situation under relaxation, it was agreed to test her reaction to injections. It was accordingly arranged that she would receive an injection of chemically pure water at the next interview.

*Interview No. 21.* After 10 min of deep relaxation, A. G. received an intramuscular water injection in the left arm. She experienced considerable pain but did not faint despite a strong feeling of "butterflies" and excessive sweating. She was relaxed for a further 16 min, but her arm continued to ache and she felt "shaken up".

The sanitary pads were now being used at will and provoked no anxiety or other untoward reactions.

*Interview No. 22.* Four days after the water injection, A. G. received her yellow fever injection at the district surgeon's rooms. She relaxed on a couch before and after the injection and experienced no disturbance despite her marked fear just prior to the event. She was extremely glad about this success and reported feeling "a lot better all round". As A. G. had been desensitized to the full hierarchies of noxious stimuli and her behavior difficulties overcome, this interview brought to an end the formal desensitization treatment. The patient was instructed to return for follow-up interviews at two-month intervals unless, of course, she felt the need to return before the stated time had elapsed.

Six weeks later, A. G. reported that she had received a smallpox vaccination in the interim and had experienced no ill-effects although she had been apprehensive for a while prior to her visit to the district surgeon's rooms. All the other improvements effected duting therapy had been maintained.

Six weeks later, A. G. reported feeling well and "over her troubles". She was given the Willoughby Neurotic Tendency Scale again. Her score was 26, a decrease of 18 points since the first interview. Therapy was terminated as A. G. seemed improved in terms of Knight's criteria (1941) of symptom improvement, improved adjustment and pleasure in sex, and increased stress tolerance. The other two criteria of improved interpersonal relationship and increased productivity were not relevant to the case as A. G.'s behaviour in these areas had never been disrupted.

## DISCUSSION

The 22 therapeutic interviews were spread over a period of three months, averaging two per week. Pehaps the most striking feature of the case was its smooth progression. The therapeutic program proceeded from interview to interview in a regular, predictable way, with behaviour changes following therapy in a manner almost perfectly consistent with theoretical expectations.

At only two points was therapy ever threatened with disruption. In Interview No. 12, A. G. arrived for her appointment depressed and perturbed about her love relationship. This mood prevented a desensitization session, and had it not cleared as rapidly as it did, it could have delayed further progress for weeks or even months. The second difficulty occurred towards the end of therapy as a result of the therapist's avoidable error in using water in the trial injection (Interview No. 21). The injection of water is ordinarily painful. The pain experienced by A. G. on this occasion fortunately did not reinforce her fear of injections unduly. She still underwent the yellow fever injection successfully a few days later. These two obstacles to progress have of course no general lesson or application other than the observation that therapeutic planning and procedure must be carried forward with considerable caution on the part of the psychotherapist.

It seems likely that the improvement in A. G.'s sexual performance resulted from a transfer of her progress in relaxation and in the sanitary pad procedure. Before the anxiety associated with the insertion of sanitary pads had been fully overcome, she unsuccessfully attempted to have intercourse (in the period between Interviews 13 and 14). By Interview 16, she was managing the sanitary pad insertions with very little anxiety and, soon after the following interview, had her first painless experience of sexual intercourse. Prior to the inhibition of the sanitary pad anxiety she had been unable to have normal sexual intercourse. Spontaneous recovery of sexual functioning accompanying general psychological improvement is not unusual, but, in the present case, the transfer effect occurred rather early. The probable reason for this occurrence was the close similarity in this case between the symptom under treatment at the time (internal sanitary pads) and the pain experienced during sex.

The present case study indicates practically the point stated elsewhere (Lazarus and Rachman, 1957) that "while a knowledge of the causative process and genesis of the individual neurosis can be of considerable value in therapy, improvement can nevertheless be obtained in many cases without such knowledge" (Rachman, 1958). In the present case, no certain "cause" could be found for the development of the anxiety and phobic reactions. A. G. said that when she was a young child she had experienced some painful injections. This may well account for her neurotic reaction to injections, but the sanitary pad and sexual difficulties were never adequately traced backwards. The possibility that these problems arose out of the fear of injections as a prototypical fear of penetration seems farfetched. The reverse explanation, that all three "reactions to penetration" were of a sexual nature, is also not supported by the evidence. The phobic response to injections antedated the sexual difficulties by 12 years, and the penetration analogy can only be assumed to be relevant if one stretches the point. In any event, A. G. was assisted without either her or the therapist's discovering adequate reasons for the development of her behavior problems.

Although the technique of desensitization is of recent origin, success with other types of psychological disturbance have been reported. Of the 122 cases reported by Wolpe in 1954, 72 were classified as anxiety states, 9 hysterics, 10 depressives, 11 obsessional-compulsives, 3 neurasthenics, and 17 mixed. He obtained cures or marked improvements in 110 cases (90 per cent). Although a fuller discussion of the applicability of this therapy is provided elsewhere (Lazarus and Rachman, 1957), it seems safe to predict that phobias are particularly amenable to the desensitization technique.

## SUMMARY

The treatment by systematic desensitization psychotherapy of a 24-year-old female patient suffering from anxiety and phobic reactions is described in detail. Several points arising out of the case history, including the development of the neurotic behavior and the "spontaneous" recovery of sexual adequacy, are discussed.

## REFERENCES

KNIGHT, R. P. (1941) Evaluation of the results of psychoanalytic therapy. *Amer. J. Psychiat.*, **98**, 434.

LAZARUS, A. A., and RACHMANN, S. (1957). The use of systematic desensitization in psychotherapy. *South African Med. J.*, **32**, 934–937.

RACHMAN, S. (1958) Objective Psychotherapy: Some theoretical considerations. *South African Med. J.*, **33**, 19–21.

WILLOUGHBY, R. R. (1934) Norms for the Clarke-Thurstone Inventory. *J. Soc. Psychol.*, **5**, 91–97.

WOLPE, J. (1948) An approach to the problem of neurosis based on the conditioned response. Unpublished doctoral dissertation, Univ. of Witwatersrand.

WOLPE, J. (1950) Genesis of neurosis: An objective account. *South African Med. J.*, **24**, 613–617.

WOLPE, J. (1952a) Experimental neurosis as learned behavior. *Brit. J. Psychol.*, **43**, 243.

WOLPE, J. (1952b) Objective psychotherapy of the neurosis. *South African Med J.*, **26**, 825–829.

WOLPE, J. (1954) Reciprocal inhibition as the main basis of psychotherapeutic effects. *A.M.A. Arch. Neurol. Psychiat.*, **72**, 205–226.

# The Treatment of Chronic Frigidity
# by Systematic Desensitization

ARNOLD A. LAZARUS, PH.D.*†

THE TERM "frigidity" is associated with a wide range of conditions, most of which refer to female hyposexuality. Frigidity need not necessarily imply deficient sexual feeling or desire *per se*, since some women who are completely frigid in all heterosexual situations are capable of orgastic experience during masturbation. Apart from organic factors (which are responsible for a minority of symptoms in young women) frigidity may generally be regarded as a learned pattern of behavior, although some females are probably genetically unequipped to respond erotically. Frigid women may be placed on a continuum extending from those who basically enjoy coitus but fail to reach orgasm, to those for whom all sexual activities are anathema.

Acute but shortlived episodes of frigidity are not uncommon during or after pregnancy and lactation, defloration, physical illness, and during periods of psychological stress. Mild or temporary frigidity may also be due to faulty sex technique and a variety of misconceptions which may usually be corrected by appropriate instruction and information. The present paper deals with the treatment of recalcitrant and persistent cases of frigidity, many of which had failed to respond to the usual run of psychiatric techniques.

While the present discussion deals with frigidity as a specific psychosexual aberration, it must be understood that several psychopathological conditions are often heralded by or result in impaired sexual functioning (e.g. endogenous depression, schizophrenia).

The patients discussed in this paper were selected from numerous cases of frigidity in our records. Excluded from the present survey are all cases in whom varying degrees of frigidity were present as a minor part of a much broader neurotic or psychotic spectrum. The 16 patients who comprise the present sample all complained of frigidity as a monosymptomatic or primary disturbance. Of the present series, five patients had been referred by general practitioners, three were referred by gynecologists, one was referred by a

* This article is reprinted with the permission of the author and the editor from the *J. Nerv. Ment. Dis.*, **136**, 272 (1963).

† Department of Psychiatry and Mental Hygiene, Witwatersrand University Medical School, Johannesburg, South Africa.

71

psychiatrist, and seven had been recommended by previous patients. Cases were only accepted for therapy when medical reports excluded organic pathology. All were married. Their mean age was 24.6 years with a standard deviation of 3.8. Of the 16 women, nine had been married for two years or less, five had been married for approximately four years, and two were married for more than ten years. The majority had always found coitus to be meaningless, somewhat unpleasant or utterly repugnant.

The educational level of these patients varied considerably and ranged from three professional women (a doctor, a lawyer and a grades teacher) to several housewives with only two or three years of secondary schooling. The patients were reasonably homogeneous with regard to socio-economic status and may be described as fairly typical of middle class, urban, white South African women.

Two of the women stated that they had been highly promiscuous premaritally. They both claimed, however, that they had never derived any sexual satisfaction whatsoever. One of these patients had also been fairly active extramaritally. A previous therapist had convinced her that these sexual exploits were a search for erotic sensations which had always eluded her. This knowledge made no appreciable difference to her condition. The remaining patients maintained that their sexual activities had been confined to their marriage partners.

In attempting to delineate reasonably clear-cut areas of causation, it was found that the basic etiological factors were very diverse. In some cases, the problem seemed to emanate from faulty attitudes and misplaced sexual emphasis in childhood, which resulted in conditioned avoidance responses to sexual activities. Many patients showed evidence of early or recently acquired feelings of hostility and resentment towards men in general and/or their husbands in particular. Only in one case was there evidence of a traumatic etiology. A few patients were completely unable to offer any explanation for their symptoms. In some, the basic reasons were apparently uncovered during therapy (these insights, although comforting, appeared to bear little relationship to therapeutic outcome), whereas in others, the pattern of causality remained speculative or enigmatic. In one case, the entire problem amounted to a hypersensitivity to extraneous auditory stimuli and a high degree of distractibility. During sexual intercourse this patient would be excessively upset by the sound of a distant motor car, an imagined footstep, a leaking tap, or the like, whereupon she would experience violent dyspareunia.

A direct fear of pregnancy appeared to be the underlying cause of chronic frigidity in yet another case. "The so-called safe period is a myth . . . no contraceptive is infallible and I refuse to play around with hormones. . . I have a rheumatic heart and doctors have warned me not to have any children, so I regard sex as a pretty risky business." When the therapist suggested that the impasse might be remedied by means of surgery, the patient revealed a

basic phobia of doctors, hospital and anesthetics, and required desensitization*
along the latter dimension. She was consequently enabled to have a salping-
ectomy and subsequently experienced sexual satisfaction for the first time
in her life.

The sexual reluctance of one patient followed a severe monilia infection
which flared up during her honeymoon. She had irrationally attributed her
illness to sexual participation and was disinclined to expose herself to the
risk of further infection. It is worth noting that she had other mild obvious
hypochondriacal tendencies, which were treated concurrently with her sexual
problems.

The following excerpt, taken from a frigid patient's notes, provides a
graphic description of the attitudes of one of the most severe cases:

"I hate every single man on this earth, bitterly. I think they are all pigs—
some smaller, some bigger. When one looks at me in the street I could shoot
him with a water pistol full of vitriol. I hate women who enjoy sex. I think
they are just animals. I hate sexy books; they are filthy. I hate to see people
kissing; it makes me feel sick. I don't want to become one of them.

"I hurt my husband's feelings whenever I can. I think he is a pig too.
I don't want to have children. I would feel too much like an animal. I have
nightmares about men—in my dreams they are just pigs and animals. I hate
sex and everything that goes with it.

"When I have intercourse I feel like spitting. I can't stand my husband's
hands on me. When I have to go to bed with him and there is no way out I
feel trapped like an animal about to be slit open with a knife. I could strangle
him and kick him. I hate to see him look at other women. I want to shout at
him 'Animal, animal'. Men are all pigs; my father, my brothers, the whole
lot!"

On studying the life histories, psychodiagnostic test profiles and similar
detailed information which was routinely obtained in each case, it became
obvious that the patients were not a homogeneous group with regard to
temperament or personality makeup. Marked individual differences and
variations in background, training and temperament were clearly noted.
There was suggestive evidence, however, that the introverted patients (i.e.
persons with an E score of less than 15 on the Maudsley Personality Inventory[3]) generally displayed straightforward *anxiety* reactions to sexual
situations— "as soon as my husband approaches me in that way I literally
feel tense if not terrified"—whereas the highly extraverted patients (i.e.
those with an E score of 35 or more) tended to complain of vaginismus and
similar reactions of a probable *hysterical* variety.

* Systematic desensitization is a technique which was developed by Dr. Joseph
Wolpe.[12,13] It consists of presenting carefully graded situations, which are subjectively
noxious, to the imagination of a relaxed patient until the most personally distressing events
no longer evoke any anxiety. A brief account of this technique is provided in the section
on therapy.

All the patients had received some form of treatment for their condition before consulting the writer. Five had received detailed instruction from their family doctors concerning sex technique. Three were treated by means of hormonal injections and topical ointments. Three other patients had consulted marriage guidance counselors who had embarked on a course of reassuring discussions with both husband and wife, supplemented by a recommended list of books on sex hygiene. One of the patients had undergone four years of psychoanalysis. Two had visited psychiatrists at weekly intervals for approximately six months, and the remaining two patients had been treated by clinical psychologists for one year, and five months respectively.

## THERAPY

The present therapeutic program was based on the assumption that frigidity is usually the result of learned habits of anxiety relating to sexual participation. As in every effective system of therapy, the basic curative mechanism would then depend on unlearning the primary neurotic stimulus configuration.

The desensitization procedure [12, 13] has proved highly effective in treating diverse neurotic reactions where specific rather than "free-floating" anxiety is present.[5] This technique has also been used in groups[7] and adapted for child therapy programs.[6, 8] Bond and Hutchison[1] have successfully employed systematic desensitization in the treatment of exhibitionism, and Lazovik and Lang[10] have scrutinized the value of desensitization therapy under controlled laboratory conditions. Rachman[11] has provided an account of a 24-year-old female who had a phobia for injections, a fear of using internal sanitary pads, and who experienced pain and anxiety in sexual situations. The elimination, by desensitization, of her sanitary pad anxiety and the injection phobia effected an improvement in her sexual adjustment.

Briefly, the desensitization method involves the following three separate sets of operations:

1) The patient is taught the essentials of Jacobson's[4] progressive relaxation. This relaxation training program seldom extends over more than six interviews. (During the past year, however, the writer has relied extensively on a long playing phonograph record of which he is the co-author.[9])

2) Graded lists are drawn up of all the definable themes into which the patient's anxieties may be grouped. This construction of anxiety hierarchies implies that all important thematic elements which engender neurotic anxiety in the patient will be identified and properly ranked according to the degree of subjective disturbance aroused.

3) The anxiety-evoking items from the hierarchy are presented verbally to the imagination of the deeply relaxed patient, commencing with the "weakest" stimuli and gradually proceeding up the hierarchy to progressively "stronger" anxiety-arousing situations. New items are introduced only when

patients are able to picture their preceding scenes without experiencing anxiety. It is impressed upon patients that if any item proves upsetting or disturbing they must raise their left forefinger.

The easiest cases to handle were those in which the normal erotic interchange between male and female constituted the essential anxiety component. "My mother warned me to keep away from boys so often that I even feel guilty when my husband kisses me." A patient who depicted less generalization along this theme said, "I actually quite enjoy kissing and necking, but when it gets more serious than that I just feel myself freezing up". Desensitization in these cases proceeded along a hierarchy of more and more intimate physical and sexual interchanges. In the most severe cases, the graded repertoire of noxious situations had to commence with the most casual and innocent contacts between the sexes. The thought of a flirtatious glance or an ephemeral embrace initially produced observable anxiety reactions in two of the patients. The "mildest" case along this dimension was a patient who could accept coitus in the "normal" position, but whose husband's erotic gratification depended on varying the sexual positions. "Frankly, I think that my husband needs treatment. He behaves just like an animal."

This patient's aversion to postural variations during coitus apparently emanated from feelings of fear and disgust when, as a young girl on the farm, she had on occasion been forced to witness animals copulating. She reported that ever since then, the sight of "animals doing it in the street" upset her unduly. Systematic desensitization was accordingly administered along dimensions of distance and size—the nearer the animals the worse; the larger the animals the worse. As soon as she became impervious to sexual activities in animals, her own behaviour underwent a change. She became free from unnecessary inhibitions which had upset her sexual relationship. Significantly, this appeared to have consolidated her marriage and according to her husband, "saved a worthwhile marriage in the nick of time".

The patient whose sex life was undermined by real or imagined extraneous sounds responded well to desensitization methods. While hypnotically relaxed, she was asked to imagine increasingly disturbing sounds while conditions for sexual relations became less and less ideal. (As an example: "I want you to imagine that you and your husband are in Cape Town on holiday. While having intercourse you can clearly hear people walking and talking in the hotel corridor.") After 14 desensitization sessions she reported that she was able to "get lost in sex". At the time of writing, she has not experienced dyspareunia for over fifteen months.

A more detailed case presentation should lend greater clarity to some of the points outlined above.

Mrs. A, aged 24 years, had been married for two and one-half years, during which time she claimed to have had coitus on less than two dozen occasions. She always experienced violent dyspareunia during intercourse as well as "disgust and anxiety at the whole messy business". She could tolerate casual kissing and caressing without anxiety and at times found these experiences "mildly pleasant". The background to her problem was clearly one of puritanical upbringing, in which much emphasis was placed on the sinful qualities of carnal desire. Mrs. A's husband had endeavoured to solve their difficulties by providing his wife with books on sex techniques and practices. Mrs. A had obligingly read these works but her emotional reactions remained unchanged. She sought treatment of her own accord when she suspected that her husband had developed an extramarital attachment.

After diagnostic interviews and psychometric tests, systematic desensitization was administered according to the following hierarchy (the most disturbing items being at the head of the list):

1) Having intercourse in the nude while sitting on husband's lap.
2) Changing positions during intercourse.
3) Having coitus in the nude in a dining room or living room.
4) Having intercourse in the nude on top of a bed.
5) Having intercourse in the nude under the bed covers.
6) Manual stimulation of the clitoris.
7) Husband's fingers being inserted into the vagina during precoital love play.
8) Caressing husband's genitals.
9) Oral stimulations of the breasts.
10) Naked breasts being caressed.
11) Breasts being caressed while fully clothed.
12) Embracing while semi-clothed, being aware of husband's erection and his desire for sex.
13) Contact of tongues while kissing.
14) Having buttocks and thighs caressed.
15) Shoulders and back being caressed.
16) Husband caresses hair and face.
17) Husband kisses neck and ears.
18) Sitting on husband's lap, both fully dressed.
19) Being kissed on lips.
20) Being kissed on cheeks and forehead.
21) Dancing with and embracing husband while both fully clothed.

Variations in the brightness of lighting played a prominent part in determining the patients' reactions. After four desensitization sessions for instance, she was without anxiety able to visualize item 14 (having her buttocks and thighs caressed) if this was occurring *in the dark*. It required several additional treatments before she was able to tolerate this imagined intimacy under conditions of ordinary lighting.

The therapist asked Mrs. A's husband to make no sexual overtures to his wife during the period of treatment (to avoid *resensitization*). Mrs. A was desensitized three times a week over a period of less than three months.

When item 17 on the hierarchy had been successfully visualized without anxiety, Mrs. A "seduced" her husband one evening and found the entire episode "disgustingly pleasant". Thereafter, progress was extremely rapid, although the first two items were slightly troublesome and each required over 20 presentations before the criterion (a 30-sec exposure without signaling) was reached. A year later Mr. and Mrs. A both said that the results of therapy had remained "spectacularly effective".

## RESULTS

Of the 16 patients, nine were discharged as "sexually adjusted" after a mean of 28.7 sessions. (The mean time was somewhat inflated by one patient, who required more than 40 sessions.)

The remaining cases were regarded as failures. Patients were usually seen once a week, so that the average time period for successful therapy was just over six months. The majority of patients listed as failures usually terminated therapy on their own initiative after less than six sessions. It can safely be said that treatment was successful for every patient who underwent more than 15 sessions.

The nine recoveries were all cases in whom reasonably clear-cut areas of inhibition could be discerned, while the seven patients who reported no improvement were nearly all individuals in whom abstruse, pervasive or extreme attitudes prevailed. Some of them were inadequately motivated for therapy. Others, although evidently eager to overcome their sexual difficulties, were unable to produce sufficiently vivid images—an essential prerequisite for effective desensitization. It is worth noting that all the successful cases were undoubtedly dysthymic in character (i.e. having high scores on neuroticism and low scores on extraversion[2]).

The criterion for "cure" was an affirmative reply to each of the following three questions:

Do you look forward to sexual intercourse?

Do you nearly always reach an orgasm?

Do you ever initiate sexual activity?

Whenever possible, patient's husbands were interviewed separately and encouraged to express their opinions concerning the outcome and effects of our therapy. (In one case, statements of a patient who claimed to be cured after eight sessions were disputed by her husband: "She still treats me like a nasty dose of castor oil." The patient in question subsequently informed the therapist that her "cure" was confined to her participation in an extra-marital relationship, but as her lover could not be interviewed—and as she was a most unreliable witness—the patient was technically regarded as a therapeutic failure.)

Follow-up inquiries were conducted in four cases after fifteen months. Two reported additional post-therapeutic improvements in sexual pleasure and adjustment. One patient stated that she still had occasional phases of sexual indifference which seldom lasted for more than a fortnight. The fourth patient stated that she had remained sexually well-adjusted for approximately four months after therapy, until she became pregnant, at which stage she again found sexual intercourse "repugnant". A few months after the birth of her baby, four additional desensitization sessions were required to regain her previously acquired level of sexual participation and enjoyment.

## DISCUSSION

From a quantitative point of view, nine recoveries of 16 cases treated is anything but spectacular, but the writer knows of no other therapeutic approach which can achieve comparable results in the treatment of chronic frigidity.

Many frigid women condescend to have treatment in order to "please" their husbands. After their own subjective assessment of "a reasonable exposure to treatment," they terminate therapy and often utilize their own sexual disinclinations as a weapon to which they add reinforced post-therapeutic hostility. Similarly, in the masochistic female, displeasure and pain during sexual intercourse may in itself afford a certain measure of anxiety relief.

The ever-present possibility of homosexuality among frigid women should not be overlooked. One of the seven therapeutic failures spoke of "revolting but exciting adolescent interludes" with members of her own sex. Whereas she regularly achieved clitoral orgasms during masturbation, she described all heterosexual activities as "locally anesthetising". It is possible that undetected homosexual proclivities were present in some of the other therapeutic failures.

In evaluating the effectiveness of systematic desensitization in the present context, the coincidence of "manipulation" and effect was observed in the fact that in nine of 16 cases, clinical improvement occurred contemporaneously with the application of the method. It seems justifiable to conclude therefore, that in the treatment of frigidity, where specific or reasonably clear-cut fears inhibit sexual pleasure, systematic desensitization is the method of choice.

## SUMMARY

An account of various cases suffering from persistent frigidity precedes a discussion of the application of Wolpe's[12, 13] technique or systematic desensitization therapy. By employing this psychotherapeutic procedure, nine of 16 recalcitrant cases of frigidity were discharged as "sexually adjusted" after a mean of 28.7 sessions. Follow-up inquires strongly suggested the durability of this method and supported the conclusion that desensitization is the method of choice in those instances where specific anxieties underly patients' frigid responses.

## REFERENCES

1. BOND, I. K. and HUTCHINSON, H. C. (1960) Application of reciprocal inhibition therapy to exhibitionism, *Canad. Med. Ass. J.*, **83**, 23–25.
2. EYSENCK, H. J. (1947) *Dimensions of Personality*, Kegan Paul, London.
3. EYSENCK, H. J. (1959) *Manual of the Maudsley Personality Inventory*, University of London Press, London.
4. JACOBSON, E. (1938) *Progressive Relaxation*, Univ. of Chicago Press, Chicago.
5. LAZARUS, A. A. and RACHMAN (1957) The use of systematic desensitization in psychotherapy, *S. Afr. Med. J.*, **31**, 934–937.
6. LAZARUS, A. A. The elimination of children's phobias by deconditioning. In EYSENCK, H. J. ed. *Behaviour Therapy and the Neuroses*, Pergamon, New York, pp. 114–122.
7. LAZARUS, A. A. Group therapy of phobic disorders by systematic desensitization, *J. Abnorm. Soc. Psychol.*, **63**, 504–510.
8. LAZARUS, A. A. and ABRAMOVITZ, A. (1962) The use of "emotive imagery" in the treatment of children's phobias, *J. Ment. Sci.*, **108**, 191–195.
9. LAZARUS, A. A. and ABRAMOVITZ, A. (1962) *Learn to Relax*—a recorded course in muscular relaxation, Troubadour Records, Wolhuter, Johannesburg,
10. LAZOVIK, A. D. and LANG, P. J. (1960) A laboratory demonstration of systematic desensitization psychotherapy, *J. Psychol. Stud.*, **11**, 238.
11. RACHMAN, S. (1959) The treatment of anxiety and phobic reactions by systematic desensitization psychotherapy, *J. Abnorm. Soc. Psychol.* **58**, 259–263.
12. WOLPE, J. (1958) *Psychotherapy by Reciprocal Inhibition*, Stanford Univ. Press, Stanford.
13. WOLPE, J. (1961) The systematic desentizitation treatment of neuroses, *J. Nerv. Ment. Dis.*, **132**, 189–203.

# Application of Reciprocal Inhibition
# Therapy to Exhibitionism*

IAN K. BOND, M.D., D.PSYCH.†

and

HARRY C. HUTCHISON, M.A., PH.D.§

*Toronto*

THE THERAPEUTIC reconditioning techniques developed by Wolpe[2] and termed "reciprocal inhibition" therapy have been applied to a diversity of neurotic disorders. To our knowledge there are no reports of the use of these techniques with the sexual perversions of exhibitionism, overt homosexuality, or pedophilia. Explorations along these lines are being undertaken at the Forensic Clinic,†† and this paper seeks to provide a detailed account of their use in a case of exhibitionism.

Psychoanalytic theory[1] considers the act of exposing the genitals a defence against the fear of castration. Experience with these patients reveals that exposure either follows some environmental stress which constitutes a challenge to the patient's sense of adequacy, or is provoked by an encounter with a female of specified age and physical appearance (blond hair, plump legs, etc.). The exposure can be thought of as an instrumental act designed to reduce an anxiety response cued off by certain classes of stimuli, and as such, the systematic desensitization techniques described by Wolpe[2] would constitute an appropriate form of treatment.

The patient under consideration is a 25-year-old, married man of average intelligence (I.Q. 106). The elder of two boys, he recalls intense antagonism towards his brother dating from an early age. Ten years separated the two.

The parents are of Anglo-Saxon stock; artisan class, and quite puritanical in outlook. The patient reports them as domineering. He recalls his

* This article is reprinted with the permission of the author and the editor from *Can. Med. Assoc. J.* **83**, (1960). The authors have extended the original paper to include further follow-up material.

† Now staff psychiatrist, Ontario Hospital, Whitby.

§ Chief Psychologist, Forensic Services, Special Lecturer, Department of Psychology, University of Toronto.

†† Forensic Clinic, Toronto Psychiatric Hospital. Supported by the Mental Health Division of the Ontario Department of Health.

mother's early admonition against childish sexual practices which she described as "evil" and "nasty", and her frequent injuctions that he conceal his genitals from the view of females. An incident which increased his sexual guilt tremendously involved punishment by his mother for engaging in a contest with another boy to see how high up the side of a wall each could urinate. He recalls at this time feeling "hurt" by the observation that his friend's penis was the larger.

His first exposure occurred at 13 following sex play with a 10-year-old neighbour girl. He had felt a desire to perform coitus, but the girl appeared indifferent to his suggestion and had refused. Her indifference hurt him; this was followed by rage, then by the exposing of his erect penis to her. During an explanatory hypnotic interview he recalled having seen this same girl urinate some five years before this episode, and his experience of astonishment at the appearance of her genitals.

Throughout adolescence he suffered feelings of inadequacy and inferiority. His exhibitionism continued, and he indulged excessively in sexual daydreams and phallic auto-erotic practices. Mild asthma and peptic ulcer appeared at this time, but he has had no symptoms of these since reaching adulthood.

At age 15 he developed a practice which served as a substitute for exposing on occasions when he could not get out in the street. He would select single females from the telephone directory, call them, and attempt to engage them in lewd conversation. A period of voyeurism occurred at this time, but disappeared after his first frank view of the adult female genitals. By the late teens and early twenties, his exhibitionism had reached bizarre proportions. Tension was constant and it was not unusual for him to expose several times during the day.

A frequent practice was to hide completely nude in a small wooded area in the centre of the town where he then lived and spring out and expose himself to the first woman who passed. Another was to hide himself in the cloakroom of a girls' school, exposing himself to the first girl to use the lavatory. If the door was latched, he would lie on the floor and thrust his erect penis under the door for the occupant's view. While driving a car, he would entertain exposure fantasies of such intensity that his driving was a public danger. These fantasies led to turning up a side street to get out of the car and expose. Passing an attractive female when driving led to exposure also.

The stimuli leading to exhibiting in this patient consisted of attractive young females of adolescent or early adult years. They were typically sophisticated and "sexy" but of respectable appearance. Particularly compelling were shapely legs and ankles, clad in sheer nylons worn with high-heeled shoes. Well-developed breasts, a trim waist and generous hips provided strong provocation also. Prostitutes or girls in bathing suits were innocuous stimuli. Fantasies of exposing to females with the appropriate attributes would lead to exhibiting.

The attack of exhibitionism was described by the patient as being preceded by a feeling of sexual excitement and dread. He would experience "a grim determination to expose, come what might". He would become tense and an erection would occur. At this time things would seem unreal, "as if watching myself doing something in a dream". He would then expose to the female usually but not always, masturbating. When the girl registered shock, "the spell would be broken" and he would flee, trembling and remorseful. His wife, often present during such an attack, described his appearance as one of being "paralyzed, with glazed eyes". On such occasions she could prevent his exhibiting only by forcefully dragging him away.

There was one interesting period of abstinence from acting out. At the age of 18 he became involved with a girl he hoped to marry and had sexual relations with her. He did not expose for six months, although his urges remained very strong. Eventually he succumbed to his urges, was apprehended, and lost the girl. At the age of 23 when courting his wife he refrained from exhibiting for two months. His exposures occurred unabated just before marriage and immediately afterwards, however. Visits to prostitutes had no effect. He would frequently expose a short distance from the brothel he had just left.

The patient's police record indicated 24 charges of indecent exposure and 11 convictions with nine prison sentences of from four months to one year.

Previous treatment had included individual and group psychotherapy and $CO_2$ abreaction therapy conducted over an 18-month period at a reformatory clinic. He had received a few weeks of individual psychotherapy and 10 months of group psychotherapy at the Forensic Clinic. During this period he wore a "chastity belt" which he decided to have made by a prosthetics manufacturer to prevent his exhibiting. His wife locked the belt in the morning and unlocked it at night. The treatment was interrupted by a conviction for indecent assault. While wearing the belt, the patient had attempted to grasp the legs and breasts of a young woman he saw in a crowd.

After his release from imprisonment for this offence, the patient sought help from a lay hypnotist. He attended four sessions, accompanied by his wife, and was given relaxation suggestions and moralistic exhortations. He found the latter useless and annoying, but he claimed some benefit from the relaxation suggestions. He renewed contact with the Forensic Clinic, and after consideration of the case, it was decided to attempt a form of reciprocal inhibition therapy. The treatment technique was discussed with the patient, who was willing to attempt anything that might help him, and it was arranged that he would attend four sessions per week, with the stipulation that his wife would continue to accompany him to avoid exposure, arrest, and interruption of treatment.

In Wolpe's[2] description of systematic desensitization of anxiety patients, the therapist establishes, initially, a hierarchy of stimulus situations in terms of their anxiety-provoking potential. Training is given in relaxation of the skeletal musculature, and while hypnosis may be used to induce such relaxation, its use is unnecessary in one who can relax readily. In a deeply relaxed state, the patient is called upon to visualize a scene which incorporates the mildest of the anxiety-provoking situations. The deep relaxation, which is anxiety-inhibiting, is thus paired with the anxiety-provoking stimulus, and after a series of presentations, anxiety ceases to dominate as a response to that situation. The next most provoking stimulus situation is dealt with in a similar manner, and the next in turn as the former ceases to become effective in provoking anxiety.

From the content of the interview in this case, the therapist established a rough hierarchy of exposure-provoking stimuli in terms of type of female, her physical attributes, and place of exposure. It is interesting to note that when the patient returned to the scene of a previous exposure, this was sufficient to elicit strong exhibitionist urges.

In the first session, the patient was relaxed by suggestions given while in a light hypnotic state. The therapist then described one of the milder situations conducive to exhibiting. A rapid mounting of tension was apparent at first. The procedure was repeated three times in the first session. After this session, the patient was instructed to practice relaxation at home, using the word "relax" as a cue for the appropriate postural adjustments. Subsequent sessions were similar to the first, with the exception that the more provoking situations were presented in progression.

After twelve sessions the patient was sent home with his wife by way of a nearby department store. These premises were replete with young women of the type to whom he usually could not resist exposing. When he arrived for the next session, he reported an involuntary relaxation when passing some of the women he had encountered. With two he did not relax involuntarily, and he used the word "relax" to initiate the process. With one woman he was unable to relax, but retained sufficient control to turn his back to her and this permitted him to recover.

The patient's wife was bedridden with duodenal ulcer for the eighth session, but he came alone and returned home without event. During the next week he went out alone to seek employment. His quest was unsuccessful and this, coupled with his wife's illness, resulted in despondency. On passing a small park, he decided to enter it and expose. He unbuttoned his trousers and hid behind a clump of bushes. But when a girl approached he went into a state of involuntary relaxation and lost his erection. He then adjusted his clothing and continued on his way, "feeling foolish".

From this point, improvement was rapid. His exhibitionistic urges became weaker and less frequent and he felt quite confident of his ability to handle them. As his sexual fantasies diminished, exhibiting was involved in them to a much lesser degree. The patient was able to engage in mixed group activities without tension for the first time, and he astonished his wife by attending a party and dancing with women attired in low-cut gowns. After the party, rather than experiencing tension and desire to expose, he felt "relaxed and at peace". Sexually he became more virile and he reported considerable enjoyment in his sex-relationships with his wife.

After 20 sessions, an unusual event occurred. He was at home, alone, and had an urge to telephone a female in order to engage her in prurient conversation, a practice he had given up four years previously. The urge was relatively weak, and he called his wife at her work and indulged in amorous discussions. This behaviour did not alarm the patient, and he felt no urge to repeat this activity.

It was decided to terminate treatment after the 20th session. The patient continued practising relaxation at home. In following up contacts over the next month, thoughts of exposing were reported as occurring about once per week in very mild form. However, one day while walking through a department store he found himself stimulated by a young female. He followed her for a time; then another, and another, finding his excitement increasing. After three hours of following women shoppers through the store and masturbating through his trouser pocket, he arrived in the lingerie department. He then exposed in what was for him an uncharacteristic manner: he was unable to achieve an erection; he felt no urge to speak to the woman to whom he exposed; nor did he look to observe the effect he had upon her. He did not try to escape, and was arrested.

The court was lenient, and the patient was returned to the Clinic for treatment. This was resumed on a once-weekly basis by the second writer.

However, four sessions after this exposure, while walking up the street in broad daylight, he felt an uncontrollable urge to look up the skirts of a woman who was standing at a bus stop. He carried out the act and was promptly arrested. Once again the court returned the patient to the Clinic. Systematic desensitization to females was continued on a once-weekly basis for 5 months, and the patient, on reporting that he was free of symptoms, was terminated with a once-monthly follow-up arrangement. A total of 46 sessions had been completed at this time.

Following cessation of treatment, the patient was completely free of symptoms for a period of 13 months. He obtained heavy manual employment with a municipal agency, and, although slight of stature, earned a permanent staff position and a promotion within six months. During the period of the follow-up, he commented on how the lewd jokes told by his fellow-workmen had no effect upon him, although they would have "set him off on a rampage before". Social and sexual adjustment was excellent.

Ten months after termination of treatment, he was called into the municipal office by the personnel officer, informed that the nature of his past offences was known, and he was summarily dismissed from employment.

This experience was disheartening to him. He was unable to find employment, and within a month was under severe financial stress. The therapist suggested a resumption of treatment, but the patient expressed the wish to carry on without treatment to see whether his symptoms returned. Two months later, thirteen months after his last sexual offence, the patient was refused financial assistance in a welfare office. He left the building feeling depressed. He saw a woman on the street and found himself following her. She went into an office building and eventually to a washroom. The patient followed her inside, with urges to look under the door and perhaps expose as he had done in the past. The woman had heard him enter, and she shouted in alarm, frightening the patient away. He felt that these urges were on the borderline of control, and he castigated himself for this episode. However, a week later, still in dire financial straits, as he passed by the door of an office building where he had exposed in the past, he felt an urge which he acted on again. He went in the building to a locker-room and exposed to a woman whose back was turned to him. He made good his escape without the woman knowing of his presence. The third incident in the series occurred when he was passing the building of the first incident on his way to the welfare office. He entered and went to the same washroom. As he entered, a woman screamed. He ran, and was apprehended. When interviewed by the therapist regarding these three incidents, he observed that he was in no danger of exposing to women on the street or in department stores (the setting of the desensitization sessions) but that women's washrooms made him tense and excited, and that a woman in the washroom was a strong provocation.

The case presents certain interesting features. As noted at the outset, two broad classes of stimuli initiate the exhibitionistic response in the writers' experience with such cases; situations involving a threat to the adequacy of the individual; and females of specified age and appearance. There are of course individual differences in the matter of the relative strength of these two classes of stimuli.

In the case reported here, the stimulus of the female seemed the obvious point of attack, and the writers addressed their efforts to this hierarchy to exclusion of others. This was successful in that provocative females in public places as for example streets, parks, or department stores, ceased to be effective stimuli insofar as initiation of tension concerned. Situations giving rise to feelings of inadequacy were ignored, and these were allowed to retain their strength, as had weaker stimuli of washrooms which had been associated with the stimulus complex on previous instances of exposure. Under conditions which favoured the summation of these stimuli, the patient was rendered prone to exposure. A thorough application of Wolpe's technique would have consisted of establishing a complete inventory of the situations in which the patient had exposed or had experienced urges, followed by a progressive desensitization of all the stimulus hierarchies represented. This is being carried out at the time of writing.

While this case demonstrates the value of systematic desensitization technique in the treatment of exhibitionism of a non-psychotic type, it should be noted that other forms of reciprocal inhibition therapy might be more suitable in a particular case. In a more recent and less severe case than that reported here, although similarly resistive to group or individual therapy, exposure followed a slowly mounting tension which was initiated by situations giving rise to feelings of inadequacy. The second writer spent but 26 sessions in teaching the patient to relax to a verbal cue whenever he felt his tension mounting. Over a 22 month follow-up, he has never been in danger of exposing.

While single case presentations of the kind offered here are usually interesting and often instructive, what is required is an amassing of results with the technique over a wide range of severity of exhibitionistic conditions, coupled with appropriate comparisons of results with patients who have been treated by conventional methods. This may well prove reciprocal inhibition techniques the treatment of choice in exhibitionism.

## REFERENCES

1. LORAND, A. S. and BALINT, M. eds. (1956) *Perversions: Psychodynamics and Therapy*, Random House, New York.
2. WOLPE, J. D. (1954) *A.M.A. Arch. Neurol. Psychiat.*, **72**, 205.

# Group Therapy of Phobic Disorders by Systematic Desensitization*†

### Arnold A. Lazarus

*Psychiatric Unit, Witwatersrand University Medical School*

THE INCREASING demands for psychological and psychiatric services dictate the need for effective short-term therapeutic techniques and the extension of the existing services. Consequently, group techniques have grown in clinical stature, and the past decade has witnessed the development of numerous divergent procedures. A most promising variety of short-term therapy is Wolpe's (1958) system of "reciprocal inhibition", by which he achieved the recovery of 188 out of 210 neurotic cases in an average of 34·8 sessions.

A double economy can be achieved by combining the advantages of Wolpe's (1958) expedient clinical procedures with the additional time- and effort-saving properties of group therapy. This paper describes the adaptation of Wolpe's most important therapeutic procedure—the technique of systematic desensitization based on relaxation—to the group treatment of phobic disorders. In addition, the therapeutic effects of group desensitization were compared with more conventional forms of interpretive group psychotherapy on matched pairs of phobic subjects.

## METHOD

### General Procedure

The sample consisted of 35 middle-class urban white South Africans who were handicapped by phobic disorders.§ Social class membership was defined in terms of education, vocation, and income. There were 7 university graduates, 16 matriculants, and 12 patients

* This article is reprinted with the permission of the author and the editor from *J. Abnorm. Soc. Psychol.* **63**, 504–510 (1961).

† This paper is an outline of the experimental section of a thesis entitled "New Group Techniques in the Treatment of Phobic Conditions", which was accepted by the University of the Witwatersrand in December 1960, for the degree of Doctor of Philosophy.

§ The sample was not drawn from psychiatric hospitals or institutions as it was felt that extraneous variables would be introduced. Since the rules of the South African Psychological Association forbid registered psychologists to advertise in the press, the patients were obtained with the generous aid of friends and colleagues who made announcements at lectures and contacted their own associates.

with at least 3 years of secondary schooling. Apart from 3 professional women, the majority of female patients were housewives whose husband's average earnings were the equivalent of $550 a month. The mean income for the rest of the group was approximately $600 a month. In all, there were 12 men and 23 women, the mean age being 33·2 years with a standard deviation of 9·87.

The entire group included 11 acrophobics, 15 claustrophobics, 5 impotent men (treated as suffering from sexual phobia), and a mixed group of 4 phobic patients. The latter comprised a girl with a fear of sharp objects, a man with a fear of physical violence, a woman who was afraid to be a passenger in a moving vehicle, and a woman with a phobia for dogs.

The basic experimental design was to compare group desensitization therapy with more conventional methods of group treatment (or therapy based on "group dynamics"). The group desensitization technique consisted of systematically counterposing by relaxation graded lists of anxiety evoking stimuli which the separate groups of patients were asked to imagine.

The efficacy of group desensitization was first compared with group interpretation. The same therapist (the investigator) conducted all the therapeutic groups.

The initial comparison was made on a group of five acrophobic patients, two of whom received desensitization therapy, and three who were treated by interpretive group procedures.

Throughout the experiment, pairs of phobic patients were matched in terms of sex, age (within a 4-year range), and the nature and objective severity of the phobic disorders. A coin was tossed to decide whether a given member of each matched pair would be treated by desensitization therapy or by group interpretation. Extra (unmatched) individuals were always placed in the interpretive groups because it is generally agreed that these groups require a minimum of three members (Corsini, 1957).

When, after six sessions, treatment with the acrophobic groups was well under way, the next group (five impotent men) was selected and similarly subdivided into two additional groups, treated by desensitization and interpretation, respectively.

Three months later, the group of six claustrophobic patients was selected and equally subdivided to form a third separate desensitization-interpretation comparison.

Thus, at the end of 6 months, a total of seven patients had received group desensitization and nine had been treated by group interpretation.

Seven months later, additional acrophobic and claustrophobic patients were obtained in order to investigate the effects of relaxation per se. It was hypothesized that individuals who received training in relaxation at the end of each interpretive session would show a greater diminution of phobic reactions than those patients who had been treated solely by group interpretation. The suggestion that interpretation-plus-relaxation might be more effective than desensitization was also tested.

Accordingly, an additional six acrophobic patients were equally divided into two matched groups, the one receiving desensitization therapy and the other receiving interpretation-plus-relaxation. The latter group was trained in an accelerated version of Jacobson's (1938) progressive relaxation for about 15 min at the end of each interpretive therapeutic discussion.

A few weeks later, an additional nine claustrophobic patients were similarly subdivided. Group desensitization was administered to four patients and group interpretation-plus-relaxation was applied to five.

Finally, the mixed phobic group was treated by desensitization in order to determine whether desensitization could be successfully applied to a heterogeneous phobic group.

Thus, group desensitization was applied to 18 patients; group interpretation was applied to 9 patients, and 8 patients were treated by group interpretation-plus-relaxation.

## Selection of Phobic Patients

Although there were numerous volunteers for inclusion in the investigation, only those people whose phobias imposed a severe limitation on their social mobility, jeopardized their interpersonal relationships, or hindered their constructive abilities were admitted to the therapeutic groups.

Several people who were greatly handicapped by phobic disorders were excluded because they had received previous psychiatric treatment, ranging from psychoanalysis to electroconvulsive therapy. These people were given individual treatment in order to avoid ambiguity concerning the effects of the therapeutic groups.

The character and severity of the phobias were assessed in the following manner: Patients reporting acrophobic symptoms were privately and individually required to climb a metal fire escape. The experimenter climbed the stairs directly behind the patients and urged them to see how high they could climb. Few of the patients were able to proceed higher than the first landing (approximately 15–20 feet from ground level). The patients who were admitted to the acrophobic groups were all able to achieve a pretherapeutic height of between 15 and 25 feet.

Similarly, patients with claustrophobic traits were admitted individually into a well-ventilated cubicle with large French windows which opened on to a balcony. The patient sat facing the open windows. To the left of the patient was a movable screen which could be pushed as far as the center of the cubicle, thus, creating a sensation of space constriction. The patients were told that the experimenter would first shut the French windows and then proceed to push the screen towards the centre of the room. They were urged to remain in the cubicle for as long as possible and to reopen the windows only when they felt that the need for air had become unbearable. Most of the patients showed visible signs of discomfort as soon as the windows were shut, and no one was able to tolerate the screen at a distance of less than 20 inches.

Detailed information regarding the purpose of the investigation was withheld from the patients to avoid possible prejudice to the results. They were merely informed that the experimenter was conducting research into the alleviation of phobic disorders by group methods.

Apart from the initial screening procedures, individual contact with the patients was avoided in order to exclude the influence of any additional therapeutic factors. It is thought, for instance, that history taking and psychometric investigations may in themselves be therapeutic. In order to determine the value of group therapy *per se*, it was considered necessary to eliminate as many of these extraneous variables as possible. Attention was deliberately focused, therefore, on the specific techniques under investigation, avoiding the use of any supplementary measures which might facilitate therapeutic progress. For instance, in clinical practice it is customary to precede the application of systematic desensitization by a brief outline of the theoretical rationale behind the technique. Since it could be argued that this practice has a direct bearing on the results, the patients were directly desensitized without any preliminary explanation.

## Group Desensitization

Anxiety hierarchies (graded lists of stimuli to which the patients reacted with unadaptive anxiety) were constructed (Wolpe, 1958). In preparing these hierarchies, the experimenter extracted common elements from remarks which individual patients wrote on the questionnaires they filled out, and a group hierarchy was constructed. It must be emphasized that the hierarchical situations were imaginary ones, listed on paper and presented only symbolically to the patients.

The acrophobic group hierarchy, for example, consisted of the following situations: looking down from a very high building, seeing films taken from an airplane, looking down from a height of 80–100 feet, looking down a well, sitting high up on a grandstand during a football game, looking down from a 60-foot balcony, sitting on a narrow ledge at a height of 60 feet with a safety net a few feet away, looking down from a height of about 55 feet, seeing someone jump from a 50-foot diving board, sitting on a wide ledge about 35 feet from the ground, looking down from a height of approximately 20 feet, looking down from a height of about 10 feet.

The claustrophobic group hierarchy consisted of 16 situations ranging from "sitting in a large and airy room with all the windows open", to "sitting in front of an open fire in a small room with the doors and windows shut". The group hierarchy applied to the impotent men contained 10 items referring to progressively intimate sexual situations requiring increasing amounts of initiative.

The first therapeutic session was devoted entirely to training the patients in intensive muscular relaxation. At the end of the session, the patients were instructed to practise specific relaxation exercises for about 15 min morning and night.

The second session was held 3 days later, when further training in relaxation was provided. Towards the end of this session, desensitization commenced with the presentation (in imagination) of the two weakest items of the relevant anxiety hierarchy. The acrophobic patients, for example, were first told to picture themselves looking out of a window about 10 feet from the level of the street. It was impressed upon them that if any scene proved upsetting or disturbing, they were to indicate this by raising their left hand When any patient signaled in this manner, the scene was "withdrawn" immediately.

When the two least disturbing items in the relevant anxiety hierarchy had been presented, each of the patients was asked to report on the clarity of the imagined scenes and their accompanying levels of disturbance. The second session ended after the patients had been told to practise relaxation twice daily for periods of about 10 min.

The subsequent desensitization sessions followed a set pattern. The therapist named the various muscle groups to be relaxed. When a deep level of relaxation was reached, the patients were presented with successive items from the hierarchical series. The desensitization procedure was conducted at the pace of the "slowest" (i.e. most anxious) subject.

The third session was terminated only when all the patients were able to tolerate an exposure of about 10 sec to the first three items on the hierarchy without signaling anxiety. Thereafter, new items were introduced only when a 10-sec tolerance to the preceding item had been achieved. It took several sessions before the entire group was able to visualize a given item for as long as 10 sec without one or another member's signaling some disturbance.

Apart from occasional restlessness in those who were ready for more "difficult" anxiety items but who were constantly re-exposed to stimuli which they had long since mastered, no harm seemed to ensue from proceeding at a pace that was obviously too slow for part of the group. On the other hand, experience has shown that too rapid a pace can prove extremely antitherapeutic and lead to increased levels of anxiety.

Therapy in the desensitization groups was terminated when the final item on the hierarchy was tolerated by the patients for 10 sec without signaling. Patients often reported a marked amelioration of their phobic responses when the anxiety hierarchies were only half completed. It was insisted that each member would nevertheless have to undergo desensitization of the entire hierarchy in order to consolidate and reinforce their therapeutic gains.

The treatment of the claustrophobic groups was conducted out of doors. The patients in the mixed phobic group were handed the items of their relevant anxiety hierarchies on slips of paper. Here, the relaxation procedure adopted was as previously outlined, but instead of describing the items, the therapist handed a typewritten anxiety scene to each group member and instructed him to read the description of the scene, to close his eyes and to try to imagine the situation with tranquility. The patients were instructed to signal in the usual manner when a given situation became disturbing, and then immediately to stop imagining the scene and to continue relaxing. After about 10 sec, all the patients were told to stop picturing the scene and remain relaxed. Those who had successfully imagined their item without undue disturbance were then handed a new anxiety situation. In this manner, each group member was able to proceed at his own pace. No more than two successive items were presented at any one session.

## Group Interpretation

The approach used in the interpretive groups was a form of insight therapy with re-educative goals (Wolberg, 1954). Leadership was basically democratic, and the therapist's primary role was that of a participant observer. The groups passed through two phases: First, there was an introductory period during which the group situation was structured with the emphasis on a free and permissive emotional atmosphere. Feelings of initial tension and reticence were dealt with by open discussion, emphasizing group tolerance and acceptance and clarifying numerous misconceptions. Second, descriptions of phobic symptoms preceded intensive discussions which focused attention on emotions and on current interpersonal relationships. The emphasis shifted from a situational to a personal exploration. A considerable amount of historical data emerged and frequently provided abreactive and cathartic responses. The recall of forgotten memories was often accompanied by violent emotional reactions.

The group of impotent men displayed a high degree of empathy for one another, and frequently expressed feelings of hostility and resentment towards the therapist. These feelings were accepted by him and clarified for the patients; they were followed by discussions of the effects of frustration.

At the end of each session, the therapist provided a summary of the proceedings. He attempted not only to recapitulate the remarks of the subjects and to reflect back to the group the emotional significance of their statements, but also to suggest possible connections between their symptoms and their feelings. Interpretive remarks dealt mainly with possible motives behind the façade of manifest behavior. Premature interpretations were vigilantly avoided. Obvious rationalizations, as well as statements of overprotesta-tion, were challenged by the therapist only when he sensed a readiness on the part of the group.

Both the interpretive groups and the desensitization sessions were usually conducted three times a week. The desensitization groups were disbanded when all the patients were able to tolerate the most severe anxiety producing stimulus in the hierarchy without undue disturbance.

Members of the interpretive groups were given the same number of sessions as the corresponding desensitization groups. Since very few patients recovered from their phobias by means of the interpretive procedures, the ones whose phobic symptoms persisted were provided with an opportunity of undergoing group desensitization. (There were too few desensitization failures to satisfy the minimum numerical requirements for comparable interpretive groups.) Although the main response was an immediate willingness to introduce the "different group technique", the group of impotent men decided to continue employing interpretive procedures a while longer. Group desensitization was then administered to those patients who were not rendered symptom-free by the interpretive methods.

## RESULTS

### Assessment of Recovery

One month after therapy had terminated, the acrophobic and claustrophobic patients who claimed to have recovered from their phobias were required to undergo additional stress tolerance tests.

The acrophobic subjects were required to climb to the third landing of a fire escape (a height of about 50 feet). From the third story, they were required to go by elevator with the experimenter to the roof garden, eight stories above street level, and then to count the number of passing cars for 2 min.

The claustrophobic subjects were required to remain in the cubicle with the French windows shut and the movable sreen a few inches away. Those who were able to endure the situation with no apparent distress for 5 min were regarded as recoveries, provided that they were also able to present satisfactory evidence that they were no longer handicapped in their life situations. The tests were conducted individually in the presence of a witness.

With two exceptions, all the patients who stated that they had recovered from their phobias were able to face the tolerance tests with outward tranquility, although some of the acrophobic patients later admitted that they had felt "a trifle anxious" when looking down from the edge of the roof garden.

Neither the impotent men nor the members of the mixed phobic group were objectively tested.

The most rigorous criteria were used in assessing therapeutic results. For instance, only those patients who displayed and unambiguous post-therapeutic freedom from their respective phobic disorders were classified as recoveries. These criteria were, of course, essentially symptomatic. If a claustrophobic patient for instance, was still unable after therapy to visit the cinema for fear of suffocation, his treatment was considered a failure, regardless of any *ex parte* testimony to the contrary. Merely to enable a patient to "accept his neurosis" or to achieve a so-called "personality reintegration" without symptomatic relief was considered not good enough. Recovery from a phobic condition implies total neutrality or indifference to the formerly anxiety generating stimulus constellation. The present study made no provision for moderate or slight improvements. The latter were all classified as failures.

*Statistical Analysis of the Results*

Results are summarized in Table 1. As shown, there were 13 recoveries and 5 failures for desensitization, 2 recoveries and 15 failures for other forms of treatment. The resulting chi square is 10·69, which is highly significant ($p < 0.01$).

Additional statistical comparisons were computed for the matched pairs of acrophobic and claustrophobic patients who received group desensitization or group interpretation, respectively. There was a total of five matched pairs in these groups. Both members remained unimproved in one pair; in four, the desensitization patients recovered but the interpretation cases failed. There were no pairs in which both recovered or in which only interpretive methods succeeded. By applying the null hypothesis that the two methods are equally effective, the probability of obtaining this result is 0·0625.

In the case of the impotent men, no matching was carried out. Fisher's (1946, p. 97) exact test, which gave a probability of 0·1, was employed for testing significance. When the two probabilities, 0·0625 and 0·1, were

TABLE 1

*Number of patients assigned to each condition and the therapeutic outcome*

| Patients | Treated by desensi- tization | Re- covered | Treated by interpre- tation | Re- covered | Treated by inter- pretation and relaxation | Re- covered |
|---|---|---|---|---|---|---|
| Acrophobics | 5 | 4 | 3 | 0 | 3 | 1 |
| Claustro- phobics | 7 | 4 | 3 | 0 | 5 | 1 |
| Impotence | 2 | 2 | 3 | 0 | – | – |
| Mixed group | 4 | 3 | – | – | – | – |
| Total | 18 | 13 | 9 | 0 | 8 | 2 |

combined (Fisher 1946, p. 99), the resulting level of significance was 0·03, favoring desensitization.

It is interesting to note that when comparisons were made between the matched pairs of acrophobic and claustrophobic patients who received group desensitization as opposed to group interpretation-plus-relaxation, the level of significance in favor of desensitization was only 12·5 per cent. There were three matched pairs in which desensitization proved successful and interpretation-plus-relaxation failed. There were no cases where group inter-pretation plus-relaxation succeeded while group desensitization failed. Both methods failed with three matched pairs and both methods succeeded with one matched pair.

Since a significance level of 12·5 per cent falls outside the conventional limits, the obvious conclusion is that there is no evidence of differences bet-ween the desensitization and interpretation-plus-relaxation conditions. Of course, seven matched pairs provided one with little leverage and the stati-stical analysis of such a small number cannot be conclusive. It is worth noting, however, that of the six individuals who were initially unsuccessfully treated by interpretation-plus-relaxation, four later recovered from their phobias after a mean of 9·8 group desensitization sessions.

Of the total of 15 patients who had derived no apparent benefit from the interpretive procedures, 10 recovered from their phobias after a mean of 10·1 group desensitization sessions, as compared with the mean of 20·4 sessions which were necessary for effective group desensitization when only this procedure was employed.

*Follow-up Studies*

Follow-up studies were conducted by means of the following question-naire:

1. Has your original phobic disorder returned?
2. If you have had a relapse, is it slight, moderate, or severe?
3. Since receiving treatment have you developed any new symptoms? (If so, please elaborate.)
4. Please underline all the following complaints which apply to you:
Tension Depression Anxiety Palpitations
Dizziness Insomnia Nightmares Headaches
Tremors Sexual problems Fatigue Stomach
trouble Other symptoms (specify)
5. Please indicate whether any of the above complaints commenced *after* your participation in the therapeutic groups.
6. Are you still handicapped in any area of your daily living? (Specify.)
7. Have you consulted another therapist?

The duration of after-study history varied from group to group, and ranged from 15 months to 1·5 months with a mean of 9·05 months. All those subjects whose follow-up reports revealed even slight phobic recurrences were considered to have relapsed. Particular attention was devoted to the question of possible symptom substitution, but no evidence of this phenomenon was encountered.

When the follow-up evaluations were taken into account, 10 of the 13 patients who had recovered by means of group desensitization still maintained their freedom from phobic symptoms. Thus, 3 patients were regarded as having relapsed.

Of the 2 patients who had recovered after undergoing group interpretation-plus-relaxation, 1 maintained his recovery.

Eight of the 10 patients who recovered after undergoing post-interpretive group desensitization maintained recovery.

*Summary of Findings*

Group desensitization was applied to 18 patients of whom 13 initially recovered and three subsequently relapsed.

Group interpretation was applied to 9 patients. There were no recoveries in this group.

Group interpretaion-plus-relaxation was applied to 8 patients of whom 2 recovered and 1 subsequently relapsed.

The 15 patients who had not benefited from the interpretive procedures were then treated by group desensitization. There were 10 recoveries of whom 2 subsequently relapsed:

## DISCUSSION

Wolpe (1958) has expressed the basis of his "reciprocal inhibition" therapy as follows.

If a response incompatible with anxiety can be made to occur in the presence of anxiety-evoking stimuli so that it is accompanied by a complete or partial suppression of the anxiety-responses, the bond between these stimuli and the anxiety-responses will be weakened.

His method of systematic desensitization based on relaxation incorporates Jacobson's (1938) finding that muscular relaxation inhibits anxiety and that their concurrent expression is physiologically impossible.

The deliberate use of the parasympathetic accompaniments of skeletal muscular relaxation to inhibit neurotic anxieties reciprocally may be termed "specific reciprocal inhibition". There is, however, a broad range of stimuli which have *nonspecific* properties for inhibiting neurotic responses reciprocally. The more usual clinical medium of verbal interchange, for instance, may in itself bring about the incidental or nonspecific reciprocal inhibition of neurotic responses. In other words, it is postulated that *interview situations* can sometimes evoke autonomic responses similar to those of deep muscle relaxation.

The fact that far fewer sessions were required to desensitize those subjects in the present sample who had previously received interpretive therapy may be explicable by the notion that interpretive group situations evoked appropriate emotional responses in most of the subjects to inhibit some of their anxieties. In other words, it is probable that some of the anxiety responses evoked by the group discussions underwent a measure of nonspecific reciprocal inhibition. Furthermore, those patients who received post-interpretive group desensitization had the advantage of having established a therapeutic relationship with the experimenter. It is postulated that "the therapeutic atmosphere of empathy and acceptance may in itself reciprocally inhibit neurotic anxieties" (Lazarus, 1959).

It should be mentioned that the interpretive groups apparently enabled many of the patients to achieve a constructive modification of their self-evaluation, often clarified their evaluation of others, and enhanced their potentialities of interpersonal integration. These gains, however, appeared to have little bearing on their phobic symptoms, which usually persisted until desensitization procedures were administered.

The comparatively high relapse rate in the present series is probably related to the fact that the treatment was rather narrowly confined to a single range of stimuli which could in some cases have been a small part of a broad constellation, other elements of which may have afforded additional and possibly more useful bases for desensitization. In a proper clinical setting, the group desensitization procedures would have been preceded by individual history taking and the compilation of detailed clinical information for use either individually or in the group situations. Consequently, the conditions for the application of desensitization therapy were far less than optimum, a point which suggests that the experimental outcomes are only minimally indicative of the utility of this therapeutic approach to phobic symptoms.

The concept of "experimenter bias" is a relevant consideration in any study of this kind. It is difficult to determine the extent to which the present results were influenced by the therapist's theoretical affiliations. In terms of subjective interest, however, it should be noted that the experimenter's preferences were decidedly in favor of the interpretive methods. Fortunately, the ennui which is generated while applying desensitization procedures is adequately offset by the gratifying results.

If another therapist had treated the interpretive groups, a significant difference in the results might merely have reflected the superiority of the individual therapist rather than the methods employed. The treatment of phobias by interpretive methods, however, is well known to be difficult. Curran and Partridge (1955), for instance, state that "phobic symptoms are notoriously resistant to treatment, and their complete removal is rarely achieved". Similar views are expressed by Maslow and Mittelmann (1951), Henderson and Gillespie (1955), and Mayer-Gross, Slater, and Roth (1955). By contrast, phobias respond to desensitization exceedingly well (Eysenck, 1960; Lazarus and Rachman, 1957; Wolpe, 1958). It is contended, therefore, that the superior results achieved by group desensitization are not a function of the therapist's disproportionate skills (or unconscious prejudices) but a reflection of the intrinsic value of desensitization *per se* in the treatment of phobic disorders.

The point may legitimately be raised as to whether desensitization achieves any result other than the elimination of the phobic symptom. Comments on the general repercussions of desensitization are not possible in the context of the present study. No attempt was made to study changes in personality or general adaptation. Many patients, however, made remarks which suggested that the elimination of a phobic symptom is not an isolated process, but has many diverse and positive implications. As Eysenck (1959) states:

> The disappearance of the very annoying symptom promotes peace in the home, allays anxiety, and leads to an all-round improvement in character and behavior.

The extent to which desensitization is a method of *general* applicability (i.e. whether this method would benefit any neurotic patients other than those suffering from phobic disorders) is also worthy of mention. The value of desensitization is limited to those conditions wherein appropriate hierarchies can be constructed and where specific rather than pervasive anxiety is present. In other words, it is only where reasonably well-defined stimulus configurations can be identified that desensitization techniques should be applied. For example, patients whose interpersonal relationships are clouded by specific fears of rejection, hypersensitivity to criticism, clear-cut areas of self-consciousness, or similar specific anxiety evoking stimuli often derive benefit from desensitization procedures. By contrast, desensitization cannot readily be applied in such cases as character neuroses, hysterical disorders, and chronic inadequacy. A further prerequisite for the effective application of desensitization is the ability to conjure up reasonably vivid visual images which elicit emotional reactions comparable to the feelings evoked in the real situation.

While dealing with the limitations of desensitization procedures, one should not lose sight of the fact that systematic desensitization appears to be a most valuable technique in the alleviation of phobic disorders. The fact that this method can be effectively administered in *groups* suggests greater availability with little loss in economy or effectiveness for phobic sufferers.

## SUMMARY

Wolpe's (1958) technique of systematic desensitization based on relaxation was adapted to the treatment of phobic disorders in groups. Of the 18 subjects who were treated by direct group desensitization, 13 recovered in a mean of 20·4 sessions. Follow-up inquiries after an average of 9·05 months revealed that 3 of the subjects had relapsed. With a more traditional form of interpretive group psychotherapy applied to 17 subjects, after a mean of 22 therapeutic meetings, it was found that only 2 patients were symptom-free. Both these patients had attended groups in which relaxation was employed as an adjunct to the interpretive procedures. The 15 subjects who were not symptom-free after interpretive group therapy were then treated by group desensitization. After a mean of 10·1 sessions, 10 of them recovered. The very much shorter time required to effect a recovery by desensitization in those patients who had previously received interpretive therapy suggests that the therapeutic relationship and additional non-specific factors may have facilitated the reciprocal inhibition of neurotic anxieties motivating the phobic symptoms. There is some basis for the idea that therapists of every persuasion could helpfully employ systematic desensitization as an adjunct to their traditional techniques in the management of phobic disorders.

## REFERENCES

CORSINI, R. J. (1957) *Methods of group psychotherapy* McGraw-Hill, New York.
CURRAN, D., and PARTRIDGE, M. (1955) *Psychological medicine*. Livingstone, Edinburgh and London.
EYSENCK, H. J. (1959) Learning theory and behavior therapy, *J. Ment Sci.*, **105**, 61–75.
EYSENCK, H. J. (Ed.) (1960) *Behaviour therapy and the neuroses*. Pergamon, Oxford.
FISHER, R. A. (1946) *Statistical methods for research workers*. Oliver and Boyd, Edinburgh.
HENDERSON, D. and GILLESPIE, R. D. (1955) *A text-book of psychiatry*. Oxford University Press.
JACOBSON, E. (1938) *Progressive relaxation*. Chicago University Press (1938).

LAZARUS, A. A. (1959) The elimination of children's phobias by deconditioning, *S. Afr. Med. Proc.*, **5**, 261–265.

LAZARUS, A. A. and RACHMAN, S. (1957) The use of systematic desensitization in psychotherapy, *S. Afr. Med. J.*, **31**, 934–937.

MASLOW, A. H. and MITTELMANN, B. (1951) *Principles of abnormal psychology*. Harper, New York.

MAYER-GROSS, W., SLATER, E. and ROTH, M. (1955) *Clinical psychiatry*, Cassel, London.

WOLBERG, L. R. (1954) *The technique of psychotherapy*, Grune and Stratton, New York.

WOLPE, J. (1958) *Psychotherapy by reciprocal inhibition*, Stanford University Press.

# Isolation of a Conditioning Procedure as the Crucial
# Psychotherapeutic Factor: A Case Study*

JOSEPH WOLPE, M.D.†

IN A considerable number of publications e.g. [1, 5, 7, 9, 11-13] it has been shown that methods based on principles of learning achieve strikingly good results in the treatment of human neuroses. Neuroses are usually characterized by persistent habits of anxiety response to stimulus situations in which there is no objective danger—for example, the mere presence of superiors, being watched working, seeing people quarrel, riding in an elevator. Since these habits of emotional response have been acquired by learning [10, 11] it is only to be expected that they would be overcome by appropriate procedures designed to bring about unlearning. Most of the procedures that have been used have depended upon inhibition of anxiety through the evocation of other responses physiologically incompatible with it (reciprocal inhibition); for each occasion of such inhibition diminishes to some extent the strength of the anxiety response habit. [11]

When "dynamic" psychiatrists are confronted with the therapeutic successes of behavioristic therapy they discount them on the ground that the results are "really" due to the operation of "mechanisms" postulated by *their* theory: transference, insight, suggestion, or de-repression. Despite the fact that it is now manifest [14, 15] that the basic "mechanisms" of psycho-analysis have no scientifically acceptable factual foundations, their pro-ponents can still content themselves with saying that the *possibility* of their operation has not been excluded. Resort to this kind of comfortable refuge would be undermined if study of the therapeutic course of individual cases were to show *both* that there is a direct correlation between the use of conditioning procedures and recovery and that "dynamic mechanisms" are *not* so correlated, either because they cannot be inferred from the facts of the case or because even when they might be inferred they have no temporal relation to the emergence of change.

* This article is reprinted with the permission of the author and the editor, from *J. Nerv. Ment. Dis.*, **134**, 316–329 (1962).

† Department of Neurology and Psychiatry, University of Virginia School of Mede-cine, Charlottesville, Virginia.

The case described below was made the subject of variation of several of the factors that are alleged from various standpoints to have therapeutic potency. A patient with a single severe phobia for automobiles was selected for the experiment because the presence of a single dimension of disturbance simplifies the estimation of change. It was found that a deconditioning technique—systematic desensitization[9, 11, 13]—alone was correlated with improvement, which was quantitatively related to the number of reinforcements given. At the same time, activities that might give any grounds for imputations of transference, insight, suggestion, and de-repression were omitted or manipulated in such a way as to render the operation of these "mechanisms" exceedingly implausible. Furthermore, the conduct of therapy in several series of interviews separated by long intervals had results incompatible with "spontaneous recovery"—a possibility that might have been entertained if improvement during the intervals had been as great as during the treatment periods; but in fact virtually no change occurred during the intervals.

This case incidentally illustrates how difficult it can be to find stimulus situations that evoke sufficiently low anxiety to enable *commencement* of desensitization, and how the details of procedure must be tailored to the needs of the case.

### THE CASE OF MRS. C

The patient, a 39-year-old woman, complained of fear reactions to traffic situations. Dr. Richard W. Garnett, Jr., a senior staff psychiatrist, had referred her to me after interviewing her a few times. I first saw the patient at the University Hospital on April 6, 1960. Briefly her story was that on February 3, 1958, while her husband was taking her to work by car, they entered an intersection on the green light. On the left she noticed two girls standing at the curb waiting for the light to change, and then, suddenly, became aware of a large truck that had disregarded the signal, bearing down upon the car. She remembered the moment of impact, being flung out of the car, flying through the air, and then losing consciousness. Her next recollection was of waking in the ambulance, seeing her husband, and telling him that everything was all right. She felt quite calm and remained so during the rest of the journey to the hospital. There she was found to have injuries to her knee and neck, for the treatment of which she spent a week in the hospital.

On the way home, by car, she felt unaccountably frightened. She stayed at home for two weeks, quite happily, and then, resuming normal activities, noticed that, while in a car, though relatively comfortable on the open road, she was always disturbed by seeing any car approach *from either side*, but not at all by vehicles straight ahead. Along city streets she had continuous anxiety, which, at the sight of a laterally approaching car less than half a block away, would rise to panic. She could, however, avoid such a reaction by closing her eyes before reaching an intersection. She was also distressed in other situations that in any sense involved lateral approaches of cars. Reactions were extraordinarily severe in relation to making a left turn in the face of approaching traffic on the highway. Execution of the turn, of course, momentarily placed the approaching vehicle to the right of her car, and there was a considerable rise in tension even when the vehicle was a mile or more ahead. Left turns in the city disturbed her less because of slower speeds. The entry of other cars from side streets even as far as two blocks ahead into the road in which she was traveling also constituted a "lateral threat". Besides her reactions while in a car, she was anxious while walking across streets, even at intersections with the traffic light in her favor, and even if the nearest approaching car were more than a block away.

During the first few months of Mrs. C.'s neurosis, her panic at the sight of a car approaching from the side would cause her to grasp the driver by the arm. Her awareness of the annoyance this occasioned subsequently led her to control this behaviour, for the most part successfully, but the fear was not diminished.

Questioned about previous related traumatic experiences, she recalled that ten years previously a tractor had crashed into the side of a car in which she was a passenger. Nobody had been hurt, the car had continued its journey, and she had been aware of no emotional sequel. No one close to her had ever been involved in a serious accident. Though she had worked in the Workmen's Compensation Claims office, dealing with cases of injury had not been disturbing to her. She found it incomprehensible that she should have developed this phobia; in London during World War II, she had accepted the dangers of the blitz calmly, without ever needing to use soporifics or sedatives.

She had received no previous treatment for her phobia. During the previous few days, she had told her story to Dr. Garnett; and then a medical student had seen her daily and discussed various aspects of her life, such as her childhood and her life with her husband—all of which she had felt to be irrelevant.

The plan of therapy was to confine subsequent interviews as far as possible to the procedures of *systematic desensitization*, and to omit any further history-taking, probing, and analyzing. Systematic desensitization[1,3-5,9-13] is a method of therapy that has its roots in the experimental laboratory. It has been shown experimentally[6,8,11] that persistent unadaptive habits of anxiety response may be eliminated by counteracting (and thus inhibiting) individual evocations of the response by means of the simultaneous evocation of an incompatible response (reciprocal inhibition). Each such inhibition leads to some degree of weakening of the anxiety response habit.

In systematic desensitization, the emotional effects of deep muscle relaxation are employed to counteract the anxiety evoked by phobic and allied stimulus situations presented to the patient's *imagination*. Stimulus situations on the theme of the patient's neurotic anxiety are listed and then ranked according to the intensity of anxiety they evoke. The patient, having been relaxed, sometimes under hypnosis, is asked to imagine the weakest of the disturbing stimuli, repeatedly, until it ceases to evoke any anxiety. Then increasingly "strong" stimuli are introduced in turn, and similarly treated, until eventually even the "strongest" fails to evoke anxiety. This desensitizing to imaginary situations has been found to be correlated with disappearance of anxiety in the presence of the actual situation.

In the second interview, training in relaxation and the construction of hierarchies were both initiated. To begin with, Mrs. C. was schooled in relaxation of the arms and the muscles of the forehead. Two hierarchies were constructed. The first related to traffic situations in open country. There was allegedly a minimal reaction if she was in a car driven by her husband and they were 200 yards from a crossroads and if, 400 yards away, at right angles, another car was approaching. Anxiety increased with increasing proximity. The second hierarchy related to lateral approaches of other cars while that in which she was traveling had stopped at a city traffic light. The first signs of anxiety supposedly appeared when the other car was two blocks away. (This, as will be seen, was a gross understatement of the patient's reactions.) The interview concluded with an introductory desensitization session. Having hypnotized and relaxed Mrs. C., I presented to her imagination some presumably neutral stimuli. First she was asked to imagine herself walking across a baseball field and then that she was riding in a car in the country with no other cars in sight. Following this, she was presented with the allegedly weak phobic situation of being in a car 200 yards from an intersection and seeing another car 400 yards on the left. She afterwards reported no disturbances to any of the scenes.

The third interview was conducted in the presence of an audience of five physicians. The Willoughby Neuroticism Test gave a borderline score of 24. (Normal, for practical purposes, is under 20.) About 80 per cent of patients have scores above 30.[11] Instruction in relaxation of muscles of the shoulder was succeeded by a desensitization session in which the following scenes were presented:

1) The patient's car, driven by her husband, had stopped at an intersection, and another car was approaching at right angles two blocks away.

2) The highway scene of the previous session was suggested, except that now her car was 150 yards from the intersection and the other car 300 yards away. Because this produced a finger-raising (signaling felt anxiety), after a pause she was asked to imagine that she was 150 yards from the intersection and the other car 400 yards. Though she did not raise her finger at this, it was noticed that she moved her legs. (*It was subsequently found that these leg movements were a very sensitive indicator of emotional disturbance.*) Consequently, at the fourth interview, I subjected Mrs. C. to further questioning about her reactions to automobiles, from which it emerged that she

was continuously tense in cars but had not thought this worth reporting, so trifling was it beside the terror experienced at the lateral approach of a car. She now also stated that *all* the car scenes imagined during the sessions had aroused anxiety, but too little, she had felt, to deserve mention. While relaxed under hypnosis, Mrs. C. was asked to imagine that she was in a car about to be driven around an empty square. As there was no reaction to this, the next scene presented was being about to ride two blocks on a country road. This evoked considerable anxiety!

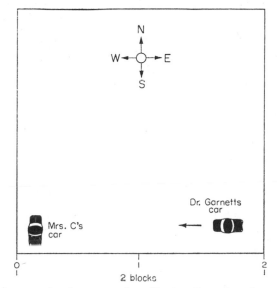

FIG. 1. Imaginary enclosed square where Doctor Garnett makes progressively closer advances to Mrs. C.'s car. (See text.)

At the fifth interview, it was learned that even the thought of a journey raised Mrs. C.'s tension, so that if, for example, at 9 a.m. her husband were to say, "We are going out driving at 2 p.m.", she would be continuously apprehensive, and more so when actually in the car. During the desensitization session (fourth) at this interview, I asked her to imagine that she was at home expecting to go for a short drive in the country in four hours' time. This scene, presented five times, evoked anxiety that did not decrease on repetition. It was now obvious that scenes with the merest suspicion of exposure to traffic were producing more anxiety than could be mastered by Mrs. C.'s relaxation potential.

A new strategy therefore had to be devised. I introduced an artifice that lent itself to controlled manipulation. On a sheet of paper I drew an altogether imaginary completely enclosed square field, which was represented as being two blocks (200 yards) long (see Fig.1). At the southwest corner (lower left) I drew her car, facing north (upwards), in which she sat with her husband,

and at the lower right corner another car, supposed to be Dr. Garnett's, which faced them at right angles. Dr. Garnett (hereafter "Dr. G.") was "used" because Mrs. C. regarded him as a trustworthy person.

This imaginary situation became the focus of the scenes presented in the sessions that followed. At the fifth desensitization session, Mrs. C. was asked to imagine Dr. G. announcing to her that he was going to drive his car a half-block towards her and then proceeding to do so while she sat in her parked car. As this elicited no reaction, she was next made to imagine him driving one block towards her, and then, as there was again no reaction, one and a quarter blocks. On perceiving a reaction to this scene, I repeated it three times, but without effecting any decrement in the reaction. I then "retreated", asking her to imagine Dr. G. stopping after traveling one block and two paces towards her. This produced a slighter reaction, and *this decreased on repeating the scene, disappearing at the fourth presentation.* This was the first evidence of change, and afforded grounds for a confident prediction of successful therapy.

At the sixth session, the imagined distance between Dr. G.'s stopping point and Mrs. C.'s car was decreased by two or three paces at a time, and at the end of the session he was able to stop seven-eighths of a block short of her (a total gain of about 10 paces). The following are the details of the progression. In parentheses is the number of presentations of each scene required to reduce the anxiety response to zero:

1) Dr. G. approaches four paces beyond one block (3).
2) Six paces beyond one block (3).
3) Nine paces beyond one block (2).
4) Twelve paces beyond one block, i.e., one and one-eighth block (4).

At the seventh session, Mrs. C. was enabled to tolerate Dr. G.'s car reaching a point half a block short of her car without disturbance; at the eighth session, three-eighths of a block (about 37 yards); at the tenth, she was able to imagine him approaching within two yards of her without any reaction whatsoever.

The day after this, Mrs. C. reported that for the first time since her accident she had been able to walk across a street while an approaching car was in sight. The car was two blocks away but she was able to complete the crossing without quickening her pace. At this, the eleventh session, I began a new series of scenes in which Dr. G. drove in front of the car containing Mrs. C. instead of towards it, passing at first 30 yards ahead, and then gradually closer, cutting the distance eventually to about three yards. Desensitization to all this was rather rapidly achieved during this session. Thereupon, I drew two intersecting roads in the diagram of the field (Fig. 2). A traffic light was indicated in the middle, and the patient's car, as shown in the diagram, had "stopped" at the red signal. At first, Mrs. C. was asked to imagine Dr. G.'s car passing on the green light. As anticipated, she could at once accept this without anxiety; it was followed by Dr. G.'s car passing one way and a resident physician's car in the opposite direction. The slight anxiety this aroused was soon eliminated. In subsequent scenes, the resident's car was followed by an increasing number of students' cars, each scene being repeated until its emotional effect declined to zero.

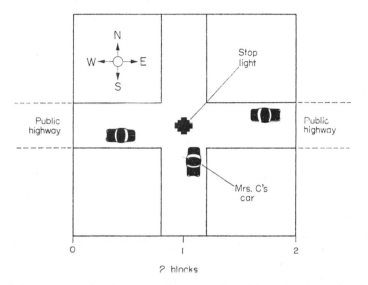

FIG. 2. Imaginary enclosed square with crossroads and traffic light added. Other cars pass while Mrs. C.'s car has stopped at the red light. (See text.)

At the twelfth session, the roadway at right angles to Mrs. C.'s car was made continuous with the public highway system (as indicated by the dotted lines) and now, starting off again with Dr. G., we added the cars of the resident and the students, and subsequently those of strangers. Imagining two unknown cars passing the intersection produced a fair degree of anxiety and she required five presentations at this session and five more at the next before she could accept it entirely calmly. However, once this was accomplished, it was relatively easy gradually to introduce several cars passing from both sides.

We now began a new series of scenes in which, with the traffic light in her favor, she was stepping off the curb to cross a city street while a car was slowly approaching. At first, the car was imagined a block away, but during succeeding sessions the distance gradually decreased to ten yards.

At this point, to check upon transfer from the imaginary to real life, I took Mrs. C. to the Charlottesville business center and observed her crossing streets at an intersection controlled by a traffic light. She went across repeatedly with apparent ease and reported no anxiety. But in the car, on the way there and back, she showed marked anxiety whenever a car from a side street threatened to enter the street in which we drove.

Soon afterwards, the opportunity arose for an experiment relevant to the question of "transference". A medical student had been present as an observer during four or five sessions. Early in May I had to leave town for a week to attend a conference. I decided to let the student continue therapy in my absence. Accordingly, I asked him to conduct the fifteenth desensitization session under my supervision. I corrected his errors by silently passing him written notes. Since he eventually performed quite well, he agreed to carry on treatment during my absence, and conducted the eighteenth to the twenty-third sessions entirely without supervision. His efforts were directed to a new series of scenes in which, while Mrs. C. was being driven by her husband along a city street, Dr. G.'s car made a right turn into that street from a cross street on their left. At first, Dr. G. was imagined making this entry two blocks ahead, but after several intervening stages it became possible for her to accept it calmly only half a block ahead. The student therapist then introduced a modification in which a student instead of Dr. G. drove the other car. The car was first visualized as entering two blocks ahead and the distance then gradually reduced to a half-block in the course of three sessions, requiring 63 scene presentations, most of which were needed in a very laborious advance from three-quarters of a block.

At this stage, the therapist experimentally inserted a scene in which Mrs. C.'s car was making a left turn in the city while Dr. G.'s car approached from the opposite direction four blocks ahead. This produced such a violent reaction that the therapist became apprehensive about continuing treatment. However, I returned the next day. Meanwhile, the point had been established that a substitute therapist could make satisfactory progress. (Under the writer's guidance, but not in his presence, the student therapist went on to conduct two entirely successful sessions the following week.)

I now made a detailed analysis of Mrs. C.'s reaction to left turns on the highway in the face of oncoming traffic. She reported anxiety at doing a left turn *if an oncoming car was in sight*. Even if it was two miles away she could not allow her husband to turn left in front of it.

To treat this most sensitive reaction, I again re-introduced Dr. G. into the picture. I started by making Mrs. C. imagine (while hypnotized and relaxed) that Dr. G.'s car was a mile ahead when her car began the turn. But this was too disturbing and several repetitions of the scene brought no diminution in the magnitude of anxiety evoked. It seemed possible that there would be less anxiety if the patient's husband were not the driver of the car, since his presence at the time of the accident might have made him a conditioned stimulus to anxiety. Thus I presented the scene with Mrs. C.'s *brother* as the driver of the car. With this altered feature, Dr. G.'s making a left turn a mile ahead evoked much less anxiety, and after four repetitions it declined to zero; we were gradually able to decrease the distance so that she could eventually imagine making the turn with Dr. G.'s car only about 150 yards a way (see Table 1). Meanwhile, when she was able to "do" the turn with Dr. G. three-eighths of a mile away, I introduced two new left-turn series: a strange car approaching with her brother driving, and Dr. G. approaching with her husband driving—both a mile away initially. Work on all three series went on concurrently. When Mrs. C. could comfortably imagine her brother doing a left turn with the strange car five-eighths of a mile ahead, I resumed the original series in which her husband was the driver, starting with a left turn while the strange car was a mile ahead. This now evoked relatively little anxiety; progress could be predicted, and ensued. The interrelated decrements of reaction to this group of hierarchies are summarized in Fig. 3.

Other series of related scenes were also subjected to desensitization. They are listed in Table 1, in order of commencement, but there was much overlapping of incidence. One comprised left turns *in the city* in front of oncoming cars. Since cars in the city move relatively slowly, she felt less "danger" at a given distance. At first, we dealt with left turns while an approaching car was about two blocks away, and in the course of several sessions gradually decreased the distance until Mrs. C. could comfortably "do" a left turn with the other car slowly moving 15 yards ahead. The series where Mrs. C. was crossing streets as a pedestrian was extended, and she was enabled in imagination to cross under all normal conditions. She reported complete transfer to the reality. A series that was started somewhat later involved driving down a through street with a car in a side street slowing to a stop. At first, the side street was "placed "two blocks ahead. The distance was gradually decreased as desensitization progressed, and eventually she could without anxiety drive past a car slowing to a stop. A series intercurrently employed to desensitize her in a general way to the feeling that a car was "bearing down upon her", was not part of any real situation. In our imaginary square field (Fig. 1), I "placed" two parallel white lines, scaled to be about 20 feet long and 10 feet apart. During the session I said, "You are walking up and down along one white line and Dr. G. drives his car up to the other at one mile per hour..." This was not disturbing; but at subsequent visualizings the speed was gradually increased and at an early stage the distance between the lines decreased to five feet. At four miles per hour there was some anxiety. This was soon eliminated, and several presentations of scenes from this series during each of 10 sessions made it possible for Mrs. C. calmly to imagine Dr. G. driving up to his white line at 18 miles per hour while she strolled along hers.

The total effect of desensitization to these interrelated series of stimulus situations was that Mrs. C. became completely at ease in all normal traffic situations—both in crossing streets as a pedestrian and riding in a car. Improvement in real situations took place in close relation with the improvements during sessions. A direct demonstration of the transfer of improvement with respect to crossing streets at traffic lights has been described above.

The patient's progress was slow but consistent. Because she lived about 100 miles away, her treatment took place episodically. At intervals of from four to six weeks she would come to Charlottesville for about two weeks and be seen almost every day. Noteworthy reducing in the range of real situations that could disturb her occurred in the course of each period of active treatment, and practically none during the intervals. She was instructed not to avoid exposing herself during these intervals to situations that might be expected to be only slightly disturbing: but if she anticipated being very disturbed to close her eyes, if feasible, for she could thus "ward off" the situation. Every now and then, particular incidents stood out as landmarks in her progress. One day in late August, driving with her brother in a through street in her home town, she saw a car slowing down before a stop sign as they passed it. Though the car did not quite stop, she had no reaction at all, though gazing at it continuously. This incident demonstrated the transfer to life of the desensitization to the relevant hierarchy (No. 23) which had been concluded shortly before. Since then, similar experiences had been consistently free from disturbance.

At the conclusion of Mrs. C.'s treatment, she was perfectly comfortable making a pedestrian crossing even though the traffic was creeping up to her. Left turns on a highway were quite comfortable with fast traffic up to about 150 yards ahead. When the closest approaching car was somewhat nearer, her reaction was slight anxiety, and not panic, as in the past. In all other traffic situations her feeling was entirely normal. Another effect of the treatment was that she no longer had headaches due to emotional tension.

In all, 57 desensitization sessions were conducted. The number of scene presentations at a session generally ranged from 25 to 40. Table 1 records a total of 1491 scene presentations, which does not include a small number of test scenes that were not continued because they were too disturbing when presented. The last session took place on September 29, 1960. It was followed by the taking of Mrs. C.'s history, given below. It will be seen that it contains nothing to suggest that there were sexual problems underlying the automobile phobia.

When Mrs. C. was seen late in December, 1960, she was as well as she had been at the end of treatment. Her sexual relations with her husband were progressively improving. At a follow-up telephone call on June 6, 1961, she stated that she had fully maintained her recovery and had developed no new symptoms. Her relationship with her husband was excellent and sexually at least as satisfying as before the accident. A further call, on February 19, 1962, elicited the same report.

## LIFE HISTORY

The patient was born in a small town in Virginia, the eldest of a family of five. Her father had died of heart disease in June, 1957. He had always been good to her as a child, and had never punished her. He had often embarrassed his family by getting drunk on weekends. The patient had felt very close to her mother, who was still living and had always been kind and loving, and punished the patient only occasionally. Mrs. C. had always got on well with her siblings. She could recall no traumatic childhood experiences. She had always been a good student and had liked school very much, participating in games and making friends easily. The only person whom she had especially disliked was a teacher who had once put a tape over her mouth for speaking in class. She graduated from high school at 17, spent two years in an office and then a year in college. In 1942, when 21, she had joined the U.S. Armed Forces and gone to England, where she had become engaged to an Air Force navigator who was later killed in action. She reiterated that during the blitz she had often been in danger, witnessed destruction and seen the dead and injured without any great distress. In December, 1945, returning to the United States, she had worked at an office job until 1957, when she had married.

Her first sexual feelings were experienced at the age of 12. She reported that she had never masturbated. From the age of 13 she had gone out in groups and at 17 begun individual dating. Her first serious attachment was to the airman who was killed, but she had seen little of him because of war conditions. After his death, she had lost interest for a time in forming other associations. On returning to the United States, she had resumed casual dating. Her next serious association was with her husband, whom she had met in 1955. They had married in May, 1957, about nine months before the accident. Until the accident, the marital relationship had been good. Sexual relations had been satisfactory, most often with both partners achieving orgasm. Since the accident, however, she had been negatively influenced by adverse comments that her husband had made about her disabilities, so shat sexual behavior had diminished. Nevertheless, when coitus occurred, the still had orgasm more often than not.

## DISCUSSION

Laboratory studies[6, 8, 11] have shown that experimental neuroses in animals are learned unadaptive habits characterized by anxiety that are remarkable for their persistence (resistance to the normal process of extinction). These neuroses can readily be eliminated through repeatedly inhibiting the neurotic responses by simultaneous evocations of incompatible responses (i.e. by reciprocal inhibition of the neurotic responses.[6, 8, 11]) The effectiveness of varied applications of this finding to human neuroses[1–5, 7–13] gives support to the view that human neuroses too are a particular category of habits acquired by learning.

In the systematic desensitization technique the effects of muscle relaxation are used to produce reciprocal inhibition of small evocations of anxiety and thereby build up conditioned inhibition of anxiety-responding to the particular stimulus combination. When (and only when) the evocations

TABLE 1

*Summary of data concerning hierarchies*

| No. of hierarchy | Content of hierarchy | No. of presentations of scenes from each hierarchy | Result |
|---|---|---|---|
| 0 | Baseball field (control scene) | 1 | No reaction |
| 1 | Approaching highway crossroads which another car approaches laterally (two distance variables—own distance and that of other car) | 15 | Nil |
| 2 | Stationary at city intersection while other cars approach (two blocks maximum) | 2 | Nil |
| 3 | About to be driven from country lodge—starting from distance of two blocks (temporal variable) | 9 | Nil |
| 4 | Approached by Dr. G.'s car on imaginary field (Fig. 1) starting two blocks away | 41 | + |
| 5 | As No. 4, but Dr. G. starts each advance from one block away | 50 | + |
| 6 | Dr. G. drives his car to pass in front of hers (decreasing passing distance, 30 yards to 3 yards) | 10 | + |
| 7–8 | Mrs. C. stopped by red in imaginary field (Fig. 2) and increasing variety and number of medical school cars pass on green | 10 | + |
| 9–10 | As No. 7 but the crossroad now continuous with public highway and increasing variety and number of strange cars pass (Fig. 2) | 27 | + |
| 11 | Walking across road at intersection while a car moves towards her (decreasing distances from $1\frac{1}{2}$ blocks to 10 yards) | 30 | + |
| 12 | Goes through on green with increasing number of strange cars stationary at right and left | 4 | No disturbance from outset |
| 13 | As her car passes on green, Dr. G.'s car advances at side (decreasing distance from $\frac{1}{2}$ block to 10 yards) | 25 | + |
| 14 | While Mrs. C.'s car moves slowly in town, Dr. G.'s car turns into her lane from side street (2 blocks to $\frac{1}{4}$ block) (Sessions by student, see text) | 39 | + |
| 15 | As No. 14, but strange car (2 blocks to $\frac{1}{2}$ block) (Sessions by student, see text) | 62 | + |
| 16 | Dr. G.'s car makes left turn across path of her slowly moving car (2 blocks to $\frac{3}{4}$ block) (Sessions by student, see text) | 22 | + |
| 17 | As No. 16, but student's car (2 blocks to $\frac{3}{4}$ block) (Sessions by student, see text) | 26 | + |
| 18 | Mrs. C.'s car in city turns left while Dr. G. advances (Handled alternately by student and author) (6 blocks to $3\frac{3}{4}$ blocks) | 22 | + with difficulty |

TABLE 1—*Continued*

| No. of hierarchy | Content of hierarchy | No. of presentations of scenes from each hierarchy | Result |
|---|---|---|---|
| 19 | On highway (Fig.2) turns left in front of tractor moving 5 m. p. h. (1 mile to $1/_4$ block) | 36 | + |
| 20 | Turns left in car while at fixed distance of $1/_2$ block a car whose driver is instructed by Dr. G. is advancing. Its speed was gradually increased from 5 to 30 m.p.h. | 93 | + |
| 21 | Turns left while two strange cars advance a block ahead. Speed of the cars increased gradually from 15 m.p.h. to 26 m.p.h. | 25 | + |
| 22 | While driving in taxi in through street, sees a car moving very slowly to stop at intersection ahead. Distance decreased from 1 block to $5/_{16}$ block | 35 | + |
| 23 | As No. 22, but the other car decelerates from normal speed. Distance gradually decreased from $1/_2$ block to zero from line of intersection | 102 | + |
| 24 | Walking across intersection at green light, while car a block away approaches. Increasing speeds 10–20 m.p.h. | 5 | + |
| 25 | Stepping off curb to cross at unguarded intersection while car on left approaches at 10 m.p.h. Decreasing distance 1 block to $3/_8$ block | 137 | + very difficult progress from $1/_2$ block on |
| 26 | Does left turn in city while a car approaches at 10 m.p.h. Decreasing distance from $7/_8$ to $5/_8$ block | 67 | + very difficult from $3/_4$ block on |
| 27 | She walks back and forth in the imaginary enclosed field parallel to a white line up to which Dr. G. drives his car at 1 m.p.h. Her distance from the line decreases from 10 yds. to $4^1/_2$ yds. | 23 | + |
| 28 | While she keeps constant parallel distance of 5 yds. from white line, Dr. G.'s speed increases from 1 to 18 m.p.h. | 68 | + |
| 29 | Steps off curb at unguarded intersection while car on *right* approaches at 10 m.p.h. Distances 1 block to $5/_7$ block | 14 | + |
| 30 | On highway in car driven by brother, does left turn in face of approaching car driven by Dr. G. Distance between them decreases from 1 mile to 350 yards | 70 | + |

TABLE 1—*Continued*

| No. of hierarchy | Content of hierarchy | No. of presentations of scenes from each hierarchy | Result |
|---|---|---|---|
| 31 | As 30, but stranger drives other car. Distances from 1 mile to 150 yds. | 126 | + |
| 32 | As 30, but Mrs. C.'s husband drives her car. Distances from 1 mile to 175 yds. | 117 | + |
| 33 | As 30, but Mrs. C.'s husband drives her car and stranger drives the other. Distances from 1 mile to 150 yds. | 100 | + |
| 34 | In taxi that does U-turn while a car approaches in city. Distances 2 blocks to 1 block | 6 | + |
| 35 | Driven by husband does left turn in city in face of slowly oncoming car. Distances of $1/2$ block to 15 yds. | 29 | + |
| 36 | In sight of oncoming car, enters highway from side road after stopping. Distances $1/4$ to $1/8$ mile | 43 | + |
| | Total Scenes | 1491 | |

of anxiety are weakened by the counterposed relaxation does the anxiety response *habit* diminish. By systematic use of stimulus combinations whose anxiety-evoking potential is or has become weak, the habit strength of the whole neurotic theme is eliminated piecemeal.

The case of Mrs. C. illustrates with outstanding clarity how the course of change during systematic desensitization conforms to the expectations engendered by the reciprocal inhibition principle. Whenever a scene presented to the patient aroused a good deal of anxiety, that scene could be re-presented a dozen times without diminution of the anxiety. On the other hand, if the initial level of anxiety was lower, decrements in its intensity were achieved by successive presentations. It is a reasonable presumption that, as long as evoked anxiety was too great to be inhibited by the patient's relaxation, *no change* could occur; but when the anxiety was weak enough to be inhibited, repeated presentations of the scene led to progressive increments of *conditioned inhibition* of the anxiety-response habit, manifested by ever-weakening anxiety-responding. At every stage, each "quantum" of progress in relation to the subject matter of the desensitization sessions corresponded in specific detail to a small step towards recovery in an aspect of the real life difficulty. The fact that change occurred in this precise way in itself almost justifies the elimination of various "alternative explanations".

Mrs. C. had a total of 60 interviews, at each of which, except the first two and the last, a desensitization session was conducted. Including the initial three which proved to be unusable, 36 hierarchies entered into the sessions. All of these, tabulated in Table 1, share the common theme of "car-approaching-from-the-side", but each has its own unique stimulus

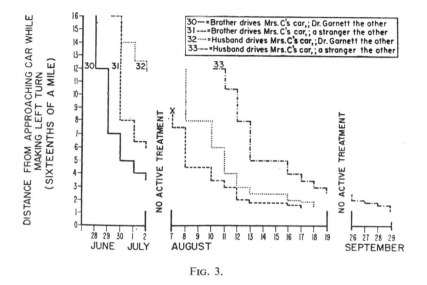

FIG. 3.

elements calling for separate desensitizing operations. The amount of attention a hierarchy needs is diminished by previous desensitization of other hierarchies that have elements in common with it. This is graphically illustrated in Fig. 3. Hierarchies 30, 31, 32 and 33, each of which relates to turning left on the highway while another vehicle advances, differ, one from the next, in respect of a single stimulus condition and are in ascending order of anxiety arousal. Desensitization in overlapping sequences, starting with Hierarchy 30, shows parallel progressions. Now, desensitization of Hierarchy 33 was in fact first attempted before Hierarchy 30, from which it has three points of difference. At that time, presenting the approaching car at a distance of *one mile* evoked more anxiety than could be mastered by the patient's relaxation. But after Hierarchy 30 had been dealt with, and in Hierarchies 31 and 32, the "other car" could be tolerated at about one-half mile, it was possible to introduce Hierarchy 33 at three-quarters of a mile with very little anxiety. The increase in toleration was clearly attributable to desensitization to the stimulus elements that Hierarchy 33 *shared* with the three foregoing ones.

Figure 3 also illustrates the significant fact that *therapeutic change did not develop during the intervals when the patient was not receiving treatment,* and this was true even of reactions that were the main focus of treatment at the time. There is no drop, following the intervals, in the reactive level of any of the hierarchies represented. However, it is interesting to note that between July 2 and August 7 the reactive level of Hierarchy 31 has risen somewhat. This was not a "spontaneous" endogenously determined relapse, but due to the fact that, late in July, Mrs. C. had ridden in a taxi whose driver, despite her protests, had persisted in weaving among traffic at high speed. Immediately after this she was aware of increased reactivity. As can be seen, the lost ground was soon regained.

A question that may come to mind is this. What assurance did the therapist have of a correspondence between distances as imagined by Mrs. C. and objective measures of distance? The first, and most important answer is that rough correspondence was necessary, since what was always at issue was *distance as conceived by the patient*. The second answer is that a firm anchoring referent was the agreement between patient and therapist that a city block in Charlottesville would be considered 100 yards in length. Similar considerations apply to Mrs. C.'s conceptions of speed.

Among other explanations that may be brought forward to account for the recovery, the only one that, even at face value, would seem to deserve serious consideration in this case is *suggestion*. We shall take this usually ill-defined term to mean the instigation of changes in the patient's behavior by means of verbal or nonverbal cues from the therapist. In all psychotherapy there is at least an implied suggestion of, "This will make you well". Getting well under the impulse of such a general suggestion would not be related to particular therapeutic maneuvers, as was the case with Mrs. C. Another kind of suggestion has the form, "You will get well if. . . ." In commencing Mrs. C.'s desensitization, the therapist was careful to say no more than, "I am going to use a treatment that may help you". He did not say under what conditions it would help. During the first few sessions (and also several times later) when the scenes presented aroused considerable anxiety, repetition brought about no decrement of reaction. Decrement was noted consistently when anxiety was less. To sustain a hypothesis that suggestion was behind this would require evidence of the very specific instruction—"You will have decreasing anxiety only to situations that produce little anxiety in the first place". In fact, no such instruction was in any form conveyed. The patient could only have become aware *a posteriori* of the empirical relations of her changing reactions.

The relevance of the other "processes"—insight, de-repression, and transference—commonly invoked to explain away the effects of conditioning methods of therapy is negated by the absence of significant opportunity for such processes to have occurred. Any possible role of insight may be excluded by the fact that the only insight given to the patient was to tell her she was suffering from a conditioned fear reaction—and no change followed this disclosure . The possibility of de-repression may be ruled out by the non-emergence of forgotten material, and the de-emphasis of memory, even to the exclusion of the taking of a history during treatment—other than the history of the phobia's precipitation two years earlier and brief questioning about previous similar events, none of which had any effect on the neurosis.

The action of anything corresponding to "transference" is rendered implausible by the fact that interviews with the therapist led to improvement *only* when conditioning procedures were carried out in accordance with the requirements of reciprocal inhibition, and improvement was limited to the subject matter of the procedures of the time. Also, for a week, when the therapist was away, progress was effected by a medical student (20 years younger than the therapist) using the same conditioning techniques. In addition, the rather mechanical manner in which the sessions were conducted could hardly by said to favor the operation of transference effects; and certainly, the patient-therapist relationship was in no way ever analyzed. The third to the tenth interviews (and many others irregularly later) were conducted with the patient in full view of an unconcealed audience, without adverse effects on therapeutic progress.

The possibility of "spontaneous" recovery could be excluded with unusual confidence, since clinical improvement was a consequence of each of the periods of one to three weeks when the patient was being treated in Charlottesville, and was never noted during the four to six-week intervals the patient spent at home.

"Secondary gain", so often invoked in explanations of post-traumatic neurotic reactions, can have no credence as a factor in this case, either as a maintaining force or as determining recovery by its removal, for the patient did not receive any financial benefit, came for treatment eight months before litigation, became well two months before litigation, and did not relapse after a disappointing decision by the court.

## SUMMARY

The treatment by systematic desensitization is described of a severe case of phobia for laterally approaching automobiles. The initiation of desensitization required the introduction of imaginary situations in a fictitious setting in order to procure anxiety responses weak enough to be inhibited by the patient's relaxation. Recovery was gradual and at every stage directly correlated with the specific content of the desensitization procedures. Certain operations that are usually performed in most systems of therapy were excluded or modified in order to remove any basis for arguing that the successful outcome was "really" due to insight, suggestion, de-repression, or transference.

## REFERENCES

1. BOND, I. K. and HUTCHINSON, H. C. (1960) Application of reciprocal inhibition therapy to exhibitionism, *Canad. Med. Assoc. J.*, **83**, 23–25.
2. EYSENCK, H. J. (1960) *Behavior Therapy and the Neuroses*, Pergamon Press, New York.
3. LAZARUS, A. A. New group techniques in the treatment of phobic conditions, *J. Abnorm. Soc. Psychol.* In press.
4. LAZARUS, A. A. and RACHMAN, S. (1957) S. The use of systematic desensitization in psychotherapy, *S. Afr. Med. J.*, **31**, 934–936, 1957.
5. LAZOVIK, A. D. and LANG, P. J. (1960) A laboratory demonstration of systematic desensitization psychotherapy, *J. Psychol. Stud.*, **11**, 238–247.
6. NAPALKOV, A. V. and KARAS, A. Y. (1957) Elimination of pathological conditioned reflex connections in experimental hypertensive states, *Zh. Vyss. Nerv. Deiat. Pavlov.*, **7**, 402–409.
7. RACHMAN, S. (1961) Sexual disorders and behavior therapy, *Amer. J. Psychiat.*, **118**, 235–240.
8. WOLPE, J. (1952) Experimental neuroses as learned behavior, *Brit. J. Psychol.*, **43**, 243–268.
9. WOLPE, J. (1954) Reciprocal inhibitions as the main basis of psychotherapeutic effects, *A.M.A.Arch. Neurol. Psychiat.* **72**, 205–226.
10. WOLPE, J. (1956) Learning versus lesions as the basis of neurotic behavior, *Amer. J. Psychiat.*, **112**, 923–927.
11. WOLPE, J. (1958) *Psychotherapy by Reciprocal Inhibition*, Stanford Univ. Press, Stanford, Calif.
12. WOLPE, J. (1959) Psychotherapy based on the principle of reciprocal inhibition. In BURTON, A. *Case Studies in Counseling and Psychotherapy*, Prentice-Hall, Englewood Cliffs, New Jersey.
13. WOLPE, J. (1961) The systematic desensitization treatment of neuroses. *J. Nerv. Mental Dis.*, **132**, 189–203.
14. WOLPE, J. (1961) The prognosis in unpsychoanalyzed recovery from neurosis, *Amer. J. Psychiat.*, **118**, 35–39.
15. WOLPE, J. and RACHMAN, S. (1960) Psychoanalytic evidence: A critique based on Freud's case of Little Hans. *J. Nerv. Ment. Dis.*, **131**, 135–148.

# The Application of Learning Principles to the Treatment of Obsessive-Compulsive States in the Acute and Chronic Phases of Illness*

D. WALTON† and M. D. MATHER§

## INTRODUCTION

On the basis of the successful treatment of a seriously disturbed obsessive-compulsive state, it was decided to apply the same principles of learning to the treatment of similar obsessionals. In this first study (Walton, 1960) only the motor conditioned reactions were initially treated. Although the patient responded positively, he was re-admitted to hospital some seven months later, suffering from excessive handwashing. This was one of his previous major compulsions. It was considered that his relapse was due to failure to treat the more basic conditioned autonomic drive (C.A.D.) from which the motor reactions developed. Eysenck (1960) has similarly warned against the partial cures that might be expected should only the motor reaction be extinguished and the historically earlier C.A.D. mediating these be ignored. In other words, should only the instrumental acts be removed, the drive tendencies will remain, and either new instrumental acts will emerge, become both reinforced and habitual, or the old ones will once more become manifest.

Yates (1960) has, however, argued that it does not seem to be important whether one treats the motor habit or the C.A.D. He suggests that if the motor habit is extinguished, this will in turn reduce the learned anxiety. Certainly in the case of the above obsessional, recourse to the treatment of the motor components temporarily resulted in a remission. His subsequent relapse however would seem to offer support for the contentions of Eysenck and of Jones that untreated C.A.D. may later be reduced by the exercise of instrumental motor responses. This would then serve to reinforce the development of these or different motor habits.

A further inference from this case was that length of illness might dictate whether to treat the C.A.D. alone or in conjunction with the instrumental

* This paper was written specially for publication in this book.
† Late Principal Clinical Psychologist, Winwick Hospital, Warrington.
§ Senior Clinical Psychologist, Hollymoor Hospital, Birmingham.

117

motor acts. In long-standing obsessive-compulsive states, the motor habits may have become "functionally autonomous" and so independent of the initial C.A.D. Thus the treatment of the original C.A.D. would not be expected to remove the motor compulsions, because the original stimuli, said to be associated with the C.A.D. would be different from those now evoking the motor habits. In other words, in long standing obsessive-compulsive states, the initial stimuli associated with the C.A.D. would continue to arouse anxiety. The various instrumental motor responses would however be related, through a process of generalization and possibly secondary rewards, to a variety of other conditioned stimuli. Behaviour therapy might therefore require, in the chronic phase, the extinction of both the initial autonomic conditioned responses and the motor reactions. In contrast, in the acute phase, the relationship between anxiety and the motor habit would be more apparent and there would be less need to consider treating the motor component.

The following cases illustrate how these various hypotheses were tested out and their validity ascertained.


## CASE STUDIES

CASE 1—A young man in his early thirties was referred to the Psychology Department for the treatment of compulsive handwashing. This compulsion had started some seven months previously.

He stated that he continually washed his hands all day and that it prevented him from keeping a job. If ever he cleaned anything he always felt it would never be cleaned adequately.

Other compulsions had been evident for some years. These included repeatedly switching electric lights on and off, shaving for long periods and turning water-taps on and off. It was, however, his compulsive handwashing which necessitated hospital treatment.

The patient was of above average intelligence and had won a scholarship to a university. His studies were interrupted by National Service. Whilst in the army he suffered his first mental breakdown. He had the feeling that there were "two me's, a lower and a higher me" and these two parts of his mind were "back to back". He also had the presentiment that he would die. This frightened him so much that he sought a physical examination by the Army M.O. to reassure him. He volunteered the explanation that he was afraid of dying because he had committed "mortal sin" and would go to hell. He was also over-concerned about his physical appearance. His skin and his teeth were particular sources of worry because of a horror of blemishes and of false teeth.

The "mortal sins" included masturbation in which he had indulged only once, and possibly homosexual feelings. He had been attracted to a young man of his own age whilst in the army, though he denied having gratified his homosexual urge in any way. The one thing preventing this was, he claimed, his Roman Catholic beliefs.

On leaving the Army he returned to the university. For some unstated reason he left after a few months and took a labouring job. Here he became involved in a row with another labourer and the latter punched him on the mouth. This revived the fear that damage may be done to his teeth and that he may have to have false teeth. This was associated with intense aggression towards the man who may have caused this harm. The next day he took to work a hammer and a sharpening steel for the purpose of battering the man. The fact that he realized for the first time he was capable of such hatred and violence generated considerable guilt. He considered that having the intention to do harm was as bad as actually doing it. In fact, he never carried out his intentions.

After several months had elapsed he began to feel he was "less human" and afraid of the sadistic tendencies he believed he possessed. Simultaneously his aggression generalized from one man to other people of the same social class and also to his own relatives and family. These feelings might have been at least partly mixed with some resentment against his intellectually inferior job. He was very dissatisfied with his vocational life and the fact that he made no progress.

About one year after the incident with the labourer he developed the handwashing ritual. He attended a psychiatric day-hospital for a short time but was eventually referred to another hospital for full in-patient treatment. He was diagnosed as an obsessive-compulsive neurotic.

CASE 2—A young man in his early thirties was referred for the investigation and treatment of an obsessional neurosis. This consisted of two compulsive urges. Firstly, he felt compelled to write, "I am a queer" on any piece of paper or on a wall. Whenever he wrote a letter he could never be certain that he had not written in the body of the letter "I am a queer". This doubt evoked compulsive checking of anything he wrote. Similarly he imagined he had written it on blank walls and that people could read it. He also felt compelled to tell people. "I am a queer." He had, however, never repeated the phrase aloud to anyone. Secondly, he had the urge to harm people and was afraid of knives and scissors lest he might pick them up and do damage.

He was one of a family of three brothers. Up to the age of six he had suffered from enuresis. At school he proved to be bright and won two scholarships. He never showed much interest in the opposite sex and, according to his mother, was a "lone wolf type".

After leaving school he did not seek further education but took a clerical job. He began courting a young girl, who subsequently jilted him. This disturbed him greatly. He was admitted to hospital where he was certified and diagnosed as a catatonic schizophrenic. He received deep insulin therapy. Following his discharge he joined an art school. There followed several homosexual experiences which provoked considerable guilt. The compulsion to tell people that he was "a queer" and to write it down then began. He suffered an additional trauma in the death of his father. He became very tense and anxious. Once more he was admitted to hospital and diagnosed as an anxiety-depressive with obsessional features. He was also stated to have suicidal ruminations and to show evidence of depersonalization. He was very sullen and withdrawn. He received a course of E.C.T., though he remained diffident and worried. At this point he was referred to the Psychology Department for the treatment of his persistent obsessional ideas.

## PROPOSED THEORETICAL MODEL

The autonomic drive in both cases had been conditioned by social pressures to the expression of aggressive and sexual drives. Subsequent environmental conditions had been such as to increase the intensity of these socially inacceptable urges and thus to increase the anxiety associated with them. The obsessional symptoms which had developed later were considered to be instrumental in reducing the anxiety related to both these drives.

In Case 1, the handwashing served to reduce the guilt or anxiety evoked by the intense aggression he had felt towards the labourer.

In Case 2, his compulsive checking and thoughts were similarly reinforced by anxiety-reduction. Since he had satisfied himself that he had not in fact written "I am a queer", the probability of his discovery was less and so his anxiety became less. Whenever worried about discovery he would then resort to the most efficient drive-reducing agent he knew, namely his compulsion.

### Derivation of Method of Treatment

One common feature of these two cases was the acute onset of the obsessional symptoms at the time of referral. Since these were advanced by their drive-reducing properties, it was considered that treatment should concentrate on the removal of the historically earlier conditioned autonomic drives. The obsessive-compulsions, being dependent on these would then extinguish through a lack of reinforcement.

### Case 1—Method of Treatment

The method of reciprocal inhibition by self-assertion was adopted (Wolpe, 1958). This would decrease the anxiety associated with the aggressive behaviour. It would thus dissipate suppressed aggressive tendencies and reduce the probability of "explosive" and impulsive outbursts. Reduction in the intensity of both anxiety and aggression and therefore a lowering of his general level of emotionality might be expected. The necessity for the anxiety-reducing compulsion, handwashing, would then be removed.

*Response to treatment.* This treatment was carried out over a period of three months. During this time, he was seen very little by the authors since periodic encouragement to be more self-assertive was considered adequate. The M.M.P.I. results obtained during this three month period demonstrated a striking reduction in symptomatology. This was mirrored by a reported improvement in his compulsions. The handwashing compulsion had completely disappeared by the end of the three months' treatment. One month later, he left hospital "relieved".

*Minnesota Multiphasic Personality Inventory Results* (T scores)

| | Sept '58 | Oct '58 | Nov '58 | Dec '58 |
|---|---|---|---|---|
| Hypochondriasis | 72 | 53 | 47 | 58 |
| Depression | 72 | 49 | 66 | 71 |
| Hysteria | 75 | 57 | 66 | 71 |
| Psychopathy | 84 | 58 | 60 | 60 |
| Masculinity/Femininity | 71 | 51 | 63 | 58 |
| Paranoia | 79 | 51 | 68 | 56 |
| Psychasthenia | 99 | 60 | 78 | 65 |
| Schizophrenia | 92 | 67 | 65 | 69 |
| Hypomania | 63 | 55 | 58 | 48 |

| Validity Scales | Sept '58 | Oct '58 | Nov '58 | Dec '58 |
|---|---|---|---|---|
| ? | 67 | 89 | 47 | 49 |
| L | 50 | 57 | 56 | 59 |
| F | 62 | 55 | 60 | 53 |
| K | 64 | 62 | 59 | 67 |

A follow-up was attempted. It is however impossible to report his sub-sequent progress or otherwise, since he failed to reply to several enquiries.

## Case 2—Method of Treatment

Reciprocal inhibition of the conditioned anxiety was again attempted by the development of self-assertive responses (Wolpe, 1958). In this case it was hypothesized that it would increase his confidence with people and reduce his anxiety over social reactions to his behaviour. One might also assume that if he wished to be rid of his homosexuality, the development of self-asser-tive attitudes might help him to resist the homosexual advances of others.

*Response to treatment.* He carried out the instructions over a period of three weeks. During this time, the compulsive thoughts and checking disappeared. He claimed that he was far more confident and that he did not experience guilt over his homosexuality. "I have never felt better for years." He left hospital "recovered" one month after the commencement of treatment.

During a one-year follow-up, there was no recurrence of either guilt feelings for obsessional symptoms, although he was apparently still a practising homosexual.

Four months after discharge, he was readmitted to hospital, having been sacked from his job. This time he complained that his mother was telephon-ing people to tell them he was mad. He gave this as the reason for his re-admission. A few days later, he left hospital against medical advice. He then moved to another part of the country where he was again admitted to hospital some three months later. The events which led to his readmission were not certain. It appeared he had been hypomanic and subsequently suffered from a state of exhaustion. A few months later he returned to his home county and entered hospital again. This time he had feelings of un-reality, depersonalization and auditory hallucinations. He was reported to be still anxious about the presence of his homosexual urges, though there was no return of guilt, compulsive thoughts, or compulsive behaviour. His conversation was reported to be more fluent than previously. During his stay, however, he absconded and attempted suicide by slashing his wrists. On return to hospital he was admitted to a more disturbed ward, where another suicidal attempt was made by trying to stuff the sheets down his throat. He had a course of E.C.T. and a course of deep insulin. This time he left hospital "relieved".

It is apparent from this follow-up that there was no real remission of the psychotic symptoms from which he had initially suffered and that he was still a homosexual. However the specifically treated guilt and the compulsions mediated by it never returned throughout the total period under review.

### Discussion of Cases 1 and 2

The present two cases tentatively confirm the conclusions drawn from the successful treatment of the obsessive-compulsive state previously reported.

Removal of drive tendencies in the acute phase of illness appear to result in the rapid extinction of both compulsive motor and thinking habits dependent upon them. The fact that Case 2 suffered subsequently from a full psychotic breakdown does not appear to invalidate the argument and inferences drawn from these two studies, that treatment of the conditioned autonomic drive will result in rapid amelioration of compulsive habits dependent on this drive in obsessive-compulsive neuroses of acute onset.

The following two cases of obsessional neuroses differ from Cases 1 and 2 in that their symptoms are long-standing.

CASE 3—A single woman teacher had for the past six years endured an obsessive-compulsion, which was evoked whenever she went to the toilet. The compulsion was apparently motivated by a fear of faeces and urine. It consisted of changing the clothes she was wearing for washable ones and removing her corset and stockings. This was followed by a careful scrutiny of the toilet bowl and seat lest they should be soiled in any way. Whenever she urinated she was preoccupied with the thought that she may also have defecated. Doubts also existed about her clothes having touched the toilet. She would spend altogether half an hour going to the toilet. This included the careful examination and arrangement of her clothes. Sometimes she was forced to wear slacks since there was less probability of these touching the toilet seat than a skirt. Associated with these fears was a fear of animal faeces. She would therefore avoid park seats, brushing against walls and lamp-posts, and she was afraid of sitting in peoples' houses where animals were kept as pets. She also insisted upon having a bath every night. This would prove very stressful to her because she could not convince herself that she was thoroughly clean.

Another aspect of her problem concerned her sexual and social life. She was afraid of being in the company of men, lest one should touch her or make advances to her. Even if no such incident occurred, doubts existed in her mind, and she experienced great difficulty in distinguishing between her preoccupation and actuality. She was a very religious person and overconcerned with moral issues. The company of men was potentially dangerous to her since it created the opportunity for temptation and "sinful" behaviour. To get married, she claimed, would make her feel she had committed a sin. Sexual intercourse and pregnancy even within wedlock were perceived as sinful. Being touched by a man would also evoke guilt, though to a lesser degree. If she experienced affection for or anger towards anyone, she had guilt feelings, since both these emotions could lead to what she considerered sinful acts.

Her social activities were very much curtailed by her inability to make use of public seats or public toilets or to enter male company or even to pass a man in the street. She was in fact unable to pursue her profession of teaching for these reasons.

According to her parents, she had had a very religiously-biased education. She had attended a Roman Catholic convent school and had been taught by nuns, who were "bell, book and candle" in their approach. A rigid discipline and code of morals were imposed upon the girls. The patient had apparently been a very "sensitive" child and had interpreted their teaching seriously and literally. Her parents professed more liberal views.

At the age of fourteen she developed religious "scruples". She became concerned about the idea of original sin and the possibility that she had sinned in her behaviour. Attending confession in no way reduced the guilt and she gave up going to church. There was no evidence that she had behaved in any socially or morally unacceptable way, though she claimed that indulging in masturbation once had been sufficient to produce such guilt feelings.

At the age of fifteen she was told the facts of life by a rather prudish aunt. This only served to increase her guilt feelings over sexual urges, rather than enlightening her in any way. For ten weeks she became pre-occupied with thoughts of sex and began looking at people and the outline of their sex organs. She said she experienced great "sexual tension", and she had to stay away from Grammar school. She wanted to be on her own all the time and was afraid of people.

It was not until the age of eighteen, that other symptoms developed. She began to feel dirty when going to the toilet, and her fear of faeces with the associated toilet rituals and avoidance of animals and public seats became evident.

She entered hospital and was given E.C.T. to no avail. Shortly following this carbon dioxide therapy was administered. There was still no improvement. At the age of twenty-four further help was sought.

## PROPOSED THEORETICAL MODEL

During childhood, she was apparently subjected to strong social and religious pressures to which she over-reacted. The intensity of these pressures and her highly labile autonomic nervous system (high neuroticism on the M.P.I.) would seem to account for the excessive response. This response became conditioned to a wide range of pleasurable stimuli, which occurred in conjunction with the punishing ones, namely the religious pressures. The pleasurable stimuli were those from her sexual and aggressive urges. Suppression of these became rewarding through the reduction of the anxiety conditioned to them.

By a process of generalization all stimuli potentially capable of evoking sexual behaviour acquired avoidance drive properties. Similarly all functions of the uro-genital organs became conditioned to the anxiety. Urinating and subsequently defecating were anxiety-provoking. The fear of all faeces and urine of both animals and humans was a result of further stimuli generalization. Park seats and lamp-posts which appeared to have nothing in common with the sexual drive then evoked avoidance behaviour apparently through secondary generalization. The rituals of changing her clothes, etc., prior to using the toilet developed as instrumental acts to reduce the conditioned avoidance drive in those situations.

### Derivation of Method of Treatment

If the hypothesis already stated is correct that in the chronic phase of obsessional illness, the instrumental motor responses are evoked by a variety of conditioned stimuli other than those associated with the initial C.A.D., the removal of this C.A.D. should fail to abolish completely the motor responses. An attempt was made to validate this. The same method of treatment was adopted therefore for this chronic case as for the previous two acute cases.

In Case 1, the development of more self-assertive responses reciprocally inhibited the anxiety associated with aggression and the anxiety-reducing act of handwashing was extinguished through the absence of a reinforcing agent. In this case (3) the anxiety was conditioned initially to the sexual drive and behaviour. According to the above hypothesis in this chronic case reduction of the anxiety conditioned to sex should not extinguish the motor habit or toilet ritual.

*Method of treatment.* An "anxiety" hierarchy of sexual behaviour was constructed for systematic desensitization (Wolpe, 1958). Relaxation was at first achieved by intravenously administered sodium amytal (5 grains). Other methods of relaxation proved unsatisfactory, particularly in the early stages when her anxiety response even to the earliest items was intense. Half-way through the treatment oral administration of the drug seemed adequate. Sixty-four sessions were required for completion of the following hierarchy..This covered a period of nine months.

HIERARCHY

1. Seeing man at a distance on the other side of the road.
2. Passing man in garden (hedge between them).
3. Passing man in street (several yards separating them).
4. Passing man in street.
5. Passing by a mixed group.
6. Goes into room full of people (both sexes), all of whom are seated. She gives them a message.
7. Goes into room full of people (both sexes), all of whom are seated. She gives them a message and receives a reply.
8. Same as 7, though in addition on receiving their reply she gives them an answer.
9. Same as 7, though one now specifies that it is a young man who gives her the initial reply to her message. Item 9 was changed so as to include the young man—she had been interpreting the last two items as a young man speaking to her.
10. Goes into room full of people (both sexes) and stays at one end of room away from the group for one minute.
11. Goes into room full of people (both sexes) and enters into a brief discussion with them for one minute (though still at other end of room).
12. Same as 10 except spends two minutes in room.
13. Same as 11 except spends two minutes in discussion.
14. Hands a message on paper to men in the room.
15. Hands a message on paper to men in the room and waits for reply.
16. Sitting for one second with men (chairs some distance apart).
17. Sitting for one minute with men (chairs some distance apart).
18. Sits for several minutes with men (chairs some distance apart).
19. Talks for one minute sitting in men's company (chairs apart).
20. Talks for a few minutes sitting there (chairs apart).
21. Talks for 5–10 min sitting there (chairs apart).

22. Talks for $^1/_4$ hr sitting there (chairs apart).
23. Talks for 20–30 min sitting there (chairs apart).
24. Talks for 45 min sitting there (chairs apart).
25. Sits next to one of the group (male) for 1 min.
26. Sits next to one of the group (male) for few minutes.
27. Sits next to one of the group (male) for 5–10 min.
28. Sits next to one of the group (male) for 15 min.
29. Sits next to one of the group (male) for 20 min.
30. Sits next to one of the group (male) for 30 min.
31. Sits next to one of the group (male) for 45 min.
32. Walking next to man for a few minutes (implying friendly relationship).
33. Walking next to man for 5–10 min.
34. Walking next to man for 15 min.
35. Walking next to man for 20 min.
36. Walking next to man for 30 min.
37. Walking next to man for 45 min.
38. Sits next to two men for 1 min.
39. Sits next to two men for a few minutes.
40. Sits next to two men for 10 min.
41. Sits next to two men for 20 min.
42. Sits next to two men for 30 min.
43. Sits next to two men for 45 min.
44. Shakes hands with one man (stranger).
45. Shakes hands with two men (strangers).
46. Shakes hands with one man who is a friend.
47. Holds hands with a man who is a friend.
48. Goes out with man and holds hand with him (friend again).
49. Goes out with man and he puts arm round her (friend again).
50. Goes to dance and dances with man (a friend).
51. Goes out with man she is fond of (affectionate relationship).
52. Holding hands with man she is fond of.
53. He puts his arm round her.
54. Goes to dance with man she is fond of—dances with him.
55. Man she is fond of kisses her goodnight on cheek.
56. Man she is fond of kisses her goodnight on cheek and embraces.
57. Man she is fond of kisses her goodnight on mouth.
58. Man she is fond of kisses her goodnight on mouth and embraces her.
59. Man she is fond of, whose moral standards she does not know, kisses her on cheek.
60. Same as 59, in addition embraces.
61. Same as 59, except kisses her on mouth.
62. Same as 61, in addition embraces.
63. Husband takes off his top clothing whilst she is in the bedroom.
64. Husband in pyjamas.
65. Husband in pyjama trousers goes into bathroom.
66. Husband in underpants only goes into bathroom.
67. Husband in bath.
68. Husband in pyjamas kisses and embraces her.
69. Husband in pyjama trousers kisses and embraces her.
70. Husband in underpants kisses and embraces her.
71. Both undressing together.
72. Kissing husband passionately in pyjamas.
73. Kissing husband passionately in pyjama trousers.

74. Kissing husband passionately in underpants.
75. Kissing husband passionately, both in state of undress.
76. Same as 75, though sitting on a bed.
77. Both getting into bed together at night.
78. Both sleeping together.
79. Both lying awake before going to sleep.
80. Husband kisses her whilst lying in bed.
81. Husband kisses and embraces her in bed.
82. Tongue kiss and embrace in bed.

*Response to treatment.* Her response during this period of treatment was in many ways encouraging. Her anxiety response to sexual stimuli was very much less. She could pass men in the street, sit next to them on public vehicles, wait in shop or bus queues with them and speak to them. Two incidences she related with considerable satisfaction. She had waited with a stranger, a young man, for half an hour at a bus stop and had become engaged in a lengthy conversation. This almost resulted in a date. On a second occasion, she renewed a childhood acquaintanceship (a young man of her own age). Her general behaviour was more assertive and she stated she could at least express affection to her parents without experiencing guilt.

Her generalized fear of urination, defecation and excreta was partially reduced. She could walk past lamp-posts without experiencing the urge to scrutinize her clothes. The toilet ritual however was unimproved as hypothesized. It was her opinion that it had become worse. It seemed at least that she was more concerned over this symptom than she had been at the commencement of treatment.

CASE 4—A married American lady, aged 48, was referred for the treatment of a severe, longstanding obsessive-compulsive state.

Her one compulsion consisted of the repeated reading and checking of long and detailed instructions of what should happen to her body following her death. She had composed and typed in capital letters three foolscap sheets of instructions and made several copies of them. These copies were distributed in various drawers and cupboards around the house. Consequently, should she die, the possibility of these copies being discovered and the instructions contained therein being carried out, was increased. The content, of the instructions was very morbid; it demanded that the patient's body should be completely dissected. All the details as to how this should be done were included. Many sentences and qualifying adjectives and adverbs were repeated to guarantee that the people reading the instructions would be able to carry them out absolutely according to her wishes.

The reading and checking of these copies was always performed before retiring to bed at night. Not only every word but every letter had to be checked and rechecked. At its worst this ritual might take her all night to complete. Sometimes it might take her several hours and at best only $^3/_4$ hr. She never resorted to the compulsion during the day.

She stated that the reason for this compulsion was her intense fear of being buried alive. In order to avert this possibility it was necessary, she claimed, for her instructions to be carried out immediately by any person who might assume her to be dead. The assurance of a final confirmation of her death by a doctor was not sufficient to allay the fear, uor was the assurance of cremation adequate for her.

Associated with this problem was her claustrophobia. This was, however, more long-standing and pre-dated both the obsessive-compulsive habit and her fear of being buried alive. She was unable to go into an elevator, to travel underground or to sit in a room with the door locked. Fear of being in a confined space seemed to be common to both her phobias: her claustrophobia and her fear of being buried alive. The smaller and darker the space in which she was confined the more terrified she became. The thought of being enclosed in a coffin thus represented to her the maximum stress.

The patient maintained that she had always had a dislike of being in an underground railway or in any enclosed space, that is as long as she could remember. A number of incidents had occurred, however, which aggravated this dislike until it developed ultimately into the proportions of a phobia.

At the age of 22 she underwent an operation. The anaesthetic was administered by inhalation, which she recalled produced an unpleasant sensation and she felt she was going to suffocate. This she claimed had some influence on the development of her claustrophobia since restriction in breathing would be an inevitable part of being enclosed. She felt, however, that fear of suffocation was not basic to her problem, though perhaps a facet of it.

Shortly following this operation and before she had completely regained her strength, she walked through an underground tunnel which had just been opened for pedestrians in New York. She apparently collapsed. In her own opinion this did not occur because of fear but because she had been feeling physically unwell. It nevertheless served to reinforce the anxiety she already possessed in relation to confined spaces.

She eventually sought treatment in a mental hospital where she stayed for nine years. It is doubtful that the severity of her claustrophobia alone had prevented her from coping outside hospital during the whole of this period. There may have been some secondary gain for her to remain in hospital. She had married an alcoholic. No improvement in her claustrophobia took place whilst she was in hospital until she had a leucotomy. Following this there was some relief for a short time, but the phobia ultimately returned in all its original intensity.

She left hospital and no further significant event occurred until some years later (and two years prior to being seen by the authors). She caught sight of the heading of an article in a newspaper. It read, "Man put in coffin Alive". She was so horrified by the statement that she dared not read further. The possibility of this happening to herself occurred to her. This fear grew as did her obsessional compulsions.

She was seen by a psychiatrist as an out-patient. He obtained a copy of the newspaper article. He tried to convince her that the story was fictitious and that it had a happy ending. This failed to destroy her doubts and some time later she was admitted into another hospital. She was unable to read any newspaper lest it contained any other similar material.

The fact that her husband was unreliable exacerbated her condition. She felt he could not be trusted to carry out her instructions, should he at any time take her for dead. The following is an extract from the patient's instructions:

Before my body is moved from the bed I die on, that is while my body is still on the bed I die on, all and everyone of all the main arteries of all and every kind in the whole of my body and all and everyone of all and every artery of all and every kind in the whole of my body definitely must all and everyone definitely all be completely and absolutely severed right through in fullest detail so that every single drop of blood in the whole of my body is definitely all completely and absolutely drained right out of the whole of my body, and definitely not a single drop of blood is left in the whole of my body, and my heart must also definitely be pierced the whole way right through my heart in fullest detail and this piercing of my heart the whole way right through my heart in fullest detail must also definitely all be done in fullest detail several times in each and everyone of definitely all and everyone of definitely all the exactly very most vital spots in the whole of my heart which make absolutely and positively sure beyond all possible shadow of doubt that I am absolutely and positively and completely dead.

## PROPOSED THEORETICAL MODEL

There had been a number of traumatic experiences in her history which reinforced what was already a seemingly mild anxiety response to enclosed spaces; firstly, the restricted breathing during the administration of an anaesthetic; collapsing in an underground tunnel and finally the reading of a newspaper headline concerning confinement in a coffin. These so aggravated the claustrophobia that some drive-reducing measure became essential to her. This consisted of the repeated writing and checking of instructions concerning what should happen to her body after death, in order to prevent burial and enclosure.

### Derivation of Method of Treatment

This was a second case of a long-standing obsessional illness for which the same method of treatment was proposed as for Case 3 in an attempt to test the same hypothesis. The initial C.A.D. in this case was the claustrophobia. This was treated by the method of reciprocal inhibition.

*Method of treatment.* Stage 1. A graded series of rooms were planned for her to enter alone. These decreased in size and increased in darkness, that is contained fewer windows. The first time she was required to enter any room, it was for a relatively short period of time (a few seconds) with the door first opened wide. On each subsequent session, the door was closed a little more until she was able to sit in the room with the door fully closed but not locked. The next stage involved locking the door for increasing periods of time. The time was gradually increased to one hour. Five rooms and one large cupboard were included in the hierarchy. She was seen twice a day for two and a half months.

This method of treatment resulted in a marked improvement in her claustrophobia. She reported that she could travel in elevators and had no fear of enclosed spaces. In spite of the significant reduction in her claustrophobia, her fear of confinement in a coffin still remained.

Stage 2. It was decided to extend the graded programme to include material related to such confinement. Due to her extreme anxiety response to this and practical difficulties, the programme constituted only verbal material for her to read. She was first required to read emotionally-charged words in a neutral context. The context was gradually modified and extended to become more anxiety-provoking.

She was first required to read aloud in one session the following words:

| Coffin | Buried | Alive | Grave | Dead |
|--------|--------|-------|-------|------|
| Underground | Funeral | Dark | Locked | Confined |

Some of these words were then introduced into four sentences, which she read aloud in five sessions. More sentences containing these words were then added at subsequent phases of the treatment, until finally four complete paragraphs had been complied (see below). At each phase, she read aloud the sentences which were then constituting each of the four sections. The end of each phase is indicated by dotted lines and the number of sessions spent in the phase is in parenthesis.

1. The doors to banks are always locked at night ..... (5) They are locked to prevent robberies ..... (3) Banks contain many thousands of pounds confined usually in underground vaults ..... (5) These vaults are usually buried deep in the earth ..... (6) It is a specialized job to build a vault. It must be so strong that when locked no one can force an entry to steal the money so carefully protected inside ..... (11) Vaults are so air-conditioned that bank-tellers can work within the locked vaults for several hours without strain ..... (4) On one occasion it was known for a person to have been locked in one of the vaults accidentally ..... (3) During this time there was a power-failure and the air-conditioning also failed, leaving the vault in complete darkness and insufficient air-supply ..... (6)
2. During winter-time it is dark early in the evening ..... (5) Such darkness curtails the amount of time children can play in the parks, etc. ..... (3) Park gates are always locked thus preventing the children from entering ..... (5) Sometimes children are locked in in the parks. They manage to get out of the park by climbing over the park wall ..... (6) This is not always accomplished without hazard—and many is the time a child has called "snakes alive, there's a cop waiting for me". Such children, caught in the act, do not lightly under take such again in the future. They do not want to be locked up in an approved school or confined to a certain area on probation. It is admitted, however, that there are some children who never respond to discipline from the cradle to the grave ..... (11), and in consequence spend the greater part of their young lives "buried alive" in institutions and schools of correction ..... (4) Severe misdemeanours are punished by solitary confinement to small, dark cells for indefinite periods of time ..... (3) The length of time may be so long they wonder if they are forgotten ..... (6)
3. In the army disobedient soldiers are sometimes punished by being confined to barracks ..... (5) This restriction to their movements and liberty is an effective deterrent to future disobedience on the part of a high percentage of soldiers ..... (3) Soldiers always receive such punishment with the gravest of expressions ..... (5) They feel liberty is one of the most precious things in their lives and to be deprived of it indefinitely, as were prisoners of war, it would be much better to be dead. So they conform to army discipline ..... (6), and undertake whatever tasks the army orders, even bringing to camp under escort dangerous rebels of the "Dead-or-alive" category ..... (11), or pretending to be dead after a mock ambush ..... (4) This act may be so convincing that they may find themselves being carried to a burial ground ..... (3) In order to avoid detection, they allow themselves to be buried with the intention of digging their way out when the "coast is clear " ..... (6)
4. Electricity is sometimes transferred from power-station to user by means of underground systems of cables ..... (5) These cables are especially re-inforced to withstand the damp and pressure ..... (3) Any damage to such cables necessitates the electrician working below ground level. Because of the poor lighting and darkness often encountered under such conditions, portable electric lights are used ..... (5) In digging into the earth, the electrician often finds objects which have been buried for many years. One such person is said to have found some Roman ruins ..... (6) and what appears to have been the remains of an ancient cemetery. In such cemeteries ancient funeral rites were performed before burial, such as the slaughter of a lamb in the sacrifice to the gods in the presence of the dead body in the coffin ..... (11) and the oldest surviving relative of the deceased lying in an open coffin in the "preparation for death" ceremony ..... (4) Before the coffin of the deceased is lowered into the grave the relative's coffin is also closed ..... (9)

The next part of Stage 2 of the treatment was aimed at helping her to cope with factual material. Extracts from a newspaper cutting were written out for her to read. These extracts were graded into what seemed an anxiety hierarchical order. At each session she was required to read one additional extract, so that twelve sessions were required to complete the hierarchy. Finally, she read the whole of the newspaper cutting itself.

1. Trapped under bricks. Then yesterday he was home again to tell his story.
2. It felt like a week to Mr. X—trapped under bricks in a hospital site at—. Then yesterday he was home again to tell his story.
3. It felt like a week to Mr. X, the 44 hours he was buried alive trapped under bricks in a hospital site at—. Then yesterday he was home again to tell his story.
4. It felt like a week to Mr. X, the 44 hours he was buried alive trapped under half a ton of bricks in a hospital site at—. Then yesterday he was home again to tell his story.
5. It felt like a week to Mr. X, the 44 hours he was buried alive, trapped under half a ton of bricks in the dark, dank, bitterly cold basement of a hospital site at—. Then yesterday he was home again to tell his story.
6. My Lost Weekend—buried alive.
    It felt like a week to Mr. X the 44 hours he was buried alive, trapped under half a ton of bricks in the dark, dank, bitterly cold basement of a hospital site at—. Each slight movement brought another shower of bricks crashing down on him. Then yesterday he was home again to tell his story.
7. "Every now and again I could hear footsteps only a few yards away. But either my voice was too weak from yelling for help or the machinery would start up and drown my shouts.
8. I tried to imagine how long it would be before they missed me. The men at ground level might have thought I had walked off because I had only been there a couple of weeks.
    My landlady at—would not have bothered because I had only been with her a few days and I was paid up. I had to pin my hopes on my widowed mother up in—.
9. Remember I thought I had been there several days. I should have phoned her on Saturday night. By Wednesday or Thursday she would have been worried and reported me missing.
    I could imagine the police calling at the site and a big search starting.
    But would they find me in that vast place? Would they even think of looking in the basement? I had no idea.
10. No one knew where I had gone.
    It was black down there. I brushed against this pile of bricks and they clattered down around me, knocking me to the ground."

*The Pain.*

    "The cramp was hell. The pain was so bad sometimes that I passed out.
    When I woke up, I started shouting again, but no one heard. I thought my leg was broken.
11. I tried to think of the Cup matches. That kept my mind occupied for some time until I blacked out again.
    When I came to, I thought of my folks at home.
    I wondered that they would think when I was released, if ever they found me.
    I got scared that no one would find me, and I would rot away in the basement.
12. On Sunday morning I really began to get scared. There was water in the basement and it started trickling into my Wellington boots. I was afraid the level was rising and that I might be drowned. My thoughts began to wander after that, and I can't recall anything more."

Fifty-five sessions were devoted to reading this material aloud. Once she was able to read it without experiencing anxiety, further desensitization was attempted by visualization of situations more directly related to her own death and burial.

### HIERARCHY

1. Doctor examines her whilst she is unconscious.
2. Doctor examines her breathing whilst she is unconscious.
3. Doctor examines her heart-beat whilst she is unconscious.
4. She lies dead and is examined by a doctor. She is left for a few days so there is absolute certainty of death. He examines her again.
5. She lies dead and is examined by a doctor. Her head has been cut from her body only one minute after the doctor has left. She is then cremated.
6. Lies dead. Examined once by doctor. Left for a few minutes before decapitation and cremation.
7. Same as 6 except 15 min delay between examination and decapitation.
8. Same as 6 except 30 min delay between examination and decapitation.
9. Same as 6 except 60 min delay between examination and decapitation.
10. Same as 6 except few hours delay between examination and decapitation.
11. Lies dead and is examined once by the doctor. She is left for a few days followed by decapitation and cremation.
12. Same as 11 except left for one week.
13. Is taken to morgue following death, i.e. before doctor examines her. Is examined by doctor in the morgue. She is then left in the morgue for a few minutes before decapitation and cremation.
14. Same as 13, except left in morgue for 15 min before decapitation and cremation.
15. Same as 13, except left in morgue for 30 min before decapitation and cremation.
16. Same as 13, except left in morgue for 60 min before decapitation and cremation.
17. Same as 13, except left in morgue few hours before decapitation and cremation.
18. Same as 13, except left in morgue a day before decapitation and cremation.
19. Same as 13, except left in morgue a few days before decapitation and cremation.
20. She is taken to morgue and examined there by a doctor. She is decapitated and covered with a sheet 1 sec before cremation.
21. Same as 20, except covered with sheet 5 sec before cremation.
22. Same as 20, except covered with sheet 1 min before cremation.
23. Same as 20, except covered with sheet 5 min before cremation.
24. Same as 20, except covered with sheet 15 min before cremation.
25. Same as 20, except covered with sheet 30 min before cremation.
26. Same as 20, except covered with sheet 1 hr before cremation.
27. Same as 20, except covered with sheet 1 sec before decapitation and cremation.
28. Same as 27, except covered with sheet 5 sec before decapitation and cremation.
29. Same as 27, except covered with sheet 1 min before decapitation and cremation.
30. Same as 27, except covered with sheet 5 min before decapitation and cremation.
31. Same as 27, except covered with sheet 15 min before decapitation and cremation.
32. Same as 27, except covered with sheet 30 min before decapitation and cremation.
33. Same as 27, except covered with sheet 60 min before decapitation and cremation.
34. Same as 27, except covered with sheet a few hours before decapitation and cremation.
35. Same as 27, except covered with sheet a day before decapitation and cremation.
36. In morgue covered with sheet up to shoulders 1 sec before doctor's examination.
37. In morgue covered with sheet up to shoulders 5 sec before doctor's examination.

38. In morgue covered with sheet up to shoulders 1 min before doctor's examination.
39. In morgue covered with sheet up to shoulders 5 min before doctor's examination.
40. In morgue covered with sheet up to shoulders 15 min before doctor's examination.
41. In morgue covered with sheet up to shoulders 30 min before doctor's examination.
42. In morgue covered with sheet up to shoulders 60 min before doctor's examination.
43. In morgue covered with sheet up to shoulders a few hours before doctor's examination.
44. In morgue covered with sheet up to shoulders 1 day before doctor's examination.
45. In morgue covered with sheet up to shoulders a few days before doctor's examination.
46. Examination in morgue by doctor, put in open coffin (i.e. prior to cremation not burial) and to lie there for 1 sec before being decapitated.
47. Same as 46, except to lie there for 5 sec.

*Response to treatment.* The improvement in her claustrophobia was apparently maintained. The extended programme relating to burial, however, failed to have any benefical effect. Although she was able to advance in the hierarchies and to comply with the requirements of this therapeutic technique, she nevertheless reported no decrease in the fear of burial. Throughout the whole period of treatment, there was also no improvement in her compulsive checking.

### Discussion of Cases 3 and 4

It appears that when one is dealing with the treatment of chronic compulsive symptomatology, treatment of the original C.A.D. is not directly relevant to the removal of the terminal motor symptoms. In Case 3 particularly, it appears that as one problem was removed she became more bothered and preoccupied with the residual motor habits. The motor responses in both these cases were apparently related by a process of generalization to conditioned stimuli other than those evoking the initial C.A.D. In Case 3, the stimuli generalization might have constituted faeces, urine and dirt.

In Case 4, one must also consider whether there were secondary rewards available to the patient, and that she preferred to remain in hospital. It was certainly the case that she had had a most difficult life with her husband.

A further problem that might be raised is whether her leucotomy had significantly impeded learning. This seems unlikely because it did not appear to impede learning with respect to overcoming her claustrophobia. Also Case 6 (to follow) showed a very rapid response to a deconditioning programme (hierarchical approach) after a leucotomy. Assuming therefore that the hierarchies were relevant, one might consider that her failure to respond might have been partly attributable to a lack of desire to be better. This has previously been commented upon with respect to stammering (Lehner, 1960).

CASE 5—A single woman had suffered from symptoms of an obsessive-compulsive type for some ten years. She was admitted to hospital mainly because of her symptoms of depression which seemed to be reactive to her incapacitating obsessions.

The main feature of her obsessional illness was compulsive handwashing which appeared to arise from doubts about contamination of herself by dirt. In order to convince herself that she was clean she had to wash her hands four or five times. She was forced to use her "own" bar of soap and her own towel. The whole process would take fifteen minutes.

It was necesary for her to wash her hands after every daily activity for she believed that everything she touched might have been handled by someone before her whose habits were not clean. Door-knobs and taps were particularly anxiety-provoking since these were frequently handled by many people and her chances of "being contaminated" were therefore increased. The toilet was an added stress and after use her nails had to be scrubbed. This was in addition to the usual handwashing. Public conveniences were considered far too contaminating and were never used.

Whenever she took a bath and washed her hair the whole operation used to last several hours. This was because the bath and the washbasin had to be cleaned thoroughly until they were "spotless" and every part of herself had to be washed several times. Fresh water for rinsing was also essential. Furthermore she required her mother to sit by her in order to reassure her continually that she had thoroughly washed every inch of herself.

Other precautions were taken to avoid contamination. She carefully avoided brushing against walls or other people's clothes. Her own articles of clothing were always stored in a place especially preserved for the purpose and untouched either by anyone else or their belongings. Should any of her possessions be handled by other than herself she was compelled to wash them.

Walking down any street or thoroughfare was an effort since she had to examine each place where she trod for patches of dirt.

On speaking to people she could never be certain that they had not spat in her face. She was therefore compelled to wash her face after every conversation.

Other repetitive actions had previously been apparent although at the time of admission to hospital they were not evident. This was chiefly because she used to delegate to her mother many activities that were particularly stressful. For instance, continually checking and rechecking a door once it was closed was no longer necessary since her mother used to open and close all doors for her. In addition, she would never turn a tap on herself and hardly ever ventured outside the house alone lest she were required to handle something with no facilities available for washing. She also had difficulty sitting on any seats which were used by other people.

Some of her history was difficult to elicit since she appeared "defensive" and was not forthcoming with information. It seemed she had lived with her uncle, mother, father and two younger brothers since being a child. Her father died when she was twenty-five years old. This was very disturbing for her. She appears to have been an anxious person who was also subject to fits of depression. She had, for instance, been employed in many jobs leaving one as soon as she had a depressive episode and taking up another. She had been employed in three factories and in one hotel as a chambermaid. In this last post she had contracted scabies which she believed was due to having handled the visitors' towels. Her next job was that of a shop-assistant.

During this time she began courting and became very attracted towards a man. She nevertheless disapproved morally of some of his love-making. Furthermore she found out that the man was already married. This was a shock to her and she felt she ought to break off her affair with him. However, she still continued to go out with him. This particular incident seems to have had the most significance in the development of her obsessional symptoms. She experienced considerable guilt and felt "dirty" when she went back to her work serving in the store. Anxiety was aroused whenever she went to the toilet because she was afraid of faeces getting on to her clothes and making her dirty. The handwashing and other obsessional features did not develop until some time later. She could not be explicit about the time interval.

It was several years later that she sought psychiatric help and entered hospital for a course of E.C.T. Whilst in hospital she contracted an infection of the kidney. This only increased her already existing fears of contamination and dirt. After seven weeks she left hospital. There was little improvement in her condition. Four years later she was readmitted to hospital for the investigation and treatment of depression and obsessional symptoms. The latter had become incapacitating.

## PROPOSED THEORETICAL MODEL

Through a process of socialization, anxiety had become conditioned to sexual behaviour. The incident with the married man had evoked a strong anxiety response which appears to have generalized from the sexual drive to a wide range of stimuli, including the uro-genital organs and their product and all forms of dirt. Where avoidance of these stimuli was not possible, excessive washing was adopted as a means of anxiety-reduction.

### Derivation of Method of Treatment

One of the hypotheses posed in the introduction appears to have been borne out by the treatment of the last two cases, namely that removal of the original C.A.D. has virtually no effect upon the long-standing motor habit. The treatment of this case was designed to assess on the other hand whether removal of this motor component alone would be sufficient to effect a complete and permanent remission.

*Method of treatment.* Stimuli *now* evoking the handwashing compulsion were graded into "anxiety" hierarchies. She was required to perform rather than to visualize these hierarchies. It was hoped to reciprocally inhibit the anxiety which had generalized to these stimuli such that the anxiety-reducing compulsion was not now evoked. A negative habit of not washing should then be reinforced. A similar method of treating a compulsive habit of stone-kicking has been reported (Walton, 1960).

### HIERARCHY A. (Door Knob)

1. Touches the door handle which has been first wiped with a cloth washed in hot water.
2. Touches the door handle which has been wiped with a hot, damp cloth.
3. Touches the door handle which has been wiped with a cold, wet cloth.
4. Touches the same handle which has been wiped with a dry cloth.
5. Touches the same handle which has not been wiped.
6. Touches a door-handle which is more frequently used.
7. Touches the handle of an outside door.
8. Touches a ward door-handle which is not used frequently.
9. Touches a ward door-handle which is used more frequently, but which is first wiped with a hot, wet cloth.
10. Touches the same door-handle as no. 9, but wiped with a dry cloth.

## HIERARCHY B. (Chair)

1. Sits on a wooden chair which is first wiped with a hot, wet cloth.
2. Sits on a different wooden chair, which has been used more, and which is first wiped with a hot, wet cloth.
3. Sits on the same wooden chair as No. 2, which is wiped with a cold, wet cloth.
4. Sits on a wooden chair which is first wiped with a dry cloth.
5. Sits on a wooden chair which is not wiped.
6. Sits on an upholstered chair, not used by patients.
7. Sits on an upholstered chair which is used by the patients in the department.
8. Sits on an upholstered chair which is in a ward.
9. Sits on the same chair as No. 8 but leans back in it.
10. Sits on the same chair as No. 8 and left to relax for an indefinite length of time.
11. Sits on this chair which has first been touched by the psychologist.
12. Sits on this chair, on which has been placed a piece of paper from the floor.

## HIERARCHY C. (Walls)

1. Touches toilet wall with right hand.
2. Touches toilet wall with both hands.
3. Touches a part of the toilet wall near the light switch.
4. Touches a part of the toilet wall on a level with the hip.
5. Touches a part of the toilet wall on a level with the toilet seat.
6. Touches a part of the toilet wall under the toilet roll.
7. Touches the toilet door.
8. Touches the part of the wall immediately next to the toilet seat.
9. Touches the toilet roll-holder.
10. Touches the toilet roll after a full round of paper has been torn off.
11. Touches the toilet roll after half the outer portion has been torn off.

## HIERARCHY D. (Picking up objects from the floor)

1. Picks a clean piece of paper from a clean floor, without touching the floor.
2. Picks a crumpled piece of paper from a clean floor, without touching the floor.
3. Picks a piece of paper with ink on, from a clean floor, without touching the floor.
4. Picks a clean piece of paper from a washed part of the floor, and touches the floor.
5. Same as 4, but using a part of the floor only wiped with a dry cloth.
6. Same as 4, but using a part of the floor which is neither wiped nor washed.
7. Picks a clean piece of paper from a more used part of the floor, and touches the floor.
8. Picks a clean piece of paper from a wiped part of the floor on the ward, and touches the floor.
9. Same as No. 8, but using an unwiped part of floor.
10. Picks a clean piece of paper from a more used part of the floor on the ward, and touches the floor.
11. Picks a clean piece of paper from the floor near the ward door.

## HIERARCHY E. (Walking)

1. Walks along the corridor leading to the psychology department, without looking down.
2. Walks along a relatively infrequently used hospital corridor.
3. Walks along a hospital corridor frequently used by patients.

4. Walks along a path outside which is clean.
5. Walks along a dirtier path outside.
6. Walks up the side of the stairs, without lifting her skirt.
7. Walks up the centre of the stairs without lifting her skirt.
8. Walks along a muddy path.

## HIERARCHY F. (Toilet)

1. Uses departmental toilet after the seat has been wiped with a hot, wet cloth.
2. Same as 1 except that toilet is wiped with hot, damp cloth.
3. Same as 1 but toilet is wiped with a cold, wet cloth.
4. Same as 1 but toilet is wiped with a dry cloth.
5. Uses departmental toilet without it having been wiped at all.

## HIERARCHY G. (Washing Hands)

1. Washes her hands after the water has been run into the basin for her.
2. Washes her hands and runs her own water into the basin after the tap and plug have been washed for her.
3. Washes her hands and runs her own water into the basin, without the tap and plug having been washed.
4. The same as 3, but required to perform within the time limit of 1 min 45 sec.
5. The same as 3, but given time limit of 1 min 30 sec.
6. The same as 3, but given time limit of 1 min 15 sec.

Phase 1 of the treatment consisted of Hierarchies $A_1$, $B_1$, $C_1$, $D_1$, $E_1$, $F_1$, $G_1$ (27 sessions).
Phase 2 of the treatment consisted of Hierarchies $A_2$, $B_2$, $C_2$, $D_2$, $E_2$, $F_2$, $G_1$ (5 sessions).
Phase 3 of the treatment consisted of Hierarchies $A_3$, $B_3$, $C_3$, $D_3$, $E_3$, $F_3$, $G_1$ (3 sessions).
Phase 4 of the treatment consisted of Hierarchies $A_4$, $B_4$, $C_4$, $D_4$, $E_4$, $F_4$, $G_1$ (4 sessions).
Phase 5 of the treatment consisted of Hierarchies $A_5$, $B_5$, $C_5$, $D_5$, $E_5$, $F_5$, $G_1$ (4 sessions).
Phase 6 of the treatment consisted of Hierarchies $A_6$, $B_6$, $C_6$, $D_6$, $E_6$, $F_5$, $G_2$ (8 sessions).
Phase 7 of the treatment consisted of Hierarchies $A_7$, $B_7$, $C_7$, $D_7$, $E_7$, $F_5$, $G_3$ (11 sessions).
Phase 8 of the treatment consisted of Hierarchies $A_8$, $B_8$, $C_7$, $D_8$, $E_8$, $F_5$, $G_3$ (14 sessions).
Phase 9 of the treatment consisted of Hierarchies $A_8$ (18 sessions), $B_9$ (18 sessions), $C_7$ (8 sessions) and $C_8$ (10 sessions), $D_8$ (18 sessions), $E_8$ (10 sessions) and $E_9$ (8 sessions), $F_5$ (18 sessions), $G_3$ (10 sessions) and $G_4$ (8 sessions).
Phase 10 of the treatment consisted of Hierarchies $A_9$, $B_{10}$, $C_9$, $D_9$, $E_9$, $F_5$, $G_5$ (15 sessions).
Phase 11 of the treatment consisted of Hierarchies $A_{10}$, $B_{11}$, $C_{10}$, $D_{10}$, $E_9$, $F_5$, $G_6$ (6 sessions).
Phase 12 of the treatment consisted of Hierarchies $A_{10}$, $B_{12}$, $C_{11}$, $D_{11}$, $E_9$, $F_5$, $G_6$ (8 sessions).

She was encouraged to decrease the time spent in performing items of hierarchies D, E, F and G, since these situations usually evoked lengthy scrutinization. On the other hand, she was encouraged to spend longer touching objects and sitting on chairs (i.e. hierarchies A, B and C) since she usually avoided these activities. Between Stages 11 and 12 an attempt was made to speed up her progress by requesting her to perform hierarchies A, B, C, D and E of phase 11 by herself three times a day. This she did for seven days.

*Response to treatment.* Such treatment continued for two months. The mother was interviewed and it was her opinion that the patient did not now avoid passing her mother and brother at home nor did she mind brushing past coats hanging in the hall. She also did not spend as long washing her hands and was more prepared to leave the wash-basin (after a few minutes there). She spent less time washing her hair and shared the soap used by the rest of the family. When the mother had volunteered to turn on taps for her, the patient had refused the offer. On buses she did not shrink back as she passed people.

This improvement was maintained for a few weeks. However the hierarchies could not be completed as she could not advance any further in them. Similarly no further improvement was noted outside the hospital. She began complaining about the patients on the ward and their "dirty" habits, which she was finding increasingly intolerable. It is unlikely that this was due to a real deterioration in their ways, but rather an increase in her own anxieties. She did in fact admit that the ward was not objectively becoming less clean, but that she herself could no longer live in the conditions.

### Discussion of Case 5

It would seem that even in the chronic obsessive-compulsive state treatment of the motor compulsion *per se* is inadequate. It gives support to Eysenck's contention (1960) mentioned earlier that only a partial cure may be expected should only the motor reaction be extinguished and the historically earlier conditioned autonomic responses ignored.

The inference that may be drawn from the treatment of these three chronic obsessionals (Cases 3, 4 and 5) is that the extinction of *either* initial conditioned autonomic drives alone (Cases 3 and 4) or the motor habits mediated by these (Case 5) does not effect a permanent cure of long-standing symptomatology.

As hypothesized in the introduction, therapy in the chronic case should constitute the reduction of both the drive tendencies and the motor reactions developing from them.

CASE 6—A middle-aged man with a long history of mental illness was referred for the psychological treatment of a severe obsessive-compulsive habit which had persisted for many years. It has grown steadily worse over the past three years.

He was compelled to wash his hands everytime he touched either "an animate or inanimate object". This handwashing would last from two to twenty minutes. If for any reason he could not wash his hands the anxiety would be so great it "would block his mental state". He would then be unable to do anything and would literally become immobile. This symptom was seen at its worst in the morning when he had to get dressed or at any time when he was forced to change his clothes. After putting on every article of clothing he had to go the bathroom to wash his hands. On each occasion that he returned to wash, the time he would spend over his hands would increase until, at the final stage of dressing, he would take a full twenty minutes washing. He stated that the whole process would take three to five hours. He would use one large bar of soap per day.

Although he could touch nothing without subsequently resorting to his compulsion some objects, he admitted, aroused more anxiety than others. He felt that some people and things would contaminate him more than others. "Contamination" to him was not synonymous with dirt or infection. He defined it rather as "hypocrisy and pretence". Persons whom he thought were adopting a façade of high morals, religious scruples and conservatism would be considered the most contaminating—"they were not spontaneous or at harmony within themselves". He could never ascertain whether or not any person answered this description or whether they had or had not touched any particular object. He therefore became reluctant to touch anything or to speak to anybody. He was reticent in his general behaviour and said he had difficulty in expressing himself. He also claimed that he had experienced the greatest difficulty with his father who represented for him the most hypocritical person.

Every action was a considerable effort for him, whether or not it necessitated objects being touched. He would invariably hesitate for several seconds before entering a room, walking upstairs or getting up from a chair.

According to the patient his problems started early in his life. They mainly revolved around his father who was a very strict and religious man and whose discipline was described as "puritanical" and reminiscent of the Victorian era. His religious persuasion was Evangelical. The father never deviated from a strict code of ethics and expected his son to do the same.

At the age of seventeen the patient began to experience homosexual urges. He went out with a young boy and admitted to having had homosexual relations with him, though he denied believing this was either unlawful or immoral at the time. He later became aware of the potential harm in what he had done when he read of a boy who had had hospital treatment following a homosexual assault. He then wondered whether he also had hurt the young boy. This guilt generalized and soon he began to be afraid of talking to people lest he should hurt their feelings.

The guilt was aggravated by his father's attitude to the problem. According to the patient his father had never learned to face the unpleasant realities of life and turned his back on anything that was not socially respectable. He therefore considered the patient's behaviour too repulsive even to discuss. The patient gave up all his social activities as well as his homosexual practices. He began to read philosophy and obtained a considerable amount of literature on the social condemnation of homosexuality. Although his homosexual activities had never been discovered he became very disturbed about the social implications. He felt he would be ostracized by society and that he would lose his friends and his job. His feelings were a mixture of guilt about himself and hostility towards society in general. These developed to severe proportions. By the time he was twenty he had paranoid ideas that people were going to lynch him. His guilt was so intense that "every motor outlet was guilt-ridden". To enjoy himself or to derive pleasure from any outlet was perceived as sinful. He deliberately adopted the life of a "hermit". This constituted more and more withdrawal from people and an increased pre-occupation with religion. He managed to hold a very routine clerical job until the age of twenty-three when he was discharged from it.

A year later he attemped suicide by taking 125 aspirins. He was admitted to a general hospital. On recovery he returned home. His mental condition in no way improved. He was then admitted to a mental hospital. Within a few months he was discharged. For the next two years his activities became even more restricted. He never went further than one hundred yards from his home and remained fearful of meeting anyone. At about this time his compulsive handwashing and sense of contamination were in the early stages of development.

He was again admitted to a mental hospital and received a course of E.C.T. Following this he discharged himself. Considerable deterioration in his mental condition then took place. The guilt increased and he felt he was not worthy to live. He therefore deprived himself of food and drink. For a third time he was admitted to the same mental hospital where he was certified and diagnosed as a schizophrenic. In addition to his mental symptoms he suffered from malnutrition because of his refusal to take food. He absconded from hospital but was brought back again. He remained for another three years. During this time he attempted suicide a second time by trying to pierce his heart with a pair of scissors. His treatment consisted of forty-eight insulin comas. He was then placed in a less disturbed ward, where he reported some improvement. The handwashing and fear of contamination gradually became worse, however, and he received a cylocaine infiltration into the frontal lobes. Although he himself reported that he gained no benefit from this operation he was discharged from hospital.

Two months later he attemped suicide a third time by taking 108 grains of sodium amytal and two tots of whisky. This resulted in a fourth admission to a mental hospital. Following discharge he noted some improvement. He started to go to the cinema once a week. However, he could not take a job, his handwashing was completely incapacitating and his fear of contamination severe, particulary in relation to his father. He found it almost impossible to speak to his father and took great pains to avoid any physical or social contact with him. There was also a fear of "being hemmed in", by his father or people like him. He stated that he felt they were going to "crush" his individuality and force him to adopt once more the religious hermit-like existence. He admitted, moreover, that the guilt he had experienced over his homosexuality was unjustifiable as was the approach of his father and that he no longer had guilt feelings. He had been functioning at this poor level outside hospital for several years and attending an out-patient clinic. He was then referred for the psychological treatment of the compulsive handwashing, by far the most distressing and handicapping feature of his condition.

## PROPOSED THEORETICAL MODEL

The trauma which seemed to be originally responsible for precipitating the first symptoms at the age of 17, was the threat of punishment and ostracism for his offending behaviour, namely the homosexual assault. Intense anxiety was evoked in this and other similar punishing situations. His autonomic response became conditioned to two sets of stimuli: (1) the presence of people with high moral standards including his father (they were the punishing agents); and (2) the stimuli involved in the subject's own behaviour, namely his homosexual, agressive tendencies. His high autonomic drive was such as to prevent an adaptive response to the traumatic situations. His neurotic solution was twofold: (1) to avoid the threatening stimuli; and (2) to inhibit the offending behaviour. A process of stimuli generalization took place, such that all assertive responses became conditioned to the anxiety and everbody in society represented a potential punishing agent. This would seem to explain his statement that "every motor outlet was guilt-ridden" and that all social contact was avoided by increased withdrawal. Some of the initial punishing stimuli were however more highly conditioned to the anxiety than later stimuli generalizations, i.e. his avoidance response was most apparent to religious fanatics—"contamination is synonymous with the over-religious".

The motor habit of handwashing which developed later was an instrumental act to reduce this conditioned avoidance drive. The intensity of the motor habit increased in proportion to the intensity of the C.A.D. evoked.

Thus the length of time he would spend washing his hands would increase after contact with religious fanatics and would be correspondingly less after contact with the less religious. The same motor habit also appeared related to the autonomic response conditioned to the expression of aggression. Any assertive behaviour on his part would be followed by handwashing.

### Derivation of Method of Treatment

On the basis of the experience with previous cases, it was postulated that:

(1) Reduction of the historically early C.A.D. by reciprocal inhibition would be necessary to remove the need for any instrumental motor act (Case 5).

(2) Independent removal of the instrumental motor act would also be necessary in the chronic case. The motor act might, by the process of secondary generalization, be associated with stimuli apparently unrelated to those initially evoking the C.A.D. (Cases 3 and 4).

### Method of treatment

*Phase I.* This consisted of reducing the initial conditioned autonomic response to religious people. The method adopted was that of systematic desensitization (Wolpe, 1958). The following hierarchies were constructed for visualization.

Prior to each session, $7\frac{1}{2}$ grains of sodium amytal were administered intravenously, since the use of muscular relaxation (Wolpe, 1958) seemed impossible in this case. The patient was unable to sit back in an armchair or lie on a bed during the day-time, since adopting these positions evoked too much anxiety. He would be placed in a position inferior to another person, a factor in common with the traumatic punishing situation. "I will be submerged" were his own words.

HIERARCHY RELATING TO THE RELIGIOUS AND THE
HYPOCRITICAL.—1.

1. Sits next to child who comes from unconventional background.
2. Sits next to an adult who comes from an unconventional background.
3. Touches a child who is spontaneous.
4. Shakes hands with an adult who is spontaneous.
5. Touches personal belongings of a child from an unconventional background.
6. Touches personal belongings of a spontaneous adult.
7. Passes down a road and sees a "warm" church (many flowers in it and no grey stone walls) which only Church of England people of a "non-puritanical" type frequent.
8. Goes into this church and comes out again.
9. Sits down on one of the pews in this church.
10. Sits next to a spontaneous adult in this church.
11. Touches this adult.
12. Sits down in this church with other people of a sincere type.
13. Listens to a sincere religious service.

14. Accepts newly-printed pamphlets at the church door from a sincere member.
15. Reads the titles of these pamphlets.
16. Reads the content—a religious but non-Biblical story.
17. Sings from a hymn-book and reads from a prayer-book.
18. Passes an Evangelical church in the distance.
19. Goes to a service in a Church of England with no stained glass on one side.
20. Goes to the same church but there is no stained glass on two out of the four sides.
21. Goes to the same church but there is no stained glass on three out of the four sides.
22. Attends a service in the cemetery of this church with flowers on the graves.
23. Attends this service in cemetery with no flowers on the graves.
24. Reads from his pamphlet a quotation from the Bible.
25. Reads from a modern version of the Bible.
26. Shares the Bible with a sincere person next to him.
27. Attends same Church of England service in church ruins.
28. Attends same service in church ruins with one stone wall erected.
29. Attends same service in ruins with 2 stone walls erected.
30. Attends same service in ruins with 2 stone walls and stone archways.
31. Attends service in ruins with 2 stone walls, stone archways and a stone floor.
32. Attends service in same structure with part of the roof complete also.
33. Attends service within the whole stone structure of the church.
34. Attends service within the same church which is inhabitable and renovated.
35. Attends service in the church which also contains stone benches.
36. Attends service in same church with plain glass windows installed.
37. Jostles with sincere people to get into the service.
38. Sees notice to announce official conversion of this stone church to a Protestant church.
39. Sits with differing types of Church of England people in the Protestant church.
40. Sits near to Church of England members who might not be sincere in the same church.
41. Sits next to these people in the same church.
42. Sees a nonconformist notice outside the church.
43. Sings nonconformist hymns in the service in this church.
44. Attends the same service in this church, where there are some nonconformists.
45. Attends the same church service and sees nonconformists sitting around him.
46. Attends the same church service and sits next to nonconformist.
47. Attends the same church service with a complete congregation of nonconformists.
48. Attends the same church service with a few Methodists in the congregration.
49. Attends the same church service with a few Methodists sitting around him.
50. Attends the same church service with a few Methodists sitting next to him.
51. Attends the same church service with a complete congregation of Methodists.
52. Attends the same church service with one or two Gospel Hall people sitting in the congregation.
53. Attends the same church service with few Gospel Hall people sitting around him.
54. Attends the same church service, sitting next to the Gospel Hall people.
55. Uses the book belonging to a Church of England member.
56. Uses a book belonging to a Congregationalist.
57. Uses a book belonging to a Methodist.
58. Uses a book belonging to a Gospel Hall person.

## HIERARCHY OF FATHER—2.

1. Looks into room where father has been.
2. Walks into room where father has been.
3. Walks round room where father has been.

4. Looks into room where father's cup and saucer are on table.
5. Walks into room where father's cup and saucer are on table.
6. Looks into room where father's cup, saucer and plate are on table.
7. Walks into room where father's cup, saucer and plate are on table.
8. Looks into room where father's cup, saucer and plate have just been used by father.
9. Walks into room where father's cup, saucer and plate have just been used by father.
10. Looks into room where father's infrequently used jacket is on a chair.
11. Walks into room where father's infrequently used jacket is on a chair.
12. Looks into room where father's frequently used jacket is on a chair.
13. Walks into room where father's frequently used jacket is on a chair.
14. Looks into room where father's frequently used jacket is on a chair and he has left used crockery on the table.
15. Walks into this room.
16. Looks into room where father's jacket and trousers (frequently used) are on chair.
17. Walks into this room.
18. Looks into room with father's jacket, trousers, shirt on chair.
19. Walks into room with father's jacket, trousers, shirt on chair.
20. Looks into room with father's jacket, trousers, shirt and underwear on chair.
21. Walks into room with father's jacket, trousers, shirt and underwear on chair.
22. Walks into same room and sits on a chair.
23. Walks into same room and sits on a chair and touches table.
24. Walks into same room and sits on a chair and touches table and chair seat.
25. Walks into same room and sits on a chair and touches father's overcoat.
26. Walks into same room and sits on a chair and touches father's overcoat and infrequently used jacket.
27. Walks into same room and sits on a chair and touches father's overcoat and frequently used jacket.
28. Walks into same room and sits on a chair and touches father's overcoat, jacket and trousers.
29. Walks into same room and sits on a chair and touches father's overcoat, jacket, trousers and shirt.
30. Walks into same room and sits on a chair and touches father's overcoat, jacket, trousers, shirt, and underwear.
31. Touches chair-seat which father uses infrequently.
32. Touches chair-seat which father uses regularly.
33. Sits on chair-seat which father does not often use.
34. Sits on chair-seat which father uses regularly.
35. Sits on chair a few feet away from father.
36. Sits on chair at arm's length away from father.
37. Sits on chair near to father (but not touching).
38. Sits on chair near to father and touches him with one hand.
39. Sits on chair near to father and touches him with two hands.
40. Sits on sofa next to father so that they are touching.


*Phase II.* It was proposed to decrease the frequency of the instrumental act by the method of reciprocal inhibition. "Performance" hierarchies were constructed which involved contact with objects evoking increasing degrees of anxiety and which would usually be followed by increased handwashing. By leading him into these graded series of situations and requiring him not to wash (see Case 5), one hoped to reinforce the negative habit of not washing.

At each session he commenced at the beginning of the following hierarchies and proceeded through the items as far as he could go without experiencing anxiety. Time lapses between the end of a session and ultimately washing his hands varied from four to seven hours.

In the construction of these hierarchies, it was not always possible to determine the anxiety-provoking factors which dictated the order. Hierarchy 3 was to some extent determined by the increasing chances of religious people having touched certain objects. Hierarchy 6 was graded according to the inferior positions in which he was placed. The patient himself could not give the reasons for the order of the other two hierarchies. Secondary generalization had apparently played a large role in the development of his compulsions.

## HIERARCHY 3

1. Touches two books that have not been handled by patients.
2. Touches a table-top occassionally used by patients.
3. Touches the back of a chair occasionally used by patients.
4. Touches the back of a chair mostly used by patients.
5. Touches the arms of a chair occasionally used by patients.
6. Touches the seat of this chair with right hand only.
7. Touches the seat of this chair with both hands.
8. Touches the seat of a chair mostly used by patients with right hand only.
9. Touches the seat of a chair mostly used by patients with both hands.
10. Touches the seat of the chair he uses himself with right hand only.
11. Touches the seat of the chair he uses himself with both hands.
12. Touches a magazine handled by the patients.
13. Touches the side of a row of drawers with right hand only.
14. Touches the side of a row of drawers with both hands.
15. Touches a drawer with right hand only.
16. Touches a drawer with both hands.
17. Touches the bolt which screws in the drawer-handle with right hand only.
18. Touches the bolt which screws in the drawer-handle with both hands.
19. Touches the handle of the middle drawer with right hand.
20. Touches the handle of the middle drawer with both hands.
21. Touches the handle of the top drawer with right hand.
22. Touches the handle of the top drawer with both hands.
23. Touches the side of a coal-scuttle near the handle with right hand.
24. Touches the side of a coal-scuttle near the handle with both hands.
25. Touches the side of the coal-scuttle handle with right hand.
26. Touches the side of the coal-scuttle handle with both hands.
27. Touches the handle of the coal-scuttle with right hand.
28. Touches the handle of the coal-scuttle with both hands.
29. Sits on a chair in the patient's waiting-room.
30. Touches the arm of this chair with right hand.
31. Touches the arm of this chair with both hands.
32. Touches the seat of this chair with right hand.
33. Touches the seat of this chair with both hands.
34. Sits on this chair after touching the seat.
35. Touches a door of the department near the handle with right hand.
36. Touches a part of the same door nearer the handle with right hand.
37.1 Touches the metal ring into which the door-handle is fixed with the right hand.

38. Touches the door-handle itself with right hand.
39. Touches a door (used less frequently) near the handle with left hand.
40. Touches a part of the same door nearer the handle with left hand.
41. Touches the metal ring into which this door-handle is fixed with the left hand.
42. Touches the door-handle itself with left hand.
43. Touches the metal ring around the door-handle with left hand, after he has opened the door with the right hand.
44. Touches the same door handle with left hand after he has touched it with the right hand.
45. The same as 42 except using a door-handle more frequently touched.
46. The same as 43 using a door-handle more frequently touched.
47. Touches his clothes with right hand.
48. Touches his clothes with left hand.
49.1 Touches his clothes with left hand in the same place' that he has touched with his right hand.

## HIERARCHY 4 (Clothes)

1. Lifts front of pullover up and down with each hand separately and then with both hands.
2. Touches trousers with both hands (placing left hand where right hand has been).
3. Rolls up both sleeves of pullover.
4. Pulls pullover partly over his head.
5. Takes off pullover—puts it on again and puts jacket over pullover and then takes jacket off again at the end of the session.
6. Same as 5 but takes jacket off in middle of session.
7. Same as 6, when he takes pullover off he puts it on the bed before putting it on again.
8. Same as 6 puts pullover on the back of the chair he often uses.
9. Same as 6 puts pullover on the seat of this chair.
10. Same as 6—puts pullover on the seat of psychologist's chair.
11. Same as 6—puts pullover on the seat of patients' chair.
12. Same as 6—puts pullover on the seat of patients' chair and puts jacket over the back of the chair.
13. Same as 6—puts pullover on the chair where his jacket has previously been.
14. Same as 6—puts sleeve of pullover on the arm of the patient's "waiting" seat.
15. Same as 6—puts one sleeve of pullover against the back of his jacket.
16. Touches his trousers near the turn-ups.
17. Touches the top of his trouser turn-ups.
18. Touches his shirt near the collar.
19. Touches his tie and collar (at the back).
20. Touches the side of his jacket with his pullover.
21. Touches the front of his jacket with his pullover.
22. Touches the bottom of his trouser turn-ups.
23. Touches the front of his collar and part of his tie near the knot.
24. Touches the collar of his jacket with his pullover.
25. Touches the knot of his tie.
26. Touches the top of his socks.
27. Touches the back of his shoes.
28. Touches the top of his shoes.

## HIERARCHY 5 (Traversing Thresholds)

1. Walks from a small room to a large room.
2. Turns the corner of a corridor.
3. Steps up on to a rug.

4. Steps up on to a door mat.
5. Walks over a door mat in passing from the small room, to the large room and back again.
6. Turns two corners of a corridor.
7. Goes up and down two steps.
8. Goes up and down three steps.
9. Goes up and down four steps.
10. Goes up and down five steps.
11. Goes up and down six steps.
12. Goes up and down seven steps.
13. Goes up and down eight steps (one flight of the stairs).
14. Walks from the corridor down one step into a very small room (the door being opened for him).
15. Turns two corners of a corridor, opening a door half-way.
16. Same as 14 except that he opens the door for himself.
17–23 Same as 7–13 of the second flight of stairs (each item includes also the whole of the first flight).
24–30 Same as 7–13 of the third flight of stairs (each item includes also the whole of the first and second flights).
31. Descends all three flights and goes out of a door at the bottom which leads outside. He then returns and ascends the stairs.

## HIERARCHY 6 (Lying Down)

1. Sits on a high bed and leans back on one elbow.
2. Same as 1, but leans back on two elbows.
3. Same as 2, and puts one leg up on to the bed.
4. Same as 3, but puts two legs on to the bed.
5. Same as 4, and straightens his legs out on the bed.
6. Lies on the bed with hands clenched.
7. Same as 6, but relaxes right hand.
8. Same as 6, but relaxes both hands.
9. Sits on a long low table.
10. Sits on the table and leans back on both elbows.
11. Lies full length on the table.
12. Sits on a much lower armchair.
13. Sits on a stool.
14. Sits on a low box.
15. Sits on two cushions on the floor.
16. Sits on one cushion on the floor.
17. Sits on a rug on the floor.
18. Sits on the bare floor.
19. Sits on the floor and leans back on one elbow.
20. Lies full length on the floor.

## STAGE I*

*Response to treatment.* Phase I of the treatment was continued to the end of the first hierarchy (the hypocritical). This required 17 sessions over a period of two months. The intensity of his anxiety in response to the "father" items, however made it impossible to proceed. A finer grading of the items

* A distinction is made between "Stages" and "Phases". "Phases" refer to methods of treatment and "Stage I" to pre-leucotomy and "Stage II" to post-leucotomy.

did not reduce the anxiety. He also experienced increasing difficulty in visualizing.

Phase II of the treatment was commenced just before the introduction of the "father" hierarchy. The same resistance was met; he was unable to proceed in the "performance" hierarchies 3 and 5 beyond the first two items. Hierarchies 4 and 6 were not attempted.

During this treatment he did show limited improvement. More assertive responses were evident. He took the initiative to go to the seaside for a day, which he had not done for many years. He stated that he could sit next to people and talk to them without experiencing anxiety. His handwashing, however, did not improve. His father also remained a severe problem. The patient maintained he could no longer live in the same house with him and came into hospital as an in-patient. He was in an extremely tense and anxious state.

Since attempts had been made to reduce both the initial conditioned autonomic response and later motor reactions in this case other reasons had to be sought to explain his failure to improve. Two possibilities seemed feasible. Firstly he might have been gaining some secondary rewards from his symptoms. Secondly very powerful autonomic lability or neuroticism might have disrupted learning at a relatively early stage on the continuum of stress represented by the hierarchies.

The first point did not seem to apply though it was difficult to assess exactly. The second point seemed of some importance in this case.


STAGE II

It appeared, that, if any progress was to be expected, some measure should be taken to reduce his excessive autonomic lability more effectively and more permanently. On the basis of previous evidence (Petrie, 1952) it was considered that a leucotomy operation would be the most likely to decrease neuroticism and so facilitate learning. It was also postulated that the subsequent application of learning principles would be necessary to remove the conditioned responses (both autonomic and motor), since in the chronic phase, these might be partly functioning autonomously of the unconditioned autonomic response. It was noted that in Case 4, the conditioned fears and instrumental act were not improved by the leucotomy she received, though there was an apparent lessening in the intensity of her emotions.

Six months following the leucotomy operation of Case 6, he was again referred to the psychology department for the treatment of his compulsive handwashing. This had remained unchanged. During this six-month period, he had in fact once more had the intention of committing suicide. He had decided to take a trip to the seaside at night with a view to throwing himself in the sea. Circumstances had, however, aborted the attempt.

Shortly following this incident, he was interviewed for the purpose of assessing the severity of the compulsion. Although the length of time spent washing his hands was the same, he was, in his own words, "less emotionally involved" in it. He likened himself to "a robot performing an act without any feeling behind it". His father and religious people still provoked considerable anxiety. This appears to confirm the opinion that a leucotomy fails to abolish learned emotional responses, even though it appears to reduce emotional responsiveness.

Phase I of the treatment was recommenced. Muscular relaxation was used this time. His fear of sitting back no longer seemed to interfere significantly with this procedure.

Phase II of the treatment was again introduced at the fourteenth session after item 46 had been reached on the "hypocritical" hierarchy.

It would be impossible to make any therapeutic claims for the role played by the application of learning principles without first being able to assess the benefits obtained solely from the leucotomy. It was decided to omit Hierarchies 5 and 6 which pertained to situations evoking the responses of extreme slowness and hesitancy rather than avoidance of physical contact. His untreated obsessional behaviour related to these two hierarchies was used as control data to assess the effects of the leucotomy alone.

Before Hierarchies 5 and 6 were introduced, fifty-two sessions over a period of three months had been devoted to Hierarchies 1, 2 and 3. Hierarchy 4 could not be commenced until Hierarchy 3 had been completed. At this point he had completed Hierarchy 1, reached item 36 on Hierarchy 2 and item 20 on Hierarchy 3.

He stated that his handwashing had improved greatly. He could touch all furniture on the ward, magazines and newspapers, he could do cleaning jobs without resorting to his compulsion. He only washed 2 or 3 times a day for 2 min each time, instead of 20 min. He had reduced the amount of soap used from one bar in one day to one bar in four days. He only spent 40 min in the bath instead of 2 hr. The only objects now inducing the handwashing were door knobs and the personal belongings of religious people of the Evangelical order. He could, however, converse freely with everyone of any religious views. In short, all symptoms relating to the hierarchies so far commenced, had been alleviated.

The untreated psychomotor slowness had however in no way improved over this period of 3 months (i.e. 9 months after the leucotomy). He still could not walk spontaneously across a threshold, up steps or round corners. Rising from chairs and lying down still presented the same difficulty. This would appear to confirm that without the subsequent application of learning principles, a leucotomy fails to remove conditioned responses. The inference is that his handwashing would also have remained unaffected by a leucotomy alone.

At this point, Hierarchies 5 and 6 were introduced.

*Response to the complete programme of treatment*

Another five months were required to complete all the hierarchies and conclude the treatment (8 months in all). Complete recovery of all aspects of his obsessional behaviour was apparently effected. There were no objects or persons that he could not touch. When he did so, no anxiety was evoked and no handwashing compulsion followed.

He was able to talk to anyone, even of Evangelical persuasion. When asked to read an Evangelical pamphlet concerning hell-fire and damnation, he responded with amusement rather than anxiety. The relationship with his father greatly improved; both physical and social contact with him no longer presented any problem and the patient spent long week-ends at home with him. The attitude of the father also changed. Recognizing the absence of any psychiatric symptoms in his son he had in the patient's own words "opened his heart and his pocket to me". A completely new wardrobe of clothes for him had been financed by the father.

His handwashing was within normal proportions. He only washed for 2 min before breakfast, before dinner and before going to bed at night. Dressing and undressing never took longer than 5 min in contrast with the 5 hr he would spend prior to treatment.

Both the Hierarchies 5 and 6, which were introduced later, appeared to have had similar therapeutic effect. He could turn corners, walk into rooms, get up from a supine position and from armchairs immediately and without hesitation. He could also go up and down stairs without any difficulty.

In his own words, "There is a tremendous difference. I can relax more easily and am completely at ease. I can converse with anyone. Handwashing is down to once or twice a day. I am far more optimistic than I was".

Arrangements were made for him to attend a rehabilitation course for six weeks, and a clerical training course for six months.

It is of some importance that on discharge, his homosexual desires were still present, but he stated that he no longer experienced guilt over them.

A follow-up has not been possible as yet, since the patient has only been discharged a few weeks.


*Discussion on Case 6*

Three factors appear to have contributed to this successful outcome:

(1) The removal of the initial conditioned avoidance response to punishing stimuli (the over-religious).

(2) Independent removal of the drive-reducing compulsion of hand-washing, and other motor habits (i.e. hesitation and psychomotor slowness).

(3) The reduction of emotional lability to an optimal level for learning in this retraining programme.

## CONCLUSIONS

The inferences made in the introduction of this chapter appear to be borne out by the results of these six cases.

(1) Firstly in the acute phase of breakdown, removal of the basic conditioned autonomic drive is sufficient, to remove also the motor reactions mediated by it. This has been demonstrated by Cases 1 and 2.

(2) Secondly, in the long-standing obsessive-compulsive, treatment of *either* the conditioned drives or the motor compulsion *alone* results in only a partial recovery.

In Cases 3 and 4 particularly the persistence of the compulsion was evident in spite of a marked reduction in the original conditioned drives. There appeared to be two possible reasons for this:

(i) The compulsion itself had become conditioned by secondary generalization to many stimuli apparently unrelated to those initially evoking the autonomic response. Case 3 seems to be an illustration of this. The lamp-posts and park seats evoking an avoidance response were apparently far removed from the original sexual stimuli. In this way the drive-reducing compulsion had become partly autonomous of the original cause.

(ii) The possibility of the development of secondary rewards perpetuating an otherwise handicapping obsessional motor habit was raised by Case 4. The incentive to remain in hospital away from domestic and marital difficulties may have played a part in the continuance of her symptoms.

(3) Case 5 on the other hand, supports the contention that even in the chronic phase the motor component is probably not *completely* autonomous of historically earlier conditioned drives. At least treatment effecting a considerable remission of the motor compulsion was only temporary and autonomic reactions increased.

Further support for this is offered by another obsessive-compulsive state being treated at present. He is a middle-aged South African engineer who has always taken more interest in medicine than engineering and who for the past 2 years has become involved in detailed physical examination of himself. These have lasted for as long as three hours at a time, and he has had recourse to them at least once a day. This compulsion has served to reduce the fear that he might die of some incurable disease and leave his family (wife and two children) without any financial support. He had suffered from financial difficulties during his own education and feared his children might suffer similarly, should anything happen to him. The incurable diseases he feared included cancer of any part of the body, heart disease and nephritis. The examination always centred round the possible presence or absence of signs of these diseases. He could never convince himself for instance that there were not uneven bumps on himself and he would become involved in detailed comparisons of the two sides of his body. Similarly he could never ascertain to his own satisfaction whether or not he had abnormal heart beats. He was most fearful lest he should excrete blood and was compelled to examine his faeces for long periods of time. Looking in a mirror would also result in long examinations. He had therefore avoided using a miror for the past two years lest he should submit to his compulsion. Slight pressure on any part of his body would also be sufficient to provoke the compulsion.

Treatment was directed towards the removal of this motor compulsion alone. This consisted of a performance hierarchy requiring him to touch without examining an increasingly larger area of his body for an increasingly longer period of time. (See Case 5 method of treatment.) No attempt was made to reduce the conditioned fear of illness nor the primary and earlier conditioned anxiety over family dependence. Over a period of four months he improved greatly, seldom resorting to his compulsion outside hospital. A major relapse occurred, however, upon the third pregnancy of his wife. This increased the number in the family dependent on him and thus exacerbated the original conditioned fear relating to his family.

Some months later he was again referred to the psychology department for the treatment of his compulsions which had returned in all their original severity. For six months, treatment has proceeded along the same lines, i.e. purely symptomatic removal of the motor compulsion. Once more improvement has taken place to the point where he seldom resorts to examination and then only for five minutes at a time. He has never seen a consultant physician for confirmation of his health since treatment recommenced. He states however that he still fears for the welfare of his family and therefore for his own health. The conditioned fears have remained and should these be left untreated, the symptomatic relief that has been obtained so far would presumably only be temporary. The initial relapse following his wife's pregnancy would support this view.

(4) The fourth factor of importance in the treatment of the chronic obsessional relates to the unconditioned autonomic response. As has been suggested by Case 6, hyperemotional responsiveness may interfere with learning in any retraining programme, whether or not the latter is concerned with the removal of the learned drive or the drive-reducing habits. The leucotomy which decreased the intensity of the unconditioned autonomic reactivity seemed to be responsible for his being able to progress in the learning programme in Stage II. It was, however, confirmed by leaving some symptoms untreated, that the decrease in neuroticism or autonomic lability was not in itself sufficient to remove the maladaptive habits (both autonomic and motor).

Some method of reducing neuroticism, as well as the manifest symptoms of a neurosis, may be just as important in the treatment of the acute case. In the retraining programme of the two acute cases 1 and 2, emotional lability did not appear to arrest the learning of more adaptive behaviour. Since, however, no attempt had been made to reduce the inherent neuroticism and thus to increase the stress tolerance, over-reactivity to future stresses and the development of new neurotic responses might therefore be expected. Extensive follow-up of acute obsessionals following behaviour therapy would be required to validate this argument.

## ACKNOWLEDGEMENTS

We are most grateful to Dr. P. M. O'Flanagan, Dr. C. M. Holden, and Dr. H. Fleming (Winwick Hospital, Warrington) for their permission to publish the present report concerning patients under their care.

## REFERENCES

EYSENCK, H. J. (1960) Learning Theory and Behaviour Therapy. In *Behaviour Therapy and the Neuroses*, Pergamon Press, Oxford.

LEHNER, G. F. J. (1960) Negative Practice as a Psychotherapeutic Technique. In *Behaviour Therapy and the Neuroses* (Ed. H. J. Eysenck) Pergamon Press, Oxford.

PETRIE, A. (1952) *Personality and the Frontal Lobes*, Routledge and Kegan Paul, London.

WALTON, D. (1960) The Relevance of Learning Theory to the Treatment of an Obsessive-compulsive State. In *Behaviour Therapy and the Neuroses* (Ed. H. J. EYSENCK) Pergamon Press, Oxford.

WOLPE, J. (1958) *Psychotherapy by Reciprocal Inhibition*, Stanford University Press, Calif.

YATES, A. J. (1960) Symptoms and Symptom Substitution. In *Behaviour Therapy and the Neuroses* (Ed. H. J. EYSENCK) Pergamon Press, Oxford.

# Behaviour Therapy, Spontaneous Remission and Transference in Neurotics*

H. J. EYSENCK

*Institute of Psychiatry (Maudsley Hospital), University of London*

ANY GENERAL theory of neurotic behaviour must attempt to account for the main phenomena in this field of psychology, and its acceptability must in part depend on its success in thus creating a "nomological network" within which otherwise isolated events can be ordered and understood. One of the most important, most universal, and most widely acknowledged of these phenomena is that of *spontaneous remission*; as is well documented in several research reports (Denker, 1946; Landis, 1938; Shepherd and Gruenberg, 1957; Barendregt, 1961) neurotics tend to get better without any form of specific psychiatric treatment. This improvement appears to be a function of time; Eysenck (1960a) has suggested the following formula as descriptive of the situation:

$$X = 100 \, (1 - 10^{-0 \cdot 0045 \, N})$$

where $X$ stands for the amount of improvement achieved in per cent and $N$ for the number of weeks elapsed. He comments that "while the exact values in this formula should not be taken too seriously, its general form is of course that of the typical learning curve with which psychologists are familiar" (p. 711).

It is also well known that psychotherapeutic treatment, whether psychoanalytic or eclectic, does not accelerate this rate of recovery (Eysenck, 1952, 1960; Levitt, 1957; Barendregt, 1961; Landis, 1938; Zubin, 1953; Wolpe, 1958). Under these circumstances it may be worthwhile to take a closer look at the phenomenon of spontaneous recovery from a theoretical point of view, in order to determine possible causative factors; it is clearly impermissible to implicate "time" as such, because it can only be *events* happening in time which can exert a causal influence, and our formula does not tell us very much about the possible nature of these events. It is the purpose of this article to present a theory of "spontaneous remission"; this theory is derived from a general body of knowledge sometimes referred to as

* This article is reprinted with the permission of the editor from *Amer. J. Psychiat.*, (1963), **119**, 867–871.

"learning theory" (Hilgard, 1956; Kimble, 1961). It also links up with a rational theory of diagnosis and treatment in neurosis which has been called "behaviour therapy" (Eysenck, 1960b; Eysenck, 1960c) and which purports to achieve results superior to those for which "spontaneous remission" can be held responsible (Wolpe, 1958; Eysenck 1963).

Before proceeding to a discussion of this theory, we may note with some surprise that what may be called the currently prevailing "orthodox" set of psychiatric hypotheses, which are closely identified with psychoanalytic and "dynamic" notions, have nothing to say about spontaneous remission; indeed, they seem to suggest that such remission cannot occur, or that, where it does, it can only be of very short-term duration. This follows directly from the Freudian notion that neurotic behaviour is motivated by some underlying complex or complexes, and that the treatment of the symptom without some form of "uncovering" of the underlying complexes must lead to a recrudescence of the same, or the appearance of some other symptom. The evidence is decisively opposed to this belief (Yates, 1958; Wolpe, 1961) and it is notable that no adequate documentation has ever been put forward by psychoanalytic writers, who seem entirely to rely on anecdotal evidence, on repetition of doctrinal pronouncements, and on uncontrolled studies incompletely presented. Such an important point, one might have imagined, should have been established a little more securely before being accepted and interpreted as ruling out of court *a fortiori* all non-psychoanalytic methods of treatment. As the evidence stands now, we may perhaps say that the failure of symptoms to recur after spontaneous remission, or after some form of behaviour therapy, is a decisive argument against the Freudian theory.

How does behaviour therapy deal with spontaneous remission? In order to answer this question we must first state the main tenets of the general theory, without however being able here to bring forward all the supporting evidence; this task has been attempted elsewhere (Eysenck, 1960a; Metzner, 1961; Wolpe, 1958). For convenience, we may number the points in order. (1) Neurotic behaviour consists of maladaptive conditioned responses of the autonomic system, and of skeletal responses made to reduce the conditioned (sympathetic) reactions. (2) While the term "symptom" may be retained to describe neurotic behaviour, there is no implication that such behaviour is "symptomatic" of anything. (3) It follows that there is no underlying complex or other "dynamic" cause which is responsible for the maladaptive behaviour; all we have to deal with in neurosis is conditioned maladaptive behaviour. (4) Treatment consists of the *deconditioning*, by reciprocal inhibition, extinction, conditioned inhibition, or in some other way, of the maladaptive behaviour, and the *conditioning*, along orthodox lines, of adaptive behaviour. (5) The treatment is a-historical and does not involve any "uncovering" of past events. (6) Conditioning and deconditioning will usually proceed through behavioural channels, but there is no reason why verbal methods should not also be used; there is good evidence that words are conditioned stimuli which have an ascertainable position on the stimulus and response generalization gradients of the patients (Shoben, 1949).

Consider now a typical case history involving the establishment and cure of a cat phobia (Freeman and Kendrick, 1960). A traumatic event involving the patient's favourite cat produces a conditioned fear of cats; this develops to such an extent that she is effectively home-bound for many years, refusing to go out for fear of encountering cats. Treatment is by means of graduated presentations of cats (first symbolically, i.e. by words and pictures, then bodily, but at a distance, etc.) under conditions of relaxation and para-sympathetic stimulation (desensitization, reciprocal inhibition). After a few weeks treatment is completely successful, and a permanent cure achieved (no relapse for several years). In this case history there is no spontaneous remission, and we may enquire (a) why such a remission might have occurred and (b) why in fact it did not do so.

First, we have a traumatic event which, by means of classical conditioning, produces a conditioned fear reaction to a previously neutral set of objects, i.e. cats. It is easy to see how this conditioned fear arose, but it is not so easy to see just why it should have persevered so long. Solomon and Wynne (1954), on the basis of their work with dogs, have offered the principle of "partial irreversibility" in avoidance conditioning, but it should be noted that the aversive stimuli in their case were probably stronger than in the case of the patient, and also that they report no single-trial learning, as seems to have occurred in this patient. On general learning-theory principles one would have expected the gradual *extinction* of the conditioning fear response in the course of time. Each time the patient saw a cat (the CS), without a recurrence of the traumatic events which precipitated her original fear (the UCS), this unreinforced presentation of the CS should lead to an increment of inhibition potential leading to extinction. Similarly, each time she discussed her troubles with a sympathetic listener this should have had an effect similar to that of "reciprocal inhibition", also leading to extinction of the fear response. In other words, behaviour theory seems to have no difficulty in explaining the extinction of neurotic symptoms by "spontaneous remission"; this extinction is the natural result of the inevitable recurrence of the CS in the absence of reinforcement. We may thus reinterpret our formula for the time course of spontaneous remission by saying, not that it resembles the typical learning curve, but rather that it resembles (and indeed is nothing but) the typical extinction curve. Our hypothesis, then, is that *all neurotic symptoms are subject to extinction*, and that this process of extinction is reflected in observable behaviour in the form of "spontaneous remission". The theory would appear to fit the facts reasonably well, but it would also appear to assert too much; not all cases of neurosis do in fact remit, and a theory predicting universal remission is clearly in need of an extension.

Such an extension is indeed implied in the first of our numbered postulates of behaviour therapy, given above, in which attention was drawn to the importance of "skeletal responses made to reduce the conditioned (sympathetic) reaction". What is asserted here is that in many cases of neurosis the original stage of classical conditioning is followed by a stage of instrumental conditioning, and that it is this secondary development which makes impossible the process of extinction by removing the conditions of its occurrence, i.e. the presentation of the CS under conditions of non-reinforcement. Consider the events in the laboratory during the extinction of a conditioned response. The dog, lashed to his stand, is presented with the CS a number of times; his conditioned responses get weaker and weaker until finally they cease altogether. This paradigm differs profoundly from that of our patient encountering a cat in the street after her conditioned fear has been established. The patient is not lashed to a stand, and thus forced to witness the conjunction: CS–non-reinforcement; she is free to turn her back and run away. This course of conduct produces an entirely different paradigm, one favourable to the growth of an instrumental response of running away from cats. Simplifying the situation grossly, we may say that what happens is something like this. The patient approaches the cat and experiences a conditioned sympathetic response (fear) which is profoundly disturbing and (negatively) reinforcing. She turns and runs, thus excluding the cat from her field of vision, and also increasing the distance between herself and the feared object. This behaviour reduces the sympathetic arousal, and is thus reinforced by the resulting lessening of fear. The next time the patient encounters a cat, the newly-acquired habit of running away will again, and more easily, be brought into play, until finally an instrumental conditioned response of running away is developed to such an extent that it permanently excludes the possibility of encountering the CS at all. In this way the secondary process of instrumental conditioning "preserves" the primary conditioned response; putting the whole matter into psychiatric terminology, instrumental conditioning makes impossible the "reality testing" of the classically conditioned response.

There is no doubt, of course, that in most cases the situation is much more complex than this. The original conditioning is not always, and perhaps not even usually, a traumatic, single trial event; repeated sub-traumatic trials may produce an even stronger conditioned fear response than a single traumatic event. Little is known about the precise dynamics of this process in individual cases, largely because psychiatric attention has not usually been directed at these events from the point of view of learning theory. Again, few neuroses are mono-symptomatic, and there may be a very complex interweaving of several different habit-family hierarchies (Hull, 1943; Wolpe, 1958), each subject to extinction at different rates, and by exposure to different events (CSs). Lastly, experience indicates, and theory suggests, that extinction of conditioned fear responses in one habit family hierarchy facilitates (through a process of generalization) extinction in others, whether this extinction is occurring during "spontaneous remission" or during behaviour therapy. To mention these complications, to which many others could have been added, is simply to remind the reader that while in principle the explanation of spontaneous remission here given is perhaps correct, nevertheless much experimental and observational work remains to be done before the details of the process can be said to be at all well understood.

It is interesting to note that several observationally well attested phenomena can be brought into this theoretical framework. Consider the pilot who has crashed his plane, or the cowboy who has been thrown by his horse. It has often been stated that if the pilot, or the cowboy, is allowed to walk away from the plane, or the horse, he will never fly, or ride, again. If, however, he makes himself fly or ride again immediately, then there will be no such disastrous after-effect. We may regard the original event as productive of a conditioned fear reaction to planes or horses; this by itself would not be strong enough to preclude future resumption of the particular activity which produced the traumatic event. However, bodily removal from the now feared object produces instrumental conditioning, along the lines indicated above, and it is this additional process of avoidance conditioning which, when superadded to the original classical conditioning, makes the total aversive forces too great to be overcome.

Much the same explanation could be given to the well-known fact that psychiatric casualties during the war tend to go back to combat easily and readily if treated in front-line conditions, but hardly ever if sent back to base hospitals first and then treated. Here also the part played by classical conditioning is fundamental, but can be counteracted by a process of extinction in the front-line situation; if instrumental conditioning is allowed to add its share, i.e. through removal of the patient to a base-line hospital, prognosis is poor because now *extinction is made almost impossible*! Other applications of this general theory will easily occur to the reader.

This may be an appropriate place to consider another event which is frequently claimed to be an almost invariable concomitant of the therapeutic process, namely *transference*. Here there is indeed a psychoanalytical theory to explain the phenomena alleged to occur, namely the development of certain strong emotional feelings on the part of the patient for the analyst (and perhaps vice versa). This theory depends on the *transfer* of certain childhood emotions originally attached to the parents; these, it is suggested, are transferred to the analyst. Now there is little doubt that such emotional dependence does in fact occur, although there is very little well-established evidence to suggest just how frequent, how strong and how lasting such emotions are. Indeed, similar facts have been known to occur in the Catholic confession for many hundreds of years, and the priest taking the confessional is taught how to deal with these feelings. How does behaviour theory account for the facts?

In the first place, it is important to dissociate $T_F$ (the facts conveniently summarized under the heading "transference" and $T_T$ (the psychoanalytic theory of literal "transference"). The writer would hold that $T_F$ is a real phenomenon requiring an explanation, but that $T_T$ is a speculative theory without any sound experimental background. It is unfortunate that the name for $T_F$ immediately suggests the truth of $T_T$; it might be better if a more neutral name were to be chosen. In any case, it will be clear from what has been said that when it is stated that behaviour therapists reject the notion of transference, what is meant is a rejection of the speculative theory, and not of the facts themselves.

As for an alternative theory, consider the position of the therapist in his relation to the patient. Whether because of spontaneous remission, or because of the reciprocal inhibition produced by the permissive attitude of the therapist, there is a tendency for the patient to improve. Consider the therapist as a CS in this situation, consider the unknown cause of the improvement as the UCS, and consider the improvement and its attendant emotions and feelings as the response. It will be clear that there will be a tendency for the therapist to be credited with the properties of the UCS, through a process of classical conditioning, and that attitudes and emotions appropriate to the latter are shifted to the former. A wellknown example is given by Pavlov, who reports that when an electric light was used as the CS for a feeding–salivation experiment, the dog after a while licked the light bulb! In other words, there is a transfer of reactions appropriate to the UCS to the CS. As an example of such a transfer in a human subject, consider Connie, a 5-year-old girl being treated for enuresis by means of the well-known bell-and-blanket method (Gwynne Jones, 1960). When the first signs of a cure became noticeable after 4 applications, she spontaneously kissed and hugged the red light on the apparatus which illuminated the switch activating the bell, saying "The ting-a-ling is my best friend". No doubt it would seem almost sacrilegious to many psychiatrists to consider this analogous to full-blown "transference", but the fundamental identity or lack of identity of the processes involved must be established in a more experimental basis than mere shocked disbelief. The explanation here given accounts for the facts as well as does the Freudian, and in addition it is based on well-documented laboratory experiments; nevertheless it would be most desirable to submit it to direct experimental investigations before regarding at as anything but an hypothesis.

This paper has been kept short on purpose, being purely theoretical in the first place, and lacking direct experimental support in the second. It would be idle guesswork to extend speculation beyond the points raised, although promising extensions do suggest themselves in considerable number. Its primary purpose, however, will have been served if it reawakens interest in the phenomena of spontaneous remission and transference, and leads to more experimental investigations of these interesting and perhaps even crucial events in the life-history of the neurotic. The formulation of an explanation in terms of learning theory here given is not the only one possible, and it may not be the one preferred by other psychologists; it may nevertheless repay investigation. But primarily it is hoped that the reconsideration of these phenomena will serve to raise doubts about the adequacy of that "premature crystallization of spurious orthodoxy" which is present-day psychoanalytic theory.

## REFERENCES

BARENDREGT, J. T. (1961) *Research in psychodiagnostics*, Mouton, The Hague.

DENKER, R. (1946) Results of treatment of psychoneuroses by general practitioners, *N.Y. State J. Med.* **46**, 2164–2166.

EYSENCK, H. J. (1952) The effects of psychotherapy: an evaluation, *J. Consult. Psychol.* **16**, 319–324.

EYSENCK, H. J. (1957) *Dynamics of anxiety and hysteria*, Praeger New York.

EYSENCK, H. J. (1960a) The effects of psychotherapy. In EYSENCK (Ed.): *Handbook of abnormal psychology*, Basic Books, New York.

EYSENCK, H. J. (Ed.) (1960b) *Behaviour therapy and the neuroses*, Pergamon Press, New York.

EYSENCK, H. J. (1960c) A rational system of diagnosis and therapy in mental disease. In ABT *and* RIESS (Eds.): *Progress in Clinical Psychology*, IV, 46–64, Exune and Stratton, New York.

EYSENCK, H. J. (Ed.) (1963) *Experiments in behaviour therapy*, Pergamon Press, New York.

FREEMAN, H. J. and KENDRICK, D. C. (1960) A case of cat phobia, *Brit. Med. J.* **2**, 497–502.

GWYNNE JONES, H. (1960) The behavioural treatment of enuresis nocturna. In EYSENCK, H. J. (Ed.): *Behaviour therapy and the neuroses*, Pergamon Press, New York.

HILGARD, E. A. (1956) *Theories of learning*, Appleton-Century-Crofts, New York.

HULL, C. L. (1943) *Principles of behavior*, Appleton-Century-Crofts, New York.

KIMBLE, G. A. (1961) *Conditioning and learning*, Appleton-Century-Crofts, New York.

LANDIS, C. (1938) Statistical evaluation of psychotherapeutic methods. In HIMIE (Ed.) *Concepts and problems in psychotherapy*, Heinemann, London.

LEVITT, E. E. (1953) The results of psychotherapy with children: an evaluation, *J. Consult. Psychol.* **21**, 189–196.

METZNER, R. (1961) Learning theory and the therapy of neuroses, *Brit. J. Psychol. Mon. Suppl.* **33**.

SOLOMON, R. L. and WYNNE, L. C. (1954) Traumatic avoidance learning: the principles of anxiety conservation and partial irreversibility, *Psychol. Rev.* **61**, 353–385.

SHEPHERD, M. and GRUENBERG, E. M. (1957) The age for neuroses, *Millbank Mem. F. Quart. Bull.* **35**, 258–265.

SHOBEN, E. J. (1949) Psychotherapy as a problem in learning theory, *Psychol. Bull.* **46**, 346–392.

WOLPE, J. (1958) *Psychotherapy by reciprocal inhibition*, Stanford Univ. Press.

WOLPE, J. (1961) The prognosis in unpsychoanalysed recovery from neuroses, *Amer. J. Psychiat.* **117**, 35–39.

YATES, A. J. (1958) Symptoms and symptom substitution, *Psychol. Rev.* **65**, 731–374.

ZUBIN, J. (1953) Evaluation of therapeutic outcome in mental disorders, *Nerv. Ment. His.* **117**, 95–111.

# Case of Homosexuality Treated
# by Aversion Therapy*

BASIL JAMES, M.B., B.CH., B.SC., D.P.M.

*Registrar, Glenside Hospital, Stapleton, Bristol*

HADFIELD (1958), in an interesting paper on the cure of homosexuality, defines "cure" as meaning that the patient "loses his propensity to his own sex and has his sexual interests directed towards those of the opposite sex, so that he becomes in all respects a sexually normal person". He quotes the Wolfenden report— "none of our medical witnesses were able, when we saw them, to provide any reference in medical literature to a complete change of this kind". He further maintained that the process of cure was a long one, and that the main benefit of investigating cases of homosexuality is that the cause of the condition may be ascertained and that means of prevention may be found.

The report by Curran and Parr (1957) of a series of 100 homosexuals seen in private practice, in which those patients treated psychotherapeutically derived no apparent benefit in terms of changed sexual preference or behaviour as compared with those matched patients not so treated, adds to the feeling of therapeutic impotence which the practitioner so often feels when faced with the problem of homosexuality.

A special Committee of the Council of the B.M.A. (1955), in a memorandum on homosexuality and prostitution, laid stress on the need for research into the treatment of homosexuals.

The case here reported is thought to be of special interest in that to some extent the patient acts as his own control as previous methods of treatment had been unsuccessful.

## CASE REPORT

Male, single, aged 40 years. Mother alive and well. Father, who had been married before, died of cancer when patient was aged 16. There is one half-sister and one half-brother.

His homosexual drive was first apparent at the age of 15, and his first homosexual experiment was at 18. Since then he had been exclusively homosexual, girls having no physical attraction whatever, physical contact with them inducing a feeling of revulsion.

* This article is reprinted with the permission of the author and editor from *Brit. Med. J.* 1962, **1**, 768–770.

The impulse was very strong and extremely difficult to resist. He was attracted by young men aged 18–25, and had had no heterosexual experiences. The affairs were on an emotional basis, a series of monogamous relationships, the other man usually breaking it off. He would be upset for a while, and then find somebody else. The tendency was to increasing promiscuity. The pattern was usually one of mutual masturbation, kissing and occasional intercrural activity.

He was rated "six" on the Kinsey scale (Kinsey et al., 1948).

The patient was a university graduate (I.Q. 133), had been commissioned in the Army with a good Service record. On demobilization he had taken an executive post with an oil company, but his employment was terminated owing to his known homosexuality. After this his family had set him up in a retail business, but he had mismanaged the finances to such a degree that his business was on the verge of bankruptcy.

He had been under psychiatric in-patient care previously, for three months in 1953, and he was given group and individual psychotherapy and stilboestrol. This latter treatment he describes as "worse than useless", for while the drive remained he was impotent and the resulting frustration increased his homosexual desire, which was difficult to tolerate. He had spontaneously stopped taking the tablets, and continued his homosexual practice.

The present admission was via the general hospital where he had been admitted after a serious attempt at suicide by barbiturate overdosage. He described his suicidal bid as an intellectual one and maintained that this was logical as his homosexual activities had started a train of behaviour which he described as "psychopathic and quite beyond control". In order to attract partners and maintain relationships it had been necessary to impress with a display of wealth. He had spent beyond his means to acquire clothes, a car, drink, etc., and in order to obtain more money and other support from the family he had found it necessary to lie repeatedly. Relations with the family had for many years become progressively more strained, and although this fact worried him a great deal and although he had excellent intellectual insight he was quite unable to do anything about it. He felt that the cornerstone of his problem was his homosexuality, and that all available treatment for this condition had failed to help him.

The theory of aversion therapy was explained to him and he was frankly sceptical, but nevertheless he agreed to undergo the treatment.

## Treatment

Treatment was carried out in a darkened single room, and during this time no food or drink other than the prescribed alcohol was allowed. At regular two-hourly intervals he was given an emetic dose of apomorphine by injection followed by 2 oz (57 ml) of brandy. On each occasion when nausea was felt a strong light was shone on a large piece of card on which were pasted several photographs of nude or near-nude men. He was asked to select one which he found attractive, and it was suggested to him that he re-create the experiences which he had had with his current homosexual partner. His fantasy was reinforced verbally by the therapist on the first two or three occasions.

Thereafter a tape was played twice over every two hours during the period of nausea. This began with an explanation of his homosexual attraction along the lines of father-deprivation occurring at a time when awareness of homosexual attraction was not abnormal, this being reinforced by his first homosexual experiences, a learned pattern thus being established. The adverse effect of this pattern on him and its consequent social repercussions was then described in slow and graphic terms ending with words such as "sickening", "nauseating", etc., followed by the noise of one vomiting. This invariably accentuated the emetic effect of apomorphine. After 30 hr the treatment was terminated because of acetonuria, and the patient was allowed up and about.

After a period of 24 hr the treatment was restarted with another tape, which concentrated more wholly upon the effect his practices had had on him, again ending histrionically. Again the treatment was stopped because of acetonuria, this time after 32 hr.

The following night the patient was awakened every 2 hr and a record played which was frankly congratulatory and which explained in optimistic terms what would have been accomplished if, in fact, his homosexual drive had been reversed. At this stage no other treatment was given and next morning the patient was allowed up and about. On each of the third, fourth, and fifth days after the apomorphine treatment had finished a card was placed in his room, pasted on to it being carefully selected photographs of sexually attractive young women. Each morning he was given an injection of testosterone propionate and told to retire to his room when he felt any sexual excitement. He was provided with a record-player and records of a female vocalist whose performance is generally recognized as "sexy".

## Results

Since the treatment his whole demeanour has altered. His relatives describe him as "a new man", and his relations with them as wholly satisfactory and better than at any time in his life. He himself has felt no attraction at all to the same sex since the treatment, whereas previously this attraction had been present throughout every day. Sexual fantasy is entirely heterosexual and he soon acquired a regular girl friend. Kissing and strong petting occurs regularly, and is entirely pleasurable, in contrast with the revulsion with which he had previously regarded any heterosexual contact. In these situations he achieves strong erections and has the desire to make further sexual advances. He has ejaculated on several occasions in this situation. He no longer finds it necessary to lie or spend beyond his means. He feels generally at ease and happier than at any time since his childhood, and describes the treatment as "fantastically successful" and comments on its swiftness. In addition his hobby, writing, has been productive for the first time for very many years, and in the 20 weeks since his treatment he has written several short stories, some of which have been accepted by publishers, and has completed a full-length novel.

This is the first time in his life that he has lost his propensity to his own sex and has his sexual interests directed towards those of the opposite sex so that he has become in all respects a sexually normal person.

## DISCUSSION

Curran (1947) said "it is very easy for habit formation to occur in the sexual sphere, and the longer these habits persist the more difficult they are to break." Also, "little evidence has been put forward that intensive psychotherapy is of special value in the treatment and cure of sexual disabilities in themselves." It is only recently that the concept of learned behaviour patterns, their unlearning and relearning, has been given prominence as a therapeutic method (Eysenck et al., 1960). Few reports of the method as applied to sexual abnormalities have been published.

Raymond (1956) reports a case of fetishism treated by aversion therapy, and when one considers his quotation of Binet that the form taken by a sexual perversion was determined purely by an external event, stating that "the man who can love only men could easily have been a nightcap fetishist or a shoe-nail fetishist," his reported case and the one under consideration bear many points of similarity. It would appear that Raymond's patient underwent physiological (Pavlovian) ultraparadoxical inhibition, with the complete reversal of his former likes and dislikes as described by Sargant (1957).

Our patient did not experience such a dramatic phenomenon, but it may be that he would have done so if the treatment had been more prolonged.

Freund (1960) has published a series of cases of homosexual patients treated by aversion therapy, and finds that his results vary according to the external pressure brought to bear on them before referral for treatment. Those who sought assistance because of threatened police action, for example, were the worst prognostic group, whereas those who spontaneously sought help responded most satisfactorily.

The administration of alcohol does not appear to be part of the therapeutic technique as described by Raymond or Freund. The theoretical aspects of the action of alcohol on the sexual response is discussed by Franks (1960). In the case under consideration, however, two main factors influenced its use. Firstly, although the patient was not an alcoholic, drinking was part of the behaviour pattern associated with his homosexual activity. Secondly, the consumption of alcohol under the therapeutic conditions appeared to accentuate the emetic effect of the apomorphine.

The introduction of tape recordings during the treatment was another modification of the techniques previously described. The content of the tape had been carefully composed in terms of the patient's personal history and background, in order to give the recording as personal a quality as possible.

## SUMMARY

The case is described of a 40-year-old 100 per cent homosexual treated by aversion therapy. The results fulfil the criteria of cure as defined by Hadfield. The treatment is brief, is in no way analytical, and can be adapted to the individual patient. Although the period of follow-up is comparatively short, the patient's heterosexual attraction is increasing with time rather than decreasing, and it would be easy to give a "booster" course of treatment should he show signs of relapse. The method depends very largely on the co-operation of the patient and his desire to be rid of his homosexual feelings. In his case other methods of treatment had completely failed.

I thank Dr. Donal F. Early, consultant psychiatrist, Glenside Hospital, for permission to treat and publish this case, and express my appreciation of the way in which the nursing staff co-operated so fully in the treatment.

## REFERENCES

B.M.A. (1955) *Homosexuality and Prostitution*, Memorandum of evidence by special Committee of the Council of the B.M.A. B.M.A., London.
CURRAN, D. (1947) *Practitioner*, **158**, 343.
CURRAN, D. and PARR, D. (1957) *Brit. med. J.*, **1**, 797.

EYSENCK, H. J., *et al.* (1960) In *Behaviour Therapy and the Neuroses*, ed. H. J. Eysenck, Pergamon Press, Oxford.

FRANKS, C. M. (1960) *Ibid.*, p. 278.

FREUND, K. (1960) *Ibid.*, p. 312.

HADFIELD, J. A. (1958) *Brit. Med. J.*, **1**, 1323.

KINSEY, A. C., POMEROY, W. B. and MARTIN, C. E. (1948) *Sexual Behaviour in the Human Male*, Saunders, Philadelphia.

RAYMOND, M. J. (1956) *Brit. Med. J.*, **2**, 854.

SARGANT, W. (1957) *Battle for the Mind*, Heinemann, London.

# Behaviour Therapy in Transvestism*

## J. D. GLYNN and P. HARPER

*Whittingham Hospital, near Preston, Lancashire*

A MAN of 27 had been in the habit of dressing in female clothes since the age of 14. While his wife was away at work he dressed as usual in her clothes and went out shopping. He was apprehended by the police and referred for psychiatric examination. Over 4 years the marriage had never been consummated owing to his wife's frigidity.

He was admitted to hospital and treated along the lines outlined by Raymond.† Apomorphine hydrochloride (gr. $^1/_{20}$–$^1/_8$) was injected intramuscularly 2-hourly for 4 days and nights. After injection he was asked to dress entirely in women's clothing, and he wore this throughout the period of nausea and vomiting. Apart from losing 1 lb in weight he remained in good physical condition.

After 4 day's treatment the patient exhibited marked revulsion at the sight of female clothes and flatly refused to put them on. He no longer felt any desire to wear them, and this was still so when he was examined 7 months later.

His wife's frigidity, which was coincidental and unconnected with his transvestism, was treated in outpatients by reciprocal inhibitions as described by Wolpe§; the success achieved can be gauged by the fact that she is now pregnant, and the marriage is happily stabilized.

Aversion therapy may seem time-consuming and temporarily unpleasant for the patient, but it appears to be effective.

Our purpose has not been to explain how aversion therapy works, but to confirm that with it transvestism can be successfully treated. The condition is adequately described in most psychiatric textbooks, but its treatment is not.

* This note is reprinted with the permission of the authors and the editor from the *Lancet* (4. 3. 61) p. 619.

† Raymond, M. J. *Brit. Med. J.*, 1956, ii, 854.

§ Wolpe, J. Psychotherapy by Reciprocal Inhibition. 1958.

# The Application of Behaviour Therapy
## to a Sexual Disorder*

C. B. BLAKEMORE

*Institute of Psychiatry, Maudsley Hospital, London*

## INTRODUCTION

Transvestism, the wearing of clothes of the opposite sex as a means of sexual outlet, may be regarded as a habitual pattern, in terms of a behavioural analysis, involving a distortion of stimulus and response relations. Although this condition can be found in both males and females, with the latter represented by such historical figures as the Chevalier d'Eon and Georges Sand, in our own culture the principal social concern is with the male transvestist. While most authorities would contend that transvestism does not exist in pure culture, without some additional disorders of behaviour, neurotic personality traits, or latent homosexuality being present, nevertheless it can occur in individuals who show no other overt signs of sexual abnormality. Many transvestists are in most respects heterosexual, without any significant homosexual history, and the majority of those reported on in the literature are found to be married men with families. In this respect it is important to add that while the transvestist may derive sexual stimulation and satisfaction from being identified with, and taken for, a member of the opposite sex, this does not necessarily imply a general belief on his part that he is a member of the opposite sex in terms of psychological make-up, or a desire to change sex by surgical procedures. Here the transvestist differs from the transsexualist, for whom crossdressing is just one symptom of a more generalized psychosexual disorder.

The literature on transvestism has been the subject of a very detailed and thorough review by Lukianowicz (1959), and is further summarized by Lavin *et al.* (1961), with regard to both the theoretical arguments put forward to account for the condition and the methods of treatment employed up to that time. Environmental, psychodynamic, and endocrine factors have each been suggested as possible aetiological variables. Some writers on the subject have argued that the parents' desire for a child of the opposite sex, and the subsequent favouring of the child when it behaves accordingly, is

* This paper was written specially for publication in this book.

165

an important variable, while others have suggested that sexual exhibitionism by the mother or a sister is the main aetiological factor. From the standpoint of Freudian psychodynamic theory transvestism is a defence against castration fears, by means of identification with an imaginary phallic woman of one's own creation. Again, it has been suggested that genetic and endocrine factors may be responsible for the condition, but the findings of Barr and Hobbs (1954) that male transvestists bear the male $xy$ chromosome complex would appear to weaken this contention. Each of these arguments is supported by only slight empirical evidence, usually based on a very small number of cases, and, for the most part, without any adequate provision of control data. In spite of these differences of opinion regarding the causative factors underlying transvestism, most authorities do appear to agree, however, that the first manifestations of this pattern of behaviour occur during childhood or early adolescence.

Differences of opinion exist also in respect of the treatment to be employed in cases of transvestism, with the proposed methods covering a wide range of psychological and physical procedures. Some authorities, such as Ostow (1953) and Peabody et al. (1953), have argued that intensive psychotherapy, preferably along the lines of classic psychoanalysis, offers the only hope of a lasting cure, while others would claim that more superficial psychotherapy can produce fairly rapid changes in behavioural adjustment (Lukianowicz, 1959). The value of psychotherapy in the treatment of transvestism is difficult, if not impossible, to assess, for the cases reported upon may be highly selective, and against these there are no control data. In this respect it is worth noting, perhaps, that in many of those treated cases that are in the literature, the transvestism appears to be a secondary symptom to some other psychiatric disturbance, and that in such cases it was brought under therapeutic control if, or when, the more basic disorder responded to treatment. As an alternative to psychotherapy a variety of physical and surgical treatments have been suggested, and some evidence produced in favour of their possible usefulness. These suggestions range from reports of the disappearance of transvestist symptoms in psychotics and depressives after treatment with E.C.T. or chemotherapy, to hormone treatments and recommendations of castration if the patient desires it. The same criticisms that have been put forward against the therapeutic claims of psychotherapy could be applied also to each of these proposed physical and surgical methods.

An evaluation of the literature on transvestism suggests that, in most instances, there is an insufficiently clear and rationally established relationship between assumed aetiological variables on the one hand, and, on the other hand, the various methods employed in treatment. As a result each authority tends to arrive at conclusions, with respect to both aetiology and treatment, by means of retrospective reasoning from the small number of cases which he has successfully treated. Because of the few transvestists which each clinician is likely to see, the problem of setting up adequately controlled experiments is bound to be a difficult one. If, however, the treatment has been derived directly from a simple aetiological model, then it should be possible to experimentally manipulate certain of the treatment variables in a systematic fashion, thus testing hypotheses pertaining to both the treatment itself and the underlying causative factors involving the symptom.

The possibilities for the development of such an approach may be seen in the few reports to have appeared on attempts to treat transvestism by means of behaviour therapy. Here the assumption is that the cross-dressing pattern of behaviour is essentially a learned response, and that the treatment should be based on our existing knowledge regarding the modification of learned patterns of behaviour. Each of the cases reported upon has relied on aversion conditioning, in which an attempt is made to disrupt the learned behaviour by substituting an unpleasant response for the existing pleasurable response associated with the given stimulus–response relationship. Attempts to treat alcoholism by this type of aversion therapy, with varying degrees of success, have been reported for many years. One of the earliest applications of the technique to a sexual abnormality was made by Raymond (1956), who reported on the successful use of aversion therapy in the treatment of a handbag and pram fetishist. Raymond employed as his noxious response the vomiting resulting from the injection of an emetic drug, such as apomorphine or emetine hydrochloride. This vomiting was controlled in such a way that it occurred always while the patient was in the presence of handbags and/or prams, or was viewing pictures of these stimulus objects. The aim in such a procedure is to establish a conditioned response along classical Pavlovian lines, in which the symptom-related stimuli (the conditioned stimulus) become associated with the onset of the unpleasant vomiting response (the unconditioned response).

Davies and Morgenstern (1960) attempted to employ a similar approach to Raymond's in the treatment of a transvestist. They abandoned this, however, when it was found that the patient's symptoms were associated with cysticercosis and temporal lobe epilepsy. Glynn and Harper (1961) briefly report on the treatment by aversion therapy of a 27-year-old male transvestist who had been in the habit of cross-dressing since he was 14 years of age. After a short treatment session with the use of emetic drugs, lasting only four days, this patient remained symptom free up to at least a seven-months' follow-up. Another example of the application of behaviour therapy to transvestism is reported by Oswald (1962). His patient, a 37-year-old male who had been cross-dressing from an early age, was treated by aversion therapy using emetic drugs, together with a tape-recording of male and female voices making comments on the patient's existing and desired responses to transvestism. Shortly after treatment this patient became depressed and somewhat suicidal. After this had cleared he was able to return to his wife and family, and to take up his previous employment as a telephone engineer.

Eight months after treatment he still dressed-up in female clothes on occasions, but reported that there had been a striking change in his fantasy-life, especially in the apparent disappearance of the dressing-up and masochistic fantasies in which he had previously indulged.

Among the most detailed accounts of the application of behaviour therapy to the treatment of transvestism, are the two cases reported by a group of workers from Banstead Hospital, Surrey. This group, with which the present author was closely associated, consisted of both psychiatrists and psychologists working in close collaboration. Both of these cases were treated by aversion therapy, but the approach adopted with the second one was considerably modified in the light of experience gained with the earlier case.

## THE FIRST CASE

This is briefly commented upon by Barker *et al.* (1961) and is reported in detail by Lavin *et al.* (1961). The following is a short summary of this report.

1. *The patient* was a young man of 22, who had been married for less than a year. He was the third child of a coal-miner's family, in which there was no history of mental illness. He had received an elementary school education, was currently employed as a lorry-driver, and was found to be of average intelligence. He was a man of athletic build who practised weight-lifting and physical culture.

He reported that he had been dressing in female clothes recurrently since the age of eight. This practice had originally centred around the wearing of his older sister's dresses. Cross-dressing had been accompanied by erotic satisfaction since the age of fifteen. Although he masturbated infrequently, this was always accompanied by transvestist fantasies.

Both the patient and his wife reported that their marital relations were satisfactory, and he denied transvestist fantasies during intercourse. However, his wife had only recently learned of his abnormality, and this was one of the factors which strongly motivated him in seeking treatment.

2. *The treatment procedure* was modelled on that employed by Raymond (1956). As this patient was not affected by actually handling female clothes, but obtained his main satisfaction from the total effect of cross-dressing and admiring himself in a mirror, the conditioned stimulus was made up of a series of twelve 35 mm coloured transparencies of the patient dressed in various items of female clothing, ranging from the wearing of panties only to being completely dressed and with make-up. This aspect of the conditioned stimulus was augmented by a tape-recording of the patient's own voice giving his name and stating the various items of female clothing which he was wearing. The introduction of this tape-recording was designed to facilitate the generalization of any conditioned response that might be established.

The treatment took place in a small room in which there was a bed with a white screen set up at the foot of it, a projector mounted behind the head, and a tape-recorder. Sixty-eight treatment sessions were given at two-hourly intervals over a period of six days and six nights. Each treatment session commenced with the administration of the drug by intramuscular injection; as soon as the patient reported the onset of nausea, headache, etc., then one of the slides was flashed on to the screen and the tape-recorder was started, and these were kept running until he vomited. The main drug used was apomorphine, but the patient tended to develop a tolerance for this, and despite considerable variation of the dosage he failed to vomit on a number of occasions. In an attempt to counter this tolerance a variety of other preparations were administered, either by injection or orally, at different times during the treatment, including emetine hydrochloride, mustard, and salt in water.

At the outset and during the course of the treatment a small number of injections of sterile water were administered, to test for possible pseudo-conditioning and for the establishment of a conditioned response to the pictures and tape recording. None of these produced any clearly significant reactions, although in the case of one, given about half way through the treatment, the patient experienced slight discomfort and retching when the conditioned stimulus was presented.

Throughout the entire course of the treatment the patient was kept awake by oral administration of dexamphetamine sulphate, on the assumption that the additional cerebral stimulation might facilitate the conditioning process.

Despite signs of physical strain which appeared towards the end of the sixth night, the patient remained well, and was both co-operative and highly motivated during this course of treatment.

3. *Progress* was first noted when, after a number of trials, he began to refer to the pictures of himself in female clothing as a "disfigurement", and stated that he could not understand how cross-dressing had at one time been pleasurable. Six months after the completion of this treatment the patient reported that he was symptom-free, and expressed every confidence in remaining so in the future. Since this report was published Lavin and his associates have stated that an eighteen-month follow-up revealed that this patient had, in fact, remained free from relapse up to that time (see footnote in Blakemore *et al.* (1963)).

In their discussion of this case the authors make a number of critical comments on the procedure which they employed, mainly in respect of the value of emetic drugs in aversion therapy. The first of these is that the duration of the nausea and headache prior to vomiting varied considerably between injections. As the onset of these unpleasant effects was their only cue for the introduction of the symptom-related conditioned stimulus, they found it impossible to hold constant the interval between the presentation of this stimulus and the vomiting response. They point out that if the treatment is to achieve its results by means of classical Pavlovian conditioning this interval is of critical importance, and that optimal conditioning should take place within the range of from 0·5 sec to 2·5 sec between the conditioned stimulus and the unconditioned response—a range in which they were able to operate for very few of their sixty-eight treatment sessions. Secondly, they point out that on many occasions, especially towards the end of the course of treatment, the patient failed to vomit, and that under these conditions it was impossible to define accurately what response was being made. Their final criticism is that the headache and nausea experienced prior to vomiting appeared to fluctuate in intensity, and it is possible that the conditioned stimulus was being associated with the relief of unpleasant symptoms for part of the time. As a result of these considerations, all of which have an important bearing on the principles underlying aversion therapy itself, the authors are led to suggest that some learning process other than Pavlovian respondent conditioning may be responsible for the apparent efficacy of their treatment of this patient.

Similar criticisms of the use of emetic drugs in aversion therapy have been made by Eysenck (1960) and Rachman (1961), both of whom suggest that most of these difficulties may be overcome by the use of electric shock as a noxious stimulus. Such a procedure was adopted by the same group of workers in their second application of behaviour therapy to the treatment of transvestism.

## THE SECOND CASE

The treatment of a transvestist by means of faradic aversion conditioning has been reported in detail by Blakemore *et al.* (1963). The following is a short summary of this report.

1. *The patient* was a 33-year-old engineer, who had been married for four years and had one son. He had received a good education, and was pursuing a successful career in the Civil Service. At the time of treatment his physical health was good, although while serving with the R.A.F. between eighteen and twenty he had developed a duodenal ulcer which had subsequently perforated.

He stated that his neurotic father, a coal-miner, and a "highly strung" older sister had been responsible for him having an unsettled childhood. He had been indulging in transvestism, so far as he could recollect, since about the age of four years. During childhood he often derived pleasure from secretly dressing in his mother's or sister's clothing. At the age of twelve he experienced an emission while wearing a corset, and thereafter cross-dressing was usually, but not invariably, accompanied by masturbation. National Service prevented him from cross-dressing, although during this period he frequently masturbated with transvestist fantasies. On his return to civilian life he indulged regularly in transvestism, and developed a compulsion to appear in public at night dressed as a woman complete with make-up and a wig.

During the early part of his marriage he had found it necessary to cross-dress in order to obtain an erection during intercourse. He gave up this practice because of his wife's opposition, however, and came to prefer normal intercourse to transvestism as a form of sexual outlet, although he still indulged frequently in his older pattern of cross-dressing behaviour.

Before being treated by behaviour therapy he had received six years of supportive psychotherapy, which had done little to modify his symptom. He had, however, become addicted to sodium amytal during this time, which was initially prescribed to reduce tension.

2. *The treatment procedure* adopted with this patient has much in common with the paradigm involved in instrumental or operant conditioning, as well as with the more orthodox classical conditioning employed in earlier studies of aversion therapy. This procedure was partly dictated by the fact that the patient derived little pleasure from the handling of female clothes, and while he enjoyed admiring himself in his cross-dressed state in front of a mirror, his main source of stimulation and satisfaction came from the actual act of dressing-up and feeling these clothes next to his skin.

The treatment was carried out in a small room which was screened off in the middle. Behind the screen were a chair, a full-length mirror, and an electric floor grid. This grid was made of a corrugated rubber mat, to which were stapled strips of tinned copper wire. Alternate wires of this grid were then connected to the two poles of a hand-operated electric current generator. This was capable of giving a sharp, unpleasant electric shock to the feet and ankles of anyone standing on the grid at the time of the generator being operated.

At the start of each of the trials into which the treatment was divided, the patient stood naked on the grid and when instructed began to dress in his own "favourite outfit" of female clothing. This had been only slightly modified for use during the treatment, in that slits had been cut in the feet of nylon stockings and a thin metal plate to act as a conductor had been fitted into the sole of each shoe. At some point during his dressing in these female clothes the patient either received an electric shock or heard a buzzer. Each of these was a signal to begin undressing, and this signal, either shock or buzzer, was repeated at regular intervals until he was completely undressed. With the commencement of each new trial the patient had no idea whether it would end in him receiving an electric shock or hearing the buzzer.

Five such trials, with a one-minute rest interval between each one, were administered at half-hourly intervals from 9·00 a.m. until late afternoon over a six-day period. These six days were not consecutive, however, for a weekend break of two days intervened between the fourth and fifth treatment days. At the end of the treatment a total of 400 trials had been given. In half of these trials the signal to undress was an electric shock, while in the remainder it was the sound of the buzzer. In order to avoid the same number of garments being put on during each trial and stereotyped undressing behaviour, both the amount of time before the signal to undress and the interval between repetitions of this signal during undressing were varied from trial to trial.

3. *Progress* had been followed-up, at the time of the report, for the first six months after treatment. At this time the patient claimed that he had no desire to indulge in transvestism, and that during this period his relationship with his wife had improved. He stated also that he was taking less sodium amytal than at any time for a number of years. It is reported, however, that he experienced at times a dull testicular pain while in certain situations which would previously have acted as a stimulus for cross-dressing, and that this could only be relieved by intercourse with his wife or by masturbation.

The authors point out that this procedure resembles in certain important respects escape learning in the absence of a warning stimulus. They had predicted, prior to the commencement of treatment, that the patient would come to discriminate in his undressing behaviour between those trials which involved repeated electric shocks and those which only involved the buzzer. It was thought that he would take longer to undress when the buzzer was being sounded, and that during such trials he would experience reduction of tension and anxiety while undressing (i.e. while avoiding female clothes) from his knowledge that this was to be a non-shock trial. This prediction was not borne out, however, by a study of the patient's behaviour over the last 75 of the 400 trials, for there was no significant difference in his undressing behaviour during shock or buzzer trials.

In their final discussion of this case these authors suggest that their study may provide some evidence in support of the claim that instrumental conditioning could have played a more important role than Pavlovian classical conditioning in the success of this treatment. This they base on the fact that the introduction of the buzzer resulted in the aversive shock being administered for only half of the trials, and that such 50 per cent partial reinforcement could impair the process of classical responded conditioning, but facilitate that of operant instrumental conditioning during the later stages of the treatment.

## DISCUSSION

The outcome of these few studies reporting upon the application of behaviour therapy to transvestism would appear to be encouraging in a number of ways, and it is to be hoped that future work will provide additional control data against which to assess its therapeutic efficacy and make possible comparisons with other psychological and physical methods. At the present time, however, the evidence would seem to indicate that this treatment has resulted in a marked modification of behaviour in the three patients who are reported to be symptom-free. In the one reported failure (excluding the case in which treatment was terminated) there was also some change in the general pattern of transvestist behaviour, and it is only fair to add that Oswald (1962) has pointed out that this patient was never considered wholly suitable for behaviour therapy. While it might be argued that these improvements may be only temporary, nevertheless, those patients who have benefited from treatment appear to have remained symptom-free for longer periods after treatment than for a number of years prior to treatment. It is possible that they may relapse, but the same must be said of the results obtained by any other form of treatment, and indeed, our knowledge of the extinction of learned patterns of responses would suggest that in certain cases there is some likelihood of this happening. We have no reason to believe, however, that a short course of behaviour therapy at this time will not restore the patient to a symptom-free state, either for a similar or longer period than before.

Even if the value of behaviour therapy in the treatment of transvestism could be accepted as having been demonstrated, many problems calling for further research would still remain, especially in relation to the practical details of aversion therapy and the learning process underlying its efficacy. Such problems as the significance of the conditioned stimulus, and the identification of the behavioural response to be modified, have barely been touched upon in the studies which have appeared so far in the literature. The relevance of these problems has been stressed, however, by Lavin *et al.* (1961), who point out that the selection of an appropriate conditioned stimulus is of great importance. It would seem inappropriate, for example in their own case, to have the patient handle female clothing during treatment if this had no significance for him in relation to his symptom, but, on the other hand, highly appropriate for him to see pictures of himself dressed as a woman if the pleasurable aspects of his symptom are mainly centred around viewing himself in a mirror. Another transvestist may also enjoy seeing himself in a mirror while dressed as a woman, but his main source of satisfaction may be derived from the actual act of cross-dressing and feeling the clothes next to his skin. It is obvious that such individual differences are important from the point of view of the behavioural responses we wish to modify, and we should not be surprised, therefore, if a patient failed to respond to a treatment in which the symptom-related stimulus was not an integral part of the habitual stimulus–response pattern which formed the basis of his symptom. What we do not know, however, are the limits of stimulus generalization for an aversion response to other untreated stimulus–response relationships. Information on such problems as this could possibly be obtained by experimental investigation of the relative values of various symptom-related stimuli obtained from a number of individual patients, and also by systematic attempts to modify the transvestist behaviour by manipulating verbal behaviour related to the symptom. In respect of this last possibility it would seem true to say that while there is now a sizable literature on the operant conditioning of verbal behaviour and the direct manipulation of statements of attitudes and belief (Krasner, 1958; Salzinger, 1959), very little has been done to investigate the generalization of these manipulations to non-verbal behaviour in such clinical situations as those being discussed here. Attempts to set up experiments and manipulate variables *within* the behaviour therapy situation could lay the basis for extensive research on these problems, which may, as a consequence, result in the extensive modification and improvement of aversion therapy itself.

Many of the problems concerned with the nature of the aversive unconditioned response have already been touched upon. It would seem that the use of electric shock as a noxious stimulus has many advantages over the emetic drugs for aversion therapy in general, not only because of the greater control which the behaviour therapist has over the timing of the various stimulus and response contingencies, but also because it permits greater flexibility of the patient's behaviour in the treatment situation. An alternative to electric shock as an aversive stimulus might be found in the use of white noise played through earphones. This could have many advantages over electric shock, especially in instrumental learning situations, for the same stimulus can be used as a positive as well as a negative reinforcement. In such a procedure the noise would be played throughout the treatment session at a sufficiently high volume to irritate without being very unpleasant or painful; this noise could then be cut out as a positive reinforcement for "anti-symptom" behaviour, and increased in volume to an unpleasant level as a negative reinforcement for "pro-symptom" behaviour.

Another series of problems on which we need more information are those related to the learning process involved in aversion therapy, and here again, the entire behaviour therapy approach to the treatment of transvestism could be radically modified by the findings of such research. An example of how treatment by behaviour therapy might be analysed to provide such information can be seen in the study reported by Blakemore *et al.* (1963). In their discussion of the possible learning processes involved in the treatment of their patient they say:

> It is difficult to establish exactly how this conditioned aversion was brought about. Of the two possible explanations which most readily present themselves, either separately

or in combination, one would utilize a learning process associated with the act of dressing, while the other would involve aversion developed during undressing and escape from female clothing. In the first of these the patient received an unpleasant electric shock during the actual act of putting on female garments; this provides us with the basic essentials for the development of a conditioned aversion response along classical Pavlovian lines. The variation of the time allowed for dressing would ensure that the patient was not handling or wearing the same garments on each trial, and thus the aversion would be generalized. In the second of the possible processes responsible, the patient was repeatedly shocked during the act of undressing, and therefore was positively reinforced, by the cessation of these shocks, for behaviour which involved the escape from and avoidance of female clothing. Here we have the basic requirements for the development of an instrumental conditioned avoidance response.

From such an analysis it is possible to set up a number of hypotheses, to be tested during the treatment, whose results would add to our understanding of the relative contributions of these alternative learning models. Indeed as we have seen already, these authors go on to say that a further analysis of their procedure, regarding the use of 50 per cent partial reinforcement with the noxious stimulus, also might imply that the learning process contributing to the efficacy of their treatment could have involved instrumental as well as classical conditioning. If this suggestion is followed up by further research, and instrumental conditioning is shown to be important in the treatment of such cases, then the earlier emphasis on the blocking of existing behaviour by the establishment of a classical conditioned aversion response would be changed to one of extinction by directly manipulating the reinforcement following the existing and alternative responses. Contained within such a change of emphasis would be the utilization of positive reinforcement for responses incompatible with the symptomatic behaviour, either in combination with, or instead of, the negative reinforcers which have been employed in the past. A further change in procedure under such circumstances could be the more extensive use of schedules of partial reinforcement, for the systematic introduction of such procedures during operant conditioning tends to increase the resistance of instrumental responses to extinction (Kimble, 1961). From the point of view of behaviour therapy, as Eysenck (1963) has pointed out, the value of such scheduling of reinforcement could be related to relapse rates. In this respect it is worth noting that Lovibond (1961) has demonstrated this in another context, for he was able to show that in the case of patients treated for enuresis by conditioning techniques, the relapse rate could be considerably reduced by having the treatment based on schedules of partial reinforcement.

From this discussion it will be seen that the employment of behaviour therapy in the treatment of such conditions as transvestism offers almost limitless opportunities for experimental research, in that numerous modifications of the technique are possible, and therefore variables can be systematically studied during the actual treatment. Its apparent efficacy would seem to justify the recommendation of its application in further cases, and the research findings derived from such studies should add to our better understanding of the treatment, the learning process by which it obtains its results, and environmental variables which contribute to the maintenance of the symptom. We might conclude by saying, that as a hope for the future, the investigation of such techniques in the treatment of transvestists, fetishists, homosexuals, exhibitionists, and so on, could provide the evidence on which an empirically based theory of sexual disorder could be established.

## ACKNOWLEDGEMENTS

I would like to thank my former colleagues Dr. J. C. Barker, Dr. C. G. Conway, Dr. N. I. Lavin, and Dr. J. G. Thorpe for their permission to summarize in detail the material contained in the publications which we worked on jointly while at Banstead Hospital. I would also like to thank the editor of *Behaviour Research and Therapy*, for his permission to quote the extract from the paper which appears in that journal.

## REFERENCES

BARKER, J. C., THORPE, J. G., BLAKEMORE, C. B., LAVIN, N. I. and CONWAY, C. G. (1961) Behaviour therapy in a case of transvestism, *Lancet*, i, 510.

BARR, M. L. and HOBBS, G. N. (1954) Chromosomal sex in transvestites, *Lancet*, i, 1109–1110.

BLAKEMORE, C. B., THORPE, J. G., BARKER, J. C., CONWAY, C. G. and LAVIN, N. I. (1963) The application of faradic aversion conditioning to behaviour therapy in a case of transvestism, *Behav. Res. Therapy.* 1, 29–34.

DAVIES, B. M. and MORGENSTERN, F. S. (1960) Temporal lobe epilepsy and transvestism, *J. Neurol, Neurosurg. Psychiat.* 23, 247–249.

EYSENCK, H. J. (1960) Summary and conclusions, in *Behaviour Therapy and the Neuroses*, Pergamon Press, London.

EYSENCK, H. J. (1963) Behaviour therapy, extinction, and relapse in neurosis. Brit. J. Psychiat., 109, 12–18.

GLYNN, J. D. and HARPER, P. (1961) Behaviour therapy in a case of transvestism, *Lancet*, i, 619–620.

KRASNER, L. (1958) Studies of the conditioning of verbal behavior, *Psychol. Bull.* 55, 148–170.

KIMBLE, G. A. (1961) *Hilgard and Marquis' Conditioning and Learning*, Appleton-Century-Crofts, New York.

LAVIN, N. I., THORPE, J. G., BARKER, J. C., BLAKEMORE, C. B. and CONWAY, C. G. (1961) Behaviour therapy in a case of transvestism, *J. Nerv. Ment. Dis.* 133, 346–353.

LOVIBOND, S. H. (1961) Conditioning and Enuresis. Ph. D. thesis, Univ. of Adelaide.

LUKIANOWICZ, N. (1959) Survey of various aspects of transvestism in the light of our present knowledge, *J. Nerv. Ment. Dis.*, 128, 36–64.

OSTOW, M. (1953) Transvestism, *J.A.M.A.*, 152, 1553.

OSWALD, I. (1962) Induction of illusory and hallucinatory voices with considerations of behaviour therapy, *J. Ment. Sci.*, 108, 196–212.

PEABODY, G. A., ROWE, T. and WALL, G. M. (1953) Fetishism and transvestism, *J. Nerv. Ment. Dis.*, 118, 339–350.

RACHMAN, S. (1961) Sexual disorders and behavior therapy, *Amer. J. Psychiat.*, 118, 235–240.

RAYMOND, M. J. (1956) Case of fetishism treated by aversion therapy, *Brit. Med. J.*, ii, 854–856.

SALZINGER, K. (1959) Experimental manipulation of verbal behavior: A review, *J. Gen. Psychol.*, 61, 65–94.

# Behaviour Therapy, Extinction and Relapse in Neurosis*

H. J. EYSENCK

*Institute of Psychiatry, University of London*

BEHAVIOUR therapy is defined as the application of the principles of modern learning theory to the treatment of neurotic disorders (Eysenck, 1960a, 1963). It defines neurotic "symptoms" as unadaptive conditioned autonomic responses, or the skeletal and muscular activities instrumental in moderating these conditioned autonomic responses. Treatment consists essentially in the extinction of autonomic, skeletal and muscular responses of this type. This extinction may be produced in a great variety of ways, but experience has shown that the most useful and important is probably the method of counter-conditioning or "reciprocal inhibition" (Wolpe, 1958). This method takes two forms, according to the nature of the symptom. (1) When the symptom is of a dysthymic character (anxieties, phobias, depression, obsessive-compulsive reactions, etc.) it is assumed that the disorder consists of conditioned *sympathetic* reactions, and the treatment consists of reconditioning the stimulus (or stimuli) to produce *parasympathetic* reactions which, being antagonistic to the sympathetic ones, will weaken and finally extinguish them. These disorders we will here call "disorders of the first kind". (2) When the symptom is of a socially disapproved type in which the conditioned stimulus evokes parasympathetic responses (alcoholism, fetishism, homosexuality), or where there is an entire absence of an appropriate conditioned response (enuresis, psychopathic behaviour), treatment (aversion therapy) consists of the pairing of the stimulus in question with strong aversive stimuli producing sympathetic reactions. These disorders we will call "disorders of the second kind". (In putting the distinction between these two types of treatment in this very abbreviated form, we have used the terms "sympathetic" and "parasympathetic" on a rather inexact shorthand notation to refer to hedonically positive and negative experiences respectively; the reader familiar with the complexities of autonomic reactions will no doubt be able to translate these blanket statements into more precise language appropriate to each individual case. We have retained this use of the terms here because

---

* This article has been reprinted with the permission of the editor from *Brit. J. Psychiat.*, (1963), **109**, 12–18.

176

it aids in the general description given, and indicates the physiological basis assumed to exist for the hedonic reactions.)

It has always been emphasized that behaviour therapy is *purely symptomatic*; behaviour therapy is based on a theory regarding neurotic behaviour which maintains that "there is no neurosis underlying the symptom, but merely the symptom itself" (Eysenck, 1960a, p. 9). The most frequent objection to purely symptomatic treatment has always been based on an alternative hypothesis, viz. one which regards the symptom merely as the manifestation of some "unconscious" and "repressed" complex which is the true base from which symptoms spring; the "complex" is the "illness", and the symptom cannot be cured in any permanent form without "uncovering" the "complex". (Quotation marks are used to indicate those terms and concepts for which the writer has been unable to find any experimental evidence in the literature.) It would follow directly from such an hypothesis that treatment of symptoms only would result in speedy relapse, and one would predict that behaviour therapy, in any of its forms, might produce some initial amelioration, only to be followed by a recrudescence of the same, or emergence of some other symptom. That this is a crucial point has been universally recognized by behaviour therapists and their critics alike; psychoanalysis seldom makes clear-cut and empirically verifiable predictions, and the fact that on this point its many practitioners are unanimous makes it a valuable testing-stone for experimentally-minded psychiatrists and psychologists. The evidence (Wolpe, 1961; Yates, 1958) suggests strongly that the looked-for recrudescence of symptoms has signally failed to materialize. This is true not only in relation to behaviour therapy; it has also been found in relation to spontaneous remission (which according to psychoanalytic thinking should not occur) that permanence of recovery, rather than relapse, is the rule (Denker, 1946). Nevertheless, the writer does not feel that this problem should be dismissed too easily; the available evidence is suggestive, but by no means conclusive. There undoubtedly are instances in the literature where relapses have been found to take place, and even if the total number should not be very large, it may be useful to look at the problem from the theoretical point of view. Protagonists tend to take an all-or-none point of view in these matters; a more objective approach might indicate some less extreme position to be more in accord with the facts, and might also lead to suggestions for improvements in the methods of treatment used.

Let us first consider the fact that behaviour therapy posits the occurrence of classical and instrumental conditioning as crucial elements in the genesis of neurotic disorders of the first kind, and frequently also of the second kind, and that it assumes these two kinds of conditioning to play a central part in the treatment of both kinds of neurosis. Such a statement has many important theoretical consequences, and it seems curious that so little work has been done to investigate theoretically the sets of deductions which can be made from these basic premises. In this paper we shall be concerned in the main with a particular phenomenon universally found in conditioning experiments and entitled "extinction" by Pavlov. This is defined by Kimble (1961) as "the specific procedure of presenting the conditioned stimulus unaccompanied by the usual reinforcement; also the decrement in a conditioned response which results from that procedure". It is our belief that in tracing the fate of those conditioned responses we call neurotic symptoms, too little attention has been paid to the facts of extinction, and the conditions giving rise to them. It is suggested that extinction affects in a profoundly different manner neurotic disorders of the first and second kind respectively, and that the problem of relapse cannot be discussed in any satisfactory manner without paying attention to these differences.

Consider neurotic disorders of the first kind, i.e. the dysthymic disorders. Here it is hypothesized that the original cause of the symptom is a conjunction of a single traumatic event (or several repeated subtraumatic experiences) with the presence of a previously neutral stimulus. Through classical conditioning the previously neutral stimulus (CS) now acquires the properties properly belonging to the traumatic event (UCS), itself, and produces the autonomic disturbances originally produced by the UCS. As I have argued elsewhere (Eysenck, 1962) this account would lead us to expect spontaneous remission to occur in practically all cases of neurosis, due to the fact that on subsequent occasions the presentation of the CS would not be followed by reinforcement, so that in due course extinction should take place. It is, of course, well known that in the great majority of neurotic disorders spontaneous remission does in fact supervene within a relatively short period of time (Eysenck, 1960b), so that the facts are in good accord with our hypothesis.

Those cases where spontaneous remission does *not* occur can be explained in terms of a subsequent *second* stage of instrumental conditioning. If the patient withdraws from the CS upon encountering it there will be a lowering of sympathetic arousal which should act as a reinforcement for the act of avoidance; and this reinforcement should gradually lead to the building up of a new habit of avoiding the CS, thus making extinction impossible (Eysenck, 1962).

In relation to symptoms of the first kind, therefore, we find that the role of extinction is a very important one. In a large number of cases it effectively performs the function of therapy without the intervention of any particular therapist, leading to the spontaneous remission (and nonrecurrence!) of the symptom. As the events producing extinction may, on a first approximation, be assumed to be randomly distributed over time, one would expect the curve of recovery to be a simple exponential function of time, and as I have shown this is in fact so (Eysenck, 1960b). It appears that recovery from neurotic disorders roughly follows the course given by the formula

$$X = 100(1 - 10^{-0.00435\,N})$$

where $X$ stands for the amount of improvement and $N$ the number of weeks elapsed. While the exact values in this formula should not, of course, be taken too seriously, its general form is that of the typical extinction curve with which psychologists are familiar from the laboratory. It is clear, then, that in the case of neurosis of the first kind, extinction works in favour of the therapist and may even unaided lead to improvement and cure. Where the random events of life, acting in this fashion, do not produce a cure, the therapist can aid the process along the lines laid down by Wolpe (1958) and others. Relapses should not occur in the ordinary way unless a new, repeated traumatic event occurs to produce a new symptom and a new neurotic disorder. This, of course, could not be considered a relapse, just as we would not consider it a relapse if a patient with a broken scapula should years after recovery suffer a Pott's fracture! Cure from one set of symptoms does not confer immunity on the patient.

Now consider the situation in relation to disorders of the second kind. Here the situation is clearly exactly the opposite to that which we have encountered so far. The patient is suffering from a maladaptive habit which is either itself an unconditioned response ($_sU_R$), as in the case of enuresis, or where the conditioned stimulus has become associated with consequences which are immediately pleasurable to the patient, although they may be socially undesirable and highly unpleasant in their long term consequences for the individual himself (fetishism, alcoholism, etc.). Some types of disorder, such as homosexuality, may pertain to either one or the other of these two categories, i.e. homosexual disorders may be entirely due to an accidental conditioning process, or they may be innate response tendencies ($_sU_R$), or they may be a mixture of both. In any case what is true in all these types of disorder is that a strong bond has been created between a previously neutral stimulus and a strong positive reinforcement. Ordinary events of life occurring randomly are not likely to lead to extinction as they are not likely to associate the conditioned stimulus with lack of reinforcement.

It might be objected that surely punishment in its various forms has been designed specially by society to produce precisely such a dissociative effect and that by imprisonment, beating or torturing homosexuals, fetishists, etc. we are substituting a negative reinforcement for a positive one. That such an objection is not tenable has been shown in practice by the failure of these methods throughout recorded history; no one nowadays assumes that the habits of the homosexual are altered by putting him into prison, even though such punishment may restrain the expression of these habits for a while (in other words punishment may affect $_sE_R$ but not $_sH_R$). Even more important, Mowrer has shown (1950) both theoretically and experimentally

... that the consequences of a given act determine the future of that act not only in terms of what may be called the quantitative aspects of the consequences but also in terms of their temporal pattern. In other words, if an act has two consequences—the one reward-ing and the other punishing—which would be strictly equal if simultaneous, the in-fluence of those consequences upon later performances of that act will vary depending on the *order* in which they occur. If the punishing consequence comes first and the reward-ing one later the difference between the inhibiting and the reinforcing effects will be in favour of the inhibition. But if the rewarding consequence comes first and the punishing one later the difference will be in favour of the reinforcement.

It is with respect to this temporal sequence that aversion therapy differs from punishment in the ordinary sense of the term. Punishment is a relatively arbitrary and long delayed consequence of action which, according to the principle just considered, should have very little if any influence upon the habit in question. Aversion therapy attempts to apply the aversive stimulus *immediately* after the conditioned stimulus, and in such a way that it eliminates, or at least precedes, the positive reinforcement resulting from the act. This is often difficult to do, as clearly split-second timing is of the utmost importance; as has been pointed out before, many people who attempt aversion therapy do so without a full appreciation of the complexities of conditioning, and failure easily results from the haphazard manipulation of time relationships.

Consider now a case where aversion therapy has been successful and where the conditioned stimulus has been successfully linked with the aversive stimulus; we will call this link "aversive conditioning". Now clearly aversive conditioning, like all other types of conditioning, is subject to extinction, and we must consider how extinction can arise, and how it would influence the future course of the symptom. The first point to be borne in mind is that aversive conditioning tends to stop when conditioning has only just been achieved, i.e. without any considerable degree of overlearning. As an example, take the treatment of enuresis by means of the bell-and-blanket method. According to the theoretical analysis of Lovibond (1961), urinating in bed is the conditioned stimulus which becomes linked with the aversive stimulus, the bell, which in turn produces the immediate reflex cessation of urination. Now it is clear that conditioning can only proceed while the patient still produces the conditioned stimulus, i.e. while conditioning is still far from complete. The moment the patient ceases to urinate in bed further conditioning becomes impossible. With modifications the same argument would hold for other types of aversion therapy. Where the conditioned stimulus can be voluntarily applied, as in the case of consump-tion of alcoholic beverages, consideration of time, expense and great dis-comfort produced usually limits the number of conditioning trials to a relatively small proportion of what may be required to produce any con-siderable degree of overlearning.

After successful aversion therapy, the patient emerges with a central nervous system into which has been built a certain amount of "aversive conditioning" which is subject to what has been called oscillation by

Spearman (1927) and Hull (1943); this is usually designated as $_sO_R$. Oscillation is a feature of all biological systems and produces random variations in the strength of inhibitory and excitatory potential; these oscillations may be quite considerable in relation to the total amount of potential under consideration.

Consider now an individual who has submitted to a course of aversion conditioning, and whose degree of conditioning is just at the point where the original behaviour does not occur in relation to the stimuli which used to set it off before the course of aversive conditioning. Due to the process of oscillation the effectiveness of aversive conditioning will be much weaker on certain occasions than on others, and if by accident the original stimuli are present at a time when the excitatory potential of the aversive conditioning is low, then he is liable to give way to temptation. If he does, then the extinction process phase of the aversive conditioning will have begun because the conditioned stimulus has been presented without the (negative) reinforcement. It would follow that on subsequent occasions the excitatory potential ($_sE_R$) would already be weaker to begin with, even without the action of oscillation, so that further extinction trials are even more likely to occur. We thus find that in neurotic disorders of the second kind the random events of everyday life, far from leading to spontaneous remission will rather lead to relapse, other things being equal. Thus our prediction, on theoretical grounds, would be that relapse should be rare or even non-existent in disorders of the first kind, but relatively frequent with disorders of the second kind. There are no empirical studies, the results of which could be used to support this deduction in any conclusive manner, but it is noteworthy that those who have denied the occurrence of relapse, like Wolpe (1958), have concentrated largely on disorders of the first kind. Writers dealing with disorders of the second kind, like Gwynne Jones (1960), Oswald (1962), Freund (1960) and others, have drawn attention to the frequency of relapse in patients of this type. It would seem, therefore, that the distinction made is a potentially fruitful one, although the reasons for the difference in relapse rates may be due, in part at least, to other causes as well. Thus the symptoms of disorders of the first kind are usually such as to motivate the patient very strongly to undergo a process of therapy, in order to get relief from these symptoms. The symptoms of disorders of the second kind, however, are much less painful to bear as far as the individual is concerned; indeed they may appear quite pleasant and agreeable to him. It is society, through one of its various agencies, which provides the motivation for therapy, and this imposed drive is likely to be much weaker. This is important because it is well known that the strength of conditioned responses is very much determined by the strength of the drive under which the individual is working. Here we may have, therefore, an additional principle accounting for the high relapse rate predicted for disorders of the second type.

If we are right in assuming that aversion therapy is less effective than it might be because of the reasons given, then we should look to learning theory for suggestions which might lead to more effective methods of conditioning, and to a lessening of the degree of extinction or "relapse". The most obvious suggestion which emerges from laboratory studies appears to be that the process of aversive conditioning should make use of *partial* rather than complete 100 per cent reinforcement, as is the most usual practice at the moment. The discovery that partial reinforcement, i.e. the random reinforcement and non-reinforcement of conditioned stimuli, leads to a much greater resistance to extinction, was made in 1939 by Humphries, and is sometimes known as "Humphries' paradox". A lengthy discussion of this phenomenon and its theoretical interpretation is given by Kimble (1961). We need not here concern ourselves with the theoretical explanations or with the details of the experimental procedures; it is sufficient to note that the evidence for the phenomenon is surprisingly unanimous and leaves little doubt about its reality. Whilst apparently contrary to common sense, the efficacy of partial reinforcement in delaying extinction is not entirely inexplicable even on the commonsense level itself. One hundred per cent reinforcement during the acquisition phase marks this phase off obviously and completely from the extinction phase, so that not only is the change obvious to the subject, but also there will be a change in a number of the more remote conditioned stimuli, including the drive stimuli, which together set the stage for the occurrence of the conditioned response. In the case of partial reinforcement the two phases are much more difficult to mark off from each other and the pattern of internal stimulation is very much less different as we go from one phase to the other.

However that may be, the crucial test of a theoretical prediction must inevitably lie in the experimental demonstration that the phenomenon predicted does actually occur. Fortunately there is a very carefully controlled experimental study comparing the relapse rates of children treated by means of the bell-and-blanket method for enuretic disorders by S. H. Lovibond (1961). In half the cases partial reinforcement was used, and 100 per cent reinforcement with the other half. He found that significantly greater tendency to relapse was found in the latter group as compared with the former. We may, therefore, conclude that this deduction has some empirical support, although it would, of course, be desirable to study it in connexion with many other types of disorder of the second kind in addition to the enuretic ones worked on by Lovibond.

It is noteworthy that many investigators in the use of aversion therapy go directly counter to this principle. Thus in the deconditioning treatment of alcoholism patients are often told not to take drinks on their own and outside the treatment situation, as this would interfere with the treatment. Every precaution is taken to ensure 100 per cent reinforcement—thus also ensuring, if our hypothesis be correct, that relapse should be the more likely to occur! (It is likely, incidentally, that the massing of conditioning trials leads to an increase in inhibition and, therefore, raises the probability of extinction and relapse. Oswald (1962, p. 211) has argued in favour of a method in which alcohol is given even after nausea has begun. This not only goes counter to the principle of the inefficiency of backward conditioning, but also ensures a quite unusual massing of conditioning trials such as would not be expected to aid in the prevention of extinction.)

Whilst partial reinforcement presents one way of avoiding the difficulties of extinction and relapse, it is of course not the only one. A second method is that of "overlearning", i.e. the continuation of the conditioning process, preferably through the use of widely-spaced trials, well beyond the point where conditioning occurs to an apparently satisfactory degree. It is impossible on *a priori* grounds to lay down any general rules as to the precise number of reinforced trials required; this obviously depends on such factors as the subject's drive, his conditionability, the urgency of the situation, facilities present at the time and so on. It might be said in parentheses, however, that practitioners appear often to have used reinforcements in aversion therapy, the strength of which was much greater than would be required for satisfactory conditioning. The use of strong doses of apomorphine can be defended in that, as is well known, the strength of the unconditioned stimulus in part determines the efficacy of the conditioning process. However, the acute misery induced puts many people off the treatment altogether, and it also tends to reduce the number of conditioning trials to an absolute minimum. The number of reinforced trials, however, is probably a more important factor in determining the strength of the conditioned response, and more numerous trials with a weaker UCS would probably be more effective than a small number with the strong UCS. The precise effects of varied combinations of conditions must, of course, be determined by experimental investigations; it can only be hoped that these will in the future be more closely geared to existing knowledge than has been the case in the past.

Even with partial reinforcement and overlearning the dynamics of the situation in the case of disorders of the second type are such that relapse is an ever-present danger. It can be guarded against by widely-spaced conditioning trials administered throughout the life history of the individual, perhaps once or twice a year; it seems likely that such a programme would prevent relapse quite efficiently, particularly when used in conjunction with the other methods outlined. Again the call must be for experimental investigations, properly designed, executed and evaluated according to the most rigorous criteria of modern statistical and experimental method.

## SUMMARY

In this paper a distinction has been drawn on theoretical lines between two types of neurotic disorders, and the consequences have been traced of the extinction process on the symptoms of these two types of disorders. It was shown that while extinctions occurring naturally during the life history of the individual should produce *spontaneous remission* in patients suffering from disorders of the first kind, it should produce a *relapse* after successful treatment in the case of patients suffering from disorders of the second kind. Certain deductions were made from modern learning theory suggesting that the occurrence of extinction and relapse could be lessened by using treatment processes emphasizing partial reinforcement, overlearning, spaced trials and supportive conditioning. It was argued that the distinction between these types of disorder is from the practical point of view a fundamental one, and that generalizations about the recrudescence of symptoms after treatment by behaviour therapy are quite unjustified unless they specify the type of disorder to which they are meant to apply. It is also argued that current methods of aversion therapy tend to violate precisely those principles which would ensure a lessening of the relapse rate, and that widespread experimentation should be encouraged in which these principles would be put to the test of clinical success.

## REFERENCES

DENKER, R. (1946) Results of treatment of psychoneuroses by general practitioners, *New York State J. Med.* **46**, 2164–2166.

EYSENCK, H. J. (1960a) *Behaviour Therapy and the Neuroses*, Pergamon Press, Oxford.

EYSENCK, H. J. (1960b) *Handbook of abnormal psychology*, Pitman, London.

EYSENCK, H. J. (1962) Behaviour therapy, spontaneous remissions and transference in neurotics. *Amer. J. Psychiat.*

EYSENCK, H. J. (1963) *Experiments in Behaviour Therapy*, Pergamon Press, Oxford.

FREUND, K. (1960) Some problems in the treatment of homosexuality. In EYSENCK, H. J. (Ed.) *Behaviour Therapy and the Neuroses*. Pergamon Press, Oxford, 312–326.

HULL, C. L. (1943) *Principles of behaviour*, Appleton-Century Crofts, New York.

GWYNNE JONES, H. (1960) The behavioural treatment of enuresis nocturnal. In Eysenck, H. J. (Ed.) *Behaviour Therapy and the Neuroses*. Pergamon Press, Oxford, 377–403.

KIMBLE, A. A. (1961) *Hilgard and Marquis' Conditioning and Learning*, Appleton-Century Crofts, New York.

LOVIBOND, S. H. (1961) The theory and method of conditioning in relation to enuresis and its treatment. Unpublished Ph.D. thesis Adelaide.

MOWRER, O. H. (1950) *Learning theory and personality dynamics*, Ronald, New York.

OSWALD, I. (1962) Induction of illusory and hallucinatory voices with consideration of behaviour therapy, *J. Ment. Sci.* **108**, 196–212.

SPEARMAN, C. (1927) *Abilities of man*, Macmillan, London.

WOLPE, J. (1958) *Psychotherapy by reciprocal inhibition*, Stanford University Press.

WOLPE, J. (1961) The prognosis in unpsychoanalysed recovery from neurosis, *Amer. J. Psychiat.*, **117**, 35–39.

YATES, A. (1958) Symptoms and symptom substitution, *Psychol. Rev.* **65**, 371–374.

# PART II

# OPERANT CONDITIONING

THE METHODS of reciprocal inhibition discussed in the first part of this book derive essentially from the experimental and theoretical work of Pavlov; the methods of operant conditioning discussed in this part derive essentially from the experimental and theoretical work of Bechterev. Just as Pavlov was followed by many learning theorists who translated his concepts and empirical findings into modern learning theory, so Bechterev also found many successors, the main one being probably B. F. Skinner. It is only relatively recently that the Skinnerian approach has spread from the field of rats and pigeons into that of human beings, and its success does not perhaps as yet come up to its promise. Yet this promise is undoubtedly immense, and it is unfortunate that few psychiatrists are sufficiently acquainted with Skinner's contributions to enable them to adapt his methods and formulations to their problems. It is in the hope that a few worked-out examples would inspire readers to search out other contributions in this quickly developing field that the papers here reprinted were selected; they constitute examples of many different types of application of operant conditioning to psychiatric problems.

It will be clear to the reader, after perusing these examples, that they differ in certain quite important ways from those reprinted in the preceding section. Primarily these differences arise from the fact that the methods of treatment associated with reciprocal inhibition aim to cure the patient; while his symptoms are considered as inappropriate conditioned reflexes, the hope and expectation is that the desensitization and deconditioning of these reactions will lead to the disappearance of the "neurosis", which is conceived merely as the sum total of all these symptoms. Operant conditioning usually focuses on one specific symptom, frequently one which is central, and attempts to "shape" the patient's behaviour in such a way that the annoying symptom disappears, but without either the hope or the expectation that the disorder as such will be eliminated. There is no obvious reason why operant conditioning should not be used in exactly the same way as reciprocal inhibition, or why it should not also be successful in deconditioning the symptoms which together constitute the neurosis; no doubt within the next year or two such attempts will be made, and their success or failure will teach us much about the practical and also the theoretical contribution which the thinking of Bechterev and Skinner can make to modern psychiatry.

One possible reason why Skinnerians have restricted themselves in this fashion may be related to the fact that their major research effort has been concentrated on psychotic, rather than on neurotic patients. It is not clear why this should be so, but the practical corollary has clearly been to make

187

them concentrate on the manipulation of individual symptoms, which is feasible, rather than on total cure, which is probably not. Again, we may confidently expect a transfer of attention from the psychotic to the neurotic field, with many useful practical and theoretical consequences. It is with these possible applications in mind that some of the papers in this section should be read; until their inherent promise is realized, operant conditioning cannot be regarded as being as central to psychiatry as is reciprocal inhibition.

# Reinforcement and Punishment in the Control
# of Human Behavior by Social Agencies*

C. B. FERSTER, PH.D.

*Indiana University Medical Center, 1100 West Michigan St.,
Indianapolis, Indiana*

CLINICAL psychiatry and psychology depend on fundamental experimental analyses of behavior just as other fields of medicine depend on the basic sciences of physiology, biochemistry, and pharmacology. The slow development of basic natural-scientific analyses of behavior has resulted in clinical practices developed by rule of thumb or in terms of special theories unrelated to a fundamental or systematic behavioral analysis. Behavioral experimentation with animals has been a continuous, although small contribution, to clinical theory and practice. The work of Pavlov on the conditioned reflex has provided the main source for much of the extensions to clinical problems. John B. Watson and his students first applied the conditioned reflex to the experimental development, elimination, and generalization of phobic reactions in children.[8] Later, N. E. Miller, S. Dollard, and O. H. Mowrer and others extended the conditioned reflex to a wider range of human performances and clinical problems.[2, 5, 6] The work of B. F. Skinner has given further impetus to applications to problems of psychiatric rehabilitation and therapy by an experimental analysis of "operant" behavior: the behavior of organisms which exists because of its effect on the environment in contrast with the reflex behavior analyzed by Pavlov.[1, 7] Using the framework of Skinner's theoretical and experimental analysis, this paper outlines a program to change the behavior of psychiatric patients or generate new behavior by manipulating the actual environmental events maintaining a performance. The manipulatable events in the present and past environment of an organism are used to analyze the current performance in terms of the general processes already dealt with experimentally in animals and humans. The role of positive reinforcement and its corollaries in determining behavior is emphasized over aversive control.

* This article is reprinted with the permission of the author and editor from *Psychiat. Res. Rep.* **10**, 101–118 (1958).

## THE NATURE OF THE SOCIAL AGENCY

Most of the behavior of organisms exists because of its effect on the environment (operant reinforcement). The paradigm is: An event following a given instance of behavior subsequently increases the frequency of occurrence of that behavior. The verbal response "good morning" is maintained because it produces a reply from most audiences. In the absence of a reply, the response would disappear. Not all events have this property, and those that do are called reinforcement. Most human behavior is social because it has its effect on other organisms, which in turn arrange the reinforcements; this is in contrast to the physical environment, which reinforces directly. The same reinforcement paradigm may be extended to larger groups of people, such as social institutions and agencies; less well-defined groups involved in social practices, codes of conduct, etc.; small groups, such as the milieu in a certain factory, or neighborhood "gang" of children. These social practices ultimately refer to a set of reinforcements and punishments which the people who constitute the social agency or social practice apply to the behavior of an individual. The social situation is unique only in so far as other organisms mediate the reinforcements, punishments, or other important environmental effects.

A fundamental psychological analysis must deal with the behavior of the individual, and the functional dimensions of social behavior appear only when they are expressed in terms of the consequences that the members of a group of people arrange for an individual. Social approval, for example, refers to a high disposition to supply favorable consequences to a wide range of specific behaviors of the individual; and conversely, a low disposition to arrange punishments. Similarly, an individual with "social prestige" is one whose repertoire is reinforcing to members of a group, and will maintain the behavior of listening, reading, seeking close contact, and supplying reinforcements designed to maximize further performances.

Other social institutions such as law, government, religious agencies, and the family arrange very specific consequences which are somewhat easier to specify. The law and government, for example, have effects on the individual, largely by punishing specified forms of behavior by fines and incarceration. The religious agencies have some of their effects on the behaviors of the individual by similar processes. The punishments of hell and the rewards of heaven, as well as the more usual contingencies involved in the approval and disapproval by the membership of the religious agency, are used to maintain or suppress various behaviors.

## THE LARGE ORDER OF MAGNITUDE OF SOCIAL CONTROL

The importance of social behavior in human affairs is heightened by the fact that the majority of human reinforcements are mediated by another individual. Many of the reinforcements deriving their effect from groups of people have a larger order of magnitude of effect than reinforcements supplied only by a single individual or the physical environment. The heightened control by social reinforcement comes about because:

(1) Some reinforcements are possible only when a performance is carried out in connection with other individuals. The appeal of the parade and uniform comes primarily from the prestige which the individual can share only by being a member of a group which in turn is important to the community. The process referred to here is similar to *identification* in dynamic psychology. Other examples in which the individual can have an effect in the community only when he behaves in concert with other individuals include the "gang", the revival meeting, and the cooperative action of three men lifting an object too heavy for any one of them.

(2) Large numbers of individuals can potentially arrange reinforcements and punishments contingent on the behavior of the individual. The potential of an audience in rewarding or punishing depends in turn on the relevance of the reinforcements and punishments for the behavioral repertoire of the individual. The larger the number of individuals who can potentially reward, punish, or discontinue reinforcing behavior, the greater the effect is likely to be. Also, as the social agency involves more persons, there is less chance that an individual can avoid the punishment by escaping to another social group or to another environment for the reinforcements to maintain his existing repertoire. The control on the speaker by a relevant and effective audience illustrates this property of social reinforcements. When the audience has only a few members, the speaker may react to punishment or non-reinforcement by turning to other audiences. As the size of the audience increases, however, the effect of the contingencies they arrange on the behavior of the speaker becomes more and more inevitable. The control achieved in brain washing illustrates the large order of magnitude of effect from controlling all of the audiences affecting an individual. Similarly, a group practice or a set of cultural mores has a large order of magnitude of control because the larger number of individuals who will arrange the reinforcements and punishments which constitute the social practice make this almost inevitable.

## CHARACTERIZATION OF THE BEHAVIOR OF THE PSYCHIATRIC PATIENT IN TERMS OF A FUNCTIONAL ANALYSIS

Many psychiatric patients or potentially psychiatric patients may be characterized as having repertoires whose performances are not producing the reinforcements of the world: because too much behavior is being punished; because nearly all of the individual's behavior is maintained by avoiding aversive consequences rather than producing positive effects; of a combination of all of these. A potential reinforcing environment exists for every individual, however, if he will only emit the required performances on the proper occasions. One has merely to paint the picture, write the symphony, produce the machine, tell the funny story, give affection artfully, and the world will respond in kind with prestige, money, social response, and love. Conversely, a repertoire which will make contact with the reinforcements of the world will be subsequently maintained because of the effect of the reinforcement on the performance. The problem is social because most of the reinforcements are mediated by other individuals.

A deficient behavioral repertoire may arise because:

## 1. *Inadequate Reinforcement History*

Under this category belong individuals who are not making contact with important parts of their environment simply because their history did not include a set of experiences (educational) which could develop these performances during the normal maturation of the individual. Especially in the area of everday social contacts, considerable skill is necessary for producing social reinforcements, and the absence of this skill either results in an individual without a social repertoire or one who achieves affects on his social environment by indirect means, as, for example, using aversive stimulation to gain attention. It is possible that this latter behavior would disappear if the individual had a repertoire which would be effective in producing positive reinforcements. The existence of weak, positively reinforced repertoires, particularly in the field of ordinary social contacts, could result in "unsocial behavior" designed to affect the behavior of others by generating aversive conditions which are strong enough to produce avoidance, escape, and punishment. The reinforcing effect of these "anti-social" reactions might be large only in respect to the weak, positively reinforced repertoire.

## 2. *Schedule of Reinforcement*

The schedule of reinforcement of a given performance might also produce a weakened disposition to engage in this performance so that the normal reinforcements do not occur. This kind of absence of behavior would be produced particularly in situations where large amounts of work are required for reinforcements, as, for example, in the case of the writer, housewife, student, or salesman, where reinforcement depends on a fixed amount of work. The individual's repertoire contains the required performances, but the existing schedule of reinforcement is such as to weaken the repertoire and thereby prevent its occurrence even though the correct form of the behavior would be available if the schedules of reinforcement were more optimal.

## 3. *Punishment may Distort a Performance which otherwise would be Reinforced*

The absence of adequate repertoires in the individual could result from the distortion of the form of the behavior so that the performance does not have its customary effect. Excessive punishment may also generate avoidance behavior which is strong enough to be prepotent over the currently positively reinforced repertoires of the individual.

## TECHNIQUE AVAILABLE TO THE THERAPIST

The basic principles governing the development and maintenance of behavior are relevant to the task of generating new performances in an individual whose existing repertoire is not making contact with the reinforcements potentially available to him. The same principles are also relevant to the problem of generating adequate repertoires which will escape punishment.

Some of the reasons for a currently inadequate behavioral repertoire may be found in the history of the organism, perhaps even in the early infancy. In many cases, however, the behavioral history of an individual is inaccessible. To the extent, however, that a current environment exists which can potentially maintain performances in all of the important segments in the individual's life by positive reinforcement, the history of the individual is relevant only in so far as it is useful in assessing the current repertoire of the individual. A functional program of therapy relying on the manipulatable factors in the patient's environment may have important therapeutic effects, without reference to speculative accounts of the patient's history, the current verbal reports of his feelings, and attitudes. Little more is to be desired if a patient is content with his lot, works productively in a job, achieves affection and respect from this fellows, has an adequate sexual and home life, enjoys food and drink in moderation, and has diversions and adequate social relations.

If the therapist is ultimately to be successful, he must alter the relationship between the patient's performance in a wide variety of social situations and the reinforcement and punishment which will result. The therapist initially has the prestige of his profession and social position and the potential reinforcing effect involved in transference. These properties of the therapist, initially at least, give him the ability to change the patient's performance in at least some situations outside of the room in which the therapy is conducted. Ultimately, the reinforcement of these performances in the patient's environment will maintain the continued attention of the patient to the therapist's advice.

## THE PROCESSES BY WHICH SOCIAL AGENCIES AFFECT
## THE BEHAVIOR OF THE INDIVIDUAL

The major processes of behavior provide the technology for generating and eliminating behavior in the individual and are basic to the analysis of social effects. In the final analysis, the agency can have an effect on the individual only by arranging some environmental event contingent on the behavior of the individual. The social situation differs from the nonsocial one by the mediation of another organism in the delivery of the reward, punishment, or other consequence. It must be assumed, in the absence of contrary evidence, that the processes and laws operating in social situations are the same ones which are the basis for all behavioral processes.

## Reinforcement

Reinforcement is the most important process by which behavior is generated and maintained. Most of an organism's behavior exists because of the effect on the environment, perhaps with the exception of the psychotic whose repertoire reflects the absence of behavior maintained with positive reinforcement. Reinforcement differs from the colloquial reward in its specificity; it is the immediate environmental consequences of a specific performance. The major effect of reinforcement needs to be distinguished from the classical or Pavlovian-type conditioning where the conditioned response is some elicited reflex, usually autonomic. The increase in the frequency of occurrence of the performance that is reinforced is the property of reinforcement that permits the tremendous variety and subtlety that occurs in the field of "voluntary" behavior as opposed to reflex and autonomic behavior.

Most reinforcements of everyday life are social rather than involving immediately important biological conditions. These social-maintaining-events operate as reinforcements because they are in a chain of events leading ultimately to a more basic consequence. Money provides an example of a conditioned reinforcer—*par excellence*—which derives its effect because its possession is a condition under which other performances will produce basic environmental effects. The important social consequences of money occur because the reinforcing properties of money nearly always depend immediately or ultimately upon the behavior of other individuals. Similarly, a smile can reinforce behavior because an individual who is smiling is more likely to supply subsequent reinforcements than one who is not.

As with money, many reinforcements in human behavior can be effective in the absence of any specific deprivation, unlike most reinforcements demonstrated in animal experiments. These "generalized" reinforcements maintain much of human behavior, and have large order of magnitudes of effect because their reinforcing power comes from a variety of reinforcements and deprivations and does not depend upon a current level of deprivation. This is especially true of nearly all reinforcements mediated by other organisms, because the mediation by another organism, in general, permits the application of a wider range of reinforcements. Other examples of generalized reinforcers include paying attention, affection, saying "right", or "correct", smiling, etc. These are important reinforcements because they are the usual conditions under which another organism will reinforce a behavior of an individual.

## The Development of Complex Forms of Behavior: "Shaping"

A major corollary of reinforcement is a procedure by which a reinforcing agency can produce progressively complex forms of behavior by small increments from a preceding simpler form. A commonly used animal-demonstration experiment illustrates the process. If we wish to teach a pigeon to peck at a small disc on the wall of his chamber, we first establish a reinforcer by presenting grain to the bird whenever the grain hopper is illuminated. The bird soon comes to approach the hopper only when it is illuminated, and it is then possible to use the lighted hopper as a reinforcement. The bird faces in the direction of the small disc, is reinforced, and the effect is an immediate increase in the tendency to face the disc. Reinforcement is then withheld until the bird nods slightly in the direction of the disc, and the reinforcement of this slightly more complex form increases its frequency. When the bird is nodding in the direction of the disc, the variation in the magnitude of the nod is noted and the reinforcement is shifted in the direction of those nods bringing the bird's head closer to the disc. By continuing the process, the pigeon can soon be made to strike the disc.

The same process occurs in the development of human behavior, particularly in the formative years. The process by which complex forms are generated is relevant to the therapy situation whenever a patient is lacking parts of the complex repertoire necessary to achieve reinforcement from the complicated social environment. Simply telling a patient what kind of performance is necessary for reinforcement will seldom generate the required complex performance. The situation is analogous to the golfer who would like to drive the ball 250 yards. The necessary performance must be acquired in small steps, beginning with an existing repertoire and approximating the final performance with intermediate, temporary reinforcements.

The therapist is in a position to "shape" behavior in a patient by beginning with a performance already in his repertoire and exposing him to selected portions of his environment designed to generate the new, more complex form. The therapist can select an environment accessible to the patient in which a reinforcing agent is operating which will reinforce with a high degree of probability a variation in the patient's performance in the direction of the desired, more complicated form.

For example, consider the hypothetical case of an individual who has never acquired the performances necessary for facile enough social contact. The patient's current repertoire contains enough verbal behavior to permit him to talk to the therapist. A first step in this hypothetical case might be to send the patient to a college campus one morning and have him say "Good morning" to several people he passes. The environment of the campus is chosen to almost guarantee the reinforcement of this response. This kind of exercise would also illustrate to the patient general verbal processes in human behavior where it is possible to command a verbal response from an audience. In a similar vein, the complexity of the verbal repertoire of the individual could be increased further. Commands, such as "Could you please tell me the time", also produce almost inevitable responses in most situations; and if the rate of development of the new behavior is made small enough from the preceding forms which the patient is emitting successfully, there would be no difficulty from nonreinforcement because of inaudible remarks, mumbling, or other distortion of the behavior which would prevent the reinforcement.

Group therapy or psychodrama could also be adapted to the task of generating new performances as an intermediate step to be used between "office therapy" and exercises using outside environments accessible to the patient. Patients could use each other, under the direction of a therapist, to develop skills necessary in normal social practice. The therapist would set tasks for each patient carefully graded so as to be within the range of the existing behavioral repertoire. Groups of patients would provide an environment potentially capable of supporting at least some kinds of performances, and the exercises would be designed to take advantage of these reinforcements which are possible within the hospital environment. Exercises could be designed, for example, to illustrate and develop behaviors which makes it possible to command behavior from another individual: the effect of saying "please", kinds of performances which will engender conversation, cooperation in projects, techniques for achieving nonsocial reinforcements as in reading, and developing productive skills as in occupational therapy. Many of these goals are already present in many hospital situations. What is required is a program of administration which will maintain motivation during the development of the complex repertoire and establish the behavior firmly enough to provide a basis to go on to a next, more complex form.

Another example on a slightly more complex level might be the behavior of a shy boy or girl having difficulty in social and sexual relations with the opposite sex. The first task is to specify the necessary performances for achieving the potential social reinforcements. A practical program requires the development of a repertoire capable of getting a date and carrying it through adequately. The practical program would include the development of auxiliary skills such as dancing, skating, card-playing, and various sports which would provide performances predominately nonsocial which could be carried out in the company of the opposite sex and provide opportunities for the reinforcements of other kinds of behavior. As in the previous example, it would be necessary to begin with the existing repertoire and develop a situation in which the audience composed of the opposite sex can reinforce the appropriate behavior whenever it occurs. The situation is a potentially difficult one because any nonreinforcement will have large effects on an initially weak verbal repertoire. A series of exercises could be constructed beginning, for example, with a situation in which little is required verbally, such as playing cards, and the emission of only those responses whose reinforcements are guaranteed, such as a command, reading, trite sayings, etc. The development of a repertoire leading to sexual activity would begin with performances designed to extend physical contact; for example, shaking hands, help over minor obstacles, congratulatory pat on the shoulder, etc.

To the extent that enough major performances in enough important areas can be generated, the fundamental historical reason behind the original disincliniation to associate with the opposite sex, or avoid contact with the opposite sex, is no longer essential to the correction of the situation. So long as the individual as spending the time with the opposite sex, enjoying adequate sexuo-social relations, and engaged in normal social give-and-take, the historical factors are no longer relevant.

## Intermittent Reinforcement

Social reinforcements are intermittent because the reinforcements mediated by another organism are less reliable than those produced by the physical environment. This arises because the social reinforcement depends upon behavioral processes in the reinforcer which are not always under good control by the reinforcee. For example, if one is asked to look outside and report whether it is raining, many factors in the repertoire of the listener could interfere with the successful completion of the report: the listener is afraid of height, some more urgent audience catches the attention of the listener, the listener happened not to be attentive at the moment the request is made, the listener's eye glasses are off at the moment, etc. In contrast, the effects of most behavior on the physical environment is almost inevitable.

The nature of the intermittency has a great influence on the disposition to engage in a given behavior. It is possible to produce an almost complete cessation of some behavior which the individual has emitted literally thousands of times by alteration of the schedule of reinforcement. Similarly, identical frequencies of reinforcements on different reinforcement schedules produce widely differing dispositions to engage in the behavior.

The history by which the individual is exposed to many schedules is also of great importance. Certain schedules of reinforcement will sustain behavior normally if approached in gradual steps but will produce complete cessation (abulia) if the individual is exposed to the final schedule at once. In the most prevelant schedule of reinforcement found in human affairs (ratio reinforcement), the reinforcement occurs as a function of a certain number of instances of a performance. One of the major properties of this schedule of reinforcement is a decline in the disposition to emit the behavior when the amount of work for reinforcement becomes too large. This lessened disposition occurs particularly as inability to begin work just after a reinforcement. The disinclination of the novelist to begin a new novel just after completing one is a pure example of this effect. There is some suggestion that there are inductive effects among the various repertoires of the individual.

An optimal schedule of reinforcement in one area will help sustain a performance under a less optimal schedule of reinforcement in another area; and, conversely, reinforcement on unoptimal schedules of reinforcement may have the opposite effect of weakening a repertoire whose reinforcement schedule is more optimal. These "ratio" or piecework schedules of reinforcement are contrasted with another major schedule class where the reinforcement of a response becomes more likely with passage of time since the previous reinforcement. These schedules are less prevalent in human affairs than ratio schedules, and tend to produce a level of performance more appropriate to the frequency of reinforcement regardless of the history of the individual. Examples of this latter class of schedules of reinforcement include looking in the mailbox when the mail delivery occurs somewhat unpredictably (variable-interval reinforcement), and looking into the pot on the stove as the water is being boiled.

Optimum parameters of a schedule of reinforcement may also result in very large amounts of behavior and a strong disposition to engage in the reinforced behavior. The behavior of the gambler is an excellent example where an explicit program of reinforcement (technically classified variable-ratio) generates a strong disposition to gamble, even though the individual operates at a loss over a longer period of time. Here the heightened disposition to gamble arising from the optimal variable-ratio schedule of reinforcements (even the loser wins frequently) overrides the over-all low net reinforcement.

*Applications to therapy.* To the extent that a patient's difficulties result from inadequate or unoptimal reinforcement of important repertories, there is little in the immediate therapy situation which can change his performance. The salesman, for example, whose ratio of "selling" to sales becomes too high and suffers from irritability, moodiness, and the disinclination to work, needs more sales for "less selling" before his situation can improve. Arthur Miller's play *Death of a Salesman* provides an excellent example of the deterioration in a performance that can come about under a "piecework" schedule of reinforcement.

It is possible that the general condition of an individual whose behavior is weak because of too much behavior emitted with too little reinforcement resembles conditions arising from aversive control. This may be especially true when the "strained" repertoire is supplemented by aversive conditions such as threats which can be avoided only by emitting more of the "strained" behavior. For example, the factory worker on a piecework pay schedule may be threatened, lose his job, or be fined when he stops working even though his rate of pay is proportional to the amount of work he does. Secondary factors may also influence the way in which a given repertoire is maintained on a schedule of reinforcement. Physical exhaustion, poor health, and inductive effects from other repertoires may produce strain under a schedule of reinforcement which under other conditions might have been satisfactory.

*Early exposure to intermittent reinforcement.* Many behavioral repertoires are weak because of an accidental history which supplied an inadequate reinforcement at an early stage. This could come about especially when punishment produces forms of behavior which go unreinforced because they are distorted. An optimal schedule of reinforcement of a repertoire is essential at an early stage of development if a strong disposition to engage in the performance is to be maintained later under less optimal schedules. The genesis of avid gamblers illustrates the importance of the schedule of reinforcement during the initial acquisition of the repertoire. Professional gamblers, for example, will arrange a high frequency of reinforcement for the beginner in order to provide conditions under which the beginner will continue to gamble later when the schedule of reinforcement is less adequate. Similarly at least a part of the difference between the person who continues to gamble, and those who failed to continue after a brief exposure, lies in the initial "luck". The fisherman is on the same schedule of reinforcement as the gambler, and the result is the same. The avid interest of the fishing devotee is extreme compared with others and probably represents the result of an optimal schedule of reinforcement during the initial fishing experiences.

The community maximizes the frequency of reinforcement during the educational phase of an individual by providing reinforcements for rough approximations to the ultimately effective forms. For example, a young child emitting the response "wawer" is likely to be reinforced by a glass of water, while the same response at a later stage of development will be unreinforced, or even punished. Thus, in the early stages of development of the repertoire a higher frequency of reinforcement is more easily achieved than later, when the community demands a more differentiated and closely specified form of behavior and environmental control. Whether newly developing behavior will persist depends upon whether the initial frequency and manner of reinforcement will sustain the performance as it comes under the control of the relevant stimuli, as the form of the behavior becomes more and more differentiated, and as the audience selectively reinforces more effective forms. Whenever a repertoire becomes weakened because of accidental non-reinforcement during the early development of the repertoire it becomes more difficult to reinstate the repertoire because the form of the behavior must now be more exact and under more precise environmental control than during the early stages of development.

Compare, for example, the successful and unsuccessful adult in his sexuo-social relations with the opposite sex. Very highly differentiated behavior under close stimulus control is required. Once an individual matures beyond a given age without developing the performances in respect to the opposite sex which will be reinforced, it becomes more difficult to acquire effective performances. The situation is comparable to the difficulties of the algebra student who tries to learn factoring without being facile in algebraic multiplication and division.

In cases where the individual's repertoire is inadequate because of an unoptimal schedule of reinforcement, it should be possible to do therapy by directing the individual to situations where some approximation to the effective form of the behavior will be reinforced. Only after the repertoire is acquired in a form that is maximally effective in achieving reinforcement, would the individual be directed into situations where progressively more nonreinforcement could occur.

### Superstitious Reinforcement

A reinforcing event will increase the disposition to engage in the behavior reinforced even though the reinforcement is spurious or accidental. As in the case of the gambler, the chance history of reinforcement is important in determining whether accidental or spurious reinforcements will sustain the behavior. Once there is some tendency to emit the behavior as the result of some accidental reinforcements, the resulting tendency to continue behaving increases the likelihood that the behavior will be in progress subsequently when another reinforcement occurs. These superstitious performances are most likely to occur under high motivation, as for example the gambler addressing the dice "come seven" or the "posturing" of the bowler. These spurious reinforcements are probably even more effective in the field of aversive control. If the aversively maintained behavior is conditioned strongly enough, the behavior may never extinguish because the avoidance behavior prevents the occurence of the conditioned aversive stimuli which now would no longer be followed by the aversive event.

Here again the therapist is in a position to select special situations in the patient's environment where the positive reinforcement occurs even though the superstitious behavior is withheld; or in those cases where the superstition is maintained by "avoiding" an aversive event, the behavior is withheld in a situation where the primary aversive event will not occur. Some preliminary experients in the latter case by English workers have shown large effectiveness of this manner of therapy in dealing with phobic behavior in selected individuals.[4]

### Stimulus Control of Behavior

The reinforcement or punishment of a verbal or nonverbal response depends upon the nature of the audience. Not all performances of an individual are reinforced on all occasions, and the situation characteristically present when a given kind of behavior is reinforced comes to control the likelihood that the performance will occur. Nearly all of the behavior of the normal adult comes under very close stimulus control of the various audiences to which he is exposed. Details of speech as subtle as vocabulary and intonation change with different audiences. The thematic material of a conversation varies widely depending upon the audience, from shop talk to a co-worker to the "baby-talk" maximally effective in producing a reaction from an infant. Poor development of stimulus control will result in a lower net frequency of reinforcement. The nonreinforcement of behavior that occurs during the development of stimulus control is tantamount to intermittent reinforcement until the stimulus control develops. To the extent that performances are reinforced only on specific occasions and by particular audiences, a failure of stimulus control results in an increase in the proportion of an individual's behavior which goes unreinforced.

The normal maturation of an individual into childhood and adulthood illustrates the interrelation between intermittent reinforcement and stimulus control. We reinforce almost any form of behavior in infants and very young children so long as there is a remote resemblance to the required performance. As the child grows older, however, the reinforcement is continually shifted in the direction of forms which approximate the normal cultural practices. Many members of the community will reinforce the behavior of the young child even though it has little importance for the listener. As the child develops through school-age, however, the audience becomes more selective and now properly differentiated forms of behavior will go unreinforced if they are not reinforcing for the listener. Hence, a further possibility of nonreinforcement arises whenever a performance is inappropriate for a given audience. The better an individual's performances are controlled by the environment, therefore, the more optimal will be the schedule of positive reinforcement. Inadequate stimulus and audience control of behavior could be one of the conditions under which an inadequate repertoire would develop because of performances occuring where they will not be reinforced and not occuring when they will be reinforced.

Just as accidental reinforcements may generate forms of behavior which is superstitious in the sense that the behavior is not a necessary condition for the occurrence of the reinforcement, it is possible for irrelevant aspects of a situation to acquire stimulus control of a performance. Every occasion on which a reinforcement occurs has multiple dimensions, and the aspects which come to control are somewhat undetermined until there are differential consequences in terms of the various elements. For example, an individual has a history in which many of the people who have given good advice have worn double-breasted suits, bow-ties, and spoken with a cosmopolitan accent. There will, therefore, be a heightened disposition to follow advice from persons exhibiting these characteristics until enough individuals have been encountered who shared some of these properties but have given bad advice. In a similar manner, an audience resembling a parent may increase the likelihood of occurrence of performances previously reinforced by a parent, even though that audience is not a potential reinforcer. This kind of inadequate stimulus control may simply be an accident of the historical conditions under which past reinforcements have occurred in situations which have multiple dimensions, some of which are irrelevant. More adequate stimulus control can develop only by exposure to the irrelevant aspect of the situation and the corresponding nonreinforcement. General motivational factors may also heighten the control by irrelevant aspects of a situation or audience. The man lost on the desert without water is more likely to mistake irrelevant stimuli for water.

It should be possible to sharpen the stimulus control of behavior by alternately exposing the individual to situations containing the various elements separately and allowing the resulting reinforcement and nonreinforcement to strengthen the tendency to emit the performance on the relevant occasions and weaken the disposition to emit the behavior when the irrelevant aspects are present.

It may be possible to design exercises using the principles governing the development of stimulus control of behavior to increase the sharpness of the stimulus control of a patient's behavior. What is required is to teach the patient to attend to the differential effects his performances have on the environment. The earlier example of the patient learning to say " Good morning" provides an example of the type of exercise that may be possible. After the patient is saying "Good morning" successfully in situations where the reinforcement as all but inevitable, the therapist points up situations where the likelihood of a verbal response of this kind being reinforced is near zero and explains the relevant factors responsible. For example, the patient is instructed to say "Good morning" to a man running to catch a train or to workers entering a factory a few minutes after the official starting time. Further exercises would include alternating between the situations where "Good morning" will be reinforced and those which "Good morning" will go unreinforced. The complexity of the exercises could be gradually increased as more and more complex forms were available as a result of the "shaping" from the earlier exercises. Eventually exercises would be carried out in which the thematic material of a conversation would be manipulated in respect to the interest of the audience.

## Aversive Control

In social situations most control by aversive stimuli involves the removal or discontinuation of positive reinforcement rather than some kind of primary aversive stimulation. The usual social punishments are (1) *disapproval:* a state of affairs where the reinforcer is not likely to continue reinforcements for specific performances; (2) *fines:* a loss of money or privilege effectively reduces the amount of various kinds of behavior that can be reinforced; (3) *criticism:* an indication of specific performances which will not be reinforced, or which will bring about nonreinforcement in other spheres, and (4) *incarceration:* the extreme case where large portions of the repetoire of the individual can no longer produce their characteristic rein-forcement.

While the discontinuation of positive reinforcement can be used as a punishment, it is important to distinguish between the effect of nonreinforce-ment *per se* and its use as a punishment. As noted earlier, the nonreinforce-ment of a performance on one occasion and its consistent reinforcement on a second occasion is the main process by which environmental control of behavior takes place. The decline of frequency of occurrence of a performance as a function of nonreinforcement has very different properties from punish-ment by the discontinuation of reinforcement. In the latter case, the punish-ment is carried out by presenting a stimulus which is already correlated with a low probability of response because of previous nonreinforcement. Its aversive effect probably derives from the over-all importance in the reper-toire of the individual of the behavior being blocked. The simple discontinu-ation of positive reinforcement shares some of the properties of an aversive stimulus, particularly during the transient phase while the frequency of the nonreinforced performance is still falling. Once the stimulus control is established, however, the resulting low disposition to engage in the extin-guished behavior allows concurrent repertoires to take over. The salient feature of punishment is that an aversive stimulus is applied to some per-formance which is maintained by a positive reinforcement; thus the original source of strength of the performance is still present and the performance can reappear in some strength when the punishment is discontinued. This is to be contrasted with simple extinction or nonreinforcement where the main-taining event for the behavior is discontinued and the performance no longer occurs simply because it no longer had its characteristic effect on the environment.

A second major effect of an aversive stimulus is the disruption of substan-tial segments of the repertoire of the individual by the situation characteristi-cally preceding the aversive event. The pre-aversive situation (anxiety) has an emotional effect in the sense that it produces a state of affairs where there is a disruption of parts of the individual's repertoire not directly related to the aversive event. For example, the student just before the crucial exami-nation, the patient in the dentist's waiting room, the child just before the parent discovers the broken ash tray, and the soldier just before the battle will all show considerable disruption of the normal repertoire; marked changes in the frequency of occurrence of all of the performances which might normally occur under these situations without the aversive event.

The third function of the aversive stimulus is in maintaining behavior be-cause it terminates or postpones (escapes or avoids) the aversive event. The examples of these kinds of reinforcements in a normal repertoire include opening or closing a window to alter an extreme in temperature; buying fuel in advance of cold weather, or making an apology to reduce the threat of punishment.

The clinical effects of excess of punishment have been fairly widely recognized an analyzed, and much of current therapy is analyzed as eliminating the aversive effects of situations which no longer are associated with punishment.

The disruptive effects of aversive control will interfere with the development of the precise forms of behavior being generated by positive reinforcement. This would be particularly true in the area of social contact such as sexual behavior where punishment is widely applied, and where complex and precise forms of behavior are required. A practical program would be designed to develop forms of behavior which would avoid punishment as well as maximize reinforcement. Situations which would disrupt positively maintained reportoires because of a history of punishment would have to be approached in small steps so that strength of the positively maintained behavior is large in respect to the disruptive effect and the aversive history.

Another corollary of aversive control is its prepotency over positively reinforced behavior. The use of aversive control generates immediate escape and avoidance behavior, and the wide use of punishment and aversive stimulation as a technique of control probably stems from the immediate effects which this kind of stimulation achieves as opposed to the slower development of behavior by a positive reinforcement. When an aversive condition is set up in order to generate some performance which must ultimately be maintained by positive reinforcement (for example, nagging), the control often backfires when the individual terminates the nagging by counter aversive control rather than emitting the performance which will reinforce the "nagger" and terminate the nagging. It is possible that some psychiatric patients have repertoires almost entirely composed of immediate reactions to threats and punishments which are entirely prepotent over positively reinforced repertoires. To the extent that this is true, the development of strong positively reinforced repertoires would provide an avenue of therapy.

## SUMMARY

The present analysis of the psychiatric patient characterizes him in terms of the reinforcements immediately available in his environment, or potentially available if changes can be brought about in his repertoire. The general plan is to bring to bear toward the rehabilitation of the patient whatever techniques are available for generating new behavior and eliminating existing performances. Potential reinforcements for almost any kind of behavioral repertoire exists in some environment. By selectively directing the patient into currently accessible reinforcing environments, it may be possible to build almost any kind of repertoire by proceeding in small steps from a performance that is currently maintained in one part of the patient's environment to a slightly more complex performance which could be reinforced in another situation accessible to the patient. All the known principles by which behavior is generated, differentiated, brought under stimulus control, and eliminated would be used. The major processes appealed to were: (1) Reinforcement; those environmental events which produce an increase in the frequency of occurrence of a specific performance they follow. (2) Differentiation of complex forms; a major corollary of reinforcement which makes it possible to begin with a performance which is currently reinforced and then gradually increase the complexity of the performance by reinforcing progressively more complex forms. (3) The long-term maintenance of a performance by manipulating the occurrence of instances of nonreinforcement of the performance. (4) The stimulus control of behavior; deliberate nonreinforcement of the performance on one occasion coupled with reinforcement of that same performance on another occasion in order to sharpen the environmental or stimulus control of the performance. (5) Elimination of behavior by choosing an environment in which the behavior can occur without punishment or reinforcement, whichever is relevant.

It is possible that many of the symptoms which bring the patient to therapy are largely a by-product of inadequate positively reinforced repertoires; that the disposition to engage in the psychotic, neurotic, and pathological behaviors may seem strong when compared to weak existing repertoires but would disappear as soon as alternative effective ways of dealing with some accessible environment are generated.

The examples of exercises designed to generate positively reinforced repertoires and eliminate debilitating performances are intended only as suggestive. A satisfactory protocol for generating new performances can come about only from experience in an experimental program with patients carried out by persons with sufficient clinical skill.

The present analysis emphasizes the manipulatable aspects of environments potentially available to the patient. The behavior of the patient is treated directly as the subject matter of therapy rather than as a symptom of inner cause. Just as the current behavior of an individual developed as a result of the past exposure to some environment, the current repertoire should be amenable to a similar process in the current environment. To the extent that behavioral processes are reversible, it should be possible to change any performance by manipulating the relevant factor within the context of the same process in which it was originally generated.

## REFERENCES

1. FERSTER, C. B. and SKINNER, B. F. (1957) *Schedules of Reinforcement*, Appleton-Century-Crofts, N.Y.
2. HULL, C. L. (1953) *Principles of Behavior*, Appleton-Century-Crofts, N.Y.
3. LINDSLEY, O. R. (1956) Operant conditioning methods applied to research in chronic schizophrenia, *Psychiat. Res. Repts.*, **5**, 118–139.

4. MEYER, V. (1953) The treatment of two phobic patients on the basis of learning principles, *J. Abnorm. Soc. Psychol.*, **55**, 261–266.
5. MILLER, N. F. and S. DOLLARD (1950) *Personality and psychotherapy*, McGraw-Hill, N. Y.
6. MOWRER, O. H. A stimulus response analysis of anxiety and its role as a reinforcing agent, *Psychol. Rev.*, **46**, 553–566.
7. SKINNER, B. F. (1953) *Science and Human Behavior*, MacMillan, N.Y.
8. WATSON, J. B. and R. RAYNER Conditioned emotional reactions, *J. Exp. Psychol.*, **3**, 1–14.

# *Application of Operant Conditioning to Reinstate Verbal Behavior in Psychotics**

WAYNE ISAACS†, JAMES THOMAS and ISRAEL GOLDIAMOND

IN OPERANT conditioning, behavior is controlled by explicitly arranging the consequences of the response, the explicit consequence being termed reinforcement. For example, a lever-press by a rat activates a mechanism which releases food. If the rat has been deprived of food, lever-pressing responses will increase in frequency. If this relationship between food and response holds only when a light is on, the organism may discriminate between light on and light off, that is, there will be no lever-pressing responses when the light is turned off, but turning it on will occasion such responses. From this simple case, extensions can be made to more complicated cases which may involve control of schedules of reinforcement. These procedures have recently been extended to the study of psychopharmacology,[5] controlled production of stomach ulcers,[4] obtaining psychophysical curves from pigeons,[3] conditioning cooperative behavior in children,[2] programming machines which teach academic subjects,[11] analyzing the effects of noise on human behavior,[1] and decreasing stuttering,[7] to mention a few examples.

The following account is a preliminary report of the use of operant conditioning to reinstate verbal behavior in two hospitalized mute psychotics. Patient A, classified as a catatonic schizophrenic, 40, became completely mute almost immediately upon commitment 19 years ago. He was recorded as withdrawn and exhibiting little psychomotor activity. Patient B, classified as schizophrenic, mixed type, with catatonic features predominating, was 43, and was committed after a psychotic break in 1942, when he was combative.

* This article is reprinted with the permission of the authors and editor from *J. Speech Hearing Disord.* **25**, 8–12 (1960).

† Wayne Isaacs (M.S., Southern Illinois University, 1951) is Assistant Clinical Director of Anna State Hospital, Anna, Illinois. James Thomas (M.A., University of Texas, 1953) was a clinical psychologist at the hospital during this experiment and is currently at Central State Hospital, Indianapolis. Israel Goldiamond (Ph.D., The University of Chicago, 1955) is Associate Professor of Psychology at Southern Illinois University and is Director of the Perception and Conditioning Laboratory. This report stems from projects connected with a weekly seminar on operant conditioning conducted at the hospital by the third author. Responsibility for the authorship and the *post hoc* analysis is the third author's; the first two authors are responsible for application of experimentally based procedures to shape the verbal behaviors of the patients.

He completely stopped verbalizing 14 years ago. Each $S$ was handled by a different $E$ (experimenter). The $E$s were ignorant of each other's activities until pressed to report their cases. This study covers the period prior to such report.

## CASE HISTORIES

### Patient A

The $S$ was brought to a group therapy session with other chronic schizophrenics (who were verbal), but he sat in the position in which he was placed and continued the withdrawal behaviors which characterized him. He remained impassive and stared ahead even when cigarettes, which other members accepted, were offered to him and were waved before his face. At one session, when $E$ removed cigarettes from his pocket, a package of chewing gum accidentally fell out. The $S$'s eyes moved toward the gum and then returned to their usual position. This response was chosen by $E$ as one with which he would start to work, using the method of successive approximation. [9] (This method finds use where $E$ desires to produce responses which are not present in the current repertoire of the organism and which are considerably removed from those which are available. The $E$ then attempts to "shape" the available behaviors into the desired form, capitalizing upon both the variability and regularity of successive behaviors. The shaping process involves the reinforcement of those parts of a selected response which are successively in the desired direction and the nonreinforcement of those which are not. For example, a pigeon may be initially reinforced when it moves its head. When this movement occurs regularly, only an upward movement may be reinforced, with downward movement not reinforced. The pigeon may now stretch its neck, with this movement reinforced. Eventually the pigeon may be trained to peck at a disc which was initially high above its head and at which it would normally never peck. In the case of the psychotic under discussion, the succession was eye movement, which brought into play occasional facial movements, including those of the mouth, lip movements, vocalizations, word utterance, and finally, verbal behavior.)

The $S$ met individually with $E$ three times a week. Group sessions also continued. The following sequence of procedures was introduced in the private sessions. Although the weeks are numbered consecutively, they did not follow at regular intervals since other duties kept $E$ from seeing $S$ every week.

Weeks 1, 2. A stick of gum was held before $S$'s face, and $E$ waited until $S$'s eyes moved toward it. When this response occurred, $E$ as a consequence gave him the gum. By the end of the second week, response probability in the presence of the gum was increased to such an extent that $S$'s eyes moved toward the gum as soon as it was held up.

Weeks 3, 4. The $E$ now held the gum before $S$, waiting until he noticed movement in $S$'s lips before giving it to him. Toward the end of the first session of the third week, a lip movement spontaneously occurred, which $E$ promptly reinforced. By the end of this week, both lip movement and eye movement occurred when the gum was held up. The $E$ then withheld giving $S$ the gum until $S$ spontaneously made a vocalization, at which time $E$ gave $S$ the gum. By the end of this week, holding up the gum readily occasioned eye movement toward it, lip movement, and a vocalization resembling a croak.

Weeks 5, 6. The $E$ held up the gum, and said, 'Say *gum, gum*', repeating these words each time $S$ vocalized. Giving $S$ the gum was made contingent upon vocalizations increasingly approximating *gum*. At the sixth session (at the end of Week 6), when $E$ said, "Say *gum, gum*," $S$ suddenly said, "Gum, please". This response was accompanied by reinstatement of other responses of this class, that is, $S$ answered questions regarding his name and age.

Thereafter, he responded to questions by $E$ both in individual sessions and in group sessions, but answered no one else. Responses to the discriminative stimuli of the room generalized to $E$ on the ward; he greeted $E$ on two occasions in the group room. He read from signs in $E$'s office upon request by $E$.

Since the response now seemed to be under the strong stimulus control of $E$, *the person*, attempt was made to generalize the stimulus to other people. Accordingly, a nurse was brought into the private room; $S$ smiled at her. After a month, he began answering her questions. Later, when he brought his coat to a volunteer worker on the ward, she interpreted the gesture as a desire to go outdoors and conducted him there. Upon informing $E$ of the incident, she was instructed to obey $S$ only as a consequence of explicit verbal requests by him. The $S$ thereafter vocalized requests. These instructions have now been given to other hospital personnel, and $S$ regularly initiates verbal requests when nonverbal requests have no reinforcing consequences. Upon being taken to the commissary, he said, "Ping pong", to the volunteer worker and played a game with her. Other patients, visitors, and members of hospital-society-at-large continue, however, to interpret nonverbal requests and to reinforce them by obeying $S$.

## Patient B

This patient, with a combative history prior to mutism, habitually lay on a bench in the day room in the same position, rising only for meals and for bed. Weekly visits were begun by $E$ and an attendant. During these visits, $E$ urged $S$ to attend group therapy sessions which were being held elsewhere in the hospital. The $E$ offered $S$ chewing gum. This was not accepted during the first two visits, but was accepted on the third visit and thereafter. On the sixth visit, $E$ made receipt of the gum contingent upon $S$'s going to the group room and so informed $S$. The $S$ then altered his posture to look at $E$ and accompanied him to the group room, where he seated himself in a chair and was given the gum. Thereafter, he came to this room when the attendants called for him.

Group Sessions 1–4. Gum reinforcement was provided for coming to the first two weekly sessions, but starting with the third, it was made contingent upon $S$'s participation in the announced group activity. The group (whose other members were verbal) was arranged in a semicircle. The $E$ announced that each $S$ would, when his turn came, give the name of an animal. The $E$ immediately provided gum to each $S$ who did so. The $S$ did not respond and skipped his turn three times around. The same response occured during the fourth session.

Group Session 5. The activity announced was drawing a person; $E$ provided paper and colored chalk and visited each $S$ in turn to examine the paper. The $S$ had drawn a stick figure and was reinforced with gum. Two of the other patients, spontaneously and without prior promting by $E$, asked to see the drawing and complimented $S$. Attendants reported that on the following day, $S$, when introduced to two ward visitors, smiled and said, "I'm glad to see you". The incident was followed by no particular explicit consequences.

Group Session 6. The announced activity was to give the name of a city or town in Illinois. The $S$, in his turn, said, "Chicago". He was reinforced by $E$, who gave him chewing gum, and again two members of the group congratulated him for responding. Thereafter, he responded whenever his turn came.

After the tenth session in the group, gum reinforcement was discontinued. The $S$ has continued to respond vocally in the situations in which he was reinforced by $E$ but not in others. He never initiates conversations, but he will answer various direct questions in the *group sessions*. He will not, however, respond vocally to questions asked *on the ward*, even when put by $E$.

## DISCUSSION

Both $S$s came from special therapy wards of patients selected because of depressed verbal behavior and long stay in the hospital; tranquilizing drugs were not used. The extent to which reinstatement of verbal behavior was related to the special treatment offered the patients in the special wards set up for them cannot readily be assayed. Among the special treatments accorded them were group therapy sessions. Nevertheless, the similarities between the pattern of reacquisition of verbal behavior by the patients and the patterns of learning encountered in laboratory studies suggest that the conditioning procedures themselves were involved in the reinstatement of verbal behavior.

In the case of Patient A, the speaking response itself was gradually shaped. The anatomical relation between the muscles of chewing and speaking probably had some part in $E$'s effectiveness. When a word was finally produced, the response was reinstated along with other response members of its class, which had not been reinforced. The economy of this process is apparent, since it eliminates the necessity of getting $S$ to produce *every* desired response in order to increase his repertoire. In this case, $E$ concentrated on one verbal response, and in reinstating it, reinstated verbal responses in general. On the stimulus side, when the response came under the stimulus control of $E$, the stimulus could be generalized to other members of $E$'s class of discriminative *stimuli*, namely, people. This may have relevance for the clinical inference of the importance for future interpersonal relations of prior identification with some person. In the case of Patient B, the stimulus control involved a *given setting*, the rooms where he had been reinforced. The discrimination of $E$ in one case, and not in the other, may be explained in terms of the establishment of operant discrimination, which also involves extinction.[9] Operant discrimination is established when a response in the presence of $S^D$, a discriminative stimulus, is reinforced, and a response in the presence of $S^\Delta$, a stimulus other than $S^D$, is not. After some time, the response will occur when $S^D$ is presented, but not when $S^\Delta$ is presented; the response discriminates $S^D$ from it having been extinguished when $S^\Delta$ was presented. In the case of Patient A, $E$ was with $S$ on the ward, in the group room, and privately. Reinforcement occurred in all occasions. But $S$ was on the ward (and other rooms) without $E$, and therefore without reinforcement for those responses which were occasioned by the ward and which only $E$ reinforced. Hence, these responses would extinguish in the ward alone, but would continue in the presence of $E$, defining discrimination of $E$ from other stimuli. In the case of Patient B, this process may have been delayed by the fact that $E$ and the other patients reinforced only in a specific room. It will be recalled that attendants rather than $E$ brought $S$ to the group room.

Interestingly, in the group sessions, when Patient B emitted the responses which $E$ reinforced, other psychotic patients also reinforced Patient B. They were thereby responding, on the occasion of $S$'s responses (discriminative stimuli for them), in the same way that $E$ did. The term *identification*, used as a label here, shares some behavioral referents with the term as used in the preceding paragraph and might be explained behaviorally in terms of the *generalized reinforcer*.[10] These behaviors by the patients are similar to behaviors reported in client-centered group sessions, where clients increase in reflective behaviors as counseling progresses, and in psychoanalytic group sessions, where patients increasingly make analytic interpretations of each other. Here, the patients are also behaving like the therapist. While this parallel lends itself to the facetious thought that operant group sessions may produce operant conditioners, it does suggest that psychotics are behaving, with regard to responses by the major source of reinforcement in the group, according to the same laws which govern such group behaviors of nonhospitalized *S*s.

The various diagnostic labels applied to psychotics are based to a considerable extent upon differences between responses considered abnormal, for example, hallucinations, delusions of persecution, and the like. The therapeutic process is accordingly at times seen in terms of eliminating the abnormal behaviors or states. Experimental laboratory work indicates that it is often extremely difficult to *eliminate* behavior; extinction is extremely difficult where the schedule of reinforcement has been a variable interval schedule,[6] that is, reinforcement has been irregular, as it is in most of our behaviors. Such behaviors persist for considerable periods without reinforcement. Experimental laboratory work has provided us quite readily with procedures to *increase* responses. In the case of psychotics, this would suggest focusing attention on whatever *normal* behaviors *S* has; an appropriate operant, no matter how small or insignificant, even if it is confined to an eye movement, may possibly be raised to greater probability, and shaped to normal behavior.[8] Stated otherwise, abnormal behaviors and normal behaviors can be viewed as reciprocally related, and psychotics as exhibiting considerable abnormal behavior, or little normal behavior. Normal behavior probability can be increased by decreasing probability of abnormal behaviors, or abnormal behaviors can be decreased by the controlled increase of normal behaviors. This preliminary report suggests that a plan of attack based upon the latter approach may be worth further investigation.

## SUMMARY

Verbal behavior was reinstated in two psychotics, classified as schizophrenics, who had been mute for 19 and 14 years. The procedures utilized involved application of operant conditioning. The relationship of such procedures, based on controlled laboratory investigations with men and animals, to procedures based on clinical with human patients was discussed and was considered as directing our attention to shaping and increasing the probability of what normal behaviors the psychotic possesses.

## ACKNOWLEDGMENTS

The authors wish to express their appreciation to Dr. Leonard Horecker, Clinical Director of Anna State Hospital, and to Dr. Robert C. Steck,

Hospital Superintendent, for their encouragement and facilitation of the project. This investigation was supported in part by a grant from the Psychiatric Training and Research Fund of the Illinois Department of Public Welfare.

## REFERENCES

1. AZRIN, N. H. (1958) Some effects of noise on human behavior, *J. Exp. Anal. Behavior*, **1**, 183–200.
2. AZRIN, N. H. and LINDSLEY, O. R. (1956) The reinforcement of cooperation between children, *J. Abnorm. Soc. Psychol.*, **52**, 100–102.
3. BLOUGH, D. S. (1958) A method for obtaining psychophysical thresholds from the pigeon, *J. Exp. Anal. Behavior*, **1**, 31–44.
4. BRADY, J. V. (1958) Ulcers in "executive" monkeys, *Sci. Amer.*, **199**(4), 95–100.
5. DEWS, P. B. (1958) The effects of chlorpromazine and promazine on performance on a mixed schedule of reinforcement, *J. Exp. Anal. Behavior*, **1**, 73–82.
6. FERSTER, C. B. and SKINNER, B. F. (1957) *Schedules of Reinforcement* (Appleton-Century-Crofts) New York.
7. FLANGAN, B., GOLDIAMOND, I. and AZRIN, N. H. (1958) Operant stuttering: the control of stuttering behavior through response-contingent consequences, *J. Exp. Anal. Behavior*, **1**, 173–178.
8. GOLDIAMOND, I. (1958) Research which can be done in a mental hospital. Address delivered to Illinois State Mental Hospitals Conference, Giant City State Park, Illinois.
9. KELLER, F. and SCHOENFELD, W. (1950) *Principles of Psychology*, Appleton-Century-Crofts, (New York).
10. SKINNER, B. F. (1953) *Science and Human Behavior*, Macmillan, New York.
11. SKINNER, B. F. (1958) Teaching machines, *Science*, **128**, 969–977.

# Intensive Treatment of Psychotic Behavior
# by Stimulus Satiation and Food Reinforcement*†

T. AYLLON

*Anna State Hospital*

## INTRODUCTION

Until recently the effective control of behavior was limited to the animal laboratory. The extension of this control to human behavior was made when Lindsley successfully adapted the methodology of operant conditioning to the study of psychotic behavior (Lindsley, 1956). Following Lindsley's point of departure other investigators have shown that, in its essentials, the behavior of mental defective individuals (Orlando and Bijou, 1960), stutterers (Flanagan, Goldiamond and Azrin, 1958), mental patients (Hutchinson and Azrin, 1961), autistic (Ferster and DeMyer, 1961), and normal (Bijou, 1961; Azrin and Lindsley, 1956) children is subject to the same controls.

Despite the obvious implications of this research for applied settings there has been a conspicuous lag between the research findings and their application. The greatest limitation to the direct application of laboratory principles has been the absence of control over the subjects' environment. Recently, however, a series of applications in a regulated psychiatric setting has clearly demonstrated the possibilities of behavioral modification (Ayllon and Michael, 1959; Ayllon and Haughton, 1962). Some of the behaviors studied have included repetitive and highly stereotyped behaviors such as complaining, pacing, refusal to eat, hoarding and many others.

What follows is a demonstration of behavior techniques for the intensive individual treatment of psychotic behavior. Specific pathological behavior patterns of a single patient were treated by manipulating the patient's environment.

* This article is reprinted with the permission of the author and editor from *Behav. Res. Ther.* (1963). **1**, 53–62.

† This report is based, in part, on a 2 year research project (1959–1961), conducted by the author at the Saskatchewan Hospital, Weyburn, Saskatchewan, Canada, and supported by a grant from the Commonwealth Fund. Grateful acknowledgment is due to H. Osmond and I. Clancey of the Saskatchewan Hospital. The author also thanks E. Haughton who assisted in the conduct of this investigation, and N. Azrin and W. Holtz for their critical reading of the manuscript.

## The Experimental Ward and Control over the Reinforcement

This investigation was conducted in a mental hospital ward, the characteristics of which have been described elsewhere (Ayllon and Haughton, 1962). Briefly, this was a female ward to which only authorized personnel were allowed access. The ward staff was made up of psychiatric nurses and untrained aides who carried out the environmental manipulations under the direction of the experimenter. Using a time-sample technique, patients were observed daily every 30 min from 7·0 a.m. to 11·0 p.m.

The dining room was the only place where food was available and entrance to the dining room could be regulated. Water was freely available at a drinking fountain on the ward. None of the patients had ground passes or jobs outside the ward.

## Subject

The patient was a 47-year-old female patient diagnosed as a chronic schizophrenic. The patient had been hospitalized for 9 years. Upon studying the patient's behavior on the ward, it became apparent that the nursing staff* spent considerable time caring for her. In particular, there were three aspects of her behavior which seemed to defy solution. The first was stealing food. The second was the hoarding of the ward's towels in her room. The third undesirable aspect of her behavior consisted in her wearing excessive clothing, e.g. a half dozen dresses, several pairs of stockings, sweaters, and so on.

In order to modify the patient's behavior systematically, each of these three behaviors, stealing food, hoarding, and finally excessive dressing was treated separately.

## EXPERIMENT I

### Control of Stealing Food by Food Withdrawal

The patient had weighed over 250 pounds for many years. She ate the usual tray of food served to all patients, but, in addition, she stole food from the food counter and from other patients. Because the medical staff regarded her excessive weight as detrimental to her health, a special diet had been prescribed for her. However, the patient refused to diet and continued stealing food. In an effort to discourage the patient from stealing, the ward nurses had spent considerable time trying to persuade her to stop stealing food. As a last resort, the nurses would force her to return the stolen food.

---

* As used in this paper, "nurse" is a generic term including all those who actually work on the ward (attendants, aides, psychiatric and registered nurses).

PLATE A. The early stages of satiation. As the patient received the towels she folded them properly and stacked them around her bed. Notice that the towels on her bed are also kept neatly.

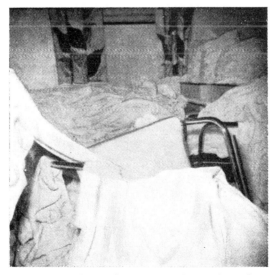

PLATE B. The patient's room just before she started to rid herself of the towels. Notice that there are still a few stacks of folded towels, but now the chairs, bed and floor are literally covered with them.

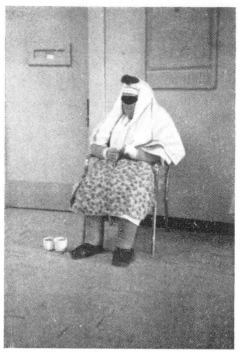

PLATE C. The patient as she appeared before
the start of Experiment III. The thickness of
her legs is enhanced by approximately 2
dozen pairs of stockings that she wore.
Notice the bandages she wears on her wrists
as well as the cups beside her.

PLATE D. The patient eating in the dining room in the initial stages
of Experiment III.

PLATE E. The patient after she started to discard a few items of clothing.

PLATE F. The patient during the final stages of the experiment.

To determine the extent of food stealing, nurses were instructed to record all behaviors associated with eating in the dining room. This record, taken for nearly a month, showed that the patient stole food during two thirds of all meals.

## Procedure

The traditional methods previously used to stop the patient from stealing food were discontinued. No longer were persuasion, coaxing, or coercion used.

The patient was assigned to a table in the dining room, and no other patients were allowed to sit with her. Nurses removed the patient from the dining room when she approached a table other than her own, or when she picked up unauthorized food from the dining room counter. In effect, this procedure resulted in the patient missing a meal whenever she attempted to steal food.

## Results

Figure 1 shows that when withdrawal of positive reinforcement (i.e. meal) was made dependent upon the patient's "stealing", this response was eliminated in two weeks. Because the patient no longer stole food, she ate only the diet prescribed for her.

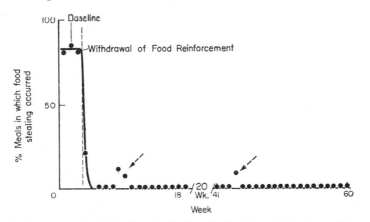

FIG. 1. A response, food stealing, is eliminated when it results in the withdrawal of food reinforcement. The dotted arrows indicate the rare occasions when food stealing occurred. For purposes of presentation a segment comprising 20 weeks during which no stealing occurred is not included.

The effective control of the stealing response is also indicated by the gradual reduction in the patient's body weight. At no time during the patient's 9 years of hospitalization had she weighed less than 230 pounds. Figure 2 shows that at the conclusion of this behavioral treatment her weight stabilized at 180 pounds or 17 per cent loss from her original weight. At this time, the patient's physical condition was regarded as excellent.

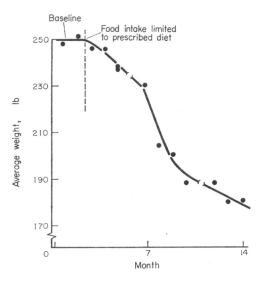

FIG. 2. The effective control of food stealing results in a notable reduction in body weight. As the patient's food intake is limited to the prescribed diet her weight decreases gradually.

## Discussion

A behavioral principle used in the laboratory shows that strength of a response may . be weakened by the removal of positive reinforcement following the response (Ferster, 1958). In this case, the response was food stealing and the reinforcer was access to meals. When the patient stole food she was removed from the dining room and missed her meal.

After one year of this behavioral treatment two occasions of food stealing occurred. The first occasion, occurring after one year of not stealing food, took the nurses by surprise and, therefore the patient "got away" with it. The second occasion occurred shortly thereafter. This time, however, the controlling consequences were in force. The patient missed that meal and did not steal again to the conclusion of this investigation.

Because the patient was not informed or warned of the consequences that followed stealing, the nurses regarded the procedure as unlikely to have much effect on the patient's behavior. The implicit belief that verbal instructions are indispensable for learning is part of present day psychiatric lore. In keeping with this notion, prior to this behavior treatment, the nurses had tried to persuade the patient to cooperate in dieting. Because there were strong medical reasons for her losing weight, the patient's refusal to follow a prescribed diet was regarded as further evidence of her mental illness.

## Control of one Form of Hoarding Behavior through Stimulus Satiation

During the 9 years of hospitalization, the patient collected large numbers of towels and stored them in her room. Although many efforts had been made to discourage hoarding, this behavior continued unaltered. The only recourse for the nursing staff was to take away the patient's towels about twice a week.

To determine the degree of hoarding behavior, the towls in her room were counted 3 times a week, when the patient was not in her room. This count showed that the number of towels kept in her room ranged from 19 to 29 despite the fact that during this time the nurses continued recovering their towel supply from the patient's room.

### Procedure

The routine removal of the towels from the patient's room was discontinued. Instead, a program of stimulus satiation was carried out by the nurses. Intermittently, throughout the day, the nurses took a towel to the patient when she was in her room and simply handed it to her without any comment. The first week she was given an average of 7 towels daily, and by the third week this number was increased to 60.

### Results

The technique of satiation eliminated the towel hoarding. Figure 3 shows the mean number of towels per count found in the patient's room. When the number of towels kept in her room reached the 625 mark, she started taking a few of them out. Thereafter, no more towels were given to her. During the next 12 months the mean number of towels found in her room was 1·5 per week. A few pictures are included to illustrate this procedure (see plates A and B).

### Discussion

The procedure used to reduce the amount of towel hoarding bears resemblance to satiation of a reinforcer. A reinforcer loses its effects when an excessive amount of that reinforcer is made available. Accordingly, the response maintained by that reinforcer is weakened. In this application, the towels constituted the reinforcing stimuli. When the number of towels in her room reached 600, continuing to give her towels seemed to make their collection aversive. The patient then proceeded to rid herself of the towels until she had virtually none.

During the first few weeks of satiation, the patient was observed patting her cheeks with a few towels, apparently enjoying them. Later, the patient was observed spending much of her time folding and stacking the approximately 600 towels in her room. A variety of remarks were made by the patient

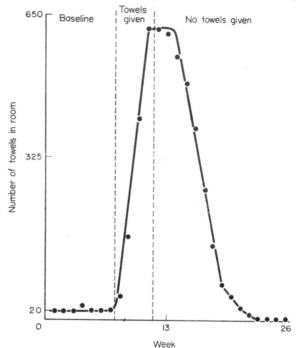

FIG. 3. A response, towel hoarding, is eliminated when the patient is given towels in excess. When the number of towels reaches 600 the patient starts to discard them. She continues to do so until the number found in her room averages 1·5 compared to the previous 20 towels per week.

regarding receipt of towels. All verbal statements made by the patient were recorded by the nurse. The following represent typical remarks made during this experiment. First week: As the nurse entered the patient's room carrying a towel, the patient would smile and say, "Oh, you found it for me, thank you". Second week: When the number of towels given to patient increased rapidly, she told the nurses, "Don't give me no more towels. I've got enough." Third week: "Take them towels away . . . I can't sit here all night and fold towels." Fourth and fifth weeks: "Get these dirty towels out of here. . ." Sixth week: After she had started taking the towels out of her room, she remarked to the nurse, "I can't drag any more of these towels, I just can't do it!"

The quality of these remarks suggests that the initial effects of giving towels to the patient was reinforcing. However as the towels increased they ceased to be reinforcing, and presumably became aversive.

The ward nurses, who had undergone a three-year training in psychiatric nursing, found it difficult to reconcile the procedure in this experiment with their psychiatric orientation. Most nurses subscribed to the popular psychiatric view which regards hoarding behavior as a reflection of a deep "need" for love and security. Presumably, no "real" behavioral change was possible without meeting the patient's "needs" first. Even after the patient discontinued hoarding towels in her room, some nurses predicted that the change would not last and that a worse behavior would replace it. Using a time-sampling technique the patient was under continuous observation for over a year after the termination of the satiation program. Not once during this period did the patient return to hoarding towels. Furthermore, no other behavior problem replaced hoarding.

## EXPERIMENT III

*Control of an Additional Form of Hoarding through Food Reinforcement*

Shortly after the patient had been admitted to the hospital she wore an excessive amount of clothing which included several sweaters, shawls, dresses, undergarments and stockings. The clothing also included sheets and towels wrapped around her body, and a turban-like headdress made up of several towels. In addition, the patient carried two to three cups on one hand while holding a bundle of miscellaneous clothing, and a large purse on the other.

To determine the amount of clothing worn by the patient, she was weighed before each meal over a period of two weeks. By subtracting her actual body weight from that recorded when she was dressed, the weight of her clothing was obtained.

*Procedure*

The response required for reinforcement was stepping on a scale and meeting a predetermined weight. The requirement for reinforcement consisted of meeting a single weight (i.e. her body weight plus a specified number of pounds of clothing). Initially she was given an allowance of 23 pounds over her current body weight. This allowance represented a 2 pound reduction from her usual clothing weight. When the patient exceeded the weight requirement, the nurse stated in a matter-of-fact manner, "Sorry, you weigh too much, you'll have to weigh less". Failure to meet the required weight resulted in the patient missing the meal at which she was being weighed. Sometimes, in an effort to meet the requirement, the patient discarded more clothing than was required. When this occurred the requirement was adjusted next weighing time to correspond to the limit set by the patient in the preceding occasion.

*Results*

When food reinforcement is made dependent upon the removal of superfluous clothing the response increases in frequency. Figure 4 shows that the patient gradually shed her clothing to meet the more demanding weight requirement until she dressed normally. At the conclusion of this experiment her clothes weighed 3 pounds compared to the 25 pounds she wore before this treatment.

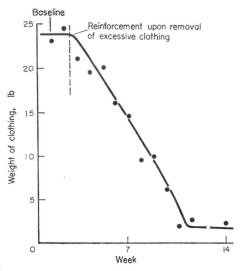

FIG. 4. A response, excessive dressing, is eliminated when food reinforcement is made dependent upon removal of superfluous clothing. Once the weight of the clothing worn by the patient drops to 3 pounds it remains stable.

Some verbal shaping was done in order to encourage the patient to leave the cups and bundles she carried with her. Nurses stopped her at the dining room and said, "Sorry, no things are allowed in the dining room". No mention of clothing or specific items was made to avoid focusing undue attention upon them. Within a week, the patient typically stepped on the scale without her bundle and assorted objects. When her weight was over the limit, the patient was informed that she weighed "too much". She then proceeded to take off a few clothes, stepped on the scale again, and upon meeting the weight requirement, gained access to the dining room. A few pictures are shown to illustrate this behavioral modification (see plates C, D, E and F).

## Discussion

According to the principle of reinforcement a class of responses is strengthened when it is followed by reinforcement. A reinforcer is such when it results in a response increase. In this application the removal of excessive clothing constituted the response, and the reinforcer was food (i.e. access to meals). When the patient met the weight requirement she was reinforced by being given access to meals.

At the start of this experiment, the patient missed a few meals because she failed to meet the weight requirement, but soon thereafter she gradually discarded her superfluous clothing. First, she left behind odd items she had carried in her arms, such as bundles, cups, and handbags. Next she took off the elaborate headgear and assorted "capes" or shawls she had worn over her shoulders. Although she had worn 18 pairs of stocking at one time, she eventually shed these also.

During the initial part of this experiment, the patient showed some emotional behavior, e.g. crying, shouting, and throwing chairs around. Because nurses were trained to "ignore" this emotional behavior, the patient obtained no sympathy or attention for them. The withholding of social reinforcement for emotional behavior quickly led to its elimination.

At the conclusion of this behavior treatment, the patient typically stepped on the scale wearing a dress, undergarments, a pair of stockings, and a pair of light shoes. One of the behavioral changes concomitant with the current environmental manipulation was that as the patient began dressing normally she started to participate in small social events in the hospital. This was particularly new to the patient as she had previously remained seclusive spending most of the time in her room.

About this time the patient's parents came to visit her and insisted on taking her home for a visit. This was the first time during the patient's 9 years of hospitalization that her parents had asked to take her out. They remarked that previously they had not been interested in taking her out because the patient's excessive dressing in addition to her weight made her look like a "circus freak".

## Conclusion

The research presented here was conducted under nearly ideal conditions. The variables manipulated (i.e. towels, food) were under full experimental control. Using a time-sample technique the patient was observed daily every 30 min from 7·00 a.m. to 11·00 p.m. Nurses and aides carried out these observations which were later analyzed in terms of gross behavior categories. These observations were in force for over a year during which time these 3 experiments were conducted. The results of these observations indicate that none of the three pathological behavior patterns (i.e. food stealing, hoarding and excessive dressing) exhibited by the patient was replaced by any undesirable behavior.

The patient displayed some emotional behavior in connection with each experiment, but each time it subsided when social reinforcement (i.e. attention) was not forthcoming. The patient did not become violent or seclusive as a consequence of these experiments. Instead, she became socially more accessible to patients and staff. She did not achieve a great deal of social success but she did begin to participate actively in social functions.

A frequent problem encountered in mental hospitals is overeating. In general this problem is solved by prescribing a reduction diet. Many patients, however, refuse to take a reduction diet and continue overeating. When confronted with this behavior, psychiatric workers generally resort to two types of explanations.

One explanation of overeating points out that only with the active and sincere cooperation of the patient can weight reduction be accomplished. When the patient refuses to cooperate he is regarded as showing more signs of mental illness and all hopes of eliminating overeating come to an end.

Another type of explanation holds that overeating is not the behavior to be concerned with. Instead, attention is focused on the psychological "needs" of the patient. These "needs" are said to be the cause of the observable behavior, overeating. Therefore the emphasis is on the removal of the cause and not on the symptom or behavior itself. Whatever theoretical merit these explanations may have, it is unfortunate that they fail to suggest practical ways of treating the behavior itself. As a consequence, the patient continues to overeat often to the detriment of his health.

The current psychiatric emphasis on the resolution of the mental conflict that is presumably at the basis of the symptoms, is perhaps misplaced. What seems to have been forgotten is that frequently behavioral deficits such as those reported here, prevent the patient from being considered for discharge not only by the hospital personnel but also by the patient's relatives. Indeed, as far as the patient's relatives are concerned, the index of improvement or deterioration is the readily observable behavior, and not a detailed account of the mechanics of the mental apparatus.

Many individuals are admitted to mental hospitals because of one or more specific behaviors, and not always because of a generalized "mental" disturbance. For example, an individual may go into a mental hospital because he has refused to eat for several days, or because he talks to himself incessantly. If the goal of therapy were behavioral rehabilitation, these behaviors would be treated to reinstate normal eating and normal talking. However, because the current emphasis in psychotherapy is on "mental-conflict resolution" little or no attention is given to dealing directly with the very behavioral deficits which prevent the patient from returning to the community.

In summary, this investigation demonstrates that extensive and effective behavioral modification is feasible without a costly and lengthy psychotherapeutic treatment. In addition, the often heard notion that another undesirable behavior will replace the original problem behavior is not supported by the findings to date.

## REFERENCES

AYLLON, T. and MICHAEL, J. (1959) The psychiatric nurse as a behavioral engineer, *J. Exp. Anal. Behav.* **2**, 323–334.

AYLLON, T. and HAUGHTON, E. (1962) Control of the behavior of schizophrenic patients by food, *J. Exp. Anal. Behav.* (In press.)

AZRIN, N. and LINDSLEY, O. (1956) The reinforcement of cooperation between children, *J. Abnorm. Soc. Psychol.*, 52.

BIJOU, S. (1961) Discrimination Performance as a Baseline for Individual Analysis of Young Children, *Child Develpm.* **32**, 163–170.

FERSTER, C. B. (1958) Control of behavior in chimpanzees and pigeons by time out from positive reinforcement, *Psychol. Monogr.*, **72**, 1–38.

FERSTER, C. and DEMYER, M. (1961) The development of performances in autistic children in an automatically controlled environment, *J. Chron. Dis.*, (1961) **13**, 312–345.

FLANAGAN, B., GOLDIAMOND, I. and AZRIN, N. (1958) Operant stuttering: The control of stuttering behavior through response-contingent consequences, *J. Exp. Anal. Behav.*, **56**, 49–56.

HUTCHINSON, R. R. and AZRIN, N. H. (1961) Conditioning of mental hospital patients to fixed-ratio schedules of reinforcement, *J. Exp. Anal. Behav.*, **4**, 87–95.

LINDSLEY, O. R. (1956) Operant conditioning methods applied to research in chronic schizophrenia, *Psychiat. Res. Rep.*, **5**, 118–139.

ORLANDO, R. and BIJOU, S. (1960) Single and multiple schedules of reinforcement in developmentally retarded children, *J. Exp. Anal. Behav.*, **3**, 339–348.

# Experimental Analysis of Hysterical Blindness*

## Operant Conditioning Techniques

JOHN PAUL BRADY, M.D. and DETLEV L. LIND, A.B.

*Indianapolis*

## INTRODUCTION

The viewpoint adopted for experimental purposes in this study was that the behavior of an organism is generated and maintained chiefly by its consequences on the environment. Over a wide range of conditions, a hungry rat, placed in a so-called "Skinner box", will persist in pressing a bar if, as a consequence of this response, a pellet of food is delivered to it at least some of the time. This exemplifies the principle of reinforcement which is at the core of current behavior theory. Conditioning of this type is termed operant (instrumental) to distinguish it from respondent (classical Pavlovian) conditioning. The probability of a given response in relation to the conditions of reinforcement of that response has been the subject of much study of Skinner,[4] Ferster and Skinner,[2] and others. Recently, controlled experiments conducted with human subjects using cubicles analogous to the "Skinner box" have demonstrated the existence of these same relationships in human behavior and the feasibility of analyzing human behavior within this methodological framework.[3] However, the relationships between an organism's behavior, its environmental consequences, and the disposition or probability of the organism to repeat a particular response often is obscure in so complex a psychobiological unit as man. For example, when a man behaves in a given way, the most important consequence of his activity, from the standpoint of reinforcement, may be its effect on some part of his intricate social or intrapersonal environment. Further, the given behavior or its effect may be readily understood only in terms of its "symbolic meaning". Nevertheless, much of man's behavior, both normal and

* This article is reprinted with the permission of the authors and editor from *Arch. Gen. Psychiat.* **4**, 331–339 (1961).

From the Institute of Psychiatric Research, Indiana University Medical Center.

This paper was read at the Irish Division Meetings of the Royal Medico-Psychological Association in Dublin, July 20, 1960.

Research psychiatrist, Indiana Medical Center (Dr. Brady) and research assistant, Veterans' Administrations Hospital, Indianapolis (Mr. Lind).

aberrant, can be analyzed in terms of these general principles and influenced by their systematic application.[5]

The present report concerns the application of operant conditioning methodology in the study of a patient with hysterical blindness. In the course of this study, the patient, who had been totally blind for 2 years, regained his sight. It is not the primary purpose of the present report to argue the utility of these techniques for the removal of hysterical symptoms or for psychiatric therapy generally. Rather, the intent is to demonstrate unique advantages this methodological approach offers for the systematic analysis of symptomatic behavior within a controlled, experimental context. In the present instance, some of the variables of which the patient's seeing or not seeing were a function were studied by operant conditioning techniques. An attempt was made to influence his disposition to see by manipulating some of these variables in accordance with experimentally demonstrable principles. In the course of the study, note was taken of the patient's verbal and social behavior in addition to the operant response (pressing a button) being measured. Some of these clinical observations, elicited in part by the conditioning procedure, were quite understandable in terms of the conventional psychodynamic concept of hysteria.

## REPORT OF CASE

The patient, now 40 years of age, was born on a farm in rural Indiana, the youngest of 4 children in a poor family. The father was described as an irresponsible man, who quit the family group entirely when the patient was 11, and has not been heard from since. He depicts his mother as the strong and determining force in the family group especially with respect to him during his early years. It is of interest that the patient had 2 maternal aunts who were totally blind during their last years. He refers to them as "nice old ladies."

The patient was shy and retiring during his childhood and left school (the eighth grade) at the age of 16 because he "liked work better". He held a variety of jobs, chiefly unskilled, but never stayed at any more than a few months.

He was married in 1942, after a very brief courtship, to a woman who worked as a welder in the factory at which he also was employed. The patient describes her as "often nervous and upset", but it is clear that she makes the important decisions in the house and that he is greatly dependent on her. From his description of his married life, one gets the picture of almost constant harassment from his wife and mother-in-law. Nonetheless, he speaks of his wife only in the most endearing terms. They have 2 children, a boy 13 and a girl 17.

Shortly after his marriage, the patient, then 23, was drafted into the Army where he served for 3 years. He did not see active combat, but worked as a teletype operator and truck driver in the United States and England. One incident is of interest. While driving an Army truck in England, he had an accident with a civilian driving a sports car in which the civilian was seriously injured. He states that he can now recall nothing of the accident scene or the period of investigation by civilian and military authorities which immediately followed, although he himself was not injured in any way. This is one of several examples of the patient's ability to repress large areas of experience, visual and other, with remarkable facility. While still in the Army, the patient developed dendritic keratitis of the right eye, following a tonsillectomy. Corneal scarring resulted, and the visual acuity of the right eye was reduced to 20/80. Shortly after this, he was given a medical discharge from the Army and was awarded a small pension because of the loss of vision.

After release from service, the patient had a succession of semiskilled jobs, remaining at none for more than a year. He seemed to tolerate responsibility poorly and was very sensitive to criticism. During this period, there were 3 minor recurrences of his eye infection which were treated conservatively in the hospital. On each occassion, he requested an increase in his pension, but this was denied since the visual acuity of the affected eye had not decreased. Between his discharge from the Army in 1945 and the occurrence of his total blindness 12 years later, his general adjustment was poor. He depended greatly on public assistance and financial aid from relatives because of frequent periods of unemployment and poor planning in general.

Three days before Christmas in 1957, the patient, while shopping in a supermarket with his wife and mother-in-law, suddenly became totally blind in both eyes. He is able to recall few details of the episode, and no immediate precipitating event is apparent. It did occur at a time when his wife and mother-in-law were being more demanding than usual, requiring him to work nights and weekends at various chores under their foremanship. One immediate consequence of his blindness was, then, partial escape from this situation. The family group first interpreted the blindness in theurgic rather than medical terms and sought counsel from its Fundamentalist minister. Several days later, however, the patient was admitted to a veteran's hospital, where he remained for 2 weeks. Neurological and ophthalmological examinations were negative except for the small corneal scar in the right eye described previously. A diagnosis of total hysterical blindness was made. At the time, the patient did not seem greatly alarmed by his loss of sight, but instead had an attitude of patient forbearance. The obvious discrepancy between his report of total blindness and his ability to get about on the ward was apparant. He was not concerned with this, but felt hurt and unjustly accused when other patients pointed out this discrepancy to him. The nature of his illness was explained to him, and interviews under sodium pentothal were conducted in an effort to increase his vision. Blindness persisted, however. Immediately after release from the hospital, the patient applied for training for the blind through an appropriate public agency. Several months later, he was admitted to a veterans' diagnostic center, where several additional neurological and ophthalmological examinations were conducted with similar negative results, and the diagnosis of hysterical blindness was confirmed. Although the blindness was not considered service-connected, a special pension was awarded because of his total disability. During the 18 months which intervened between his discharge from the diagnostic center and the beginning of the present treatment program, the patient was treated at an outpatient psychiatric clinic 2 hours weekly, without results. Various drugs were used as adjuvant treatments, as well as sodium pentothal interviews, but to no avail.

Because of the long history of generally poor adjustment, the fixity and duration of the symptoms, and the patient's resistance to psychotherapeutic intervention, a program of rehabilitation for the totally blind was recommended. His subsistence was derived from his government pension, financial aid from the local community to his underage children, some financial assistance from relatives, and other community resources on which he came to depend more and more. During these 18 months, he seldom left his house, but spent most of his time listening to radio or recorded reading supplied to him by an agency for the blind. Although he made some effort to learn Braille and to rehabilitate himself in other ways, he gradually came to depend on his wife more and more to meet his ordinary needs.

In summary, this is a man who developed total hysterical blindness which proved refractory to psychiatric intervention of various sorts for 2 years. Although the immediate precipitating cause of his blindness is not clear, one might conjecture, in dynamic terms, that somatically converted angry feelings toward a controlling wife upon whom he was greatly dependent were an important factor. Several items from the history could well support hysterical blindness as a symptom choice in this man: his exposure as a child to his 2 totally blind aunts; a recurrent eye infection which did leave him with some loss of vision and for which he was compensated financially; his immaturity, and his tendency to use amnesic repression as a means of adjustment. The long duration of the symptom despite psychiatric treatment may be accounted for, in part, by his passivity, the dependency needs which the symptom helped him satisfy, and the sizeable pension he was receiving for the disability.

## BEHAVIORAL PRINCIPLES

A patient with total hysterical blindness is generally able to get around better than a patient with total blindness from an organic lesion. He states he can see nothing, yet is able to avoid large obstacles in walking, handle eating utensils, reach accurately for small objects, etc. This indicates that the hysterical patient does "see" in some sense. *Dynamically*, one would say that the patient reports being blind because he is consciously unaware of seeing. *Behavioraly*, one would say that the patient is not making full use of visual cues as evidenced by the fact that his behavior is not adequately under control. In order to study experimentally the effects of visual cues on the control of behavior, it is necessary first to generate some relatively stable behavior upon which the effect of visual stimuli can be measured. For this purpose, an operant-conditioning situation was selected in which the behavioral requirement for reinforcement (reward) would be the spacing of responses (button-pressing) in a prescribed way. Specifically, the patient would be required to space his responses between 18–21 sec. In other words, a response which followed the preceding response by less than 18 sec or more than 21 sec would not be reinforced, but would simply reset the apparatus for the start of another period. A response which followed the preceding response within the specified time interval (18–21 sec) would be reinforced. Technically, such a schedule of reinforcement is termed a differential reinforcement of low rate (DRL) of 18 sec, with a limited hold of 3 sec.

It is convenient to study the performance of an individual on such a schedule by recording the actual intervals between responses (the interresponse times) over class intervals of 3 sec each. The number of responses in each 3-sec interval is recorded automatically and the number falling in the 18–21 sec interval constitutes the patient's "score" for that session. After a stable distribution of interresponse times had been generated in this way, visual stimuli could be introduced to serve as cues for the correct spacing of responses, i.e. the patient can acquire more reinforcements (improve his score) by making use of visual cues. Hence, the effects of such cues on his operant performance and behavior in general can be systematically studied. One might wonder how so fixed a symptom as this man's blindness could be manipulated by simply differentially reinforcing responses that are contingent upon his making use of visual cues. However, use can be made of several behavioral principles demonstrable by the controlled study of operant behavior in lower animals.

*Choice of reinforcers.*—The potency of a reinforcer in maintaining behavior is a function of its importance to the organism. Rather than a single specific reinforcer, such as candy, multiple, generalized reinforcers were used. Use was made of the patient's great need for approval and sensitivity to criticism in bringing his behavior under experimental control. When he did well during testing, i.e. made a high score, he was given praise and approval. Conversely, when he did poorly, i.e. made a low score, disapproval and criticism were expressed toward him. These social reinforcers were supplemented by more tangible rewards and punishments, such as special privileges and trips to the hospital canteen, or withdrawal of these when he did poorly.

*Immediacy of reinforcement.*—The effectiveness of a reinforcer is a function also of the temporal proximity of the behavior and the reinforcing event. This is seen especially in the child who repeatedly eats green apples for the immediate pleasure it gives, although he knows they will give him a stomach-ache several hours later. Such behavior is characteristic also of the immature adult. Much of the present patient's financial and social difficulties are related to this. Hence, maximum use can be made of approval, praise, and other reinforcers by delivering them immediately after each testing session. The environmental consequences of his blindness which tend to favor its continuation are more remote in time.

*Successive approximation.*—This is the technique of developing complex responses in an organism by starting with some behavior in his present repertoire, and, by a series of small steps and the use of appropriate reinforcement, gradually approaching the desired behavior. Very complex responses involving difficult discriminations can be developed in lower animals by this technique. In the present study, the patient would be expected to show small but steady improvement in his score on successive sessions. His behavior first would come under the control of gross visual stimuli, and, later, after a series of small steps, under the control of finely discriminative stimuli.

*Stimulus generalization.*—After a stimulus has been conditioned to evoke a given response, similar stimuli tend to evoke the same response. In the present instance, it was anticipated that the control exerted over the patient's behavior by the visual stimuli in the experimental room would gradually generalize to visual stimuli produced in other situations (on the ward, home on visits, etc.). These visually cued responses then would be reinforced outside the testing room by the consequences of seeing which generally support this behavior in the community (e.g. enjoying television, ambulating easily, sight of a friend, etc.).

## TESTING PROCEDURE

The present program was started 2 weeks after the patient entered the hospital for the fourth time since the onset of his blindness. At this time, he was complaining not of his blindness, but of a variety of minor gastrointestinal symptoms, without structure change. He was told that his digestive symptoms and blindness were related and that both would be treated by "reconditioning therapy". With no further explanation, the patient was started on a program of operant conditioning entailing two $^1/_2$ hr sessions daily, 5 days a week.

At the start of each session, the patient was led into a small rectangular room and seated alone at a desk. His hand was placed on a small button mounted in a box (Fig. 1). He was instructed to try to space his responses between 18 and 21 sec as described earlier.

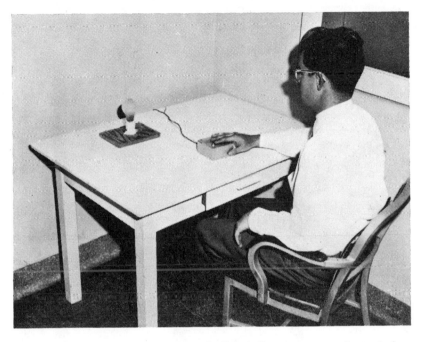

FIG. 1. Subject in experimental room. The light bulb was present as shown during Phases III and IV only.

For the remainder of the session, he was then left alone in the room. A correctly spaced response (18–21 sec since the previous) caused a buzzer to sound, while an incorrectly spaced response (less than 18 or more than 21 sec) caused no buzzer to sound but merely reset the apparatus for the start of another interval. After several practice sessions, visual stimuli of varying intensity and topography were introduced in the room in a manner described below. The entire experimental procedure was programmed automatically by appropriately designed switching circuits. This equipment, along with devices for recording the inter-response times (IRT's) automatically was housed in an adjoining room.

## RESULTS

It will be convenient to discuss the results of the study in 5 phases corresponding to 5 experimental conditions.

I. (*Sessions 1 through 6*).—During Phase I, the illumination of the testing room was held constant and there were no visual cues for the 18 to 21 sec intervals.

After several days, the patient's performance became stable. Most responses fell within the correct interval, i.e. spaced 18–21 sec apart, which rang the buzzer (reinforcement) and added to the patient's score for that day. Figure 2 shows the distribution of inter-response times (IRT's) for the sixth session. Note that in addition to the peak in the 18–21 sec interval a

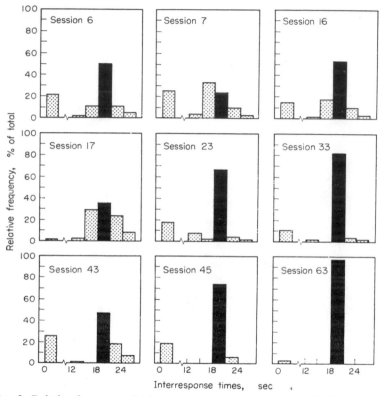

FIG. 2. Relative frequency distributions of inter-response times (IRT's) grouped into class intervals of 3 sec each. Responses falling in the 18–21 sec interval (black) are reinforced. IRT's between 3 and 12 sec (occurring only rarely) have been omitted.

second peak appears in the first or 0–3 sec interval. These first interval responses do not represent gross inaccuracies in the patient's effort to space his responses 18–21 sec apart, but rather, "multiple" responses. On these occasions, the patient has pressed the button 2 or more times in rapid succession instead of making one discrete response. In some animal experiments, "multiple" responses on a schedule of this type (DRL) are considered to be related to the "emotionality" of the animal during testing. In the present study, they appeared to correlate with the patient's manifest anxiety.

Indeed, the percentage of responses falling in this first interval may serve as an independent behavioral measure of the patient's affective state.

Clinically, the patient was moderately anxious during this phase of the study. The gastrointestinal symptoms which occasioned his admission to the hospital gradually disappeared, but there was no change in his blindness.

II. (*Sessions 7 through 16*).—During this phase, a light bulb was present in the room located where it could not be seen directly by the seated patient. The voltage delivered to the bulb was reduced by means of a variable voltage transformer so that, when lit, the illumination in the room was increased by a barely perceptible amount. The light was programmed to go on after 18 sec had elapsed since the last response and to go off again 3 sec later. In other words, the appearance of the light corresponded exactly with the period during which a response would be reinforced (causing the buzzer to sound and adding to the patient's score for that session). The patient could greatly improve his score by making use of the visual cue thus provided.

Introducing this barely perceptible light has a profound influence on the patient's operant responding. Note the marked deterioration in the percentage of correct responses when the light was first introduced (Session 7 of Fig. 2). The introduction of this visual cue, then, was accompanied by deterioration rather than improvement in score. The greatest number of responses was made prematurely, in the 15–18 sec interval. Premature responses reset the apparatus and hence postponed the appearance of the light. In other words, the approach of the crucial 18–21 sec interval, now accompanied by a light, constituted a *preaversive situation*. By responding prematurely, the patient precluded the appearance of the light and thereby avoided an aversive experience. Note also the large number of responses in the first interval (multiple responses).

The *clinical* effect of introducing visual cues was equally dramatic. The patient came out of the seventh session trembling and perspiring and reported feeling "very frightened". He was unable to account for his marked distress, but reported simply that he suddenly became very afraid during the testing session. He gave no indication of being consciously aware of a light in the room. While still very apprehensive, at the end of the session, the patient made some spontaneous comments regarding his relationship with his wife. He recounted several episodes in which he became extremely angry at her.

With reassurance, the patient returned to the testing situation the next day, and his score gradually improved again in the sessions which followed. By the 12th session, the percentage of correct responses was back to the level obtained before the light was introduced (Phase I). There was also less anxiety. He then seemed to reach a plateau, with about 50 per cent of his responses correctly spaced (as in Session 16, Fig. 2). In an effort to account for the patient's failure to improve his score beyond that obtained when no light was present (Phase I), he was observed directly during Session 16.

This was done without his knowledge by means of a peephole drilled in the wall of a closet in the room. He was observed to be resting his head on the table, his eyes covered by his forearm, during the entire session. In other words, he learned to avoid the now aversive and anxiety-provoking light by the simple expedient of covering his eyes. Since he was not told that a visual cue would be provided, and was not "consciously aware" of the light, this was acceptable and appropriate behavior in the situation.

III. (*Sessions 17 through 23*).—It was decided to place the light at its full intensity (about 100 watts) in clear view in front of the patient and to tell him of its presence (Fig. 1). He was told that the light would help him determine when to press the button and eventually enable him to make a perfect score and to see normally again. He expressed doubt about regaining his sight, but agreed to the new testing arrangements. Again, the light went on only during the 3 sec interval during which a response would be reinforced.

Figure 2 shows the distribution of IRT's for the first session under these conditions (Session 17). Again, the number of correctly spaced responses fell (36 per cent of total). The patient expressed concern over his poor performance and sought approval; he did not appear more anxious than usual, however. In the new situation making the presence of the visual cues known to the patient seemed to avoid the recurrence of anxiety, even though the performance was disrupted as before. The percentage of multiple (first-interval) responses was small, again in keeping with the level of overt anxiety present.

By making continued approval and acceptance contingent upon a continually improving score, the patient's percentage of correct responses gradually increased. In Session 23, 67 per cent of his responses were correctly spaced (Fig. 2), but he was still unaware of seeing. He accounted for his high percentage of correctly spaced responses by reporting that he could feel the heat thrown off by the light bulb when it came on. This was clearly an unconscious rationalization for his use of visual cues, however, since the temperature changes were too small to be detected. There was some return of anxiety, again reflected in the percentage of 0–3 sec IRT's.

IV. (*Sessions 24 through 45*).—It was decided to decrease the intensity of the light by means of the variable voltage transformer in the circuit. The patient was told that this would be done gradually, so that he would switch over from feeling the heat of the bulb (which he admitted would become too small to be detected) to seeing it. As rewards continued to be delivered or withdrawn in accordance with his performance the patient's score continued to improve while the intensity of the light was reduced in small decrements. Eighty-two per cent of his responses were correctly spaced in Session 33 (Fig. 2).

The patient's score continued to improve in the sessions which followed.* His adjustment on the ward and his relationships with others also improved. He became less defensive about his blindness and less guarded in his behavior, entering into ward activities and aiding the nurses in various chores. Although he still reported seeing nothing, he used visual metaphors with increasing frequency, especially in the context of angry feelings toward his wife or mother-in-law. For example, he frequently spoke of not "seeing eye to eye" with his wife or having felt so angry toward her he "couldn't see straight".

The patient's operant behavior changed abruptly in Session 43 (Fig. 2). The percentage of responses during the correct interval dropped to half its previous value (48 per cent), and the number of multiple responses (first-interval) rose sharply. At the end of the session, the patient came out of the room exclaiming that he could see the light. He appeared both anxious and exhilarated, and sought praise and approval for his accomplishment. He accounted for his poor score during this session despite his awareness of visual cues by stating that he felt almost paralyzed by the light. His score improved rapidly over the next 2 sessions, however, and he became less anxious (Session 45, Fig. 2).

V. (*Sessions 46 through 63*).—Now that the patient was able to make use of the visual cues provided by the 40-watt bulb on the desk in front of him, it was decided to introduce more difficult discriminative stimuli. At first, a stimulus board of 4 small lights mounted in a row was substituted for the single large bulb. This was programmed so that a change in pattern of the lights (the end two going off and the middle two coming on) signaled that 18 sec had elapsed since the previous response. After this, a stimulus panel was used which consisted of a small pane of translucent glass on which various geometrical designs could be projected. With each change in experimental conditions, the correct spacing of responses was contingent upon making finer visual discriminations. With each new discriminative problem, the patient's performance was poorer for a few sessions and then gradually improved. Figure 2 shows the distribution of IRT's for the patient's last session (No. 63), in which a difficult visual discrimination was used. Except for a few multiple responses, all the presses were separated by 18–21 sec, indicating a reinforcement on each occasion. The formal operant sessions were discontinued at this point.

During this phase of the study, the patient's clinical condition continued to improve. He used the visual modality (and was aware of seeing) more and more on the ward and at home during visits. After operant conditioning

---

* During four of the sessions (No.'s 34, 40, 49 and 55) the interval that was reinforced, and the corresponding visual cues was varied randomly among the 15–18, 18–21 and 21–24 sec intervals to ascertain that the patient was not relying on the temporal cue of 18 sec to guide his responses. Since the patient obtained a high score during these sessions also, reliance on a temporal cue was ruled out.

was discontinued, more conventional therapy was instituted. This consisted largely of support and efforts to rehabilitate him socially and vocationally.

## COMMENT

In this study a chronic hysterical symptom has been analyzed and manipulated by operant conditioning techniques. The experimental program was such that the number of correctly spaced responses served as an index of the patient's use of visual cues and the number of multiple (first interval) responses a behavioral measure of his anxiety.

When visual cues were first introduced in the testing situation, profound effects were noted in the patient's clinical condition and operant behavior which are of interest from a psychodynamic point of view. Modern psychoanalytic theory would regard the patient's blindness as a manifestation of repression and his relative freedom from overt anxiety as an indication of the "success" of this repression. Put another way, anxiety maintains the repression, and any threat to this repressive defense would be accompanied by an increase of anxiety. In the present study, the patient was only moderately anxious in the testing situation when the spacing of responses was not cued by visual stimuli (Phase I). However, when such cuing was first introduced in Phase II, the responses were reinforced only in the presence of a visual stimulus, the coincidence of light and response simulated the visual *control* of his responses, and intense anxiety was observed. It may be argued that the patient's repression was weakened momentarily and anxiety was generated. As mentioned earlier, the aversive property of the light is evidenced by the shift in mode of the distribution of the IRT's to the earlier 15–18 sec interval (Session 7 of Fig. 2). The patient's spontaneous remarks at this time suggested the areas of life experience and feelings which occasioned the development of the neurosis. This was confirmed by later clinical observations. These findings would seem to corroborate experimentally the dynamic view of hysterical blindness as a manifestation of repression, which, in turn, is maintained by anxiety.

In Phase III the patient was told that visual cues would be present. Again a disruption in performance was seen but little anxiety. It appears that alerting the patient to the presence of the light facilitated its repression and little anxiety was generated. In the sessions that followed the patient's behavior came more and more under control of visual cues; anxiety gradually mounted again and he defended himself for a time against conscious awareness of the cues by the rationalization that he could feel the bulb's heat. When he finally reported seeing, he was intensely anxious for a short time. After this it was possible to bring the patient's responding under finer and finer visual stimulus control until a high degree of visual acuity was demonstrated. This generalized to outside the testing situation.

The issue of therapy *per se* has been largely omitted by intention, but a few comments are in order. Eysenck[1] has recently reviewed the treatment of neurotic symptoms by techniques derived from learning theory, and Walton and Black[6, 7] have reported on the treatment of hysterical aphonia and other disorders by conditioning techniques, but within a different theoretical framework than the present essay. The treatment of psychiatric disorders by operant conditioning techniques is being studied at several centers in the United States. In the present study, it might be argued that the whole testing procedure constituted "psychotherapy" in the broad sense of the term, and that the specific conditioning procedures were incidental. This argument would be more persuasive, however, had the patient not proved so refractory to the many, but more usual, psychotherapeutic measures that were taken over a long period. Further, the systematic reappearance of anxiety, the occurrence of preaversive avoidance behavior, and the evolution of behavior clearly under the control of environmental cues support the authors' contention that return of visual function was specifically related to the events programmed in the testing procedure. Once visual function was regained by the process of successive approximation described earlier, the patient was amenable to more conventional rehabilitative techniques. For a time he worked at a community rehabilitation center during the day and stayed at the hospital at night. Seven months ago he was discharged from the hospital and returned to his own community.

He now returns to the hospital laboratory at monthly intervals for follow-up evaluation and general support; he is in on other treatment at this time. For several months his visual ability has been unchanged. On testing he is able to read small case newspaper print, to identify geometrical patterns, and to identify small objects. In a social situation, his performance is more variable. Sometimes he is slow to recognize the faces of persons who knew him when he was blind. Also, in the presence of these same persons, he walks with the awkward gait he exhibited when totally blind. Perhaps a more meaningful index of his present clinical condition, however, is his performance in the everyday business of living. He is gainfully employed in his community (as a switchboard operator), and is managing his family responsibilities and other affairs in a satisfactory manner. It is now 13 months since he first reported seeing.

## SUMMARY

An experimental analysis of hysterical blindness by operant conditioning techniques is reported to illustrate the utility of this method for the study of psychiatric conditions. Clinical data, in part evoked by the conditioning procedure, also are reported. These are usually conceptualized within a "psychodynamic" framework. Some areas of *rapprochement* between concepts derived from dynamic theory and operant conditioning are suggested. Brief comments are made on some therapeutic aspects of the study.

## REFERENCES

1. EYSENCK, H. J. (1959) Learning Theory and Behaviour Therapy, *J. Ment. Sci.* **105,** 61–75.
2. FERSTER, C. B. and SKINNER, B. F. (1957) *Schedules of Reinforcement,* Appleton-Century-Crofts, New York.
3. LINDSLEY, O. R. (1960) Characteristics of the Behavior of Chronic Psychotics as Revealed by Free-Operant Conditioning Methods, *Dis Nerv. Syst.* **22,** 66–78.
4. SKINNER, B, F. (1938) *The Behavior of Organisms,* Appleton-Century-Crofts, New York.
5. SKINNER, B. F. (1953) *Science and Human Behavior,* Macmillan, New York.
6. WALTON, D. and BLACK, D. A. (1958) The Application of Learning Theory to the Treatment of Stammering. *J. Psychosom. Res.* **3,** 170–179.
7. WALTON, D. and BLACK, D. A. (1959) The Application of Modern Learning Theory to the Treatment of Chronic Hysterical Aphonia, *J. Psychosom. Res.* **3,** 303–311.

# Reduction in Rate of Multiple Tics
# by Free Operant Conditioning Methods*

BEATRICE H. BARRET, PH.D.

*Department of Psychiatry, Behavior Research Laboratory, Harvard Medical School*

THE experimental investigation of neuromuscular tics has probably been most limited by difficulties in developing sensitive and reliable behavioral measurement techniques. The closest approximation to an experimental study of tics, by Yates,[18] was based on a patient's records of her ability to reproduce her tic symptoms. Yates did not attempt to obtain *objective* records or measurement of the patient's tics.

The method of free operant conditioning, originally developed by Skinner[15] to study animal behavior and later modified by Lindsley,[9] to study the behavior of chronic psychotics, has provided precise techniques of behavioral measurement and control. These techniques have been extended to the investigation of such pathological behaviors as vocal hallucinatory episodes,[10, 11, 12] pressure of speech,[13] and stuttering.[7] By the application of free operant techniques, Ferster[5] succeeded in expanding the very limited behavioral repertoires of two autistic children, and Brady and Lind[3] performed an experimental analysis with therapeutic results in a patient with hysterical blindness.

The basic datum of the free operant method is the frequency of a specific and reliably defined response within a controlled experimental environment. The method is most readily applied, therefore, in cases where changes in the rate of a repeated movement are of primary concern. The present report describes an application of free operant methods to the control of multiple neuromuscular tics.

* This article is reprinted with the permission of the author and editor from the *J. Nerv. Ment. Dis.*, (1962). **135**, 187–195.

† Department of Psychiatry, Havard Medical School, Behavior Research Laboratory, Metropolitan State Hospital, Waltham, Massachusetts. Ogden R. Lindsley, Ph.D., Director of the Laboratory, generously supplied the diagrammatic sketch in Figure 1 and the controlling and recording equipment. His advice and encouragement were invaluable in the conduct of this experiment. This research was supported by Research Training Grant 2 M–7084 and Research Grant MY-2778 from the National Institute of Mental Health, U.S. Public Health Service.

METHOD

*Patient*

The patient in this experiment was a 38-year-old veteran, hospitalized in the Neurology Service of a local VA hospital.* His extensive multiple tics started approximately 14 years ago, during his term of duty in the armed services. Although a medical discharge was available to him, the patient chose to continue in the service, eventually serving overseas, until regular discharge. Since then he has been employed as an accountant by a single firm.

An interview prior to the experiment revealed that the patient knew of no traumatic experience preceding the abrupt onset of tics. He told of awakening during the night with a choking sensation accompanied by a momentary inability to breathe or swallow. He recalled this as a frightening experience and was puzzled by the subsequent development of tics. Within a few months, spasmodic movements had developed in much of his body. At the time of this experiment, his major movements included contractions of neck, shoulder, chest, and abdominal muscles, head nodding, bilateral eye blinking, opening of the mouth, and other comparatively mild facial movements.† The patient complained of difficulty in swallowing, hence of slow ingestion. His clear, intelligent speech was marked only occasionally by barely noticeable hesitation.

In recent years the patient was not fully aware of the presence of his tics. On occasion, when the thought himself relatively free of them, his wife reported that there was no reduction in his twitching. The patient did feel, however, that his movements were reduced in frequency while he was playing his saxophone in a local band on weekends. His greatest concern was the extent to which his tics made him conspicuous to strangers and limited his business advancement. In general, little was known of the patient's personal history.

The patient had undergone psychological counseling for a number of months and had received pharmacological treatment which included a variety of tranquilizing and muscle-relaxing drugs. Neither treatment had afforded symptomatic relief. The patient displayed no outstanding symptoms of psychopathology. His tics were considered symptomatic of an extrapyramidal system disturbance and untreatable by conventional methods.

Since he had experienced no success with other methods, the patient was highly motivated to participate in this experiment. Although he was soon discharged to return to work in a neighboring state, he voluntarily rehospitalized himself two months later for continuation of the experiment.

---

* The author is grateful to Norman Geschwind, M.D., Department of Neurology, Boston VA Hospital, who suggested the experimental behavioral study of this patient and who arranged for space and the loan of various apparatus components.

† Some of the patient's movements were so strong that, when he was seated in a chair on casters, they caused slight rolling.

## Arrangement of Apparatus

*Patient's enclosure:* A quiet, well ventilated room with observation facilities was equipped with a comfortable swivel-tilt armchair, an ashtray, a set of comfortable earphones which the patient wore throughout all experimental sessions, and a Grass EEG console (see Figure 1).

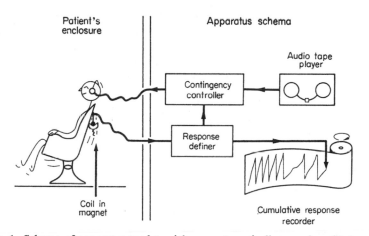

FIG. 1. Schema of apparatus used to pick up, automatically record, and program the contingent consequences of multiple tics.

*Operandum:* A large U-shaped magnet, securely attached to the outside of the chair back, served as a convenient device for summating multiple tics. Although the swivel arc of the chair was restricted and the chair's casters removed, its tilt was freely operative. An induction coil rested in a "nest" of electrical tape strung between the poles of the magnet.* Slack in the tape was adjusted so that when the patient was seated in the chair his most noticeable spasmodic movements, regardless of locus or amplitude, created a slight movement of the coil in the magnetic field.

*Response definition and recording:* The current induced in the moving coil was amplified by one channel of an EEG recorder to operate a sensitive relay. The operations of this relay were directly recorded as tics. The duration and amplitude of the recorded tics were determined by setting the amplifier gain so that each strong and obvious tic would operate the response relay and cumulative response recorder. After initial selection, this amplifier gain was held constant throughout the experiment.

## Response-contingent Events

In free operant conditioning, the frequency of a response is altered by programing particular consequences contingent upon the emission of that

* Michael J. Malone, M.D., offered the general idea of the "tic chair" and magnetic pickup.

response. Generally this method has been used to generate steady rates of responding or to increase the frequency of a given response. When *reduction* in the frequency of a symptom is desired, the event contingent upon symptom occurrence may be 1) the removal of a positive stimulus or 2) the presentation of an aversive stimulus. In this experiment, both types of tic-contingent events were used.

By the use of a tape recorder, a positive stimulus (music) could be removed or an aversive stimulus (noise) presented when a tic occured. Pulses from the response relay were transmitted through a timer to a circuit which controlled the tape recorder output to the patient's earphones (see schema Fig.1). All recording and controlling equipment was located in a nearby room.*

*Music:* In order to maximize the patient's interest, the music used in the experiment was selected by the patient himself from the hospital's library. Boredom and satiation were minimized by using several selections with no repetitions.

The contingency arrangement was programed so that each tic produced a 1·5 sec interruption of music. If the patient did not tic for at least 1·5 sec, he could hear the music until it was automatically interrupted by the next tic. In effect, this schedule differentially reinforced time intervals between tics of 1·5 sec or more.†

*Noise:* Azrin[1] found that responses could be eliminated by making the presentation of white noise contingent upon their occurrence; and Flanagan, Goldiamond, and Azrin[7] successfully reduced chronic stuttering by presentation of a stutter-produced loud tone. In the present experiment a tape loop of white noise (60 db) was used as a tic-produced aversive stimulus.

The contingency was arranged so that each tic produced 1·5 sec of noise over the patient's earphones. When the patient was tic-free for at least 1·5 sec, the noise was automatically interrupted and did not recur until the next tic.

### Contingency Testing

As a control to test the effect of the contingencies described above, periods of continuous music and continuous noise were used. This amounted to removal of the contingency requirement which, in the case of music, more nearly approximated the conditions of music therapy.

### Self-control

The effects of music and noise were compared with the patient's own efforts to control his tics. A signal light (60 watt bulb) was introduced and the patient was instructed to control his tics by his most frequently used methods for as long as the light was on.

    * The cooperation, assistance, and patience of Dave Adkins and the staff of the EEG laboratory at the Boston VA Hospital made possible the occupancy of sufficient space to approximate good environmental control.

    † In technical terms, this schedule is a time contingent crf drl of 1·5 sec with an unlimited hold[6].

*Experimental Sessions*

The patient was informed that we would be studying the effects of various conditions on his tic rate. He had selected a lasting supply of music tapes with the understanding that he would hear them at least some of the time during the experiment. He was instructed to make himself comfortable and to remain seated in the chair, with earphones on, throughout the sessions. Aside from previously mentioned instructions concerning the signal light, no further explanation was given. The experimental room was closed, and recording was begun. Experimental conditions were changed without interruption by adjusting the controlling equipment. The duration of sessions varied from two to three hours depending on meal schedules and other hospital routines. No attempt was made to set up predetermined time intervals for each experimental condition. With a few exceptions due to time limits, each condition was run long enough to show its maximal effect when compared with the normal tic rate or operant level.

## RESULTS

Cumulative records of the first four sessions showing the effects of music and noise on tic rate are shown in Fig. 2.* These sessions were conducted during a 48-hr period prior to the patient's discharge. The remaining sessions were held two months later when the patient voluntarily rehospitalized himself for continuation of the experiment.

To facilitate comparison of tic rates under the various experimental conditions, the continuous records in all figures have been telescoped and grouped. The steeper the slope of the curves, the higher the tic rate. Rate estimates may be made by reference to the grid showing rates for representative slopes.

*Operant Level Determinations*

The patient's normal tic rate (operant level) ranged between 64 and 116 tpm (tics per minute),† with some decrease in the short run at 4 E during the last session in Fig. 2. No diurnal variations in tic rate were noted.

---

\* The cumulative response recorder feeds paper at a constant speed while each tic impulse moves the recording pen one step in a vertical direction. After 450 tics have been recorded, the pen automatically resets to the base and is ready to step up with the next tic (see Fig. 1). Horizontal lines in the curves are periods when no tic impulses occurred.

† For example, the first four pen excursions labeled 1 A were continuously recorded tics during a 26-min period at the start of the first session to get an operant level. Without interruption, the 1 B curves follow, showing 27 min of tics under continuous music. The two curves labeled 1 C record a return to the operant level for 10 min, followed immediately by the 1D period of 34 min with each tic producing interruption of the music. The 2 A curves show operant level rates at the start of session 2, followed by 25 min of continuous music (2B), then 21 min of tic-contingent interruption of music (2C), and so on. The same identification system is used in Fig. 4 for sessions 7 and 8.

Although sessions were run during various hours of the day and evening to capitalize on limited time, neither fatigue nor hunger affected tic rate of response to experimental conditions.*

*Effects of Noise*

There was a very slight increase in the tic rate during a brief 7-min period when continuous white noise (60 db) was played ("noise" in Fig. 2). However, when made tic-contingent, noise reduced the tic rate to about 40 tpm ("con-

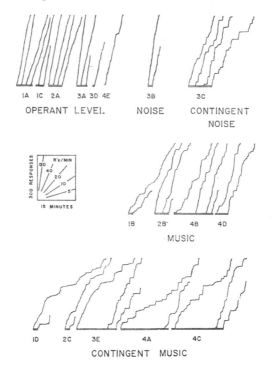

FIG. 2. Cumulative response records of the first four experimental sessions showing changes in tic rate under conditions of tic-contingent noise and tic-contingent interruption of music and control runs of both noise and music without the contingency requirement. The experimental sessions are numbered and the sequence of conditions within each session identified by letters. Double bars connect all immediately successive curves under designated conditions. Breaks in double bars indicate a change of conditions.[8]

tingent noise" in Fig. 2). The long tic-free intervals toward the end of the contingent noise period may have been due to dozing which the patient later reported. Because of its apparent soporific effect, noise was not used further.

* Sessions 2, 4, and 8 were run in the morning and terminated for the patient's lunch; sessions 1 and 3 occurred in the afternoon; sessions 5 and 7 were conducted in the evening.

## Effects of Music

Continuous music ("music" in Fig. 2) reduced the tic rate about as much as did contingent noise (40 tpm). However, when each tic interrupted the music ("contingent music"), the rate was lowered to 15 to 30 tpm. During every period of contingent music, the effect of the contingency was an additional reduction of 40 to 50 per cent in tic rate. After the first session there was no overlap between the range of rates under continuous music and under tic-contingent interruption of music. The differential magnitude of these effects on this patient thus requires no statistical test.

The fact that contingent music produced a greater reduction in rate of ticing than did continuous music appears to be the result of longer, more frequent ticfree periods when the contingency was in effect. The improbability of fatigue effects is indicated by a comparison of the 4A rate under contingent music obtained at the start of a morning session with the 1D, 2C and 3E rates under this condition recorded at the end of the three previous sessions.

## Effects of Self-control

The tic-reducing effect of contingent music is compared with the patient's sustained efforts at self-control in Fig. 3 (fifth session). In response to instructions and a signal light, the patient reduced his tic rate to 50 to 60 per min.

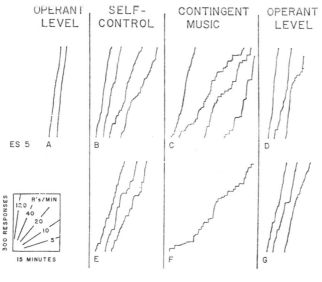

FIG. 3. A continuous cumulative record of the fifth experimental session showing rate changes under sustained self-control compared with the greater reduction under tic-produced interruption of music. The sequence of conditions is indicated by letters.

This rate is only slightly higher than that previously obtained with contingent noise and non-contingent music. Under the condition of tic-contingent interruption of music, however, rates were considerably lower, ranging from 20 to 35 per min.* Again there was no overlap between the range of rates under the three conditions (operant level, self-control, and contingent music). Note the initial rapid tic rate at the beginning of the C period of contingent music. This increase in rate following a period of self-control (B) parallels what clinicians have observed in tiqueurs.[17] It appears that this effect was strong enough to counteract temporarily the effect of the contingent music (C).

In addition to the differential effects on tic rate of self-control and the music contingency condition, there was also a difference in the patient's general behavior topography. In the B period of self-control, the patient was observed to engage in head-holding and general prolonged contraction. In contrast, during the E period of self-control, he engaged in relaxed tapping with finger or foot and occasional singing. This new form of behavior was first observed as the patient accompanied contingent music in the C period.

These differences in behavior topography shown during the B and E periods of self-control may account for the longer tic-free intervals in E than in B. They may also explain the differential response to contingent music in C and F. In other words, it appeared that the patient used two different methods of reducing his tics and that these two methods had different effects on subsequent tic reduction under contingent music. During B, self-control was effected by a generalized rigid contraction which was followed in C by an initial increase in rate despite the availablility of contingent music. In contrast, during E self-control was achieved through release methods with the subsequent rapid and marked rate reduction under contingent music (F).

## Reliablility of the Effect of Contingent Music

The previously described data from six experimental sessions showed that tic-contingent interruption of music reduced the patient's tic rate far more than did non-contingent music, tic-produced white noise, or the patient's efforts at self-control. During those sessions, the patient had approximately six hours' exposure to contingent music. Following a two-month interruption of the experiment, the reliablity of the tic-reducing effect of contingent music was subjected to empirical test by a series of replications on the same patient.†
The result of alternating operant level control periods (7 A, 7 C, 7 E, and 8 A, 8 C, 8 E, and 8 G) with periods of tic-produced interruption of music (7 B, 7 D, and 7 F; and 8 B, 8 D, and 8 F) are shown in Fig. 4. The effect

* This differential effect was reproduced repeatedly in session 6, which is not shown here.
† Both Claude Bernard, in 1865 ([2]), and Murray Sidman, in 1961 ([14]). have pointed out that the most convincing test of reliability of an "effect" is the demonstration of its reproducibility in a series of replications.

of contingent music on tic-free intervals was dramatically and reliably demonstrated by reductions of from 55 to 85 per cent below the operant rate on each of these six replications.

The tic-reducing effect of contingent music was more immediate and prolonged than in earlier sessions. Tic-free intervals were, for the most part, considerably longer and more frequent than previously, and only brief

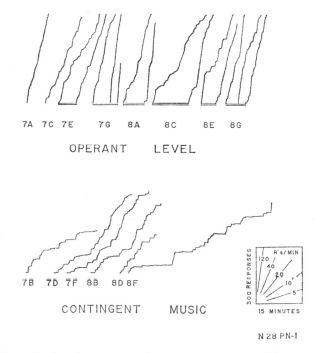

FIG. 4. Records of sessions 7 and 8 demonstrating reproducibility of the marked tic-reducing effect of tic-contingent interruption of music in six replications. Letters designate the sequence of conditions within numbered sessions.

bursts of tics occurred with high local rate. The patient expressed irritation at the end of session 8 because he had wanted to hear the remainder of a jazz concert being played during 8 F (the period with lowest tic rate; 9 per min). He commented that he was concentrating on the musical ideas and became annoyed when his brief bursts of tics interrupted it. During most of the 44 min 8 F period of contingent music he was observed to be almost motionless as he listened to the music.

The pattern of tic-free intervals followed by brief intervals of heightened local rate which developed in response to contingent music appeared to generalize to the operant ticing rate as early as session 4. If this was a true generalization, it may have therapeutic implications. On the other hand, it may simply represent a minor shift of unknown nature in the tic rate.

Because of possible operandum unreliability (discussed below), the most valid comparisons should be limited to the differential effects of self-control, non-contingent music, and contingent music relative to the operant tic rate.

Intrasession decrease in operant level rate did appear with regularity during the last two sessions (Fig. 4). Operant tic rates 7C, 7E, 8C and 8E, which were recorded between periods of contingent music, showed somewhat longer tic-free intervals than those recorded at the beginning of these sessions (7A and 8A) or those recorded at the end of these sessions (7G and 8G). The reasons for this decrease are far from clear, but the decrease may have something to do with attention. The patient reported that during these sessions he was anticipating more music and knew he would not hear it if he had many tics.

## DISCUSSION

The results of this experiment clearly demonstrate that non-contingent music and tic-contingent white noise reduced the tic rate to a level comparable with that produced by self-control. A far more powerful reduction was produced by tic-contingent interruption of music.

In evaluating the differential control of tic rate shown in these data and the possible extensions of the basic method to other symptoms for either therapeutic or research purposes, the most pertinent consideration is the design of the operandum, the device which permits the symptom to operate a switch.[16] Two major requirements of a good operandum are the reliability of its operation and the specificity of the response class which actuates it.* The fragile tape arrangement of our crude operandum does not insure reliable operation for continued general application. It is not stable enough to maintain accurate calibration during repeated use. A more stable operandum might have permanently fixed pickups, preferably embedded in upholstery in different areas of a chair.

Although a chair operandum provided a relatively comfortable situation for the patient, it did restrict his motility more than might be desired. Moreover, it was not specific to tic movements alone. A more tic-specific operandum would be operated solely by tic movements. Improved specificity of tic measurement without restrictions on motility may be obtained by pickups placed at the loci of various tics which would be telemetered by transmitters worn on the patient's belt or in a pocket.[8] The patient could then engage in routine daily activities while effects of interest are continuously recorded.

---

* Ferster [4] has discussed in some detail the general requirements of an accurate operandum (manipulandum). This device, which is manipulated by the subject's behavior, also defines the response being conditioned or attenuated. It is the point of contact between the subject and the automatic recording equipment. For these reasons its operating characteristics are of utmost importance.

Once the operandum requirements have been refined, therapeutic effects can be more reliably evaluated. The use of tic-contingent interruption of music could be extended in time or otherwise modified. For example, the duration of the tic-free interval necessary to produce music could be progressively lengthened. With remote recording, the long-term effects of an appropriate contingency arrangement could be evaluated by furnishing the patient with a portable contingency controller to plug into his home radio or television set for relief of his symptom. The contingencies for music and noise, already demonstrated to be effective, could be combined in a multiple contingency whereby each tic would bring 1·5 sec of noise and pauses greater than 1·5 sec would bring music, until the next tic impulse simultaneously interrupted the music and restored the white noise.

The observed behavior changes offered as possible explanations for differential tic rates recorded under self-control could be objectively measured to evaluate the interaction between symptomatic and non-symptomatic responses. For example, if operanda had been provided for simultaneously recording the patient's finger-tapping and singing, it might have been possible to show an inverse relationship between the rate of vocalizing and finger-drumming and the tic rate. In addition, experiments could be run to determine whether tic movements may be diminished or even eliminated by differentially reinforcing another more circumscribed and more socially acceptable motor response which serves the same discharge function as tics.

A free operant conditioning analogy to the negative practice technique used by Yates[18] could be readily investigated by positively reinforcing the patient for each tic. If this variation of the method is therapeutic, positive reinforcement of the symptom should be followed by reduction in the operant tic rate.

The general aspects of the pickup and continuous recording system described here provide a method for direct and objective behavioral measurement of motor symptom frequency which would be useful in studying the effects of drugs, the influence of attention, and variations in tic rate during diagnostic or therapeutic interviews.

## SUMMARY

A method for continuous automatic recording of the rate of multiple tics has been used in a demonstration of differential control of tic rate by free operant conditioning procedures.

The results showed that the multiple tics of a neurological patient, previously refractory to pharmacological and psychological therapies, could be reduced in rate by self-control, by tic-produced white noise, and by continuous music. The most dramatic, rapid, and reliable reduction resulted from tic-produced interruption of music. The power of tic-contingent enviromental consequences in controlling this patient's symptom was shown, and suggestions were offered for extending and refining the basic method for more definitive investigations of this and other motor disturbances.

## REFERENCES

1. AZRIN, N. H. (1958) Some effects of noise on human behavior, *J. Exp. Anal. Behav.*, **1**, 183–200.
2. BERNARD, C. (1957) *Introduction to the Study of Experimental Medicine*, Paris, 1865, translated 1927. Dover Publications, New York.
3. BRADY, J. P. and LIND, D. L. (1961) Experimental analysis of hysterical blindness, *Arch. Gen. Psychiat.*, **4**, 331–339.
4. FERSTER, C. B. (1953) The use of the free operant in the analysis of behavior, *Psychol. Bull.*, **50**, 263–274.
5. FERSTER, C. B. (1961) The development of performances in autistic children in an automatically controlled environment, *J. Chron. Dis.*, **13**, 312–345.
6. FERSTER, C. B. and SKINNER, B. F. (1957) *Schedules of Reinforcement*, Appleton-Century-Crofts, New York.
7. FLANAGAN, B., GOLDIAMOND, I. and AZRIN, N. H. (1958) Operant stuttering: the control of stuttering behavior through response-contingent consequences, *J. Exp. Anal. Behav.*, **1**, 173–177.
8. HEFERLINE, R. F. (1962) Learning theory and clinical psychology—an eventual symbiosis? In A. J. BACHRACH (Ed.) *Experimental Foundations of Clinical Psychology*, Basic Books, New York.
9. LINDSLEY, O. R. (1956) Operant conditioning methods applied to research in chronic schizophrenia, *Psychiat. Res. Rep.*, **5**, 118–139.
10. LINDSLEY, O. R. (1959) Reduction in rate of vocal psychotic symptoms by differential positive reinforcement, *J. Exp. Anal. Behav.*, **2**, 269.
11. LINDSLEY, O. R. (1960) Characteristics of the behavior of chronic psychotics as revealed by free-operant conditioning methods, *Dis. Nerv. Syst. Monogr. Suppl.*, **21**, 66–78.
12. LINDSLEY, O. R. (1961) Direct measurement and functional definition of vocal hallucinatory symptoms in chronic psychosis. Paper presented at Third World Congress of Psychiatry, Montreal, Canada, June.
13. SHEARN, D., SPRAGUE, R. L. and ROSENZWEIG, S. (1961) A method for the analysis and control of speech rate, *J. Exp. Anal. Behav.*, **4**, 197–201.
14. SIDMAN, M. (1961) *The Tactics of Scientific Research*, Basic Books, New York.
15. SKINNER, B. F. (1938) *The Behavior of Organisms*, Appleton Century, New York.
16. SKINNER, B. F. (1962) Operandum, *J. Exp. Anal. Behav.*, **5**, 224.
17. WECHSLER, I. S. (1952) *Clinical Neurology*, Saunders, Philadelphia.
18. YATES, A. J. (1958) The application of modern learning theory to the treatment of tics, *J. Abnorm. Soc. Psychol.*, **56**, 175–182. Reprinted in H. J. EYSENCK (Ed.) *Behavior Therapy and the Neuroses*, Pergamon, New York 1960.

# Conditioning of Mental-hospital Patients
# to Fixed-ratio Schedules of Reinforcement\*†

R. R. HUTCHINSON§   and   N. H. AZRIN

*Southern Illinois University*      *Anna State Hospital*

THE PRESENT investigation is an analysis of the responding of mental-hospital patients to fixed-ratio schedules of reinforcement.

## SUBJECTS

The subjects in these experiments were seven male patients of a mental hospital who were diagnosed as schizophrenic. Their ages ranged from 26 to 69 years, with a median of 47 years. These subjects were long-term or "chronic" patients; with only one exception, they had been hospitalized for at least 14 years. Their length of hospitalization ranged from 2 to 36 years, with a median of 19 years. Aside from the usual hospital medication, none of the subjects was undergoing formal therapy during this study; nor did medical diagnosis indicate organic involvement. In order to insure regular participation by the subjects, no patients were selected who had frequent visitors to the hospital, who were allowed home visits, or who had grounds passes or jobs in the hospital. Only those patients were selected who accepted cigarettes and candy, since those reinforcers could be most easily programmed with available equipment. Each patient was receiving thorazine regularly as treatment.

## APPARATUS

*Experimental Chamber*

The experimental room was a sound-attenuated and temperature-controlled enclosure 7 feet wide, 10 feet long, and 12 feet high. The door to this room could be closed securely, but was never locked. The subjects could

\* This article is reprinted with the permission of the authors and editor from *J. Exper. Anal. Behav.* **4**, 87–95 (1961).

† This paper is based in part on a thesis submitted by the senior author in partial fulfillment of the M.A. degree at Southern Illinois University. The investigation was supported by a grant from the Psychiatric Training and Research Fund of the Illinois Department of Public Welfare. The advice and assistance of R. C. Steck, W. Holz and D. Sauerbrunn are gratefully acknowledged.

§ Now at Yale University.

be observed through a window of one-way glass which was effectively concealed from the patient by a ventilator grill and which allowed no mirrored reflection. The manipulandum and vending magazine were placed on the wall opposite this window. An electric cigarette lighter and ashtray were mounted nearby.

## Response and Reinforcement Apparatus

The manipulandum was of the type designed by Lindsley (1956), and consisted basically of a brass knob mounted on a shaft. When a subject pulled this knob through a distance of 1 cm with a force of 300 g, a concealed switch closed. Closure of this switch constituted the measured response. An enclosed magazine with a capacity of 100 reinforcements was located above the response knob. Reinforcement consisted of the delivery of a single cigarette or piece of candy into a tray which was located 7 in. from the response knob. At the time of reinforcement, the delivery tray was lighted and a soft buzzer sounded for 3 sec. Typically, the reinforcer was obtained by the patient within a second or two after its delivery into the tray. In other instances, the reinforcers were simply allowed to accumulate in the tray until the end of the session. In both instances, the receipt of reinforcement required negligible time and produced little or no interruption of the ongoing responding. For this reason, all of the programming apparatus as well as the recorders and counters remained functional during the delivery of reinforcement. The response panel and vending magazine appeared self-contained to the subject, but in fact were connected by a concealed cable with the controlling and recording apparatus located in another room.

## PROCEDURE

### Patient Handling and Programming Procedure

The experimental sessions for a given patient were conducted daily, Monday through Friday, and at the same time each day. The sessions ended after the delivery of a fixed number of reinforcements. Assistants who were naive about the purposes, objectives, or expectations of the study escorted the patients to and from the experimental room. When the door of the experimental room was closed, an electrical switch automatically started the session. The use of this door switch to initiate the sessions proved to have two advantages. First, no extinction period could occur between the time the patient entered the room and the time the "authorized" session began. Second, the patient considered the reinforcement schedule to be less under the control of the experimenter because no waiting period was necessary while the assistant was starting the session.

*Instructions to Subjects*

On the first occasion that a patient was brought to the experimental room, he was asked, "Would you like some candy and cigarettes?" The assistant would obtain a cigarette or piece of candy for himself by moving the response knob and would encourage the subject to do the same saying: "You can get as many as you want to take back to the ward with you." He then left the room saying,"Get all you want; I'll be back in a little while." If the subject did not respond within 20 or 30 min, the assistant again entered the room and further demonstrated the apparatus. If necessary, he even placed the subject's hand on the manipulandum. Although minimal instruction had been desired, in some cases responding began only if the above instructions were used.


## RESULTS AND DISCUSSION

Of the seven patients initially selected for these experiments, five were studied for a period of over 3 months. The response curves of two of the subjects, shown in Fig. 1, demonstrate the typical changes in performance which occured during the initial weeks of conditioning. At the start of conditioning, every response was reinforced. To the extent that responding was sustained under this continuous reinforcement, progressively larger numbers of responses were required. Both subjects in Fig. 1 had an extremely low response rate of only 4 or 5 responses per minute during the first several experimental sessions. Gradually, however, responding increased to a level greater than 100 per minute at the higher ratio requirements. All five subjects initially showed these same low rates of less than 6 responses per minute during the first two experimental sessions. The time required to produce high rates of responding varied among subjects. Indeed, with two subjects, over 40 experimental sessions were required before response rates above 100 per minute were observed. All subjects consistently maintained the level of final performance such as that shown in Fig. 1 over consecutive experimental sessions.

The reason for the day-to-day increase in responding is not clear from the above data. Possibly, responding was increased because of the successively higher number of responses required for reinforcement. On the other hand, the same increase might have been simply a function of time. This question is partially answered by Fig. 2, which presents the average rate of responding of Subject C over a 26-day period. The response rate appears to increase moderately each time the number of responses required for reinforcement increases. An even more evident effect is in the day-to-day increase in the rate of responding when the number of responses required for reinforcement is not changed. This increase in time is particularly noticeable at the higher ratios. Boren (1956) and Skinner (1938), using

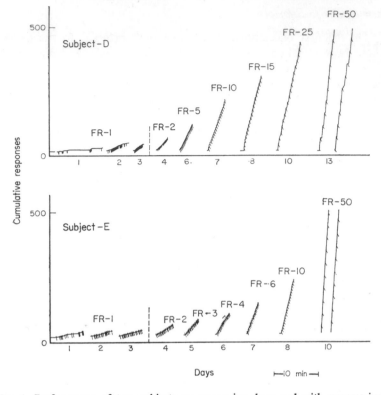

FIG. 1. Performance of two subjects on successive days and with progressively higher numbers of responses required for reinforcement. Each diagonal mark on the cumulative-response curves indicates the delivery of a reinforcement. Each curve represents the response record of one entire session (except for FR 50, which contains two curves).

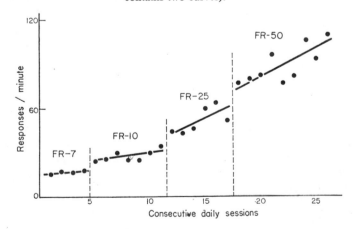

FIG. 2. Changes in daily response rate for one subject over 26 days.

animal subjects, have also found that the overall rate of responding increases as the number of responses required for reinforcement is raised. On the other hand, the observed increase in response rate over time has not been found in studies with animals, but has been noted by Ellis *et al.* (1960) in a study of mental defectives.

Figure 3 illustrates the typical performance of each subject on an FR 50 schedule. Responding under fixed-ratio schedules of reinforcement was observed to take place in a characteristic temporal pattern. The pattern

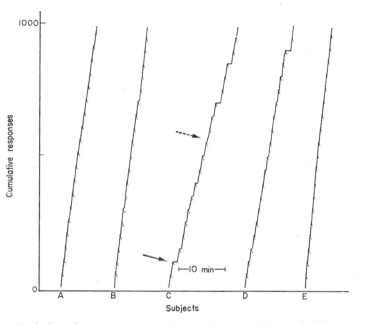

FIG. 3. Typical performance by each of five subjects during an FR 50 schedule of reinforcement. The solid arrow indicates the characteristic pause following reinforcement. The dotted arrow indicates one of the rare instances in which the pause occurs after responding has begun.

of responding was essentially bi-valued: either responding occurred at a high rate or not at all. Pausing, or the absence of responding, occurred immediately after reinforcement (solid arrow). Pauses occurred only rarely once responding had begun (dotted arrow); the frequency of such pauses was found to be no greater than is commonly observed with animal subjects in this laboratory. As is also true of animal subjects, the differences observed among subjects in overall response rates appear largely due to differences in the duration of pausing following reinforcement. These findings are quite similar to those reported by other investigators in work with normal humans

(Holland, 1958) mental defectives (Ellis, 1960), psychotic children (Lindsley, 1956), as well as with animal subjects (Ferster and Skinner, 1957).

Ordinarily, the number of responses required for reinforcement was increased only when a stable pattern of responding was well-established. Under this procedure, fixed-ratio requirements as great as 300 were maintained with no disruption of performance. In several cases, however, the ratio requirement for a particular subject was raised to a value much greater than had previously been programmed. Figure 4 illustrates the

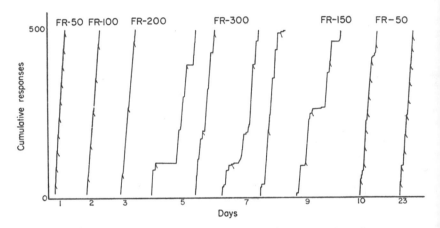

FIG. 4. Ratio strain resulting from rapid increases in the number of responses required for reinforcement and subsequent recovery when the ratio requirement is reduced to the former value. Typical segments of the response record are shown for each day.

effect of such "ratio strain" for one subject. Responding was successfully maintained as the number of responses required for reinforcement was raised from 50 to 100 on Day 2, and then to 200 on Day 3. On Day 4 the ratio was further increased to 300, where it was held through Day 7. The performance deteriorated severely on Day 5, although pausing was still partially localized after reinforcement. However, the subject ceased responding entirely after 15 reinforcements (not shown). By the fourth day at FR 300 (Day 7 in Fig. 4), deterioration was even more severe, and the subject stopped responding entirely after only 11 reinforcements (also not shown). On Days 8 and 9 the ratio requirement was reduced to 150. Even though performance was previously sustained at a ratio of 200, responding at FR 150 was now very erratic and terminated after reinforcements. When the ratio requirement was lowered to the original value of 50 (Day 10), sustained performance was again observed. However, pausing did not immediately localize after reinforcement, but it appeared at many points in the ratio. Over a period of 14 experimental sessions, normal performance gradually returned (Day 23). It may be noted that before the ratio requirement produced disturbance in normal performance, no increase was evident in the pause following reinforcement as a function of the ratio requirement. This absence of pausing at higher ratios is characteristic of the results observed throughout this investigation but differs from the results obtained with

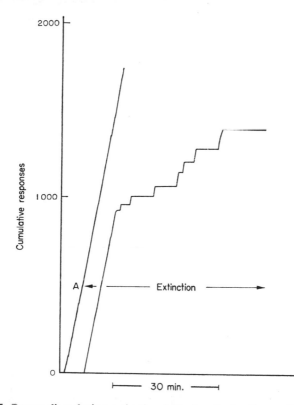

FIG. 5. Responding during extinction following fixed-ratio conditioning. Extinction begins at *A.*

animals (Boren, 1956; Ferster and Skinner, 1957). However, this same absence of increased pausing at higher fixed ratios can be noted in Holland's (1957) study of normal humans as well as in Ellis' (1960) study of mental defectives.

Occasionally, reinforcement was deliberately withheld. Figure 5 illustrates the typical pattern of responding which resulted during this extinction procedure. Prior to extinction, every 50th response had been reinforced. The reinforcements were then withheld for the remainder of the session (starting at *A*). The subject continued to respond at the usual high fixed-ratio rate for over 2000 responses before any pausing occurred. Periods of responding then began to alternate with progressively more frequent periods of no responding. The same bi-valued rate was obtained during extinction as was seen during reinforcement (Ferster and Skinner, 1957). Eventually, responding ceased entirely and the patient often left the room at this time. Extinction was attempted with all subjects, each showing this same response pattern and the same eventual cessation of responding.

Figure 6 shows the control of behavior exerted by conditioned reinforcement. Reinforcement was withheld beginning at *A*. As in Fig. 5, the

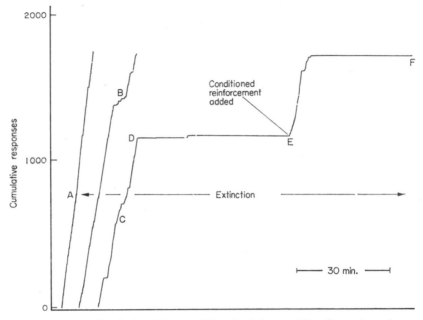

FIG. 6. Responding induced by conditioned reinforcers. The diagonal marks on the response record up to *A* indicate the delivery of the reinforcer and its accompanying stimuli. At *E* the conditioned-reinforcing stimuli were scheduled alone. Typical changes in rate during extinction are indicated at *B*, *C*, and *D*. (See text.) Neither the reinforcement nor conditioned reinforcement was delivered from *A* to *E*.

responses during this extinction procedure continue at the same rate as during reinforcement. The first major disruption in responding occurred at *B*. Occasionally, intermediate rates of responding appeared, such as at *C*, and the performance ceased almost entirely at *D*. The controlling apparatus was then set (prior to *E*), so that the next response and every 50th response thereafter would be followed by the buzzer sound and light change that normally accompanied the delivery of reinforcement. A response occurred at *E* which resulted in the rapid emission of over 600 more responses before responding again extinguished. The behavioral control exerted by these conditioned reinforcers is quite similar to that obtained in studies of animal behavior (Skinner, 1938).

It had been anticipated that great variability from day to day, as well as within each day, would characterize the performance of these chronic patients. As has been noted above, however, responding consistently occurred at the high rates that normally characterize fixed-ratio performance. Even more surprising is the consistency that was observed in the overall rate of response from day to day. In no case did the overall rate on any one day differ by more than 20 per cent from that of the previous day. Typically, the overall rate did not change by more than 10 per cent.

## SUMMARY

Five mental-hospital patients, diagnosed as schizophrenic, were conditioned under fixed-ratio schedules of reinforcement. Low rates of responding were initially observed in all subjects. Over a period of from 5 to 40 experimental sessions and at progressively larger ratio requirements, all subjects came to respond much more rapidly.

Much less day-to-day variation was present than might be expected of the behavior of psychotic patients. The overall response rate for a given patient usually varied less than 10 per cent from one day to the next.

The temporal pattern of responding which developed was found to be essentially bivalued: the subjects either responded at a very high rate or they did not respond at all. Periods of no responding typically occurred after reinforcement and only rarely at any other time. When the number of responses required for reinforcement was drastically increased, the usual pattern of performance was disrupted severely and responding ceased entirely after a short period. When the ratio requirement was then reduced to the original value, the disruption persisted for a number of experimental sessions. During extinction, responding was reduced, because of progressively more frequent periods of no responding, with little change in the local response rate. It was found that responding could be reinstated temporarily through the use of conditioned reinforcers.

The results of these experiments are highly similar to those obtained in studies of infra-humans and normal humans. The one exception to this essential similarity is the extended period of time necessary to produce high rates of responding.

## REFERENCES

BOREN, J. (1956) Response rate and resistance to extinction as functions of the fixed ratio, *Diss. Abst.*, **14**, 8, 1261.

ELLIS, N. R., BARNETT, C. D. and PRYER, M. W. (1960) Operant behavior in mental defectives: exploratory studies, *J. Exp. Anal. Behav.*, **1**, 63–69.

FERSTER, C. B. and SKINNER, B. F. (1957) *Schedules of reinforcement*, Appleton-Century-Crofts, New York.

HOLLAND, J. G. (1958) Human vigilance, *Science*, **128**, 61–67.

LINDSLEY, O. R. New techniques of analysis of psychotic behavior. Annual Technical Report No. 3 to the Group Psychology Branch, Office of Naval Research, September 1955–November 1956.

SKINNER, B. F. (1938) *The behavior of organisms*, Appleton Century, New York.

# The Psychiatric Nurse as a Behavioral Engineer*†

TEODORO AYLLON§ and JACK MICHAEL

*University of Houston*

THE BEHAVIOR which leads to a person's admission to a mental hospital often involves danger to himself or others, withdrawal from normal social functions, or a dramatic change from his usual mode of behaving. The professional staff of the psychiatric hospital directs its major efforts toward the discovery of the flaw in the patient's mental apparatus which presumably underlies his disturbing and dangerous behavior. Following the medical paradigm, it is presumed that once the basic disfunction has been properly identified the appropriate treatment will be undertaken and the various manifestations of the disfunction will disappear.

While diagnosis is being made and during subsequent treatment, the patient is under the daily care of the psychiatric nurses** in the ward. There, he often exhibits annoying and disrupting behavior which is usually regarded as a further manifestation of his basic difficulty. This behavior is sometimes identical with that which led to his admission; but at other times it seems to originate and develop within the hospital setting. Although it is still regarded as a reflection of his basic problem, this disruptive behavior may become so persistent that it engages the full energies of the nurses, and postpones, sometimes permanently, any effort on their part to deal with the so-called basic problem.

Disrupting behaviors usually consist in the patient's failure to engage in activities which are considered normal and necessary; or his persistent engagement in activities that are harmful to himself or other patients, or disrupting in other ways. For example, failures to eat, dress, bathe, interact

* This article is reprinted with the permission of the authors and editor from the *J. Exper. Anal. Behav.* **2**, 323–334 (1959).

† This paper contains a portion of the data from a doctoral dissertation submitted to the Department of Psychology, University of Houston, in partial fulfillment of the requirements for the Ph.D. degree, in August, 1959. Grateful acknowledgment is due to the members of the doctoral committee for their help and encouragement, and also to Drs. H. Osmond and I. Clancey, Superintendent and Clinical Director of the Saskatchewan Hospital, for making research at this institution possible.

§ Now at Saskatchewan Hospital, Weyburn, Saskatchewan.

** As used in this paper, "psychiatric nurse" is a generic term including all those who actually work on the ward (aides, psychiatric nurses, and registered nurses).

socially with other patients, and walk without being led are invariably disruptive. Hoarding various objects, hitting, pinching, spitting on other patients, constant attention-seeking actions with respect to the nurses, upsetting chairs in the dayroom, scraping paint from the walls, breaking windows, stuffing paper in the mouth and ears, walking on haunches or while in a squatting position are disruptive when they occur frequently and persistently.

At present, no systematic approach to such problems is available to the nurses. A psychodynamic interpretation is often given by psychiatrists and psychologists; and, for that matter, the nurses sometimes construct "depth" interpretations themselves. These interpretations seldom suggest any specific remedial actions to the nurses, who then have no other recourse than to act on the basis of common sense, or to take advantage of the physical therapy in vogue. From the point of view of modern behavior theory, such strong behaviors, or behavioral deficits, may be considered the result of events occurring in the patient's immediate or historical environment rather than the manifestations of his mental disorder. The present research represents an attempt to discover and manipulate some of these environmental variables for the purpose of modifying the problem behavior.

## RESEARCH SETTING

The research was carried out at the Saskatchewan Hospital, Weyburn Saskatchewan, Canada. It is a psychiatric hospital with approximately 1500 patients. Its most relevant features in terms of the present experiment are:

(1) The nurses are trained as psychiatric nurses in a 3-year program.

(2) They are responsible for the patients in their wards and enjoy a high degree of autonomy with respect to the treatment of a patient. The psychiatrists in the hospital function as advisers to the nursing staff. This means that psychiatrists do not give orders, but simply offer advise upon request from the psychiatric nurses.

(3) The nurses administer incoming and outgoing mail for the patients, visitor traffic, ground passes, paroles, and even discharge, although the last is often carried out after consultation with a psychiatrist. The nurses also conduct group therapy under the supervision of the psychiatric staff.

The official position of the senior author, hereafter referred to as $E$, was that of a clinical psychologist, who designed and supervised operant-conditioning "therapy" as applied by the nurses. Once his advice had been accepted, the nurses were responsible for carrying out the procedures specified by $E$. It was the privilege of the nurses to discontinue any treatment when they believed it was no longer necessary, when they were unable to implement it because of lack of staff, or when other ward difficulties made the treatment impossible. Whenever termination became necessary, $E$ was given appropriate notice.

## SUBJECTS

The subjects used in this investigation were all patients in the hospital. Of the total 19 patients, 14 had been classified as schizophrenic and 5 as mentally defective. Except for one female patient who was resident for only 7 months, all patients had been hospitalized for several years. Each subject presented a persistent behavior problem for which he had been referred to $E$ by the nursing staff. None of the $S$s was presently receiving psychotherapy, electroconvulsive therapy, or any kind of individual treatment.

The behaviors which were studied do not represent the most serious problems encountered in a typical psychiatric hospital. They were selected mainly because their persistence allowed them to survive several attempts at altering them.

## PROCEDURE

Prior to a systematic observational study of the patient's behavior the nurses were asked about the kind and frequency of naturally occurring reinforcement obtained by the patient, the duration and frequency of the problem behavior, and the possibility of controlling the reinforcement. Next, a period of systematic observation of each patient was undertaken prior to treatment. This was done to obtain objective information on the frequency of the behavior that was a problem to the nurses, and to determine what other behaviors were emitted by the patient.

Depending on the type of behavior, two methods were used for recording it. If the behavior involved interaction with a nurse, it was recorded every time it occurred. Entering the nurses' office, and eating regular meals are examples of such behavior.

Behavior which did not naturally involve contact with the nurse was recorded by a time-sampling technique. The nurse who was in charge of the program was supplied with a mimeographed record form. She sought out the patient at regular intervals; and without interaction with him, she recorded the behavior taking place at that time. She did not actually describe the behavior occurring, but rather classified it in terms of a pre-established trichotomy: (a) the undesirable behavior; (b) incompatible behavior which could ultimately displace the undesirable behavior; and (c) incompatible behavior which was not considered shapeable, such as sleeping, eating, and dressing. (Although these latter acts are certainly susceptible to the influence of reinforcement, they were regarded as neutral behaviors in the present research.) The period of observation varied from 1 to 3 min. After making an observation, the nurse resumed her regular ward activities until the next interval was reached, whereupon she again sought out the patient. Except for one patient, who was observed every 15 min, such observations were made every 30 min.

The relevant aspect of the data obtained by the time-check recording is the proportion of the total number of observations (excluding observations of neutral behavior) during which the patient was engaging in the behavior being altered. This will be called the relative frequency of the behavior. As an example, on the first day of the program of extinction for psychotic talk in the case of Helen (see below), 17 nonneutral behaviors were recorded. Of these, nine were classed as psychotic talk and eight as sensible talk; the relative frequency of psychotic talk was 0·53.

Although it would have been desirable, a long pretreatment period of observation was precluded by the newness of this approach and the necessity of obtaining the voluntary cooperation of the nurses.

After the pretreatment study had been completed, E instructed the ward nurses in the specific program that was to be carried out. On all cases the instruction was given at ward meetings and usually involved the cooperation of only two shifts, the 7 a.m. to 3 p.m., and 3 p.m. to 11 p.m., since the patients were usually asleep during the 11 p.m. to 7 a.m. shift.

The pretreatment studies indicated that what maintained undesirable behavior in most of the patients was the attention or social approval of the nurses toward that behavior. Therefore, the emphasis in instructing the nursing staff was on the operation of giving or withholding social reinforcement contingent upon a desired class of behavior. What follows illustrates the tenor of E's somewhat informal instructions to the nurses. "Reinforcement is something you do for or with a patient, for example, offering candy or a cigarette. Any way you convey attention to the patient is reinforcing. Patients may be reinforced if you answer their questions, talk to them, or let them know by your reaction that you are aware of their presence. The common-sense expression 'pay no attention' is perhaps closest to what must be done to discourage the patient's behavior. When we say 'do not reinforce a behavior', we are actually saying 'ignore the behavior and act deaf and blind whenever it occurs'."

When reinforcement was given on a fixed-interval basis, the nurse was instructed to observe the patient for about 1 to 3 min at regular intervals, just as in the pretreatment observation period. If desirable behavior was occuring at the time of observation, she would reinforce it; of not, she would go on about her duties and check again after the next interval had passed. Strictly speaking, this is fixed interval with a limited-hold contingency (Ferster and Skinner, 1957). During a program of extinction the nurse checked as above; however, instead of reinforcing the patient when he exhibited the behavior being altered, she simply recorded it and continued her other work. Except for specific directions for two patients, the nurses were not given instructions on the operation of aversive control.

The programs requiring time-sample observations started after breakfast (around 9 a.m.) and ended at bedtime (around 9 p.m.), and were usually carried out by only one of the 6 to 12 nurses on each shift. Because of the daily shift changes, the monthly ward rotations, and a systematic effort to give everyone experience at this new duty, no patient's program was followed by any one nurse for any considerable length of time. Nineteen, as a minimum, different nurses were involved in carrying out each patient's program. Over 100 different nurses participated in the entire research project.

Most social ward activities took place in the dayroom, which was a large living room containing a television set, card tables, magazines, and games. It was here that reinforcement was given for social behaviors toward patients, and for nonsocial behaviors which were strengthened to compete with undesirable behaviors. The fact that the research was carried out in five wards distributed far from each other in a four-floor building made it impossible for $E$ to observe all the nurses involved in the research at any one time. Because of the constant change in nursing personnel, most of $E$'s time was spent in instructing new people in the routines of the programs. In addition, since $E$ did not train the nurses extensively, he observed them, often without their knowledge, and supervised them in record keeping, administering reinforcement, extinction, etc. That the nurses performed effectively when $E$ was absent can be at least partially determined by the ultimate results.

## RESULTS

The results will be summarized in terms of the type of behavior problem and the operations used in altering the behavior. In general, the time required to change a specific behavior ranged from 6 to 11 weeks. The operations were in force for 24 hours a day, 7 days a week.

### Strong Behavior Treated by Extinction, or Extinction Combined with Reinforcement for Incompatible Behavior

In the five cases treated with this program, the reinforcer was the attention of the nurses; and the withholding of this reinforcer resulted in the expected decline in frequency. The changes occurring in three of the behavior problems, scrubbing the floor, spending too much time in the bathroom, and one of the two cases of entering the nurses' offices, were not complicated by uncontrollable variables. Lucille's case is presented in detail as representative of these three. The interpretation of the changes occuring in the other two behavior problems, entering the nurses' offices, and psychotic verbal behavior, is not so clearcut. Helen's case illustrates this point. For details concerning the cases not discussed in this paper, see Ayllon (1959).

*Lucille.* Lucille's frequent visits to the nurses' office interrupted and interfered with their work. She had been doing this for 2 years. During this time, she had been told that she was not expected to spend her time in the nurses' office. Frequently, she was taken by the hand or pushed back bodily into the ward. Because the patient was classified as mentally defective, the nurses had resigned themselves to tolerating her behavior. As one of the nurses put it, "It's difficult to tell her anything because she can't understand—she's too dumb".

The following instructions were given to the nurses: "During this program the patient must not be given reinforcement (attention) for entering the nurses' office. Tally every time she enters the office."

The pretreatment study indicated that she entered the office on an average of 16 times a day. As Fig. 1b shows, the average frequency was down to two entries per day by the seventh week of extinction, and the program was terminated. Figure 1a shows the same data plotted cumulatively.

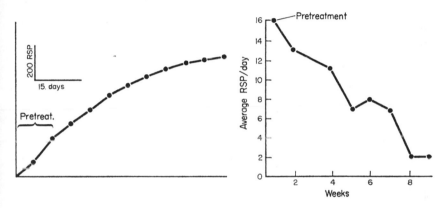

FIG. 1. Extinction of the response "entering the nurses' office"; (a) cumulative record; (b) conventional record.

*Helen.* This patient's psychotic talk had persisted for at least 3 years. It had become so annoying during the last 4 months prior to treatment that other patients had on several occasions beaten her in an effort to keep her quiet. She was described by one of the psychiatrists as a "delusional" patient who "feels she must push her troubles onto somebody else, and by doing this she feels she is free". Her conversation centered around her illegitimate child and the men she claimed were constantly pursuing her. It was the nurses' impression that the patient had "nothing else to talk about".

A 5-day pretreatment observation of the patient was made at 30-min intervals to compare the relative frequencies of psychotic and sensible content in her talk. Some of the nurses reported that, previously, when the patient started her psychotic talk, they listened to her in an effort to get at the "roots of her problem". A few nurses stated that they did not listen to what she was saying but simply nodded and remarked, "Yes, I understand", or some such comment, the purpose of which was to steer the patient's conversation on to some other topic. These reports suggested that the psychotic talk was being maintained by the nurses' reaction to it. While it is recognized that a distinction between psychotic and normal talk is somewhat arbitrary, this case was included in the research because of its value as a problem involving primarily verbal behavior.

The following instructions were given to the nurses: "During this program the patient must not be given reinforcement (attention) for her psychotic talk (about her illegitimate child and the men chasing her). Check the patient every 30 min, and (a) tally for psychotic talk; and (b) reinforce (and tally) sensible talk. If another patient fights with her, avoid making an issue of it.

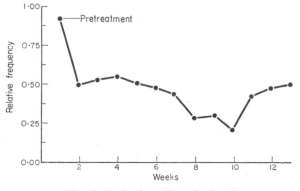

FIG. 2. Extinction of psychotic talk.

Simply stop the other patient from hurting her, but do so with a matter-of-fact attitude."

The 5-day observation period resulted in a relative frequency of psychotic talk of 0·91. During treatment (Fig. 2), the relative frequency dropped to less than 0·25; but, later on, it rose to a value exceeded only by the pretreatment level. The sudden increase in the patient's psychotic talk in the ninth week probably occurred because the patient had been talking to a social worker, who, unknown to the nurses, had been reinforcing her psychotic talk. The reinforcement obtained from the social worker appeared to generalize to her interaction with other patients and nurses. The patient herself told one of the nurses, "Well you're not listening to me. I'll have to go and see Miss _____ (the social worker) again, 'cause she told me that if she would listen to my past she could help me."

In addition to the reinforcement attributable to the social worker, two other instances of bootleg reinforcement came to light. One instance occurred when a hospital employee came to visit the ward, and, another, when volunteer ladies came to entertain the patients. These occasions were impossible to control, and indicate some of the difficulties of long-term control over verbal behavior.

It is of interest to note that since the reinforcement program began, the patient has not been attacked by the other patients and is only rarely abused verbally. These improvements were commented upon by the nurses, who were nevertheless somewhat disappointed. On the basis of the improvement shown in verbal behavior, the nurses had expected a dramatic overall change which did not occur.

*Strong Behavior Treated by Strengthening Incompatible Behavior*

This case represented an attempt to control violent behavior by strengthening an incompatible class of responses, and to recondition normal social approaches while the violence was under control. The first phase was quite successful; but errors in strategy plagued the last half of the program, and it was terminated by the nurses because the patient became more violent.

The immediate reason for referral was that the patient, Dotty, had become increasingly violent over the last 5 years, and recently attacked several patients and hospital personnel without any apparent reason. Since admission and up to the present, she had received many electroconvulsive-therapy treatments aimed at reducing this violence, with little or no success. In 1947, a physician recommended her as a good case for psychosurgery. In December of the same year, she attempted to strangle her mother who was visiting her at the time. In July 1948, the patient had a leucotomy. The situation had recently become so serious that at the least suspicious move on her part the nurses would put her in the seclusion room. She spent from 3 to 12 hr daily in that room.

A 5-day pretreatment study, at 15-min intervals, indicated that one of the nonviolent behaviors exhibited fairly often was "being on the floor" in the dayroom. The response included lying, squatting, kneeling, and sitting on the floor. Strengthening this class of responses would control the violence and, at the same time, permit the emotional behavior of other patients and nurses toward her to extinguish. To strengthen the patient's own social behavior, her approaches to the nurses were to be reinforced. The response "approach to nurse" was defined as spontaneous requests, questions or comments made by the patient to the nurse. Ultimately, the plan was to discontinue reinforcing being on the floor once the patient–nurse social interaction appeared somewhat normal. Presumably, this would have further increased the probability of approach to the nurses.

For the duration of the program, continuous social reinforcement was to be available for her approach to the nurses. Social reinforcement was to be available for the first 4 weeks only, on a fixed interval of 15 min, contingent on the response being on the floor. For the last 4 weeks, social reinforcement was to be withheld for being on the floor.

The following instructions were given to the nurses for the first 4 weeks of the program: "Reinforce (and tally) her approaches to you every time they occur. Check the patient every 15 min, and reinforce (and tally) the behavior being on the floor."

From the fifth week on the instructions were modified as follows: "Continue reinforcing (and tallying) her approaches to you every time they occur. Check the patient every 15 min, and tally but do not reinforce the behavior being on the floor."

During the period of reinforcement, as shown in Fig. 3, the relative frequency of the response being on the floor increased from the pretreatment level of less than 0·10 to a value of 0·21. During the succeeding 4 weeks of extinction, the frequency of being on the floor returned to the pretreatment level.

It was clear that being on the floor was incompatible with the fighting behavior and that the latter could be controlled by reinforcing the former.

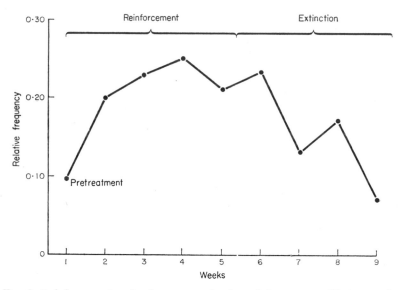

FIG. 3. Reinforcement and subsequent extinction of the response "being on the floor"

During the period of reinforcement for being on the floor, she attacked a patient once; but during the period of extinction, she made eight attacks on others. Her approaches to nurses increased overall during the 4 weeks of reinforcement, but they decreased during the last 4 weeks, even though they were still being reinforced. This decrease paralleled the decrease in being on the floor. While being on the floor was undergoing extinction, attacks on the patients and nurses increased in frequency, and the nurses decided to return to the practice of restraining the patient. The program was terminated at this point.

The patient's failure to make the transition from being on the floor to approaching the nurses suggests that the latter response was poorly chosen. It was relatively incompatible with being on the floor. This meant that a previously reinforced response would have to be extinguished before the transition was possible, and this, too, was poor strategy with a violent patient.

## Weak Behavior Strengthened by Escape and Avoidance Conditioning

Two female patients generally refused to eat unless aided by the nurses. One, Janet, had to be forcefully taken to the dining room, where she would permit the nurses to spoonfeed her. The other patient, Mary, was spoonfed in a room adjacent to the dining room. Both patients had little social contact with others and were reported to be relatively indifferent to attention by the nurses. Both were also reported to care only for the neat and clean appearance of their clothing. Mary had been at the hospital for 7 months, and Janet had been there for 28 years. These two patients were in different wards and apparently did not know each other.

The program involved a combination of escape and avoidance conditioning, with food spilling as the aversive stimulus. All spoonfeeding was to be accompanied by some food spilling which the patient could escape by feeding herself after the first spilling, or avoid by feeding herself the entire meal. Social reinforcement was to be given contingent on feeding herself.

It was hoped that once self-feeding began to occur with some regularity, it would come under the control of environmental variables which maintain this behavior in most people, such as convenience, social stimulation at meal time, etc. In both cases, the program ultimately resulted in complete self-feeding, which now has been maintained for over 10 months. Janet's behavior change was complicated by a history of religious fasting, and her change took a little longer. Mary's case will be given here in detail.

The following instructions were given to the nurses: "Continue spoonfeeding the patient; but from now on, do it in such a careless way that the patient will have a few drops of food fall on her dress. Be sure not to overdo the food dropping, since what we want to convey to the patient is that it is difficult to spoonfeed a grown-up person, and not that we are mean to her. What we expect is that the patient will find it difficult to depend on your skill to feed her. You will still be feeding her, but you will simply be less efficient in doing a good job of it. As the patient likes having her clothes clean, she will have to choose between feeding herself and keeping her clothes clean, or being fed by others and risking getting her clothes soiled. Whenever she eats on her own, be sure to stay with her for a while (3 min is enough), talking to her, or simply being seated with her. We do this to reinforce her eating on her own. In the experience of the patient, people become nicer when she eats on her own."

During the 8-day pretreatment study, the patient ate 5 meals on her own, was spoonfed 12, and refused to eat 7. Her weight at this time was 99 pounds.

Her typical reaction to the schedule was as follows: the nurse would start spoonfeeding her; but after one or two "good" spoonfuls, the nurse would carelessly drop some food on her dress. This was continued until either the patient requested the spoon, or the nurse continued spoonfeeding her the entire meal. The behavior the patient adopted included (a) reaching for the spoon after a few drops had fallen on her dress; (b) eating completely on her own; (c) closing her mouth so that spoonfeeding was terminated; or (d) being spoonfed the entire meal. Upon starting the schedule, the most frequent of all these alternatives was the first; but after a while, the patient ate on her own immediately. The relevant data are shown in Fig. 4. On the 12th day, the patient ate all three meals on her own for the first time. Four

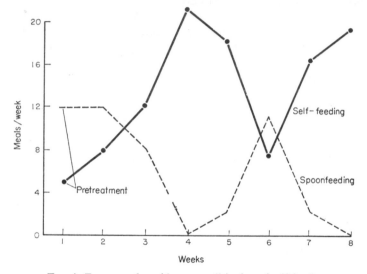

FIG. 4. Escape and avoidance conditioning of self-feeding.

meals were refused out of the last 24: one meal was missed because she stated she didn't like "liver" and the other three because she said she was not hungry. Her weight when she left the hospital was 120 pounds, a gain of 21 pounds over her pretreatment weight.

Mary's relapse in the fifth week, after she had been eating well for 2 weeks, was quite unexpected. No reasonable explanation is suggested by a study of her daily records; but, after she had been spoonfed several meals in a row, the rumor developed that someone had informed the patient that the food spilling was not accidental. In any event, the failure to feed herself lasted only about 5 days.

Since the patient's hospital admission had been based on her refusal to eat, accompanied by statements that the food was poisoned, the success of the program led to her discharge. It is to be noted that although nothing was done to deal directly with her claims that the food was poisoned, these statements dropped out of her repertoire as she began to eat on her own.

*Strong Behavior Weakened through a Combination of Extinction for Social Attention and Stimulus Satiation*

For 5 years, several mentally defective patients on the same ward, Harry, Joe, Tom and Mac, had collected papers, rubbish, and magazines and carried these around with them inside their clothing next to their body. The most serious offender was Harry, whose hoarding resulted in skin rashes. He carried so much trash and so persistently that for the last 5 years the nurses routinely "dejunked" him several times during the day and before he went to bed.

An analysis of the situation indicated that the patient's hoarding behavior was probably maintained by the attention he derived because of it and by the actual scarcity of printed matter. There were few papers or magazines in the ward. Some were brought in occasionally; but since they were often torn up and quickly disappeared, the nurses did not bring them in very often.

It was expected that flooding the ward with magazines would decrease the hoarding behavior after the paradigm of satiation. Similarly, the availability of any magazines was expected to result in their being the major object of hoarding. The latter would facilitate an easier measurement of this behavior.

In addition, social reinforcement was to be withheld for hoarding magazines and rubbish. The results for all patients were essentially similar: a gradual decrease in hoarding. After 9 weeks of satiation and extinction, the program was terminated, since hoarding was no longer a problem. This improvement has been maintained for the last 6 months.

The following instructions were given to the nurses: "During this program the patients Harry, Mac, Joe and Tom must not be given reinforcement (attention) for hoarding. There will be a full supply of magazines in the dayroom. Every night, after all patients have gone to bed, replenish the magazine supply in the dayroom. Every night while the patients are in bed, check their clothes to record the amount of hoarding. Do not, however, take their hoarding from them!"

The original plan was to count the number of magazines in the patient's clothing after they had gone to bed. This is, in fact, the dependent variable shown in Fig. 5 for Joe, Tom and Mac. The recording for Harry had to be changed, however; after 4 days of the program, he no longer carried the rubbish or magazines in his clothing. Instead, he kept a stack of magazines on his lap while he was sitting in the dayroom. The number of magazines in his stack was counted when he left the dayroom for supper, and this is the dependent variable shown for Harry in Fig. 5. (Mac was out of the ward for 3 weeks because of illness.)

Prior to the program, one of the nurses questioned the possibility and even advisability of changing Harry's behavior. Her argument was that "behavior has its roots in the personality of the individual. The fact that he hoards so much indicates that Harry has a strong need for security. I don't see how are we going to change this need, and I also wonder if it is a good thing to do that." This was a point of view commonly encountered, especially regarding relatively nonverbal patients.

It would seem in this case that Harry transferred his security needs from hoarding rubbish and magazines to sitting in the dayroom and looking at magazines, especially during T.V. commercials. The transfer occurred with no apparent signs of discomfort on his part.

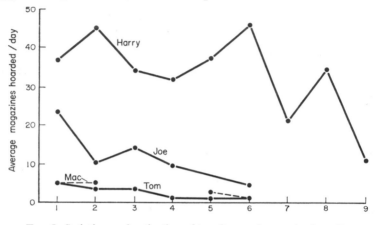

FIG. 5. Satiation and extinction of two forms of magazine hoarding.

### Other Cases

Combinations of extinction, reinforcement, and avoidance programs were set up for three patients; in two of these problem behavior was eliminated in only a few weeks. The program of the third patient was followed for 20 days and then terminated since he had shown no changes by that time. An interpretation of the outcome of each of these programs is rendered questionable by the number of controlling variables involved and the nature of the changes.

The pretreatment study of four additional patients showed that the problem behavior of three of them did not occur often enough to justify carrying through a program; and in the fourth case, no easily controllable variables were available and, again, no program was undertaken.

### DISCUSSION

On the basis of this work, further research along the same lines is now under way.* The present results are presented in this preliminary form in the

* This new project is supported by a grant from the Commonwealth Fund, and is being conducted under the auspices of the Saskatchewan Hospital, Weyburn, Saskatchewan, Canada.

hope that they will provide encouragement to those who are in a position to conduct similar research. Therefore, it will be useful to mention a few other aspects of this work.

A major problem concerns the use of nurses as experimental assistants as well as substitutes for the recording and programming apparatus of the laboratory. There is no question as to the greater reliability of the ordinary laboratory component. In large part, however, the nurses' failures in carrying out $E$'s instructions were unsystematic with respect to the results obtained, and although undesirable, they do not by any means render this kind of work uninterpretable. Systematic errors in observation can be reduced to some extent by dealing with response classes that are relatively easily identified. But, of course, this problem will become more serious as efforts are made to alter more subtle aspects of behavior. Perhaps the only solution is to be dissatisfied with one's techniques and principles until the behavioral changes are so obvious as to render statistical analysis superfluous.

Another question concerns the acceptability of this approach to the hospital staff. The nurses and psychiatrists who were familiar with the "reinforcement programs", as they were called, were given questionnaires and interviews to determine their attitudes toward this work. The results indicate a mildly favorable reception in general, with some enthusiastic support from both nurses and psychiatrists.

Regarding time actually spent in carrying out the programs, it might seem unreasonable to expect the already overworked nurse to devote 2 or 3 min every half-hour to observation and recording. However, this is only about 40 min of an 8-h shift; and, besides, much of her work stems from patient's behavior problems, the elimination of which would make the 40 min an excellent investment of time.

Two sources of possible misunderstanding between $E$ and nurses should be pointed out. First, when nurses were asked about the sort of problems they had in the ward, if no dramatic behaviors, such as attempts at suicide, or violent acts, had been recently reported, they often denied having any problems. Problems also went unrecognized because they were considered unsolvable. For example, since most nurses attributed the behavior of a patient to his diagnosis or age, little or no effort was made to discover and manipulate possibly relevant environmental variables.

Second, even after a behavior had been modified, it was not uncommon to hear nurses remark, "We've changed her behavior. So what? She's still psychotic." It seemed that once a persistent problem behavior was eliminated, its previous importance was forgotten and other undesirable aspects of the patient's repertoire were assumed to be the most important ones. In general, their specific expectations were unclear or unverbalized, and they tended to be somewhat dissatisfied with any change less than total "cure".

Finally, an objection often raised against this approach is that the behavior changes may be only temporary. However, permanent elimination of ward behavior problems requires a permanent elimination of the environmental variables that shape them up and maintain them. The clinical belief that a favorable behavioral change, if properly accomplished, will be permanent probably rests on a faulty evaluation of the role of environmental variables in controlling behavior. Certainly, it is not based on any actual accomplishments in the field of mental health.

## REFERENCES

AYLLON, T. (1959) The application of reinforcement theory to ward behavior problems. Unpublished doctoral dissertation, University of Houston.

FERSTER, C. B. and SKINNER, B. F. (1957) *Schedules of reinforcement*, Appleton-Century-Crofts, New York.

# Operant Stuttering: The Control of Stuttering
# Behavior through Response-contingent Consequences*†

BRUCE FLANAGAN, ISRAEL GOLDIAMOND

*Southern Illinois University*

and NATHAN AZRIN

*Anna State Hospital*

THE ATTEMPT to understand and control stuttering has received considerable attention in both clinic and laboratory. The concept of anxiety has played a major role in formulations in both areas; stuttering is considered "an anxiety-motivated avoidant response that becomes 'conditioned' to the cues or stimuli associated with its occurrence".[5]

This study reports a preliminary investigation designed to explore the extent to which stuttering can be brought under operant control.

Three male stutterers from the speech clinic, ages 15, 22 and 37, served as Ss. The S read from loose printed pages; every time he stuttered, E pressed a microswitch which activated an Esterline–Angus recorder. A check was run by turning the microswitch over to another E, who had not been informed of the nature of the experiment, and instructing him to press upon each moment of stuttering. The E observed S through a one-way mirror in a room adjoining the experimental room, and heard him through a sound-amplification system.

When a curve of stuttering frequency considered smooth was obtained, E turned a switch which initiated a 30 min period of response-contingent stimuli. After this period, S was observed for another 30 min without such stimuli following each press of the microswitch. No specific $S^D$s were introduced to differentiate periods. A constant noise level of 60 db was present throughout the experiment.

Response-contingent periods were of two kinds. During the *aversive period*, every depression of the microswitch which activated the recorder also produced a 1-sec blast of a 6000-cycle tone at 105 db in S's earphones.

* This article is reprinted with the permission of the authors and editor from the *J. Exper. Anal. Behav.* 1, 173–177 (1958).

† The authors wish to express their appreciation to Dr. Chester J. Atkinson, of Southern Illinois University, for his assistance with equipment problems and active interest during the course of the study.

During the *escape period*, such a blast was constantly present; every depression of the microswitch shut off the tone for 5 sec. Such use of noise as an aversive stimulus which was contingent upon responding or which could be escaped by responding followed a procedure used by Azrin.[1]

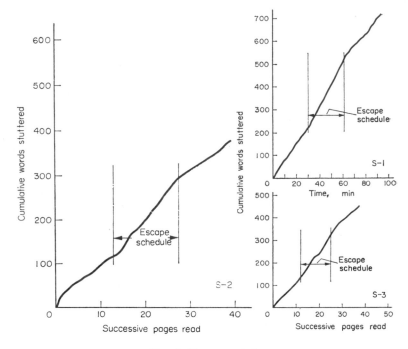

FIG. 1. Escape periods.

Each *S* was run on two consecutive days. For *S-1*, the escape period was presented on the first day, and the aversive on the following day. For *S-2* and *S-3*, the order was aversive-escape.

Record was kept not only of stuttering frequency, but also of elapsed time and number of pages of copy read. Data are presented in the accompanying figures. For all *S*'s, the ordinate is cumulative words stuttered. For *S-1*, the abscissa is time, producing rate curves. For *S-2* and *S-3*, however, the abscissa is number of pages read, and the curves depict stutters per page read.

Curves for sessions containing escape periods are presented in Fig. 1. For all *S*s, stuttering increases when escape from the tone is made contingent upon stuttering. When the tone is turned off, stuttering is no longer followed by such consequences, and the rate drops. All *S*s display short interludes of diminished rate, characterized by irregularities in the curves. All sessions open with a high-burst stuttering activity. This concurs with findings of "adaptation" studies in stuttering.[7]

Curves for sessions containing aversive periods for *S-1* and *S-3* are presented in Fig. 2. Making presentation of a blast contingent upon stuttering tends to depress the rate of stuttering during each period in a marked manner; *S-1* seems to have been moving toward an asymptote of complete suppression. The compensatory rise previously noted [2, 8] following cessation of aversive consequences is pronounced in both *S*s. The adaptation burst is again present.

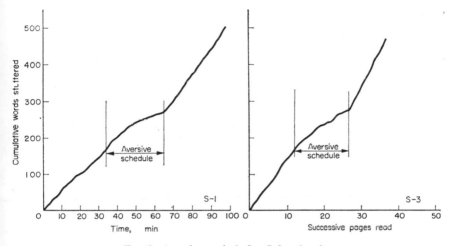

FIG. 2. Aversive periods for *S-1* and *S-3*.

The aversive-period session for *S-2* is presented in Fig. 3, which depicts total suppression of stuttering during the aversive period, and beyond. The period during which definition of stuttering was turned over to another *E* is designated under the heading, Control *E*.* There is no discernible effect on response rate, arguing for the validity of the major *E*'s judgment of stuttering. The adaptation burst is again present.

Comparisons of the various figures tend to indicate that number of pages read can apparently be equated with time as a component of rate. Such an equation would follow if rate of reading itself, that is, pages per unit of time, were constant. For *S-2* and *S-3*, the mean reading times in minutes per page are:

|       | Base line | Escape | Final | Base line | Aversive | Final |
|-------|-----------|--------|-------|-----------|----------|-------|
| *S-2* | 2·20      | 2·12   | 2·07  | 2·28      | 2·10     | 2·30  |
| *S-3* | 2·48      | 2·30   | 2·42  | 2·50      | 2·65     | 2·75  |

* Both *E*s are speech therapists. The major *E* is a stutterer who has had 7 years of experience as a speech therapist specializing in stuttering.

The only safe conclusion seems to be that *S-3* reads more slowly than *S-2*; the apparent randomness of the data suggests constancy in reading rate.

The data presented suggest that the stuttering response is an operant which occurs in the context of another operant, namely, verbal behavior. Although one cannot stutter without talking, neither can one limp without walking, and limping can be controlled separately from walking. Reading

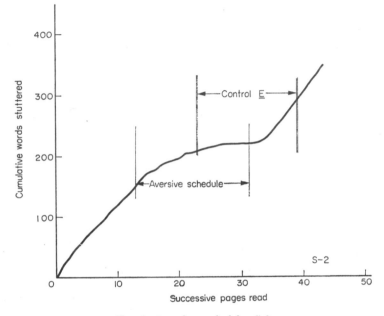

Fig. 3. Aversive period for *S-2*.

rate was apparently not systematically affected by the response-contingent stimuli which controlled stuttering, hence the two are separable responses. The operant nature of reading has been discussed elsewhere;[9] the way in which stuttering responses reacted to operant controls in this study cannot be distinguished from reactions of other operant behaviors, and suggests that they are in this class of behaviors.

When termination of a noxious stimulus was made contingent upon stuttering, response rate rose. When onset of a noxious stimulus was made contingent upon stuttering, response suppression occurred, displaying compensation upon cessation of such consequences. For one *S*, the response was completely suppressed, and this suppression continued beyond the termination of the aversive contingency. Where *S* avoids certain consequences by suppressing a response, the suppresssion will be maintained by absence of the consequences. Accordingly, elimination of the consequences by *E* will tend to maintain the suppression. The adaptation effects reported in the speech literature were found here. These consist of an initial burst of stuttering, which then "adapts out", that is, drops to a base-line rate. These curves have been considered similar to respondent extinction curves,[10] although classical extinction is not obtained.[7] Consideration of conditions related to the establishment of an operant base line would involve a stuttering response being occasioned by $S^D$s. Placing a stutterer in a speech clinic with instructions to speak is not a procedure calculated to diminish generalization of the $S^D$s to new stimuli present in the experimental session. The response rate should rise. As the experiment progresses, and no new consequences are applied to response occasioned by the new $S^D$s, we are establishing conditions for discrimination of new from old $S^D$s; the new stimuli lose their control; the situation is "perceived as familiar", or "perceived as non-threatening". Operant discrimination involves *operant* extinction of responses to $S$, the new $S^D$s.

Concerning the relationship of stuttering to anxiety, presumably of a respondent type, anxiety is associated with the suppression of operant behavior;[3] stuttering behavior was both suppressed and intensified, and these changes are explainable on an operant basis. Since the stuttering response can be isolated from regular speech as a unit of response, we might speculate that such isolation would come about through differential consequences applied to breaks in speech, and smooth speech. Such differentation might relate to the anxiety of the parent (rather than the child) upon hearing a stuttering response. She may reinforce the behavior by becoming attentive, and should she later decide to extinguish by ignoring, the usual burst of increased stuttering behavior during onset of extinction[4, 6] might increase *her* anxiety, lead to remorse, reinstatement of reinforcement—and the establishment of a variable-interval schedule making extinction all the more difficult.

If further research supports the operant analysis presented here, then it would seem that controlled alteration of such behavior, that is, therapy, would involve application of procedures from the experimental analysis of operant behavior, notably of responses reinforced on a variable-interval schedule.

## REFERENCES

1. AZRIN, N. (1958) Noise and human behavior, *J. Exp. Anal. Behav.*, **2**, 183–200.
2. ESTES, W. K. (1944) An experimental study of punishment, *Psychol. Monogr.*, **57**, No. 263.
3. ESTES, W. K. and SKINNER, B. F. (1941) Some quantitative properties of anxiety, *J. Exp. Psychol.*, **29**, 290–400.
4. FERSTER, C. B. (1957) Withdrawal of positive reinforcement as punishment, *Science*, **126**, 509.
5. JOHNSON, W. J. (1955) *Stuttering in children and adults*, University of Minnesota (Minneapolis).

6. KELLER, F. S. and SCHOENFELD, W. N. (1950) *Principles of psychology*, Appleton-Century-Crofts, New York.
7. ROUSEY, C. L. (1958) Stuttering severity during prolonged spontaneous speech, *J. Speech and Hearing Res.*, 1, 40–47.
8. SKINNER, B. F. (1938) *The behavior of organisms*, Appleton Century New York.
9. SKINNER, B. F. (1958) *Verbal behavior*, Appleton-Century-Crofts, New York.
10. WISCHNER, G. J. (1950) Stuttering behavior and learning: a preliminary theoretical formulation, *J. Speech and Hearing Dis.*, 15, 324–325.

# Conditioning against Silences in Group Therapy*

R. V. HECKEL, S. L. WIGGINS and H. C. SALZBERG

*Veterans Administration Hospital, Augusta, Georgia*

## PROBLEM

Auditory stimuli ranging from white noise to high frequency, high intensity sounds have been used to produce change in the operant levels of behavior in both human and animal subjects, chiefly as masking, distracting, interfering and in some cases avoidant stimuli associated with tasks having varying degrees of motivation for the subjects.[1, 2, 4] There have also been a series of studies on verbal reinforcement which date from Thorndike and Rock's[7] work on learning without awareness and developed by Greenspoon,[3] Philbrick and Postman,[5] Postman and Jarrett,[6] and elaborated on by studies in which certain verbal behaviors are instituted or changed by activities on the part of the experimenter, in most instances without the subject's awareness of these activities. The purpose of this study was to determine the effectiveness of an "unpleasant" auditory stimulus for eliminating silences in a group therapeutic setting.

## METHOD

*Subjects.* The subjects for this experiment were white, male in-patients varying on each experimental day between seven and nine.

*Apparatus.* An air-conditioned, soundproofed experimental room was equipped with an observational one-way mirror and two microphones for listening and recording purposes. A speaker hidden in an air conditioning vent was used for transmission of the auditory stimulus. The auditory stimulus was produced by a standard Maico audiometer and consisted of a continuous tone of 85 db at 4000 c/s.

*Procedure.* The group chosen for this experiment consisted of patients in a continuing psychotherapy group which had been in operation for several months meeting for a one-hour session twice a week with two therapists present. In the initial stage of the experiment the total number and duration

* This article is reprinted with the permission of the authors and editor from the *J. Clin. Psychol.* **28**, 216–217 (1962).

279

of silences following a ten-second period of silence, for the first fifteen minutes of the hour, were recorded for four group meetings. This served as the control data and yielded an operant level of responding.

The experimental treatment consisted of four group meetings in which the auditory stimulus was presented after each ten-second period of silence, in the first fifteen minutes of each session. The stimulus was continued until some member of the group "broke" the silence by speaking.

The last four meetings served as extinction trials and again the number and duration of silences were recorded. During each phase of the experiment the therapists refrained from initiating comments or statements for the first fifteen minutes of each group meeting. The subjects were given no information about the experiment nor the sound other than to inform them, in response to their questions, that the sound was probably some malfunctioning of the recording apparatus used in the room.

## RESULTS AND DISCUSSION

The effectiveness of the auditory stimulus in reducing the number and duration of silences is illustrated in Fig. 1. A Spearman rank order correlation of 0·79 was found between the number and duration of silences. The

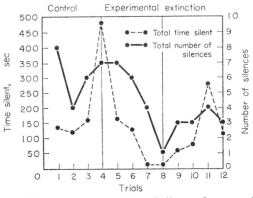

FIG. 1. Total time silent and total number of silences for control, experimental and extinction trials.

greatest total time spent in silence was exhibited in the control trials followed by a decrement in total time almost to the point of a complete absence of silence in the third and fourth trials of the experimental treatment. During the extinction trials, there was a slight increase in total time and number of silences but at a much lower level of responding than was found during the control trials.

These results indicate that though none of the subjects of the experiment recognized nor stated the principle governing the correct response or the purpose of the auditory stimulus, they did learn to make the correct response.

This supports Thorndike's hypothesis suggesting that learning can be automatic and independent of the subject's awareness.

It also suggests that a standard laboratory technique can operate effectively in reinforcing or altering verbal responses. For example, an auditory stimulus could be introduced into group therapy sessions to reduce the number and duration of silences. This is particularly useful in groups which are characterized by prolonged "warm-up" periods during each therapy session. A longer period of silence on the part of the therapist was not used since investigation of this particular group indicated that few silences occurred after the first fifteen minutes or warm-up period. The shorter time period also lessened the possibility of group members becoming aware of the experimental procedure.

Another point of interest is the type of stimulus used in the study. As was mentioned previously it was felt that the stimulus employed in the experiment was "unpleasant" since it was sustained in duration for a period of time and several members of the group complained about its annoying qualities. In light of the results obtained it now seems desirable to test a series of other combinations of frequency and intensity to determine the optimum stimulus conditions in eliminating prolonged periods of silence, and also to perhaps generate an auditory stimulus of a more pleasant nature, such as music, to determine what effects, if any, these will have as reinforcers of verbal responses in group therapy.

## SUMMARY

An unpleasant auditory stimulus was introduced into a continuing psychotherapy group to determine the effect of the stimulus in eliminating silences during the first fifteen minutes of each session. A reduction in both number and duration of silences was found during the treatment trials of the experiment and after the stimulus was discontinued the number and duration of silences did not reach the former operant level.

## REFERENCES

1. BARNES, G. W. and KISH, G. B. (1957) Reinforcing properties of the termination of intense auditory stimulation, *J. Comp. Physiol. Psychol.*, **50**, 40–53.
2. BARNES, G. W. and KISH, G. B. (1960) Reinforcing properties of the onset of auditory stimulation. National Science Foundation Research Terminal Report, No. NSF-G 8609.
3. GREENSPOON, J. (1955) The reinforcing effect of two spoken sounds and the frequency of two responses. *Amer. J. Psychol.*, **68**, 409–416.
4. HEISE, G. A. and MILLER, G. A. (1951) Problem solving by small groups using various communication nets, *J. Abnorm. Soc. Psychol.* **46**, 327–335.
5. PHILBRICK, E. B. and POSTMAN, L. (1955) A further analysis of 'learning without awareness'. *Amer. J. Psychol.*, **68**, 417–424.
6. POSTMAN, L. and JARRETT, R. F. (1952) An experimental analysis of 'learning without awareness', *Amer. J. Psychol.*, **65**, 244–255.
7. THORNDIKE, E. I. and ROCK, R. T., JR. (1934) Learning without awareness of what is being learned or intent to learn it, *J. Exp. Psychol.* **17**, 1–19.

# PART III

# OTHER METHODS

RECIPROCAL inhibition and operant conditioning are not the only methods available to behaviour therapists, and this section of the book presents selected examples to demonstrate that learning theory contains many other concepts and methods which can be used with advantage. Such methods may aspire to be complete therapies of major neuroses in themselves, as for instance Ellis's "rational psychotherapy", or more frequently they constitute the application of some law of learning theory to a specific symptom under well-controlled conditions. The symptoms most frequently attacked in this connexion have been tics, bedwetting, stammering and similar monosymptomatic disorders; the reason for their selection has probably usually been simply the ease with which the dependent variable (the symptom) could be shown to depend in a quantitative fashion upon the independent variable (the treatment). This preference should of course not be interpreted to mean that these are the only types of disorders to be so treated; in principle there is no restriction whatever upon the universality of the laws of learning involved in the treatment. It is natural that in demonstrating the validity of a theoretical deduction, such as that involved in extinction with reinforcement, the research worker would select a symptom which would show directly, and without argument or ambiguous interpretation, the results of the experimental manipulation. The time will no doubt come fairly soon when the experimental paradigms can be extended to less clear-cut and obvious types of symptom.

Hypnosis has been put into this group, in spite of the fact that few people would perhaps regard it as deriving in any sense from modern learning theory. I believe that a good case could be made out, and has indeed been made by Platanov, that hypnosis may be regarded as being a phenomenon dependent very much on *verbal conditioning*; our own demonstration that a person's facility for forming conditioned responses (eye-blink conditioning) is closely related to his facility for becoming deeply hypnotized seems to point in the same direction as the Russian work. It seems unfortunate that hypnosis has fallen into disrepute, quite without any objective reason, and is now hardly used at all in Western psychiatric practices. It may be true that when inappropriately used it may lead to recovery, speedily followed by recrudescence of symptoms; even this is by no means certain, however, as the literature on the subject is so poor, anecdotal and lacking in even the most elementary form of control that it would almost be true to say that literally nothing can be asserted with reasonable certainty other than that hypnosis is occasionally followed by remission of symptoms, and that these symptoms may occasionally return.* Psychiatry is notoriously given to fads, and the present ostracism of hypnosis, just like its one-time prevalence, is not based on either theoretical or experimental foundations which can stand up to scrutiny. Its integration with behaviour therapy would appear to be one of the most worth-while developments of the future; perhaps one might also express the hope that in the course of this development some light might be thrown on the psychological and physiological nature of the state of hypnosis itself.

* A good summary is available in HILGARD *et al.*, *J. Nerv. Ment. Dis.* (1961) **133**, 461–418.

# Rational Psychotherapy*

### ALBERT ELLIS

### I

THE CENTRAL theme of this paper is that psychotherapists can help their clients to live the most self-fulfilling, creative, and emotionally satisfying lives by teaching these clients to organize and discipline their thinking. Does this mean that *all* human emotion and creativity can or should be controlled by reason and intellect? Not exactly:

The human being may be said to possess four basic processes—perception, movement, thinking, and emotion—all of which are integrally interrelated. Thus, thinking, aside from consisting of bioelectric changes in the brain cells, and in addition to comprising remembering, learning, problem-solving, and similar psychological processes, also is, and to some extent has to be, sensory, motor, and emotional behavior.[1,4] Instead, then, of saying, "Jones thinks about this puzzle", we should more accurately say, "Jones perceives-moves-feels-THINKS about this puzzle". Because, however, Jones' activity in relation to the puzzle may be *largely* focused upon solving it, and only *incidentally* on seeing, manipulating, and emoting about it, we may perhaps justifiably emphasize only his thinking.

Emotion, like thinking and the sensori-motor processes, we may define as an exceptionally complex state of human reaction which is integrally related to all the other perception and response processes. It is not *one* thing, but a combination and holistic integration of several seemingly diverse, yet actually closely related, phenomena.[1]

Normally, emotion arises from direct stimulation of the cells in the hypothalamus and autonomic nervous system (e.g. by electrical or chemical stimulation) or from indirect excitation via sensori-motor, cognitive, and other conative processes. It may theoretically be controlled, therefore, in four major ways. If one is highly excitable and wishes to calm down, one may (*a*) take electroshock or drug treatments; (*b*) use soothing baths or

* This is a group of four papers, grouped together by the editor, and slightly abridged to remove duplications. Changes have been approved by the author. The articles are reprinted with permission from the author and the editors of the following journals:

*J. Gen. Psychol.* **59**, 35–49 (1958); *J. Clin. Psychol.* **15**, 338–343 (1959); *J. Psychol.* **51**, 141–150 (1961); *J. Clin. Psychol.* **13**, 344–350 (1957).

relaxation techniques; (c) seek someone one loves and quiet down for his sake; or (d) reason oneself into a state of calmness by showing oneself how silly it is for one to remain excited.

Although biophysical, sensori-motor, and emotive techniques are all legitimate methods of controlling emotional disturbances, they will not be considered in this paper, and only the rational technique will be emphasized. Rational psychotherapy is based on the assumption that thought and emotion are not two entirely different processes, but that they significantly overlap in many respects and that therefore disordered emotions can often (though not always) be ameliorated by changing one's thinking.

A large part of what we call emotion, in other words, is nothing more or less than a certain kind—a biased, prejudiced, or strongly evaluative kind—of thinking. What we usually label as thinking is a relatively calm and dispassionate appraisal (or organized perception) of a given situation, an objective comparison of many of the elements in this situation, and a coming to some conclusion as a result of this comparing or discriminating process.[4] Thus, a thinking person may observe a piece of bread, see that one part of it is mouldy, remember that eating this kind of mould previously made him ill, and therefore cut off the mouldy part and eat the non-mouldy section of the bread.

An emoting individual, on the other hand, will tend to observe the same piece of bread, and remember so violently or prejudicedly his previous experience with the mouldy part, that he will quickly throw away the whole piece of bread and therefore go hungry. Because the thinking person is relatively calm, he uses the maximum information available to him—namely, that mouldy bread is bad but non-mouldy bread is good. Because the emotional person is relatively excited, he may use only part of the available information—namely, that mouldy bread is bad.

It is hypothesized, then, that thinking and emoting are closely interrelated and at times differ mainly in that thinking is a more tranquil, less somatically involved (or, at least, perceived), and less activity-directed mode of discrimination than is emotion. It is also hypothesized that among adult humans raised in a social culture thinking and emoting are so closely interrelated that they usually accompany each other, act in a circular cause-and-effect relationship, and in certain (though hardly all) respects are essentially the *same thing*, so that one's thinking *becomes* one's emotion and emoting *becomes* one's thought. It is finally hypothesized that since man is a uniquely sign-, symbol-, and language-creating animal, both thinking and emoting tend to take the form of self-talk or internalized sentences; and that, for all practical purposes, the sentences that human beings keep telling themselves *are* or *become* their thoughts and emotions.

This is not to say that emotion can under *no* circumstances exist without thought. It probably can; but it then tends to exist momentarily, and not to be sustained. An individual, for instance, steps on your toe, and you spontaneously, immediately become angry. Or you hear a piece of music and you instantly begin to feel warm and excited. Or you learn that a close friend has died and you quickly begin to feel sad. Under these circumstances, you may feel emotional without doing any concomitant thinking. Perhaps, however, you do, with split-second rapidity, start thinking "This person who stepped on my toe is blackguard!" or "This music is wonderful!" or "Oh, how awful it is that my friend died!"

In any event, assuming that you don't, at the very beginning, have any conscious or unconscious thought accompanying your emotion, it appears to be difficult to *sustain* an emotional outburst without bolstering it by repeated ideas. For unless you keep telling yourself something on the order of "This person who stepped on my toe is a blackguard!" or "How could he do a horrible thing like that to me!" the pain of having your toe stepped on will soon die, and your immediate reaction will die with the pain. Of course, you can keep getting your toe stepped on, and the continuing pain may sustain your anger. But assuming that your physical sensation stops, your emotional feeling, in order to last, normally has to be bolstered by some kind of thinking.

We say "normally" because it is theoretically possible for your emotional circuits, once they have been made to reverberate by some physical or psychological stimulus, to keep reverberating under their own power. It is also theoretically possible for drugs or electrical impulses to keep acting directly on your hypothalamus and autonomic nervous system and thereby to keep you emotionally aroused. Usually, however, these types of continued direct stimulation of the emotion-producing centers do not seem to be important and are limited largely to pathological conditions.

It would appear, then, that positive human emotions, such as feelings of love or elation, are often associated with or result from thoughts, or internalized sentences, stated in some form or variation of the phrase "This is good!" and that negative human emotions, such as feelings of anger or depression, are frequently associated with or result from thoughts or sentences which are stated in some form or variation of the phrase "This is bad!" Without an adult human being's employing, on some conscious or unconscious level, such thoughts and sentences, much of his emoting would simply not exist.

If the hypothesis that sustained human emotion often results from or is directly associated with human thinking and self-verbalization is true then important corollaries about the origin and perpetuation of states of emotional disturbance, or neurosis, may be drawn. For neurosis would appear to be disordered, over- or under-intensified, uncontrollable emotion; and this would seem to be the result of (and, in a sense, the very same thing as) illogical, unrealistic, irrational, inflexible, and childish thinking.

That neurotic or emotionally disturbed behavior is illogical and irrational would seem to be almost definitional. For if we define it otherwise, and label as neurotic *all* incompetent and ineffectual behavior, we will be including actions of *truly* stupid and incompetent individuals—for example, those who are mentally deficient or brain injured. The concept of neurosis only becomes meaningful, therefore, when we assume that the disturbed individual is *not* deficient or impaired but that he is theoretically capable of behaving in a more mature, more controlled, more flexible manner than he actually behaves. If, however, a neurotic is essentially an individual who acts significantly below his own potential level of behaving, or who defeats his own ends though he is theoretically capable of achieving them, it would appear that he behaves in an illogical, irrational, unrealistic way. Neurosis, in other words, consists of stupid behavior by a non-stupid person.

Assuming that emotionally disturbed individuals act in irrational, illogical ways, the questions which are therapeutically relevant are: (*a*) How do they originally get to be illogical? (*b*) How do they keep perpetuating their irrational thinking? (*c*) How can they be helped to be less illogical, less neurotic?

Unfortunately, most of the good thinking that has been done in regard to therapy during the past 60 years, especially by Sigmund Freud and his chief followers,[5, 6, 7] has concerned itself with the first of these questions rather than the second and the third. The assumption has often been made that if psychotherapists discover and effectively communicate to their clients the main reasons why these clients originally became disturbed, they will thereby also discover how their neuroses are being perpetuated and how they can be helped to overcome them. This is a dubious assumption.

Knowing exactly how an individual originally learned to behave illogically by no means necessarily informs us precisely how he *maintains* his illogical behavior, nor what he should do to change it. This is particularly true because people are often, perhaps usually, afflicted with *secondary* as well as *primary* neuroses, and the two may significantly differ. Thus, an individual may originally become disturbed because he discovers that he has strong death wishes against his father and (quite illogically) thinks he should be blamed and punished for having these wishes. Consequently, he may develop some neurotic symptom, such as a phobia against dogs because, let us say, dogs remind him of his father, who is an ardent hunter.

Later on, this individual may grow to love or be indifferent to his father; or his father may die and be no more of a problem to him. His fear of dogs, however, may remain: not because, as some theorists would insist, they still remind him of his old death wishes against his father, but because he now hates himself so violently for *having* the original neurotic symptom—for behaving, to his mind, so stupidly and illogically in relation to dogs—that every time he thinks of dogs his self-hatred and fear of failure so severely upset him that he cannot reason clearly and cannot combat his illogical fear.

In terms of self-verbalization, this neurotic individual is first saying to himself: "I hate my father—and this is awful!" But he ends up by saying: "I have an irrational fear of dogs—and this is awful!" Even though both sets of self-verbalizations are neuroticizing, and his secondary neurosis may be as bad as or worse than his primary one, the two can hardly be said to be the same. Consequently, exploring and explaining to this individual—or helping him gain insight into—the origins of his primary neurosis will not necessarily help him to understand and overcome his perpetuating or secondary neurotic reactions.

If the hypotheses so far stated have some validity, the psychotherapist's main goals should be those of demonstrating to clients that their self-verbalizations have been and still are the prime source of their emotional disturbances. Clients must be shown that their internalized sentences are illogical and unrealistic at certain critical points and that they now have the ability to control their emotions by telling themselves more rational and less self-defeating sentences.

More precisely: the effective therapist should continually keep unmasking his client's past and, especially, his present illogical thinking or self-defeating verbalizations by (*a*) bringing them to his attention or consciousness; (*b*) showing the client how they are causing and maintaining his disturbance and unhappiness; (*c*) demonstrating exactly what the illogical links in his internalized sentences are; and (*d*) teaching him how to re-think and re-verbalize these (and other similar) sentences in a more logical, self-helping way. Moreover, before the end of the therapeutic relationship, the therapist should not only deal concretely with the client's specific illogical thinking, but should demonstrate to this client what, *in general*, are the main irrational ideas that human beings are prone to follow and what more rational philosophies of living may usually be substituted for them. Otherwise, the client who is released from one specific set of illogical notions may well wind up by falling victim to another set.

It is hypothesized, in other words, that human beings are the kind of animals who, when raised in any society similar to our own, tend to fall victim to several major fallacious ideas; to keep reindoctrinating themselves over and over again with these ideas in an unthinking, autosuggestive manner; and consequently to keep actualizing them in overt behavior. Most of these irrational ideas are, as the Freudians have very adequately pointed out, instilled by the individual's parents during his childhood, and are tenaciously clung to because of his attachment to these parents and because the ideas were ingrained, or imprinted, or conditioned before later and more rational modes of thinking were given a chance to gain a foothold. Most of them, however, as the Freudians have not always been careful to note, are also instilled by the individual's general culture, and particularly by the media of mass communications in this culture.

What are some of the major illogical ideas or philosophies which, when originally held and later perpetuated by men and women in our civilization, inevitably lead to self-defeat and neurosis? Limitations of space preclude our examining all these major ideas, including their more significant corollaries; therefore, only a few of them will be listed. The illogicality of some of these ideas will also, for the present, have to be taken somewhat on faith, since there again is no space to outline the many reasons *why* they are irrational. Anyway, here, where angels fear to tread, goes the psychological theoretician!

1. The idea that it is a dire necessity for an adult to be loved or approved by everyone for everything he does—instead of his concentrating on his own self-respect, on winning approval for necessary purposes (such as job advancement), and on loving rather than being loved.

2. The idea that certain acts are wrong, or wicked, or villainous, and that people who perform such acts should be severely punished—instead of the idea that certain acts are inappropriate or antisocial, and that people who perform such acts are invariably stupid, ignorant, or emotionally disturbed.

3. The idea that it is terrible, horrible, and catastrophic when things are not the way one would like them to be—instead of the idea that it is too bad when things are not the way one would like them to be, and one should certainly try to change or control conditions so that they become more satisfactory, but that if changing or controlling uncomfortable situations is impossible, one had better become resigned to their existence and stop telling oneself how awful they are.

4. The idea that much human unhappiness is externally caused and is forced on one by outside people and events—instead of the idea that virtually all human unhappiness is caused or sustained by the view one takes of things rather than the things themselves.

5. The idea that if something is or may be dangerous or fearsome one should be terribly concerned about it—instead of the idea that if something is or may be dangerous or fearsome one should frankly face it and try to render it non-dangerous, when that is impossible, think of other things and stop telling oneself what a terrible situation one is or may be in.

6. The idea that it is easier to avoid than to face life difficulties and self-responsibilities—instead of the idea that the so-called easy way is invariably the much harder way in the long run and that the only way to solve difficult problems is to face them squarely.

7. The idea that one needs something other or stronger or greater than oneself on which to rely—instead of the idea that it is usually far better to stand on one's own feet and gain faith in oneself and one's ability to meet difficult circumstances of living.

8. The idea that one should be thoroughly competent, adequate, intelligent, and achieving in all possible respects—instead of the idea that one

should *do* rather than always try to do *well* and that one should accept oneself as a quite imperfect creature, who has general human limitations and specific fallibilities.

9. The idea that because something once strongly affected one's life, it should indefinitely affect it—instead of the idea that one should learn from one's past experiences but not be overly-attached to or prejudiced by them.

10. The idea that it is vitally important to our existence what other people do, and that we should make great efforts to change them in the direction we would like them to be—instead of the idea that other people's deficiencies are largely *their* problems and that putting pressure on them to change is usually least likely to help them do so.

11. The idea that human happiness can be achieved by inertia and inaction—instead of the idea that humans tend to be happiest when they are actively and vitally absorbed in creative pursuits, or when they are devoting themselves to people or projects outside themselves.

12. The idea that one has virtually no control over one's emotions and that one cannot help feeling certain things—instead of the idea that one has enormous control over one's emotions if one chooses to work at controlling them and to practice saying the right kinds of sentences to oneself.

It is the central theme of this paper that it is the foregoing kinds of illogical ideas, and many corollaries which we have no space to delineate, which are the basic causes of most emotional disturbances or neuroses. For once one believes the kind of nonsense included in these notions, one will inevitably tend to become inhibited, hostile, defensive, guilty, anxious, ineffective, inert, uncontrolled, or unhappy. If, on the other hand, one could become thoroughly released from all these fundamental kinds of illogical thinking, it would be exceptionally difficult for one to become too emotionally upset, or at least to sustain one's disturbance for very long.

Does this mean that all the other so-called basic causes of neurosis, such as the Oedipus complex or severe maternal rejection in childhood, are invalid, and that the Freudian and other psychodynamic thinkers of the last 60 years have been barking up the wrong tree? Not at all. It only means, if the main hypotheses of this apper are correct, that these psychodynamic thinkers have been emphasizing secondary causes or results of emotional disturbances rather than truly prime causes.

Let us take, for example, an individual who acquires, when he is young, a full-blown Oedipus complex: that is to say, he lusts after his mother, hates his father, is guilty about his sex desires for his mother, and is afraid that his father is going to castrate him. This person, when he is a child, will presumably be disturbed. But, if he is raised so that he acquires none of the basic illogical ideas we have been discussing, it will be virtually impossible for him to *remain* disturbed.

For, as an adult, this individual will not be too concerned if his parents or others do not approve all his actions, since he will be more interested in his *own* self-respect than in *their* approval. He will not believe that his lust for his mother is wicked or villainous, but will accept is as a normal part of being a limited human whose sex desires may easily be indiscriminate. He will realize that the actual danger of his father castrating him is exceptionally slight. He will not feel that because he was once afraid of his Oedipal feelings he should forever remain so. If he still thinks it would be improper for him to have sex relations with his mother, instead of castigating himself for even thinking of having such relations he will merely resolve not to carry his desires into practice and will stick determinedly to his resolve. If, by any chance, he weakens and actually has incestuous relations, he will again refuse to castigate himself mercilessly for being weak but will keep showing himself how self-defeating his behavior is and will actively work and practice at changing it.

Under these circumstances, if this individual has a truly logical and rational approach to life in general, and to the problem of Oedipal feelings, in particular, how can he possibly *remain* disturbed about his Oedipal attachment?

Take, by way of further illustration, the case of an individual who, as a child, is continually criticized by his parents, who consequently feels himself loathsome and inadequate, who refuses to take chances at failing at difficult tasks, who avoids such tasks, and who therefore comes to hate himself more. Such a person will be, of course, seriously neurotic. But how would it be possible for him to *sustain* his neurosis if he began to think in a truly logical manner about himself and his behavior?

For, if this individual does use a consistent rational approach to his own behavior, he will stop caring particularly what others think of him and will start primarily caring what he thinks of himself. Consequently, he will stop avoiding difficult tasks and, instead of punishing himself for being incompetent when he makes a mistake, will say to himself something like: "Now this is not the right way to do things; let me stop and figure out a better way." Or: "There's no doubt that I made a mistake this time; now let me see how I can benefit from making it."

This individual, furthermore, will if he is thinking straight, not blame his defeats on external events, but will realize that he himself is causing them by his illogical or impractical behavior. He will not believe that it is easier to avoid facing difficult things, but will realize that the so-called easy way is always, actually, the harder and more idiotic one. He will not think that he needs something greater or stronger than himself to help him, but will independently buckle down to difficult tasks himself. He will not feel that because he once defeated himself by avoiding doing things the hard way that he must always do so.

How, with this kind of logical thinking, could an originally disturbed person possibly maintain and continually revivify his neurosis? He just couldn't. Similarly, the spoiled brat, the worry-wart, the ego-maniac, the autistic stay-at-home—all of these disturbed individuals would have the devil of a time indefinitely prolonging their neuroses if they did not continue to believe utter nonsense: namely, the kinds of basic irrational postulates previously listed.

Neurosis, then, usually seems to originate in and be perpetuated by some fundamentally unsound, irrational ideas. The individual comes to believe in some unrealistic, impossible, often perfectionistic goals—especially the goals that he should always be approved by everyone, should do everything perfectly well, and should never be frustrated in any of his desires—and then, in spite of considerable contradictory evidence, refuses to give up his original illogical beliefs.

Some of the neurotic's philosophies, such as the idea that he should be loved and approved by everyone, are not entirely inappropriate to his childhood state; but all of them are quite inappropriate to average adulthood. Most of his irrational ideas are specifically taught him by his parents and his culture; and most of them also seem to be held by the great majority of adults in our society—who theoretically should have been but actually never were weaned from them as they chronologically matured. It must consequently be admitted that the neurotic individual we are considering is often statistically normal; or that ours is a generally neuroticizing culture, in which most people are more or less emotionally disturbed because they are raised to believe, and then to internalize and to keep reinfecting themselves with, arrant nonsense which must inevitably lead them to become ineffective, self-defeating, and unhappy. Nonetheless: it is not absolutely *necessary* that human beings believe the irrational notions which, in point of fact, most of them seem to believe today; and the task of psychotherapy is to get them to disbelieve their illogical ideas, to change their self-sabotaging attitudes.

This, precisely, is the task which the rational psychotherapist sets himself. Like other therapists, he frequently resorts to the usual techniques of therapy which the present author has outlined elsewhere,[2,3] including the techniques of relationship, expressive-emotive, supportive, and insight-interpretive therapy. But he views these techniques, as they are commonly employed, as kinds of preliminary strategies whose main functions are to gain rapport with the client, to let him express himself fully, to show him that he is a worthwhile human being who has the ability to change, and to demonstrate how he originally became disturbed.

The rational therapist, in other words, believes that most of the usual therapeutic techniques wittingly or unwittingly show the client *that* he is illogical and how he *originally* became so. They often fail to show him, however, how he is presently *maintaining* his illogical thinking, and precisely what he must do to change it by building general rational philosophies of living and by applying these to practical problems of everyday life. Where most therapists directly or indirectly show the client that he is behaving illogically, the rational therapist goes beyond this point to make a forthright, unequivocal *attack* on the client's general and specific irrational ideas and to try to *induce* him to adopt more rational ones in their place.

Rational psychotherapy makes a concerted attack on the disturbed individual's irrational positions in two main ways; (a) the therapist serves as a frank counter-propagandist who directly contradicts and denies the self-defeating propaganda and superstitions which the client has originally learned and which he is now self-propagandistically perpetuating; (b) the therapist encourages, persuades, cajoles, and at times commands the client to partake of some kind of activity which itself will act as a forceful counter-propagandist agency against the nonsense he believes. Both these main therapeutic activities are consciously performed with one main goal in mind: namely, that of finally getting the client to internalize a rational philosophy of living just as he originally learned and internalized the illogical propaganda and superstitions of his parents and his culture.

The rational therapist, then, assumes that the client somehow imbibed illogical ideas or irrational modes of thinking and that, without so doing, he could hardly be as disturbed as he is. It is the therapist's function not merely to show the client that he has these ideas or thinking processes but to persuade him to change and substitute for them more rational ideals and thought processes. If, because the client is exceptionally disturbed when he first comes to therapy, he must first be approached in a rather cautious, supportive, permissive, and warm manner, and must sometimes be allowed to ventilate his feeling in free association, abreaction, role playing, and other expressive techniques, that may be all to the good. But the therapist does not delude himself that these relationship-building and expressive-emotive techniques in most instances really get to the core of the client's illogical thinking and induce him to think in a more rational manner.

Occasionally, this is true since the client may come to see, through relationship and emotive-expressive methods, that he *is* acting illogically, and he may therefore resolve to change and actually do so. More often than not, however, his illogical thinking will be so ingrained from constant self-repetitions, and will be so inculcated in motor pathways (or habit patterns) by the time he comes for therapy, that simply showing him, even by direct interpretation, *that* he is illogical will not greatly help. He will often say to the therapist: "All right, now I understand that I have castration fears and that they are illogical. But I *still* feel afraid of my father."

The therapist, therefore, must keep pounding away, time and again, at the illogical ideas which underlie the client's fears. He must show the client that he is afraid, really, not of his father, but of being blamed, of being disapproved, of being unloved, of being imperfect, of being a failure. And such fears are thoroughly irrational because (a) being disapproved is not half so terrible a one *thinks* it is; because (b) no one can be thoroughly blameless or perfect; because (c) people who worry about being blamed or disapproved essentially are putting themselves at the mercy of the opinion of *others*, over whom they have no real control; because (*d*) being blamed or disapproved has nothing essentially to do with one's *own* opinion of oneself; etc.

If the therapist, moreover, merely tackles the individual's castration fears, and shows how ridiculous *they* are, what is to prevent this individual showing up, a year or two later, with some *other* illogical fear—such as the fear that he is sexually impotent? But if the therapist tackles the client's *basic* irrational thinking, which underlies *all* kinds of fear he may have, it is going to be most difficult for this client to turn up with a new neurotic symptom some months or years hence. For once an individual truly surrenders ideas of perfectionism, of the horror of failing at something, of the dire need to be approved by others, of the notion that the world owes him a living, and so on, what else is there for him to be fearful of or disturbed about?

To give some idea of precisely how the rational therapist works, a case summary will now be presented. A client came in one day and said he was depressed but did not know why. A little questioning showed that he had been putting off the inventory-keeping he was required to do as part of his job as an apprentice glass-staining artist. The therapist immediately began showing him that his depression was related to his resenting having to keep inventory and that this resentment was illogical for several reasons:

(*a*) The client very much wanted to learn the art of glass-staining and could only learn it by having the kind of job he had. His sole logical choice, therefore, was between graciously accepting this job, in spite of the inventory-keeping, or giving up trying to be a glass-stainer. By resenting the clerical work and avoiding it, he was choosing neither of these two logical alternatives, and was only getting himself into difficulty.

(*b*) By blaming the inventory-keeping, and his boss for making him perform it, the client was being irrational since, assuming that the boss was wrong about making him do this clerical work, the boss would have to be wrong out of some combination of stupidity, ignorance, or emotional disturbance; and it is silly and pointless blaming people for being stupid, ignorant, or disturbed. Besides, maybe the boss was quite right, from his own standpoint, about making the client keep the inventory.

(*c*) Whether the boss was right or wrong, resenting him for his stand was hardly going to make him change it; and the resentment felt by the client was hardly going to do him, the client, any good or make him feel better. The saner attitude for him to take, then, was that it was too bad that inventory-keeping was part of his job, but that's the way it was, and there was no point in resenting the way things were when they could not, for the moment, be changed.

(*d*) Assuming that the inventory-keeping was irksome, there was no sense in making it still *more* annoying by the client's continually telling himself how awful it was. Nor was there any point in shirking this clerical work, since he eventually would have to do it anyway and he might as well get this unpleasant task out of the way quickly. Even more important: by shirking a task he knew that, eventually, he just had to do, he would lose respect for himself, and his loss of self-respect would be far worse than the slight, rather childish satisfaction he might receive from trying to sabotage his boss's desires.

While showing this client how illogical was his thinking and consequent behavior, the therapist specifically made him aware that must be telling himself sentences like these: "My boss makes me do inventory-keeping. I do not like to do his. . . . There is no reason why I have to do it . . . . He is therefore a blackguard for making me do it. . . . So I'll fool him and avoid doing it. . . . And then I'll be happier." But these sentences were so palpably foolish that the client could not really believe them, and began to finish them off with sentences like: "I'm not really fooling my boss, because he sees what I'm doing. . . . So I'm not solving my problem this way. . . . So I really should stop this nonsense and get the inventory-keeping done. . . . But I'll be damned if I'll do it for him! . . . . However, if I don't do it, I'll be fired. . . . But I still don't want to do it for him! . . . . I guess I've got to, though. . . . Oh, why must I always be persecuted like this? . . . And why must I keep getting myself into such a mess? . . . I guess I'm just no good. . . . And people are against me. . . . Oh, what's the use?"

Whereupon, employing these illogical kinds of sentences, the client was becoming depressed, avoiding doing the inventory-keeping, and then becoming more resentful and depressed. Instead, the therapist pointed out, he could tell himself quite different sentences, on this order: "Keeping inventory is a bore. . . . But it is presently an essential part of my job. . . . And I also may learn something useful by it. . . . Therefore, I had better go about this task as best I may and thereby get what *I* want out of this job."

The therapist also emphasized that whenever the client found himself intensely angry, guilty, or depressed, there was little doubt that he was then thinking illogically, and that he should immediately question himself as to what was the irrational element in his thinking, and set about replacing it with a more logical element or chain of sentences.

The therapist then used the client's current dilemma—that of avoiding inventory-keeping—as an illustration of his general neurosis, which in his case largely took the form of severe alcoholic tendencies. He was shown that his alcoholic trends, too, were a result of his trying to do things the easy way, and of poor thinking preluding his avoidance of self-responsibilities. He was impressed with the fact that, as long as he kept thinking illogically about relatively small things, such as the inventory-keeping, he would also tend to think equally illogically about more important aspects, such as the alcoholism.

Several previous incidents of illogical thinking leading to emotional upheaval in the client's life were then reviewed, and some general principles of irrational thought discussed. Thus, the general principle of blamelessness was raised and the client was shown precisely why it is illogical to blame anyone for anything. The general principle of inevitability was brought up and he was shown that when a frustrating or unpleasant event is inevitable, it is only logical to accept it uncomplainingly instead of dwelling on its unpleasant aspects. The general principle of self-respect was discussed, with the therapist demonstrating that liking oneself is far more important than resentfully trying to harm others.

In this manner, by attempting to show to teach the client some of the general rules of logical living, the therapist tried to go beyond his immediate problem and to help provide him with a generalized mode of thinking or problem solving that would enable him to deal effectively with almost any future similar situation that might arise.

The rational therapist, then, is a frank propagandist who believes wholeheartedly in a most rigorous application of the rules of logic, of straight thinking, and of scientific method to everyday life, and who ruthlessly uncovers every vestige of irrational thinking in the client's experience and energetically urges him into more rational channels. In so doing, the rational therapist does not ignore or eradicate the client's emotions; on the contrary, he considers them most seriously, and helps change them, when they are disordered and self-defeating, through the same means by which they commonly arise in the first place—that is, by thinking and acting. Through exerting consistent interpretive and philosophic pressure on the client to change his thinking or his self-verbalizations and to change his experiences or his actions, the rational therapist gives a specific impetus to the client's movement toward mental health without which it is not impossible, but quite unlikely, that he will move very far.

Can therapy be effectively done, then, with *all* clients mainly through logical analysis and reconstruction? Alas, no. For one thing, many clients are not bright enough to follow a rigorously rational analysis. For another thing, some individuals are so emotionally aberrated by the time they come for help that they are, at least temporarily, in no position to comprehend and follow logical procedures. Still other clients are too old and inflexible; too young and impressionable; too philosophically prejudiced against logic and reason; too organically or biophysically deficient; or too something else to accept, at least at the start of therapy, rational analysis.

In consequence, the therapist who *only* employs logical reconstruction in his therapeutic armamentarium is not likely to get too far with many of those who seek his help. It is vitally important, therefore, that any therapist who has a basically rational approach to the problem of helping his clients overcome their neuroses also be quite eclectic in his use of supplementary, less direct, and somewhat less rational techniques.

Admitting, then, that rational psychotherapy is not effective with all types of clients, and that it is most helpful when used in conjunction with, or subsequent to, other widely employed therapeutic techniques, I would like to conclude with two challenging hypotheses: (*a*) psychotherapy which includes a high dosage of rational analysis and reconstruction, as briefly outlined in this paper, will prove to be more effective with more types of clients than any of the non-rational or semi-rational therapies now being widely employed; and (*b*) that a considerable amount of—or, at least, proportion of—rational psychotherapy will prove to be virtually the only type of treatment that helps to undermine the basic neuroses (as distinguished from the superficial neurotic symptoms) of many clients, and particularly of many with whom other types of therapy have already been shown to be ineffective.

## REFERENCES

1. COBB, S. (1950) *Emotions and Clinical Medicine*, Norton, New York.
2. ELLIS, A. (1955) New approaches to psychotherapy techniques, *J. Clin. Psychol. Monog. Suppl.*, No.11. Brandon, Vermont: *J. Clin. Psychol.*
3. ELLIS, A. (1955) Psychotherapy techniques for use with psychotics, *Amer. J. Psychother.*, **9**, 452–476.
4. ELLIS, A. (1956) An operational reformulation of some of the basic principles of psychoanalysis, *Psychoanal.. Rev.*, **43**, 163–180.
5. FENICHEL, O. (1945) *The Psychoanalytic Theory of Neurosis*, Norton, New York.
6. FREUD, S. (1938) *Basic Writings.*, Modern Library, New York.
7. FREUD, S. (1924–1950) *Collected Papers*, Hogarth Press, London.

## II. A HOMOSEXUAL TREATED WITH RATIONAL PSYCHOTHERPHY

### Presenting Problems

The client came for psychotherapy primarily because he had been exclusively homosexual all his life and thought that it was about time he settled down and married. He had read about the therapist's work with homosexuals in a magazine and was self-referred. In addition to his homosexual problem, he suffered from heart palpitations which had been consistently diagnosed as being of purely psychogenic origin, and he wondered whether something could be done about them, too. He vaguely thought that he might have other problems, but was not certain what they were.

### Background Data

The client was a thirty-five year old male, living in Brooklyn with his parents, and operating his disabled father's toy factory. He had been raised as a Catholic, but no longer considered himself a believer. He was the only son of what he described as a "very religious and very neurotic" mother and an "exceptionally weak, dominated father" who had been disabled by a serious stroke two years before the client came for treatment. He had always been quite close to his mother, and usually did her bidding, even though he bitterly resented her persistent attempts to control himself and his father. He liked but did not respect his father.

The client, whom we shall call Caleb Frosche, was born and raised in Brooklyn; had a shy, uneventful childhood; spent three unhappy years in the Navy; always did well in school; did some college teaching for a short time after obtaining his doctorate in zoology; and reluctantly took over his father's business, and was carrying it on successfully, after the father had had a serious stroke. Caleb had a few dates with girls when he went to high school, but was afraid to make any sexual overtures, for fear of being rejected, and consequently had not even ever kissed a girl. While in the Navy he was plied with liquor by two other sailors and induced to have his first homosexual experience at the age of nineteen. Since that time he had engaged in homosexual acts every two or three weeks, always making his contacts at public urinals and never having any deep relationships with his partners. He occassionally dated girls, mainly to show others that he was heterosexual, but he was not particularly attracted to any of them and never made any advances or got seriously involved.

Shortly after his father began to have difficulties with his heart (10 years ago) Caleb began to experience sudden attacks of heart palpitations and chest pain. These would spontaneously subside a few minutes after they began, but he would be left in a shaken condition for several hours or days afterward. Continual medical examinations had revealed no heart pathology, and he referred to himself as a "cardiac neurotic".

*Therapeutic Approach*

Caleb was one of the first clients treated with a special therapeutic approach which the therapist developed after many years of practicing orthodox psychoanalysis and psychoanalytically-oriented psychotherapy. *Rational psychotherapy*,[1, 2, 3, 4] as the technique is called, stems from the hypothesis that most significant human emotions and actions, including neurotic feelings and behavior, stem from basic assumptions, beliefs, or philosophies which the individual consciously or unconsciously holds. Neurotic symptoms, it is held, are caused and maintained by illogical or irrational ideas and attitudes, and tend to reinforce these illogical beliefs. To accomplish effective psychotherapy, the basic irrational philosophies or value systems of the disturbed individual not only have to be brought to conscious attention, and their origins interpreted (as is done in all analytically-oriented therapies) but, even more importantly, the client must be shown how he is now, in the present, wittingly or unwittingly *maintaining* his irrational beliefs by continually re-indoctrinating himself, through self-verbalization or autosuggestion, with the nonsensical philosophies he originally acquired. The client must also be shown, most specifically and concretely, how to depropagandize or de-indoctrinate himself from his self-defeating philosophies and how to substitute more rational value judgments in their place. Depropagandization is taught the client by the therapist, inducing him (*a*) to assume that all his exaggerated fears, anxieties, hostilities, guilts, and depressions must be grounded in illogical beliefs and attitudes; (*b*) to trace these illogical beliefs to their assumptions; (*c*) to question these assumptions; (*d*) to attack them in the light of logical and rational methodologies; (*e*) to counter them, in action, with behavior that directly contradicts them; and (*f*) to replace them, ultimately, with rational, non-defeating values and beliefs which, when they are ultimately accepted, will automatically encourage non-neurotic behavior.

### Attacking the Client's Fixed Homosexuality

The first major symptom of the client which was attacked by the therapist was his pattern of exclusive homosexuality, as this was the aspect of his behavior with which he was most concerned when he came to therapy. In tackling the client's homosexual pattern, the therapist first carefully explained why this mode of behavior was neurotic. He showed the client that although homosexual activity is not in itself a product of emotional disturbance, its *fixed* or *exclusive* form is invariably a neurotic symptom because it rigidly, prejudicedly, and fetishistically eliminates *other* modes of sexual fulfillment, notably heterosexuality. This means that the homosexual arbitrarily, out of some illogical fear or hostility, forfeits sexual desire and satisfaction in connection with half the population of the world; and, to make his behavior still more illogical in our culture, confines himself to sex acts with those partners with whom he is most likely to get into serious legal and social difficulties, including arrest and blackmail.

Caleb was shown, at the start of therapy, that there would be not attempt on the therapist's part to induce him to surrender his homosexual desires or activities—since there was no logical reason why he should not, at least, maintain inverted *desires*—but that the goal of therapy would be to help him overcome his irrational blocks against heterosexuality. Once he overcame those, and actively desired and enjoyed sex relations with females, it would be relatively unimportant from a mental health standpoint, whether he still had homosexual leanings as well.

The basic assumptions behind Caleb's homosexual pattern of behavior were then quickly brought to light. From questioning him about his specific homosexual participation, it was revealed that he invariably would enter a public urinal or a gay bar, would wait around until some male approached him, and then, whether this male appealed to him or not, would go off to have sex relations. On never a single occasion, in sixteen years of homosexual activity, had he ever actively approached a male himself.

On the basis of this and allied information, it was made clear to Caleb that his outstanding motive for remaining homosexual was his strong fear of rejection by (*a*) all women and (*b*) most males. He was so convinced that he might be rejected if he made sexual approaches to either women or men, that he had arranged his entire sex life so that no active approach, and consequently no possibility of rejection, was necessary. He had obviously acquired his fear of rejection, as further questioning soon brought out, at an early age, and it was probably related to the fact that he had been a rather chubby and unattractive boy, and that even his own mother had kept remarking that he would have trouble finding and winning an attractive girl.

Rather then spend much time belaboring the point that Caleb's fear of rejection probably stemmed from his childhood, the therapist convinced him, on purely logical grounds, that this was so since he had apparently feared being rejected by girls when he was in his early teens, and his fear must have originated sometime prior to that time. The therapist, instead, tried to get, as quickly as possible, to the source of his fear of rejection: namely, his illogical *belief* that being rejected by a girl (or a fellow) was a terrible thing. Said the therapist:

T: Suppose, for the sake of discussion, you had, back in your high school days, tried, really tried, to make some sexual passes at a girl, and suppose you had been unequivocally rejected by her. Why would that be terrible?

C: Well—uh—it just would be.

T: But *why* would it be?

C: Because—uh–I–I just thought the world would come to an end if that would have happened.

T: But *why*? Would the world *really* have come to an end?

C: No, of course not.

T: Would the girl have slapped your face, or called a cop, or induced all the other girls to ostracize you?

C: No, I guess she wouldn't.

T: Then what *would* she have done? How would you—*really*—have been hurt?

C: Well, I guess, in the way you mean, I wouldn't.

T: Then why did you think that you would?

C: That's a good question. Why did I?

T: The answer, alas, is so obvious that you probably won't believe it.

C: What is it?

T: Simply that you thought you would be terribly hurt by a girl's rejecting you merely because you were *taught* that you would be. You were raised, literally raised, to believe that if anyone, especially a girl, rejects you, tells you she doesn't like you, that this is terrible, awful, frightful. It isn't, of course: it isn't in any manner, shape, or form awful if someone rejects you, refuses to accede to your wishes. But you *think* it is, because you were *told* it is.

C: Told?

T:   Yes—literally and figuratively told. Told literally by your parents, who warned you, time and again, did they not, that if you did wrong, made the wrong approaches to people, they wouldn't love you, wouldn't accept you—*and that would be awful, that would be terrible.*

C:   Yes, you're right about that. That's just what they told me.

T:   Yes—and not only they. Indirectly, figuratively, symbolically, in the books you read, the plays you saw, the films you went to—weren't you told the same thing there, time and again, over and over—that if anyone, the hero of the book, you, or anyone else, got rejected, got rebuffed, got turned down, they *should* think it terrible, should be hurt?

C:   I guess I was. Yes, that's what the books and films really say, isn't it?

T:   It sure is. All right, then, so you *were* taught that being rejected is awful, frightful. Now let's go back to my original question. Suppose you actually did ask a girl for a kiss, or something else; and suppose she did reject you. What would you *really* lose thereby, by being so rejected?

C:   Really lose? Actually, I guess, very little.

T:   Right: dammed little. In fact, you'd actually gain a great deal.

C:   How so?

T:   Very simply: you'd gain experience. For if you tried and were rejected, you'd know not to try it with that girl, or in that way, again. Then you could go on to try again with some other girl, or with the same girl in a different way, and so on.

C:   Maybe you've got something there.

T:   Maybe I have. Whenever you get rejected—as you do, incidentally, every time you put a coin in a slot machine and no gum or candy comes out—you are merely learning that this girl or that technique or this gum machine doesn't work; but a trial with some other girl, technique, or machine may well lead to success. Indeed, in the long run, it's almost certain to.

C:   You're probably right.

T:   O.K. then. So it isn't the rejection by girls that *really* hurts, is it? It's your *idea*, your *belief*, your *assumption* that rejection is hurtful, is awful. *That's* what's really doing you in; and that's what we're going to have to change to get you over your silly homosexual neurosis.

Thus, the therapist kept pointing out, in session after session, the illogical fears behind the client's fixed homosexual pattern of behavior—and *why* these fears were illogical, how they were merely learned and adsorbed from Caleb's early associates, and, especially how *he* now kept re-indoctrinating himself with these fears by parroting them unthinkingly, telling himself over and over that they were based on proven evidence, when obviously they were completely arbitrary and ungrounded in fact. His fear of rejection, of losing approval, or having others laugh at him or criticize him, was examined in scores of its aspects, and revealed to him again and again. It was not only revealed, but scornfully, forcefully *attacked* by the therapist, who kept showing Caleb that it is necessarily silly and self-defeating for anyone to care too much about what *others* think, since then one is regulating one's life by and for these others, rather than for oneself; and, moreover, one is setting up a set of conditions for one's own happiness which make it virtually impossible that one ever will be happy.

Caleb's homosexual pattern of behavior, then, was consistently, forthrightly assailed not on the grounds of its being immoral or wrong, but solely on the grounds of its being self-defeating and limiting—and of its stemming from basic, largely nonsexual assumptions which had ramifications in all the rest of his life, and kept him from enjoying himself in many other ways as well.

## Activity Homework Assignments

At the same time that the philosophic assumptions underlying Caleb's fear of rejection, and his consequent homosexual behavior, were being directly questioned and attacked, he was encouraged by the therapist to date girls, so that he could, in actual practice, overcome his fears concerning them. He was warned that his first attempts at dating might well result in embarrassment, awkwardness, and failure; but was told that only by working through such situations, with the help of the therapist, was he likely to overcome his irrational fears in these connections.

On his first date, which he made the week following his first therapy session, Caleb saw a girl who was very nice and refined, but who was quite cold, and who obviously had severe problems of her own. On his second attempt, he met a librarian, a year younger than he, who was warm and accepting, and with whom he immediately began to pet heavily, but who also turned out to be severely disturbed. While still going with her, he went to a party with a girl whom he had known in a friendly way for some time, but whom he had never actually dated; and he wound up by having intercourse with her, which he thoroughly enjoyed. The girl, however, moved to another town shortly thereafter, and he did not see her again.

While Caleb was seeing these girls, the therapist went over with him in detail his behavior with and his reactions to them. He was given specific information and instruction in regard to how to make dates; what to expect from the girls; how to understand them and their problems; how to avoid being discouraged when he was rebuffed; what kinds of sexual overtures to make and when to make them, etc. His mistakes and blunders were gone over in an objective, constructive manner; and he was shown how, instead of blaming himself for these mistakes, he could put them to good self-teaching uses.

After he had seen the therapist seven times, on a once a week basis, Caleb met a girl whom he thought was most desirable, and was at first sure that he would not be able to get anywhere with her. The therapist consistently encouraged him to keep seeing her, even when things looked rather black in their relationship, and insisted that he not give up too easily. Largely because of the therapist's encouragement, Caleb did persist, and soon began to make headway with this girl. He not only managed to win her emotional allegiance; but in spite of the fact that she had a history of sexual indifference, he gradually awakened her desires and, through heavy petting, was able to give her, much to her surprise, tremendous orgasmic release. She was the one who finally insisted that they have intercourse: and this, too, proved to be supremely enjoyable for her and Caleb. The thing that most impressed Caleb, however, was not his sexual prowess with the girl but his ability to win her emotional responsiveness against initial great odds, after he had first convinced himself that he could never succeed. His basic philosophy of his own worthlessness, or the necessity of his failing at anything he really wanted very badly, was rudely shaken by this practical lesson in the value of continuing to fight against odds.

Although Caleb's homosexual proclivities were barely mentioned after the first two sessions, and no direct attempt was made to get him to forego them, he completely and voluntarily renounced homosexuality as soon as he began to be sexually and emotionally successful with females. By the time the twelfth week of therapy had arrived, he had changed from a hundred per cent fixed homosexual to virtually a hundred per cent heterosexual. All his waking and sleeping fantasies became heterosexually oriented, and he was almost never interested in homosexual outlets.

### Attacking the Client's Psychosomatic Symptoms and Vocational Problems

Since this paper largely focuses on the treatment of homosexual symptomatology, only a short summary will be given of how this client's nonsexual problems, particularly his psychosomatic and vocational symptoms, were attacked and overcome by the application of principles of rational psychotherapy. He was shown how he had originally begun to tell himself fear and hostility-creating nonsense, bringing on his cardiac neurosis and then, once his symptoms arose, reinforcing them with more illogical ideas. Thus, he kept propagandizing himself with two basic irrational philosophies of living: first, the idea that he must be perfectly competent, achieving, and successful in everything he did; and second, the idea that when he failed or made a mistake at any task, he should blame himself severely. These philosophies, of arrant perfectionism and self-blame, the therapist clearly showed Caleb, necessarily *had* to lead him to acquire some kind of symptoms, such as his heart palpitations, in the first place, and induce him to aggravate and perpetuate them in the second place.

When Caleb, in the course of the ninth session, finally began to see that his having his heart palpitations was originally related to intense dislike for having to take over his father's factory, instead of pursuing his own chosen career, and that they were enormously exaggerated by his fear that he would not be strong and competent enough to control them, his heart symptoms quickly began to abate and within a few more weeks he was entirely free of them. As he lost his hostility to his parents and himself, his strong desire to be a professor of zoology came to the fore, and he began to prepare himself for that vocation.

*The Close of Therapy*

Caleb unexpectedly said he thought he would discontinue therapy and try to go it on his own at the end of the nineteenth session; and, although the therapist thought this was a rather premature closing, he went along with the client's wish, on the assumption that Caleb would soon get into difficulty and return for further therapy later. As it happens, however, almost three years have now passed and Caleb has not returned. He has written two long letters, and it appears that he has married the fourth girl he dated and is getting along nicely in this marriage. He is teaching zoology in a midwestern university and is getting along well, if not perfectly, in most respects. He is completely disinterested in homosexual relations at present and is free from the psychosomatic heart symptoms with which he came to therapy.

One of the most interesting aspects of this case is that some basic issues in Caleb's life were virtually never discussed during the entire therapeutic procedure—partly because the therapist thought that some of them would be analyzed in more detail later, and partly because he thought that some of the issues were largely irrelevant to Caleb's basic problems. Thus, the therapist felt that Caleb's homosexual pattern of behavior was, at least in part, caused by his over-attachment to his mother, and by his unconsciously feeling incest guilt. In the entire course of therapy, however, relatively little reference was made to Caleb's relations with his mother, and no detailed analysis of this relationship was effected. Nonetheless, Caleb's deviated pattern of homosexuality completely changed in the course of therapy—largely, in all probability, because the *main* cause of this homosexuality was *not* his Oedipal attachment to his mother but his severe feelings of inadequacy and fear of rejection—which *were* thoroughly analyzed and attacked in the course of therapy.

By the same token, although Caleb's hostility to his father, and his probable jealousy of the father's hold over his mother, was never, largely because of lack of time, thoroughly interpreted to him, he wound up by being, on the one hand, much less hostile toward and, on the other hand, more able to break with his father. This was because his basic philosophies of blaming both himself and others were steadily and powerfully attacked in the course of therapy; and, once these philosophies started to change, he had no need of being jealous of and hostile toward his father.

*Summary*

In this case of a thirty-five year old male who entered therapy because he was severely troubled by a fixed pattern of homosexuality, a swift frontal attack was made by the therapist on the basic assumptions or philosophies illogically underlying the client's symptoms. In the course of this attack the client was shown, by the therapist's rigorously unmasking and then inducing the client himself to contradict and act against his irrational beliefs, that his homosexual pattern of behavior and his other neurotic symptoms were not hopelessly ingrained and that he himself could control his own destiny by changing his assumptions. Specifically, the client was helped to see that it was not overly-important if others did not love or approve him; that failing at a task was not a crime; and that perfect achievement is a silly goal for a human being to strive for. As he began to change the fundamental irrational beliefs that motivated his homosexual and neurotic behavior, the client's symptoms almost automatically began to disappear and he was able to change from a fixed, exclusive homosexual to a virtually hundred per cent heterosexually oriented individual.

## REFERENCES

1. ELLIS, A. (1956) The effectiveness of psychotherapy with individuals who have severe homosexual problems, *J. Consult. Psychol.*, **20**, 191–195.
2. ELLIS, A. (1957) Rational psychotherapy and individual psychology, *J. Individ. Psychol.*, **13**, 38–44.
3. ELLIS, A. (1957) Outcome of employing three techniques of psychotherapy, *J. Clin. Psychol.*, **13**, 344–350.
4. ELLIS, A. (1958) Rational psychotherapy, *J. Gen. Psychol.*, **59**, 35–49.

## III. THE TREATMENT OF A PSYCHOPATH WITH RATIONAL PSYCHOTHERAPY

So-called psychopaths, or individuals suffering with a severe character disorder whose behavior is distinctly antisocial, are exceptionally difficult to treat with psychotherapy. They only rarely come for treatment on a voluntary basis; and when they are treated involuntarily, they tend to be resistant, surly, and in search of a "cure" that will involve no real effort on their part. Even when they come for private treatment, they are usually looking for magical, effortless "cures", and they tend to stay in treatment only for a short period of time and to make relatively little improvement.

Psychoanalytic techniques of approaching psychopaths are particularly ineffective for several reasons: These individuals are frequently non-introspective and non-verbal; they tend to be not overly-bright or well-educated; they are impatient of long-winded procedures; and they are highly sceptical or afraid of involved psychological analysis or interpretation. It is therefore only the exceptional psychopath who can be helped with analytic methods such as those employed by Lindner (1944) in his *Rebel Without a Cause*. Considerably modified techniques of interpretation, such as advocated by Cleckley (1950) and Schmideberg (1956) are often recommended instead.

Before attempting to treat any young delinquents or older criminals in my present private practice of psychotherapy, I had considerable experience in examining and treating them when I was Chief Psychologist at the New Jersey State Diagnostic Center and later Chief Psychologist of the New Jersey Department of Institutions and Agencies. At that time I became impressed with the fact that whether the offender was a thief, a sex deviate, a dope addict, or a murderer, about the very worst way to try to help him rehabilitate himself was to give him a moral lecture, appeal to his superego, or in any way blame him for his misdeeds. For I began to see at that time that, in their own peculiar ways, virtually all these offenders really were anxious and guilty underneath their façade of psychopathic bravado; and that, in fact, their criminal acts were frequently committed as a defensive attempt to protect them against their own feelings of low self-esteem. In other words, many of them were already being compulsively driven to psychopathic behavior by underlying guilt and anxiety; and to endeavor to make them more guilty and anxious, as is often at first attempted in psychoanalytic technique, would hardly help them lose their need for their compulsive defenses.

Instead, I found that if I temporarily showed the offender that I was *not* critical of his behavior, and if I at first allied myself with him (if necessary) against the authorities of the institution in which he was incarcerated (and whom he almost invariably saw as being persecutory), a notable degree of rapport could be established between us. Then, once the prisoner felt that I was really on his side, it was often possible to show him that his pattern of criminal behavior was not merely immoral and antisocial (which he of course knew without my telling him so) but that, more importantly, it was *self-defeating*. If I could convince him, which I often could, that however much society might be (from his standpoint, justifiably and revengefully) harmed by his crimes, he *himself* was invariably even more self-sabotaged by these acts and their usual consequences, then I had a fairly good chance of getting him to change his behavior in the future.

My many investigatory and therapeutic relationships with criminals taught me, then, that so-called hardened psychopaths, like other disturbed human beings, act in an irrational and self-defeating manner because they believe, quite falsely, that they are helping themselves thereby; and when they are calmly, unblamefully, and yet vigorously disabused of this belief, they are often capable of radically changing their philosophic orientation and their antisocial behavior which springs from that orientation. Because many or most of the classic psychopaths are, as Cleckley points out, basically psychotic, they are often most difficult to treat; and one must usually be contented with reasonably limited gains. Nonetheless, remarkable improvements in their general living patterns, and particularly in the reduction of their antisocial behavior, may result from proper treatment.

A case involving the rational therapeutic treatment of a psychopath will now be described. The patient was a 25-year-old son of a well-to-do family and had been engaging in antisocial behavior, including lying, stealing, sexual irresponsibility, and physical assaults on others since the age of 14. He had been in trouble with the law on five different occasions, but had only been convicted once and spent one year in a reformatory. He displayed no guilt about his offences and seemed not at all concerned about the fact he had once helped cripple an old man whose candy store he and his youthful comrades had held up. He had two illegitimate children by different girls, but made no effort to see them or contribute to their financial support. He came for psychotherapy only at the insistence of his lawyer, who told him that his one chance of being put on probation, instead of being sent to prison, for his latest offence (rifling several vending machines) was for him to plead emotional disturbance and convince the court that he was really trying to do something to help himself in regard to this disturbance.

For the first few sessions the patient was only moderately cooperative, kept postponing appointments without good cause, and came 10 or 15 minutes late to almost every interview. He would listen fairly attentively and take an active part in the sessions; but as soon as he left the therapist's office he would, in his own words, "forget almost everything we said", and come in for the next session without giving any thought to his problems or their possible alleviation. It was not that he resentfully was resisting therapy; but he quite frankly was doing little or nothing to "get with it".

During the first several sessions, little attempt was made by the therapist to get the full details of the patient's history. It was merely determined that he was the only son of a doting mother, who had always given him his way, and of a merchant father who had ostensibly been friendly and permissive, but who actually had held up to him almost impossibly high standards of achievement and who was severely disappointed whenever he fell below these standards. The patient—whom we shall call Jim—had been a spoiled brat with other children, over whom he was always trying to lord it; had never lived up to his potentialities in school; had started to gain attention from his peers and his teachers at an early age by nasty, show-off behavior; and had only been able to get along reasonably well with girls, one or more of whom he usually managed to have serve him while he sadistically exploited her masochistic tendencies.

Although the patient was quite intelligent, and could easily understand psychodynamic explanations of his behavior—such as the possible connection between his failing to satisfy his father's high standard of excellence and his trying to prove to others, by quite opposite antisocial actions, how "great" he was —no attempt to interpret or clarify such connections was made. For one thing, he stoutly opposed such "psychoanalytic crap" whenever the psychodynamics of his situation were even hinted at; for another thing, the rational therapist frequently makes relatively little use of this kind of historical clarification, since he deems it highly interesting but not necessarily conducive of basic personality change.

Instead, the patient's current circumstances were first focused upon, and he was quickly and intensively shown that he kept defeating himself in the present—as well as in the past. Thus, he kept discussing with the therapist the possibility of his violating the terms of his bail and "skipping out of town". The therapist, without being in the least moralistic about this notion or taking any offence at the implied concept that therapy was not going to help the patient and that therefore he might as well go on living the kind of life he had always lived, calmly and ruthlessly showed Jim that (a) he had very little likelihood of being able to skip town without being caught in short order; (b) he would only lead a life of desperate evasion during the time he would remain free; and (c) he would most certainly know no mercy from the court if and when he was recaptured. Although, at first, the patient was most loath to accept these grim facts, the therapist patiently persisted in forcing him to do so.

At the same time, the therapist kept showing Jim the silly and totally unrealistic philosophies behind his self-defeating notions of trying to skip bail. He was shown that he was grandiosely and idiotically telling himself that he *should* be able to do what he wanted just because he wanted to do so; that it was totally unfair and unethical for others, including the law, to stand in his way; and that it was utterly catastrophic when he was frustrated in his one-sided demands. And these assumptions, the therapist kept insisting, were thoroughly groundless and irrational.

"But why," asked Jim at one point in the fourth session, "shouldn't I want things to go my way? Why *shouldn't* I try to get what I want?"

*Therapist*: No reason at all. To want what you want when you want it is perfectly legitimate. But you, unfortunately, are doing one additional thing—and that's perfectly illegitimate.

*Patient*: What's that? what's the illegitimate thing?

*Therapist*: You're not only *wanting* what you want, but *demanding* it. You're taking a perfectly sane desire—to be able to avoid standing trial for your crimes, in this instance—and asininely turning it into an absolute *necessity*.

*Patient*: Why is that so crazy?

*Therapist*: For the simple reason that, first of all, *any* demand or necessity is crazy. Wanting a thing, wanting any damned thing you happen to crave, is fine—as long as you admit the possibility of your not being able to get it. But as soon as you demand something, turn it into a necessity, you simply won't be able to *stand* your not getting it. In that event, either you'll do something desperate to get it—as you usually have done in your long history of antisocial behavior—or else you'll keep making yourself angry, exceptionally frustrated, or anxious about not getting it. Either way, *you* lose.

*Patient*: But suppose I *can* get what I want?

*Therapist*: Fine—as long as you don't subsequently defeat your own ends by getting it. As in this case. Even assuming that you could skip bail successfully—which is very doubtful, except for a short while—would you *eventually* gain by having to live in terror of arrest for the remainder of your life or by having to give up everything and everyone you love here to run, let us say, to South America?

*Patient*: Perhaps not.

*Therapist*: Perhaps? Besides, let's assume, for a moment, that you really could get away with it—you really could skip bail and that you wouldn't get caught and wouldn't live in perpetual fear. Even then, would you be doing yourself such a great favor?

*Patient*: It seems to me I would! What more could I ask?

*Therapist*: A lot more. And it is just your *not* asking for a lot more that proves, to me at least, that you are a pretty sick guy.

*Patient*: In what way? What king of crap are you giving me? Bullshit!

*Therapist*: Well, I could get highly "ethical" and say that if you get away with things like that, with rifling vending machines, jumping bail, and such things, that you are then helping to create the kind of a world that you yourself would not want to live in, or certainly wouldn't want your friends or relatives to live in. For if you can get away with such acts, of course, others can too; and in such a pilfering, bail-jumping world, who would want to live?

*Patient*: But suppose I said that I didn't mind living in that kind of world—kind of liked it, in fact?

*Therapist*: Right. You might very well say that. And even mean it—though I wonder whether, if you really gave the matter careful thought, you would. But let us suppose you would. So I won't use that "ethical" argument with a presumably "unethical" and guiltless person like you. But there is still another, and better argument, and one that you and people like you, generally overlook.

*Patient*: And that is?

*Therapist*: That is—your own skin.

*Patient*: My own skin?

*Therapist*: Yes, your own thick and impenetrable skin. Your guiltless, ever so guiltless skin.

*Patient*: I don't get it. What the hell are you talking about?

*Therapist*: Simply this. Suppose, as we have been saying, you are truly guiltless. Suppose you, like Lucky Luciano and a few other guys who really seem to have got away scot-free with a life of crime, really do have a thick skin, and don't give a good goddam what happens to others who may suffer from your deeds, don't care what kind of a world you are helping to create. How, may I ask, can you—you personally, that is—manufacture and maintain that lovely, rugged, impenetrable skin?

*Patient*: What difference does it make how I got it, as long as it's there?

*Therapist*: Ah, but it does!—it does make a difference.

*Patient*: How the hell does it?

*Therapist*: Simply like this. The only practical way that you can get guiltless, can maintain an impenetrable skin under conditions such as we are describing, where you keep getting away with doing in others and reaping criminal rewards, is by hostility—by resenting, hating, loathing the world against which you are criminally behaving.

*Patient*: Can't I get away with these things without hating others? Why can't I?

*Therapist*: Not very likely. For why would a person do in others without hating them in some manner? And how could he not be at least *somewhat* concerned about the kind of dog-eat-dog social order he was creating unless he downed his potential concern with defensive resentment against others?

*Patient*: I don't know—. Why couldn't he?

*Therapist*: Have *you?*

*Patient*: Have I, you mean, managed not to—?

*Therapist*: Exactly! With your long history of lying to others. Leading them on to do all kinds of things they didn't want to do, really, by your misleading them as to your feelings for them. The girls you got pregnant and deserted, for instance. The partners in crime you double-crossed. The parents whose help you've always run back for after breaking promise after promise to them? Would you call that *love* you felt for these people? Affection? Kindliness?

*Patient*: Well—uh—no, not exactly.

*Therapist*: And the hostility, the resentment, the bitterness you felt for these people—and must keep perpetually feeling, mind you, as you keep "getting away" with crime after crime—did these emotions make you feel good, feel happy?

*Patient*: Well—at times, I must admit, they did.

*Therapist*: Yes, at times. But really, deep down, in your inmost heart, *does* it make you feel good, happy, buoyant, joyous to do people in, to hate them, to think that they are no damned good, to plot and scheme against them?

*Patient*: No, I guess not. Not always.

*Therapist*: Even most of the time?

*Patient*: No—uh—no. Very rarely, I must admit.

*Therapist*: Well, there's your answer.

*Patient*: You mean to the thick skin business? You mean that I thicken my skin by hating others—and only really hurt myself in the process.

*Therapist*: Isn't that the way it is? *really* is? Isn't your thick skin—like the lamps made of human skin by the Nazis, incidentally—built of, nourished on little but your own corrosive hatred for others? And doesn't that hatred mainly, in the long run, corrode you?

*Patient*: Hm. I—. You've given me something to think about there.

*Therapist*: By all means think about it. Give it some real, hard thought.

In similar manner, the therapist, in session after session with this intelligent psychopath, kept directly bringing up, ruthlessly examining, and forthrightly attacking some of his basic philosophies of living, and showing him that these philosophies underlay his antisocial thoughts and behavior. No criticism of or attack on the patient *himself* was made; but merely on his ideas, his thoughts, his assumptions which (consciously and unconsciously) served as the foundation stones for his disordered feelings and actions.

After 22 sessions of this type of rational therapy, the patient finally was able to admit that for quite a long time he had vaguely sensed the selfdefeatism and wrongness of his criminal behavior, but that he had been unable to make any concerted attack on it largely because he was afraid that he *couldn't* change it—that (a) he had no ability to control his antisocial tendencies; and (b) he felt that he would not be able to get along satisfactorily in life if he attempted to live more honestly. The therapist then started to make a frontal assault on the philosophies behind these defeatist feelings of the patient. He showed Jim that an individual's inability to control his behavior mainly stems from the *idea* that he cannot do so—that long-standing feelings are innate and unmanageable and that one simply *has* to be ruled by them. Instead, the therapist insisted, human feelings *are* invariably controllable—if one seeks out the self-propagandizing sentences (e.g. "I must do this," "I have no power to stop myself from doing this," etc.) which one unconsciously uses to create and maintain these "feelings".

Jim's severe feelings of inadequacy—his original feelings that he never could gain the attention of others unless he was a problem child and his later feelings that he could not compete in a civilized economy unless he resorted to lying or thieving behavior—were also traced to the self-propagated beliefs behind them (to the sentences, "I am utterly worthless unless I am always the center of attention, even though I gain this attention by unsocial behavior"; "If I competed with others in an honest manner, I would fall on my face, and that would be utterly disgraceful and unforgivable", etc.). These self-sabotaging beliefs, and the internalized sentences continually maintaining them, were then not merely traced to their source (in Jim's early relations with his parents, teachers, and peers) but were logically analyzed, questioned, challenged, and counter-attacked by the therapist, until Jim learned to do a similar kind of self-analyzing, questioning, and challenging for himself.

After 31 sessions (mainly on a once-a-week basis) of this type of highly active rational psychotherapy, Jim (who by that time had been placed on probation) voluntarily gave up the fairly easy, well-paying, and unchallenging job which his family, because of their financial standing, had been able to secure for him, and decided to return to college to study to be an accountant. "All my life", he said during the closing session of therapy, "I have tried to avoid doing things the hard way—for fear, of course, of failing and thereby 'proving' to myself and others that I was no damned good. No more of that crap any more! I'm going to make a darned good try at the hard way, from now on; and if I fail, I fail. Better I fail that way than 'succeed' the stupid way I was 'succeeding' before. Not that I think I *will* fail now. But in case I do—so what?"

Jim is now (two years later) finishing up college and doing quite well at his school work. There is every reason to believe that he will continue to do so at his chosen field of endeavor. A self-defeating psychopath has finally turned into a forward-looking citizen. In this case, the patient's high intelligence and good family background unquestionably contributed to making him a more suitable prospect for psychotherapy than the average psychopath would usually be. The same technique of rational psychotherapy, however, has recently been used with several other individuals with severe character disorders and symptoms of acute antisocial behavior and it appears to work far better than the classical psychoanalytic and psychoanalytically oriented methods which I formerly employed with these same kind of patients. While rational therapy is no quick panacea for all human ills, it can be a remarkably effective technique when adequately and forcefully used with a wide variety of severely and moderately disturbed patients.

### REFERENCES

1. CLECKLEY, H. (1950) *The Mask of Sanity*, Mosby, St. Louis.
2. ELLIS, A. (1957) Rational psychotherapy and individual psychology, *J. Individ. Psychol.*, **13**, 38–44 (a).
3. ELLIS. A. (1957) Outcome of employing three techniques of psychotherapy, *J. Clin. Psychol.*, **13**, 344–350 (b).
4. ELLIS, A. (1958) Neurotic interaction between marital partners, *J. Counsel. Psychol.*, **5**, 24–28 (a).
5. ELLIS, A. (1958) Rational psychotherapy, *J. Gen. Psychol.*, **59**, 35–49 (b).
6. ELLIS, A. (1958) Hypnotherapy with borderline schizophrenics, *J. Gen. Psychol.*, **59**, 245–253 (c).
7. LINDNER, R. (1944) *Rebel Without a Cause*, Grune and Stratton, New York.

## IV. OUTCOME OF EMPLOYING THREE TECHNIQUES OF PSYCHOTHERAPY

*Introduction*

Considering the many claims that have been made for the effectiveness of several major techniques of psychotherapy, and the stated or implied conviction that one method is superior to another, it is surprising that almost no studies can be found in the literature where two or more modes of therapy have been tried with similar groups of patients and their results objectively compared. Studies such as that of Fiedler,[9] comparing some aspects of therapeutic relationships in psychoanalytic, nondirective, and Adlerian therapy, are rare; and they usually skirt the ticklish question of therapeutic outcome. The paucity of investigations in this area can partly be attributed to the unusual difficulties involved in doing studies of therapy. Evaluation of outcome of even a single technique, as Mosak,[10] Porter,[11] Rogers and Dymond,[12] Zubin,[14] and others have shown, is a formidable undertaking. It is even harder to compare outcomes of two or more methods: since how are patients, therapists, and conditions of therapy to be fairly matched, to insure each technique's being given an equal chance to prove its worth?

One means of comparing the effectiveness of two or more techniques is for the same therapist to employ, with similar types of clients, each of the methods to be compared: thus largely eliminating the important factor of the therapist's experience and skill. Even this experimental procedure, however, has a serious possible flaw: as there is no certainty that therapists using different methods will be equally enthused and open-minded about the possibilities of each one employed. By a fortunate accident, a situation arose during the last several years where a single therapist, the present writer, was in turn favorably disposed toward three different techniques of therapy: first, orthodox psychoanalysis; then, psychoanalytically-oriented psychotherapy; and finally, rational psychotherapy. In 1949, after seven years of training and experience in clinical psychology, especially in the areas of psychotherapy and marriage counseling, and after the completion of a personal analysis, the writer began, under control, to do orthodox psychoanalysis, employing the sofa, free association, extensive dream analysis, and resolution of the transference neurosis. This was continued for the next three years, when it was gradually abandoned in favor of a face-to-face, highly active and interpretative psychoanalytically oriented technique. From this evolved, at the beginning of 1955, a radically different method called rational psychotherapy.[6, 7]

*Method*

Since it has been the writer's custom, for the last several years, to keep summary records on all clients seen, including information relating to diagnosis, number of sessions, and therapeutic outcome,[5, 8] 78 closed cases were taken from the therapist's files, consisting of individuals who had been treated for at least ten sessions with rational analysis. These were matched with 78 cases of individuals who had been treated for at least ten sessions with psychoanalytically oriented psychotherapy. As a result of matching procedures, each group included 61 neurotics and 17 borderline psychotics.

In the rational therapy group, the mean age was 30·8 years; 36 clients were female; and 83 per cent had some amount of college training. In the psychoanalytically oriented therapy group, the mean age was 30·5 years; 35 clients were female; and 81 per cent had college training. Thus, both groups were closely matched as to diagnosis, age, sex, and education. The group treated with rational techniques, however, left therapy after an average of 26 sessions, while those treated with psychoanalytically oriented techniques left after an average of 35 sessions.

In addition, 16 cases were taken from the therapist's files, consisting of clients who had been treated with orthodox psychoanalysis. The patients included in these cases were 12 neurotics and 4 borderline psychotics; had a mean age of 26·3; consisted of ten females and six males; had some amount of college training in 82 per cent of the cases; and left therapy after an average of 93 sessions.

Each of the individuals in the three groups studied had routinely been rated by the therapist, soon after his or her case had been closed, in terms of whether he or she had made (a) little or no progress while being seen; (b) some distinct improvement; or (c) considerable improvement. These ratings were used in the comparisons listed below.

## Results

The results of this study, in terms of outcome of therapy for the three groups investigated, are listed in Table 1. Examination of the data in this table reveals that therapeutic results appear to be best for clients treated with rational analysis and poorest for those treated with orthodox analysis. When

TABLE 1

*Outcome of employing three psychotherapy techniques*

| Outcome of Therapy | Orthodox psycho-analysis N = 16 | Psycho-analytically oriented psy-chotherapy N = 78 | Rational psycho-therapy N = 78 | Total N = 172 |
|---|---|---|---|---|
| Little or no improvement: | 8 (50%) | 29 (37%) | 8 (10%) | 45 (26%) |
| Neurotic clients | 5 | 19 | 2 | 26 |
| Borderline psychotic clients | 3 | 10 | 6 | 19 |
| Distinct improvement: | 6 (37%) | 35 (45%) | 36 (46%) | 77 (44%) |
| Neurotic clients | 5 | 31 | 30 | 66 |
| Borderline psychotic clients | 1 | 4 | 0 | 11 |
| Considerable improvement: | 2 (13%) | 14 (18%) | 34 (44%) | 50 (30%) |
| Neurotic clients | 2 | 11 | 29 | 42 |
| Borderline psychotic clients | 0 | 3 | 5 | 8 |

tested with Chi-square procedures, the observed differences between the group treated by rational therapy and that treated by orthodox psychoanalysis, as well as those between the group treated by rational therapy and that treated by psychoanalytically oriented technique, prove to be highly significant ($p = 0.001$). The observed differences, however, between the group treated by orthodox psychoanalysis and that treated by psychoanalytically oriented therapy does not prove to be statistically significant. Otherwise stated: significantly more clients treated with rational analysis showed considerable improvement and significantly fewer showed little or no improvement than clients treated with the other two techniques.

The study included too few individuals diagnosed as borderline psychotic to warrant statistical comparison between these and neurotic clients. The data in Table 1 indicate, however, that there may have been a less successful outcome with borderline clients no matter which technique was employed; and that borderline clients treated with rational analysis may have improved more frequently than those treated with the psychoanalytic methods.

In addition to the clients listed in Table 1, the records of another group were examined who first were seen for one of the psychoanalytic therapies and who, a year or more later, returned to be treated with rational analysis. It was found that of 9 clients who received some orthodox analytic treatment and who later were seen for rational analysis, 3 maintained their previous level of improvement and 6 achieved a greater degree. Of 20 clients originally seen for psychoanalytically-oriented therapy, one made a worse adjustment, 5 maintained their previous level of improvement, and 14 achieved a greater degree of improvement when seen for rational analysis.

In an effort to see more precisely what elements of rational technique were effective, the cases of the 59 neurotic clients listed in Table 1 who seemed to show distinct or considerable improvement were analyzed. The main irrational ideas found in these clients, as well as the more rational views replacing these in the course of therapy, were categorized as shown in Table 2.

The data of Table 2, with some additional information gathered from the cases on which the data were gathered, would seem to indicate that (a) each client tended to have several basic illogical ideas rather than one or two main ones; (b) the cluster of irrational notions held by one client was by no means indentical with the cluster held by another client; (c) clients who improved with therapy tended to change many, but hardly all, their irrational attitudes; (d) the degree of improvement of a given client tended to vary directly with the proportion of basic illogical philosophies that he changed; (e) some irrational beliefs were held by nearly all the clients while other beliefs were held by considerably fewer, though still a high percentage, of the 59 individuals who improved with therapy; (f) some irrational beliefs, even after a course of effective therapy, were held more firmly than other self-defeating assumptions.

TABLE 2

*Basic irrational ideas held by 59 clients and their more rational replacements in the course of psychotherapy*

| Basic irrational idea | No. of clients originally holding | More rational replacement | No. of clients finally acquiring |
|---|---|---|---|
| It is a dire necessity for an adult to be approved or loved by almost everyone for almost everything he does. It is most important what others think of one. It is better to depend on others than on oneself.     55 | | It is pleasant, but not necessary, for an adult to be approved or loved by most others. It is better to win one's own respect than others' approval. It is more desirable to stand on one's own feet than to depend mainly on others.     38 | |
| One should be thoroughly competent, adequate, talented and intelligent in all possible respects. The main goal and purpose of life is achievement, success. One is worthless if one is incompetent.     53 | | It is better to focus on *doing* than on doing *well*; to accept oneself as an imperfect creature, who has definite human limitations and fallibilities; to consider oneself worthwhile whether or not one is competent or achieving.     28 | |
| One should severely blame oneself for one's mistakes and wrongdoings. Punishing oneself for one's errors will help prevent future mistakes.     48 | | One should acknowledge and accept one's mistakes and wrongdoings and use them as guides for self-improvement. Punishing oneself for one's errors will usually detract from and sabotage action necessary to eliminate them.     42 | |
| One should blame others for their mistaken or iniquitous behavoir. One should get upset by others' errors and stupidities. One should spend considerable time and energy trying to reform others. One can best help others by roundly criticizing them and sharply pointing out the errors of their ways.     46 | | People who make mistakes or act iniquitously are unintelligent, ignorant, or disturbed, and blaming them is neither just, nor effective. Getting upset by others' errors and stupidities will neither help them nor oneself. It is better to focus on rectifying one's own mistakes than on trying to reform others. One can best help others by serving as a good model of behavior.     34 | |
| Because something once strongly affected one's life, it should indefinitely affect it. Because one was once weak and helpless, one must always be. Because one's parents or society raised one to accept certain traditions, one must always unthinkingly accept them.     45 | | One should learn by one's past experiences but not be overly-attached to or prejudiced by them. Even though one was once weak and helpless, one need not, as an adult, continue to be. One should thinkingly consider and question alternative modes of present behavior rather than act in a purely traditional or customary manner.     38 | |

TABLE 2. *Continued*

| Basic irrational idea | No. of clients originally holding | More rational replacement | No. of clients finally acquiring |
|---|---|---|---|
| It is terrible, horrible, and catastrophic when things are not the way one would like them to be; they *should* be better than they are. Others should make things easier for one, help with life's difficulties. One should not have to put off present pleasures for future gains. | 44 | It is too bad when things are not the way one would like them to be, and one should try to change conditions for the better; but when this is impossible, one had better be resigned to the way things are and stop telling oneself how awful they are. It is nice when others help one with life's difficulties; but if they don't, that is too bad and one can confront these difficulties oneself. If one does not often put off present pleasures for future gain, one sabotages one's own well-being. | 40 |
| It is easier to avoid than to face life's difficulties and self-responsibilities. Inertia and inaction are necessary and/or pleasant. One should rebel against doing things, however necessary, if it is unpleasant to do them. | 43 | The so-called easier way is usually the much harder way in the long run and the only way to solve difficult problems is to face them squarely. Inertia and inaction are generally unnecessary and relatively unpleasant: humans tend to be happiest when they are actively and vitally absorbed in creative pursuits. One should do necessary things, however unpleasant they may be, without complaining and rebelling | 36 |
| Much unhappiness is externally caused or forced on one by outside people and events. One has virtually no control over one's emotions and cannot help feeling badly on many occasions. | 42 | Most human unhappiness is caused or sustained by the view one takes of people and events rather than by the people and events themselves. One has enormous control over one's emotions if one chooses to work at controlling them by saying logical and unself-defeating sentences to oneself. | 36 |
| If something is or may be dangerous or injurious one should be terribly concerned about it. Worrying about a dire possibility will help ward it off. | 31 | If something is or may be dangerous or injurious one should face it and try to render it undangerous or uninjurious; and, when that is impossible, focus on other things and stop telling oneself what a terrible situation one is in. Worrying over a dire situation possibility will rarely ward it off and often will prevent one's effectively counteracting it. | 21 |

*Discussion*

Although the results of this study distinctly favor the hypothesis that a clinician can help his clients improve in a significantly greater number of instances through employing rational therapy than psychoanalytic techniques, they must be taken with due caution. The data only demonstrate that certain clients seemd to improve *with* therapy and not necessarily *because of* it. Only a single therapist's results were investigated, and he could have been prejudiced in his ratings of outcome, the energy and zeal he devoted to different types of treatment, etc. And since the three techniques overlap in some respects, it might be contended that, to the degree that any one of them worked, its success was attributable to some factor common to the other techniques.

Moreover, the fact that clients who previously had psychoanalytic therapy and later, under rational analysis, usually held or increased their level of improvement may merely indicate that clients who secure an extra amount of any type of psychotherapy do better than those who receive only a single ration. The therapist's impression was that most of the clients who did better under rational than psychoanalytic techniques received vital therapeutic ingredients that are normally lacking in the psychoanalytic methods and therefore improved. But this may have been a purely subjective judgement.

More to the point, perhaps, is the observation that, in addition to the clients used in the main comparisons made in this study, another 22 individuals who were treated with rational therapy for from one to five sessions appeared to benefit considerably from their treatment. During a comparative period of time, only 7 clients seemed to benefit similarly from one to five sessions of psychoanalytically oriented psychotherapy and no clients similarly benefited from a few sessions of orthodox psychoanalysis.

Still another interesting sidelight on the relative values of the three techniques surveyed is the fact that whereas the therapist's psychoanalytically-treated clients frequently (as perhaps most clients do) started talking to their friends about their therapy and amateurishly analyzing these friends; and whereas in many or most cases they largely succeeded in antagonizing and confusing these friends with their analyses; the clients treated with rational analysis appeared to have much more success in using some of their newly discovered insights and philosophies with their friends, and in many instances apparently helped these friends considerably.

The obtained evidence relating to specific irrational ideas held by the clients studied would provide reason for believing that neurotics frequently have several basic illogical philosophies of living and that, as they improve in therapy, these philosophies significantly change. It would appear that neurotics *perceive* such things as lack of approval, failure, incompetence, and their own and others' wrongdoing as utterly dreadful, and that they *view* change, self-control, decision- making, effort, and responsibility-taking as terribly difficult or impossible. When, by a fullfledged attack on the irrationality of their beliefs about the horror of disapproval, failure, and wrongdoing, and by a concomitant urging them to make decisions and perform acts which they think are difficult or impossible, they are persuaded to surrender their basic irrational ideas for more rational replacements, they thereby become less neurotic.

From the list of basic irrational ideas obtained in this survey, it would appear that psychoanalytic writers are partly correct in stressing the influence of parent-imposed prejudices: since the adult neurotic's pronounced belief that he must be widely loved, that he must blame himself severely for his wrongdoings, and that he must be strongly affected by his past are fairly obviously related to views that he tends to learn from his parents. On the other hand, it would seem likely that some of the neurotic's most widely held irrational biases, especially those he may continue to hold even after successful therapy, are as much society- as parent-promulgated, and for that very reason may be more difficult to change.

Thus, the present study showed that the one idea which improved neurotics who seem to have the greatest difficulty in replacing in the course of therapy is that of the necessity of their being thoroughly competent and perfectly successful. This idea, of course, is exceptionally indigenous to our culture and is probably as much or more promulgated by non-parental agencies (schools, advertisements, biographies, business mores, etc.) as by parent teachings.

A final word about the use of a rational technique of psychotherapy: from a purely clinical and statistically unsubstantiated standpoint, it may be noted that although, like most other forms of psychotherapy, rational analysis appears to work best with individuals who are not too psychotic, who are fairly intelligent, and who are reasonably young when they come for treatment, it does not necessarily work in relation to any specific psychodiagnostic sub-category. Anxiety neurotics, obsessives, and even seriously schizoid individuals may all benefit by it—providing that they have certain traits that are not necessarily related to any diagnostic category. These traits especially seem to include a willingness to work, intellectual curosity, and a willingness to accept direction from the therapist at the beginning. Among those who benefit least from rational therapy are clients who will not accept hard work and discipline, who refuse to try to think for themselves, and who dogmatically insist on adhering to some absolutist creed—such as orthodox Freudianism.

*Summary*

Data are presented on therapeutic outcome when the same therapist employed orthodox psychoanalysis, psychoanalytically-oriented psychotherapy, and rational psychotherapy with groups of matched clients. It was found that individuals treated with orthodox psychoanalysis showed little or no improvement in 50 per cent of the cases, distinct improvement in 37 per cent, and considerable improvement in 13 per cent. Those treated with psychoanalytically-oriented therapy showed little or no improvement in 37 per cent of the cases, distinct improvement in 45 per cent, and considerable improvement in 18 per cent. Those treated with rational psychotherapy showed little or no improvement in 10 per cent of the cases, disinct improvement in 46 per cent, and considerable improvement in 44 per cent.

Although the observed differences between the groups treated with orthodox psychoanalysis and psychoanalytically oriented therapy did not prove to be statistically significant, those between the groups treated with rational psychotherapy and the other two techniques did reach statistical significance. While the obtained data of the study do not offer incontrovertible proof of the superiority of the technique of rational psychotherapy, they strongly indicate that neither orthodox nor liberal psychoanalytic procedures may be the very last word in effective technique.

Data are also presented on the basic irrational ideas held by neurotic clients and their tendency to give way to more rational replacements with therapeutic improvement.

## REFERENCES

1. ANSBACHER, H. L. and ANSBACHER, ROWENA R. (1956) *The individual psychology of Alfred Adler*, Basic Books, New York.
2. DUBOIS, P. (1907) *The psychic treatment of nervous disorders*. Funk and Wagnalls, New York.
3. ELLIS, A. (1955) *New approaches to psychotherapy techniques*. Brandon, Vermont: *J. Clin. Psych. Monogr. Suppl.*
4. ELLIS, A. (1955) Psychotherapy techniques for use with psychotics, *Amer. J. Psychother.*, **9**, 452–476.
5. ELLIS, A. (1956) The effectiveness of psychotherapy with individuals who have severe homosexual problems, *J. Consult. Psychol.*, **20**, 191–195.
6. ELLIS, A. (1956) Rational psychotherapy. Paper presented at the Annual Meeting of the American Psychological Association, Aug. 30, 1956. To be published in *J. Gen. Psychol.*
7. ELLIS, A. (1957) Rational psychotherapy and individual psychology. *Amer. J. Indl. Psychol.*, **13**, 38–44.
8. ELLIS, A. The private practice of psychotherapy: a clinical psychologist's report. *J. Gen. Psychol.* in press.
9. FIEDLER, F. E. (1950) A comparison of therapeutic relationships in psychoanalytic, nondirective and Adlerian therapy, *J. Consult. Psychol.*, **14**, 436–445.
10. MOSAK, H. (1950) Evalutions in psychotherapy: a study of some current measures. Ph.D. dissertation, University of Chicago.
11. PORTER, E. H. JR. (1943) The development and evalution of a measure of counseling interview procedures. *Educ. Psychol. Msmt.*, **3**, 105–26, 215–238.
12. ROGERS, C. R. and DYMOND, ROSALIND, F. (1954) *Psychotherapy and personality change*, University of Chicago Press,
13. THORNE, F. C. (1950) *Principles of personality counseling*, Brandon, Vermont: *J. Clin. Psych.*
14. ZUBIN, J. A. (1953) Evaluation of therapeutic outcome in mental disorders, *J. Nerv. Ment. Dis.*, **117**, 95–111.

# Behavior Modification in Chronic Schizophrenics*

*Veterans' Administration Hospital, Perry Point, Maryland*

STUDIES of hospitalized schizophrenic patients have begun to shed a somewhat more optimistic light on the prediction and treatment of chronicity, long a problem in neuropsychiatric hospitals. Recent research has suggested that potentially chronic patients may be detected, within reasonable limits of error, shortly following admission (Anker, 1961, 1962; Lindemann *et al.*, 1959). The ability to make such predictions, and an understanding of the bases upon which they are made, may lead to more effective treatment methods designed to reduce the probability of patients becoming long term wards of the hospital. This paper will deal with the treatment of patients already long established in the hospital who have proved generally refractory to conventional therapies. A discussion of the theoretical considerations which prompted this study will be followed by a presentation of the procedures employed and the results obtained.

It was the author's fundamental assumption that any situation producing a change in behavior is a learning situation, and that "therapeutic" effects are phenomena of learning, subject to the principles governing that process. This general viewpoint is compatible with the position taken by numerous authors during recent years, notable among whom are Dollard and Miller (1950), Eysenck (1960), and Wolpe (1959). Bandura (1961) has written an excellent brief review of the literature dealing with psychotherapy viewed as a learning process.

Behavioral reactions to experimental insoluble conflict situations bear a striking similarity to the clinically observed behavior of neuropsychiatric patients. These conflicts usually have been learned discrimination problems with animal subjects (e.g. Gantt, 1953; Richter, 1953; Masserman and Pechtel, 1953; Maier, 1948, 1949). Bizarre and inappropriate behavioral stereotypy, for example, is extremely common in both situations, and equally resistant to extinction. Hovland and Sears (1938), in their experiments on conflict, report similar behavioral disturbances in normal human subjects, albeit less severe. Grinker and Spiegel (1945) observed that the reactions

---

* This paper is a modified and extended version of a study by Anker, J. M. and Walsh, R. P., Group Psychotherapy, a Special Activity Program, and Group Structure in the Treatment of Chronic Schizophrenics, *J. Consult. Psych.*, **25**, 476–481 (1961).

of persons subjected to the more general stresses and/or conflicts of combat at times may be difficult to differentiate from schizophrenic reactions. Such observations suggest the possible advantage in applying principles manipulated in the experimental learning situation to the understanding and modification of naturally occurring clinical behavior deviations.

It has been demonstrated that behavioral disturbances are produced most conspicuously in the "double approach-avoidance" conflict situation (Hovland and Sears, 1938; Dollard and Miller, 1950). Such conflicts involving multiple ambivalence seem to be most typical of problems in human adjustment. Although most certainly an oversimplification, one may take the point of view that symptoms of "mental disorders" are the behavioral result of conflicting ambivalent motives in a multiple approach-avoidance conflict.

It might be assumed, as many authors have in the past, that all humans intrinsically are motivated toward self-realization, self-actualization, and gratification from adequate interpersonal relationships. In functional psychological disorders such adient motivation is thought to be mitigated by extreme avoidance motives learned from damaging interpersonal experience; a life-long pattern of avoiding the potential dangers of human relationships.

On the other hand the schizophrenic may be assumed to have a positive motivation toward intrapersonal protective isolation and "unreal" gratifications of fantasy which are tension-reducing in their own right; the schizophrenic process. This process, however, has been described as posing to the patient the threat of complete ego annihilation, the ultimate destruction of "self" (Fenichel, 1945). This threat initiatcs attempts to re-establish object relations directed at holding or reversing the schizophrenic process. Thus, Fenichel views delusions and hallucinations as attempts to restore contact with reality, from within the psychotic frame of reference. Briefly, the schizophrenic may be viewed as being engaged in a conflict between the ambivalent goals of adequate interpersonal behavior on the one hand and the ultimate outcome of schizophrenic behavior on the other.

Responses to ambivalent goals have been considered as outcomes of approach and avoidance gradients in relation to "distance" from the goal (Dollard and Miller, 1950; Miller 1944). Increasing motivation, the approach gradient, results in a maximal increase in tension with minimal gains toward the goal. A lessening of the avoidance gradient, however, should produce maximal gains toward the goal with minimal increases in tension. The therapies studied and reported in this paper were devised with these principles in mind, and were directed toward increasing effective and rewarding interpersonal relationships among chronic schizophrenics. The treatments, which will be described in detail below, were constructed so as to maximize the potential for reducing avoidance of interpersonal exchange. Interaction with peers was elicited, on a verbal level in group psychotherapy, and primarily on a behavioral level in a special activity group. Responsibility for productivity remained with the patients and there was little or no outside pressure. The only censures experienced by the subjects in the study came from peers within their own group as was true also of the experiences which positively reinforced "normal" behavior. No attempt was made to reinforce approach behavior, to "build" motivation.

This paper reports an experimental study of therapies developed within this theoretical framework but has only indirect relevance to the body of theory itself. It is possible the procedures to be described could have been derived from another theoretical orientation; consequently the study is not "crucial" in this respect. It was not intended either to challenge or to support directly the constructs upon which these treatments were based. They were, rather, simply the springs from which specific procedures, capable of evaluation, were derived.

## THE EXPERIMENTAL VARIABLES

The use of activity programs in neuropsychiatric hospitals received its major impetus from Myerson's "total push" method in the treatment of chronic NP hospital patients (Myerson, 1939). Many authors since have reported varying degrees of success with this treatment method and progressive variations upon it (e.g. Cohen, 1959; Murray and Cohen, 1959; Pace, 1957; Peters, 1955). Patients in such programs usually have been assigned to a group and given or offered a relatively specific "job". Responsibility for performance typically rests with the supervisor or therapist and slightly, if at all, with the patient members. Generally this approach might be thought of as a systematized attempt to increase drive level by stimulation and encouragement.

Scher (1957a, 1957b) extended this concept considerably with his emphasis upon the "task orientation" of the patient. When response to the task was *demanded* rather than being requested Scher concluded that significant therapeutic changes were produced. A controlled study by DiGiovanni (1958) failed to replicate Scher's results when the activity group was compared with a psychotherapy group and a control group, and all groups were compared before and after. The treatment procedures were conducted for only 4 months, however, as compared with 12 months in Scher's study.

Members of groups occurring naturally adopt responsibility and/or develop ways of delegating it to themselves and other members. They participate in a general division of labor. Kretch and Crutchfield (1948) state this mutual cohesiveness, as opposed to external pressure, is what constitutes a group. It was presumed that this type of social organization could occur in a chronic schizophrenic group under appropriate conditions and, to the extent that it did occur, behavior alteration would be possible through the extinction of interpersonal avoidance responses. This kind of group may be distinguished from many extant hospital activity groups by the locus of responsibility, the patient members themselves.

The activity program evaluated in this study was designed to promote this "normal" type of social organization. The criteria chosen for it were as follows: (a) the group should have a definite goal or finished product which may be achieved in a relatively short period of time; (b) the goal should be periodic so that once the immediate goal is achieved another similar one, but one presenting new challenges, takes its place; (c) there must be a sufficient range of demand so that patients at all levels of adjustment may contribute meaningfully to the goal; (d) the activity must be complex enough so that it will pose *meaningful* problems to be resolved by the group; and (e) this activity must be of such a nature that patients are capable of maintaining it with a minimum of staff intervention, particularly professional staff.

After evaluating a number of possible programs, the activity chosen for study was the production of plays for hospital patients and personnel. The characteristics of this activity are described in more detail under "Method".

It would be insufficient to describe the type of group psychotherapy studied as "orthodox". A review of pertinent literature reveals a rather widespread range of approaches to group psychotherapy with schizophrenics (E. G. Bach, 1954; Grauer, 1955; Klapman, 1946, 1947; Kramer, 1957; Lazell, 1954; Peyman, 1956; Powdermaker and Frank, 1953; Schnadt, 1955). The technique used in this study very closely resembles that described by Kramer with the possible exception of less emphasis being placed upon the role of interpretation by the therapist. The atmosphere was permissive and designed to promote a growing sense of "belongingness" by fostering a comfortable "family quality". During the sessions attention was focused upon nonpsychotic verbal interactions between patients. Interaction was encouraged and implemented by the therapist but not demanded. The therapist patterned his orientation after that described by Frank (1952) by being "a perspicacious, strong, accepting person who structured the situation clearly for the patients and supported them in their emotional turmoil". Any level of nonpsychotic verbal interaction was encouraged. This included topics like the difficulty in keeping personal belongings identified in the hospital laundry and the problem of saving enough money for passes. These techniques might be contrasted to the didactic or pedagogical approach suggested by Lazell and Klapman.

A number of authors (Hoffman, 1959; Kramer, 1957; Powdermaker and Frank, 1953), writing on group structure, have speculated on the therapeutic advantages of group homogeneity or heterogeneity. While there is active disagreement in this area, the consensus favors some type of heterogeneity. Group structure, because of its implications for group treatment methods generally was included as a main effect in this study.

It was hypothesized that significant improvement in behavioral adjustment would occur as a result of group psychotherapy, the special activity program (drama group), and heterogeneous group structure. The analysis of these independent variables and of their interactions constitutes the study reported here.

## DESIGN OF STUDY

The three independent variables and their interactions were analyzed by a $2 \times 2 \times 2$ factorial design, each variable being dichotomized. The unique combinations of the three dichotomous variables resulted in eight distinct "treatment" groups. The effectiveness of group therapy was evaluated by contrast with a comparable group not receiving group therapy, the effectiveness of the drama group by contrast with a comparable group not in the special activity program, and the effectiveness of heterogeneity by contrast with a comparable homogeneous group. Because a patient's original level of behavioral adjustment could influence the degree of change in adjustment the data were adjusted for this effect by covariance. Additionally, it was impossible to insure that all patients would remain in the study until its conclusion. Because the length of exposure to the treatment procedures could affect the degree of change in adjustive behavior this effect was covaried as well. Thus the design was a $2^3$ factorial analysis of multiple covariance.

## PROCEDURE

*Selection of Subjects and Groups*

One hundred and thirty-four male schizophrenic patients on a continued treatment ward of a 1500 bed Veterans' Administration neuropsychiatric hospital were rated in the Multidimensional Scale for Rating Psychiatric Patients (Lorr, 1953). A pilot study of interrater reliabilities produces an average reliability coefficient of 0·85 taken over II ward personel. The average interrater reliability coefficient for three raters on the interview section was 0·91. Coefficients in the total matrix ranged from 0·66 to 0·96. This level of reliability was considered sufficient to allow ratings by different raters to be considered as comparable. The protocols were scored for each patient and each profile was compared with the hypothetical normal profile by means of the D statistic (Osgood and Suci, 1952). A distribution of Ds thus was generated, one end of the distribution reflecting maximum congruence with normal behavior, the other end reflecting maximum divergence, or pathological behavior. This distribution was normalized. Subjects for the four homogeneous groups were chosen randomly from patients having $T$ scores between ± 1 standard deviation. The four heterogeneous groups each were comprised of two patients with $T$ scores of $< -1$ S.D., two patients with $T$ scores of $> +1$ SD, and three patients with $T$ scores in the midrange. Based on evidence presented by Bales and Borgatta (1955) and experience in group psychotherapy group size was limited to seven. Each of the four homogeneous and heterogeneous groups was assigned randomly to the treatment combinations of group psychotherapy and the drama group. All eight groups had the same average level of pathology as measured by the Lorr scale. There were no significant differences between groups regarding age, duration of hospitalization, or the taking of ataractic drugs. Median age was 38·9 years. Median duration of hospitalization was 9·2 years. Fifty-three of the 56 experimental subjects were on ataractics.

*Measures*

The principal dependent variable, behavioral adjustment, was measured by the MACC Behavioral Adjustment Scale (Ellsworth, undated). The MACC produces scores entitled Motility, Affect, Cooperation, and Communication, and a Total Adjustment score, the sum of the Affect, Cooperation, and Communication scores. This scale has been shown to differentiate significantly between open ward patients and closed ward patients on a continued treatment service, to be correlated significantly with the Hospital Adjustment Scale, and to be associated significantly with other measures of improved behavioral adjustment such as length of time spent on pass. The scale is short, 14 items, and can be rated with high reliability. Pilot study data on ratings by pairs of raters used in the experiment produces interrater reliabilities ranging from 0·82 to 0·99 with an average coefficient of 0·92, taken over the 15 combinations of six rater pairs. These levels are consistent with reliabilities previously reported for the scale.

Ancillary measures of group cohesiveness and social choice were taken in the hope that the experimental groups would produce measurable changes in peripheral social behavior. The Semantic Differential profile given by each patient on himself was compared with the average profile he gave for other members of his group. A $D$ statistic was calculated and interpreted as a measure of cohesion. As his attitude toward himself and his attitude toward the group converged it was expected the value of $D$ would decrease.

Social choice data were obtained in a free choice situation. All patients on the experimental ward ate at the same time in the same area of the dining hall. They were seated four to a table but had complete freedom to choose any table in the area and any companions from among their fellow patients. Actual choice of companions at the noon meal was recorded for the 56 patients in the study. These choices were then categorized as "in group" or "out group" choices.

*Method*

Following the pilot study on reliability and the selection of groups, all subjects which were rated on the MACC, were given the Semantic Differential (which included their name and the names of the other members of their group), and were observed at their noon meal for three consecutive days and their choice of companions recorded. Sleeping arrangements were changed so that group members has adjacent beds. Simultaneously the experimental procedures began. The four groups in group psychotherapy were seen twice each week for one and one-half hours; a total of three hours a week. All groups were seen by the same therapist, the author.

The four drama groups were formed into two groups of 14, one homogeneous and one heterogeneous. In each group half of the patients were in group psychotherapy and half were not. These groups met three times a week for an hour. Generally they met in the Recreation Hall with a staff moderator, a recreational therapist from Special Services. This moderator had been instructed to supply the groups with all the material and information requested or needed by them for the production of plays, but to avoid taking over the "Leadership" of the group. The role of the moderator might best be characterized as a "Nondirective resource person". This role proved to be a difficult one to assume and was maintained only by frequent consultations between the experimenters and the moderator. Difficulties appeared too from the moderator's identification with the group himself. Thus, when a group once decided to put on a play reading from the scripts, he became personally concerned over the adequacy of their decision. The moderator was present for all of the earlier meetings of the groups but missed some as time went on and occasional conflicting duties prevented his attendance. On those occasions the groups met without him. At the beginning of the study all patients in the drama groups were told individually that they had been chosen for a detail to provide plays for the entertainment of the staff and follow patients. They were "assigned", not given a choice. Some patients protested at leaving present details or simply engaging in an activity for which they did not care. Most patients, however, accepted the new "detail" with characteristic indifference. When complaints occurred about belonging to the group patients were told that their dissatisfaction was understandable but nothing could be done. Further, it was pointed out that they were obliged to meet.this challenge but were free to do it in whatever way they decided as a group.

The study continued for one full year with measures taken every six weeks. The nurses and nursing assistants rating subjects on the MACC were not made aware of the specific hypotheses of the study or of the subgroups into which their patients fell. Two raters from different shifts rated each subject for each rating period. Ratings were based on observations of the subjects for the week immediately preceding the date the ratings were due. It was agreed that any subject leaving the hospital within two months after the beginning of the study was to be replaced by another randomly selected subject. Patients who left after longer than two months were counted as subjects but were replaced in groups by another "equivalent" patient. No data were collected on these subjects which were used only to maintain the groups at their full strength.

## RESULTS

Because the primary dependent variable, the MACC, consisted of four subscores and a summary score, five separate analyses were done. In each case the analysis of the final scores was adjusted by multiple covariance for the effect of initial level and the length of time the subject was in the study. These results are presented in Table 1.

Analysis of the Semantic Differential distance measures between self-rating and the average rating of other group members revealed no difference between original and final measures that could be attributed to any treatment or treatment combination. This measure produced very high attrition because of blank, incomplete, or obviously invalid protocols. It is interesting to note, however, that *all* distance measures decreased over time and that this difference was significant at the 0·02 level.

Changes in choice of luncheon companions from outgroup to ingroup were practically nil. These social choices showed a remarkable consistency over time and no significant differences were obtained, either between treatment groups and combinations of treatment groups or between original and final choices over all subjects.

## DISCUSSION AND CONCLUSIONS

The most compelling result of this study is the consistency with which the activity group showed significant change on the various categories of the MACC Behavioral Adjustment Scale. Changes were significant on all but the Affect subscale where the $F$ missed significance at the 0·05 level by a value of only 0·08. These changes uniformly were in the direction of improved behavioral adjustment. The significant change in the Motility subscale reflected a lessening of motility. The data suggest this was a decrease in behavioral agitation and restlessness. Group psychotherapy showed a significant decrease in motility as well, but the data did not reach significance on the other subscales or on Total Adjustment score. No significant results were attributable to the homogeneity–heterogeneity variable. During the study 18 patients left on trial visit or discharge, two of which returned within six months. No group or treatment showed a significant difference in this regard.

TABLE 1

*Factorial analyses of multiple covariance for MACC behavorial adjustment scale data*

| Source of variation | $R_{x_1 x_2}{}^a$ | $R_{x_1 y}$ | $R_{x_2 y}$ | $R^2_{y \cdot x_1 x_2}$ | $M^2$ error of estimate | $F^b$ | $p$ |
|---|---|---|---|---|---|---|---|
| **Motility** | | | | | | | |
| Act$^c$ | 0·01 | 0·62 | −0·12 | 0·40 | 7·286 | 4·647 | <0·05 |
| GpRx$^d$ | −0·02 | 0·59 | −0·28 | 0·41 | 8·618 | 5·496 | <0·01 |
| GpStr$^e$ | −0·03 | 0·61 | −0·21 | 0·41 | 6·055 | 3·862 | NS |
| Act-GpRx | 0·03 | 0·65 | −0·14 | 0·44 | 2·557 | 1·631 | NS |
| Act-GpStr | −0·05 | 0·60 | −0·19 | 0·39 | 5·650 | 3·603 | NS |
| GpRx-GpStr | −0·03 | 0·62 | −0·22 | 0·42 | 4·218 | 2·690 | NS |
| Act-GpRx-GpStr | −0·03 | 0·62 | −0·22 | 0·43 | 0·770 | 0·491 | NS |
| Within | −0·08 | 0·62 | −0·27 | 0·43 | 1·568 | | |
| **Affect** | | | | | | | |
| Act | −0·54 | 0·48 | −0·39 | 0·25 | 12·669 | 3·681 | NS |
| GpRx | −0·56 | 0·47 | −0·42 | 0·26 | 0·054 | 0·017 | NS |
| GpStr | −0·56 | 0·46 | −0·41 | 0·24 | 6·665 | 2·086 | NS |
| Act-GpRx | −0·55 | 0·46 | −0·43 | 0·26 | 1·188 | 0·372 | NS |
| Act-GpStr | −0·53 | 0·47 | −0·36 | 0·24 | 7·988 | 2·500 | NS |
| GpRx-GpStr | −0·56 | 0·46 | −0·41 | 0·24 | 0·027 | 0·008 | NS |
| Act-GpRx-GpStr | −0·56 | 0·46 | −0·41 | 0·25 | 0·784 | 0·245 | NS |
| Within | −0·51 | 0·41 | −0·37 | 0·20 | 3·195 | | |
| **Communication** | | | | | | | |
| Act | 0·56 | 0·63 | 0·31 | 0·40 | 57·367 | 11·407 | <0·01 |
| GpRx | 0·55 | 0·67 | 0·35 | 0·45 | 4·606 | 0·916 | NS |
| GpStr | 0·57 | 0·68 | 0·40 | 0·46 | 1·272 | 0·253 | NS |
| Act-GpRx | 0·55 | 0·69 | 0·38 | 0·47 | 0·034 | 0·007 | NS |
| Act-GpStr | 0·60 | 0·69 | 0·40 | 0·47 | 0·006 | 0·001 | NS |
| GpRx-GpStr | 0·58 | 0·67 | 0·40 | 0·45 | 9·078 | 1·805 | NS |
| Act-GpRx-GpStr | 0·59 | 0·69 | 0·40 | 0·47 | 5.298 | 1.053 | NS |
| Within | −0·56 | 0·66 | −0·35 | 0·44 | 5·029 | | |
| **Cooperation** | | | | | | | |
| Act | −0·56 | 0·67 | −0·44 | 0·45 | 51·195 | 9·249 | <0·01 |
| GpRx | −0·59 | 0·71 | −0·43 | 0·51 | 3·183 | 0·575 | NS |
| GpStr | −0·57 | 0·71 | −0·39 | 0·50 | 12·161 | 2·197 | NS |
| Act-GpRx | −0·58 | 0·71 | −0·42 | 0·51 | 1·157 | 0·209 | NS |
| Act-GpStr | −0·54 | 0·71 | −0·37 | 0·51 | 0·984 | 0·178 | NS |
| GpRx-GpStr | −0·57 | 0·70 | −0·40 | 0·49 | 3·943 | 0·712 | NS |
| Act-GpRx-Gp-Str | −0·57 | 0·71 | −0·40 | 0·50 | 11·065 | 1·999 | NS |
| Within | −0·52 | 0·67 | −0·32 | 0·45 | 5·535 | | |

[a] $x_1$ = initial level, $x_2$ = length of stay in study, $y$ = final score on dependent variable.
[b] An $F$ of 4·05 is significant at $p = 0.05$, 7·21 at $p = 0.01$.
[c] Act = Activity program (drama groups).
[d] GpRx = Group psychotherapy.
[e] GpStr = Group structure (homogeneity vs. heterogeneity).

TABLE 1. *Continued*

| Source of variation | $R_{x_1 x_2}$ | $R_{x_1 y}$ | $R_{x_2 y}$ | $R^2_{y \cdot x_1 x_2}$ | $M^2$ error of estimate | $F^b$ | $p$ |
|---|---|---|---|---|---|---|---|
| Total Adjustment (Affect ÷ Communication + Cooperation) | | | | | | | |
| Act | −0·53 | 0·63 | −0·42 | 0·41 | 234·073 | 9·496 | <0·01 |
| GpRx | −0·57 | 0·68 | −0·45 | 0·46 | 5·025 | 0·147 | NS |
| GpStr | −0·55 | 0·67 | −0·42 | 0·45 | 56·815 | 1·665 | NS |
| Act-GpRx | −0·57 | 0·68 | −0·44 | 0·47 | 2·074 | 0·061 | NS |
| Act-GpStr | −0·54 | 0·68 | −0·40 | 0·46 | 28·324 | 0·830 | NS |
| GpRx-GpStr | −0·56 | 0·67 | −0·43 | 0·45 | 34·289 | 1·005 | NS |
| Act-GpRx-GpStr | −0·56 | 0·68 | −0·43 | 0·46 | 41·710 | 1·222 | NS |
| Within | −0·52 | 0·64 | −0·37 | 0·41 | 34·126 | | |

The fact that the significant differences found on the MACC for the activity group were not found in the Semantic Differential and social choice data for the same group reinforces earlier questions about these measures. A satisfactory method for screening invalid Semantic Differential protocols was not found. While some protocols were obviously invalid, e.g. those showing an invariant response pattern on the test form, in many cases this judgment was difficult to make. When the validity of a protocol remained in question it was accepted as data and treated as valid. This is an arbitrary procedure at best. Reliabilities on this instrument, using only the "valid" protocols, calculated from immediate test-retest by replicated items in the test form, ranges from − 0·25 to 0·96 with an average of 0·58. The overall change from pre- to post-test, if interpretable at all, most likely reflects a change in therapeutic procedures on the ward which occurred simultaneously but independently of the study. Overall rates of leaves, trial visits, and discharges also increased.

Although choice of luncheon companions was intended to be a measure of the formation of "real" groups resulting from the artificial experimental groupings, it became obvious that this behavior was extremely stable and insensitive to change. Use of a behavioral measure which did not have a previously stereotyped pattern would have been advantageous.

The results of the study are encouraging. While only one treatment produces significant changes, it did so with compelling strength and consistency. The activity variable was responsible for most of the change in behavioral adjustment that occurred. It should be pointed out, however, that a difference existed between the therapy and the drama groups in addition to the differences in "treatment". The group psychotherapist was a different person from the resource person associated with the drama groups. Thus, it is possible that the results document differences between the skills of these two people rather than between treatments as such. While this interpretation is possible it does not seem most parsimonious. This problem was evaluated when the study was designed and there appeared no feasible way of separating person effect from treatment effect and maintaining an adequate design. Additionally, the results favor the activity effect—a treatment wherein the resource person has only minimal contact. The amount and nature of contact with the subjects was specified as carefully as possible before the study began and every effort was made to insure they were maintained as such. Thus this problem does not affect the interpretation of the activity effect, which reached overall significance in any event. One could question the nonsignificance of the results in most areas for group psychotherapy, however. It is possible that a more skilled therapist, using the same procedures, might have produced significant results. It was decided to spell out the group psychotherapy procedures as clearly as possible and have all groups seen by the same therapist to avoid confounding intertherapist differences.

The aim of both the activity and the group psychotherapy programs was to provide the participating patients with a controlled opportunity to reduce the interpersonal avoidance which typifies the chronic schizophrenic. On the bases of the theoretical formulations described earlier it was felt that re-reduction of interpersonal avoidance would result in demonstrable change in behavioral adjustment as measured by the MACC. The fact that such change occurred clearly in the activity program and only slightly in the group psychotherapy program suggest the necessity of examining the differences between these techniques. Although theoretically both were designed to achieve the same end, actual operations were markedly different. A number of alternative explanations might be suggested but it seems most important to the author that the interactions in psychotherapy were primarily verbal, while patient in the activity program interacted on a motoric level as well, and in a "real" context of problem solving. Feedback from behavior would be much more immediate and meaningful in the latter situation and, hence, would tend to have stronger reinforcement value as well as increasing the tendency to generalize.

Because the drama activity had its own discrete characteristics, in addition to the criteria specified in the study, it is impossible to state with certainty the source of the significant differences. It is clear, however, that the activity studies produced significant results in the predicted direction and there is reason to expect that it would do so again at another time or in another place.

This latter finding taken alone should be of significance to those in mental hospitals concerned with the treatment of chronic schizophrenics. The activity program studied here produced consistent and significant behavioral change with a minimum of staff intervention and expenditure of time. The "personnel efficiency" of such a treatment method is unquestionably of value. Of much greater significance, however, it the fact that this inexpensive technique produces results which, in this study, were incomparably better than the more expensive and time consuming group psychotherapy requiring a highly trained therapist. The implications of this study for the systematic use of nonprofessional personnel in the active treatment of chronic schizophrenics are compelling, as well as being attractive.

A number of refinements present themselves for future study. Activity programs should be varied by content, holding basic selection criteria constant, to evaluate the generality of the criteria. It would be expected, of course, that any activity program constructed to conform to the basic criteria and administered as the one currently studied would produce equivalent results. The difficult problem of therapist "effects" in group psychotherapy requires further attention. Although the homogenity-heterogenity variable did not produce significant results as it was studied, it is likely that the method of study could be improved. In this study it was advantageous to make the central tendency in the types of group structure equivalent, varying only the dispersion. It is likely, however, that an effect due to group structure may interact with levels of pathology. Thus a study varying both effects systematically would provide informative data.

## SUMMARY

Group psychotherapy, a specially designed activity program, and the homogeneity or heterogeneity of groups were evaluated as therapeutic modalities in the treatment of chronic schizophrenic patients. These variables were studied in a $2 \times 2 \times 2$ factorial design with multiple covariance of initial level of behavioral adjustment and length of stay in the therapeutic program. The primary dependent, variable was the NACC Behavioral Adjustment Scale and its subscales. Measures of group cohesion and social choice also were obtained. The activity variable produced significant and consistent results in the predicted direction. Group psychotherapy produced relatively minor positive results and the group structure variable produced none. None of the interactions were significant. The ancillary measures of group cohesion and social choice showed no systematic change. The implications of this study for the use of this kind of activity program involving nonprofessional personnel in the treatment of chronic schizophrenic patients are positive and compelling. Refinements in design and suggestions for future research were presented.

## REFERENCES

ANKER, J. M. (1961) Chronicity of neuropsychiatric hospitalization: A predictive scale, *J. Consult. Psychol.*, **25**, 425–432.

ANKER, J. M. (1962) A note on the factor structure of the neuropsychiatric chronicity scale. *J. Consult. Psychol.*, **26**, 198.

BACH, G. R. (1954) *Intensive group psychotherapy*, Ronald, New York.

BALES, R. F. and BORGATTA, E. F. (1955) Size of a group as a factor in the interaction profile. In A. P. HARE, E. F. BORGATTA and R. F. BALES (Eds.), *Small Groups*, Knopp, New York, Pp. 396–413.

BANDURA, A. (1961) Psychotherapy as a learning process, *Psychol. Bull.*, **58**, 143–159.

COHEN, L. B. (1959) The use of extramural activities in group psychotherapy with hospitalized female chronic schizophrenics, *Group Psychother.*, **12**, 315–321.

DIGIOVANNI, P. (1958) Orthodox group psychotherapy and activity group therapy with regressed schizophrenics. Unpublished doctoral dissertation, University of Illinois.

DOLLARD, J. and MILLER, N. E. (1950) *Personality and psychotherapy*, McGraw-Hill, New York.

ELLSWORTH, R. B. *MACC Behavioral Adjustment Scale*, Los Angeles: Western Psychological Services, undated.

EYSENCK, H. J. (Ed.) (1960) *Behaviour therapy and the neuroses*, Pergamon Press, New York.

FENICHEL, O. (1945) *The psychoanalytic theory of neurosis*, Morton, New York.

FRANK, J. D. (1952) Group psychotherapy with chronic hospitalized schizophrenics. In E. B. BRODY and F. C. REDLICH (Eds.), *Psychotherapy with schizophrenics*, International Univer. Press, New York. Pp. 216–230.

GANTT, W. H. (1953) Principles of nervous breakdown—schizokinesis and Autokinesis, *Ann. N. Y. Acad. Sci.*, 143–163.

GRAUER, D. (1955) Problems in psychotherapy with schizophrenics, *Amer. J. Psychother.*, **9**, 216–233.

GRINKER, R. R. and SPIEGEL, J. P. (1945) *War neurosis*, Blakiston, New York.

HOFFMAN, L. R. (1959) Homogenity of member personality and its effect on group problem-solving, *J. Abnorm. Soc. Psychol.*, **58**, 27–32.

HOVLAND, C. I. and SEARS, R. R. (1938) Experiments on motor conflict. I. Types of conflict and their modes of resolution, *J. Exp. Psychol.*, **23**, 477–493.

KLAPMAN, J. W. (1946) *Group psychotherapy*, Grune & Stratton, New York.

KLAPMAN, J. W. (1947) Didactic group psychotherapy with psychotic patients. In S. R. SLAVSON (Ed.), *The practice of group therapy*. International Univer. Press, New York.

KRAMER, M. C. (1957) Group psychotherapy with psychotic patients, *J. Nerv. Ment. Dis.*, **125**, 36–43.

KRETCH, D. and CRUTCHFIELD, R. S. (1948) *Theory and problems of social psychology*, McGraw-Hill, New York.

LAZELL, E. W. (1945) Group psychotherapy. In J. L. MORENO (Ed.), *Group psychotherapy: A symposium*, Beacon, New York.

LINDEMANN, J. E., FAIRWEATHER, G. W., STONE, G. B., SMITH, R. S. and LONDON, I. T. (1959) The use of demographic characteristics in predicting length of neuropsychiatric hospital stay, *J. Consult. Psychol.*, **23**, 85–89.

LORR, M. (1953) Multidimensional scale for rating psychiatric patients, *VA Tech. Bull.*, No. 10–507.

MAIER, N. R. F. (1948) Experimentally induced abnormal behavior, *Sci. Monthly*, **67**, 210–216.

MAIER, N. R. F. (1949) *Frustration: The study of behavior without a goal*, McGraw-Hill, New York.

MASSERMAN, J. H. and PECHTEL, C. (1953) Neuroses in monkeys: A preliminary report of experimental observations, *Ann. N. Y. Acad. Sci.*, **56**, 253–265.

MILLER, N. E. (1944) Experimental studies of conflict. In J. McV. HUNT (Ed.), *Personality and the behavior disorders*, Ronald, New York.

MURRAY, E. J. and COHEN, M. (1959) Mental illness, milieu therapy, and social organization in ward groups, *J. Abnorm. Soc. Psychol.*, **58**, 48–54.

MYERSON, A. (1939) Theory and principles of the "total push" method in the treatment of chronic schizophrenia, *Amer. J. Psychiat.*, **95**, 1197–1204.

OSGOOD, C. E. and SUCI, G. J. (1952) A measure of relation determined by mean difference and profile information, *Psychol. Bull.*, **49**, 251–262.

PACE, R. E. (1957) Situational therapy, *J. Pers.*, **25**, 578–588.

PETERS, H. N. (1955) Learning as a treatment method in chronic schizophrenia, *Amer. J. Occup. Ther.*, **9**, 185–189.

PEYMAN, D. A. R. (1956) An investigation of the effects of group psychotherapy on chronic schizophrenic patients, *Group Psychother.*, **9**, 35–39.

POWDERMAKER, FLORENCE B. and FRANK, J. D. (1953) *Group Psychotherapy*, Harvard Univer. Press, Cambridge.

RICHTER, C. P. (1953) Experimentally produced behavior reactions to food poisoning in wild and domesticated rats, *Ann. N. Y. Acad. Sci.*, **56**, 225–239.

SCHER, J. M. (1957) Perception: Equivalence, avoidance, and intrusion in schizophrenia, *AMA Arch. Neurol. Psychiat.*, **77**, 210–217 (a).

SCHER, J. M. (1957) Schizophrenia and task orientation: The structured ward setting, *AMA Arch. Neurol. Psychiat.*, **78**, 531–538 (b).

SCHNADT, F. (1955) Techniques and goals in group psychotherapy with schizophrenics, *Int. J. group Psychother.*, **5**, 185–193.

WOLPE, J. (1958) *Psychotherapy by reciprocal inhibition*, Stanford Univer. Press.

# Asthma Conceived as a Learned Response*†

JOHN W. TURNBULL

HYPERSENSITIVITY has been demonstrated as an aetiological factor in bronchial asthma, but various authors[6, 14, 34] have pointed out that individuals with skin sensitivity do not always have symptoms when the allergic substances are inhaled, while at other times symptoms may be present without exposure to the substances. In other individuals with asthma, skin sensitivities cannot be demonstrated. These observations suggest that allergic variables alone cannot completely explain the production and development of asthma, and suggest the possibility that psychological variables may help to explain the residual variance.

The way in which psychological variables operate in asthmatic behavior is not clear, but the literature offers some suggestive leads. Dollard and Miller,[5] in discussing the development of physical symptoms as a result of psychological variables, state, "There are two main kinds of symptoms: (1) those that are learned responses to a state of high drive, and (2) those that are innate physiological reactions to a state of high drive or to some consequence of a learned response".[5] Alexander[1] makes a comparable division of symptoms, differentiating between what he terms vegetative neuroses and conversion symptoms. He asserts that vegetative neuroses occur in the vegetative organ system and are the physiological concomitants of a chronic emotional state, while conversion symptoms occur in the voluntary neuromuscular and sensory perceptive systems. Conversion symptoms are regarded as substitute expressions of repressed emotions, and serve to give the organism partial relief through symbolic expression of the underlying need. Alexander states, "Asthma ... has components of a hysterial conversion symptom since it can serve as the direct expression and partial substitute for a suppressed emotion such as the wish to cry. Breathing—although an automatic function—is also under the control of voluntary innervations."[1] Alexander, then, interprets clinical evidence to indicate that asthma is not simply a physiological concomitant of intense emotion, but is a substitute response which serves the needs of the organism.

If asthma can be viewed as substitute behavior which the organism has learned to meet its needs, then it should be possible to apply principles of

* This article is reprinted with the permission of the author and editor from *J. Psychosom. Res.* **6**, 59–70 (1962).

† From the Jewish National Home for Asthmatic Children, Denver, Colorado, U.S.A.

learning in understanding the psychological variables which are involved. The purpose of this paper is to explore the possibility that asthmatic behavior can be produced through learning, and to consider some of the ways in which important learning variables may operate. The emphasis will be upon *molar* breathing patterns. The term *asthma-like* behavior will be used in discussing what is learned, and it will refer to behavior which "looks like" asthma. This term is used with the intent of temporarily avoiding response definition difficulties, so that a preliminary approach to the problem can be made from the point of view of general behavior theory. Genetic and allergic variables will not be dealt with in this paper, but these factors can be conceptualized as dimensions of individual differences in susceptibility to the acquisition of asthmatic behavior.

## HOW CAN ASTHMA BE LEARNED?

At first glance the classical conditioning paradigm seems admirably suited for explaining the learning of asthma-like behavior. Dekker and Groen,[3] for example, reported that with certain asthmatic patients it was possible to provoke reproducible attacks of asthma-like behavior with "obviously innocuous" stimuli. They interpreted these findings as suggesting "acquired conditioning". Laboratory conditioning studies [4, 22 - 24, 26, 27] have also demonstrated that asthma-like behavior can be learned as a conditioned reponse. The typical method has been to expose pre-sensitized animals or sensitive humans to allergic inhalants, thus inducing an asthmatic attack. It is then determined whether stimuli present in the original situation will elicit an asthma-like response on the basis of conditioning. Sufficient evidence is presented in these studies to suggest that asthma-like behavior can be conditioned, but the conditioned response extinguishes quite rapidly, failing to appear within relatively few trials after withdrawal of the unconditioned stimulus. Since the response extinguishes rapidly, these studies do not seem to explain how learned asthma-like behavior can persist.

Respiratory conditioning has also been studied under procedures in which the conditioned stimulus has been paired with noxious stimulation capable of eliciting breathing changes, such as shock. Various types of conditioned respiratory responses have been obtained this way, and several of these studies seem to have relevance for the learning of asthma-like respiratory behavior. Kappauf and Schlosberg[12] conditioned sharp inspirations to a buzzer in rats by following the buzzer with shock. Freedman[7] studied respiratory conditioning accompanying the learning of an avoidance leg flexion response in dogs. He found a conditioned enhancement of respiration which consisted of inspiratory gasps with or without hyperpnea or polypnea. Liddell[16] reported that respiratory disturbance, established through conditioning, is an invariable result of exposing an animal to training for the development of experimental neurosis. A study comparing the ease of respiratory and flexor conditioning was done by Walker and Kellogg.[33] With a buzzer as the conditioned stimulus and shock as the unconditioned stimulus, a highly consistent respiratory conditioned response was established in dogs in half the number of trials required for a highly consistent flexor response. On the other hand, complete extinction of respiratory conditioning was not attained in more than twice the number of trials required for the extinction of flexor conditioning.

Studies in which the respiratory response to be learned is elicited with an allergic unconditioned stimulus show the learning of an asthma-like breathing pattern, but rapid extinction occurs. Conditioning studies utilizing eliciting stimulus (i.e. shock) usually fail to produce a pattern of respiration closely resembling asthmatic breathing, but these respiratory responses show much greater resistance to extinction. The problem seems to be one of explaining how asthma-like behavior conditioned with allergic inhalants can persist, and how a pattern of respiratory behavior more closely resembling asthma can be developed in the presence of emotion eliciting stimuli. An experiment by Brogden[2] suggests an approach to this problem. Brogden performed a conditioning study using classic Pavlovian procedures. He trained dogs to make leg withdrawal responses to a bell, shock as the unconditioned stimulus. He also rewarded each correct response with food, and then shock was omitted to test the Pavlovian principle that the necessary strenghtening operation was the pairing of the conditioned stimulus with the unconditioned stimulus. The conditioned reaction was maintained for as many as 1000 trials (when the tests were concluded) in the absence of shock, as long as food was regularly given. This is conclusive evidence that reinforcement *in the Pavlovian sense* is not necessary for maintaining the strength of an association, since food is not an unconditioned stimulus for leg flexion.

Brogden's experiment suggests that once a response is elicited it can be maintained indefinitely if it continually leads to sufficient reinforcement. This suggests, then, that asthma-like responses conditioned with allergic stimuli could be made to persist in the absence of the unconditioned stimulus if they were followed with a sufficiently strong reinforcement. The reinforcement variable which Brogden used to produce a persistent response has also been shown[11, 18, 20, 21, 25] to be very efficacious in the shaping and development of patterns of behavior. Theoretically there is no reason to believe that an asthma-like pattern of respiration could not, under certain conditions, be shaped and developed by reinforcement, without the necessity for eliciting the response with an unconditioned stimulus of an allergic nature. Thus it seems that reinforcement should not only make conditioned responses originally elicited with allergic stimuli persist, but it could also shape respiratory behavior under conditions in which respiratory changes are elicited by emotion arousing stimuli.

Taking a two factor[20, 21] or a two stage mediation theory of learning,[25] the development of asthma-like respiratory behavior in a fear arousing situation, might, theoretically, occur as follows. When a painful stimulus, such as shock, follows a conditioned stimulus, the conditioned stimulus becomes associated with the fear reaction elicited by the shock. After a number of trials the conditioned stimulus becomes a "sign" of shock, and is able to elicit a portion of the fear reaction, including variations in respiration, prior to the occurrence of shock itself. This emotional reaction to the "sign", a concomitant of which is respiratory fluctuation, could then serve to motivate the organism to try out various instrumental activities to avoid or escape shock. If an asthma-like pattern of respiration (i.e. quick inspiration and long expiration with greater than normal amplitude) happened to be performed, and if this led to avoidance or escape from a feared stimulus, then this breathing pattern would be more likely to appear the next time the "sign" was presented. Anxiety reduction could serve as a powerful reinforcement, and several reinforced repetitions of the breathing pattern might be sufficient to fix it as the organism's most probable behavior in the presence of the conditioned stimulus. Considerable evidence[18, 21] suggests that avoidance responses, once established, are highly resistant to extinction.

One line of evidence which can be interpreted as relating anxiety reduction to asthma-like behavior is found in the reports of workers who have studied experimental neuroses. Masserman and Pechtel[17] described attacks of asthma-like behavior which lasted for several hours in a few of their neurotic monkeys. This behavior apparently appeared when the animals were brought to the experimental situation, and disappeared after they had been removed from the situation for a while. Gantt[9] described asthma-like behavior in his experimentally neurotic dog, Nick, who developed, ". . . a loud raucous breathing with quick inspiration and labored expiration . . . accompanied by a loud wheezing . . ."[9] This respiratory behavior began when the dog was brought from the paddock, increased as the experimental room was approached, and disappeared in reverse order. The experimental situation apparently became a "sign" of shock and capable of eliciting strong fear before many trials elapsed. If asthma-like behavior were simply the animal's natural reaction to intense fear (i.e. an innate physiological reaction to high drive), it should have appeared as soon as fear became strongly associated with cues in the situation. Breathing changes accompanying fear apparently developed immediately after training began, but the pattern of asthma-like respiration developed only after a period of training. Gantt's dog was trained several years before this behavior appeared. Masserman and Pechtel did not report the time period between the start of training and the appearance of an asthma-like pattern of respiration in their monkeys, but presumably this also occurred some time after the commencement of training. There seems to be a good possibility that this pattern of respiratory behavior was accidentally learned, and the fact that it was performed, in both cases, as a function of the animal's nearness to the experimental situation suggests the learning phenomenon of stimulus generalization. It could be that asthma-like respiratory behavior was actually shaped by reinforcement, in the manner suggested above. If an asthma-like pattern of breathing were followed by a marked reduction in anxiety (for example by terminating the noxious stimuli) this would strengthen the preceding behavior. A respiratory pattern could be learned in this way, could be fixated under high drive, and made to persist as an animal's stereotyped response to a stimulus situation.

Mowrer[21] and Dollard and Miller[5] have pointed out that in most forms of maladaptive learning the organism acquires self-punishing responses because they have been associated consistently with anxiety reduction. In human behavior this generally implies a conflict—a desire for something which is anxiety provoking. Without the presence of a conflict the individual would normally reduce anxiety by avoiding the anxiety provoking stimuli. Gantt's[9] dog was held in the experimental situation by a harness. In social learning situations human beings are not harnessed to prevent their avoidance of fearful stimuli, but they can, nevertheless, be trapped in anxiety provoking situations by being strongly motivated to approach a stimulus which elicits intense anxiety. Conflict in human behavior can accomplish the same result with humans that experimental restraints accomplish with animals. Since asthmatic behavior is uncomfortable, often painful and negatively reinforcing, it seems feasible to assume that this behavior, if it is learned, is behavior which is learned to resolve a conflict and reduce anxiety. Anxiety reduction could serve as an effective reinforcer in conjunction with both classical and instrumental conditioning, and it would help to explain the learning and maintenance of asthma-like behavior.

## LEARNING CONDITIONS WHICH EXPLAIN SYMPTOM CHOICE

If asthma-like behavior is learned to resolve a conflict and to reduce anxiety there must be some reason why this pattern of behavior is learned rather than another one. One feasible way in which symptom choice can be explained would be to assume that unconditioned stimuli of allergic nature elicit the response which, through learning, becomes attached to previously innocuous stimuli. Other innocuous stimuli could become capable of evoking the response through higher order conditioning, and if it were reinforced it could be maintained to a wide range of previously neutral cues. It also seems possible that the threshold intensity of unconditioned stimuli required to elicit an asthma response could be lowered , and that response probability to other intensities of the unconditioned stimulus could be increased through learning.

The previous discussion suggests ways in which individuals sensitive to allergic stimuli could learn asthma-like behavior to a range of previously neutral stimuli, but this discussion would not explain the development of asthma-like behavior in relatively insensitive individuals. The earlier discussion of behavior shaping, however, suggested that an asthma-like respiratory pattern might be shaped and developed through reinforcement, even in relatively insensitive individuals. If it is assumed that asthma-like behavior can be learned in this way, it is necessary to look for particular learning conditions which would enhance the probability that respiratory responses resembling asthma would be evoked and shaped by reinforcement.

*Early Respiratory Learning*

When a stimulus-response association is reinforced and strengthened, other similar responses are also more strongly associated with the stimulus.[11] If the initial response becomes ineffective, similar responses which are high in the response hierarchy would most probably be elicited in subsequent trial and error. If a respiratory response were performed by an organism to reduce a drive, and if this response were later rendered ineffective, other similar respiratory responses high in the response hierarchy should be evoked. The greater the similarity between the initial response and asthma-like behavior, the more readily could asthma-like behavior be learned. The previous learning of respiratory responses resembling asthma could greatly enhance the probability of subsequently eliciting asthma-like respiratory responses, and could facilitate the learning of this behavior.

Seitz[29] has reported some observations made in the course of an experiment which suggest that *early* respiratory learning may be important in producing asthma-like behavior. Seitz used the split litter technique and assigned six kittens to each of three experimental groups. Group I kittens were weaned at two weeks of age, and "cried" intensely for a week or more. Group II kittens were weaned around six weeks of age when they began spontaneously to lap milk from saucers. Group III kittens were forced to suckle until 12 weeks of age. Following weaning all kittens had standardized living experiences. In adulthood the animals were given behavioral tests, including exposure to a feeding conflict. Two of the Group I cats developed a chronic, asthma-like respiratory wheezing syndrome following exposure to feeding conflict. It seems striking that the animals which developed this behavior were those animals which had "cried" for a week following early weaning. It is tempting to speculate that, within the context of this experiment, the appearance of an asthma-like respiratory syndrome can be explained in terms of the animal's early learned association between feeding conflict and an intense respiratory response resembling asthma (i.e. crying).

Early respiratory learning is also suggested by the work of French and Alexander,[8] whose psychoanalytic investigation led them to conclude that asthma has the significance of a suppressed cry of the infant for the mother. This view, which is based on clinical observation, also suggests some hypotheses about the learning of asthma-like behavior. The French and Alexander position suggests that asthma is related to early experiences of crying for mother. From a learning point of view this has certain advantages. It brings in respiratory responding which enhances the probability that respiratory responses resembling asthma could be elicited. Secondly, it focuses on infantile experience, a time when a respiratory response (i.e. crying) is very probable, and a period when it can be strongly motivated by intense drives. In the speculative analysis which follows an attempt will be made to relate early respiratory learning to the development of asthma-like behavior.

*Learning the Crying Response*

In infancy the child is extremely dependent upon his environment, and particularly the mother, for survival. Crying is the infant's primary means of signaling for the mother, and is a response which undoubtedly becomes very significant to the child during this period of development. At first the cry is probably part of an automatic reaction to distress which brings the mother who feeds, changes, and cuddles the infant, lowering the level of noxious stimulation impinging upon him. Before long he learns to react to discomfort stimuli by making a voluntary crying response, and with continued reinforcement this is reliably learned. Since the mother provides the reduction of discomfort and the pleasures of life, she soon acquires a great deal of learned reward value through the association of her presence with rewarding circumstances.

While mother's presence is reinforcing, mother's absence or lack of maternal attention probably comes to elicit learned reactions of the opposite kind. Since the mother's absence or inattention is associated at many times with high internal drive stimuli, need frustration, pain, and probably intense fear at times when drives become exceedingly high, it seems reasonable to assume that lack of maternal attention can become associated with the anticipation of these conditions. With continued repetitions a child could learn to anticipate pain and discomfort when alone, and acquire a learned anxiety drive to the stimulus of mother's absence. This drive could serve as a stimulus as well as motivation for the crying response.

If an anxiety drive is learned to the stimulus of mother's absence it would be expected that different learning conditions would produce different intensities of it. The baby of a loving, attentive mother, being well cared for, would have less opportunity to acquire an anxiety drive associated with her absence or inattention. Such a mother seldom puts her child in a situation where he has to do much crying for help. She responds readily to his cry, his needs are often anticipated, and the child would probably feel little anxiety if mother were temporarily absent or inattentive. On the other hand a mother who ignores or disregards her child when strong drives impel him to seek her attention, could teach him to fear her absence. The baby of a rejectant mother would have a very good opportunity to acquire a high anxiety drive to the stimulus of mother's absence or inattention, and this anxiety drive could also become attached to cues indicative of maternal disapproval which in the past have been followed by mother's absence or inattention. When any of the cues to which anxiety has been learned are present, the child would be strongly motivated to make a crying response to signal for mother's attention.

While the "over-protective" mother has often been associated with the asthmatic child, this is not at all incompatible with the notion of a rejecting, unloving mother. A rejecting parental attitude can, as Levy[15] suggested, take the form of "overprotection" in certain forms of parental behavior, while the parent–child relationship still involves a basically rejecting attitude on the part of the parent.

## Learning Conditions Producing an Inhibition of Crying

The crying response could be extinguished by non-reinforcement. If the hypothetical rejected infant cries in response to the learned anxiety drive associated with mother's absence, but if the crying response no longer works (i.e. is not reinforced), the probability that the infant will cry under stimulation of the anxiety drive will become less and less, while the strength of other responses associated with the crying response, either innately or through learning, becomes relatively greater. As the strength of the crying response is reduced it would become increasingly probable that another response would be tried out in its place.

The response could also be inhibited with punishment. Since the cry is well established and its performance has been associated with the reduction of a high drive state, it could not be easily inhibited. Negative reinforcement could greatly increase the probability that the cry would be suppressed. A rejecting mother might be very annoyed to find that her crying child is not hungry, thirsty or wet, and might punish the child for crying when "nothing is wrong". If the child were actually punished for crying when he was afraid of being alone or when fear was aroused by signs of maternal disapproval, a true conflict would be created between the anxiety motivating crying and the anxiety motivating the inhibition of crying.

Interesting enough, Gerard[10] reported clinical investigations of three male and two female asthma cases whose mothers displayed a "...hypersensitiveness and irritability to the crying of the infant. Two said they 'shook the baby out of crying'; another beat him; another said she left him alone until he stopped crying." These observations together with our theoretical analysis, suggest that punishment may be particularly important in establishing early conflict, and of mediating the conflicting respiratory responses of crying and the inhibition of crying. The generality of inhibitory training could also vary. Through differential negative reinforcement the child might learn to discriminate between "times when it is all right to cry" and "times when it is not all right to cry". The more generalized the inhibitory training the more generalized and severe would be the conflict and the attendant anxiety.

### Learning a Compromise Response

In both of the situations mentioned above crying has not worked for the infant, and he would be strongly motivated to find an instrumental response to replace the cry when the drive eliciting stimuli are present. A number of respiratory responses which have a resemblance to asthmatic behavior (i.e. sighing, gasping, wheezing, and coughing) often follow severe crying spells. These responses should be high in the hierarchy of responses[11] to stimuli which are cues for the response, and should have a high probability of being tried out in the organism's search for a new instrumental response to reduce anxiety. If the child begins to make respiratory responses resembling asthma instead of the crying response, and if these responses are reinforced by the anxiety reduction associated with maternal attention, their probability of occurrence would be increased. Initially these respiratory responses might only remotely resemble clinical asthma, but with continued reinforcement they could increase in amplitude and in specificity. The mother would be most likely to respond promptly to intense respiratory responses, and through differential reinforcement could train her child to respond with increasing intensity. Responses resembling asthma could be gradually shaped by reinforcement, until a well developed asthma-like response is present to function in place of the crying response. This discussion suggests the theoretical advantage which previous respiratory learning has in explaining the learning of asthma-like behavior. The high probability of eliciting respiratory responses resembling asthma following the inhibition of a previously instrumental respiratory response (i.e. crying), would help to account for the choice of symptom.

Our earlier explanation of how asthma-like behavior could be learned with allergic unconditioned stimuli could operate together with the response generalization mechanism we have been discussing, and the combination of these conditions would seem to provide a particularly good opportunity for asthma-like behavior to be learned. If unconditioned stimuli for asthma or responses resembling asthma happened to be present during the organism's trial and error experimentation with new instrumental respiratory responses, these stimuli could further increase the probability that relevant respiratory responses would be evoked. Unconditioned stimuli could also produce greater response intensity, and improve the likelihood that the response would elicit maternal attention. Thus it would be more likely that a response resembling asthma would be reinforced and strengthened. These responses could become progressively more like clinical asthma in the manner previously suggested, and could persist with continual reinforcement.[2] While many stimuli could serve this purpose, stimuli associated with respiratory illnesses, allergic reactions, colds, bronchitis and whooping cough are common in childhood, and could serve as unconditioned stimuli for responses resembling asthma. The presence of a high anxiety level should also insure quicker establishment of the response, since various investigators, among them Taylor[32] and Spence and Farber[30, 31] have shown that a conditioned response can be more readily established in high anxiety individuals than in individuals with low anxiety.

The extent to which anxiety has been associated with the inhibition of crying could make a considerable difference in the continuation of the learned asthma-like responses. If the crying response has been inhibited by anxiety and conflict is created, the child faces a greater problem than if he simply gave up the cry because it did not work. In the latter case it would be likely, even if asthma-like responses were learned, that they could be given up for more pleasant, adaptive approach responses as the child matures. On the other hand if the mother has created a conflict by punishing crying, and made the child fearful of making approach responses toward her, he would still need the maladaptive, asthma-like responses as he grows older. With continued use and reinforcement they would become stronger, and could become one of his major means of meeting his needs.

It has been hypothesized that asthma may be related to early respiratory learning. There are, however, many patients in whom asthmatic symptoms, diagnosed as such, appear long after infancy. In these individuals something on the order of instrumental act regression[19, 28] may be involved. It could be that respiratory responses similar to those discussed previously have been learned early in life, but other more adaptive instrumental responses are subsequently learned to take their place. If these latter responses were blocked or frustrated and were no longer instrumental in producing reinforcements for the individual, they could be given up and the individual could "regress" to the earlier learned asthma-like behavior. Just as we previously suggested that the presence of unconditioned stimuli for responses resembling asthma could facilitate the shaping of an asthma-like respiratory pattern, so it also seems that unconditioned respiratory stimuli of this sort could facilitate the evocation, reinforcement, and reinstatement of "regressive" early respiratory learning. In thinking of regression to early learning as a factor which may be important in explaining late onset, something like the relationship Seitz[29] observed between intense respiratory responding in infancy and later asthma-like behavior is hypothesized.

## RESPONSE PERFORMANCE

The performance of an asthma-like response would require the presence of stimuli to which the response has been learned, and the greater the number of learned stimuli the more probable it would be that some stimulus capable of response elicitation would be present to evoke the response. The variables which affect the strength of a learned association[11] should affect the probability that a particular stimulus, whether it is an internal drive stimulus (i.e. anxiety) or a stimulus external to the organism, would be capable of response elicitation. The number of reinforced repetitions of the response in the past, and the amount and kind of reinforcement should be particularly important. Anxiety reduction would seem to be especially effective as a reinforcer. Response performance should also be increased as drive level is raised.

The stimulus generalization mechanism could also increase the organism's responsiveness to stimuli. If internal drive stimuli or external stimuli become capable of eliciting asthma-like behavior through learning, the asthma-like response could be elicited by other stimuli which lie along intensity and qualitative similarity continua with those stimuli to which the response was initially learned. Thus, generalization could increase the range of internal and external stimuli capable of evoking an asthma-like response. Increases in both the strength of original learning and in the drive level of the organism can raise the heights of stimulus generalization gradients, so both of these factors could increase the range of effective stimuli. Since intra-individual fluctuations in drive level would be likely to occur at different times and in different situations, drive level fluctuations could produce transient changes in generalization gradients for the asthma-like response. Raising the heights of generalization gradients, whether with differences in learning or with transient fluctuations in drive level, should make more stimuli capable of eliciting the response and should increase the probability of response evocation to stimuli previously capable of eliciting asthma-like responses on the basis of generalization.

If, as we previously assumed, asthma-like behavior can be learned and will persist as a means of resolving an approach-avoidance conflict, it should increase as conflict is increased, and become more probable with increments in conflict producing variables. Approach–avoidance conflict theory and stimulus displacement theory[5] should be particularly useful in analyzing some of the factors involved. A detailed analysis of asthma-like behavior within the framework of conflict theory is beyond the scope of this paper, but Knapp et al.[13] have reported a study which offers preliminary evidence that the probability of asthmatic behavior increases with degree of conflict. Forty asthmatic patients, most of whom were studied for a period of time by two psychiatrists, were independently rated on severity of pulmonary disability, and on severity of personality disturbance. The asthmatics ranged from mildly neurotic individuals with mild physical incapacity to severely disturbed individuals who had "...drastic and crippling respiratory illness". The authors reported a correlation of 0·81 between the two ratings. They also reported transient psychotic reactions in some of their subjects, and all but one of these episodes coincided with asthmatic attacks. A cause and effect relationship cannot be inferred from their correlation, but the observed relationship is in general agreement with our previous speculations, and suggests that an exploration of asthma-like behavior within the framework of conflict theory might be very fruitful.

## SUMMARY OF RESEARCH IMPLICATIONS

Since the value of a theoretical model resides in large part in its capacity to generate research ideas, some of the hypotheses implied by the theoretical discussion are listed below, and summarize some of the implications of this position.

(1) Through the use of allergic unconditioned stimuli an asthma-like response can be learned with classical conditioning methodology, and can be made to persist in the absence of the unconditioned stimulus, if the response is consistently followed by a strong reinforcement. Learning speed should be increased and speed of extinction should be reduced as drive level is raised.

(2) The threshold intensity of unconditioned stimuli capable of eliciting asthma responses can be lowered, and response probability to other intensities of the unconditioned stimulus can be increased through learning.

(3) After a learned association is established between a stimulus and an asthma-like response, new stimuli can become capable of eliciting the response through higher order conditioning (this should be particularly true in avoidance conditioning, where an asthma-like response is used as the instrumental avoidance response).

(4) A learned asthma-like response will prove more resistant to extinction if reinforced by anxiety reduction than if reinforced by reduction of positive approach drives.

(5) An asthma-like response can be learned in an instrumental learning situation through the use of behavior shaping methodology, that is, by gradually shaping respiratory behavior by reinforcing breathing patterns which are progressively closer approximations of asthmatic breathing.

(6) Asthma-like behavior can be learned more readily to replace respiratory instrumental responses (i.e. like crying) than to replace nonrespiratory instrumental responses. The greater the similarity between the original instrumental response and asthma-like behavior, the more readily could an asthma-like response be learned to take its place.

(7) If an asthma-like response is learned as an instrumental response to reduce anxiety, and if a more "adaptive" instrumental response is later learned to take its place, frustration of the more recent response should produce "regression" to the asthma-like response.

(8) When an asthma-like response is learned to a stimulus, generalization will occur to stimuli which lie along intensity and qualitative similarity continua with the initial stimulus. Learning and performance variables

which raise the height of the generalization gradients will do so in the generalization of the asthma-like response (i.e. particularly strength of original learning and drive level during performance).

## ACKNOWLEDGEMENTS

The author wishes to thank Dr. Maurice P. Smith, Psychology Department, University of Colorado, for reading an earlier draft of the manuscript, and for his helpful suggestions. Thanks are also due to Mr. Donald Loy, Psychology Department, Lookout Mountain School for Boys, Golden, Colorado, for reading and discussing the manuscript with the author. Finally, the staff members of the Psychology Department of the Jewish National Home for Asthmatic Children deserve considerable credit for their stimulating criticisms and suggestions during the entire period in which these ideas were being developed.

## REFERENCES

1. ALEXANDER, F. (1951) Fundamental concepts of psychosomatic research: psychogenesis, conversion, specificity. In *Psychological theory* (Ed. M. H. MARX) Macmillan, New York.
2. BRODGEN, W. J. (1939) Unconditioned stimulus substitution in the conditioning process. *Amer. J. Psychol.* **52**, 46.
3. DEKKER, E. and GROEN, J. (1956) Reproducible psychogenic attacks of asthma. A laboratory study. *J. Psychosom. Res.* **1**, 58.
4. DEKKER, E., PELSER, H. E. and GROEN, J. (1957) Conditioning as a cause of asthma. *J. Psychosom. Res.* **2**. 97.
5. DOLLARD, J. and MILLER, N. E. (1950) *Personality and psychotherapy*, McGraw-Hill, New York.
6. DUNBAR, H. F. (1938) Psychoanalytic notes relating to syndromes of asthma and hay fever. *Psycho-Anal. Quart.* **7**, 25.
7. FREEDMAN, B. (1951) Conditioning of respiration and its psychosomatic implications. *J. Nerv. Dis.* **113**, 1.
8. FRENCH, T. M. and ALEXANDER, F. (1941) Psychogenic factors in bronchial asthma. *Psychosom. Med. Monogr.* Vol. 4.
9. GANTT, W. H. (1944) *Experimental basis for neurotic behavior*, Harper and Brothers, New York.
10. GERARD, M. W. (1953) Genesis of psychosomatic symptoms in infancy. The influence of infantile traumata upon symptom choice. In *The psychosomatic concept in psychoanalysis* (Ed. F. DEUTSCH) Monograph series of the Boston Psychoanalytic Society and Institute, No. 1. International Universities Press, Inc., New York.
11. HULL, C. L. (1952) *A behavior system*, Yale Univ. Press, New Haven.
12. KAPPAUF, W. E. and SCHLOSBERG, H. (1937) Conditioned responses in the white rat—III. Conditioning as a function of the length of the period of delay. *J. Gen. Psychol.* **51**, 27.
13. KNAPP, H. R., NEMETZ, J. S., GILBERT, R. R., LOWELL, F. C. and MICHELSON, A. L. Personality variations in bronchial asthma. *Psychosom. Med.* **19**, 443.
14. LEIGH, D. (1952) Allergy and the psychiatrist. *Int. Arch. Allergy* **4**, 227.

15. Levy, D. M. (1943) *Maternal overprotection*, Columbia Univ. Press, New York.
16. Liddell, H. (1951) The influence of experimental neuroses on respiratory function. In *Somatic and psychiatric treatment of asthma* (Ed. H. A. Abramson) Williams and Wilkins, Baltimore.
17. Massermann, J. H. and Pechtel, C. (1953) Neuroses in monkeys. A preliminary report of experimental observations. *Ann. N.Y. Acad. Sci.* 56, 253.
18. Miller, N. E. (1950) Learnable drives and rewards. In *Handbook of experimental psychology* (Ed. S. Stevens) Wiley, New York.
19. Mowrer, O. H. (1940) An experimental analogue of "regression", with incidental observations on "reaction formation". *J. Abnorm. Soc. Psychol.* 35, 56.
20. Mowrer, O. H. (1947) On the dual nature of learning: A reinterpretation of "conditioning" and "problem solving." *Harv. Educ. Rev.* 17, 102.
21. Mowrer, O. H. *Learning theory and personality dynamics*, Ronald, New York.
22. Noelpp, B. and Noelpp-Eschenhagen, I. (1951) Die Rolle bedingter Reflexe beim Asthma bronchiale. Ein experimentaler Beitrag zur Pathogenese des Asthma bronchiale. *Helv. Med. Acta.* 18, 142.
23. Noelpp, B. and Noelpp-Eschenhagen, I. (1951) Das experimentelle Asthma bronchiale des Meerschweinchens—II. Ermittlung der Rolle bedingter Reflexe in der Pathogenese des Asthma bronchiale. *Int. Arch. Allergy* 2, 321.
24. Noelpp, B. and Noelpp-Eschenhagen, I. (1952) Das experimentelle Asthma bronchiale des Meerschweinchens—III. Studien der Bedeutung bedingter Reflexe, Bahnungsbereitschaft und Haftfähigkeit unter Stress. *Int. Arch. Allergy* 3, 108.
25. Osgood, C. E. *Method and theory in experimental psychology*, Oxford Univ. Press, New York.
26. Ottenberg, P. and Stein, M. (1958) Psychological determinants in asthma. In *Transactions of the fifth annual meeting of the Academy of Psychosomatic Medicine* (Ed. W. Dorfman) Academy of Psychosomatic Medicine.
27. Ottenberg, P., Stein, M., Lewis, J. and Hamilton, C. (1958) Learned asthma in the guinea pig. *Psychosom. Med.* 20, 395.
28. Sears, R. R. (1944) Experimental analysis of psychoanalytic phenomena. In *Personality and the behavior disorders* (Ed. J. McV. Hunt) Vol. 1. Ronald, New York.
29. Seitz, P. F. D. Infantile experience and adult behavior in animal subjects—II. Age of separation from the mother and adult behavior in the cat. *Psychosom. Med.* 21, 353.
30. Spence, K. W. and Farber, I. E. Conditioning and extinction as a function of anxiety. *J. Exp. Psychol.* 45, 116.
31. Spence, K. W. and Farber, I. E. (1954) The relation of anxiety differential eyelid conditioning. *J. Exp. Psychol.* 47, 127.
32. Taylor, J. A. (1951) The relationship of anxiety to the conditioned eyelid response. *J. Exp. Psychol.* 41, 81.
33. Walker, E. I. and Kellogg, W. N. (1929) Conditioned respiration and the conditioned flexion response in dogs. *J. Comp. Psychol.* 27, 393.
34. Wittkower, E. (1935) Studies on the influence of emotions on the function of organs. *J. Ment. Sci.* 81, 533.

# Recent Empirical and Theoretical Approaches
## to the Experimental Manipulation of Speech
## in Normal Subjects and in Stammerers*

AUBREY J. YATES

*University of Western Australia*

DURING the past ten years, considerable interest has been aroused in relation to phenomena associated with the technique known as delayed auditory feedback (D.A.F.), in which the subject (S) hears his own voice in an unnatural time relationship to his speech (the aural feedback of the voice being delayed by about one-fifth of a second). The possible relevance of findings in this area of study to the explanation and treatment of stammering has not been neglected. It is the purpose of this paper to present the main established facts in relation both to the effects of D.A.F. on speech, and in relation to stammering; to consider some recent theoretical formulations relating to the genesis and maintenance of stammering; and to discuss the extent to which the facts and the theories can be integrated. It is hoped to show that a significant break-through has been made in these areas in recent years and that rapid progress can be expected in the future, provided experimentation is directed along the crucial channels.

No attempt will be made to document in detail the basic facts to be presented. The extensive literature on D.A.F. has recently been received by the author (Yates, 1963), while many competent and thorough reviews of the facts concerning stammering have been made (see, e.g. the excellent introductory but well-documented survey by Johnson in Johnson *et. al.* (1956)). It should be carefully noted, however, that the facts to be considered in this paper represent a deliberate selection from the vast amount of material now available. Not all the established facts are necessarily crucial to the establishment of a valid theory. Indeed, since the "nature" of a fact depends on the methods by which it is obtained, some "facts" may be completely misleading in relation to the establishment of a working theory. In a sense, therefore, the chosen facts are grouped together because they appear to be directly relevant to the kind of theories which are later considered in this

* This article is reprinted with the permission of the author and editor from *Behav. Res. and Ther.*, (1963) **1.**

paper. No apology need be made for this, since the usefulness of the theory will be determined not merely by its ability to account for a given set of selected facts, but by its fruitfulness in predicting new findings and by its relevance to the successful treatment of stammering.

## A. EMPIRICAL STUDIES OF DELAYED AUDITORY FEEDBACK AND STAMMERING

### Delayed Auditory Feedback

Interest in the phenomena resulting from D.A.F. stems primarily from the work of Lee (1950a, 1950b, 1951) and Black (1951) in the United States, who apparently began their investigations independently at the same time. It is known that speech is monitored in three main ways. Kinaesthetic and sensory feedback from the speech organs provide some information. A second source is provided by the transmission of the speech sounds to the cortex via the bony structures of the body, especially the bones of the head. A third source is provided by the transmission of the speech sounds to the cortex via the air to the ear.

The airborne transmission of feedback can be interfered with in the following way. A magnetic tape recorder is modified in such a way that the voice production of $S$ may be recorded on the tape and then stored in the tape recorder for brief periods of time, after which it is returned to $S$'s ears through closely fitting headphones which occlude normal airborne feedback. The delay may be varied from very short time intervals up to about 0·30 sec, the optimal time interval for producing disturbance being 0·18–0·20 sec. It is, of course, possible to control the intensity level of the feedback at $S$'s ear, so that it can be maintained at a fixed level if desired.

The principal independent variables which have been manipulated in experiments on D.A.F. have been delay-time and the intensity of the feedback at $S$'s ear. The principal dependent variables have been duration of phrase (the time taken to read a standard passage of prose, or a phrase, or even a word) and intensity of utterance (changes in the level at which $S$ speaks). Other dependent variables (which probably overlap with the two principal ones) have included fundamental frequency, intelligibility and articulatory changes (repetitions of syllables and continuant sounds; mispronunciations; omissions; substitutions, etc.).

The task which $S$ has to accomplish under D.A.F. usually involves reading a passage of prose. The degree of standardization of the material has varied widely, from uncontrolled material to phonetically balanced passages or ones which have been equated for difficulty level, or which contain all English speech sounds. A quite different task, which has important advantages over prose material, was that used by Butler and Galloway (1957) in which five two-digit numbers were successively flashed at random on a screen in one of five different positions at a fast presentation-rate.

The principal facts concerning the effects of D.A.F. on normal speech which are considered to be of relevance in the present context may be summarized as follows:

1. *Effects of feedback delay and intensity on speech structure.* An early study by Black (1951), using specially constructed five-syllable phrases and delay times from 0·03 sec to 0·30 sec (with intensity held constant) suggested that duration of phrase increased as a function of delay up to 0·18 sec, then declined. He found a linear trend (longer delays producing greater disturbance up to

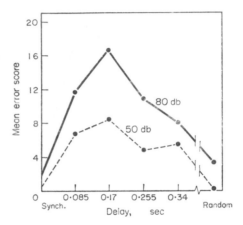

FIG. 1. Mean error score as a function of delay with different intensity levels serving as parameters (Butler and Galloway, 1957).

0·18 sec) but with a discrete increment at 0·06 sec. Tiffany and Hanley (1952) found that a reduction in reading rate resulted from an increased intensity of feedback under constant delay time, the relationship again being linear. However, a subsequent study by Butler and Galloway (1957) showed quite clearly the existence of an interaction effect between delay time and feedback intensity. As previously mentioned, their task involved the rapid naming of pairs of digits. Two intensity levels of feedback (50 db and 80 db above sensation level) and four delay times (0·085 sec; 0·17 sec; 0·255 sec; and 0·34 sec) were used. As controls, synchronous feedback and a condition they called random delay were also used. The Ss were 240 military and civilian personnel allocated at random to the various conditions and the dependent variable was the number of errors, obtained by subtracting the number of digit pairs correctly repeated under D.A.F. from the number correctly repeated without D.A.F. The results of the experiment are shown in Fig. 1. At a feedback intensity level of 50 db above sensation level, all delay times produced an equal amount of error, which was significantly higher than that found under synchronous feedback. At a feedback intensity level of 80 db above sensation level, however, a differential effect of delay was found. The number of errors increased at all delay times compared with 50 db, but a delay of 0·17 sec now produced a significantly greater effect than any other delay time. It should be noted that these results of Butler and Galloway are not inconsistent with the differential delay effects found in Black's experiment, since Black used a feedback intensity level of 85–90 db (re. 0·0002 dyn per cm²) at the reader's ear, while the linear relationship between feedback intensity and error score found by Butler and Galloway is in agreement with the results of Tiffany and Hanley (1952).

2. *Effects of feedback delay and intensity on intensity of utterance.* The results here are incomplete. Mean intensity of response has been shown to increase as a function of increased delay up to 0·09 sec and then remain constant with increased delay (Black, 1951), and these results have been confirmed by Atkinson (1953). However, Spilka (1954a) did not find any *differential* effect of delay on vocal intensity (although the intensity did increase under delay). He did, however, find a differential effect of delay on vocal intensity variance (the variance of vocal intensity peaks), but this effect was not linear. In considering these results, it should be noted that both Black and Spilka varied only delay time with intensity held constant, and that both used a very high level of feedback. Furthermore, Spilka's *shortest* delay time was 0·094 sec, whereas Black found that the increase in vocal intensity was found only up to 0 09 sec, remaining at a constant level thereafter. Thus, the results are not inconsistent. No information is at present available regarding inter-action effects of delay and intensity of feedback on intensity of utterance. Similar comments apply to Fairbank's (1955) finding of a constant increase of 10 to 12 db over the entire range of delay times which he studied.

3. *Effects of delay time and feedback intensity on fundamental frequency.* It has been shown that there is a significant rise in fundamental frequency from about 109 to 130 c/s at delay levels from 0·10 sec to 0·80 sec, with no differential effect being present (Fairbanks, 1955). However, Fairbanks investigated only delay times of 0·10 sec and above. Again, nothing is known about interaction effects.

4. *Effects of delay time and feedback intensity on intelligibility.* Increasing the intensity of D.A.F. produces a decrease in intelligibility (Atkinson, 1954), the change probably being linear (only three intensity levels were used). Differential, but non-systematic effects of delay were found, but there was no interaction between delay and feedback intensity.

5. *Effects of delay time and feedback intensity on articulation.* Various "qualitative" changes in speech have been noted under D.A.F. These include: repetition of syllables and continuant sounds; mispronunciations; omissions; substitutions and number of word endings omitted. Two findings of special interest should be noted. Korobow (1955) found that number of

intrusions *diminished* under D.A.F. Fairbanks and Guttman (1958) found
an interaction between delay time and *type* of error: while the number of
*omissions* doubled as delay changed from zero to 0·20 sec, *additions* became
twenty times as common.

6. *Adaptation to D.A.F.* Tiffany and Hanley (1956) used a 45-word prose
passage which S read under D.A.F. twelve times on two occasions separated
by a week. They found no adaptation in speed of reading, either within or
between sessions. But "fluency breaks" (repetitions and omissions) declined
significantly *between* a series of readings, although showing no adaptation

TABLE 1

*Mean and population variance of reading time (in seconds) for 60 subjects reading
ten 200-syllable sections of prose
under normal and delayed feedback conditions*

| Passage | Normal conditions | | Delayed feedback | |
|---------|-------|----------|-------|----------|
| Section | Mean | Variance | Mean | Variance |
| 1 | 52·7 | 33·6 | 70·4 | 187·7 |
| 2 | 51·7 | 38·4 | 68·5 | 182·3 |
| 3 | 51·7 | 34·8 | 65·3 | 166·4 |
| 4 | 54·5 | 50·4 | 65·9 | 179·6 |
| 5 | 52·2 | 42·3 | 64·0 | 204·5 |
| 6 | 51·0 | 42·3 | 62·1 | 134·6 |
| 7 | 51·4 | 36·0 | 62·8 | 136·9 |
| 8 | 53·4 | 54·8 | 63·1 | 116·6 |
| 9 | 50·8 | 32·5 | 59·7 | 114·5 |
| 10 | 50·1 | 38·4 | 58·8 | 114·5 |

Sources: Gibbons *et al.* (1958) and Winchester *et al.* (1959).

within a series. Reading speed and fluency correlated 0·72 for the first series,
but only 0·39 for the second series, suggesting that readers may learn to
overcome the "stuttering" effect, but not the change of rate. The latter conclusion is untenable, however. A later study by Winchester *et al.* (1959)
utilized ten 200-syllable passages (about 1600 words) read continuously.
They found no adaptation of reading rate during the first two passages
(400 syllables or about 320 words) but did find a significant increase in
reading rate during the remaining passages, the final passage being read
about 12 sec faster than the first. Taken together, these results strongly suggest that the "stuttering" effect adapts first, and this then permits an increased reading rate. However, the reading rate under D.A.F. is still significantly slower than under normal conditions at the end of the 2000-syllable
passage, as is apparent from control data collected by Gibbons *et al.* (1958).
The relevant data are shown in Table 1.

The effects of D.A.F. generally tend to disappear immediately and completely as soon as normal speech conditions are restored. Thus, Tiffany and Hanley (1952, 1956) found no difference in the characteristics of speech immediately before and immediately after the application of D.A.F. Their studies, and others, however, do suggest that some residual effect may persist for some time in the speech of Ss who are *severely* affected by D.A.F. This latter suggestion, which could be of considerable significance, has not so far been systematically investigated.

7. *Personality and delayed auditory feedback.* Work in this area will be mentioned only briefly since (a) the results are entirely inconclusive and (b) there is no reason to suppose that personality characteristics play other than a minor role in determining degree of susceptibility to D.A.F. Speakers with high verbal knowledge or high initial intelligibility are less affected by D.A.F. than speakers with low verbal knowledge or intelligibility (Arens and Popplestone, 1959; Atkinson, 1954; Beaumont and Foss, 1957). The effects of verbal fluency, though theoretically very important, have not been investigated. Spilka (1954b) hypothesized that Ss who are dependent on exteroceptive (in this case, auditory) cues will be more affected by D.A.F. than Ss who rely mainly on interoceptive (proprioceptive or kinaesthetic) cues, the underlying assumption being that all Ss rely on a combination (in differing proportions) of internal and external cues to monitor their skilled responses. Some support for this hypothesis was obtained by Spilka (1954b) and also by Goldfarb and Braunstein (1958), the latter working with normal and schizophrenic children. The correlation of various traits with susceptibility to D.A.F. does not, however, present a very clear picture. In terms of Eysenck's more parsimonious system, for example, the results could be interpreted either in relation to the introversion–extraversion dimension, or to the normal-neurotic dimension, or both. In an endeavour to clarify the situation, scores on the Maudsley Personality Inventory were correlated with indices of breakdown under seven different time delays at constant feedback intensity (Yates and Wells, to be published). The results showed that, for 35 Ss, the correlation between neuroticism and a mean error score derived from Johnson (1961) was 0·082; while the correlation of error score with extraversion was 0·117. These results should, however, be regarded with caution. A detailed examination of the relationship indicated the possibility that the relationship with neuroticism might be non-linear, with severe neurotics being either over *or* under susceptible to D.A.F. A study on a larger scale would be necessary before any firm conclusion could be drawn concerning the relationship between degree of breakdown and personality factors.

8. *Development aspects of D.A.F.* It is obvious that, from the theoretical viewpoint, study of the effects of D.A.F. at different age levels is of crucial importance. Unfortunately, only two studies have so far been published which

throw any light on these aspects. Goldfarb and Braunstein (1958) tested 25 normal children aged 8 to 10½ years under a delay of 0·16 sec, the speech of the children being rated carefully by an expert with respect to many characteristics. Under D.A.F., they found that all the children showed gross speech impairment compared with reading under normal conditions. Chase *et al.* (1961) tested ten normal children in each age group from 4 to 9 years under D.A.F. and normal conditions, the task being that of making up a story about a drawing. In spite of the unfortunate failure to use standard material, the results suggest fairly clearly that D.A.F. has a greater disrupting effect on the speech of older than of younger children. These results are therefore in agreement with those of Goldfarb and Braunstein.

9. *Varying conditions of feedback and speech.* Two important studies have thrown a good deal more light on the conditions producing breakdown in speech. Winchester and Gibbons (1957) divided 160 normally hearing

TABLE 2

*Four conditions of presentation of feedback*

| Test condition | Mode of presentation | Sensation levels | | Delay time |
|---|---|---|---|---|
| | | D.A.F. | Masking tone | |
| A | Binaural D.A.F. | 60 db | — | 0·16 sec |
| B | Uniaural D.A.F. | 60 db | — | 0·16 sec |
| C | Uniaural D.A.F. + masking | 60 db | 80 db | 0·16 sec |
| D | No D.A.F. or masking | — | — | — |

Source: Winchester and Gibbons (1957).

adults into four groups, which were allocated to one of four conditions, as shown in Table 2. As indicated in the table, D.A.F. was presented binaurally (condition A), uniaurally (condition B), and uniaurally with a masking tone in the other ear (condition C). The fourth condition (no D.A.F. or masking tone) represented a control for normal reading rate, the dependent variable. The results are shown in Table 3 and indicate that uniaural delay without masking of the other ear produced *less* disturbance than uniaural delay with masking of the other ear, although all three delay conditions produced significantly more disturbance than the control condition.

Chase and Guilfoyle (1962) presented delayed and undelayed feedback simultaneously to both ears. The gain of the undelayed feedback was varied from one-third, two-thirds or equal to that of the delayed feedback. Increasing the gain of the undelayed feedback progressively diminished the disturbance produced by the delayed feedback. However, speech was still disturbed compared with normal conditions when the gain of the undelayed feedback was made equal to that of the delayed feedback. No information is yet available as to what happens if the undelayed feedback is considerably *more* intense than the delayed feedback.

TABLE 3

*Group reading times in seconds for four feedback conditions*

| Test condition | N | Mean age | Mean time | $\sigma$ | Range |
|---|---|---|---|---|---|
| A | 40 | 37·6 | 179·8 | 24·4 | 130·6−238·2 |
| B | 40 | 32·9 | 160·3 | 19·1 | 129·0−209·4 |
| C | 40 | 39·2 | 169·8 | 26·4 | 132·7−223·6 |
| D | 40 | 31·6 | 129·8 | 21·3 | 90·5−183·8 |

Source: Winchester and Gibbons (1957).

10. *Control studies.* It is necessary to mention briefly some control studies which rule out the possible confounding effect of certain variables. Butler and Galloway (1957) have shown that random delay (defined as playing back through headphones a previous record of the task S is now performing) does not produce any increase in number of errors in the task used by them. Yates (1962a) has shown that D.A.F. does not affect performance on a highly skilled task (typewriting) where the feedback may be regarded as random noise, i.e. D.A.F. appears to affect skilled response patterns only where the feedback carries "meaning" or "rhythm". Peters (1956) showed that a speaker's production varies in intelligibility (as judged by a panel of listeners) according to the conditions under which he speaks. His speakers read lists from intelligibility tests while simultanously hearing auditory signals which varied from the same, similar but not identical, and unrelated material, to meaningful "flight-patter" phrases and babel. Speakers were more intelligible if the signals were babel or words similar to those read than if the signals were the same or unrelated words. Winchester and Gibbons (1958) found that a uniaural or binaural masking tone of high intensity did not affect the reading of a 500-syllable prose passage. Gibbons *et al.* (1958) showed that reading rate remains remarkably constant over a long period of time under normal conditions.

11. *Effects of D.A.F. on tasks other than speech.* It has been shown that rhythmic handclapping (Kalmus *et al.*, 1955), tapping (Chase *et al.*, 1959), and whistling (Hanley and Tiffany, 1954) may be severely disturbed by D.A.F. Chase *et al.* (1961) compared S's performance on two tasks (repeating [b] and tapping in groups of three) and found that similar types of error were committed in both tasks. However, they also found an insignificant correlation between error scores for the two tasks, a finding of

considerable theoretical interest. Disturbances similar to those found with speech have been noted in non-auditory tasks. Van Bergeijk and David (1959) delayed the visual feedback from handwriting by 0·50 sec while kinaesthetic feedback remained unaltered. Disturbances in handwriting resulted which were similar to those for speech. Chase *et al.* (1961) investigated the effect on tapping of presenting a delayed visual or tactile stimulus at a fixed interval of time after each tap. For example, with delayed tactile feedback, each time *S* tapped, a hard fibre dowel automatically struck *S*'s forearm 300 msec later. As the authors point out, they are here dealing with a form of delayed sensory event bearing a fixed time relationship to the tap. Nevertheless, complex (patterned) tapping was found to be quite severely affected under these conditions, compared with those involving synchronous feedback.

12. *Effects of bone-conducted D.A.F.* All of the studies dealt with so far have employed airborne feedback transmitted through headphones to the ear. However, Cherry and Sayers (1956) report that the effect of D.A.F. transmitted to the ear through a bone-conduction channel is considerably more severe than that of a correspondingly loud sound transmitted through telephones by air conduction, and, in fact, may be quite distressing.

## II. *Stammering*

The number of facts which have been established in relation to stammering must by now run into thousands. Practically every possible factor which could conceivably throw light on stammering has been subjected to examination. Here, we will present only a small selection of those facts. We will confine ourselves, for reasons stated earlier, to the facts which are particularly relevant to the theories to be discussed later. The empirical evidence to be presented may be roughly divided into two categories: the general characteristics of stammering behaviour; and the methods by which stammering can be experimentally modified.

1. *General characteristics of stammering behaviour.* (*a*) It is important to note that it is not easy to make a clear distinction between the speech of stammerers and non-stammerers. If stammering behaviour is scored for various types of non-fluency a considerable degree of overlap is found between the characteristics of the speech of individuals classified as non-stammerers and those classified as stammerers. This finding applies both to adults and children, with the differences being even less for children than they are for adults. Representative results are shown in Table 4. Recent data presented by Johnson (1961) show, in detail, the degree of overlapping in adults, for various categories. Indeed, if the records of the most fluent stammerers and the most non-fluent non-stammerers are presented in random order, even speech experts find it very difficult to classify them correctly (Johnson, 1956, p. 206). It is clear that we are dealing with a continuum of fluency–non-fluency and that while individuals labelled as stammerers

will tend to fall towards the non-fluent end of the continuum there will be many labelled stammerers whose fluency will be greater than that of individuals who have never been so labelled.

TABLE 4

*Average number of non-fluencies of various types*
*per 100 words in the speech of 42 stutterers and 42 non-stutterers*
*(average age—5 years)*

| Type of non-fluency | Stutterers | Non-stuttererers |
|---|---|---|
| Interjection | 2·9 | 2·7 |
| Part-word repetition | 4·2 | 0·4 |
| Whole-word repetition | 4·5 | 1·2 |
| Phrase repetition | 1·4 | 0·5 |
| Revisions | 1·4 | 1·5 |
| Incomplete phrases | 0·2 | 0·05 |
| Broken words | 0·1 | 0·03 |
| Prolongations | 1·5 | 0·15 |

Source: Johnson (1956).

(*b*) The incidence of stammering appears to be roughly seven per thousand of the population (Schindler, 1956). Significant cultural differences have been observed, however, and it has been suggested that the highest incidence of stammering may be found in "upwardly mobile" areas (Darley, 1955)

(*c*) The onset of stammering is usually, though not always, early in life, with ages three to four often being focal points (Johnson, 1956, p. 228).

(*d*) It seems indisputable that stammering is found more frequently in boys than in girls (Schuell, 1946). The difference varies in different studies, but the average difference may be as high as four to one.

(*e*) There is no evidence that, except for rare special cases, there is any defect of the motor structures involved in speaking; indeed, there is good evidence that stammerers are equally as good as non-stammerers in executing voluntarily skilled movements of the speaking and breathing musculature (Strother and Kriegman, 1943, 1944). This is not to deny, of course, that stammerers often exhibit quite severe motor disturbances while speaking.

(*f*) There is no evidence that stammerers are in any way different from non-stammerers in physiological or biochemical characteristics (Hill, 1944a, 1944b).

(*g*) There is no evidence that stammerers are any different from non-stammerers in personality characteristics. The notion that stammering is a symptom of some underlying *neurotic* conflict or is an indication of serious personality disturbance, appears to have no basis in fact. Rather, stammerers appear to differ in much the same way as do normals from neurotic or psychotic patients. Such differences on personality tests as are found would seem to reflect a *normal* reaction to a severe social disability. As Johnson puts it: "they differ in tending to be a bit more depressed or discouraged, a bit more anxious or uneasy or unresponsive, especially in speech situations, and somewhat more withdrawing socially. The kinds and degrees of difference indicate, not a serious personality maladjustment, but rather a normal kind and amount of emotional reaction to the sorts of frustrating, threatening, and unpleasant experience that stuttering involves" (Johnson, 1956, p. 239). In fact, it is extraordinary that more stammerers do not develop severe personality disturbances.

(*h*) Contrary to the often expressed opinion of stammerers themselves, there is no evidence that stammering increases with fatigue (Curtis, 1942).

(*i*) There is no evidence at present which will stand up to critical examination of any relationship between stammering and handedness.

(*j*) Close examination of the stammering behaviour itself has shown (in addition to the types of errors outlined earlier) that stammering tends to occur on no more than 10 per cent of the total number of words spoken; that a stammering "sequence" lasts usually no more than one to two seconds; that there is an interaction between stammering and the type of word being spoken (Brown, 1945); and that, if stammerers are asked to read a passage several times, they tend to stammer on the same words in successive readings (consistency response). It may also be noted that while interjections comprise about 35 per cent of non-fluencies of stammerers in speech, they comprise only 12 per cent of reading non-fluencies. The comparable figures for part-word repetitions are 25 per cent (speech) and 45 per cent (reading).

(*k*) Finally it may be noted that there are very considerable individual differences in the type of stammering from which different individuals suffer.

2. *The experimental modification of stammering behaviour.* There is abundant evidence that the speech of stammerers can be experimentally modified to a truly remarkable degree. The early evidence has been reviewed in detail by Bloodstein (1950). We shall concern ourselves as before, however, with only a selected portion of the evidence, i.e. that which seems to be particularly relevant to the theoretical formulations which follow.

(*a*) Stammering may be totally inhibited by a technique known as speech shadowing (Cherry and Sayers, 1956). With this method the stammerer, speaking aloud, follows as closely behind as possible another speaker who is reading from a prose passage which the stammerer does not see. Severe stammerers may achieve very high speaking speeds by this method. The present author has found that equally striking results are obtained if a tape recording or a speaker's voice on the radio are shadowed.

(*b*) Even more simply, stammering may be abolished by means of simultaneous reading, in which the stammerer and another person read from the same book. Furthermore, the stammerer will usually continue to read without fault even if the second reader switches to a different part of the passage, or starts reading gibberish. However, if the second reader stops reading, the stammerer will gradually return to his usual hesitant reading. It should be emphasized that in nearly all instances, the suppression of the stammer by shadowing or simultaneous reading is total, and the speech, if recorded, is usually indistinguishable from normal *superior* fluency. This total suppression can be achieved by not more than 40 or 50 words of practice in the case of simultaneous reading. (By the use of headphones and appropriately placed microphones, it is possible, with simultaneous reading, to record the stammerer's voice clearly with the other reader's voice heard faintly in the background. In this way, the various effects outlined above may be readily demonstrated.) Shadowing may take a little longer to master, but this is usually because of lack of skill in "pacing" the stammerer by the reader.

(c) Stammering may be abolished if the stammerer reads aloud as one of a group of normal readers or stammerers (Barber, 1939).

(d) Stammering may disappear during singing or whispering.

(e) Stammering may disappear during states of high emotion, e.g. if the stammerer becomes very angry.

(f) A series of experiments by Cherry and Sayers (1956) showed that stammering is abolished if the stammerer is prevented from hearing the low-frequency components (which are mainly bone-conducted) of his own voice while speaking. The steps in the argument were as follows:

(i) Elimination of air-conducted feedback alone does not affect stammering.

(ii) Elimination of both air-conducted and bone-conducted feedback by masking white noise approaching the pain threshold in intensity produces complete suppression of stammering.

(iii) Elimination, by means of a filter, of the high-frequency components of speech feedback only, does not affect stammering.

(iv) Elimination, by means of a filter, of the low frequency components of speech feedback only (within the range 120–180 c/s) results in the total suppression of stammering. These low frequency components are mainly bone-conducted, and emanate principally from the larynx. Cherry and Sayers (1956) also showed that the stammer was suppressed if the stammerer whispered under masking conditions, thus ruling out the possibility that the stammer disappeared merely because the intense feedback made the stammerer speak more loudly than ususal. The results for 54 cases are shown in Fig. 2. The very few breakdowns which occurred under a high energy 140 c/s masking tone arose from momentary difficulties in starting. It is again emphasized that these results were obtained with virtually no practice. They have been confirmed independently by Shane (1955) and by Maraist and Hutton (1957).

A recent study by Sutton and Chase (1961), however, sounds a caution-ary note. A voice-actuated relay controlled the presentation of white noise during reading. Nine stutterers were presented with each of the follow-ing conditions:

(i)   reading under normal conditions;

(ii)  reading under normal conditions but wearing headphones;

(iii) reading in the presence of continuous white noise (the Cherry and Sayers condition);

(iv) reading under white noise which was present only while they were speaking;

(v)  reading under white noise which was present only while they were silent.

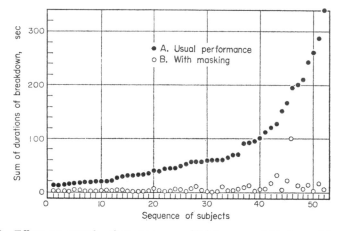

FIG. 2. Effect on speech of stammerers of high-energy 140 c/s masking tone (Cherry and Sayers, 1956).

Sutton and Chase found that conditions (iii), (iv) and (v) were equally effective in improving the speaking rate compared with conditions (i) and (ii), and they concluded that white noise did not produce its effect by pre-venting the speaker from listening to his own voice. This experiment is not conclusive, however, since there is, as we have seen, a normal delay of feedback in speech. Hence, the "white noise during silence" condition would actually mask *some* of the normal feedback of speech and this might be all that is required to effectively stop the S from listening to his own voice. Nevertheless, the results merit careful consideration.

(g) Stammering is significantly reduced (though the effects are much less dramatic than those related above) by continous reading of the same pas-sage (adaptation effect). This finding has been confirmed many times (e.g. Trotter, 1955; Golub, 1956).

(h) Stuttering is significantly reduced under a number of conditions which appear to have in common the fact that they arouse considerably less anxiety than the usual social conditions under which speech takes place. These conditions have been summarized by Bloodstein (1950) and include: reduced communicative responsibility (e.g. speaking alone or to a child); a sympathetic audience; reduced need to impress favourably; speaking in a unfamiliar way (e.g. in a foreign language); speaking rhythmically.

This concludes our survey of the empirical data we have chosen to present. It is repeated that it represents a storehouse of facts selected from a very large population. We turn now to a description and discussion of recent theoretical attempts to account for the facts relating to the effects of D.A.F., and the facts relating to stammering behaviour, and whether there is any possibility that the two sets of phenomena may ultimately be accounted for by means of a single theory relating to the self-monitoring of speech.

## B. THEORETICAL INTERPRETATIONS OF DELAYED AUDITORY FEEDBACK AND STAMMERING

### I. Delayed Auditory Feedback

It is extraordinary how little attention has been directed at the problem of how continuous speech is monitored and adjusted or corrected in relation to events occurring *within the speaker*. The majority of the standard texts on speech and hearing are completely silent on this important question, although they consider in detail the problem of the maintenance of communication (intelligibility or articulation accuracy) under changing environmental conditions, such as an increase in the level of noise. No doubt this is in part due to the very scanty amount of knowledge presently available concerning the neurological events concerned in speech and hearing. Any model of a speech control mechanism must of necessity at present be of a hypothetical nature. The neglect is the more surprising since there has been no lack of interest in the more general question of the control of high level skills. A good deal of controversy has occured, for example, over the question whether high level skilled performance is *continuously* or only *intermittently* monitored. Thus, whereas Lashley (1951) has argued that continous monitoring (in the sense that peripheral feedback from one response can influence the next response) is impossible at least in certain types of skilled performance, such as piano-playing, Gibbs (1954) has argued that continous monitoring *is* possible. Although the problem has not been solved, it is clearly of crucial importance for any theory of the self-monitoring of speech. It will be obvious that D.A.F. could be extremely useful in obtaining more empirical information about this vexed question.

Lee (1951) suggested that the speech mechanism operates like a machinegun, repeating aurally monitored units as long as the "trigger" is held down. More generally, he conceived of continuous speech as constituting a closed-loop feedback system and he argued that "a mechanism which depends on feedback for continuation or procedure into the next cycle may halt for either of two reasons: (1) the impulse or initiating phase may fail, or (2) the feedback may fail, and thus, lacking the necessary returning signal, the machine will also halt. Yet another result of feedback failure or delay might be repetition of the inititating impulse over and over until the mechanism is satisfied to proceed to the next cycle by the returned signal of feedback." (pp. 54–55).

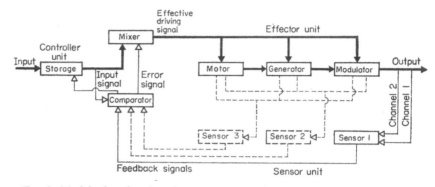

FIG. 3. Model of a closed cycle control system for speaking (Fairbanks, 1954).

Chase (1958) has argued that D.A.F. "facilitates the circulation and recirculation of speech units in the speech-auditory feedback loop" (p. 584). If this assumption is correct, it follows that it should be possible to repeat a sound more times under D.A.F. than under normal conditions. Chase found an average increase of 3·3 in the number of times the speech sound [b] could be repeated under a delay of 0·216 sec during a 5-sec period compared with a control period of similar duration. Thus, it seems that a delay in the feedback does facilitate repetition of speech units and this could well result in the kinds of disturbances which we have found to result from D.A.F.

A more comprehensive model of how a self-monitory feedback mechanism for speech might be conceptualized has been provided by Fairbanks (1954). He stresses the importance, not merely of estimating and correcting the present state of the system, but also of predicting the future course of events. The model proposed by Fairbanks is shown in Fig. 3. Essentially, his closed cycle system involves:

(i) an *effector unit* (which produces an output);

(ii) a *sensor unit* (which picks up the output);

(iii) a *storage unit* which contains the short-term instructions for a set of speech units which must be displayed through the effector unit in a definite sequence—when the sequence is completed a new set of instructions appears;

(iv) a *comparator* which matches the feedback signals from the effector unit with the input information received from the storage unit;

(v) a *mixer unit* which receives the input and error signals and combines them so as to reduce the error signal to zero.

The comparator, however, also contains a predicting device which continously indicates the future point at which the error signal will be zero. Thus, the input may be changing even before the transmission of the current speech unit is completed.

Under normal speech conditions, it may be assumed that the control system has "learned" how to correct rapidly and effectively for minor deviation (such as faults in articulation, etc.) from the normal speech pattern and for familar changes in environmental conditions (such as a sudden rise in noise level). The mechanism has, as it were, stored "experiences" against which the current output can be matched and corrected if necessary. If, however, as occurs in the case of D.A.F., the time relationship between the various types of feedback is severely distorted, the controller mechanism may not immediately be able to handle the situation. The whole system may be brought temporarily to a halt, or the signal may be repeated, or the organism may be reduced to trial-and-error behaviour. Goldiamond *et al.* (1962) have pointed out that the repetitions and prolongations characteristic of the response to D.A.F. may well represent the attempt of the organism to restore the customary overlap of output/feedback relationships in normal speech.

Fairbank's model is of particular interest in that it does seem to overcome some of the problems associated with the question of continuous monitoring of skilled behaviour. His model suggests that units of speech run off automatically and without further direct monitoring unless the error signal exceeds certain limits. Only then would the self-correcting mechanism actually be called into action. It should also be noted that it is here being suggested that the error concerns the asynchrony between air-conducted and other types of feedback. However, it is conceivable that the asynchrony also relates to the disparity between the time delay expected on the basis of previous experience and that actually being experienced. In either case the model helps to explain why there are such marked individual differences in degree of susceptibility to D.A.F. It suggests that whether or not an individual is highly susceptible to D.A.F. depends on the degree to which he utilizes *auditory* feedback in monitoring his speech. Individuals who are highly dependent on auditory feedback will be subject to severe breakdown under D.A.F.; whereas individuals who rely mainly on bone-conducted or kineasthetic feedback will show less breakdown. The experimental implications will be obvious.

However, as a recent study by Stromsta (1962) shows, the whole problem of feedback is likely to prove extremely complex. Stromsta reviewed the previous relatively scanty evidence concerning the differential transmission rates of air-, bone-, and tissue-conducted sound which suggested that there are remarkable differences in speed of transmission of sound through bone and tissue which are additional to disparities arising from spatial distances to the auditory receptors. His own study fully confirms and extends these earlier findings. He measured the minimum delay times (using male Ss only) in the following pathways: (i) a bone pathway (from the superior medial incisors to the mastoid process); (ii) a tissue pathway (from the vocal cords to the mastoid process); (iii) the internal pathway of minimum delay (from the vocal cords to the mastoid process irrespective of media); (iv) the air pathway (from the vocal cords through the pharynx and oral cavity to the tympanic membrane). His basic procedure may be illustrated by reference to the bone pathway measurements. He stimulated the incisors with each of a series of rectangular pulses representative of thirteen frequencies ranging from 125 to 2000 c/s. The transmitted impulses were picked up at the incisors and mastoid process and the arrival time difference electronically determined. Two striking findings emerged. First, there are large differences between the various media in the extent to which they resist the passage of sound, second, within a particular medium (except, of course, for air-conduction), the resistance varies according to the frequency being transmitted. The results are shown in Fig. 4a (expressed as delay-time as a function of medium and frequency) and 4b (expressed as propagation time as a function of medium and frequency).

Stromsta's results suggest that, for normal speech, the feedback via the various transmission media is delayed naturally by varying amounts, and this in turn indicates, first, that the brain must be receiving information relating to any particular speech unit spread over a time period which is greater than that involved in producing it. This further suggests that the integration of these disparate sources of information in normal speech must be central in nature, rather than peripheral.

Fairbank's model is purely fictional in our present state of knowledge of how central controlling processes operate. This is not to deny its usefulness or importance, however. But it is clear from what has been said thus far that a great deal more work of a very precise nature will be required before sufficient information of a basic kind is available which will enable a mathematical (i.e. one involving measurable qualities) model to be constructed or indeed before the essential controlling factors can be specified. This work, in relation to speech, will need to proceed along at least three lines and indeed some progress of a qualitative kind has already been made. First, the work of Stromsta, of a physical and physiological nature, needs to be continued and extended. Second, careful studies concerning the perception of successive sounds are urgently needed. Hirsch (1959, 1961) has recently carried out important studies in this area. He has shown that two brief sounds can be distinguished separately with temporal intervals as small as 2 msec. However, an interval as long as 17 msec is required if the *order* in which the sounds occured is to be correctly reported. Hirsch concluded from his studies that for temporal order judgements a peripheral mechanism is probably insufficient. Third, much more information is required concerning the time relationship involved when the organism is simultaneously receiving and transmitting information. Thus, the present author has shown (in a study to be published) that skilled operators will make many more errors on morse

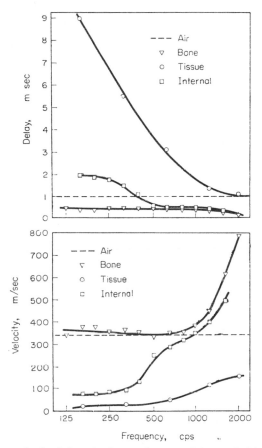

FIG. 4a. Delays obtained for air, bone, tissue, and internal sidetone pathways as a function of frequency (Stromsta, 1962).

FIG. 4b. Propagation velocity as a function of frequency for air, bone, tissue, and internal sidetone pathways (Stromsta, 1962).

code letters involving three of four symbols than on those letters involving only one or two when transmitting continuously under a delay of 0·18 sec randomly constructed lists of letters. The error score increases as a function of whether the letters are being transmitted individually, continuously at a preferred rate, and continuously as fast as possible. These results suggest that errors will not occur provided the transmission rate of a unit is so fast that the symbol is sent *before* the D.A.F. arrives back at the controlling mechanism. Further experiments are in progress to determine the effects of delays other than 0·18 sec (which, although optimal for speech disturbance, may not be for morse sending) and the effects of delay in continuous transmission of *meaningful* material. It is obvious that there is here a rich field of investigation.

Two other areas of investigation may be mentioned briefly in which the empirical results and theoretical formulations should prove to be of fundamental significance for any model of speech control. The first of these concerns the large series of investigations carried out on simultaneous reception and transmission of signals. Cherry (1953) investigated the ability of Ss to separate simultaneously presented messages. He found that, if the S were not allowed to write anything down, he had great difficulty in separating two simultaneously spoken messages emanating from a single source. However, the task could not be accomplished successfully unless the messages consisted of clichés or contained units which could be transposed with little loss of meaning from one message to another. More importantly he showed that if one message were presented through headphones to one ear and the second message simultaneously to the other (with the messages being recorded by the same voice) the S was able to reproduce, by shadowing, either of the messages without error—but he would be unable to say what was happening in the other ear and would not even perceive a change in language or be able to say what language had been spoken. It should be noted carefully that this finding applies only to continuous speech. Other studies have shown (e.g. Broadbent, 1956) that if dichotic stimulation is employed with short lists of numbers (three successively in one ear with another three successively in the other, the two sets being presented simultaneously) the S will be able to reproduce all six correctly, but will produce the three from one ear first, followed by the other three. He will not produce the digits in a mixed form. These results, and others resulting from a long series of experiments by Broadbent (reviewed in his book, 1958) on simultaneous listening and speaking, led that author to postulate a filter mechanism which enabled a subject to deal successfully with multiple information arriving simultaneously by storing or holding in a short-term memory system some of the information while other material was being processed. It is impossible to consider in detail here the large body of evidence resulting from the experiments of Broadbent and his colleagues, but it is obvious from this brief discussion that experiments of this nature will be of great significance for the elucidation of the mechanisms controlling continuous speech.

Speech, of course, is enormously complicated and difficult to analyse (it is not yet clear even what the fundamental "speech unit" is though it is evident that it will cut across such "natural" units as word length, etc.). From what has been said it will be clear that it may at this stage be more advantageous to concentrate on activities which are simpler than speech, but which are disrupted by D.A.F., such as rhythmic tapping. For this reason, as well as for others, the extensive studies of skilled tracking performance are of the greatest importance. Indeed, the present author would maintain that speech may be regarded as a form of complex tracking behaviour—and this formulation is indeed implicit in Fairbank's model. Again it is impossible to review here the extensive empirical evidence and theoretical formulations involved. Adams (1961) has recently performed this task admirably. In this author's view, however, Adams' definition of what constitutes a tracking task is unnecessarily restrictive. For Adams, a tracking task must involve an external signal which is not under the control of the operator and he explicitly rejects from his consideration self-paced tasks "where stimulus changes are a function of operator responding" (Adams, 1961, p. 62). However, this restrictive position would lead to the unnecessary distinction that Adams would regard as a tracking situation one where a pianist plays from sight a score but would not regard as a tracking situation one where the same pianist plays the same score from memory. It seems, on the contrary, perfectly reasonable, and indeed necessary, to regard as a tracking situation one where the controlling stimulus is an internalized representation of a stimulus situation, and both instrumental performance and speech are admirable examples of this kind of tracking. Of course, in many instances, the input will be partly under the control of $S$ and partly varying independently of his own output, as is the case when $S$ speaks in a noisy environment. The evidence concerning tracking behaviour is of particular interest in this context because of recent successful attempts to simulate complex performance by the use of analogue computers (e.g. Fuchs, 1962). Furthermore, in his own studies of tracking behaviour (e.g. Adams and Creamer, 1962) Adams has specifically provided evidence of an empirical kind for the necessity of postulating a perceptual anticipation mechanism which may facilitate or interfere with skilled tracking behaviour. Adams and Creamer suggest that beneficial anticipation may be based on mediating responses and response-produced cues. The similarity of this notion to Fairbank's predicting device for the control of speech will be obvious.

We may conclude, therefore, that there are many promising leads, both of a theoretical and empirical nature, available for the investigation of the fundamental mechanism involved in the self-monitoring of speech. It would, however, be premature in the present state of knowledge, to attempt to set up a general quantitative model for speech control. It is hoped that the present discussion will help to direct future empirical research along lines which will provide the essential empirical knowledge which will form the foundation of such a model.

## II. The Genesis and Maintenance of Stammering Behaviour

In this section, we shall outline and compare two of the many theoretical formulations which have been made in attempts to account for the genesis and maintenance of stammering behaviour.

*1. Stammering as learned behaviour.* The interpretation of stammering phenomena in learning theory language has been made in general terms by Johnson (1959) and others, and developed in detail by Wischner (1950) and by
Sheehan (1953, 1958).

We have already pointed out that the speech of normal young children
contains many and varied disfluencies which gradually disappear as the skill
develops. It has been argued that these non-fluencies cause the child no
concern, provided his attention is not drawn to them. However, a minority
of parents interpret these normal non-fluencies as an indication that the
child is beginning to stammer, and in their own anxiety to eliminate the
"errors", correct the child's speech, reprove him, or even punish him.
Not unexpectedly, the effect of this is to make the child aware of, and
anxious about, his speech at a critical stage in his development. This anxiety
acts as drive motivating instrumental avoidance behaviour which seeks to
reduce the anxiety-drive. Any behaviour which accomplishes this will be
reinforced. Now Johnson argued that stammering represented just such an
example of avoidance response to anxiety, in that it represented an attempt
to avoid non-fluency. An alternative type of "response" would presumably
be silence. Wischner (1950) argues, however, that the stammering respresents
an attempt to avoid the *consequences* of non-fluency, that is, parental disapproval.

Let us assume for the moment that the stammer has been successfully
established and turn to the question of its maintenance. Sheehan (1951) has
argued that, in the case of normal speech, the word as stimulus evokes a
normal speech response, the successful execution of which achieves the goal of
terminating that particular sequence (i.e. communication). Thus:

$$S_{\text{word}} \rightarrow R_{\text{normal speech response}} \rightarrow G \text{ (saying word)}$$

In stammering, however,

$$S_{\text{word}} \rightarrow R_{\text{anxiety}} \rightarrow S_{\text{anxiety}} \rightarrow R_{\text{stammering}} \rightarrow G \text{ (saying word)}$$

That is, the perception of the word (in reading) or the anticipation of saying
it produces anxiety responses which serve as stimuli for the stammering.
The stammering is reinforced *because it immediately precedes the saying
of the word correctly.*

Sheehan has significantly extended this approach by introducing the
notion of conflict in relation to stammering. Johnson and Knott (1936) described the essentials of such a theory, as did Wischner (1950) but Sheehan has
notably extended its use. We shall assume that the reader is generally familiar
with the principal features of conflict theory (see Yates, 1962b, for a review)
and proceed at once to Sheehan's application of the theory to stammering.
According to Sheehan, the two principal facts which any theory of stammering must explain are the momentary blocking (whether this involves silence
or the repetition of part of a word) and the release from the blocking, i.e.
the fact that the stammerer eventually does say the word.

The momentary blocking is accounted for by conceptualizing the stammerer as being placed in a double approach–avoidance conflict situation of increasing magnitude as he approaches a particular word. The essential features of the conflict situation are represented in Fig. 5. Two types of conflict are involved; that between speaking (approach) and not speaking (avoidance); and that between not speaking (approach) and speaking (avoidance).

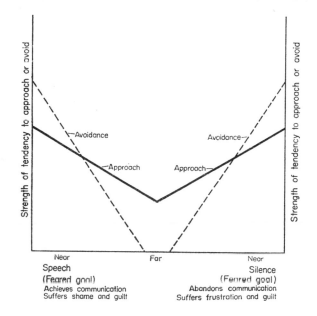

FIG. 5. Stammering as a double approach–avoidance conflict (Sheehan, 1958)

In other words, speech is *both* a desired and a feared goal; similarly, silence is *both* a feared and a desired goal. As Sheehan puts it: "Speaking holds the promise of communication, but the threat of stuttering; silence eliminates temporarily the threat involved in speaking, but at a cost of abandonment of communication. . . ." (Sheehan, 1958, p. 127).

Sheehan distinguishes five levels of conflict in stammering. At the *word-level*, the conflict is between the desire to say and avoid saying a particular word. At the *situation-level*, the conflict is between speaking and not speaking in a situation arousing anxiety about stuttering. At the *emotional-level*, the conflict relates to the content of the utterance. At the *relationship-level*, the conflict relates to conversation with particular individuals. At the *ego-protective level*, the conflict relates to speech in threatening situations involving particularly level of aspiration.

The experimental evidence in favour of the formulation of stammering as an approach–avoidance conflict, involving different levels, is presented in detail by Sheehan (1958, pp. 131–132 and 138–140) and need not be repeated here. Sheehan's formulation certainly makes "good sense" and seems to be supported by the rather meagre evidence available at present.

A more difficult question concerns the problem of accounting for the release of the stammerer from the momentary blocking. How does the equilibrium which produces blocking come to be broken? Sheehan's hypothesis is that "the occurrence of stuttering reduces the fear which elicited it, so that *during* the block there is sufficient reduction in fear-motivated avoidance to resolve the conflict, permitting release of the blocked word" (Sheehan, 1958, p. 125, italics in original). But how does the fear-reduction take place? Sheehan suggests that three factors influence the change. Firstly, the sheer occurrence of the stammering reduces the anticipatory fear, by bringing the whole process into the open. Second, the occurrence of the stammering provides more proprioceptive information about the block and reduces anxiety. Third, if we regard stammering as a form of aggression, then the occurence of the stammering reduces the aggressive drive, and hence permits speech to proceed.

It must be admitted that Sheehan's arguments are here very weak. However, in fairness, it must also be stated that the general problem of the resolution of conflict when all forces are in equilibrium has never been satisfactorily solved by any of the major theorists on conflict (Yates, 1962b). The experimental evidence purporting to support this part of the theory has also been reviewed by Sheehan (1958, pp. 132–135), though its relevance to the theory is much less obvious than in the case of the blocking itself.

We may conclude that although the *maintenance* of stammering may be satisfactorily accounted for in terms of learning theory, no satisfactory explanation has so far been put forward to account for the *genesis* of stammering. For a consideration of the theory of the genesis of stammering as presented at the beginning of this section at once reveals its total inadequacy. We may readily agree that the child's non-fluencies may be criticized by the parents or others, and that this will arouse anticipatory anxiety in relation to speech in the child. However, it is quite impossible to see why the child should successfully reduce this anxiety either by continuing to be non-fluent or developing a stammer. In either case the child is likely to receive more, not less, "punishment" (we are, of course, dealing with the *learning* of the stammer, not its maintenance). Wischner's attempts to circumvent this basic difficulty are wholly unconvincing (Wischner, 1950, pp. 329–330). The author can think of only one possible resolution of the difficulty, which runs somewhat as follows. Clearly the learned non-fluency or stammer must (in terms of the theory) reduce the anxiety by preventing the appearence of the noxious unconditioned stimulus (parental disapproval). It is possible that many parents, after initially drawing the child's attention to his non-fluencies and thus inducing anxiety, subsequently react with a policy of *withdrawing* attention to the child's speech as soon as he begins to stammer. Thus, where previously parental reproof has followed non-fluency, and while the parents observe the child's speech closely (to the discomfiture of the child) until he stammers, the act of stammering removes this embarrassing scrutiny and hence reduces the anticipatory anxiety. Hence the stammering is rewarded. While this *ad hoc* explanation is not entirely unreasonable, the author feels little confidence in it, especially as Wischner adduces what is virtually the opposite! (i.e. that the stammering is reinforced because it produces attention from the parents which was previously lacking). It must be admitted that attempts to account for the genesis of stammering in terms of learning theory have not so far been successful.

*2. Stammering as a perceptual defect.* As we have seen, the human organism reacts very rapidly to changes in external or internal stimulus conditions. Either continuously or periodically (i.e. when a significant change occurs) ongoing behaviour is modified so as to produce performance which is optimal for the current demands being made—the adjustments being effected by reference to a storehouse of information which is based on past experience. As a result of a vast amount of experience the organism builds up certain patterns of expectations. Thus, in relation to speech, the return of feedback via the shortest airborne pathway can be expected within about one-thousandth of a second. Any deviation of a marked kind from the expected pattern of feedback will lead to an attempt to restore the usual relationship. Furthermore, the brain presumably integrates the various feedback patterns arising from the triple media (air, bone and kinaesthetic) into a unitary whole. Now it is clear that the disturbance in the speech of non-stammerers under D.A.F. results primarily from a *conflict* of feedback information since (i) the *absence* of feedback does not produce these disturbances (though it does produce some changes) an (ii) the effect of D.A.F. is reduced (though not entirely abolished) in proportion as the intensity of the alternative undisturbed feedback signals approach the intensity level of the D.A.F.

It is tempting to argue that a similar asynchrony of feedback signals is present in stammering. If the stammerer is in fact suffering essentially from a perceptual defect, as Cherry and Sayers (1956) argued, that is, if he is continually receiving false or conflicting information concerning the progress of emitted speech units, then it would not be surprising if he continually repeated signals or ground to a halt from time to time. The stammerer thus has been regarded as suffering from an instability of the feedback loop, similar to that which is artificially induced in non-stammerers by D.A.F. It is important to note that, following Cherry and Sayers (as discussed earlier), the instability would be related to the bone-conducted rather than the air-conducted feedback loop (we have seen, of course, that interference with the bone-conducted feedback in non-stammerers can apparently have catastrophic effects on speech). If this reasoning is correct, then it would seem very likely that defect may ultimately be shown to have a genetic basis.

We must be careful to notice that there is not necessarily any basic incompatibility between the perceptual-defect theory and the approach–avoidance conflict theory relation to the genesis and maintenance of stammering. It could well be that the basic perceptual defect sensitizes those individuals in whom it is present and produces greater difficulty in learning to speak fluently. However, it is quite possible that such Ss only *develop* a stammer if their initial difficulties are seized on by the parents as a reason for anxiety about the child's speech. Conversely, it would follow that not all children whose normal disfluencies are punished by the parents develop a stammer—this may only be the case if the basic predisposition (in the form of feedback instability) is present. Furthermore, it will be clear that the wide variability in type of stammer which is such a striking feature of the disorder must imply a significant contribution on the part of learning.

With these points before him, it will no doubt have occurred to the reader by now to wonder what the effect of D.A.F. would be on the speech of stammerers. Would it prove possible, by varying the delay interval, to find a delay which would artificially *synchronize* the feedback for the stammerer and thus enable him to speak normally? Should this prove to be so, an important breakthrough would have been achieved, as it might well prove possible to manufacture miniature delay systems which could be permanently worn by the stammerer, in much the same way as hearing aids are worn by the deaf.

It is surprising that only one major study in this area has so far been published. Neelley (1961) tested 23 stammerers and 23 non-stammerers under no delay (N.A.F.) and under D.A.F. Under each condition, the task was to read a passage of 100 words five times. The records were scored for omissions, substitutions and additions, for correct word rate (C.W.R.—the ratio of correct words to total reading time in seconds). Measures of adaptation and consistency, as described earlier, were also taken. The delay time was 0·14 sec and the intensity level at the ear about 75 db above normal threshold for spondee words. The principal results may be summarized as follows:

1. When stammerers and non-stammerers read under D.A.F., no differences were found in omissions, substitutions, additions, or correct word rate (in the latter case, if C.W.R. under N.A.F. were controlled). If samples of speech from stammerers and non-stammerers under D.A.F. were presented in random order, they were judged on average equally disturbed.

2. Stammerers reading under N.A.F. showed significantly greater adaptation and consistency over five readings than did non-stammerers reading under D.A.F. Further, when speech records under these conditions were randomly presented, judges could identify with a good degree of accuracy the two types of speech (66 per cent of stammerers under N.A.F., and

92 per cent of non-stammerers under D.A.F.). Most of the errors involved identifying stammerers under N.A.F. as non-stammerers under D.A.F.

3. When the speech of stammerers under D.A.F. and N.A.F. was compared, it was found that omissions increased significantly, but that there was no overall change in substitutions or additions. In the latter two instances, however, extreme variability among stammerers was found. Thus, one stammerer increased in additions from 58 (N.A.F.) to 257 (D.A.F.), whereas another decreased from 256 (N.A.F.) to 6 (D.A.F.). Correct word rate was significantly lower under D.A.F., whereas the consistency effect was greater under N.A.F.

From these results, Neelley drew two major conclusions:

1. That the effect of D.A.F. on stammering behaviour varies markedly from one subject to another, at least in relation to additions;

2. That the speech changes in normal $S$s under D.A.F. do not resemble the characteristics of the speech of stammerers. In Neelley's own words: "The hypothesis that stuttering may be somehow related to a delay in auditory feedback because speech produced under conditions of delayed auditory feedback is assumed to behave like stuttering, to sound like stuttering, and to be an experience like stuttering, is discredited by the findings of this experiment" (Neelley, 1961, p. 80).

The importance, theoretically, of Neelley's conclusion, if accepted is so great that it is necessary to consider whether any weaknesses exist in the study. Two extremely important weaknesses may be pointed out, which make Neelley's conclusions quite unacceptable as they stand. In the first place, Neelley used only one delay time and one intensity level. As we have already seen there is an interaction between intensity and delay, and this may be completely obscured if a single delay and intensity is used. Furthermore, the delay time (0·14 sec) used by Neelley was not optimal for producing breakdown in normal $S$s. Thus his first finding (that stammerers do not differ from non-stammerers under D.A.F.) may be due to the fact that he used a delay time which would not affect many normal $S$s very much, combined with the fact that the speech of many stammerers did improve under D.A.F. Furthermore, it could well be that there is an optimal delay time for reducing stammering behaviour which is not the same for each stammerer. If this were so, the use of a single delay time might tend to minimize the improvement in speech, under D.A.F., of stammerers.

Secondly, Neelley lays great stress on the fact that the speech of normal $S$s under D.A.F. does not resemble that of stammerers speaking under N.A.F., and the fact that judges could distinguish samples of speech from each category. Similarly, the lack of adaptation of normal $S$s to D.A.F. compared with that of stammerers under N.A.F. is emphasized. But these empirical findings are totally irrelevant to the issue whether speech behaviour under D.A.F. is determined by the same factors which maintain stammering behaviour. The two groups are in no way meaningfully comparable in these respects. The stammerers in the experiment had presumably spent many years adapting to, and working out ways of dealing with, their perceptual defect (assuming it to exist). The Ss with normal speech were being, on the contrary, subjected to D.A.F. for the first time. Hence, it is in no way surprising that the speech of Ss subjected to D.A.F. for the first time is different from that of long-standing stammerers. The problem concerning underlying mechanism of stammering cannot in fact be resolved by the kind of experiment reported by Neelley. The problem can be solved only by a direct attack on the auditory monitoring skills of stammerers.

We may conclude, therefore, that Neelley's experiment, admirable though it is in many respects, does not lead to the conclusion Neelley drew from it. Furthermore, even the empirical results of Neelley concerning the effects of D.A.F. on stammering must be treated with great caution, since he used only a single delay time and feedback intensity level. The results of other workers suggest very strongly that the speech of some stammerers may be completely normalized by D.A.F. (Chase et al., 1961). The present author (in a study to be published) has examined the effects of different delay times and intensity levels on the speech of stammerers. In some instances, there was total suppression of stammering at all delays and intensities, in others the effect was much less striking. In this respect, there is agreement with Neelley who concludes that: "One of the most interesting and possibly important findings of the present study was the lack of homogeneity of D.A.F. effects on stutterers" (p. 78). Thus, a great deal more careful study is needed before the various issues discussed here can be resolved. We have discussed Neelley's study at length, both because of its importance, and because the bold conclusion drawn on inadequate evidence may unfortunately discourage further work along these lines.

In concluding this survey it may be pointed out that there are solid grounds both for supposing that work in the area of D.A.F. may in the immediate future throw a flood of light on the ways in which serial behaviour is controlled; and that a major breakthrough has been made in the understanding of stammering.

## REFERENCES

ADAMS, J. A. (1961) Human tracking behaviour, *Psychol. Bull.*, **58**, 55–79.
ADAMS, J. A. and CREAMER, L. R. (1962) Anticipatory timing of continuous and discrete responses, *J. Exp. Psychol.*, **63**, 84–90.
ARENS, C. J. and POPPLESTON, J. A. (1959) Verbal facility and delayed speech feedback, *Percept. Mot. Skills*, **9**, 270.
ATKINSON, C. J. (1953) Adaptation to delayed sidetones, *J. Speech Hear. Dis.*, **18**, 386–391.
ATKINSON, C. J. (1954) Some effects on intelligibility as the sidetone level and the amount of sidetone delay are changed, *Proc. Ia. Acad. Sci.*, **61**, 334–340.
BARBER, V. (1939) Chorus reading as a distraction in stuttering, *J. Speech Dis.*, **4**, 371–383.

BEAUMONT, J. T. and Foss, B. M. (1957) Individual differences in reacting to delayed auditory feedback, *Brit. J. Psychol.*, **48**, 85–89.

BLACK, J. W. (1951) The effect of delayed sidetone upon vocal rate and intensity, *J. Speech Hear. Dis.*, **16**, 56–60.

BLOODSTEIN, O. (1950) Hypothetical conditions under which stuttering is reduced or absent. *J. Speech Hear. Dis.*, **15**, 142–153.

BROADBENT, D. E. (1956) Successive responses to simultaneous stimuli, *Quart. J. exp. Psychol.*, **8**, 145–152.

BROADBENT, D. E. (1958) *Perception and Communication*, Pergamon Press, London.

BROWN, S. F. (1945) The loci of stutterings in the speech sequence, *J. Speech Dis.*, **10**, 181–192.

BUTLER, R. A. and GALLOWAY, F. T. (1957) Factorial analysis of the delayed speech feedback phenomenon, *J. Acoust. Soc. Amer.*, **29**, 632–635.

CHASE, R. A. (1958) Effect of delayed auditory feedback on the repetition of speech sounds, *J. Speech Hear. Dis.*, **23**, 583–590.

CHASE, R. A. and GUILFOYLE, G. (1962) The effect of simultaneous delayed and undelayed auditory feedback on speech, *J. Speech Hear. Res.*, **5**, 144–151.

CHASE, R. A., HARVEY, S., STANDFAST, SUSAN, RAPIN, ISABELLE and SUTTON, S. (1959) Comparison of the effects of delayed auditory feedback on speech and key tapping *Science*, **129**, 903–904.

CHASE, R. A.. HARVEY, S.. STANDFAST, SUSAN, RAPIN, ISABELLA and SUTTON. S. (1961) Studies on sensory feedback: I: Effect of delayed auditory feedback on speech and keytapping, *Quart. J. Exp. Psychol.*, **13**, 141–152.

CHASE, R. A., RAPIN, ISABELLE, GILDEN, L., SUTTON, S. and GUILFOYLE, G. (1961) Studies on sensory feedback: II: Sensory feedback influences on keytapping motor tasks, *Quart. J. Exp. Psychol.*, **13**, 153–167.

CHASE, R. A., SUTTON, S., FIRST, DAPHNE and ZUBIN, J. (1961) A developmental study of changes in behavior under delayed auditory feedback, *J. Genet. Psychol.*, **99**, 101–112.

CHASE, R. A., SUTTON, S. and RAPIN, I. (1961) Sensory feedback influences on motor performance, *J. Audit Res.*, **3**, 212–223.

CHERRY, E. C. (1953) Some experiments on the recognition of speech, with one and with two ears, *J. Acoust. Soc. Amer.*, **25**, 975–979.

CHERRY, C. and SAYERS, B. McA. (1956) Experiments upon the total inhibition of stammering by external control and some clinical results, *J. Psychosom. Res.*, **1**, 233–246.

CURTIS, J. F. (1942) A study of the effect of muscular exercise upon stuttering, *Speech Monogr.*, **9**, 61–74.

DARLEY, F. L. (1955) The relationship of parental attitudes and adjustments to the development of stuttering. In W. JOHNSON (Ed.): *Stuttering in Children and Adults*, Univ. of Minnesota Press, Minneapolis.

FAIRBANKS, G. (1954) Systematic research in experimental phonetics: 1. A theory of the speech mechanism as a servo mechanism, *J. Speech Hear. Dis.*, **19**, 133-139.

FAIRBANKS, G. (1955) Selective vocal effects of delayed auditory feedback, *J. Speech Hear. Dis.*, **20**, 333–345.

FAIRBANKS, G. and GUTTMAN, N. (1958) Effects of delayed auditory feedback upon articulation, *J. Speech Hear. Res.*, **1**, 12–22.

FUCHS, A. H. (1962) The progression–regression hypotheses in perceptual motor skill learning, *J. Exp. Psychol.*, **63**, 177–182.

GIBBONS, E. W., WINCHESTER, R. A. and KREBS, D. F. (1958) The variability of oral reading rate, *J. Speech Hear. Dis.*, **23**, 591–593.

GIBBS, G. B. (1954) The continuous regulation of skilled response by kinaesthetic feedback, *Brit. J. Psychol.* **45**, 24–39.

GOLDFARB, W. and BRAUNSTEIN, P. (1958) Reactions to delayed auditory feedback in schizophrenic children. In P. H. HOCH and J. ZUBIN (Eds.) *Psychopathology of communication*, Grune & Stratton, New York, pp. 49–63.

GOLDIAMOND, I., ATKINSON, C. J. and BILGER, R. C. (1962) Stabilization of behaviour and prolonged exposure to delayed auditory feedback, *Science*, **135**, 437–438.

GOLUB, A. (1955) The cumulative effect of constant and varying reading material on stuttering adaptation. In W. JOHNSON (Ed.) *Stuttering Children and Adults*, Univ. of Minnesota Press, Minneapolis.

HANLEY, CLAIRE, N. and TIFFANY, W. R. (1954) Auditory malingering and psychogenic deafness, *Arch. Otolaryngol.*, **60**, 197–201.

HILL, H. (1944a) Stuttering: I. A critical review of biochemical investigations. *J. Speech Dis.*, **9**, 245–261.

HILL, H. (1944b) Stuttering: II. A review and integration of physiological data, *J. Speech Dis.*, **9**, 289–324.

HIRSCH, I. J. (1959) Auditory perception of temporal order, *J. Acoust. Soc. Amer.*, **31**, 759–767.

HIRSCH, I. E. and SHERRICK, C. E. (1961) Perceived order in different sense modalities, *J. Exp. Psychol.*, **62**, 423–432.

JOHNSON, W. (1956) Stuttering. In JOHNSON, W., BROWN, S. J. CURTIS, J. J., EDNEY, C. W. and KEASTER, J. (Eds.) *Speech Handicapped Schoolchildren*, Harper, New York.

JOHNSON, W. (Ed.) (1959) *The Onset of Stuttering*, Univ. of Minnesota Press, Minneapolis.

JOHNSON, W. (1961) Measurements of oral reading and speaking rate and disfluency of adult male and female stutterers and non-stutterers, *J. Speech Hear. Dis.*, *Mongr. Suppl.* No. 7, pp. 1–20.

JOHNSON, W. and KNOTT, J. R. (1936) The moment of stuttering, *J. Genet. Psychol.*, **48**, 475–480.

KALMUS, H., DENES, F. and FRY, D. B. (1955) Effect of delayed acoustic feedback on some nonvocal activities, *Nature*, **175**, 1078.

KOROBOW, N. (1955) Reactions to stress: a reflection of personality trait organization, *J. Abnorm. Soc. Psychol.* **51**, 464–468.

LASHLEY, K. S. (1951) The problem of serial order in behaviour. In L. A. JEFFRIES (Ed.) *Cerebral Mechanisms in Behaviour*, Wiley, New York.

LEE, B. S. (1950a) Some effects of sidetone delay, *J. Acoust. Soc. Amer.*, **22**, 639–640.

LEE, B. S. (1950b) Effects of delayed speech feedback, *J. Acoust. Soc. Amer.*, **22**, 824–826.

LEE, B. S. (1951) Artificial stutter, *J. Speech Hear. Dis.*, **16**, 53–55.

MARAIST, J. A. and HUTTON, C. (1957) Effects of auditory masking upon the speech of stutterers, *J. Speech Hear. Dis.*, **22**, 385–389.

NEELLEY, J. M. (1961) A study of the speech behaviour of stutterers and non-stutterers under normal and delayed auditory feedback, *J. Speech Hear. Dis. Monogr. Suppl.* 7, pp. 63–82.

PETERS, R. W. (1956) The effect of acoustic environment upon speaker intelligibility, *J. Speech Hear. Dis.*, **21**, 88–93.

SCHINDLER, M. D. (1955) A study of educational adjustments of stuttering and non-stuttering Children. In JOHNSON, W. (Ed.) *Stuttering in Children and Adults*, Univ. of Minnesota Press, Minneapolis.

SCHUELL, H. (1946) Sex differences in relation to stuttering, *J. Speech Dis.*, **11**, 277–298.

SHANE, MARY L. S. (1955) Effect on stuttering of alteration in auditory feedback. In W. JOHNSON (Ed.) *Stuttering in children and adults*, Univ. of Minnesota Press, Minneapolis.

SHEEHAN, J. (1951) The modification of stuttering through non-reinforcement, *J. Abnorm. Soc. Psychol.*, **46**, 51–63.

SHEEHAN, J. G. (1953) Theory and treatment of stuttering as an approach–avoidance conflict, *J. Psychol.*, **36**, 27–49.

SHEEHAN, J. G. (1958) Conflict theory of stuttering. In J. EISENSON (Ed.) *Stuttering: a Symposium*, Harper, New York.

SPILKA, B. (1954a) Some vocal effects of different reading passages and time delays in speech feedback, *J. Speech Hear. Dis.*, **19**, 37–47.

SPILKA, B. (1954b) Relationships between certain aspects of personality and some vocal effects of delayed speech feedback, *J. Speech Hear. Dis.*, **19**, 491–503.

STROMSTA, C. (1962) Delays associated with certain sidetone pathways, *J. Acoust. Soc. Amer.*, **34**, 392–396.

STROTHER, C. R. and KRIEGMAN, L. S. (1943) Diadochokinesis in stutterers and non-stutterers, *J. Speech Dis.*, **8**, 323–325.

STROTHER, C. R. and KRIEGMAN, L. S. (1944) Rythmokinesis in stutterers and non-stutterers, *J. Speech Dis.*, **9**, 239–244.

SUTTON, S. and CHASE, R. A. (1961) White noise and stuttering, *J. Speech Hear. Res.*, **4**, 72.

TIFFANY, W. R. and HANLEY, CLAIRE, N. (1952) Delayed speech feedback as a test for auditory malingering, *Science*, **115**, 59–60.

TIFFANY, W. R. and HANLEY, CLAIRE, N. (1956) Adaptation to delayed sidetone, *J. Speech Hear. Dis.*, **21**, 164–172.

TROTTER, W. D. (1955) The severity of stuttering during successive readings of the same material, *J. Speech Hear. Dis.*, **20**, 17–25.

VAN BERGEIJK, W. A. and DAVID, E. E. (1959) Delayed handwriting, *Percept. Mot. Skills*, **9**, 347–357.

WINCHESTER, R. A. and GIBBONS, E. W. (1957) Relative effectiveness of three modes of delayed sidetone presentation, *Arch. Otolaryngol.*, **65**, 275–279.

WINCHESTER, R. A. and GIBBONS, E. W. (1958) The effect of auditory masking upon oral reading rate, *J. Speech Hear. Dis.*, **23**, 250–252.

WINCHESTER, R. A., GIBBONS, E. W. and KREBS, D. F. (1959) Adaptation to sustained delayed sidetone, *J. Speech Hear. Dis.*, **24**, 25–28.

YATES, A. J. (1962a) Effects of delayed auditory feedback on a skilled response (typewriting), *J. Speech Hear. Res.*, In press.

YATES, A. J. (1962b) *Frustration and Conflict*, Wiley, New York.

YATES, A. J. (1963) Delayed auditory feedback, *Psychol. Bull.*, In press.

# Learning Theory and the Treatment of Tics*†

A. ABI RAFI

YATES[1] reported a successful experiment on the extinction of four tics in a female psychiatric patient of high average intelligence. He based his method of treatment on a theoretical model treating the tic as a simple learned response which has attained its maximum habit strength. His general hypothesis was that massed practice in the tic leads to a significant decrement in the ability of the subject to respond voluntarily, and eventually leads to extinction of the tic by the process of building up a negative habit of not performing it. His results confirmed this hypothesis, i.e. the number of repeated voluntary evocations of the tic per minute declined significantly, and there was an improvement in his patient's involuntary tics. As Yates was attempting to produce maximal conditioned inhibition ($_sI_R$), he varied the conditions of practice systematically but always used a "standard procedure", by which each tic was given five 1-min periods of massed practice with one minute's rest between each period, as a control. He describes several experiments in detail but the main outcome was that very prolonged periods of massed practice, followed by prolonged rest periods, produced the largest declines.

This paper reports the outcome of similar experiments on two psychiatric patients with tics. One was given the "standard procedure" of Yates and the other the procedure of prolonged massed practice followed by prolonged rest.

## SUBJECTS

The two patients were referred to the psychology department with a view to treatment based on learning theory constructs. Before the experiments began, each patient underwent the usual neurological investigations and the possibility of an organic basic to the tics has been adequately excluded. Both patients were of high average intelligence (Wechsler Adult Intelligence Scale). One, a female, patient A, was 63 years old, and the other, a male, patient B, was 57 years old. The Maudsley Personality Inventory showed patient A to be very neurotic and slightly introverted, and patient B to be very extraverted but not neurotic.

* This article is reprinted with the permission of the author and editor from *J. Psychosom. Res.* **6**, 71–76 (1962).
† From St. Andrew's Hospital, Thorpe, Norwich, England.

382

Patient A suffered from a right foot tapping tic which appeared about two years before referral. The tapping, a seesaw-like movement of toe and heel, was continuous and forceful while she was standing up or sitting down. She was admitted to hospital on several occasions after the appearance of the tic complaining of depression and restlessness. She was treated with chlorpromazine and had modified electroconvulsive treatment. On every occasion she was discharged "relieved" but neither out-patient nor in-patient treatment, inluding E.C.T., had any influence on the tic. The tapping caused much annoyance to those who happened to be in her company. Her public life became considerably restricted because of the censure her tic evoked. She remained on chlorpromazine throughout the experiments.

Patient B was seen as an out-patient and remained one. His main complaint was a spasmodic movement of his head to the left. This began early in 1958, and gradually increased in conjunction with facial grimacing. He came to the out-patient clinic, had some physiotherapy, was given dexamphetamine and sodium amytal, also a series of pentothal abreactions, with no material progress. He continued on drugs but these were stopped with the consent of his psychiatrist after the fourth session of intensive practice.

## METHOD

The tics were considered as symptoms which had developed originally as conditioned avoidance responses, became reinforced through satisfying temporary needs and thereafter existed as learned responses separated from the original circumstances which first occasioned them. The method of treatment by massed practice was adopted.

Both patients were treated separately. Patient A was given Yates' "standard procedure", two sessions a day, one in the morning and one in the afternoon under supervision. Patient B was given very prolonged massed practice sessions, each of two hours' continuous practice, followed by prolonged rest periods (one week). The instructions were the same for both subjects, namely, to produce the tic as accurately as possible, to repeat it without pause during the practice period, and to pay attention to the tic. No stress was laid on speed.

TABLE 1

*Changes in mean frequency of two tics under condition of voluntary evocation*

| Tapping | | | | | | Head | | |
|---|---|---|---|---|---|---|---|---|
| Five 1-min sessions | | | Five 5-min sessions | | | Two-hour sessions | | |
| Sessions | M | σ | Sessions | M | σ | Sessions | M | σ |
| 1–50 | 87·68 | 11·39 | 1–10 | 40·75 | 4·35 | 1–5 | 33·50 | 2·49 |
| 51–100 | 77·81 | 5·60 | 11–20 | 41·50 | 3·52 | 6–10 | 17·80 | 2·78 |
| 101–150 | 82·36 | 6·84 | 21–30 | 47·75 | 4·07 | 11–15 | 4·86 | 3·32 |
| 151–200 | 80·44 | 5·23 | 31–40 | 45·25 | 3·77 | 16–20 | 2·68 | 4·11 |
| 201–250 | 82·40 | 7·89 | 41–50 | 40·75 | 3·63 | 21–25 | 2·51 | 3·13 |
| 251–280 | 75·47 | 9·84 | | | | | | |

Each voluntary evocation of the tic was recorded by the author for about 70 per cent of the records of patient A, and for all the records of patient B. Patient A carried out about 30 per cent of the total number of sessions at her home. These were performed under the supervision of her husband who has been adequately trained by the author in the strict procedure to be followed. He also recorded the voluntary tics. An instruction form and record sheets were provided. Patient B attended regularly at the hospital once a week. A stop watch was used.

## RESULTS

The score recorded was the number of tics per minute as counted from the record sheets.

Table 1 shows the results. In the case of patient A, the frequency of occurence of the tic per minute (under test conditions) did not show any appreciable decline either within single sessions or between sets of 50 sessions. The mean score for any one set of 50 sessions is not significantly lower than the mean score for any other set of 50 sessions (the highest value of $t$ was 1·16; the lowest, 0·46). The results of this experiment do not support the general theory propounded by Yates.

The "standard procedure" was discontinued after the 280th session and another introduced with sessions of five 5-min trials under conditions of massed practice, with one minute's rest between each period. Fifty such sessions were completed. The results of this experiment are reported in Table 1. Here again the mean score for any one set of 10 sessions is not significantly lower than the mean score for any other set of ten sessions. In neither of these two experiments was Yates' general hypothesis that massed practice leads to a significant decrement in the ability of the subject to respond voluntarily, confirmed.

Yates[2] suggests that very prolonged sessions of massed practice in terms of 6–7 hr continuous practice in one session followed by very prolonged rest, 2–3 weeks at least, could be very effective. Could it be that patient A has shown very little decline because of a simple lack of foot-pounds work? To test this, very prolonged massed practice in terms of 2 hr continuous practice in one session was introduced. Patient A was unable to tolerate this kind of stress and refused to take another session. An apparatus was therefore devised (see Fig. 1)* with a foot treadle freely pivoted on two No. 12 screws. Under the foot treadle, at the front and back, are two bell push switches. Each time the foot treadle is pressed downwards, whether by toe or by heel, a buzzer is sounded. There is a $^2/_{10}$ of an inch free play between the foot treadle and the bell push switches. Any slight pressure beyond that is enough to cause the buzzer to sound.

* Thanks are due to Mr. G. H. Tarlton, Chief Engineer, for building the apparatus to specifications.

By the conditioned-response principle, it was hypothesized that a strong connexion would be expected to develop between the stimulation arising from the desire to tap the foot and the response of hearing the buzzer and withholding the foot from tapping. Gradually this connexion should become sufficiently well-established to cause withholding of the foot from tapping in advance of the onset of the tapping, instead of afterwards. Patient A was

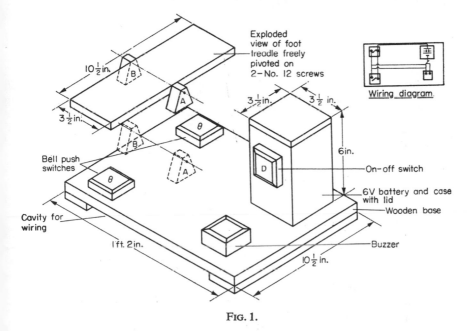

FIG. 1.

given daily practice sessions each lasting one hour. She was instructed to sit comfortably, put her right foot on the foot treadle, pay attention to the buzzers and try to balance the foot treadle and not to cause the sounding of the buzzers. There were 70 sessions in all (see Fig. 2, curve 3). The results confirm the hypothesis. The frequency of occurrence of the tic almost invariably showed steady decline. A stage was reached where she was able to keep her foot still throughout any one practice session. At the termination of the experiment she felt much improved. The foot tapping became very faint and intermittent and ceased to be a source of annoyance to her or to those around her.

In the case of patient B, the procedure of intensive practice for 2-hr periods with one week's rest between sessions, led to significant decrement in his ability to respond voluntarily (see Table 1). The frequency of occurrence of the tic per minute (under test conditions) showed a steady decline. The mean score for the second set of five sessions was significantly below that for the first set of five sessions ($t = 31.37$, $P = 0.001$). Similarly, the mean for sessions 11–15 was significantly lower than that for sessions 6–10 ($t = 18.81$, $P = 0.001$); the mean for sessions 16–20 was significantly lower than that for sessions 11–15 ($t = 3.10$, $P = 0.01$). The mean score for sessions 21–25 was not significantly below that for sessions 16–20 (value of $t$ here was 0.37). The results of this experiment confirm to the general hypothesis of Yates.

The course of decline in the frequency of voluntary responding for each tic, using the different procedures, is shown in Fig. 2. Each point on curves

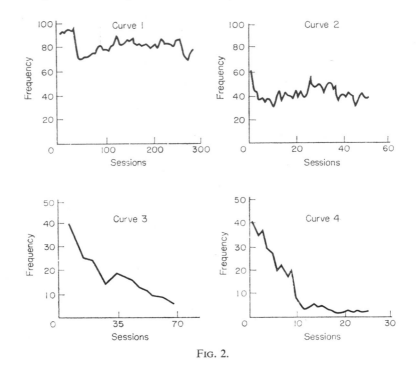

FIG. 2.

1 and 2, represents the average of five sessions (i.e. 25 1-min trials for curve 1; five 5-min trials for curve 2). Each point on curve 3 represents the total number of tics (buzzes) of seven sessions (i.e. 7 1-hr trials). Each point on curve 4, represents the average of one session (i.e. one trial of 120 min).

## CHANGES IN INVOLUNTARY TICS

Both patients reported improvement outside the test situation. Patient A felt more cheerful, started going out more frequently, and resumed her attendance at church which she stopped previously because of the annoyances her tapping caused to others; at one stage she used to put a cushion under her foot during church service, in order to make the continuous tapping inaudible. She reported total absence of the tic over three consecutive days, otherwise the frequency was sharply reduced, but complete cessation of involuntary tapping was not reported.

The condition of patient B did improve but not as dramatically as curve 4 appears to convey. The facial grimacings, which were very severely conspicuous in the early stages of treatment, completely vanished. He reported sleeping much better, whereas before treatment he used to lose a lot of sleep through the interference of the tic with any sleeping position he took. He feels much better generally, and although his head still has a tendency to move to the left, it is not so pronounced and so forceful as previously. He can now keep his head in a normal, facing-forward, position, for fairly long periods. The tic is much less frequent and very much less severe.

Towards the end of the experiment patient B was trained in the technique of systematic relaxation of muscles, with emphasis on the neck muscles. He was asked to maintain the relaxation exercises at home by devoting between fifteen and thirty minutes every day to this. He was also encouraged to try to cultivate the habit of general muscle relaxation whenever possible in the course of his everyday life. A follow-up after three months showed that he felt more relaxed and that he believed his tic had diminished.

## DISCUSSION

The results outlined above suggest that the procedure of very prolonged massed practice which was applied to patient B supports the theory proposed by Yates[1] to explain the origin of certain tics. The other two procedures applied to patient A, did not support that theory. The data further suggest that the rate of decline was steady in that tic which received the largest amount of massed practice. There is no evidence in curve 4 (see Fig. 2) of a cessation of the rate of decline in the frequency of voluntary responding to the tic, or by an initial rise in frequency, following the very prolonged rest periods. This probably indicates that the growth of the negative habit of "not doing the tic" did actually proceed at a rapid rate and contributed towards the growth of conditioned inhibition ($_sI_R$) rather than $_sH_R$.

In the case of patient A, the lack of response to repeated massed extinction trials may be ascribed to a variety of factors. Her age may very materially have increased the difficulty of development of conditioned inhibition. Yates' patient was 25 years old. She was also receiving chlorpromazine throughout the experiments. Still another factor is her position on the introversion–extraversion continuum. However, she responded favourably to the alternative method of treatment, i.e. the strengthening of one incompatible response opposite to the one to be eliminated. The foot treadle exercises resulted in the inhibition of the muscular response, the tapping of the foot, by the progressive strengthening of the connexion between the buzzer, the warning stimulus, and the withholding the foot from tapping, the response. Tapping responses became spontaneously inhibited on hearing the warning, and this inhibition, by a conditioning process, ultimately occurred spontaneously without the warning and without sounding the buzzer.

## SUMMARY

An attempt was made to treat two psychiatric patients suffering from tics by the method of treatment, proposed by Yates, based on the theoretical model that some tics may be conceptualized as drive-reducing conditioned avoidance responses, originally evoked in a traumatic situation.

Three procedures of massed practice were applied in order to build up a negative habit of "not doing the tic". Yates' "standard procedure" and a modification of this, did not confirm the hypothesis that massed practice leads to a significant decrement in the ability to respond voluntarily. His procedure of very prolonged periods of massed practice followed by very prolonged rest, supported the validity of the theory.

The patient who failed to respond favourably to Yates' method, improved significantly by exercises on an apparatus built on the basis of the classical conditioned-response principle.

## ACKNOWLEDGEMENT

The author wishes to acknowledge his indebtedness to Dr. W. J. McCulley, Medical Superintendent, St. Andrew's Hospital, for permission to publish and for making it possible for the investigation to be carried out.

## REFERENCES

1. YATES, A. J. (1958) The application of learning theory to the treatment of tics, *J. Abnorm. Soc. Psychol.* **56**, 175–182.
2. YATES, A. J. (1959) Personal communication.

# Experimental Psychology and the Treatment of a Ticqueur*

D. WALTON

*Winwick Hospital, Warrington, Lancashire*

## INTRODUCTION

In a recent book a series of new techniques for the treatment of the neuroses has been presented (Eysenck, 1960). Amongst these methods of treatment, derived from the fields of experimental psychology, is that of therapy by negative practice and conditioned inhibition "....continual repetition of a habit in the same stimulus situation will ultimately lead to the extinction of that response" (Kendrick, 1960). Nevertheless very little work has been reported so far which deals with the therapeutic application of this experimentally derived concept. Indeed, little progress appears to have been made in the treatment of tics since the publication of Meige and Feindel's classic work (1907) on the treatment of tics as examples of learned habits. It was also many years later that Dunlap (1932) claimed that tics could be eliminated by forcing the patient to repeat his tics voluntarily. An adequate theoretical rationale and experimental validation of the therapeutic efficacy of this method was, however, still lacking.

Yates (1958) was the first to report a rationale for such treatment and to carry out a series of experiments designed to determine the optimum conditions of massed practice for the extinction of tics in a young psychiatric patient. The results of this experiment, and of those of Kendrick (1958, 1959) on the role played by conditioned inhibition in the extinction of habit responses, were utilized in formulating the present method of treatment for the removal of a number of diverse tics in a young boy of eleven.

## CASE HISTORY

The patient, on referral, was 11 years and 7 months of age. Mild facial tics had been evident from the age of 5. These consisted of slight, involuntary movements of the mouth and the face. They tended to occur when he was excited, as did a mild blinking spasm. For nearly a year prior to referral for treatment several major tics were evident. Suddenly

* This article is reprinted with the permission of the author and the editor from *J. Child Psychol.* **2**, 148–155 (1961).

389

his legs and arms would jerk violently, accompanied by diverse explosive utterances such as "Good, good, good" or "Hurrah, hurrah, hurrah" or "Fool, fool, fool". If such symptoms occurred while he was in a car, their force would be sufficient to shake it. In hospital the ward-sister noted that these same tics were strong enough to move the bed. He would often be unable to eat a meal as he could not hold a glass or any cutlery. When he tried to use a knife and fork, the food and cutlery would often suddenly "shoot off" the plate, ejected by the violent hand movements. Involuntary head-turning to either side in a repetitive compulsive manner was another common symptom, as was the simultaneous raising of his eyebrows and the production of a smile-like tic. Shrugging of the shoulders accompanied by raising of an arm was a further feature. Several minor tics involved repetitive pointing at an object, or the frequent touching of his ears.

His mother admitted that he was a very emotional boy whose emotionality essentially took the form of aggression and over-confidence rather than anxiety and diffidence. She also reported that the father had always "spoiled" him, she of late being more strict. The parents often quarrelled over the way he should be handled. On the basis of the patient's history and psychological testing (Family Relations Test (Bene and Anthony, 1957)) the following hypothesis emerged. The patient was an over-privileged child who wished to claim, and was used to claiming, all the parent's attention, but of late the mother had attempted to discipline him. This constituted a threat to his over-indulged self, which produced anxiety, resentment and considerable tension. The tics could be regarded as tension-reducing phenomena. They also tended to occur at this time when he was excited or happy or when he had to meet new situations. They became much worse, for example, when he first started grammar school or when any of the nursing staff asked him how he was feeling. Any excessive emotional state appeared to produce the tics.

## SYMPTOMATIC TREATMENT OF THE TICS

### Proposed Theoretical Model

Detailed inquiry into the patient's history failed to detect traumata that might suggest how his tics initially came to coincide with drive-reduction. Perhaps the tics were originally *unconditioned* tension reducers. It is hypothesized that they had become elaborated as drive-reducing *conditioned* responses, originally evoked in a variety of situations arousing intense emotion. When such movements either produced or coincided with a reduction or cessation of the tension, the tics would become stronger by a process of reinforcement. Through a process of stimulus-generalization (Hull, 1943) a variety of stimuli similar to these original stimuli would then evoke the tic, which would become further reinforced, thus leading to the development of a powerful positive habit. Thus the reaction potential of the tics, or their readiness to become manifest, may be regarded as a multiplicative function of positive habit strength, which Hull termed $_sH_R$, and the momentary drive strength of tension ($D$).

### Derivation of Method of Treatment

According to the above model, the various tics would be viewed as simple learned habits which had reached maximum habit strength. In terms of Dunlap's (1932) and Yates' (1958) theoretical-clinical formulations, it should be possible to extinguish them by building up negative habits of "not performing the tics". For as Yates (1958) says: "If the subject is given massed practice in the tic, then reactive inhibition $I_R$ should build up rapidly. When $I_R$ reaches a certain critical point, the patient will be forced to 'rest', or not perform the tic. This habit ($_sI_R$) of not performing the tic will be associated with drive-reduction due to the dissipation of $I_R$ and hence will be reinforced. With repeated massed practice, therefore, a negative habit ('not doing the tic') will be built up, incompatible with the positive habit of doing the tic."

Yates' orientation was rather more experimental than therapeutic. He was concerned to discover the optimum conditions of massed practice for producing conditioned inhibition. As a result of considerable detailed research he came to the conclusion that: "the optimum condition for the growth of the negative habit appeared to be the combination of very prolonged massed practice followed by prolonged rest."

Unfortunately Yates was unable to apply these findings in a further, treatment-orientated study. Jones (1960) decided to do so, using the same patient, in the light of Yates' main findings. Of interest was Jones' demonstration that it is possible by persisting with massed experimental extinction trials to inhibit almost entirely the voluntary evocation of a tic. In general Yates' conclusions were confirmed. The patient showed considerable improvement, both in respect of the frequency of her tics and in her emotional state. Seventeen months after discharge, a psychiatric follow-up assessment rates the patients as "much improved".

Of particular relevance to the derivation of the present method of treatment is the modification of Hull's fundamental formula by Jones (1958). Hull regarded $I_R$ as a (negative) drive and $_sI_R$ as a negative habit. He met considerable criticism when he linked both these concepts into one formula, by addition. This was an inconsistency because in terms of his general theoretical principles he should have multiplied them, as he did for the positive drive ($D$) and positive habits ($_sH_R$). Jones (1958) has corrected this inconsistency with the following new formulation:

$$_sE_R = (D - I_R) \times (_sH_R - {_sI_R}).$$

In this formula, Jones treats the positive and negative drive-states in the same way and similarly the positive and negative habits, suggesting that they are both subject to the same laws.

Eysenck (1956) has defined the conditions under which negative habits ($_sI_R$) develop. In a recent publication Kendrick (1960) has described this process in detail:

In a situation where performance is continuous, $I_R$ builds up to a critical level, this level depending upon the strength of the primary drive (D) present at that moment. Once this critical level has been reached, an automatic resting response is produced (an involuntary rest pause, IRP). These IRP's allow the dissipation of $I_R$ below the critical level, which produces an increment of $_sI_R$. After the $I_R$ has dissipated below the critical level, performance is once again resumed. In the normal type of massed practice, where there is a slight pause between trials, as in animal experiments, or the usual 5-sec interval between trials on the pursuit rotor, $I_R$ may not have developed to a critical level. The *voluntary* rest pause, however, acts in a similar way, in that it allows some $I_R$ to dissipate, and so a further increment of $_sI_R$ is produced. Eysenck treats $_sI_R$ as a habit with all the properties of a positive habit. When performance is resumed after a rest pause and all $I_R$ has been dissipated, $_sI_R$ will undergo extinction until the next voluntary rest pause, because of the failure of reinforcement to occur. But because $_sI_R$ is a habit, there is spontaneous recovery, and so when there is a considerable gap between sets of trials, say a day, $_sI_R$ recovers and, because of this, from day to day there is an increase in the strength of $_sI_R$. It can therefore be seen that with this increase in $_sI_R$ from period to period, depending upon how quickly $_sI_R$ is accumulating, there will come a time when $_sI_R$ may equal $_sH_R$, in which case the chances of the performance of the habit are 50 : 50. Now, supposing the habit in question is at an asymptote, and therefore there is only a slight oscillation in its strength; if the habitual act is now repeated it can only lead to more $_sI_R$ being accumulated and so reducing the chances of the habit being performed. This process could be carried out to the point where the chances of the performance of the habit are very remote.

Reverting to Jones' formula (1958), when the equation is multiplied out the same drive (*D*) can activate both the positive ($_sH_R$) and negative ($_sI_R$) habits. It logically follows that once a tic has been extinguished by the above methods, then any increase in drive only serves: "to increase the potentialities of *both* habits proportionately, so no recovery would take place" (i.e. of the tic). Kendrick's experimental work (1958, 1959) with animals appears to support these inferences.

Of considerable importance also were Kendrick's findings that extinction can be brought about faster under conditions of low rather than high drive, and that there was a lowered tolerance for $I_R$ under conditions of low drive compared with states of high drive. In other words when the degree of tension is very high, the reaction potential of the tics is high, accompanied by an increased tolerance for $I_R$. If the tension can be reduced the tolerance for $I_R$ is less and extinction could be effected more quickly.

The following suggestions thus emerged for planning optimal conditions of treatment for the rapid growth of conditioned inhibition ($_sI_R$):

(1) Massed practice trials of the tics to the point where inhibition of their voluntary evocation takes place;

(2) Simultaneous reduction in drive level to produce less tolerance for $I_R$ and more rapid build-up of $_sI_R$. This could be achieved by medication with Largactil before massed practice trials.

## Method of Treatment

The subject was a patient in a general hospital ward. He received medication by Largactil (25 mg) in the general hospital approximately three quarters of an hour before he was brought by ambulance to the psychology department. In all he received Largactil 25 mg t.d.s.

## TABLE 1

*Duration of different kinds of massed practice at each session\**

| Kind of massed practice | Sessions | | | | | | | | | | | | | | | | |
|---|---|---|---|---|---|---|---|---|---|---|---|---|---|---|---|---|---|
| | 1–20 | 21 | 22 | 23 | 24 | 25 | 26 | 27 | 28 | 29 | 30 | 31 | 32 | 33 | 34 | 35 | 36 |
| 1. Major tic | 15'–27' | 30' | — | 29' | 31' | — | 31' | 31' | 31' | 15' | — | — | — | — | 31' | 31' | — |
| 2. Head turning (to right) | — | 1'40" | 1'40" | — | — | — | — | — | — | 5' | — | — | — | — | — | — | — |
| 3. Head turning (to left) | — | 1'40" | 1'40" | — | — | — | — | — | — | 10' | — | — | — | — | — | — | — |
| 4. Head movements (up and down) | — | 1'40" | 1'40" | — | — | — | — | — | — | — | — | — | — | — | — | — | — |
| 5. Head turning (to right and smiling) | — | — | — | 5' | 5' | 5' | 5' | 5' | — | — | 10' | 10' | 10' | 10' | 10' | — | 10' |
| 6. Head turning (to left and smiling) | — | — | — | 5' | 5' | 5' | 5' | 5' | — | — | 10' | 10' | 10' | 10' | 10' | — | 10' |
| 7. Head movements (up and down and smiling) | — | — | — | 5' | 5' | 5' | — | — | — | — | — | — | — | — | — | — | — |
| 8. Ear touching tic | — | — | — | — | — | — | — | 5' | — | 5' | 10' | 10' | 10' | 10' | — | — | — |
| 9. Hand withdrawal tic | — | — | — | — | — | — | — | — | — | — | 10' | 10' | 10' | 10' | — | — | — |
| Total time per session | 15'–27' | 35' | 5' | 44' | 46' | 15' | 41' | 46' | 31' | 35' | 40' | 40' | 40' | 40' | 51' | 31' | 20' |

\* Time is shown in minutes and seconds.

One session per day was carried out under supervision, the subject being instructed to reproduce the "Good, good, good" tic as accurately as possible. This involved the imitation of the total tic, including the violent simultaneous leg and arm movements and the explosive utterances. Little or no pause was allowed between each response during the massed practice sessions.

No objective measures were taken of the frequency of the tics under conditions of voluntary evocation. Reliance was placed on observation in assessing their frequency.

There were 36 treatment-sessions in all, the first lasting for 15 min. The practice of the major tic continued for 29 sessions, the remaining sessions

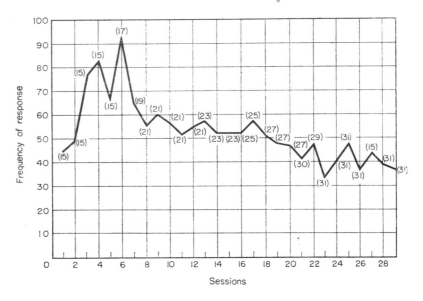

Fig. 1. Average frequency of response per minute of massed practice of the major tic. (Figures in brackets refer to time devoted to each session, in minutes.)

being devoted to the practice of the various other tics. The length of the session for the voluntary evocation of the major tics was gradually increased to 31 min of uninterrupted massed practice. Figure 1 shows the length of time devoted to each of these 29 massed practice sessions.

After 20 sessions had been completed in the practice of his major tic, the patient was then forced to practise the voluntary evocation of his remaining tics. This treatment programme is contained in Table 1.

At the general hospital, from the 18th session onwards, he practised the tics for at least a further $\frac{1}{2}$ hr per day under the supervision of a nurse.

## THERAPEUTIC RESPONSE

Figure 1 shows the average frequencies of response per minute of massed practice of the major tic. The gradual decline in the patient's ability to imitate this tic voluntarily is quite striking. More important was the generalization of this improvement to his involuntary tics. Towards the end of his stay in the general hospital, he considered that his tics very much improved both with respect to frequency and intensity. He would go for periods of up to three or four days with little evidence of their presence, something unheard of prior to treatment. In fact, in a 12-hr period of uncontrolled "observation" in the general hospital prior to treatment, there were at least 26 episodes of agitation involving his major tics.

No figures comparable to Fig. 1 are available for the other tics, as no record was kept of their frequency during the other massed practice sessions.

The patient was discharged from hospital some two months after the first treatment session as very much improved.

## FOLLOW-UP

A follow-up was carried out one year after discharge. The boy attended with his mother. There was no evidence of any tics through a half-hour interview, except for one slight facial tic.

A film was made of the follow-up interview. This was closely scrutinized to detect any tics which might have passed unnoticed, but failed to reveal any involuntary movements apart from the one mentioned above.

The mother stated that the boy had made a good general adjustment and was showing little or no evidence of tics of any kind. She also reported that before returning to grammar school (after a lapse of nearly a year) he had received private tuition for two hours a day to compensate for time lost through illness. On his return he is reported to be mixing well and studying hard. He has also joined the scouts.

## DISCUSSION

In the present paper it has been suggested that several situations appeared to be associated with an increase in $D$, and that the strength of the tics was a function both of their ability to reduce $D$ and the frequency of their evocation. Following the treatment advocated, it was also suggested that any subsequent increase of $D$ would only reactivate both the positive and negative habits proportionately. In other words, the type of therapy adopted produced a negative habit, more powerful than the positive one. Thus, any increase in $D$ would not reintroduce the previous dominance of the positive habit, but rather the negative one of not responding with tics.

However, during the follow-up period the patient was taking tranquillizers irregularly.* The question arises whether this prevented the reappear-

* At various times during the follow-up period Fentazin (4 mg t.d.s.), or Thioridazine (25–50 mg t.d.s.) were prescribed.

ance of his tics or whether it was due to the psychological treatment, based on the theoretical model just described. Tranquillizing drugs are expected to reduce $D$ (Trouton and Eysenck, 1960; Walton, 1960), and consequently the strength of any positive habit associated with such $D$ might be expected to decrease under sedation, though any subsequent increase of $D$, either through physiological adaptation to the drug, failure to take the drug as prescribed, or for any other reason might be expected, in terms of Jones' equation (1958), to result in the reactivation of the habit, unless the previous discussion on the development of negative habits was invalid. In fact the tics did not recur, in spite of the patient's *irregular* use of his tablets. He remained a very emotional and excitable boy, and family difficulties persisted (the mother still objected to the father's methods of handling him, and he was disrespectful towards his father). He also had to overcome the not inconsiderable difficulties of returning to grammar school and having to make up a year's lost ground. All these facts argue against the abolition of his tics in the follow-up period being due to a decrease of $D$ produced by drugs. The investigations of Yates (1958), Jones (1960) and Ernest (1960) are relevant. Drugs were not used in any of these studies. Significant therapeutic results were achieved, however, using methods similar to those employed in the present study, and there was no evidence of deterioration during substantial follow-up periods. The fact that Kendrick (1960) demonstrated no recovery of response under conditions of high drive suggests that the application of the tranquillizers during the follow-up period was not strictly relevant to the continued inhibition of the tics. The value of such sedation appears to lie in reducing the possibility of other symptoms being learned during the follow-up period, and not in preventing the tics from recurring.

## SUMMARY

A theoretical model is advanced to account for the development of a number of diverse tics in a young boy of eleven. A method of treatment, based on this model and on the experimental work of others, was then devised. The success of this treatment is taken as tentative support of the validity of these proposals, particularly since compatible results have been achieved by others using similar methods.

## ACKNOWLEDGEMENTS

I am most grateful to Dr. P. M. O'Flanagan, Winwick Hospital, and Mr. Gwynne Jones, Maudsley Hospital; the first for permission to publish the present report concerning a patient under his care, the second for critically reading the first draft of the paper.

## REFERENCES

BENE, E. and ANTHONY, J. (1957) *Manual for the Family Relations Test*, National Foundation for Educational Research, London.

DUNLAP, K. (1932) *Habits, Their Making and Unmaking*, Liveright, New York.

ERNEST, E. (1960) [Personal communication to H. G. Jones in] Continuation of Yates' Treatment of a Ticqueur. In *Behaviour Therapy and the Neuroses* (Ed. EYSENCK, H. J.) Pergamon Press, Oxford.

EYSENCK, H. J. (1956) "Warm-up" in pursuit rotor learning as a function of the extinction of conditioned inhibition, *Acta Psychol.* 12, 349–370.

EYSENCK, H. J. (Ed.) (1960) *Behaviour Therapy and the Neuroses*, Pergamon Press, Oxford.

HULL, C. L. (1943) *Principles of Behaviour*, Appleton-Century, New York.

JONES, H. G. (1958) The status of inhibition in Hull's system. A theoretical revision, *Psychol. Rev.* 65, 179–182.

JONES, H. G. (1960) Continuation of Yates' Treatment of a Tiqueur. In *Behaviour Therapy and the Neuroses* (Ed. EYSENCK, H. J.) Pergamon Press, Oxford.

KENDRICK, D. C. (1958) $_sI_R$ and drive level: a reply to Keehn and Sabbagh, *Psychol. Rep.* 4, 547–552.

KENDRICK, D. C. (1959) Conditioned inhibition and the drive and effort variables. *Bull. Brit. Psychol. Soc.* 38, 6A–7A (Abstract).

KENDRICK, D. C. (1960) The Theory of 'conditioned inhibition' as an explanation of negative practice effects. An experimental analysis. In *Behaviour Therapy and the Neuroses* (Ed. by EYSENCK, H. J.) Pergamon Press, Oxford.

MEIGE, H. and FEINDEL, E. (1907) *Tics and their treatment*, S. Appleton, London.

TROUTON, D. and EYSENCK, H. J. (1960) *Handbook of Abnormal Psychology* (Edited by EYSENCK, H. J.) Pitman Medical Publishing Co. Ltd., London.

WALTON, D. (1960) Drug addiction and habit formation –an attempted integration, *J. Ment. Sci.* 106, 445, 1195–1230.

YATES, A. J. (1958) The application of learning theory to the treatment of tics, *J. Abnorm. Soc. Psychol.* 56, 175–182.

# Massed Practice and Simultaneous Reduction in Drive Level—Further Evidence of the Efficacy of this Approach to the Treatment of Tics*

D. WALTON

*Principal Psychologist, Winwick Hospital, Warrington*

IN A previous paper (Walton, 1961) a theoretical model was advanced to account for the development of a number of tics in a young boy. A method of treatment, based on this model, was devised. This treatment consisted of the massed practice of his tics and of the simultaneous reduction in drive level by medication to produce less tolerance for $I_R$ and more rapid build by of $_sI_R$. Treatment was successful and a follow-up, carried out one year after discharge, failed to demonstrate a return of any of his tics.

A second boy, suffering from three clear-cut tics, provided an additional opportunity to test further the efficacy of this method of treatment. The tics involved nasal "explosion" (expiration), hiccoughing and head-shaking. He reported that these or other tics had been present for the past eleven years.

On admission to hospital the head-shaking tic occurred every minute throughout the first few days, though it occurred somewhat less frequently thereafter. Each set of such rapid side-to-side head movements lasted some five to ten seconds. His two other tics were present throughout the day, each varying from time to time in frequency of occurrence. The powerful head-shaking tic was, however, by far the most frequent.

The patient received medication by amylobarbitone, 3 grains, $1/2$ hr before appointment. There were 109 treatment sessions. Table 1 shows the duration of the different kinds of massed practice at each session. The patient made a positive response to treatment. Considerable amelioration of his symptoms occurred with some improvement in his emotional state. He became more co-operative, less mischievous and more relaxed.

Five months after the termination of this treatment considerable improvement was still evident. There was no evidence of the hiccough tic, whilst the nasal expiration tic was virtually extinct. The frequency of the head-shaking tic was also reduced to approximately three or four occasions

---

* This paper was written specially for publication in this book.

TABLE 1

*Duration of different kinds of massed practice at each session\**

| Kind of massed practice | 1 | 2 | 3 | 4 | 5 | 6 | 7 | 8 | 9 | 10 | 11 | 12 | 13 | 14 | 15 | 16 | 17 | 18 | 19 | 20 | 21 | 22 | 23 | 24 | 25 | 26 | 27 | 28 | 29—109 |
|---|---|---|---|---|---|---|---|---|---|---|---|---|---|---|---|---|---|---|---|---|---|---|---|---|---|---|---|---|---|
| 1. Head shaking | $\frac{1}{2}$ | $\frac{1}{2}$ | $\frac{1}{2}$ | $\frac{1}{2}$ | $\frac{1}{2}$ | $\frac{1}{2}$ | $\frac{1}{2}$ | $\frac{1}{2}$ | 1 | 1 | 1 | $\frac{1}{2}$ | $\frac{1}{2}$ | $\frac{1}{2}$ | – | – | – | $\frac{1}{2}$ | $1\frac{1}{2}$ | – | $\frac{1}{2}$ | $\frac{1}{2}$ | $\frac{3}{4}$ | $\frac{1}{2}$ | – | – | – | – | 1 hr at 11·0 a.m. $1\frac{1}{2}$ hr at 2·0 p.m. |
| 2. Hiccough | – | – | – | – | – | – | – | – | – | – | – | $\frac{1}{2}$ | $\frac{1}{2}$ | $\frac{1}{2}$ | 1 | $1\frac{1}{2}$ | $\frac{1}{2}$ | – | – | – | – | $\frac{3}{4}$ | $\frac{3}{4}$ | – | $1\frac{1}{2}$ | $1\frac{1}{2}$ | $\frac{1}{2}$ | – | – |
| 3. Nasal-expiration | – | – | – | – | – | – | – | – | – | – | – | – | – | – | – | – | – | – | $\frac{1}{2}$ | $\frac{1}{2}$ | – | – | – | – | – | – | – | – | – |
| Total time for session | $\frac{1}{2}$ | $\frac{1}{2}$ | $\frac{1}{2}$ | $\frac{1}{2}$ | $\frac{1}{2}$ | $\frac{1}{2}$ | $\frac{1}{2}$ | $\frac{1}{2}$ | 1 | 1 | 1 | 1 | 1 | 1 | 1 | $1\frac{1}{2}$ | $1\frac{1}{2}$ | $1\frac{1}{2}$ | $1\frac{1}{2}$ | $1\frac{1}{2}$ | $1\frac{1}{2}$ | $1\frac{1}{2}$ | $1\frac{1}{2}$ | $1\frac{1}{2}$ | $1\frac{1}{2}$ | $1\frac{1}{2}$ | $1\frac{1}{2}$ | $1\frac{1}{2}$ | 1 and $1\frac{1}{2}$ hr alternatively. |

\* Time shown in hours indicates sessions carried out on same day.

per day. The boy reported that he could now control this tic and stop it immediately, whereas originally this was impossible. There was also an apparent lessening of vigour in such head movements. He admitted that the head-shaking tic could still be exacerbated by excitement or argument, though in such situations his tics could now more easily be brought under control.

There is thus further support for the efficacy of the therapy employed. Before the soundness of this approach can be adequately assessed, however, more ticqueurs will have to be treated by similar methods.

## ACKNOWLEDGEMENTS

The author is indebted to Dr. G. CADOGEN and Dr. W. P. WALSH for their permission, encouragement and assistance in carrying out the investigation.

## REFERENCES

WALTON, D. (1961) Experimental Psychology and the treatment of a ticqueur, *J. Child Psychol. Psychiat.* **2**, 148–155.

# Objective Psychotherapy in the Treatment
# of Dysphemia*

## Arnold A. Lazarus

Since many speech therapists feel that dysphemia is already "the disorder of too many theories", they regard outside opinion as an intrusion and a usurpation of their rights. Others, imbued with a need for therapeutic teamwork (a high-sounding concept which rarely works in practice), often err by accepting contradictory and fragmentary views which only further confuse and complicate the issue. The present paper is an endeavour to increase the scope and range of the speech therapist's role by offering an objective rationale for the inclusion of certain behaviour therapeutic† techniques into the sphere of logopedics.

The study of dysphemia may be conveniently divided into three parts:

(i) The actual stutter (i.e. the analysis of clonic and tonic spasms associated with phonation, articulation and respiration which disturb the flow of speech. This would include accompanying tics and allied patterns of dysrhythmia in various areas of psychomotor activity).

(ii) The onset and underlying causes of stuttering. (In this connexion, it should be emphasized at the very outset that attempts to reveal the genesis of stuttering through biochemical analyses, psychometric investigations, medical and neurological examinations, EEG recordings and the like have all proved nonspecific for any stutterlike pattern.)

(iii) The stutterer's psychological responses, with special reference to his attitudes and feelings in various speaking situations.

In dealing with the problems associated with (iii), the speech therapist is handicapped by a paucity of effective techniques. On occasion, the anxieties which often exacerbate dysphemic responses are glossed over. In general reassurance or mild emotional support is offered, while relaxation and specific "assignments" are used as therapeutic adjuncts. On the other

---

* This article is reprinted with the permission of the author and editor from *J. South African Logopedic Soc.*, March, 1961, pp. 8–10.

† We are following Eysenck's example of subsuming the theoretical concepts and practical methods of treatment derived from modern learning theory under the heading "Behaviour Therapy".

hand, many problems are left alone on the assumption that it is highly dangerous to dabble in psychotherapy. This is a crucial gap. In most practical essentials the speech therapist is willy-nilly a psychotherapist and the treatment of specific neuroses which have a bearing on the mechanisms of speech, may legitimately be placed within the province of logopedics. The present article outlines two techniques which, in time, may conceivably form an integral part of the therapeutic *modus operandi* of every speech therapist.

Although it has not been established that dysphemia is essentially a manifestation of unresolved conflicts and anxiety, even the pure organicists cannot deny that a stutterer's speech pattern usually deteriorates in anxiety-generating situations. It is empirically demonstrable that attitudes of hypersensitivity and self-consciousness tend to further inhibit the stutterer's verbalization and result in "secondary blocking". Some stutterers, burdened by pervasive anxieties, find the mere thought of speech terrifying. The desensitization technique outlined below is not for them; it is indicated in cases where the individual is overwhelmed by anxiety and tension in *specific* speaking situations. It must be understood, however, that neither of the therapeutic techniques* dealt with is intended as a "cure" for dysphemia. When working towards a cure, the emphasis should be on a *synthesis* of different therapeutic procedures, so that consideration is given to the entire speech mechanism *per se* and to the socio-psychobiological features. But at the present stage of our knowledge, the complete elimination of a confirmed stutter is generally a therapeutic ideal rather than a practical objective. Therapeutic idealism often results in objective nihilism and fails to achieve even those modest therapeutic goals which are well within the limits of our practical skills. Those theorists (such as the psychoanalysts) for example, who insist on treating the so-called "total personality" are often so absorbed in the intricacies of their amorphous task, that they rarely achieve results comparable with those attained by therapists who use only simple vocal exercises. Thus, on the assumption that it is wise to proceed with scientific humility and caution, we shall now outline two techniques which aim to *alleviate* rather than to *eliminate* the problem of dysphemia.

## SYSTEMATIC DESENSITIZATION BASED ON RELAXATION†

Wolpe[2] has shown that specific anxieties can be eliminated if they are progressively opposed by muscular relaxation. Thus, if a stutterer becomes anxious each time he answers the telephone, this response (anxiety) must

---

* The practical application of learning theory to the treatment of tics which often accompany stutterlike patterns is dealt with towards the end of this paper. Speech therapists will easily recognize the different emphasis which is placed on the well-known technique of "negative practice".

† For a complete practical and theoretical exposition of systematic desensitization based on relaxation see Wolpe[2] Ch. 9.

be opposed by a new response (e.g. relaxation) which is physiologically incompatible with anxiety. The bond between the specific speaking situation and the anxiety will then be broken. This fact was clearly demonstrated in the case of a 19-year-old pharmacy student whose mild stutter became extremely pronounced each time he had to answer the telephone. "As soon as the 'phone starts ringing I begin to feel butterflies in my stomach," he explained. "As I get near the 'phone my fears get worse and by the time I lift the receiver to my ear, I just know that I'm going to stutter... By then I can't even open my mouth." He added that the *mere thought* of speaking on a telephone made him feel anxious. Systematic desensitization was applied as follows:

He was first trained in an accelerated version of Jacobson's[3] progressive relaxation. While fully relaxed, he was asked to imagine the sound of a telephone ringing in the distance. (He was told to signal to the therapist if he experienced any feelings of anxiety while visualizing any of the given situations.) As this failed to provoke any anxiety, he was asked to imagine the sound of a telephone ringing in the same room. This image also failed to generate any anxiety, but the thought of a telephone ringing right next to him provoked a fair measure of anxiety. His anxiety was opposed by relaxation again and again until he was able to tolerate, with complete tranquillity, the idea of a telephone ringing right beside him.

The patient was seen three days later. He reported that he no longer experienced any anxiety when he actually heard the telephone ringing... "the butterflies are completely gone in that situation". He was then desensitized to the thought of approaching a ringing telephone. It required four sessions before he was able to contemplate picking up the receiver with no feelings anxiety. At this stage he reported that his phobia for telephones had greatly dimished. "I don't panic any longer," he stated, "but I still stutter very badly over the 'phone... It's worst of all when I try checking an order over the 'phone." After nine additional desensitization sessions, there was no apparent difference between his telephonic speech and his verbalization in face-to-face situations. At the time of writing, he has maintained his improvement for over four years.

Equally good results were achieved in the case of a 19-year-old student whose stutter incapacitated her while out on a "date", while speaking in class and when answering the telephone. These three anxiety areas were treated concurrently and required 22 sessions for their complete elimination. The patient also reported an improvement in many general aspects of her speech. The follow-up in this case is also over four years.

Similarly, a 42-year-old business executive who had experienced great difficulty when talking to important clients and when ordering in a restaurant stated that "my new business contacts don't believe me when I tell them that I am a stutterer". He required only 13 desensitization sessions to effect this improvement.

A case reported elsewhere[4] was that of a 34-year-old engineer who received desensitization therapy for a speech disturbance characterized by lengthy and frequent "word blocks" accompanied by considerable tension and facial grimaces. When first interviewed he stuttered on about 12–25 per cent of words, with "blocks" averaging 3–4 seconds. His attitude towards speaking situations was poor. He received 30 hours of therapy over 9 months. Therapy sessions were usually held once a week. Training in progressive relaxation was followed by systematic desensitization. Among others the following anxiety-situations were treated: time pressures (especially speaking on the telephone as he conducted many of his occupational affairs by long-distance calls), telling jokes, public speaking, difficult "audiences", i.e. specific people who provoked added speech difficulties. Progress was gradual, but at the termination of therapy a substantial gain in speech fluency had been achieved.

One of the principal skills in the administration of systematic desensitization is to proceed at a pace which is in keeping with the patient's level of anxiety. No harm seems to ensue from proceeding at a pace that might prove too slow for a patient, but too rapid a pace can prove extremely antitherapeutic and lead to increased levels of anxiety. The desensitization procedure can be used with children[5] but, as yet no one seems to have administered it to dysphemic children.

## THE USE OF MASSED PRACTICE IN THE TREATMENT OF TICS ASSOCIATED WITH DYSPHEMIA

Yates[6] deduced a method of eliminating neurotic tics by building up a habit of "not performing the tic". According to Hullian theory[7, 8, 9] massed practice of a motor activity (e.g. a tic) causes reactive inhibition ($I_R$) to build up. When $I_R$ reaches a certain critical point the subject requires rest, i.e. he experiences a need not to perform the tic. The habit of not performing the tic becomes associated with drive reduction and is therefore reinforced. Repeated massed practice will therefore build up a negative habit ("not-doing-the-tic") which will militate against the positive habit of doing the tic.

Yates's theoretical model was applied in the case of an 18-year-old youth with an extreme stutter who invariably twisted his mouth, screwed up his eyes and jerked his head forward and back during a "block". Twelve years of intermittent speech therapy had been of no avail. He was referred to the writer for vocational guidance and was advised first to undergo therapy for the pronounced spasms and tics which seemed to impede his speech. The tics were treated concurrently but independently. Each tic was given five one-minute periods of massed practice, with one minute's rest between each period. The same order of massed practice was employed throughout the treatment. He was first required to practise the jerking of his head for five trials. After three minutes rest he was asked to perform the mouth twisting movements and finally reproduced the eye-movements. The patient was instructed to carry out two sessions daily. He was supervised by the therapist twice a week. The tendency to screw up his eyes during a "block" was eliminated in less than three weeks. The mouth-twisting response and the head-jerking required more than a month of massed practice before they entirely disappeared. To date, there has been no apparent symptom substitution, nor have any of the original tics or spasms returned. The over-all improvement in his speech is really quite remarkable. His blocks are now far more infrequent and they are usually so momentary that they often pass completely unnoticed by untrained observers. A prolonged follow-up of this case is being undertaken.

## DISCUSSION

It is premature at this stage, of course, to assess the value of the techniques outlined above in the treatment of dysphemia. The preliminary findings, however, are most encouraging and warrant further investigation. This introduces the query: "Who should carry out the treatment, speech therapist, psychologist, or both?" We therefore return to the consideration of therapeutic teamwork. In the opinion of the writer, therapeutic teamwork is tenable only where there is a clear-cut division of the skills involved. In the case of a therapeutic liaison between doctor and psychologist, for instance, the collaboration is usually fruitful. This is because the doctor remains responsible for the *physical* health of the patient and the therapeutic lines of demarcation are reasonably obvious to patients and therapists alike. It is difficult to decide whether therapeutic teamwork between speech therapist and psychologist is advisable—so much depends on their respective theoretical orientations, their therapeutic objectives, the patient's level of adjustment and so forth. By and large, it is our view that the speech therapist, given the necessary training,* would be adequately qualified to "go it alone" when confronted with cases similar to those presented above.

## REFERENCES

1. EYSENCK, H. J. (1959) Learning Theory and Behaviour Therapy, *J. Ment. Sci*, **105**, 61.
2. WOLPE, J. (1958) *Psychotherapy by Reciprocal Inhibition*, Stanford University Press and Witwatersrand University Press.
3. JACOBSON, E. (1938) *Progressive Relaxation*, University of Chicago Press.
4. LAZARUS, A. A. and RACHMAN, S. (1957) The Use of Systematic Desensitization in Psychotherapy, *S. Afr. Med. J.* **31**, 934.

* It must be understood that the desensitization technique is a highly specialized procedure. The therapist who employs desensitization requires tuition in (a) the construction of the relevant anxiety hierarchies, (b) the application of hypnotic and ordinary relaxation procedures (c) the handling of anxiety which is aroused during a session, (d) in assessing the optimal number and duration of the stimuli which should be presented in any given session.

5. LAZARUS, A. A. (1959) The Elimination of Children's Phobias by Deconditioning, *Med. Proc.*, **5**, 261.
6. YATES, A. (1958) The Application of Learning Theory to the Treatment of Tics, *J. Abnorm. Soc. Psychol.* **56**, 175.
7. HULL, C. L. (1943) *Principles of Behaviour*, Appleton-Century-Crofts (New York).
8. HULL, C. L. (1951) *Essentials of Behaviour* (Yale University Press) New Haven.
9. HULL, C. L. (1952) *A Behaviour System* (Yale University Press) New Haven.

# The Hypnotic Treatment of Asthma*

GRIFFITH EDWARDS

*Maudsley Hospital*

INTEREST in the hypnotic treatment of asthma has waxed and waned. There have been a number of reports (Kennedy, 1947; Frankland and Augustin, 1954; Magonet, 1955; Fry, 1957; Stewart, 1957) which have drawn attention to the subject, but though valuable as exciting discussion, this literature has mostly not been of a sort which can usefully be subjected to rigorous scientific study. Leigh (1953) in an authoritative discussion of the psychiatric aspects of asthma, could at that time find no evidence for the usefulness of hypnosis, except in aborting the acute attack. A recent Russian study (Bull, 1962) has reported much interesting information, but again not in such a way as readily to lend itself to critical analysis.

However, there are five papers published in the last few years, which seem to provide a sufficient body of experimental data to form a basis for critical review. The factual findings contained in these papers will be presented in the abstracts which form the first section of this review. The selection of five papers from a large literature is inevitably rather arbitrary, but they have been chosen because between them they seem to provide intelligible data relevant to most of the perplexing problems that are encountered when one tries to apply hypnosis to the treatment of a disease as complicated as asthma.

The first paper (Sinclair-Gieben, 1960) sets the stage with a detailed case-report. The second and third papers (Edwards, 1960; White, 1961) are concerned with the methodology of assessment. The last two papers (Smith and Burns, 1960; Maher-Loughnan et al., 1962) are reports of clinical trials.

## SECTION 1—FIVE PAPERS

### A Case of Status Asthmaticus Treated by Hypnosis

Sinclair-Gieben (1960) reported the case of a 60-year-old man whose status responded to hypnosis when all other methods had failed. There was a six-year history of asthma.

* This paper was written specially for publication in this book.

407

The patient was first admitted to hospital from 7th November to 7th December 1958; on that occasion, status asthmaticus responded to an energetic regime of antispasmodics and antibiotics.

The second admission was from 16th March to 1st May 1959. The patient's status failed to respond to antibiotics and antispasmodics and on 19th April, ACTH gel 80 units/day was started, but again without improvement. On 21st April, with the patient deeply cyanosed and sitting up in bed gasping for breath, hypnosis was tried. The patient was by then in a severe panic state, saying continually, "The end is near, doctor; the end is near". A deep trance was induced within 10 min, with the suggestion given: "Now you will find the wheezing stops and your breathing becomes free and easy."

The wheezing stopped almost instaneously when the suggestion was given, and within a few minutes the patient began to regain his colour. On auscultation, almost no wheezing could be heard. When the patient woke up, he declared that for 5 years he had not felt so well. Hypnosis was then given on alternate days for 10 days, and the patient was discharged. On the day of leaving hospital, he evidenced his recovery by dancing a jig in front of other patients on the ward.

A happy outcome, however, was not to be. The patient died in "acute heart failure", a few days after leaving hospital: sudden death in asthmatics has been discussed by Leigh (1953).

Not only are clinical and pathological findings well documented in this report, but psychiatric information is also provided. The patient is described as having been of stable personality, and had been successful in his work, his marriage, and interpersonal relationships.

### Respiratory Function Tests and Hypnotic Treatment of Asthma

Edwards (1960) studied serial respiratory function tests on asthmatics who had been admitted to a general hospital with symptoms of sufficient severity for the G.P. to ask for emergency admission. Asthma had not responded to antispasmodics given by the G.P. In hospital, patients were given closely-spaced (usually daily) hypnotic sessions, with respiratory function tests performed before and after each session. After discharge, follow-up was made at intervals over a year.

Several respiratory function tests were charted. The first of these was Vital Capacity (VC)—the volume of air expired from maximum inspiration to maximum expiration. Measurement of VC alone is, however, of little value; firstly because a patient's *normal* vital capacity is not always known, and secondly because even if it can be established that VC is at the subject's normal level, functional abnormality in terms of narrowing of the bronchi may still be present. Other tests than VC must, therefore, be used if increased airways resistance is to be detected: if the airways are narrowed the subject cannot expire air at the normal rate, and this abnormality can be picked up by measuring the Fast Expiratory Volume One Second ($FEV_1$), which is the volume of air that can be expired in one second, starting at full inspiration. $FEV_1$ will go on showing daily changes during the course of recovery from an asthmatic attack at a point where VC has reached a stationary maximum.

$FEV_1$ has, in one respect, the same disadvantage as VC, for again one is up against the problem of the subject's normal value not being known. The difficulty of not knowing the subject's normal values can, however, to some extent be circumvented by considering not the absolute values of VC and $FEV_1$, but rather the ratio $FEV_1 \% VC$ (Pemberton and Flanagan, 1956). This ratio is usually not less than 65 per cent when respiratory function is normal. $FEV_1$ is perphaps not so familiar a concept as Maximum Breathing Capacity (MBC), which is the total volume of air which a subject can expire on forced breathing in one minute, and which affords another indication of airways resistance. Indirect Maximum Breathing Capacity (ind. MBC) can be calculated by multiplying $FEV_1$ by 35 (Thomson and Hugh-Jones, 1958).

The content of the suggestion was that asthma would "gradually disappear", and that thenceforward any symptoms would be very minor, would cause no anxiety, and would never build up to a severe asthmatic attack.

Six patients were reported on separately. Cases 2 and 5 were poor hypnotic subjects and showed no response to treatment. The original case reports contain clinical and pathological details, but psychiatric histories were not taken.

CASE 1—A man aged 36 years, with a 7-year history of asthma. Table 1 shows the improvement during treatment (5 sessions of light hypnosis). Despite complete clinical remission when the patient was discharged 8 days after admission, tests suggested residual functional impairment. For the next 13 months, the patient did well, with ind. MBC readings of 117, 107, and 114 L/min. He was then admitted to hospital again, this time for 5 days, with a mild attack of asthma for which he himself considered admission unnecessary. Seen 16 months after the first admission (no out-patient hypnosis having been done), he said that there was "no comparison" with his previous state, and that hypnosis had been a most successful form of treatment. Yet respiratory function tests showed considerable impairment, with VC 4·75 L, $FEV_1$ 2·23 L, $FEV_1 \% VC$ 49, and ind. MBC 78 L/min.

TABLE 1

*Ventilatory function tests in Case 1 before and after course of hypnosis*
*(figures in litres)*

|  | VC | $FEV_1$ | $FEV_1\% VC$ | Ind. MBC |
|---|---|---|---|---|
| On admission | 3·1 | 1·2 | 40 | 42 |
| At discharge |  |  |  |  |
| Before final hypnotic session | 5·3 | 2·9 | 54 | 99 |
| Immediately after hypnosis | 5·4 | 3·1 | 57 | 104 |

CASE 3—A woman aged 33 years with an 18-year history of asthma. She was admitted on 30th July with a severe attack of asthma and was discharged on 9th August 1957 symptom-free, after 6 sessions of deep hypnosis. Serial respiratory function tests paralleled clinical improvement, although the final ind. MBC of 116 L/min was below a subsequent maximum of 134 L/min, showing that she was free of symptoms on discharge but not (objectively) free of asthma. Indeed, as is shown in Table 2, this woman's subjective and objective state at various times showed a striking lack of correlation. As an out-patient (no further hypnosis) she was almost symptom-free for 2 months, but was then admitted

TABLE 2

*Case 3. Showing comparison of lung-function tests with clinical state (figures in litres)*

| Date | Clinical state | VC | FEV$_1$ | FEV$_1$% VC | Ind. MBC |
|---|---|---|---|---|---|
| 1. 7. 57 | Out-patient, prior to treatment. Puffing and panting but at work | 1·8 | 0·7 | 42 | 26 |
| 8. 7. 57 | Out-patient, after 1 week's choline theophyllinate. Improved. Only slightly dyspnoeic | 2·7 | 1·8 | 65 | 65 |
| 1. 8. 57 | In-patient, very dyspnoeic, sweaty, and distressed: in bed | 2·5 | 1·5 | 61 | 53 |

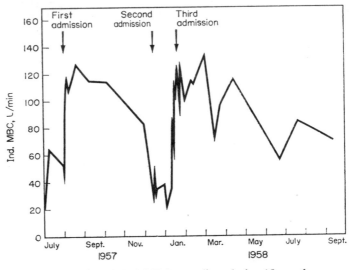

FIG. 1. Case 3. Ind. MBC recordings during 15 months.

for a second time (14th–24th December 1957), and treated with antispasmodics, and for a third time (6th–21st January 1958) on which occasion she was treated with steroids. Figure 1 shows the response in terms of ind. MBC plotted on each occasion.

CASE 4—A 33-year-old man with a 28-year history of asthma. He was admitted with moderately severe continuous dyspnoea and was discharged symptom-free 9 days later, after 5 sessions of deep hypnosis. He had been taught to induce relaxation by auto-hypnosis, but within days of returning home he developed moderately severe asthma. Five further sessions were given and though there was subjective benefit, tests showed no change; this is illustrated in Fig. 2, in which objective response as out-patient and in-patient are clearly very different. A year later the patient declared that he was "500 per cent better than in previous years", and on auscultation there was no wheeze. However, respiratory tests showed impairment: Table 3 summarizes a comparison of respiratory function tests and clinical state in this patient, the lack of correlation again being striking.

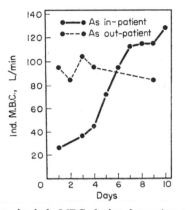

FIG. 2. Case 4. Change in ind. MBC during intermittent hypnotic treatment. Continuous line: response as in-patient. Broken line: response as out-patient.

TABLE 3

*Case 4. Showing comparison of lung-function tests with clinical state (figures in litres)*

| Date | Clinical state | VC | $FEV_1$ | $\dfrac{FEV_1\%}{VC}$ | Ind. MBC |
|---|---|---|---|---|---|
| 2. 8. 57 (day of admission) | Moderately severe dyspnoea | 2·2 | 0·8 | 35 | 27 |
| 11. 8. 57 (day of discharge) | Symptom-free | 4·8 | 3·7 | 76 | 129 |
| 23. 8. 57 (first O.P. attendance) | Slightly wheezy | 3·5 | 1·4 | 39 | 47 |
| 6. 10. 58 (O.P. attendance) | Symptom-free | 4·0 | 2·3 | 58 | 81 |

CASE 6—A woman aged 25 years, with a 15-year history of asthma. She was admitted to hospital with severe continuous dyspnoea and discharged symptom-free 12 days later, after 7 sessions of deep hypnosis. While in the ward, respiratory function continued to improve after subjective recovery was complete. This patient relapsed within a few days of returning home. She was, however, able to go about her work with respiratory function probably impaired to much the same extent as had previously necessitated admission (Table 4). Symptoms continued to fluctuate and she was put on steroids: while on steroids she developed T.B.

TABLE 4

*Case 6, showing comparison of lung-function tests with clinical state (figures in litres)*

| Date | Clinical state | VC | FEV$_1$ | FEV$_1$% VC | Ind. MBC |
|---|---|---|---|---|---|
| 24. 9. 57 (day of admission) | Moderately severe asthma. Having to stay in bed | 1·8 | 0·5 | 30 | 19 |
| 6. 10. 57. (day of discharge) | Symptom-free | 3·0 | 2·5 | 83 | 89 |
| 21. 10. 57 (first O.P. attendance) | Better than 24. 9. 57. Able to do her work | 1·7 | 0·7 | 42 | 26 |
| 6. 10. 58 (O.P. attendance) | Free from asthmatic symptoms, but with apical tuberculosis | 2·4 | 1·9 | 78 | 66 |

In all four of these patients the immediate response to hypnosis in terms of respiratory function tests before and after each hypnotic session was probably insignificant, although patient frequently reported immediate subjective improvement.

There seem to be three major factual conclusions to be drawn from this paper:

(1) Four out of six patients admitted to hospital with asthma of severity such as would normally make them candidates for steroid treatment responded to hypnotic suggestion.

(2) Subjective response to hypnotherapy (with the particular suggestion given), frequently showed an astonishing lack of relation to the patient's objective state.

(3) Brief intensive treatment of asthma by hypno-suggestion was followed by fairly rapid relapse.

### Hypnotic Treatment of Ten Asthmatics

White (1961) described the hypnotic treatment of 10 asthmatics: as the author stated, this group was heavily weighted with psychiatric abnormality. The composition of this group is shown in Table 5. All the patients except F. 9 were taking anti-spasmodic drugs when first seen and F. 5 and M. 6 were also taking steroids.

Patients were seen at an initial interview for history-taking and base-line recordings, and subsequently each patient received 7–10 hypnotic sessions over a period of 4–6 months. One patient (F.9) withdrew from the trial after 3 months. Degree of hypnosis attained was recorded as Grade 0–3: the number of patients achieving any particular depth is not stated, but the published figures seem to imply that only 2 patients achieved a deep trance. The suggestion given was of "easier breathing, lessening of tension and

TABLE 5

*Clinical details of a group of 10 asthmatics*

| Patient | Sex | Age (yrs) | Severity of asthma | Neurotic symptoms | Duration of symptoms (yrs) | Months of ttmnt | Months of follow-up | State at end of trial | | |
|---|---|---|---|---|---|---|---|---|---|---|
| | | | | | | | | Activity | Subjective state | Drug consumption |
| F 1 | F | 37 | Moderate | D | 16 | 6 | 8 | Increased | Improved | Less |
| M 2 | M | 38 | Mild | AT | 30 | 4 | 8 | Unchanged | Unchanged | Unchanged |
| F 3 | F | 32 | Severe | AD | $2\frac{1}{2}$ | 6 | 5 | Unchanged | Unchanged | Unchanged |
| M 4 | M | 32 | Moderate | D | 27 | 6 | 6 | Unchanged | Unchanged | Unchanged |
| F 5 | F | 43 | Severe | D | 8 | 6 | 6 | Increased | Improved | Less |
| M 6 | M | 30 | Severe | A | 15 | 8 | 6 | Increased | Improved | Less |
| M 7 | M | 18 | Severe | AD | 2 | 5 | 11 | Increased | Improved | Unchanged |
| F 8 | F | 57 | Severe | A | 4 | 6 | 7 | Increased | Improved | Unchanged |
| F 9 | F | 29 | Mild | Psychopathic personality | $1\frac{1}{2}$ | 3 | 0 | — | — | — |
| M 10 | M | 29 | Severe | A | 21 | 7 | 5 | Increased | Improved | Less |

A = Anxiety; D = Depression; T = Tension

TABLE 6

*The effect of different grades of hypnosis*

| Hypnosis grade | Total number of sessions | Sessions with respiratory function tests | Sessions when objective improvement possible | Respiratory state after hypnosis* | | | | | |
|---|---|---|---|---|---|---|---|---|---|
| | | | | Improved | | Unchanged | | Worse | |
| | | | | 0 | S | 0 | S | 0 | S |
| 0 | 7 | 3 | 3 | 0 | 1 | 2 | 3 | 1 | 3 |
| I | 22 | 17 | 13 | 5 | 15 | 8 | 7 | 4 | 0 |
| II | 41 | 37 | 31 | 5 | 28 | 19 | 11 | 13 | 2 |
| III | 12 | 12 | 9 | 3 | 7 | 7 | 5 | 2 | 0 |
| Totals | 82 | 69 | 56 | 13 | 51 | 36 | 26 | 20 | 5 |

* 0 = Objective state, S = Subjective state

bronchospasm, and increase in confidence". Whether the suggestion implied that the response would be rapid or gradual is not made explicit. After the period of treatment, patients were followed up for a further 6–11 months. Six subjects were initially treated as in-patients.

Assessment of results was made both in terms of the patient's report and by respiratory function tests. The tests performed were measurement of vital capatity and of peak expiratory flow rate (Wright and McKerrow, 1959), the latter being an index of airways resistance. Assessment was made

TABLE 7

*Percentage of sessions producing objective and subjective response with different grades of hypnosis*

| Grade of hypnosis | % of sessions showing improvement | |
|---|---|---|
| | Objective improvement | Subjective improvement |
| I | 38 | 68 |
| II | 16 | 68 |
| III | 33 | 58 |

before and after hypnosis at clinic visits during the subsequent follow-up. White states that a change in VC of 0·5 L and of 30 l./min in expiratory flow are significant changes, but the grounds for making this statement are not amplified.

The most important findings were as follows:

(1) There was a striking lack of correlation between immediate subjective and immediate objective response. This is shown in Table 6. Objective improvement was only considered "possible" (column 4) when the level before hypnosis was below the maximum level observed during the study of the patient. That subjective improvement occurred much more frequently than objective improvement is obvious from the table: other data showed that an objective worsening in respiratory function in 11 out of 20 sessions was accompanied by a report of decreased dyspnoea.

(2) Follow-up 12–17 months from the beginning of treatment showed that 6 patients thought they were improved and 3 thought there was no change. In no case were respiratory function tests markedly different from those at the beginning of treatment—actual figures are not given. But patients who reported subjective improvement seemed to show increased social activity. Improvement in affective symptoms was also noted.

(3) No simple relationship between response and hypnotic depth was demonstrated (Table 7). However, because response is simply reported as present or absent rather than being quantified, these figures are not sufficient to prove that depth of hypnosis is unrelated to (quantitative) therapeutic response.

*Treatment of Asthmatic Children by Hypnotic Suggestion*

Smith and Burns (1960) treated 25 asthmatic children by hypno-suggestion. These children were aged 8–15 years, with a mean age of 10·9 years, and the average age of onset of asthma was 3·5 years. Each patient was hypnotized on four occasions at weekly intervals—"the cases reported here were all satisfactory subjects in whom hypnosis was successful". The suggestion given was of "immediate and progressive relief from asthma".

Assessment of response was made in two ways:

(1) Respiratory function tests (vital capacity and forced expiratory volume one second) were done a week before treatment was started, before and after each treatment session, and finally, a week after the last treatment.

(2) Diary cards (Smith, 1958) were kept by each patient, and a record made of the patient's symptoms and use of antispasmodics.

No objective response to treatment was detected. It is stated that "a number" of the patients claimed subjective benefit. A control series was also studied, but hypnosis was thought to be so conclusively ineffective that comparison with the control series was not needed to prove the complete inefficacy of hypnotherapy.

*A Controlled Trial of Hypnosis in the Symptomatic Treatment of Asthma in Adults*

Maher-Loughnan *et al.* (1962) selected their subjects from among out-patients attending asthma clinics. Criteria for acceptance into the trial included at least a year's history of asthma, abscence of a severe bronchitic history or history of other lung disease, and absence of any history of psychotic breakdown. Patients who were on "continuous treatment" were also excluded: no patient was receiving steroids. The design, however, allowed inclusion of patients whose asthma was of various degrees of severity and on the basis of defined criteria, cases were divided into "mild", "medium", and "severe". Three hospitals (A, B, and C) participated in the trial. At A and B, a chest physician treated both hypnotic and control groups, whereas at Centre C, a chest physician treated the control group but referred the patients in the hypnotic group to a psychiatrist. A careful history was elicited from each patient, including an analysis of factors precipitating asthmatic attacks; these factors were tabulated as antigenic, infectious, physicial or emotional.

By random selection, patients were allocated to the hypnotic or to the control group. There were 27 patients in the hypnotic group and 28 in the control group. An initial period of one month's observation, to establish a base-line for the individual's symptoms, was followed by a 6-month treatment period.

Patients in the hypnosis group were given an initial hypnotic session and were then re-hypnotized at 1, 2, 4, 6, 7, 12, 16, 20, and 24-week intervals.

Hypnotic depth was recorded on a simple phenomenological scale as "light", "medium", or "deep". The suggestion given is not recorded, beyond noting that it was of "symptom removal". Hypnosis was used strictly for suggestion and not as an adjunct to other forms of psychotherapy. As well as receiving hypnotic suggestion, patients were, however, trained in auto-hypnosis—to go into a half-hour trance characterized by relaxation but not accompanied by any other therapeutic auto-suggestions. The hypnotic group was allowed to continue with their usual antispasmodics and record was made of the amount of antispasmodics used. Table 8 shows details of the degree of hypnosis achieved.

TABLE 8

*Details of hypnotherapy*

|  |  | Method of hypnosis | | | Total in hypnosis group |
|---|---|---|---|---|---|
|  |  | Hand/eye fixation | Eye fixation | Progressive relaxation | |
| Centre | | A | B | C | |
| Total no. of patients | | 14 | 6 | 7 | 27 |
| Depth of | Light | 1 | 2 | 3 | 6 |
| hypnosis | Medium | 3 | 4 | 4 | 11 |
|  | Deep | 10 | 0 | 0 | 10 |
| Auto- | Yes | 14 | 5 | 3 | 22 |
| hypnosis | No | 0 | 1 | 4 | 5 |

The control group was given, in each case, a *new* treatment—simply an antispasmodic which they had not used before. Six patients were given breathing exercises. Control group patients were seen at the same intervals and for the same length of time as patients in the treatment group.

All patients were asked to keep a simple daily diary card (as described by Waller *et al*, 1957; Francis and Spicer, 1960), on which they made a note of the amount of antispasmodics they had taken during the day and on which they also recorded the amount of wheezing they had experienced. Wheeziness was marked as absent (score 0), occasional (score 1), wheezing for 2 hr or more (score 2), or attack of asthma (score 3).

From this information on the diary cards, results of treatment were tabulated in several different ways:

(1) Number of days per month with wheezing (Table 9). It is seen that the treatment group showed considerable improvement when compared with the control group—an "average" hypnotic patient in the 6th month of treatment had 18 days clear of wheezing, 9 days occassional wheezing and 1 day with continuous or severe wheezing, this comparing with 10, 16 and 2 days respectively for an "average" control patient.

(2) "Score" of wheezing in terms of the month's total diary score for a patient averaged for each group for each month (Table 10). The average score of the hypnotic group from the third month onward differed significantly (5 per cent level) from the observation month: the control group rated in this way did not show significant change.

TABLE 9

*Condition of asthma during treatment. According to average number of days per month with wheezing*

| Month of treatment | Average no. of days per month† with | | | | | |
| | No wheeze | | Occasional wheeze | | Continuous or severe wheeze | |
| | H | C | H | C | H | C |
|---|---|---|---|---|---|---|
| Observation | 6 | 10 | 18 | 15 | 4 | 3 |
| 1 | 11 | 11 | 14 | 14 | 3 | 3 |
| 2 | 16 | 11 | 9 | 15 | 3 | 2 |
| 3 | 17 | 12 | 10 | 13 | 1 | 3 |
| 4 | 16 | 11 | 10 | 14 | 2 | 3 |
| 5 | 18 | 11 | 9 | 14 | 1 | 3 |
| 6 | 18 | 10 | 9 | 16 | 1 | 2 |

† of 28 days    H = hypnosis group (27 cases)    C = contol group (28 cases)

TABLE 10

*Condition of asthma during treatment: according to average "score" of wheezing per month*

| Month of treatment | Average score | |
| | H | C |
|---|---|---|
| Observation | 27 | 23 |
| 1 | 22 | 22 |
| 2 | 15 | 21 |
| 3 | 13 | 21 |
| 4 | 15 | 23 |
| 5 | 13 | 20 |
| 6 | 13 | 20 |

(3) Average number of times spray was used each month (Table 11). The use of the pump by the hypnotic group was greatly reduced by the 6th month.

(4) Respiratory function tests. At one hospital (C), vital capacity, fast expiratory volume one second, and peak flow were recorded at each inter-

view, but "very minor changes" were found in both control and hypnotic groups: at this centre, subjective response was less than at the other two hospitals.

In Table 12 response in the hypnotic group is analysed in relation to a number of variables. Three variables seem to have been of importance:

(i) Patients in whom auto-hypnosis was achieved showed considerable improvement in contrast to the almost total failure of response in the small group in whom auto-hypnosis could not be achieved.

TABLE 11

*Use of bronchodilators*

| Month of treatment | Average no. of times pump used | |
|---|---|---|
| | H | C |
| Observation † | 89 | 60 |
| 1 | 57 | 59 |
| 2 | 59 | 58 |
| 3 | 33 | 64 |
| 4 | 26 | 76 |
| 5 | 29 | 74 |
| 6 | 22 | 70 |

† No pump was issued to 2 control patients during the month of observation
H = hypnosis group (20 patients)   C = control group (21 patients)

(ii) The length of treatment was related to the response. Only slight improvement occured during the first month of treatment. The importance of the duration of treatment was stressed by the additional information (not tabulated) that of 18 patients, at centres A and B, who continued to be treated by hypnosis for a further 6 months, 12 became "completely free from wheezing" by the end of this additional period.

(iii) Patients at hospitals A and B (where they were treated by a chest physician) did better than patients at centre C, where they were treated by a psychiatrist.

Three other factors were also probably of some importance:

(1) Patients with mild asthma did better than those whose disease was of moderate or severe degree.

(2) Patients under 30 years of age did better than those who were older.

(3) Patients who were deeply hypnotizable or who reached medium trance depth did better at 6 months than those who were only lightly hypnotizable. At 3 months, however, the medium trance group had fared better than the deep trance subjects.

Sex was not related to response. The significance of length of asthmatic history and of particular precipitants of attacks seems dubious.

TABLE 12

*Condition of asthma during treatment, according to observations on admission and details of the hypnotherapy*

| | | Hypnotic group | | | | | | |
|---|---|---|---|---|---|---|---|---|
| | No. of patients | Average score of wheezing for month of treatment | | | | | | |
| | | Obs | 1 | 2 | 3 | 4 | 5 | 6 |
| Total no. of patients | 27 | 27 | 22 | 15 | 13 | 15 | 13 | 13 |
| A | 14 | 24 | 21 | 16 | 15 | 15 | 10 | 10 |
| Centre B | 6 | 26 | 20 | 5 | 2 | 10 | 6 | 8 |
| C | 7 | 33 | 27 | 22 | 19 | 21 | 23 | 24 |
| Sex Male | 14 | 26 | 23 | 15 | 12 | 17 | 12 | 13 |
| Female | 13 | 28 | 22 | 16 | 14 | 14 | 13 | 13 |
| 20 | 9 | 25 | 14 | 14 | 11 | 13 | 10 | 10 |
| Age (yrs.) 20–29 | 10 | 28 | 21 | 14 | 12 | 12 | 12 | 13 |
| 10+ | 8 | 27 | 22 | 19 | 18 | 22 | 16 | 17 |
| Degree of Mild | 4 | 23 | 14 | 9 | 7 | 5 | 7 | 7 |
| asthma Medium | 13 | 29 | 23 | 17 | 14 | 19 | 15 | 15 |
| Severe | 10 | 26 | 25 | 16 | 14 | 15 | 12 | 12 |
| Length of 1–9 | 9 | 26 | 19 | 15 | 9 | 17 | 10 | 12 |
| history 10–19 | 12 | 26 | 23 | 13 | 13 | 13 | 12 | 12 |
| (years) 20+ | 6 | 31 | 26 | 20 | 20 | 18 | 20 | 16 |
| Antigens | 16 | 27 | 20 | 16 | 15 | 18 | 14 | 15 |
| Type of Infections | 12 | 27 | 22 | 16 | 14 | 18 | 13 | 12 |
| trigger Physical | 16 | 28 | 25 | 18 | 15 | 16 | 14 | 13 |
| Emotional | 17 | 26 | 22 | 14 | 12 | 15 | 11 | 10 |
| Depth of Light | 6 | 26 | 20 | 18 | 15 | 22 | 16 | 18 |
| hypnosis Medium | 11 | 20 | 24 | 12 | 9 | 10 | 11 | 12 |
| Deep | 10 | 24 | 23 | 18 | 16 | 17 | 13 | 11 |
| Auto- Yes | 22 | 26 | 22 | 13 | 12 | 13 | 10 | 10 |
| hypnosis No | 5 | 29 | 27 | 24 | 18 | 25 | 26 | 27 |

## SECTION 2—DISCUSSION

*Problems in Interpreting Results*

In hypnotic treatment of asthma effective? Sinclair-Gieben's detailed report on the dramatic response to hypnosis of an asthmatic who appeared to be on the brink of death establishes a *prima facie* case for the effectiveness of hypnosis. Similarly, Edwards's report that four patients out of six admitted for emergency treatment of asthma responded to hypnosis suggests that this method of treatment deserves evalutaion—scattered reports cannot aim at proving the usefulness of hypnosis, but rather at establishing grounds for putting the question to proper therapeutic trial.

The findings of the two therapeutic trials seem to be in stark contradiction to one another. If the question put is simple, "Is hypnosis an effective treatment of asthma?" the answer seems to be a flat "No" from the results of Smith and Burns, and a straightforward "Yes" from Maher-Loughnan *et al.*

To resolve the contradiction, one must turn from an examination of the answers to an examination of the question asked. The question of the effectiveness of the hypnotic treatment cannot be assessed from any report except in the light of the following information which should be made explicit:

(1) The type of asthma being treated.

(2) The type of hypnotic treatment being given.

(3) The type of response being measured.

## The Type of Asthma

Reports on different treatment series may, in fact, be concerned with treatment of very different groups of asthmatics. Not only is some description of the kind of asthma being treated necessary if there is to be valid comparison of different series, but a breakdown in terms of type of asthma within a series may show interesting correlation with response to treatment.

"Types of asthma" are, of course, not discontinuous categories. Asthma is a disease of multifactorial aetiology and varied natural history. Rather than trying to set up a rigid typology, one must attempt to describe (in objective and communicable terms) the parameters of each case. The case cannot simply be labelled as "allergic" or "longstanding"; the aim must be to describe the factorial loading which delineates the particular patient's disease.

These factors are as follows:

(1) The fundamental elements of natural history: the patient's age: the age of onset of his asthma.

(2) Severity of asthma. Severity of symptoms may be based on the long-term or on the recent picture of the disease. The long-term description is in terms of disability over the years, whereas the short-term description is a statement of the severity of the patient's symptoms over a short observation period or at the actual time he comes for treatment.

(3) Extent of other chest disease. Some indication should be given of the extent of other chest disease, and of as much importance is that the presence of chronic bronchitis or emphysema should not be stated on the basis of inadequate examination. Disability due to these diseases is not something settled by cursory examination with a stethoscope or by observation of a barrel-shaped chest.

(4) Precipitating factors. The patient's account of his own experience is probably a fair guide to the importance of allergic or infectious precipitants of his attacks: one may question how far a brief history-taking is likely to elicit the importance of psychological factors. That allergy is far

from being a physical phenomenon to be absolutely contrasted with psychological phenomena has been demonstrated by Mason and Black (1958).

(5) Personality. There is no such entity as "the asthmatic personality";
"apart from a common core of neuroticism which may be reactive to the
dysfunction itself" (Franks and Leigh, 1959), asthmatics probably show as
wide a range of personality as the general population. Asthmatics of a greater
degree of neuroticism might perphaps be expected to cluster in series made
up of referrals to psychiatric clinics. White was treating a very different
type of asthmatic from those making up the bulk of cases in the other series
cited. Measurement of personality in objective terms is not only as important
as the other factors listed above in judging comparability of series and in
attempting correlation with intra-series response, but it is of particular
importance in hypnotic treatment series because hypnotizability and the
fundamental effects which can be produced by hypnosis may be found to
depend on personality variables.

In listing the factors which are important in delineating the individual
asthmatic, there are problems (such as estimating the extent of other chest
diseases) which are largely the province of the chest physician, and which
need not be discussed here in any further detail. The factors of most fundamental concern to the psychiatrist who is attempting to describe an asthmatic
are those which help him to decide whether he is treating a greater or a lesser
measure of panic and anxiety, as opposed to respiratory disability: the two-
way relationship of the psychological and respiratory disability is, of course,
at the very root of psychosomatic disease. An asthmatic who suffers from
chronic disability may be suffering in some degree from a primary or secondary nervous disability, while the patient in status asthmaticus is most
certainly suffering from an acute emotional disturbance as well as an acute
respiratory dysfunction.

The problem of assessing the psychological element in the disability
imposed by asthma will be considered further in the section on assessment
of the results of treatment. Here it may be noted that hypnosis applied to a
group of asthmatics in whom psychological disability is an important factor
in their everyday experience of their disease, or applied to patients at a time
(during an attack of status asthmaticus) at which psychological factors are
of importance, might well be expected to give very different results from
hypnotic treatment of asthmatics in whom psychological factors only
contribute minimally to the disability.

## Treatment

The results that can be gained by applying hypnosis to the treatment
of asthma are not only of interest to the practising physician, but also provide the research worker whose interest is in elucidating the fundamental
properties of hypnosis with an opportunity of applying pure research to

clinical experiment. What is known of the properties of hypnotic phenomena suggests that whether hypnotherapy succeeds or fails may largely depend on the skill with which the potentials of hypnosis are exploited. There is a necessity for making a very detailed appraisal of the exact manner in which hypnosis is applied to treatment. The factors which must be considered are these:

(1) Suggestion versus analysis. This review is concerned entirely with the use of hypnosis to potentiate suggestion rather than with a discussion of its use as an adjunct to therapy, by analysis of causes. The dichotomy between these two methods of treatment may be less absolute than Breuer and Freud (1895) believed, for it is almost unbelievable that the result of "analysis" are not contaminated by suggestion (Franks, 1961).

(2) Depth of hypnosis. It is often supposed that the most profound hypnotic effects are only likely to be achieved with greater depths of hypnosis (Wells, 1940) and this is a view that bodes ill for the general applicability of hypnosis to the treatment of disease, if only 10–20 per cent of the normal population will reach a somnambulistic trance (Davis and Husband, 1931). Hovever, this conclusion, though fairly derived from acute experiments on production of gross hypnotic phenomena such as post-hypnotic amnesia, age regression, etc., is not so obviously relevant to the chronic experiment such as is inherent in repeated suggestions made to the chronic asthmatic over weeks or months: whether the conclusion is valid in this situation is a matter in which the literature on hypnotic research gives little guidance. No psychologist seems to have given repeated experimental suggestions over months to normal subjects showing various lesser degrees of hypnotic susceptibility.

We are, therefore, not forced to conclude from the fact of only a relatively small proportion of subjects being deeply hypnotizable that it follows that only a small proportion of subjects will benefit fron hypnotherapy; this is a point on which the literature on hypnotic phenomena cannot yet offer conclusive evidence. Turning to the applied literature, there is considerable evidence that selected groups of patients may show a greater degree of hypnotizability than would on average be expected. Goldie, for instance (1956), noted, that, in a casualty department, hypnotic depth sufficient for minor orthopaedic operations could be obtained in 28 of 30 patients. One curious feature of the study by Maher-Loughnan et al. is that at one hospital where patients were being treated, 10 out of 14 subjects reached a deep hypnotic state, whereas at the other centre, 0 out of 6 and 0 out of 7 patients were deeply hypnotizable; this variation makes one question whether the same criterion of trance depth was being used at different centres. Smith and Burns' description of the depth of hypnosis being obtained as "adequate" needs amplification.

Maher-Loughnan's results were that deep trance subjects at the end of 6 months showed better results than subjects who achieved lighter depth

(Table 12), but the lighter trance subjects still showed considerable improvement. It would be of great interest to know whether the 18 patients who continued treatment after the initial 6-month period showed an increase or a narrowing of the gap between the response of light and deep trance subjects. White's data on the influence of hypnotic depth are difficult to interpret.

Examination of the relation between depth of hypnosis and therapeutic results in hypno-suggestion must lead at the limit to the question of what results may be obtained by repeated suggestion without any hypnosis at all. Couéism and Autogenic Training (Schultz and Luthe, 1959) are not methods which can be dismissed out of hand.

(3) Subject's expectation and the doctor's expectation. The importance of suggestion, as evinced by the placebo effect, is increasingly recognized in drug trials. Just as suggestion may influence reaction to a drug, so, it appears, may suggestion influence reaction to suggestion. Orne (1962), for example, took a group of normal volunteers who did not know much about hypnosis, and gave them a talk on hypnotic phenomena, in which they were told that "catalepsy of the dominant hand" was something which was regularly observed in the hypnotic state. When, later on, members of this audience were hypnotized, they spontaneously produced catalepsy of the dominant hand.

From this study, one might well infer that the response of an asthmatic to hypnotherapy may depend partly on whether the patient is led to believe that hypnosis is likely to be a successful method of treatment: the suggestion reinforced by hypnosis is not simply the verbal content of the therapist's suggestion, but something compounded of the patient's auto-suggestion, the therapist's covert suggestion, and the therapist's overt suggestion.

Joyce (1962), in a study of the drug treatment of patients suffering from rheumatoid arthritis, is among the authors who have shown that drug response depends not only on the drug administered, but on the doctor administering the drug. That similar differences would be found between results of hypnotic treatment by different hypnotists—explicable in terms of the hypnotist's unconscious communication of nuances of attitude rather than on any formal differences in technique—is probably to be expected. Maher-Loughnan et al. reported that one of the three hypnotists, in the series they described, achieved significantly less good results than the other two hypnotists, who, incidentally, were probably not so skilled in technique.

(4) The suggestion given. Experimental studies of hypnosis lead to the belief that suggestions may be obeyed by the subject with extraordinarily precise regard to minor details of phrasing. It seems necessary, therefore, that anyone reporting hypnotic treatment should give a full and accurate (preferably verbal) account of the suggestions which they have employed. One suspects that many hypnotists in fact make no accurate record of what they say, tending rather to hypnotize the patient and then to start impro-

vising, there being no precise preparation of what is to be said and no subsequent exact recording of what has been said.

In Maher-Loughnan's study, the suggestion given is described as "symptom removal suggestions". However, on the theme of "symptom removal" there are many possible variations. It can be suggested that wheezing will disappear, or that panic induced by wheezing will disappear. Suggestion may be given that symptoms will disappear gradually or that they will disappear quickly, and here it is relevant to note that Edwards, who gave a suggestion that symptoms would gradually disappear, found the response very gradual, whereas in the case reported by Sinclair-Gieben the suggestion was of immediate symptom relief and immediate symptom relief was seen.

Of these variations in suggestion, one suggestion may be more likely than another to produce good therapeutic results—whether indeed this is so is a conjecture which will not be settled unless we know in different series precisely what suggestion has been given.

(5) Frequency and number of hypnotic sessions. A fundamental problem underlying the design of hypnotherapy is the problem of understanding the laws that govern the duration and summation of post-hypnotic effects. The problem of using hypnosis to optimum effect is, in some ways, analogous to the proper use of drugs: to use an antibiotic effectively, one must know something about the rate of excretion of the drug and the frequency of dosage required to build up and maintain an effective blood-level. In hypnotherapy one must know the frequency of hypnotic sessions required to build up a sufficient level of therapeutic post-hypnotic effect, noting that post-hypnotic effect (like a drug which suffers excretion) may suffer decay.

The understanding of post-hypnotic effect is a complicated business. What has been discovered so far in experimental subjects suggests that the rate of decay of post-hypnotic effect varies enormously from subject to subject (Kellogg, 1929; Patten, 1930; Edwards, 1963). In one deep trance subject, post-hypnotic effect may have decayed completely within 24 hr, whereas in another deep-trance subject, a post-hypnotic effect may decay very little over the course of a year. Experiments with repeated hypnotic sessions designed to study repeated summation of post-hypnotic suggestion (Edwards, unpublished results) show similar striking differences in response among subjects who appear to reach the same depth of hypnosis.

These experimental studies, though giving only a very preliminary account of the temporal behaviour of post-hypnotic effects, can be tentatively applied to some of the problems of hypnotherapy. The great variation found in the duration and summation of post-hypnotic response to experimental suggestions presumably implies that similar variations can be expected among patients when therapeutic suggestions are given. A treatment schedule which demands that patients shall be treated at certain fixed intervals may result, therefore, in some patients being treated with insufficient frequency to produce a maintained therapeutic response, while other patients are being treated unnecessarily frequently.

Dose–response relationship in hypnotic treatment is very much a matter of the individual. Better results can be expected in a treatment series where the individual response to hypnosis is studied and treatment is given with a frequency determined by the patient's response, than in series where treatment for all patients (regardless of individual variation in response) conforms to some predetermined scheme. The studies by White, and by Smith and Burns, and the study by Maher-Loughnan *et al.* all employed a fixed interval treatment schedule.

The length of treatment is an important aspect of the treatment schedule: here the approach of different authors has been diverse. Edwards used a short intensive course of hypnosis in the acute phase of the illness, and then largely gave no further treatment; he found that patients tended to relapse quite quickly. Smith and Burns conceived the use of hypnosis as being a month's not very intensive course of treatment, and their failure to achieve results is perhaps partly an argument against the adequacy of this regime. Maher-Loughnan *et al.*, who again never gave very intensive treatment, observed little response in the first month and continuing improvement even after six months. White gave sessions spaced at 2–3 week intervals, which again is not intensive.

In designing an optimum treatment schedule, duration of treatment and frequency of treatment are not independent variables. Once more, the only guidance that the therapists can get from the literature on hypnotic research is the fact that treatment should be planned on the basis of the individual's observed response. Even to discuss whether hypnosis should be a long-term or a short-term treatment is too much of an abstraction, unless it is the individual case which is being considered—one patient will require immediate intensive treatment, and another will need long-term, widely spaced sessions, while perhaps other patients will benefit most by some combination of these two approaches.

(6) Auto-hypnosis. If patients who are being treated by hypnosis are also trained in auto-hypnosis, the problem of assessing the factors responsible for the therapeutic results is inevitably made more complicated. The series reported by Maher-Loughnan *et al.* suffers from this complication, and it is, in fact, impossible to say whether they are describing a therapeutic response to hypnotic suggestion of relief of symptoms, or a response to a form of relaxation therapy. Maher-Loughnan *et al.* found that ability to produce auto-hypnosis correlated with improvement in asthma, but this does not establish auto-hypnosis as the effective element: the ability to induce auto-hypnosis may simply be a factor which correlates with other more therapeutically effective variables such as hypnotizability. This, in any case, is not a matter which can be settled when hypnosis and auto-hypnosis are employed in the treatment of the same patient.

*Response to Treatment*

The problem of assessing response to treatment in psychosomatic illness is formidable. In measuring improvement in the asthmatic, there are, on the one hand, all the difficulties of recording change in psychiatric symptoms (change, for instance, in anxiety and in the disabilities caused by anxiety), while, on the other hand, there are the problems of assessing functional improvement in a chest disease. There is also the feeling that no analysis of improvement which makes an absolute dichotomy between psychological and physical improvement (as if each patient were two persons, a psychological and a physical being) can give anything like an adequate description of the inter-reacting improvement in a disease with inter-reacting disabilities. One may, however, accept the complexity of the problem without being forced into obscurantism. The practical approach is to abstract certain measurable aspects of improvement without supposing that these measurable aspects are a total description of the response to therapy.

(1) *The patient's subjective account of his disease.* The diary method of recording symptoms provides a way of quantifying the patient's subjective experience of his illness. There are certain obvious objections—the patient may, for instance, with an increasingly positive transference have an increasing need to please the therapist and, therefore, intentionally or unintentionally falsify his report. An apparent trend towards improvement may be contaminated by a trend towards transference. Diary cards would certainly repay sophisticated psychological investigation of reliability and validity, but it is difficult to believe that on a large enough sample of patients, transference phenomena would prevent the method providing a fair approximation to what the patient feels about his disease.

Subjective improvement, measured on diary cards, will not necessarily correlate at all closely with the state of the patient's lungs. The statement by Maher-Loughnan *et al.* that: "reasonably normal function is to be expected when the patient is not wheezing," can only be accepted if criteria of "reasonably normal function" are set low. Edwards' study of respiratory function tests in hypnotic treatment of asthma showed that the assumption that a patient is free from asthma (as defined by measurement of respiratory disability) when the patient claims to be free of symptoms, is, in many instances, not justified: this argument found further support in White's study.

There are, of course, aspects of psychological improvement not listed in a diary card which simply records the patient's awareness of disability. It could be argued by someone with psychoanalytical interests that a patient whose psychic disorganization determined the development of asthmatic symptoms might be left as disorganized, or even more disorganized, when the respiratory symptoms had been forcibly removed. Subjective improvement, it could be further argued, is only very crudely measured by subjective diminution in the symptom of wheezing, when the disease is seen as a personality disorder rather than as a respiratory disorder. Whether or not one accepts any of the psychoanalytic theories of the origin of asthma, it would certainly be of interest to devise some measure of the patient's psychological adjustment to life before and after hypnotic treatment of his asthmatic wheezing: the practical difficulty is one of devising the measuring instrument.

(2) *Objective assessment.* The objective methods of assessment ordinarily used at clinic visits (noting whether the patient is wheezing, noting whether adventitious sounds are heard with a stethoscope) provide only a rough and unquantifiable guide to the state of the patient's lungs. The development of respiratory function tests has provided much more quantifiable methods of objective recording. Indeed, in the last two decades, there have been such considerable advances in the understanding of the way in which the lungs work, as to make quite recent textbooks look like ancient archives.

The design of studies on hypnotic treatment of asthma is likely to be benefited by the advice of someone familiar with the up-to-date exploitation of these tests. A book such as Bass (1962) may be consulted for an introductory account.

### Conclusion from the Available Evidence

The argument developed in the preceding section of this review is that to ask whether the condition of the asthmatic can be improved by hypnosis is a question which can only be answered if one describes the type of asthmatic being treated, the type of hypnotic treatment employed, and the type of improvement for which one is to look. The discussion has been concerned with an appraisal of the work already done and with some suggestions as to the concepts which will have to be clarified if work on this problem is to lead to a final understanding of the place of hypnotherapy in the treatment of asthma.

However, there is still the immediate and important question whether the work so far published provides conclusive evidence for hypnosis (as so far used) benefiting, in any sense, any group of asthmatics. The clear answer comes from the study of Maher-Loughnan *et al.*: hypnosis, combined with auto-hypnosis as described in their treatment schedule, produced (in the group of asthmatics they studied) subjective improvement beyond that seen in the control group. Further than this, a conclusion as to the benefits of hypnotherapy cannot be taken; in particular, there is no justification for supposing that the correlation between subjective and objective improvement is a close one. There are neither grounds for claiming that all asthmatics are benefited by hypnotherapy, nor are there grounds (as yet) for supposing that the long-term outlook for the asthmatic is altered by hypnosis. There is evidence for the manner in which hypnosis is employed being of enormous importance.

## The Theoretical Significance of Therapeutic Response

Groen (1961) has written that "It is to be hoped that those investigators who occupy themselves with the psychotherapy of psychosomatic disorders will realize that their work can serve a double purpose: the treatment and support of patients and the scientific testing of a theory." This observation is very pertinent to the implications of hypnotic treatment of asthma, which can be divided into those relevant on the one hand to clinical practice, and on the other to psychosomatic theory.

(1) *Implications for clinical practice.* It must be inferred that hypnosis has a contribution to make in the treatment of asthma which has been insufficiently exploited in orthodox practice. Suggestion has, of course, been a potent, though unintended factor in many of the orthodox medical remedies, a point which was argued by Sir Arthur Hurst twenty years ago (Hurst, 1943), and one which was given added emphasis by patients in the Medical Research Council cortisone trial (M.R.C., 1956), showing difficulty in weaning patients from placebo. The possible value of hypnosis is specially deserving of the clinician's attention if this method of treatment is sometimes an alternative to the hazards of long-term steroid therapy. Although the proper way of applying hypnosis is a matter for skilled planning, no clinician should be daunted by erroneously supposing that the actual technique of hypnosis is a dark, mysterious and difficult art; the technique of hypnosis is, in fact, easily learned (Edwards, 1961).

Evidence on the usefulness of hypnosis in bronchial asthma should provide incentive for further critical assessment of the efficacy of hypnosis in the treatment of other diseases. Indeed, it seems a strange accident that asthma—a disease with a fluctuating and unpredictable natural history and one in which assessment of response to treatment is beset with difficulties— should so far be the condition attracting the most persuasive literature on the value of hypnosis.

(2) *Implications for psychosomatic theory.* The primary effect on the patient of the sort of hypnotherapy discussed in this review is the lessening of anxiety. The hypothesis that asthma is a psychosomatic disease in which the somatic symptoms are potentiated and perpetuated by psychic factors— anxiety directly caused by the experience of difficulty in breathing being included among these factors—cannot, of course, be naively equated with the quite untenable view that all the somatic dysfunction of the asthmatic is caused by anxiety and would, therefore, wither away if anxiety were ablated. Asthma is a multifactorial disease (Rees, 1956); and in the individual case, anxiety may be of considerable importance in perpetuating the circle

of reaction. The psychosomatic theory of asthma predicts that some asthmatics would derive considerable relief from hypno-suggestion aimed simply at the diminution of anxiety.

Interest in the response of the asthmatic to hypnotherapy is not only because of the confirmation these results provide for a psychosomatic formulation of the aetiology of the disease, but also because of the inviting opportunity that this sort of therapy offers for studying psychological and biochemical relations during the actual process of psychological and biochemical inter-reaction. Exploration of the acute and chronic biochemical changes (steroid excretion, etc.) in the asthmatic who is undergoing hypnotherapy will have to be accompanied by laboratory studies of the biochemical changes which can be induced in the normal subject by hypnosis. The time relationship of stress and the biochemical changes brought about by stress is a complex one (Grinker, 1961), and the relationship between therapy which removes anxiety and the corresponding biochemical change is undoubtedly equally complicated.

In the dissection of problems such as these, study of the hypnotherapy of asthma may provide opportunities of coming very close to the fundamental problems of mind-body relationship in illness.

## REFERENCES

BASS, B. H. (1962) *Lung function tests: an introduction*, 2nd ed., H. K. Lewis, London.
BREUER, J. and FREUD, S. (1895) *Studies in hysteria*. Vol. II of the standard edition of the *Complete Works of Sigmund Freud*, Hogarth Press, 1955).
BULL, I. (1962) In WINN R. (Ed.) *Psychotherapy in the Soviet Union*, Owen.
DAVIS, L. W. and HUSBAND, R. W. (1931) A study of hypnotic susceptibility in relation to personality traits, *J. Abnorm. Soc. Psychol.* **26**, 175.
EDWARDS, G. (1960) Hypnotic treatment of asthma: real and illusory results, *Brit. Med. J.* **2**, 492.
EDWARDS, G. (1961) A technique of hypnosis, *Med. World*, **94**, 413.
EDWARDS, G. (1963) The duration of post-hypnotic effect, *Brit. J. Psychiatry.* **109**, 259.
FRANCIS, R. S. and SPICER, C. C. (1960) Chemotherapy in chronic bronchitis, *Brit. Med. J.* **1**, 297.
FRANK, J. D. (1962) *Persuasion and healing*, Oxford University Press.
FRANKLAND, D. A. W. and AUGUSTIN, R. (1954) Prophylaxis of summer hay fever and asthma. *Lancet*, **1**, 1055.
FRANKS, C. M. and LEIGH, D (1959) The theoretical and experimental application of a conditioning model to a consideration of bronchial asthma, *J. Psychom. Res.* **4**, 88.
FRY, A. (1957) The scope for hypnosis in general practice, *Brit. Med. J.* **1**, 1323.
GOLDIE, L. (1956) Hypnosis in the casualty department, *Brit, Med. J.* **2**, 1340.
GRINKER, R. R. (1961) In: *The Physiology of Emotions* (Eds. SIMON, A. HERBERT, C. C. and STRAUS, R.) Thomas, Springfield, Ill.
GROEN, J. J. (1960) Methology of psychosomatic research, *J. Psychosom. Res.* **5**, 12.
HURST, A. (1943) Asthma in childhood, *Brit. Med. J.*, **1**, 403.
JOYCE, C. R. B. (1962) Differences between physicians as revealed by clinical trials, *Proc. Roy. Soc. Med.* **55**, 776.
KELLOGG, E. R. (1929) Duration of the effects of post-hypnotic suggestion, *J. Exp. Psychol.* **13** 502.

KENNEDY, A. (1957) The medical use of hypnotism, *Brit. Med. J.* **1**, 1317.

LEIGH, D. (1953) Asthma and the psychiatrist. A critical review, *Int. arch. Allergy*, **4**, 227.

MAGONET, A. P. (1955) *Hypnosis in asthma*, Heinemann, London.

MAHER-LOUGHNAN, G. P., MACDONALD, N., MASON, A. A. and FRY, L. (1962) Controlled trial of hypnosis in the symptomatic treatment of asthma. *Brit. Med. J.*, **2**, 371.

MASON, A. A. and BLACK, S. (1958) Allergic skin responses abolished under treatment of asthma and hay-fever by hypnosis, *Lancet I*, 877.

Medical Research Council (1956) Controlled trial of the effects of cortisone in chronic asthma, LANCET *II*, 798.

ORNE, M. J. (1962) Implications for psychotherapy derived from current research on the nature of hypnosis, *Amer. J. Psychiat.* **118**, 1097.

PATTEN, E. F. (1930) The duration of post-hypnotic suggestion, *J. Abnorm. Soc. Psychol.* **25**, 319.

PEMBERTON, J. and FLANAGAN, E. G. (1956) Vital capacity and timed vital capacity in normal men over forty, *J. Appl. Physiol.* **9**, 291.

REES, L. (1956) Physical and emotional factors in bronchial asthma, *J. Psychosom. Res.* **1**, 98.

SCHULTZ, J. H. and LUTHE, W. (1959) *Autogenic training: a psychophysiologic approach in psychotherapy*, Grune & Stratton, N.Y. Sinclair-GIEBEN, A. H. C. (1960) Treatment of status asthmaticus by hypnosis, *Brit. Med. J.* **2**, 1651.

SMITH, J. M. (1958) Hydrocortisone succinate by inhalation in children with asthma, *Lancet II*, 1248.

SMITH, J. M. and BURNS, C. L. C. (1960) The treatment of asthmatic children by hypnotic suggestion, *Brit, J. Dis. Chest.* **54**, 78.

STEWART, H. (1957) Some uses of hypnosis in general practice, *Brit. Med. J.* **1**, 1320.

THOMSON, W. B. and HUGH-JONES, P. (1958) Forced expiratory volume as a test for successful treatment of asthma, *Brit. Med. J.* **1**, 1093.

WALLER, R. E. and LAWTHER, P. J. (1957) Further observations on London fog, *Brit. Med. J.* **2**, 1473.

WELLS, W. R. (1940) The extent and duration of post-hypnotic amnesia, *J. Psychol.* **9**, 137.

WHITE, H. C. (1961) Hypnosis in bronchial asthma, *J. Psychosom. Res.* **5**, 272.

WRIGHT, B. M. and McKERROW, C. B. (1959) Maximum forced expiratory flow rate, *Brit. Med. J.* **2**, 1041.

# Some Clinical Applications of Autohypnosis*

ARNOLD A. LAZARUS, M.A. (RAND)

*Johannesburg*

ALTHOUGH hypnotic techniques have achieved considerable scientific prominence, much diversity of opinion still exists about their therapeutic value. In fact, few therapies in the history of medicine have simultaneously enjoyed such widespread acclaim and such extensive condemnation as has hypnosis. Viewed in its entirety, the history of hypnosis reveals fluctuations between short periods of intense interest and long periods of general disinterest and obscurantism.

It is relevant that Freud referred to psychoanalysis as "the administrator of the estate left by hypnotism". [1] Freud abandoned hypnotism and adopted "free association" primarily because he found that not every patient could be hypnotized and that even those who could be and were helped by direct suggestion, did not remain permanently cured. The ephemeral nature of many hypnotic cures is indeed one of the chief limitations of hypnotherapy. Hull,[2] for instance, stresses that "striking improvements in symptoms observable during the trance too often disappear disappointingly soon after its termination, and in spite of the use of vigorous post-hypnotic suggestion". The present paper, however, will endeavour to show that the application of autohypnotic techniques can completely surmount this crucial drawback. Thus the emphasis is on autohypnosis as a practical method of circumventing the temporary nature of most heterohypnotic procedures.

"By autohypnosis is meant the ability to induce, *upon oneself*, the trance of sleeping hypnosis together with such of its phenomena as may be desired." [3] This condition is of the greatest psychological interest and its uses and possible theoretical implications are almost unlimited. As Wolberg[4] states: "Self-hypnosis is a means of reinforcing indefinitely hypnotic suggestions." It enables the patient to function without the need for a dependent relationship on the hypnotist. Thus a patient's mastery of autohypnosis often contributes to his self-confidence and general independence.

Several techniques may be employed to produce autohypnosis.[3] The present writer has a preference for the following procedure:

* This article is reprinted with the permission of the author and editor from *Med. Proc.* **4**, 848–850 (1958) (South Africa).

The patient is hypnotized and told that by saying the words "deeply asleep" 5 times, he will in fact put himself into a deep hypnotic sleep. He may then give himself whatever therapeutic suggestions are indicated, and finally awaken himself by saying the words "wake up" 5 times. Innumerable variations are, of course, possible. This procedure merely amounts to a convenient post-hypnotic suggestion of autohypnosis, and is described in detail by Salter[3] and Wolberg.[4]

It is possible (although undesirable) to train a person so thoroughly in autohypnosis that he will be able to induce upon himself all the phenomena of hypnosis. This includes catalepsies, amnesias, anaesthesias, varied post-hypnotic suggestions, and even positive or negative visual and auditory hallucinations. Since patients can sometimes abuse its powers, autohypnosis should be handled like a dangerous drug and only dispensed with extreme caution and discretion. For instance, there is a risk that a patient who is proficient in the use of self-hypnotic anaesthesia, might conceivably mask physical ailments. The present writer has therefore made it a general policy to give patients heterohypnotic suggestions that block undesirable autohypnotic anaesthesias and analgesias.

A 20-year-old girl complained of excruciating menstrual pains which usually incapacitated her for 48 hr. Her gynaecologist has prescribed certain tablets which produced nausea and dizziness. She was sensitive to all salicylate compounds and her family doctor had warned her against "pain killers". e.g. morphine. Consequently, she was trained in autohypnosis and conditioned to employ the term "no pain" as an analgesic agent. When she had mastered this technique, she was again hypnotized and told that this method would only be effective in counteracting specific menstrual pain. It was emphasized that she would not be able to "switch-off" any other type of pain.

Salter[3] states that he has used autohypnosis with success in cases of stuttering, nail biting, anaesthesia for dental use, insomnia, smoking and the "will to diet". He also reports gratifying results with actors who were taught to employ self-hypnosis to combat self-consciousness. Rachman[5] reports the value of an interesting post-hypnotic procedure which closely approximates autohypnosis:

Mr. D. C., a 21-year-old student, complained of an inability to concentrate while studying. After several practical suggestions has failed to bring about an improvement, hypnotic procedures were introduced. He was hypnotized on 5 separate occasions and responded well each time. During the trances he was, in fact, able to study without being distracted, but a simple post-hypnotic suggestion that in future he would be able to concentrate without difficulty, had little effect. During the fifth hypnotic trance he was told that whenever he wished to study, he should place a particular ash-tray on his desk and that the presence of this ash-tray would re-create the non-distracting conditions experienced during the ordinary trance. This technique proved successful.

The value of autohypnosis is shown in the case of a 40-year-old woman who was cured of a crippling manifestation of "anxiety hysteria". As this case has interesting theoretical ramifications, a detailed presentation is given below:*

Mrs. M., the illegitimate daughter of a prostitute, spent her first 3 years in an atmosphere of disruption and decay. She was reared in the basement of a Parisian brothel until social welfare workers intervened and removed her to an orphanage. Her adolescent years were spent in London and, shortly before the outbreak of war, she returned to the Continent and married a rich industrialist. Her husband was killed in action and during the war she witnessed numerous atrocities and was allegedly raped by German soldiers. After the war she experienced a mental breakdown and underwent almost 5 years of psychoanalysis with a Viennese analyst. She claimed that this treatment was mildly successful in rendering her less prone to sexual recriminations, but what she termed her "panic attacks", remained unaltered.

She described herself as living in an almost perpetual state of anxiety, but at about weekly intervals she would experience a sensation of mild panic which became progressively more intense in the span of only a few minutes until this feeling became so unbearable that she would scream with sheer terror, throw herself on the floor, and attempt to render herself unconscious. The intense panic would gradually subside after 4 or 5 min.

A detail neurological examination apparently ruled out the presence of epilepsy or other cerebral pathology. She reported that her psychoanalyst had linked her "panic attacks" with previous real or imagined sexual traumata.

In 1952 she became the mistress of an English barrister and moved to London until 1955, when she became estranged from her lover. She stated that while in London, she underwent about 20 insulin coma treatments which led to an exacerbation of her condition. She came to South Africa towards the end of 1955 and consulted a psychiatrist who allegedly suggested a leucotomy.

The present writer treated her during July 1956. She was seen 15 times over a period of 4 weeks. After the initial diagnostic sessions (during which we unsuccessfully attempted to trace any specific factors which might have preceded her panic states) she was given concurrent training in relaxation and hypnotic procedures. Repeated post-hypnotic suggestions to the effect that she would no longer experience her attacks of panic had no ameliorating effect whatsoever. She was experiencing these attacks at 5–7 day intervals and became depressed and suicidal when the ordinary hypnotic therapy failed.

Autohypnotic techniques were then administered and the patient was soon able to put herself into a fairly deep hypnotic trance by saying the words "deeply asleep" 5 times. She was instructed to employ autohypnosis as soon as she felt an oncoming attack of panic and to suggest to herself that, on awakening from her trance, she would feel completely calm and relaxed. This proved highy sucessful and she was thus able to circumvent her panic states. She reported that the entire autohypnotic sequence took less than a minute. At first, this method merely succeeded in reducing the intensity of her panic states, but as she became more proficient at autohypnosis, she managed to block these attacks completely.

---

\* It should be noted that the following detailed information about each patient is obtained as a matter of routine before embarking on any therapeutic undertaking:

(a) A full report from the referring doctor;

(b) A detailed life history;

(c) Psychological tests and psychodiagnostic interviews for the purpose of obtaining comprehensive understanding of the patient as a person; and

(d) Where any doubt exists about the presence of associated or underlying latent psychotic manifestations of organic brain involvement (as may arise from the results of the physological tests and psycho-diagnostic interviews) the referring doctor is requested to seek the aid of a psychiatrist in the elucidation of the problem and his advice concerning treatment.

A follow-up enquiry, after 22 months, revealed that she was generally less anxiety-ridden and that her attacks had diminished in frequency to less than once in 2 months. She still successfully used the autohypnotic procedure when necessary. Contrary to psycho-analytic expectations, this patient did not develop alternative symptoms.

This case therefore incidentally adds to the accumulating evidence against the re-pression theory. (See especially Wolpe,[6] Eysenck,[7] Salter,[3, 8, 9] and Phillips[10].)

The main theoretical interest in this case lies in the fact that the auto-hypnotic procedure not only succeeded in reducing the *intensity* of the anxiety attacks but also diminished their *frequency* to less than one eighth of their former level. In terms of Wolpe's theoretical system,[6] it is probable that her trances reciprocally inhibited the anxiety responses to the unidentified noxious stimuli.

Despite the obvious limitations of autohypnosis, such cases as the fore-going show that it has a definite use in psychotherapy.

## ACKNOWLEDGEMENT

I wish to express my grateful thanks to the editor and his referees for their most constructive criticisms and helpful suggestions.

## REFERENCES

1. *Psychoanalysis: Exploring the Hidden Recesses of the Mind*, translated by A. A. BRILL. Encyclopaedia Britannica.
2. HULL, C. L. (1933) *Hypnosis and Suggestibility*, Appleton-Century New York.
3. SALTER, A. (1955) *What is Hypnosis?* (Farrar, Straus) New York.
4. WOLBERG, L. R. (1948) *Medical Hypnosis*, Vol. I. Grune & Stratton New York.
5. RACHMAN, S. (1958) Personal Communication.
6. WOLPE, J. (1958) *Psychotherapy by Reciprocal Inhibition*, Stanford University Press and Witwatersrand University Press.
7. EYSENCK, H. J. (1957) *The Dynamics of Anxiety and Hysteria*, Routledge and Kegan Paul (London).
8. SALTER, A. (1953) *The Case Against Psychoanalysis*, Medical Publications Limited London
9. *Idem* (1952) *Conditioned Reflex Therapy*, Allen & Unwin London.
10. PHILLIPS, E. L. (1957) *Psychotherapy: A Modern Theory and Practice*, Staples Press (London).

PART IV

# BEHAVIOUR THERAPY WITH CHILDREN

CHILDREN would appear to constitute a group of subjects almost pre-destined to provide behavior therapy with its most clear-cut applications and successes. Modification of learned behaviour patterns should be easiest when, as in children, these patterns have not been overlearned, but have only recently been established; it should also be easiest when the organism is still plastic and growing, and thus most open to modification. Why, then, one may ask, is reality exactly the opposite of expectation? Why is behaviour therapy much more widely practised in adult psychiatry than in child treatment? Because, as any unbiased review of the literature will make clear, there is no comparison between the two fields in the number of cases studied, or the number of cures reported; with the exception of enuresis nocturna, neurotic disorders of childern have only very rarely been treated by behaviour therapy.

This is clearly not so because of any outstanding success of the orthodox psychotherapeutic methods employed; as several reviews have shown, psychotherapy is perhaps even less successful with children than with adults, and its proportion of "cures" is almost certainly not greater than that attributable to spontaneous remission. Nor is it due to the greater cogency of psychoanalytic theorizing in relation to childhood disorders, as compared with the neuroses of adults; as Wolpe and Rachman have shown in their classic examination of the case of "little Hans", psychoanalytic formulations in this field are even more speculative and unsupported by evidence than in the adult field. It is difficult to think of any good reason for the present state of affairs, but whatever the reason, it seems clear that a change is urgently due. We commend the conclusions of Rachman's survey, reprinted overleaf, to the attention of all those concerned with the treatment of children.

It will be seen that the majority of those who have concerned themselves with the treatment of children have used the procedures of operant conditioning. Why this should be so is not clear either; Lazarus and others have certainly demonstrated that reciprocal inhibition is equally applicable to children as to adults. Perhaps the effect is due to irrelevant causes, temporary and purely administrative; psychiatrists often feel that the treatment of adults is their prerogative, and debar psychologists from attempting to introduce new methods, however urgently these may be needed in order to overcome the premature crystallization of spurious orthodoxy. Children are less jealously guarded, and are more frequently treated by psychologists; these are more likely, at least in the U.S.A., to be acquainted with Skinnerian formulations than with Wolpe's deductions. In Great Britain psychiatric concern over possible rivalry is less strong, and less widely felt; but in the treatment of children there has arisen a self-perpetuating group of psycho-analytically-oriented psychiatrists who insist on training in, and use of Freudian methods by all the psychologists who are appointed to child guidance clinics. Thus alternative methods of treatment, however superior in effect, are in practice barred, and so is all possibility of experimentation. The position is an interesting proof of Bertrand Russell's famous saying: "It is the fate of rebels to found new orthodoxies." Is seems unfortunate that this new orthodoxy is even more intolerant than the old.

# Learning Theory and Child Psychology:
# Therapeutic Possibilities*

S. RACHMAN

*Institute of Psychiatry, London University*

## INTRODUCTION

The applicability of modern learning theory to clinical problems has now been established. Progress in the investigation and treatment of behaviour disorders in adults has not, however, been accompanied by a similar rate of advance in child psychology. With the exception of the problems of enuresis and to a lesser extent phobias, there has been little systematic research conducted in this field by learning theorists. On purely historical grounds, this uneven development is a little surprising. The first experimental demonstration of the genesis of neurotic behaviour in a human being was carried out Watson (1920) on a young boy, Albert. Watson produced a phobia in Albert by presenting a disturbing loud noise when a white rat was brought into the boy's presence. After a few repetitions of this association Albert developed a phobia for small white furry objects. In addition to Watson's classical demonstration, the first attempt at treatment based on learning principles was also carried out on a child. In 1924 Mary Cover Jones (1924) used deconditioning methods to eliminate a rabbit phobia in a 3-year-old boy, Peter. The techniques she employed were a precursor of some of the new methods used by contemporary behaviour therapy. In particular, Wolpe's (1958) systematic desensitization method has an affinity to Jones' early study. The next significant advance in the application of learning theory to children's disorders was Mowrer and Mowrer's (1938) work on the conditioning treatment of enuresis. This disorder has continued to receive the attention of behaviour therapists, but the progress made in the treatment of adults since 1948 has not been reflected in child psychology and psychiatry.

The reason for discrepancy can probably be ascribed to an important difference in the nature of behaviour disturbances in children and adults. Most behaviour problems in children (especially in the early years) are associated with inadequate or inappropriate responses. These deficits usually

* This article is reprinted with the permission of author and editor from *J. Child Psychol. Psychiat* (1962), 3, 149–163.

441

centre around the activities of eating, sleeping, elimination and speaking. In most instances the problem arises because (in a learning theory sense) the child has failed to develop an adequate way of responding (e.g. enuresis, aphemia, anorexia, dyslexia). In adults, most problems seem to be concerned with unadaptive behaviour and the purpose of therapy is generally directed at eliminating the unwanted responses (e.g. phobias, anxiety states, compulsions, perversions). Most often the aim in therapy with adults is to break down a behaviour pattern whereas in children the therapist usually has to build up an adequate behaviour pattern.

The recent infiltration of operant conditioning procedures into clinical psychology seems to provide a tool for building up deficient responses in children. Lindsley (1956, 1960) followed up the proposals of Skinner (1959) and Skinner, Solomon and Lindsley (1954) and has already produced extremely interesting analyses of the behaviour of acute schizophrenic patients. The clinical application of this technique in child psychology is foreshadowed by the work of Ferster (1961), Lovaas (1961), Baer (1962), Spradlin (1961) and Bijou (1961) among others.

The established methods of behaviour therapy, such as Wolpe's (1958) reciprocal inhibition technique and the extinction procedures used by H. G. Jones (1960b) and Yates (1958) have already been successfully used on child patients and are described first.

## DESENSITIZATION, CONDITIONED INHIBITION, NEGATIVE PRACTICE

In his book Wolpe (1958) describes the treatment of eighty-eight patients. Of these, two were children. An 11-year-old boy, suffering from interpersonal anxiety and tic-like movements, was treated by desensitization and was markedly improved after eight treatment sessions. The second case, a 14-year-old stammerer, relapsed under stress after showing considerable improvement in the first few months of treatment. Further treatment was only able to counteract the relapse to a limited degree. The methods used in this case consisted of relaxation and breathing exercises. In a later series of thirty-nine cases treated by desensitization Wolpe (1961) decribes two further child patients. An 11-year-old boy was successfully treated for his fear of authority figures in six sessions, while another stammerer (aged 13) failed to respond. This boy, being unable to obtain vivid visual images, was unable to comply with the requirements of desensitization therapy. While the lack of success with two cases of stuttering is not conclusive, there are grounds for believing that some of the methods used in treating this condition in adults may prove more successful. The work of Case (1960) on negative practice, Sheehan (1951) and Sheehan and Voas (1957) on non-reinforcement, and of Cherry and Sayers (1960) on shadowing are among the most promising.

Lazarus and Rachman (1960) describe the treatment of a 14-year-old boy who had suffered from a fear of hospitals and ambulances for four years. The phobia had developed after the prolonged illness and suffering experienced by his mother. She had been taken from the house several times by ambulance and spent over a year in hospitals.

The boy was first trained to relax. Hierarchies of disturbing situations concerning ambulances and hospitals were then constructed, ranging from mildly upsetting to extremely upsetting items. The lowest item in the ambulance hierarchy, for example, was a mental image of a derelict ambulance in a scrap-yard, and the highest item an image of sitting beside the driver in a moving ambulance. The therapist then slowly worked up the hierarchies, desensitizing each item by relaxation responses. After ten interviews, the boy was much improved and was able to visit a hospital. Four months later he was still quite well.

Lazarus (1960) recounts the case of an 8-year-old boy who developed a fear of moving vehicles two years after having been involved in a motor accident. Initially the therapist rewarded the boy whenever he made a positive comment concerning vehicles, by giving him a piece of his favourite chocolate. By the third interview the boy was able to talk freely about all types of moving vehicles. Next a series of "accidents" with toy motor cars was demonstrated. The boy, John, was given chocolate after each accident. Later John was seated in a stationary vehicle, and slow progress (with chocolate feeding reinforcements used at each point) was made until John was able to enjoy motor travel without any anxiety. In the same paper Lazarus also reports the successful treatment of a case of separation anxiety and a case of dog-phobia. Lazarus and Abramovitz (1962) obtained marked improvements in seven out of nine children treated for phobic conditions by a modified reciprocal inhibition method.

White (1959) describes the successful treatment of a 5-year-old girl who suffered from anorexia. The child's feeding difficulties started at the age of three, and worsened after the death of her father when she was 5 years old. She had been deeply attached to her father and was extremely disturbed by his illness and death. Her father had fed her from an early age. Attempts made by her mother, relations, doctors and nurses to feed her were mainly unsuccessful. "The immediate problem", writes White, "was formulated in terms of simple conditioning, with father as the conditioned stimulus upon which the conditioned response of eating had come to depend." The reinforcement was "supplied by the satisfaction of hunger as well as by anxiety-reduction through sitting on the father's knee and being fed by him".

The method of treatment was based on this analysis and bears a strong resemblance to M. C. Jones' (1924) treatment of Peter. "The first step", says White, "was to provide a substitute for the father and to arrange a series of experiences that might gradually approximate those obtaining before the father's death." Initially the psychologist attempted to replace the conditioned stimulus provided by the father. When this was accomplished, generalization to selected relatives was undertaken (aunts, uncles and mother). This general plan of treatment (with some additions during the course of therapy) was followed for 7 months. Some marked improvements were evident after only 3–4 weeks, and when treatment concluded at the end of 7 months the girl was very much improved. This improvement has been maintained over a 3-year follow-up period. White's formulation of the problem in "terms of simple conditioning" is not entirely satisfactory. His description of the child's eating as a conditioned response is questionable, and the analysis fails to account for the onset of the feeding difficulties prior to the father's death. It may be more useful to re-set the treatment programme in terms of an operant conditioning process in which the psychologist "shaped" and expanded the range of the child's eating behaviour. While a clear theoretical explanation would be valuable, the successful outcome of this difficult case is encouraging.

Walton (1961) describes how an 11-year-old, who suffered from a complex of severe tics, was successfully treated by negative practice and conditioned inhibition methods. The treatment was carried out over 36 sessions ranging in duration from 15 min in the early stages to 30 min at the closing stages. A follow-up conducted a year later showed that the improvements had been maintained and that the boy's general adjustment had been highly satisfactory. The essence of the treatment is that the repeated evocation of the tics produces an inhibitory effect which eventually "exhausts" these movements. Williams (1959) treated temper tantrums in a 31-month-old child by a process of experimental extinction. The child displayed tantrum behaviour whenever he was put to bed in the evening. Williams argued that this unadaptive behaviour was being maintained, or reinforced, by the parental attention which it produced. The parents were instructed to refrain from re-entering the bedroom after the child had been placed in bed and to record the duration of each tantrum. The duration of the tantrums gradually decreased, and in less than 2 weeks had almost ceased. Spontaneous recovery of the tantrum pattern was later observed when one evening the maternal grandmother entered the bedroom before the child had stopped crying. The tantrum behaviour was reinstated for another few days but persistent non-reinforcement (i.e. failure to re-enter the bedroom) brought the disturbance to an end after nine days. A 2-year follow-up of this case revealed no further behaviour difficulties.

The first systematic investigation of therapy derived from learning theory was Mowrer and Mowrer's (1938) famous study of enuresis. Despite its efficiency this method was neglected for many years. Serious interest in this so-called "bell-and-pad method" has revived in the past five years, and a comprehensive evaluation of the available evidence was carried out by Gwynne Jones (1960a), who concluded that "if widely adopted, the specific conditioning method of treatment is capable of significantly reducing the incidence of *enuresis nocturna* at the later ages of childhood".

This view is borne out by the recent work of Lovibond (1961) who carried out a well planned and executed investigation. He showed that the Mowrer, Crosby and his own Twin-Signal technique of conditioning were all highly effective in arresting enuresis. The mean number of trials required to arrest the enuresis was 13·5, but the relapse rate for all three methods was unsatisfactorily high. Consequently Lovibond tried some variations of the method in an attempt to increase the stability of the newly learnt ability. He eventually developed a refined Twin-Signal method used on an intermittent reinforcement schedule. None of the fourteen subjects had experienced a relapse at the time of Lovibond's writing (i.e. from 1 to 9 months after treatment). This result is already an improvement on the earlier procedures and deserves further field trials. Lovibond's work recommends itself for two reasons. His developments of the technique promise improved results and his theoretical analysis is more convincing than either Mowrer's or Crosby's. The conditioning paradigms proposed by Mowrer and Crosby are both subject to criticism (Jones, 1960a; Lovibond, 1961) and Lovibond's reformulation of the problem in terms of conditioned avoidance training seems able to accommodate all the available information.

## Conclusions

It will be seen that with the exception of enuresis, behaviour therapy has not been systematically applied to disturbances of behaviour in children. There are reports of eleven successfully treated cases of phobias (Jones, 1924; Lazarus and Rachman, 1960; Lazarus, 1960; Lazarus and Abramovitz, 1962) and two failures (Lazarus and Abramovitz, 1962). Apart from enuresis, phobia is the only specific condition for which a detailed theoretical basis has been proposed (Wolpe and Rachman, 1960; Rachman and Costello, 1961). There are two successfully treated cases of tics on record (Walton, 1961; Wolpe, 1958), two anxiety states (Wolpe, 1961; Lazarus, 1960) and one case each of anorexia (White, 1959) and of temper tantrums (Williams, 1959). No success was obtained in the treatment of two stutterers (Wolpe, 1958, 1961).

### OPERANT CONDITIONING

"Operant behaviour usually affects the environment and generates stimuli which 'feed back' to the organism. Some feedback may have the effects identified by the layman as reward and punishment. Any consequence of behaviour which is rewarding or, more technically, reinforcing increases the probability of further responding." (Skinner, 1959.) From this acorn very large oaks indeed are growing. After nearly two decades of persistent laboratory investigations (mostly with animals) Skinner and his colleagues are now exploring the applications of operant conditioning in diverse areas of human behaviour. The topics which they have proved include the effects of drugs (Dews, 1956), attention (Holland, 1957), learning (Spiker, 1960), psychotic behaviour (Lindsley, 1956), motor behaviour (Verplank, 1956), verbal behaviour (Skinner, 1957; Krasner, 1958; Salzinger, 1959), therapy and the effects of therapy (Lindsley, 1961; King, 1956), psychological functioning in retarded children (Bijou and Orlando, 1961; Spradlin, 1961; Ellis, 1962), personality (Staats *et al.*, 1962; Brady *et al.*, 1962).

As an introduction to the research on clinical problems in child psychology, it is necessary to consider first the work of Lindley, King and Brady on adult psychopathology. Lindsley (1956, 1959, 1960, 1961a, 1961b) has made protracted observations of the operant behaviour of chronic schizophrenic patients. His research has already yielded important findings (such as the relationship between vocal, hallucinatory symptoms and motor performance) and has prepared the path for detailed functional analyses of schizophrenic behaviour. Lindsley's experiments were conducted in an indestructible room which contained only one chair and a manipulandum panel on the wall. The panel contains a lever and a small aperture through which the rewards are automatically presented. All recordings are made automatically and the $E$ (in an adjoining room) observes the patient's behaviour through a periscope or one-way screen. By using this basic situation imaginatively, Lindsley was able to investigate "motivations ranging from food to social altruism, and discriminations ranging from simple visual to time estimation and complicated concept formation". This method has already produced clinically useful results. It can be used as a sensitive evalutive device (e.g. insulin coma produced its greatest effect on operant behaviour at the time of the first insulin reaction—Lindsley, 1960). It can elucidate the characteristics of psychotic behaviour (e.g. schizophrenics develop low, erratic response rates and display stereotyping—Lindsley, 1956). Further advantages which this method offers to the experimentally-minded clinician include the possibility of tight control of experiment variables, freedom from verbal instructions, exclusion of variables associated with the clinician himself, the possibility of controlled investigations of a single case, the possibility of therapeutic control. An "unseen" advantage is provided of course by the substantial body of evidence concerning learning in human beings and operant conditioning in particular (for example, the effects of intermittent reinforcement). Each of the advantages listed here are of direct interest to child psychologists—evaluative procedures, analysis of disturbed behaviour, non-verbal instructions, control of variables, exclusion of "clinician variables", therapeutic control, single-case studies. This technique also provides the child psychologist with a suitable environment for response-building in cases of behavioural deficit, such as mutism and anorexia for example.

The possibilities of response-building are illustrated by the study of King *et al.* (1960), who shaped the behaviour of adult schizophrenics (of extreme pathology) in a Lindsley-type situation. They were able to develop the initial lever-pulling response into relatively complex problem-solving and social behaviour. In this and other studies (King, 1956; King *et al.*, 1957) attempts were made to relate operant behaviour to clinical status. The early indications are that clinical conditions and operant rate are related in a curvilinear rather than inverse manner.

While there have been no reports of behaviour disorders in children treated by operant methods, the fine case-study described by Brady and Lind (1961) is worth noting. They cured a man suffering from hysterical blindness by means of operant conditioning (see page 224). An interesting combination of reward and punishment was employed by Barrett (1961) in her treatment of an adult patient suffering from a multiple tic. As mentioned earlier, there are no reports of children being treated by operant methods for specific clinical problems. The work of Flanagan *et al.* (1958), Baer (1962), Spradlin (1961) and Ferster and de Meyer (1961), however, has a direct bearing on such problems.

Flanagan *et al.* (1958) attempt to bring the stuttering of three patients under operant control. Their preliminary analysis is encouraging, as they were able to produce total suppression of the stutter in one patient and partial suppression in the other two patients. The suppression of the stutter, which was achieved by aversive control, lasted slightly longer than the period of aversive stimulations. This stimulation was similar to that used by Barrett (1961) in her study of a patient with multiple tics and consisted of a loud 1-sec blast of noise which was triggered off the by occurrence of a stutter. Spradlin (1961) conducted a pilot study to explore the possibility of modifying the behaviour of severely retarded children by operant conditioning techniques. The indications are that this technique will prove to be of considerable value, and even in the early stages of his investigation Spradlin was able to train three children in such difficult tasks as detour, verbal and alternation behaviour. Spradlin's study also provides valuable information about procedures for adapting the children to the experimental room and the role of different types of reinforcers.

Ferster (1961) and Ferster and de Meyer (1961) have made a study of the performance of autistic children in an operant behaviour environment. Ferster and de Meyer conducted a prolonged investigation of the development of performance in two autistic children aged 8 and $9\frac{1}{2}$ years respectively. The experimental environment consisted of vending machines, a pinball machine, gramophone, kaleidoscope, and a trained pigeon. The experimenters were able to shape the behaviour of the children in relation to all of these objects, and obtained information about the effectiveness of different training schedules and different reinforcers. "Both subjects emitted more of the experimentally developed behaviour with continual exposure to the automatic equipment. Conversely, they spent less time in tantrums of inactivity while in the experimental room." This finding recalls Lindsley's observations on adult psychotic episodes.

This important study by Ferster and de Meyer shows that the behaviour of autistic children can be brought under experimental control. The next step is to develop situations and techniques of this type which can be used to induce therapeutic control and, in a general sense, to find ways of developing the behavioural repertoire of children with deficit disorders. Spradlin, and Ferster and de Meyer, have clearly demonstrated that such a programme is conceivable even with the most severe cases. Ferster and de Meyer have also demonstrated that a range of reinforcers (candy, food, music) can be effectively used, that both fixed and variable schedules of reinforcement are effective, and that certain objects (e.g. coins) can generate a variety of other reinforcers in the manner of a generalized reinforcer. They are careful to point out, however, that their study was not designed for therapeutic purposes and that it "cannot be assumed that performances developed in the experimental room will have general effects elsewhere". They suggest that social reinforcers may prove valuable in developing extra-experimental performance. These two topics, social reinforcement and the spread of experimental changes in behaviour, are likely to occupy the centre of the stage for some tine and are discussed below.

The application of operant methods to routine clinical problems has been started in a limited manner at the Institute of Psychiatry, London. To date, attempts have been made to use operant training in remedial reading cases and in the analysis of the behaviour of a child suspected of experiencing auditory hallucinations. The remedial reading method was partly derived from the work of Staats and Staats (1962) on the teaching of reading to very young children. The method used by Rachman and Loewenstein (1962) is, briefly, as follows: The child is rewarded for correctly read words an a fixed ratio of 1 : 6; each correct word is signalled on a small panel consisting of six lights; when the sixth light is reached, a buzzer sounds and a sweet is automatically delivered. Words which are incorrectly read are explained and pronounced to the subject and then placed on a subsidiary list for representation at the next coaching lesson. The cumulative record of M.R. (male, aged $9\frac{1}{2}$ years) and the number of new words learnt are illustrated in Figs. 1 and 2. Earlier attempts to teach this boy to read were unsuccessful. He quickly warmed to the operant situation and in 20 sessions (each lasting 20 min), spread over 5 weeks, he has learnt 235 new words. While it is of course too early to estimate the effectiveness of the method, the preliminary results are not discouraging.

In the substantial body of information on operant conditioning there are three topics which seem to have particular relevance for clinicians in child psychology. These selected topics are social reinforcement, intermittent reinforcement and the generalization of responses.

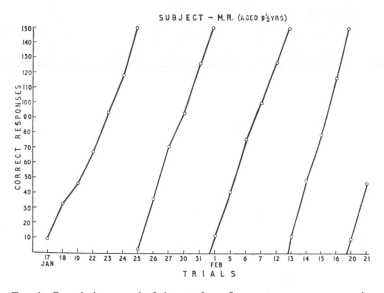

FIG. 1. Cumulative record of the number of correct responses per session

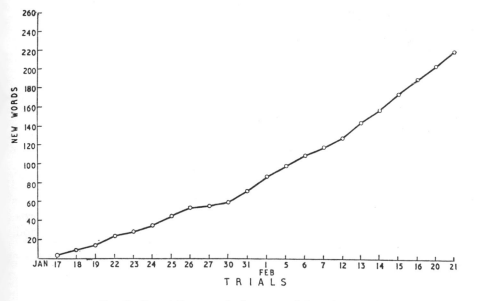

FIG. 2. Cumulative record of new words learnt per session

## Social Reinforcement

The important role of social reinforcement in child development is emphasized by some of the findings on operant conditioning. In this context social reinforcement may be regarded as any event mediated by a person which has the effect of increasing the strength of the behaviour which immediately preceded it. By definition, then, most reinforcers would be social in nature. Ferster (1958) provides a detailed discussion of the nature and significance of social reinforcement in terms of operant conditioning, and Rheingold et al. (1959) have shown its effectiveness in altering the behaviour of infants.

The exploratory studies reported by Ayllon (1960) and Ayllon and Michael (1959) indicate some of the possible applications of social reinforcers in handling disturbed patients. Although their reports deal with adult psychiatric patients, some of their techniques have a direct bearing on the care and management of both normal and disturbed children. Ayllon (1960) describes, for example, how they were able to overcome an eating difficulty in a catatonic schizophrenic patient by operant training methods. The ward staff withheld attention when the patient displayed unadaptive eating behavior (e.g. they ceased fetching her when she failed to walk to the dining-room) and reinforced satisfactory eating actions (e.g. placing candy on her tray when she served herself). These exploratory investigations are significant because they demonstrate the possibility of transferring laboratory findings into the ward, the clinic or the home. They also demonstrate that social reinforcers can be controlled and measured (albeit loosely so far) in extra-laboratory settings.

Experiments on the operation of social reinforcement in children have been reported by Gewirtz and Baer (1958a, 1958b) and Gewirtz, Baer and Roth (1958). They examined two variables affecting social reinforcement: brief social deprivation and the social availability of an adult. Their results showed that the "frequency of attention-seeking responses was greater under Low Availability than under High Availability" and that the "frequency of behaviour for approval was reliably increased by the Deprivation condition" (Gewirtz, Baer and Roth, 1958). The studies of imitative behaviour discussed by Bandura and Walters (1961) are closely related to these findings. For example, the transmission of social behaviour by imitation is facilitated by providing models of high prestige (Bandura, 1961). Individual differences in susceptibility to social influences have also received some attention. Dependent children are more easily influenced by social reinforcers than independent children (Jacubczak and Walther, 1959), and children with a history of failures are more likely to display social imitation and to respond to social reinforcement (Lesser and Abelson, 1959). Research along these avenues will eventually become incorporated in clinical work and child care.

Baer (1961) and Ferster (1958) have in fact already started the process of integration. Baer (1961) emphasizes the "reinforcement history" of the child and indicates how the analysis of individual children may be used in designing techniques for promoting their development. He also outlines some methods which can be used to present social reinforcers. In addition to the pointers derived from the research discussed above on imitation, prestige, deprivation and availability, Baer describes some gadget-like aids. One of these "gadgets" is a mechanized puppet which appeals to children and permits the experimenter to introduce and control simple and uniform social reinforcers. Lovaas (1961) used the puppet to manipulate the eating habits of nursery school children and further investigations are being conducted.

The broad guide that emerges from the available evidence is that social reinforcers should be presented intermittently, and preferably by an adult of high prestige. The use of social reinforcers in eliminating undesirable behaviour should follow a pattern of non-reinforcement rather than aversive conditioning. At the risk of oversimplifying, we may state it in this way: an undesirable response is more likely to be eliminated if it is met by no reaction at all than if it is met with a negative or punishing reaction.

## Intermittent Reinforcement

It has been found in numerous experiments on animals and humans that intermittent (partial) reinforcement produces greater resistance to the extinction of the response than does continuous reinforcement (Jenkins and Stanley, 1950; Lewis, 1960). This effect may be illustrated by two recent examples from the literature. Spradlin (1962) investigated the effects of different reinforcement schedules on the operant behaviour of twenty severely retarded children. The children were divided into four equivalent groups and trained on a Lindsley-type task with candy acting as the reinforcer. As predicted, the group which received 100 per cent reinforcement (i.e. reward for every correct response) showed faster extinction rates than the other groups of children who received intermittent rewards. Similarly, Lovibond (1961) found that the unsatisfactory relapse rate which occurs in the conditioning treatment of enuresis could be offset by the introduction of intermittent reinforcement. In other words, the high extinction rates (relapses) could be countered by altering the reinforcement schedule.

Long et al. (1958) have published extensive findings on the intermittent reinforcement of operant behaviour in over two hundred children. Their monograph details the effects of various rewards and schedules of reinforcement on children's behaviour in a Lindsley-type operant enviroment, and provides a wealth of important details for child psychologists who propose to use this technique. For example, they show that small fixed-ratios rapidly produce satiation and cessation of response, while very large fixed-ratios made experimental control difficult to obtain. They suggest that an introductory session of small fixed-ratios should then proceed gradually to ratios of up to 1 : 100.

The theoretical value of intermittently reinforced operant behaviour derives from the fact that this type of reinforcement schedule generates stable and prolonged performance. Bijou (1961) argues persuasively that the experimental analysis of the behaviour of individual children is made feasible by this method, "since a clear functional relationship has been shown between a stable baseline performance and the introduction of a special stimulus condition". If this claim is borne out by research results it will be of considerable value to clinical psychologists, who are constantly faced with the dilemma of group norms and individual patients (Meehl, 1954; Shapiro, 1961). Stable operant responding certainly lends itself to investigations designed to evaluate therapeutic (or drug) effects, or indeed any specific effect. Baer (1961) has, in fact, demonstrated its value in an experiment on the effects of reward and punishment.

## Generalization of Responses

These experimental learning techniques would be of limited interest if the changes they produce failed to generalize or spread into the patient's ordinary life and behaviour. Changes produced by the reciprocal inhibition method do spread to the patient's out-of-clinic behaviour. This is well documented, particularly in the treatment of adults (Wolpe, 1958; Eysenck, 1960).

The clinical application of operant conditioning has not yet progressed to the point where one can reach a firm conclusion. Baer (1962), for example, was able to reduce thumb-sucking in three children during experimental sessions but the habit promptly returned when the relevant conditions were withdrawn. King et al. (1960), however, were able to record significant general improvements in a group of (adult) acute schizophrenics who were treated by operant methods. By comparison with three control groups, the operant-treated patients improved in the following areas: "level of verbalization, motivation to leave the ward, less resistance to therapy, more interest in occupational therapy, decreased enuresis, and transfers to better wards". In an earlier study, King (1956) reported a "positive relationship between rate of operant motor response in schizophrenic patients and another measure of manipulative responsiveness, i.e. energy displayed in regard to the various crafts of occupational therapy".

A spread of experimentally-induced changes in behaviour was noted by Salzinger et al. (1962) in their study on the operant training of speech in young children. They found that "the application of reinforcement to the response class of first person pronouns produced an increase not only in the specific class itself but also in general speech rate". Brady and Lind (1961) obtained a dramatic change in an adult patient who had been suffering from hysterical blindness for more than two years despite numerous attempts at treatment. The patient was awarded points on a counter when he responded correctly to the presence of a light. These counterpoints were exchanged for canteen vouchers after each training session and the patient gradually learnt to respond only when the light was on. This ability then transferred to situations other than the experimental room. The patient regained his sight. This cleverly designed and simple (but highly effective) experimental procedure is a vivid example of the spread of effectiveness from the laboratory clinic to the "outside world".

The experimental work of Lovaas (1960, 1961a, 1961b) promises to elucidate the relationship between the particular response which is being conditioned and the person's general behaviour. So far Lovaas has shown that operant conditioning of verbal behaviour can transfer to other behaviour and hence influence eating habits (1961b), motor behaviour (1960) and aggressive behaviour (1961a). The trend of these results encourages the assumption that the effects of operant conditioning in the clinic will spread to the child's ordinary behaviour and environment.

Before leaving the topic of generalization of responses, it should be pointed out that there is also a technique which can be used in promoting the irradiation of newly-acquired responses. If the gap between the clinical and social environments is not surmounted spontaneously, the bridge of "successive approximation" can be used. The patient can be taught intermediate responses which will enable him to cope with non-clinical situations. A theoretical account of this technique is provided in a paper by Skinner, Solomon and Lindsley (1954), and Ayllon (1960), Bijou and Orlando (1961) and Spradlin (1961) used it in the early stages of the conditioning process. Spradlin (1961) for example used successive approximations in order to adapt his retarded patients to the experimental situation.

*Conclusions*

Operant conditioning methods can be used to generate and/or sustain stable behaviour patterns. For this reason they seem to offer child psychologists a valuable clinical tool, especially as so many disturbances of behaviour in children can be regarded as deficit disorders. The other advantages of operant methods are that they permit, when required (i) non-verbal operations, (ii) strict control of variables, (iii) quantification of operations, (iv) exclusion of "clinician-variables" and (v) single-case studies. The disadvantages are both of a practical nature. Operant methods usually demand special equipment and experimental rooms and can be time-consuming. These two factors are probably inversely related—better equipment provides for more automatic control and saves time.

In regard to further research, the three selected topics discussed above (social reinforcement, intermittent reinforcement, generalization of responses) all require further investigation. Another difficult problem concerns the effects of punishment—a subject which seems to become more complicated with the accumulation of each new piece of evidence (see Broadbent, 1961; Metzner, 1961, for example). What is needed above all, however, are clinical trials of operant methods. With very few exceptions, the applications of operant conditioning to human behaviour evade the use of these methods by active clinicians. It is perhaps time to get one's feet wet.

## SUMMARY

Advances in the application of learning theory to clinical problems in adults have not been accompanied by a similar rate of development in child psychology. A probable reason for this uneven progress lies in the fact that behaviour therapy is more obviously applicable to adult disorders. Behaviour therapy has so far provided more techniques for the elimination of unadaptive behaviour than for the development of desired behaviour The disturbances of behaviour in childhood are more often of the deficit type. Consequently it is likely that the methods of operant conditioning will increase the applications of behaviour therapy to the clinical problems of child psychology. The application of both operant conditioning and the more familiar methods of behaviour therapy may be expected to benefit child psychology.

## REFERENCES

AYLLON, T. (1960) Some behavioural problems associated with eating in chronic schizophrenic patients. Paper read at APA meeting, Chicago.

AYLLON, T. and MICHAEL, J. (1959) The psychiatric nurse as a behaviour engineer, *J. Exp. Anal. Behav.* **2**, 323–334.

BAER, D. M. (1960) Escape and avoidance response of pre-school children to two schedules of reinforcement withdrawal, *J. Exp. Anal. Behav.* **3**, 155–159.

BAER, D. M. (1961 a) Effect of withdrawal of positive reinforcement on an extinguishing response in young children, *Child Develop.* **32**, 67–74.

BAER, D. M. (1961 b) Modes of presenting social reinforcers. Paper read at APA meeting, New York.

BAER, D. M. (1962) Laboratory control of thumbsucking in three young children by withdrawal and re-presentation of positive reinforcement, *J. Exp. Anal. Behav.* (In press.)

BANDURA, A. (1961) Psychotherapy as a learning process. *Psychol. Bull.* **58**, 144–159.

BANDURA, A. and WALTERS, R. (1962) *Deviant Response Patterns.* (To be published.)

BARRETT, B. H. (1961) Reduction in rate of multiple tics by free-operant conditioning methods (unpublished paper).

BIJOU, S. W. (1961) Discrimination performance as a baseline for individual analysis of young children, *Child Develop.* **32**, 163–170.

BIJOU, S. W. and OBLINGER, B. (1960) Responses of normal and retarded children as a function of the experimental situation, *Psychol. Rep.* **6**, 447–454.

BRADY, J. and LIND, D. L. (1961) Experimental analysis of hysterical blindness, *Arch. Gen. Psychiat.* **4**, 331–339.

BRADY, J., PAPPAS, N., TAUSIG, T. and THORNTON, D. R. (1962) MMPI correlates of operant behaviour, *J. Clin. Psychol.* **18**, 67–70.

BROADBENT, D. (1961) *Behaviour*, Hodder and Stoughton, London.

CASE, H. W. (1960) Therapeutic methods in stuttering and speech blocking. In *Behaviour Therapy and the Neuroses* (Ed. EYSENCK, H. J.) Pergamon Press, Oxford.

CHERRY, C and SAYERS, B. (1960) Experiments upon the total inhibition of stammering. In *Behaviour Therapy and the Neuroses* (Ed. EYSENCK, H. J.) Pergamon Press, Oxford.

DEWS, P. B. (1956) Modification by drugs of performance on simple schedules of positive reinforcement, *Ann, N.Y. Acad. Sci.* **65**, 268–281.

ELLIS, N. (1962) Amount of reward and operant behaviour in mental defectives, *Amer. J. Ment. Def.* **66**, 595–599.

EYSENCK, H. J. (1960) *Behaviour Therapy and the Neuroses*, Pergamon Press, Oxford.

FERSTER, C. B. (1958) Reinforcement and punishment in the control of human behaviour by social agencies, *Psychiat. Res. Rep.* **10**, 101–118.

FERSTER, C. B. (1961) Positive reinforcement and behavioural deficits of autistic children, *Child Develop.* **32**, 437–456.

FERSTER, C. B. and DE MEYER, M. (1961) The development of performances in autistic children in an automatically controlled environment, *J. Chronic Dis.* **13**, 312–345.

FLANAGAN, B., GOLDIAMOND, I. and AZRIN, N. (1958) Operant stuttering—The control of stuttering behaviour through response-contingent consequences, *J. Expl. Anal. Behav.* **1**, 173–177.

GEWIRTZ, J. L. and BAER, D. M. (1958a) The effect of brief social deprivation on behaviours for a social reinforcer, *J. Abn. Soc. Psychol.* **56**, 49–56.

GEWIRTZ, J. L. and BAER, D. M. (1958b) Deprivation and satiation of social reinforcers as drive conditions, *J. Abn. Soc. Psychol.* **57**, 165–172.

GEWIRTZ, J. L., BAER, D. and ROTH, C. (1958) A note on the similar effects of low social availability of an adult and brief social deprivation on young children's behaviour, *Child Develop.* **29**, 149–152.

HOLLAND, J. G. (1957) Technique for behavioural analysis of human observing, *Science* **125**, 348 350.

JACUBSZAK, L. and WALTHER, R. H. (1959) Suggestibility as dependency behaviour, *J. Abn. Soc. Psychol.* **59**, 102–107.

JENKINS, W. O. and STANLEY, J. C. (1950) Partial reinforcement: A review and critique, *Psychol. Bull.* **47**, 193–234.

JONES, H. G. (1960a) The behavioural treatment of enuresis nocturna. In *Behaviour Therapy and the Neuroses* (Ed. EYSENCK, H. J.) Pergamon Press, Oxford.

JONES, H. G. (1960b) Continuation of Yates' treatment of a tiqueur, In *Behaviour Therapy and the Neuroses* (Ed. EYSENCK, H. J.) Pergamon Press, Oxford.

JONES, M. C. (1924) A laboratory study of fear: The case of Peter, *Pedagog. Sem.* **31**, 308–315.

KING, G. F. (1956) Withdrawal as a dimension of schizophrenia: An exploratory study, *J. Clin. Psychol.* **12**, 373–375.

KING, G. F., ARMITAGE, S. and TILTON, J. (1960) A therapeutic approach to schizophrenics of extreme pathology, *J. Abn. Soc. Psychol.* **61**, 276–286.

KING, G. F., MERRELL, D., LOVINGER, E. and DENNY, M. (1957) Operant motor behaviour in acute schizophrenics, *J. Personality* **25**, 317–326.

KRASNER, L. (1958) Studies of the conditioning of verbal behaviour, *Psychol. Bull.* **45**, 148–170.

LAZARUS, A. (1960) The elimination of children's phobias by deconditioning. In *Behaviour Therapy and the Neuroses* (Ed. EYSENCK, H. J.) Pergamon Press, Oxford.

LAZARUS, A. and ABRAMOVITZ, A. (1962) The use of "emotive imagery" in the treatment of children's phobias, *J. Ment. Sci.* (In press.)

LAZARUS, A. and RACHMAN, S. (1960) The use of systematic desensitization psychotherapy. In *Behaviour Therapy and the Neuroses* (Ed. EYSENCK, H. J.) Pergamon Press. Oxford.

LESSER, G. and ABELSON, R. (1959) Personality correlates of persuasibility in children. In *Personality and Persuasibility* (Ed. JANIS, I. L. and HOVLAND, C. I.) Yale Univ. Press, New Haven.

LEWIS, D. J. (1960) Partial Reinforcement: A selective review, *Psychol. Bull.* **57**, 1–28.

LINDSLEY, O. R. (1956) Operant conditioning methods applied to research in chronic schizophrenia, *Psychiat. Res. Repts.* **5**, 118–139.

LINDSLEY, O. R. (1960) Characteristics of the behaviour of chronic psychotics as revealed by free-operant conditioning methods, *Dis. Nerv. System* **21**, 66–78.

LINDSLEY, O. R. (1961 a) Free-operant conditioning, persuasion and psychotherapy. Paper read at APA meeting, Chicago.

LINDSLEY, O. R. (1961 b) Direct measurement and functional definition of vocal hallucinatory symptoms in chronic psychosis, Paper read at 3rd World Congress of Psychiatry, Montreal.

LONG, E. R., HAMMACK, J. T., MAY, F. and CAMPBELL, B. J. (1958) Intermittent reinforcement of operant behaviour in children, *J. Exp. Anal. Behav.* **1**, 315–339.

LOVAAS, I. O. (1960) The control of operant responding by rate and content of verbal operants: Preliminary report. (Unpublished paper.)

LOVAAS, I. O. (1961 a) Interaction between verbal and non-verbal behaviour, *Child Develop.* **32**, 329–336.

LOVAAS, O, I. (1961 b) The control of food-intake in three children by reinforcement of relevant verbal behaviour. (Unpublished paper.)

LOVIBOND, D. H. (1961) Conditioning and Enuresis. Ph.D. Thesis, University of Adelaide.

MEEHL, P. (1954) *Clinical versus statistical prediction*. University of Minnesota Press. Minneapolis.

METZNER, R. (1961) Learning Theory and the therapy of the neuroses, *Brit. J. Psychol. Monogr. Suppl.* **33**.

MOWRER, O. H. and MOWRER, W. (1938) Enuresis: A method for its study treatment, *Amer. J. Orthopsychiat.* **8**, 436–459.

ORLANDO, R. and BIJOU, S. W. (1960) Single and multiple schedules of reinforcement in developmentally retarded children, *J. Exp. Anal. Behav.* **3**, 339–348.

RACHMAN, S. and COSTELLO, C. G. (1961) The aetiology and treatment of children's phobias: A review, *Amer. J. Psychiat.* **118**, 97–105.

RACHMAN, S. and LOEWENSTEIN, L. (1962) Unpublished case data. Maudsley Hospital.

RHEINGOLD, H., GEWIRTZ, J. and ROSS, J. (1959) Social conditioning of vocalizations in the infant, *J. Comp. Physiol. Psychol.* **52**, 68–73.

SALZINGER, K. (1959) Experimental manipulation of verbal behaviour: A review, *J. Gen. Psychol.* **61**, 65–94.

SALZINGER, S., SALZINGER, K., PISONI, S., ECKMAN, J., MATHEWSON, P., DEUTSCH, M. and ZUBIN, J. (1962) Operant conditioning of continuous speech in young children, *Child Develop.* (In press.)

SHAPIRO, M. B. (1961) The single case in fundamental clinical psychological research, *Brit. J. Med. Psychol.* **34**, 255–262.

SHEEHAN, J. (1951) The modification of stuttering through non-reinforcement, *J. Abn. Soc. Psychol.* **46**, 51–63.

SHEEHAN, J. and VOAS, R. B. (1957) Stuttering as conflict. Comparison of therapy techniques involving approach and avoidance, *J. Speech Dis.* **22**, 714–723.

SKINNER, B. F. (1957) *Verbal Behaviour*, Appleton-Century-Crofts, New York.

SKINNER, B. F. (1959) *Cumulative Record*, Appleton Century, New York.

SKINNER, B. F., SOLOMON, H. C. and LINDSLEY, O. R. (1954) A new method for the experimental analysis of the behaviour of psychotic patients, *J. Nerv. Ment. Dis.* **120**, 403–406.

SPIKER, C. C. (1960) Research methods in children's learning. In *Handbook of Research Methods in Child Development* (Ed. MUSSEN, P. H.) Wiley and Sons, New York.

SPRADLIN, J. E. (1961) Operant conditioning of severely retarded children. (Unpublished paper.)

SPRADLIN, J. E. (1962) Effects of reinforcement schedules on extinction in severely mentally retarded children, *Amer. J. Ment. Defic.* **66**, 634–640.

STAATS, A. W. and STAATS, C. K., (1962) Personal communication.

STAATS, A. W., STAATS, C. K. HEARD, W. G. and FINLEY, J. R. (1962) Operant conditioning of factor analytic personality traits, *J. Gen. Psychol.* **66**, 101–114.

VERPLANCK, W. S. (1956) Operant conditioning of human motor behaviour, *Psychol. Bull.* **53**, 70–83.

WALTON, D. (1961) Experimental psychology and the treatment of a ticqueur, *J. Child Psychol. Psychiat.* **2**, 148–155.

WATSON, J. B. and RAYNER, R. (1920) Conditioned emotional reactions, *J. Exp. Psychol.* **3**, 1–14.

WHITE, J. G. (1959) The use of learning theory in the psychological treatment of children, *J. Clin. Psychol.* **15**, 229–233.

WILLIAMS, C. D. (1959) The elimination of tantrum behaviour by extinction procedures: Case report, *J. Abn. Soc. Psychol.* **59**, 269.

WOLPE, J. (1958) *Psychotherapy by reciprocal inhibition*, Stanford Univ. Press.

WOLPE, J. (1961) The systematic desensitization treatment of neuroses, *J. Nerv. Ment. Dis.* **132**, 189–203.

WOLPE, J and RACHMAN, S. (1950) Psychoanalytic evidence: A critique based on Freud's case of Little Hans, *J. Nerv. Ment. Dis.* **131**, 135–143.

YATES, A (1958) The application of learning theory to the treatment of tics, *J. Abn. Soc. Psychol.* **56**, 175–182.

# The Use of "Emotive Imagery" in the Treatment of Children's Phobias*

ARNOLD A. LAZARUS and ARNOLD ABRAMOVITZ

SOME of the earliest objective approaches to the removal of specific anxieties and fears in children were based on the fact that neurotic (learned, unadaptive) responses can be eliminated by the repeated and simultaneous evocation of stronger incompatible responses. An early and well-known example of this approach was the experiment of Jones[1] in which a child's fear of rabbits was gradually eliminated by introducing a "pleasant stimulus", i.e. *food* (thus evoking the anxiety-inhibiting response of eating) in the presence of the rabbit. The general method of "gradual habituation" was advocated by Jersild and Holmes[2] as being superior to all others in the elimination of children's fears. This rationale was crystallized in Wolpe's[3] formulation of the Reciprocal Inhibition Principle, which deserves the closest possible study:

> If a response antagonistic to anxiety can be made to occur in the presence of anxiety-evoking stimuli so that it is accompanied by a complete or partial suppression of the anxiety responses, the bond between these stimuli and the anxiety responses will be weakened.

A crucial issue in the application of this principle is the choice of a clinically suitable anxiety-inhibiting response. The most widely-used method has been that of "systematic desensitization" (Wolpe[4]) which may be described as gradual habituation to the imagined stimulus through the anxiety-inhibiting response of *relaxation*. Lazarus[5] reported several successful paediatric applications of this procedure, using both feeding and relaxation. It was subsequently found, however, that neither feeding nor relaxation was feasible in certain cases. Feeding has obvious disadvantages in routine therapy, while training in relaxation is often both time-consuming and difficult or impossible to achieve with certain children. The possibility of inducing anxiety-inhibiting *emotive* images, without specific training in relaxation, was then explored, and the results of our preliminary investigation form the subject of this paper.

Our use of the term "emotive imagery" requires clarification. In the present clinical context, it refers to those classes of imagery which are assumed to arouse feelings of self-assertion, pride, affection, mirth, and similar anxiety-inhibiting responses.

* This article is reprinted with the permission of the authors and editor from *J. Ment. Sci.* **108**, 191–195 (1962).

The technique which was finally evolved can be described in the following steps:

(a) As in the usual method of systematic desensitization, the range, intensity, and circumstances of the patient's fears are ascertained, and a graduated hierarchy is drawn up, from the most feared to the least feared situation.

(b) By sympathetic conversation and enquiry, the clinician establishes the nature of the child's hero-images—usually derived from radio, cinema, fiction, or his own imagination—and the wish-fulfilments and identifications which accompany them.

(c) The child is then asked to close his eyes and told to imagine a sequence of events which is close enough to his everyday life to be credible, but within which is woven a story concerning his favourite hero or *alter ego*.

(d) If this is done with reasonable skill and empathy it is possible to arouse to the necessary pitch the child's affective reactions. (In some cases this may be recognized by small changes in facial expression, breathing, muscle tension, etc.).

(e) When the clinician judges that these emotions have been maximally aroused, he introduces, as a natural part of the narrative, the lowest item in the hierarchy. Immediately afterwards he says, "If you feel afraid (or unhappy or uncomfortable) just raise your finger". If anxiety is indicated, the phobic stimulus is "withdrawn" from the narrative and the child's anxiety-inhibiting emotions are again aroused. The procedure is then repeated as in ordinary systematic desensitization until the highest item in the hierarchy is tolerated without distress.

The use of this procedure is illustrated in the following cases:

CASE 1—Stanley M., aged 14, suffered from an intense fear of dogs of $2\frac{1}{2}$–3 years duration. He would take two buses on a roundabout route to school rather than risk exposure to dogs on a direct 300-yard walk. He was a rather dull (I. Q. 93), sluggish person, very large for his age, trying to be co-operative, but sadly unresponsive—especially to attempts at training in relaxation. In his desire to please, he would state that he had been perfectly relaxed even though he had betrayed himself by his intense fidgetiness. Training in relaxation was eventually abandoned, and an attempt was made to establish the nature of his aspirations and goals. By dint of much questioning and after following many false trails because of his inarticulateness, a topic was eventually tracked down that was absorbing enough to form the subject of his fantasies, namely racing motor-cars. He had a burning ambition to own a certain Alfa Romeo sports car and race it at the Indianapolis "500" event. Emotive imagery was enduced as follows: "Close your eyes. I want you to imagine, clearly and vividly, that your wish has come true. The Alfa Romeo is now in your possession. It is your car. It is standing in the street outside your block. You are looking at it now. Notice the beautiful, sleek lines. You decide to go for a drive with some friends of yours. You sit down at the wheel, and you feel a thrill of pride as you realize that you own this magnificent machine. You start up and listen to the wonderful roar of the exhaust. You let the clutch in and the car streaks off. ... You are out in a clear open road now; the car is performing like a pedigree; the speedometer is climbing into the nineties; you have a wonderful feeling of being in perfect control; you look at the trees whizzing by and you see a little dog standing next to one of them—if you feel any anxiety, just raise your finger. Etc., etc." An item fairly high up on the hierarchy: "You stop at a café in a little town and dozens of people crowd around to look enviously at this magnificent car and its lucky owner; you swell with pride; and at this moment a large boxer comes up and sniffs at your heels—If you feel any anxiety, etc., etc."

After three sessions using this method he reported a marked improvement in his reaction to dogs He was given a few field assignments during the next two sessions, after which therapy was terminated. Twelve months later, reports both from the patient and his relatives indicated that there was no longer any trace of his former phobia.

Case 2—A 10-year-old boy was referred for treatment because his excessive fear of the dark exposed him to ridicule from his 12-year-old brother and imposed severe restrictions on his parent's social activities. The lad became acutely anxious whenever his parents went visiting at night and even when they remained at home he refused to enter any darkened room unaccompanied. He insisted on sharing a room with his brother and made constant use of a night light next to his bed. He was especially afraid of remaining alone in the bathroom and only used it if a member of the household stayed there with him. On questioning, the child stated that he was not anxious during the day but that he invariably became tense and afraid towards sunset.

His fears seemed to have originated a year or so previously when he saw a frightening film, and shortly thereafter was warned by his maternal grandmother (who lived with the family) to keep away from all doors and windows at nights as burglars and kidnappers were on the prowl.

A previous therapist had embarked on a programme of counselling with the parents and play-therapy with the child. While some important areas of interpersonal friction were apparently ameliorated, the child's phobic responses remained unchanged. Training in "emotive imagery" eliminated his repertoire of fears in three sessions.

The initial interview (90 min) was devoted to psychometric testing and the development of rapport. The test revealed a superior level of intelligence (I.Q. 135) with definite evidence of anxiety and insecurity. He responded well to praise and encouragement throughout the test situation. Approximately 30 min were devoted to a general discussion of the child's interests and activities, which was also calculated to win his confidence. Towards the end of this interview, the child's passion for two radio serials, "Superman" and "Captain Silver" had emerged.

A week later, the child was seen again. In addition to his usual fears he had been troubled by nightmares. Also, a quarterly school report had commented on a deterioration in his schoolwork. Emotive imagery was then introduced. The child was asked to imagine that Superman and Captain Silver had joined forces and had appointed him their agent. After a brief discussion concerning the topography of his house he was given his first assignment. The therapist said, "Now I want you to close your eyes and imagine that you are sitting in the dining-room with your mother and father. It is night time. Suddenly, you receive a signal on the wrist radio that Superman has given you. You quickly run into the lounge because your mission must be kept a secret. There is only a little light coming into the lounge from the passage. Now pretend that you are all alone in the lounge waiting for Superman and Captain Silver to visit you. Think about this very clearly. If the idea makes you feel afraid, lift up your right hand."

An on-going scene was terminated as soon as any anxiety was indicated. When an image aroused anxiety, it would either be represented in a more challengingly assertive manner, or it would be altered slightly so as to prove less objectively threatening.

At the end of the third session, the child was able to picture himself alone in his bathroom with all the lights turned off, awaiting a communication from Superman.

Apart from ridding the child of his specific phobia, the effect of this treatment appeared to have diverse and positive implications on many facets of his personality. His schoolwork improved immeasurably and many former manifestations of insecurity were no longer apparent. A follow-up after eleven months revealed that he had maintained his gains and was, to quote his mother. "a completely different child".

CASE 3—An eight-year-old girl was referred for treatment because of persistent nocturnal enuresis and a fear of going to school. Her fear of the school situation was apparently engendered by a series of emotional upsets in class. In order to avoid going to school, the child resorted to a variety of devices including temper tantrums, alleged pains and illness and on one occasion she was caught playing truant and intemperately upbraided by her father. Professional assistance was finally sought when it was found that her younger sister was evincing the same behaviour.

When the routine psychological investigations had been completed, emotive imagery was introduced with the aid of an Enid Blyton character, Noddy, who provided a hierarchy of assertive challenges centred around the school situation. The essence of this procedure was to create imagined situations where Noddy played the role of a truant and responded fearfully to the school setting. The patient would then protect him, either by active reassurance or by "setting a good example".

Only four sessions were required to eliminate her school-going phobia. Her enuresis, which had received no specific therapeutic attention, was far less frequent and disappeared entirely within two months. The child has continued to improve despite some additional upsets at the hands of an unsympathetic teacher.

## DISCUSSION

The technique of "emotive imagery" has been applied to nine phobic children whose ages ranged from 7 to 14 years. Seven children recovered in a mean of only 3·3 sessions. The method failed with one child who refused to co-operate and later revealed widespread areas of disturbance, which required broader therapeutic handling. The other failure was a phobic child with a history of encephalitis. He was unable to concentrate on the emotive images and could not enter into the spirit of the "game."

Of the seven patients who recovered, two had previously undergone treatment at the hands of different therapists. Two others had been treated by the same therapist (A.A.L.) using reassurance, relaxation and "environmental manipulation". In none of these four cases was there any appreciable remission of the phobic symptoms until the present methods were applied. In every instance where the method was used, improvement occurred contemporaneously with treatment.

Follow-up enquires were usually conducted by means of home-visits, interviews and telephone conversations both with the child and his immediate associates. These revealed that in no case was there symptom substitution of any obvious kind and that in fact, favourable response generalization had occurred in some instances.

It has been suggested that these results may be due to the therapist's enthusiasm for the method. (Does this imply that other therapists are unenthusiastic about *their* methods?) Certainly, the nature of the procedure is such that it cannot be coldly and dispassionately applied. A warm rapport with the child and a close understanding of his wish-fulfilments and identifications are essential. But our claim is that although warmth and acceptance are necessary in any psychotherapeutic undertaking, they are usually not *sufficient*. Over and above such non-specific anxiety-inhibiting factors, this technique, in common with other reciprocal inhibition methods, provides a clearly defined therapeutic tool which is claimed to have *specific* effects.

Encouraging as these preliminary experiences have been, it is not claimed that they are, as yet, anything more than suggestive evidence of the efficacy of the method. Until properly controlled studies are performed, no general inference can be drawn. It is evident, too, that our loose *ad hoc* term "emotive imagery", reflects a basic lack of theoretical systematization in the field of the emotions. In her review of experimental data on autonomic functions, Martin[6] deplores the paucity of replicated studies, the unreliability of the measures used, and the lack of operational definitions of qualitatively labelled emotions. The varieties of emotion we have included under the blanket term "emotive imagery" and our simple conjecture of anxiety-inhibiting properties for all of them is an example of the *a priori* assumptions one is forced to make in view of the absence of firm empirical data and adequately formulated theory. It is hoped that our demonstration of the clinical value of these techniques will help to focus attention on an unaccountably neglected area of study, but one which lies at the core of experimental clinical psychology.

## SUMMARY

A reciprocal inhibition[3] technique for the treatment of children's phobias is presented which consists essentially of an adaptation of Wolpe's method of "systematic desensitization".[4] Instead of inducing muscular relaxation as the anxiety-inhibiting response, certain emotion-arousing situations are presented to the child's imagination. The emotions induced are assumed, like relaxation, to have autonomic effects which are incompatible with anxiety. This technique, which the authors have provisionally labelled "emotive imagery" was applied to nine phobic children whose ages ranged from 7 to 14 years. Seven children recovered in a mean of 3·3 sessions and follow-up enquires up to 12 months later revealed no relapses or symptom substitution. An outstanding feature of this paediatric technique is the extraordinary rapidity with which remission occurs.

## REFERENCES

1. JONES, M. C. (1924) Elimination of children's fears, *J. Exp. Psychol.*, 7, 382–390.
2. JERSILD, A. T. and HOLMES, F. B. (1935) Methods of overcoming children's fears, *J. Psychol.* 1, 75–104.
3. WOLPE, J. (1958) *Psychotherapy by Reciprocal Inhibition*, Stanford Univ. Press and Witwatersrand Univ. Press.
4. *Idem* (1961) The Systematic Desensitization Treatment of Neuroses. *J. Nerv. and Mental Disease*, 132, 189–203.
5. LAZARUS, A. A. (1960) The Elimination of Children's Phobias by Deconditioning. In *Behaviour Therapy and the Neuroses*, ed. H. J. EYSENCK, Oxford: Pergamon Press.
6. MARTIN, I. (1960) Somatic Reactivity. In *Handbook of Abnormal Psychology*, ed. H. J. EYSENCK, Pitman Medical Publishing Co. London.

# The Use of Learning Theory in the Psychological Treatment of Children*

JOHN GRAHAM WHITE

*University of Liverpool, England* †

## INTRODUCTION

For some years there has been growing dissatisfaction amongst British clinical psychologists with psychoanalytically-orientated psychotherapies. On the other hand, there has been an increasing desire to derive treatment procedures from the body of general psychological theory, in particular learning theory, which will allow of more precise formulations of problem and predictions of outcome according to the specific theoretical postulate chosen. The application of conditioning and other learning techniques in the treatment of both children and adults was, of course, described thirty years ago by M. C. Jones;[5] twenty years ago, by the Mowrers;[8] and more recently by H. G. Jones,[3,4] Eysenck,[2] Walton[11,12] and Walton and Black.[13,14] The accommodation of theory and practice has been most fully attempted so far by Mowrer,[6,7] Dollard and Miller,[1] and Shoben.[9,10]

The following case study demonstrates that some forms of disordered behavior in children can be explained and treated according to well-established principles of learning,§ without any recourse to "psychodynamic" concepts and without any attempt to produce "insight" in the patient by means of verbal "interpretations" of behavior.

## CASE STUDY

Several years ago a child of five and a half was admitted to hospital in consequence of her refusal to eat and also because she was suffering from what appeared at the time to be rheumatic pains.

* This article is reprinted with the permission of the author and editor from *J. Clin. Psychol.* **15**, 227–229 (1959).

† Now at Queen's University, Belfast, N. Ireland.

§ The phrase *learning* in the context of this paper is used to cover both of Mowrer's[7] two factors, solution learning and sign learning.

*Relevant History.* The patient was the second of two girls, the only children in the family. The older child had been born during the war; for the first four years of her life the father had been with the Army abroad, and she became the "mother's baby". By the time the younger child was born the father was back home, and she became his baby. He gave her lavish attention, played with her, and almost from the time she was born fed her (she was breast-fed for only a "few weeks"). Apart from the manner in which it was carried out the history of feeding was uneventful. The child was enuretic at night until admission to hospital. From infancy, when her father was nursing her, the patient "used to hold on to and play with his collar. She would never go to bed without his collar . . . If she lost hold of the collar in the night she would call out and mother would find it for her."

Between the ages of 3 and 4 years the child's appetite became capricious. She insisted on having her main meal at 6 o'clock, when the father came in from work. She would sit on his knee throughout the meal and he would often feed her. When the father was present the mother was rejected; this younger child was the self-avowed rival of both her mother and her sister.

Father was the kind of person who would do anything to avoid "disagreeableness", such as violent scenes of any kind, and could easily be influenced by threat of this. Thus, going up to bed at night and settling for sleep were, for a long time before the child came to hospital, occasions for crises and emotional tension. Mother would put her to bed, the patient would scream, and then father would go up and read to her until she fell asleep. This went so far at times that not one, but several, books were read until the parents were exhausted.

A month before this child's fifth birthday the father spent seven weeks in hospital with an illness which was to prove fatal. The patient could not see him during this time but clung to his collar at night. When he returned home—to die—the child wanted to spend all her time in his bedroom. About two months after his discharge the father died; and the mother told the patient that he had gone to "God's hospital". The child expected that he would come back.

In September of that year the mother started to go out to work, and an aunt used to give the patient her meals. Quite fantastic antics were resorted to by her adult relatives to induce her to eat her mid-day dinner. For example, one of the relatives would put on a dance or some other performance while the grandmother tried to feed her with a spoon. Her appetite deteriorated gradually. In October she became ill with what was later diagnosed as acute rheumatism. She was confined to bed for six weeks; and during this time her appetite deteriorated to the point where she was refusing all solid foods and took only milk and fruit drinks. The family doctor himself tried to feed her with a spoon but with no success. Once the child commented to her mother, "Dr. B says if I don't eat I'll never be a big girl. If I grow into a big girl my daddy won't recognize me, will he?" By mid-December the doctor, getting worried, called in a pediatrician who took both mother and child into hospital. There the nurses tried forced feeding; but this was quite unsuccessful and was in any case stopped by the pediatrician.

*Treatment.* The most urgent need now was to revive appetite. The case was discussed in the Psychiatric Department. The immediate problem was formulated in terms of simple conditioning with father as the conditioned stimulus, upon which the conditioned response of eating had come to depend, reinforcement being supplied both by satisfaction of hunger, as well as by anxiety-reduction through sitting on the father's knee and being fed by him. The first step, therefore, was to provide a substitute for the father and to arrange a series of experiences that might gradually approximate those obtaining before the father's death. In other words, principles were to be used that involved both stimulus-substitution and the generalization continuum. The attempt was to be made to replace the father as conditioned stimulus, first by the psychologist and, later, by members of the child's own family, such as uncles, the father's sister, and finally her mother. It was decided that the psychologist, a man, should undertake this part of the treatment, and in accordance with the theortical formulation no "interpretations" were to be given to the child.

For the first week the psychologist saw the child every day for an hour and arranged a series of play sessions and tea-parties in a large play house which was equipped with miniature furniture and paraphernalia such as cooking utensils, plates and tea sets.

During the first session the child and psychologist attended to the various needs of dolls and only the dolls were fed. The mother was present on this occasion but was excluded from all subsequent sessions. On the next afternoon, while worrying considerably about "supper on the ward", the child nevertheless ate a number of miniature biscuits and drank dolls' cups full of milk laced with stout, a beverage to which her father had been partial. Play with dolls and tea parties continued every day that week with the child still refusing all meals on the ward, except once when she accepted a sausage from an uncle who was visiting her in the evening. At the weekend it was decided that the child should return home and in future attend as an out-patient.

The weekend was spent partly at home and partly at the house of a paternal aunt and uncle. (This paternal aunt was later to prove an excellent mother-surrogate, in bridging the gap between the dead father and the mother.) On Monday mother reported that the patient had eaten a little solid food both at her aunt's and at home; and while the psychologist was having his coffee the child asked for a cup, too. During the subsequent play sessions that week larger cups were substitued for the doll's cups and full sized biscuits introduced.

In the middle of the second week the mother reported an "embarrassing" experience. They were at the grandmother's house the previous day when suddenly a neighbor, an elderly Irish woman, came in with the patient and said to the mother, shaking her finger disapprovingly in her face, "Don't you tell me this child won't eat; she has just eaten two plates of spare-ribs and cabbage". That evening the mother suffered a further "embarrassment" when another neighbor, a man, called and the child told him, "I don't eat in this house. I won't eat for my mummy." By the end of the second week, although the child still refused to eat with her relatives, she had eaten fruit and nuts at this neighbor's house.

The Christmas holiday and a head cold now intervened, and the psychologist did not see either mother or child for six days. However, after a further week the patient was prepared to sit down to meals with her mother and sister but did not regularly eat anything with them. A month after referral the mother reported that the child had for the first time inquired what there was for lunch and had eaten something of everything that was available.

During this period the play sessions had continued, never less frequently than four times a week, with the patient often preparing the meals she and the psychologist ate together and determining their other activities. The psychologist played the role of submissive father and pandered to her whims, until one day, six weeks after beginning treatment, when the child had him skipping for his tea while she beat time on a hammer-peg board, he made a note to introduce at an opportune moment a little more "reality" and a little less "pleasure" into the father-child relationship.

The opportunity came in a day or two when the patient refused to stay in the playroom while the psychologist had a talk with her mother. He therefore terminated the interview and sent her home without the cup of coffee that had been promised her by the clinic secretary. Interestingly, the mother was very upset at this, fearing that the child would refuse to attend again. She attended, however, and a period of retraining was started in which a different set of responses began to be rewarded, i.e. responses other than those of exploiting the relationship with the therapist. She began to do little useful jobs about the clinic, such as mending books, as well as playing. The child continued to eat better, now taking a regular breakfast, and even to say she was hungry; but after three months of treatment she suffered a set-back when the mother had to return to work. Her diet was again reduced to fluids; and she insisted on having a collar, this time an uncle's to go to sleep with. The relapse lasted, however, only three or four days.

For the next six weeks she was unable to attend the hospital because of measles and then chicken-pox. Five months after her initial referral to the Psychiatric Department the child was showing an interest in food and developing special tastes; and a month later eating was no longer a cause for anxiety to her relatives. By this time the psychologist had managed to transfer a large part of father's mantle on to two uncles, one of whom (the husband of the paternal aunt already mentioned) the patient described as her "No. 1 uncle", saying that she loved him "nearly as much as Daddy". Nevertheless, it was learned from the aunt that the psychologist still possessed almost divine qualities for this child.

After seven months this phase of the treatment was concluded. For three years now the child has remained free of her symptoms, the nocturnal enuresis having cleared up twelve months after the feeding difficulty had been disposed of. She has been healthy and fairly well-adjusted at home, at school, and with her play friends, despite the death of a grandmother, of whom she was very fond, two years ago, and more recently, of her No. 1 uncle.

## SUMMARY

In spite of the fact that for more than thirty years psychologists have been interested in applying principles of behavior discovered in general psychology, especially those of learning, to the understanding of behavior disorders and neuroses in children, these principles have been largely neglected in treatment. In order to demonstrate that this failure of transfer need not necessarily be perpetuated, the history and treatment were described of a five and a half year old girl who for three months had resisted all attempts by her relatives, by the family doctor, and by hospital nurses to get her to take solid foods.

## REFERENCES

1. DOLLARD, J. and MILLER, N. E. (1950) *Personality and psychotherapy*, McGraw-Hill New York.
2. EYSENCK, H. J. (1957) *The dynamics of anxiety and hysteria*, Routledge & Kegan Paul, London
3. JONES, H. G. (1956) The application of conditioning and learning techniques to the treatment of a psychiatric patient, *J. Abnorm. Soc. Psychol.*, **52**, 414–419.
4. JONES, H. G. (1958) Neurosis and experimental psychology, *J. Ment. Sci.*, **104**, 55–62.
5. JONES, M. C. (1924) A laboratory study of fear: the case of Peter, *Pedag. Sem.*, **31**, 308–315.
6. MOWRER, O. H. (1950) *Learning theory and personality dynamics*, Ronald Press, New York.
7. MOWRER, O. H. (1953) *Psychotherapy. Theory and research*, Ronald Press, New York.
8. MOWRER, O. H. and MOWRER, W. M. (1938) Enuresis. A method for its study and treatment, *Amer. J. Orthopsychiat.*, **8**, 436.
9. SHOBEN, E. J. (1949) Psychotherapy as a problem in learning theory, *Psychol. Bull.*, **46**, 366–392.
10. SHOBEN, E. J. (1953) Some observations on psychotherapy and the learning process. In O. H. MOWRER, *Psychotherapy. Theory and research*. Ronald Press, New York.
11. WALTON, D. Reciprocal inhibition, sedation threshold practice, and the treatment of compulsions and schizophrenic slowness, *Bull. Brit. Psychol. Soc.*, No. 36.
12, WALTON, D. (1958) Learning theory, personality, drug-action, and the treatment of stammering, *Bull. Brit. Psychol. Soc.*, No. 36.
13. WALTON, D. and BLACK, D. A. (1958) The application of learning theory to the treatment of stammering, *J. Psychosomatic Res.*, **3**, 170–179.
14. WALTON, D. and BLACK, D. A. (1958) The application of modern learning theory to the treatment of chronic hysterical aphonia. In: EYSENCK, H. J. *Behaviour Therapy and the Neuroses*, Pergamon Press, New York (1960), pp. 259–271.

# The Elimination of Children's Phobias
# by Deconditioning*

Arnold A. Lazarus, M.A. (Rand)

*Johannesburg*

THE therapeutic properties of direct deconditioning were first demonstrated by Jones[1] in 1924. Jones eliminated fear-reactions in young children by coupling the feared objects with pleasant stimuli. She wrote:

> The hunger motive appears to be the most effective for use in this connection. During a period of craving for food, the child is placed in a high chair and given something to eat. The fear-object is brought in, starting a negative response. It is then moved away gradually until it is at a sufficient distance not to interfere with the child's eating. . . . While the child is eating, the object is slowly brought nearer to the table, then placed upon the table, and finally as the tolerance increases it is brought close enough to be touched.

Until recently, the comprehensive psychotherapeutic value of deconditioning procedures remained relatively unexplored. Sears and Cohen,[2] Guthrie,[3] Max,[4] Mowrer and Mowrer,[5] and Voegtlin[6] were among the first to provide evidence of therapeutic potentials based on this pattern. Most psychotherapists, however, have remained impervious to these and other investigations of the efficacy of techniques which stem directly from the conditioned response. The majority of clinicians appear to view conditioning techniques with suspicion and disfavour and maintain that "symptom removal" exposes the patient to the dangers of alternative symptoms, greater degrees of anxiety and numerous other undesirable manifestations of the unresolved "underlying complex". Many writers, however, notably Eysenck[7-9] and Wolpe,[10-13] have cited widespread clinical evidence which runs counter to this general viewpoint.

Eysenck's[8] lucid distinction between these opposing theories is phrased as follows:

> According to Freud, there is a "disease" which produces symptoms; cure the disease and the symptoms will vanish. According to the alternative view, there is no "disease", there are merely wrong habits which have been learned and must be unlearned. If such "unlearning" and "relearning" is efficacious, and there is no evidence of any "disease", then surely we must dismiss this additional concept as superfluous.

* This article is reprinted with the permission of the author and editor from *Med. Proc. (South Africa)* 5, 261–265 (1959).

Follow-up studies[16-19] on cases treated by a variety of methods which did not concern themselves with the uncovering of repressed material have uniformly revealed little or no tendency to relapse. These studies are directly contrary to the psychoanalytic assumption that neurotic disorders can only be resolved by delving into "unconscious, infantile, repressed material". The significance of these findings has been summed up by Wolpe[13] as follows:

> If repression were the essence of neurosis, apparently successful measures that leave "the repressed" untouched would be followed before long by relapse, i.e. the emergence of new symptoms or the recurrence of old ones. If, on the other hand, neurotic symptoms are nothing but conditioned responses, "deconditioning" measures . . . will be all that is needed to eliminate the symptoms permanently; and after thorough extinction of the neurotic responses relapse will not be expected.

Employing methods of treatment based on the hypothesis that neurotic responses can be eliminated by deconditioning, Wolpe has reported a 90 per cent level of apparent cures or marked improvements in over 200 cases. Follow-up studies on 45 patients, 2 to 7 years after the end of treatment, revealed that only one patient had suffered a moderate relapse after about a year.

Independent corroboration of Wolpe's findings on adult patients have been presented elsewhere.[14, 22] The present paper is concerned with the application of Wolpe's methods to the field of child therapy. We have already discussed how Jones employed feeding responses in overcoming neurotic anxieties in children. Wolpe has shown that there are numerous responses (apart from feeding) that are capable of inhibiting anxiety. In the main, our own child therapy programmes have made use of feeding responses, relaxation responses, conditioned avoidance responses and drugs in deconditioning. We shall illustrate these techniques by reference to actual case histories. The examples which follow have been selected from our case records of 18 phobic children who were treated by these specific deconditioning techniques.

## ILLUSTRATIVE CASE RECORDS

### Deconditioning Based on Feeding Responses

John D., 8 years old, developed a fear of moving vehicles 2 years after he and his parents had been involved in a motor car accident. He refused to enter any vehicle and on one occasion when his father had unwisely forced him into his car, the child became panic-stricken and hysterical.

Therapy consisted of first talking to John about trains, aeroplanes, buses, etc. Even this "mild exposure to the stimulus" tended to evoke anxiety in the child, but whenever he volunteered a "positive" comment, he was casually offered his favourite chocolate. During the third interview, John willingly spoke at length about types of moving vehicles and there was no longer any evidence of overt anxiety.

A series of deliberate 'accidents' with toy motor cars constituted the next phase of the treatment project. The child evidenced a fairly high level of initial anxiety. After each "accident" he was given chocolate. His anxiety was soon dissipated and he entered into the full spirit of the game.

The next step in the therapy programme consisted of sitting with the child in a stationary motor car while discussing the accident in which he had been involved. He was provided with liberal helpings of chocolate throughout this discussion. Thereafter the child was taken in a car for short distances. At the 17th session (less than 6 weeks after therapy had commenced) he willingly entered a car and, accompanied by a complete stranger, he set off for a shop $1\frac{1}{2}$ miles away where he bought chocolate. At first, he refused to go motoring with his parents unless he was given chocolate, but he soon began to enjoy motoring for pleasure.

## Systematic Desensitization Based on Relaxation

Carol M., $9\frac{1}{2}$ years old, had been an apparently healthy and well-adjusted child until about 2 months after her ninth birthday, when she became enuretic, afraid of the dark and displayed a variety of symptoms ranging from night terrors to what her doctor had labelled "psychosomatic ailments". While at school she invariably developed violent abdominal pains so that her teacher had to excuse her from class and would eventually have to send for her mother.

Immediately before the onset of her anxieties, Carol had been exposed to 3 successive traumatic incidents in the span of a few weeks. A school friend had fallen into a pond and drowned; her next-door playmate contracted meningitis and died; she had witnessed a motor car accident in which a man was killed.

During an interview with Carol's mother, Mrs. M. stated that she had read an article which stressed that one should refrain from giving a 9-year-old child any overt demonstrations of love and affection (such as hugging or kissing the child) since these practices supposedly hindered the development of "personality and maturity". The therapist vehemently condemned this contention and provided "handling instructions" which emphasized the necessity for deliberate and overt love and warmth.

A month later Mrs. M. telephoned the therapist and reported that the family had been away on vacation for over 3 weeks, during which time Carol's behaviour had been "perfectly normal". Since their return, however, Carol bedwetted each night and had become hysterical when taken to school. "She's worse than ever," Mrs. M. declared. "The child won't let me out of her sight."

When Carol returned for therapy she insisted that her mother should be present during the interviews. Her condition had deteriorated considerably. She was extremely agitated and tense and anxiously clung to her mother.

During the diagnostic interviews, it became apparent that the child's central fear was the possibility of losing her mother through death. Projective testing also suggested that she was in fact not afraid to go to school, but she was afraid that her mother might die before she returned home from school. Similarly, she was not afraid to sleep alone, but she feared that her mother might die before the night was over. Whereas psychoanalysts might have interpreted this in terms of a "death wish", we found it unnecessary to account for the child's behavior in terms of inferred constructs and simply regarded the child's neurotic reactions as having been precipitated by her sudden and harsh exposure to the traumatic realities of death. Since Carol's premature awareness of the finality of death had coincided with her mother's misinformed attitude to displays of love and affection, the child's consequent feelings of rejection finally culminated in a genuine fear of permanent maternal deprivation (i.e. death). Thus, even a brief period of separation from her mother aggravated Carol's anxieties. Our therapeutic approach involved a planned and deliberate attack on this anxiety by systematic desensitization (see below).

Wolpe's method of systematic desensitization based on relaxation makes use of Jacobson's finding[23] that muscular relaxation inhibits anxiety and that their concurrent expression is physiologically impossible. Details of the theoretical rationale and clinical application of this technique are presented elsewhere.[12, 13, 22] Briefly, the patient is given progressive training in relaxation in the course of several interviews and during the same interviews an "anxiety hierarchy" is constructed, i.e. a graded list of stimuli to which the patient reacts with unadaptive anxiety. The following anxiety hierarchy was constructed for Carol M.

> Separation from the mother for 1 week.
> Separation from the mother for 2 days.
> Separation from the mother for 1 day.
> Separation from the mother for half a day.
> Separation from the mother for 1 hour.
> Separation from the mother for 15 minutes.
> Separation from the mother for 5 minutes.

The patient, while fully relaxed, is asked to imagine the individual items of the anxiety hierarchy, starting with the least noxious situation ("Imagine that you are not going to see your mother for 5 minutes") until eventually, the most "difficult" item is presented ("Imagine that your mother is leaving you for one whole week"). Repeated reciprocal inhibition in this manner eventually leads to the development of conditioned inhibition.[13, 24]

It took 5 sessions spaced over 10 consecutive days to desensitize Carol completely to the subjective threat of maternal deprivation. Therapy had commenced on a Tuesday. On the following Friday Carol willingly went to school. This was followed by an immediate dissipation of all her other neurotic conditions. A 15-month follow-up enquiry revealed that apart from very occasional enuretic incidents, she had maintained an eminently satisfactory level of adjustment.

*The Use of Drugs in Deconditioning*

Douglas G., 3½ years old, had displayed severe phobic reactions to dogs ever since one had bitten him nearly 5 months before. His parents subsequently had obtained a puppy in the hopes that this would enable him to overcome his fears. Unfortunately the child only became hysterical whenever he saw the animal, so that his parents were forced to dispose of it. Douglas soon displayed similar phobic reactions to cats and birds, so that eventually he became afraid to venture out of doors. The child was excessively active and distracted, but a detailed medical and neurological examination revealed no organic pathology. His activity level precluded the application of relaxation techniques. Consequently, he was given small doses of amobarbital and phenaglycodol (under medical supervision) for 3 days until a satisfactory level of sedation had been achieved. He was then gradually introduced to a variety of animals without displaying any anxiety. Administration of these drugs was gradually reduced over a period of 5 weeks. A follow-up was conducted almost a year later and revealed that the child had not relapsed in any respect.

*Deconditioning Obtained by Conditioned Avoidance Responses*

Ever since he had learned to walk, Brian E., 10 years old, had made a habit of waking up and going to his mother's bed in the very early hours of the morning. An assortment of punishments, threats, bribes and rewards had each failed to modify his behavior. The child "automatically" awoke between 1 a.m. and 2 a.m. and would immediately go to his mother's bed. On one occasion, Mrs. E. had decided that if she adamantly refused to have him in her bed he might eventually sleep in his own bed. The result was that Brian spent nearly 4 hours crying outside her bedroom door and she was finally forced to allow the child into her bed.

Professional advice was sought when Mrs. E. broke her ankle and found it acutely uncomfortable to share her bed. Furthermore, at this stage Brian's behaviour was seriously disrupting personal relationships in the home. When questioned about his behavior, Brian indicated that he very much wanted to sleep in his own bed but that when he awoke, anxiety would mount within him and he would become panic-stricken unless he went to his mother's bed. Although the security of his mother's bed constituted a potent source of anxiety-relief, we endeavoured to remedy the situation by means of simple avoidance conditioning.

Max[4] was the first to show that an unpleasant electric shock in the presence of an obsessional object tends to produce a persistent avoidance reaction to the object. Conversely, it has been shown that approach responses are conditioned to a stimulus repeatedly presented at the moment of termination of an electric shock.[25-28] Consequently, the following technique was employed:

Zinc electrodes, attached to the child's left forearm, were connected to the secondary circuit of an induction coil whose primary was wired to a 6-volt dry battery. The patient was asked to imagine* himself in his mother's bed and to say the words "mother's bed" as soon as he had a clear image of the situation. A mild electric shock (at an inductorium setting of 9 cm) was then passed into his forearm. When he could no longer tolerate the shock (average duration of shock, 3·2 sec) he was instructed to say "my bed," at which point the current was immediately switched off. This procedure was repeated 14 times over a period of about 10 min.

Brian was seen again a week later and he announced with great pride that he had slept in his own bed every night. He stated that although he had awakened as usual for the first 5 nights, he had merely "turned over and gone back to sleep". He had slept right through the sixth night, however. At the time of writing, he has slept in his own bed for over 6 months.

This case affords a clear illustration of the fact that "symptom removal" *per se* is not a static or isolated process but results in a dynamic redistribution of—to use Lewin's term[29]—the relevant "field forces". Brian's new-found ability to sleep in his own bed has completely altered numerous adverse environmental pressures. His relationship with his father, e.g. had been most casual and restrained. As soon as Brian had shown that "he had the makings of a man," Mr. E.'s attitude towards him underwent a remarkable change. He began displaying an active interest in his son's activities and, whereas previously he had forbidden Brian to keep any pets, he unexpectedly brought home a dog one night. Sibling tensions have also eased considerably. In short, as Mrs. E. expressed it, "the difference in the home is nothing short of fantastic".

It might be surprising to some that the removal of a single maladaptive symptom should have had such diverse and important implications. However, this is not difficult to explain. Once the improvement occurred the dynamics of Brian's situation altered markedly in directions which served to consolidate the gain. But there is no doubt that the conditioning procedure provided a strikingly rapid initiation of change. The crucial point, however, is that techniques which reciprocally inhibit neurotic anxieties appear to have widespread and positive repercussions on diverse areas of the individual's personality.

## DISCUSSION

We have applied Wolpe's methods of direct decondioning, based on the principal of reciprocal inhibition,[13] to the field of child psychotherapy. At present, 18 phobic cases ranging in age from $3\frac{1}{2}$ years to 12 years have been treated by these techniques with gratifying results. The cases had all either recovered or were much improved according to Knight's[30] criteria; and

* Wolpe[13] has shown that it is not necessary to present the actual objects or situations.

follow-up studies conducted over periods of 6 months to $2\frac{1}{2}$ years revealed that none of the children had relapsed in any respect. Compared with other forms of psychotherapy, the duration of treatment has been exceedingly short (mean number of sessions, 9·4).

A number of non-behaviouristic therapists have tended to explain away these (to our mind) promising results in terms of "transference cures", "strengthening of the ego", and so forth. The methods have also been criticized on the ground that they are "mechanistic" and "symptom-centred," but it must be emphasized that it is a matter of routine to make a thorough preliminary study of the interpersonal dynamics of the patient as a functioning member of society. It has been suggested that our successes may simply be explained in terms of our subjective confidence in the methods employed and that the methods themselves are suspect. (Does this imply that other psychotherapists have little confidence in their own methods?) It is obvious that the therapeutic atmosphere of empathy and acceptance must in itself reciprocally inhibit neurotic anxieties. Since the deliberate deconditioning techniques were applied within the context of therapeutic warmth, the final explanation of our therapeutic successes must necessarily incorporate elements of

(*a*) Non-specific reciprocal inhibition via the relationship between patient and therapist (common to all types of psychotherapy); and

(*b*) The deliberate and specific reciprocal inhibition of neurotic anxieties as outlined above.

Wolpe's method of systematic desensitization based on relaxation[13, 22] has proved especially valuable in our treatment of childhood phobias. In some cases, modifications of this approach were necessary. For instance, we have found that very disturbed children and cases with poor "visual imagery" respond more readily to graded presentations of the actual feared objects after the child has been given post-hypnotic suggestions of calmness and relaxation.

In this connection we may also mention that we have conducted preliminary experiments utilizing pleasurable responses to music in order to inhibit neurotic anxieties reciprocally. The child's favourite music would be played while presenting him with the relevant anxiety-generating stimuli. It is still premature to report on the efficacy of this technique.

## SUMMARY

We have applied Wolpe's psychotherapeutic methods based on the principle of reciprocal inhibition to a preliminary group of 18 phobic children.

Our gratifying results indicate that these methods are eminently effective in the management of childhood phobias.

Follow-up enquiries after 6 months to $2\frac{1}{2}$ years have shown no evidence of relapse in any form.

## REFERENCES

1. Jones, M. C. (1924) *J. Exp. Psychol.*, **7**, 382.
2. Sears, R. R. and Cohen, L. H. (1933) *Arch. Neurol. Psychiat.*, **29**, 260.
3. Guthrie, E. R. (1935) *The Psychology of Learning*, Harper, New York.
4. Max, L. W. (1935) *Psychol. Bull.*, **32**, 734.
5. Mowrer, O. H. and Mowrer, W. M. (1938) *Amer. J. Orthopsychiat.*, **8**, 436.
6. Voegtlin, W. L. (1940) *Amer. J. Med. Sci.*, **199**, 802.
7. Eysenck, H. J. (1953) *Uses and Abuses of Psychology*, Pelican, London.
8. Eysenck, H. J. (1957) *The Dynamics of Anxiety and Hysteria*, Routledge and Kegan Paul, London.
9. Eysenck, H. J. (1957) *Med. World*, **86**, 333.
10. Wolpe, J. (1950) *S. Afr. Med. J.*, **24**, 613.
11. Wolpe, J. (1952) *S. Afr. Med. J.*, **26**, 825.
12. Wolpe, J. (1954) *Arch. Neurol. Psychiat.*, **72**, 205.
13. Wolpe, J. (1958) *Psychotherapy by Reciprocal Inhibition*. Stanford University Press and Witwatersrand University Press.
14. Lazarus, A. A. (1958) *S. Afr. Med. J.*, **32** ,660.
15. Meehl, P. E. (1956) In a Foreword to Phillips, E. L. *Psychotherapy*: *A Modern Theory and Practice*, Staples Press, London.
16. Luff, M. C. and Garrod, M. (1935) *Brit. Med. J.*, **2**, 54.
17. Hamilton, D. M. and Wall, S. H. (1941) *Amer. J. Psychiat.*, **98**, 551.
18. Salter, A. (1952) *Conditioned Reflex Therapy*. George Allen and Unwin, London.
19. Phillips, E. L. (1956) *Psychotherapy*: *A Modern Theory and Practice*, Staples Press, London.
20. Wolpe, J. (1948) *An Approach to the Problem of Neurosis Based on the Conditioned Response*, M.D. Thesis, Witwatersrand University.
21. Wolpe, J. (1952) *Brit. J. Psychol.*, Gen. Sect., **43**, 243.
22. Lazarus, A. A. and Rachman, S. (1957): *S. Afr. Med. J.*, **31**, 934.
23. Jacobson, E. (1938) *Progressive Relaxation*, University of Chicago Press.
24. Wolpe, J. (1952) *Psychol. Rev.*, **59**, 192.
25. Barlow, J. A. (1955) *Psychol. Rev.*, **63**, 406.
26. Coppock, H. W. (1951) *Amer. Psychologist*, **6**, 277.
27. Goodson, F. A. and Brownstein, A. (1953) *J. Comp. Physiol. Psychol.*, **48**, 381.
28. Smith, M. P. and Buchanan, G. (1954) *J. Exper. Psychol.*, **48**, 123.
29. Lewin, K. (1931) *In* Murchinson, C. (Ed.) *A Handbook of Child Psychology*, pp. 590–625. Clark University Press, Worcester, Massachusetts.
30. Knight, R. P. (1941) *Amer. J. Psychiat.*, **98**, 434.

# Clinical Implications of Relationships Between
# Verbal and Nonverbal Operant Behavior*

O. Ivar Lovaas†

*University of California, Los Angeles*

THE relationship of verbal behavior to instrumental or operant nonverbal behavior has been a neglected area of study. The absence of both empirical data and conceptual frameworks is apparent. If operant nonverbal behavior is thought to include social or interpersonal behavior, then this is an area which deserves attention, particularly from a clinical viewpiont. Almost every theory of personality alludes to modifications in nonverbal behavior which are instigated by changes in verbal behavior. Psychoanalytic theory, for example, implies that a person's language behavior controls his nonverbal behaviors. The general manner in which these interactions are stated has been a basis for numerous criticisms. Similarly, behavioristically-oriented conceptions of treatment have given limited attention to this relationship. Dollard and Miller,[2] in analyzing the relationship of language to personality and psychotherapy, limit their discussion of language largely to acquired discrimination and generalization and how these processes effect emotional behavior. They briefly mention "connecting instrumental and verbal responses" (p. 338) and state what they consider to be a most important aspect of treatment: "If therapy is to have real effect, the terminal verbal cues of the plan must be strongly connected to overt responses."

Therapy might be effective (have "real effects") because of direct operations upon the patient's emotional and social behavior and not because of operations upon his verbal behavior. Even though verbal behavior is modified in treatment, these modifications might be determined by changes in the patient's nonverbal behavior, and not *vice versa*. The data from treatment are *correlational*, and a causative relationship cannot be inferred. This paper presents some evidence from *experimentally controlled studies* to the effect that changes in a person's verbal behavior do in fact produce changes in his nonverbal operant (instrumental) behavior. Because of the dearth of research in this area, the experiments were concerned only with establishing whether

* This paper was specially written for publication in this book.
† This paper was supported by grant (M–6241) from the National Institute of Health.

verbal control over operant nonverbal behavior exists. The presentation of these studies will be followed by a discussion of a conceptual framework designed to handle the verbal-nonverbal interaction.

## EMPIRICAL WORK

The first observations of verbal control over nonverbal operant behavior were made on children in free play situations. It was observed that if $E$ (the Experimeter) reinforced a verbal response denoting behavior which $S$ (the Subject) was capable of carrying out within the situation, then $S$ would frequently engage in that nonverbal response. For example, one $S$ was reinforced for emitting "what shall I say?" As this response was repeated $S$ rose from his chair, walked across the room to an attending adult and addressed his question to her. Another $S$ was reinforced for emitting "I don't know what to say". Despite continued delivery of trinkets and small toys (events which usually would reinforce) his verbal response decreased in strength. These observations were made in a rather casual situation. They do serve to define the behaviors under investigation, namely, verbal control over nonverbal behavior (as in the first example), and the control of verbal behavior over its own occurrence (as in the second example).

These initial observations were followed by several studies which were carried out in a highly controlled setting.[4] It was found that content (what is said) of a verbal response would control rate of verbal output. For example, when $S$ repeatedly emitted the word "slower", this word would be pronounced very slowly, or "drawn out", and intervals between the words would be lengthened. The opposite took place with the word "faster". These observations probably constitute the simplest manifestations of verbal control, i.e. the word controls a dimension of its own occurrence. Several studies were subsequently carried out to investigate the control of verbal behavior over a conceptually "simple" nonverbal response, namely a lever-press. First, it was observed that the rate of verbal output would control rate of nonverbal responding. Secondly, it was observed that content of a verbal response would control latency and rate of a nonverbal response. For example, if the word "faster" was emitted by $S$ before his depression of the lever, the latency of the latter response would be shorter than the latency of the nonverbal response after $S$ emitted the word "slower". The control exerted by the "meaning" of the verbal response appears age-related as it was not observed in children below ages five to seven.

Of more direct relevance to clinical psychology are two studies involving verbal control over broader, and socially more meaningful, nonverbal behaviors. One of these,[3] dealing with symbolic aggressive behavior, gave evidence for an increase in aggressive nonverbal behavior following reinforcement of aggressive verbal behavior. In other words, some control of nonverbal aggressive behavior was achieved by manipulating verbal aggressive behavior. The other study[5] will be presented in more detail to illustrate some of the methods and procedures employed in most of these studies. The previous studies had dealt with verbal control over nonverbal behavior in a laboratory setting. This study investigated the possibility of observing control over nonverbal behavior in a situation outside the laboratory, i.e. in the child's day-to-day life. Eating behavior was selected as a nonverbal behavior that was common, significant and easily quantified.

Amounts consumed of four foods were recorded for each child in two groups of children during their morning snack in Nursery School. One week to two months after the initiation of these recordings, ten children were randomly selected for repeated sessions of verbal conditioning. The conditioning occurred from 5 to 30 min before their snack, and took place in two laboratories, one of which was located in a building some distance away from the one which housed the Nursery School. $S$s were brought to the laboratories individually and introduced to a mechanized puppet built into a stage.[1] $E$ could control various actions of the puppet from an adjoining room without being observed by $S$. During $S$'s conversation with the puppet, two kinds of reinforcement operations upon his verbal behavior about food would take place. When $S$ had emitted the name of the food that $E$ had decided to reinforce, the puppet's hand would press down a miniature lever and thereby dispense a trinket to $S$. The puppet would at the same time say: "Good", "That's fine", or "O.K.". The second kind of reinforcement operation upon the verbal behavior about the food would be initiated by the puppet stating: "Sometimes this light in here goes off. Please put it back on by saying the name of a snack." The light (in the puppet's stage) would then go off, and the puppet's head would droop forward to assume an inattentive position. As soon as $S$ emitted the appropriate food-term, the light would be turned on, the puppet's head would raise and he would state emphatically: "Oh thank you, honey, that was so good of you. I'd rather talk with you than sit here in the dark." The session with the puppet lasted about 15 min. Altogether $S$ received 23 pairings of the response, stating the food-term, with positive reinforcement. The reinforced food-term became differentiated (other food-terms occurred with decreasing frequency) and its latencies shortened.

The data give evidence that when positive reinforcement is associated with the verbal response denoting a food, the amount consumed of that food increases. Food intakes on the days of the verbal conditionings were higher than intakes on days preceeding the conditioning. There was considerable variability among $S$s in the extent to which the reinforcement of the verbal behavior controlled their food intakes. Some $S$s did not seem responsive, while others had their maximal intakes on days of the verbal conditioning. One $S$'s intake is presented in Fig. 1 for illustrative purposes. The figure gives her percentage intake of celery. She was seen for verbal conditioning on 25 January, 7 and 20 February. Her intake shows the effect of the verbal conditioning more clearly than other $S$s. Informal observations on $S$s during snack time showed that some $S$s would talk about their behavior regarding the manipulated food on the days of the verbal conditioning. For example, one $S$, on the day she was reinforced for "carrots", commented upon receiving her snack that she liked carrots (she had never eaten more than four grams in school) and that she would eat some. Her intake on that day was ten grams. During snack periods on verbal conditioning days she was overheard repeating, "Yum-yum. What's up Doc?" The phrase is identified with Bugs Bunny, the cartoon character.

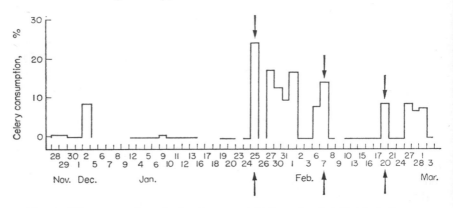

FIG. 1. $S$3's consumption of celery in per cent ($100 \times$ celery/total intake). She was positively reinforced for the word "celery" on 25 January, 7 and 20 February. Reinforcement days are indicated by arrows.

In summary, these studies show that relatively broad classes of operant nonverbal behavior can be controlled by operations upon a peron's verbal behavior. The research raises many questions, some of which are introduced within the conceptual framework that follows.

## CONCEPTUAL FRAMEWORK

Conceptual formulations designed to cover prior empirical findings on the relationship between verbal and nonverbal behavior have focused on cue-properties generated by the verbal response. All mediational hypotheses assume that cue-properties of the (hypothetical) verbal response provide the "connecting link" to the nonverbal behaviors. The verbal response, in becoming associated with an existing stimulus input, alters this input by the new stimuli this response generates. By training different kinds of verbal responses to the same original stimulus situation, changes can be observed in the discrimination-generalization behavior of the person.

In everyday life the two behaviors occur together in such ways as to suggest a number of interactions beyond those postulated for acquired discrimination and generalization. Some of these interactions have been presented in an earlier paper.[3] It might be of interest to examine two of these interactions in relationship to clinical psychology.

One conception of verbal—nonverbal interaction attributes to the verbal behavior a "directing" influence upon nonverbal behavior. This formulation presupposes that in the history of the person certain verbal and nonverbal behaviors have occurred together in such a manner that the verbal response becomes a discriminative stimulus for the nonverbal response. There are numerous historical contingencies which could bring about such control. Parents exert considerable effort in gaining verbal control over their children's behavior. When the child then emits these verbal behaviors himself, the stimulus properties of these responses, by generalization with the parent's responses, regulate his concurrent or subsequent behavior. Frequently children can be observed giving themselves instructions by imitating their parent's verbalization. Also the child might be more likely to obtain reinforcement for "doing what he is saying" than for behaving in an opposite manner or not carrying through with any actions. The acquisition of language "meanings" or "understandings" is probably based on similar reinforcement experiences. It is possible also that the sufficient conditions for verbal control may be based on contingencies lying within the person himself. It seems likely that nonverbal behavior which has been preceded by the person's own verbal behavior (or some hypothesized facsimile thereof, such as "implicit speech" or "thought") in the form of planning, rehearsal, etc., is more likely to lead to reinforcement than if this was not the case.

Because of such experiences some control over a person's nonverbal behavior should be obtained by manipulating his verbal behavior. Obviously, the control would vary from one person to another, and depend on his specific history with respect to these interactions. The psychopathic personality is probably one where little verbal control is observed. The clinical observations on "isolation" refers, in part, to the failure of language to elicit nonverbal (primarily respondent) behavior. It is more common, however, to observe a "failure" of discrimination in the other direction. The person is afraid that he would emit the nonverbal behavior if he were to talk about it. An excessive amount of control by verbal over nonverbal behavior becomes particularly noticeable in regard to certain schizophrenic or psychotic states. Many of these people will carry out elaborate conversations in the absence of a (physical) social audience, i.e. their verbal behavior is not under social control. At the same time they will engage in nonverbal interpersonal behavior, such as gestures, grimaces, and aggressions. Similar behaviors occasionally can be observed in children. Sometimes such behaviors are seen in normal adults, for example, when they gesture, smile and nod while engaged in a telephone conversation and when "talking to themselves". Instances of such behaviors are referred to as "forgetfulness" in normals, while in children and sick people they are used as descriptions of "word magic", and may in some instances be employed as indicators of inferred "hallucinatory activity", e.g. "visual hallucinations". It is not too difficult to conceptualize such excessive control in children; one could argue that they have not fully acquired discrimination of the situations in which it is appropriate to engage in interpersonal behaviors. In cases of psychosis one is probably confronted with a loss of an acquired discrimination, perhaps on the basis of disruptive respondent behavior, or a failure of society to continually reinforce appropriate social behavior. In any case, it seems premature to postulate "visual hallucinations" as the independent variable of this behavior without first exploring the more testable hypothesis of verbal control.

The second kind of verbal—nonverbal interaction which is particularly relevant to clinical psychology deals with the reinforcing stimuli held in common by the two behaviors. The common reinforcers might be primary (e.g. tension reduction) as well as secondary (e.g. other forms of self-stimulation). Frequently it appears that in everyday life verbal behavior achieves consequences similar to those of nonverbal behavior. Both behaviors may achieve the removal, or possession, of another person. Christian-ethical values (e.g. the sixth Commandment) and other cultural variables contribute to the communality of consequences. To the extent that the two response systems have reinforcing stimuli in common, it would be unlikely that an operation upon one system would not also change characteristics of responding in the other system. Both an increase and a decrease could be brought about in nonverbal responding depending upon the operations on the verbal response. For example, one could bring about a "sensitization" for a reinforcer by presenting it briefly to the verbal mode of responding. This sensitization should bring about a subsequent increase in nonverbal responding for that reinforcer. It should also be possible to "satiate" the organism on the common reinforcer by presenting it amply for the one mode of responding, whereupon one would observe a subsequent decrease in responding for that reinforcer by the other mode of responding.

Reference is frequently made in psychoanalytic writings to a "substitution" of verbal for nonverbal behavior. A common reinforcer (primary or secondary) seems implied in these statements. Substitute verbal behavior has been termed "sexualization" of speech, "pleasurable (anal) playing with words", etc. Reports are given of patients who experience pleasurable erotic sensations from talking. The contexts within which "magical" words are discussed imply partially that a potent reinforcing consequence is available, which ordinarily ("realistically") would be forthcoming only in the presence of nonverbal behavior. For example, the patient may be reluctant to emit certain verbal behaviors on the basis that these might disturb the physical world or seriously injure his therapist.

In so far as the two behaviors have reinforcing stimuli in common, it would be possible for verbal behavior to replace nonverbal behavior, by extinction of the latter, if the reinforcer which maintained the nonverbal response was consummated by verbal behavior. Perhaps the nonverbal "inactivity" of the obsessive is an example of such a state of affairs. It seems that "wish-fulfilling" daydreaming might similarly be behavior strengthened and maintained by a potent secondary reinforcer, mostly derived from social events. The elicitation of respondent behavior appropriate to a social event, independent of the social physical input, illustrates this notion. Wish-fulfilling daydreaming could then replace nonverbal interpersonal behavior if it enabled a relatively constant state of satiation for the common reinforcer.

The possibility of reducing nonverbal behavior by frequent and intensive expression of verbal behavior had been long recognized in clinical psychology. The process has usually been referred to a cathartic expression. It is in this context (of common secondary reinforcers) that one can obtain an empirical conception for the operation of catharsis.

## SUMMARY

This paper presented some evidence from experimentally-controlled studies to the effect that control over a person's nonverbal operant (instrumental) behavior can be obtained by manipulations of his verbal behavior. The studies were carried out within a conceptual framework which considers the interaction between verbal and nonverbal behavior to be an interaction between two operants. Some clinical implications of these interactions were discussed.

## REFERENCES

1. BAER, D. M. A technique of social reinforcement for the study of child behavior: 1. Behavior avoiding reinforcement withdrawal, *Child Developm.* (In press.)
2. DOLLARD, JOHN and MILLER, N. E. (1950) *Personality and psychotherapy*, McGraw-Hill.
3. LOVAAS, O. I. (1961) Interaction between verbal and nonverbal behavior, *Child Developm.* 32, 329–336.
4. LOVAAS, O. I. (1961) Cue properties of words: The control of operant responding by rate and content of verbal operants. Paper read at *WPA*, Seattle, June.
5. LOVAAS, O. I. (1961) The control of food-intake in children by reinforcement of relevant verbal behavior. Paper read at *AAAS*, Denver, December.

# Effect of Withdrawal of Positive Reinforcement
# on an Extinguishing Response in Young Children*†

DONALD M. BAER§

*University of Washington*

PUNISHMENT may be defined systematically in either of two ways: (a) as the presentation of a negative reinforcer for a response or (b) as the removal of a positive reinforcer for a response.[9] The first of these methods has seen extensive study in lower organisms.[4, 8] The second has been subject to a certain amount of discussion in psychoanalytic terminology ("loss of love"), but has seen very little experimental investigation in any species. There are only three exceptions apparent to this statement. Ferster[5] has used a withdrawal procedure ("time out") in studies with lower animals; Brackbill and O'Hare[3] have used it as a punishment technique in facilitating discrimination in young children; and Lewis[6] has used it to set up schedules of reinforcement in young children.

Yet the withdrawal of positive reinforcement as a punishing technique could prove a very significant process in the reinforcement history of the child. Punishment through the presentation of negative reinforcement is typically claimed to be ineffective in weakening responses. Estes concluded that "... a response cannot be eliminated from an organism's repertoire more rapidly with the aid of punishment than without it".[4] Sears *et al.* claim that punitiveness in a parent ".... is ineffectual over the long term as a technique for eliminating the kind of behavior toward which it is directed".[7] But they also point out that half of the parents they interviewed use punishment at least moderately often and claim that spanking does some good. In the case of the child, it will often prove impossible to present

* This article is reprinted with the permission of the author and editor from *Child Developm.* **32**, 67–74 (1961).

† The research reported herein was supported in whole by Public Health Service grant M-2208 (C1), United States Department of Health, Education, and Welfare, to whom the author is indebted. Three other debts must be acknowledged: to Mrs. Josephine Reed, director of the Seattle Day Nursery Association Schools, for gracious and generous cooperation; to Mrs. Anne Pilisdorf for her reliable and intelligent performance as *A*; and to Dr. Sidney Bijou for his continuing support, encouragement, and advice.

§ Gatzert Institute of Child Development, Department of Psychology, University of Washington, Seattle 5.

a negative reinforcer without simultaneously withdrawing positive reinforcers. The parent who slaps or spanks almost inevitably will withdraw approval and the more obvious tokens of affection at the same time. Perhaps it is this withdrawal of reinforcement which is the significant technique here.

In any case, experimental studies of the punishing effect of the withdrawal of positive reinforcement in the child should prove of systematic and practical value. The present study was designed to yield data on the effectiveness of reinforcement withdrawal for the sole purpose of weakening a response in a situation where a competitive response is not deliberately strengthened through positive reinforcement.

## METHOD

### Subjects

Children from a day care center of the Seattle Day Nursery Association were used. All Ss were experimentally naive. At the outset of the experiment, 16 Ss were divided randomly into two groups, Punishment and Control. During the course of the experiment, which required that each child participate on five different sessions, six Ss were lost, usually to their family vacation, occasionally to illness, and in one case, to withdrawal of the child from the school. There remained 10 Ss, five in each group. The average age of the Punishment group was 6–10, and of the Control group, 6–9. All Ss were within the normal range of intelligence and represented lower income groups.

### Apparatus

The entire experiment was conducted in a mobile laboratory built into a 19-foot house trailer,[2] which was parked inside the play yard of the school. The interior of the laboratory included a one-way observation booth for the experimenter and a playroom for the child. The playroom contained a small chair, two tables holding toys or apparatus, a screen on which could be projected cartoons, and a partitioned corner in which an accompanying adult (A) could sit, out of the child's sight but still present.

The experiment centered about three pieces of apparatus. The first of these was a translucent screen, on which the experimenter could project cartoons. The screen was mounted in the wall separating child and experimenter; the movie projector, a Busch "Cinesalesman", operated from the experimenter's side. The projector contained three cartoons on an "endless" reel of film and could present these in an uninterrupted sequence for an indefinite number of cycles. The cartoons were of the Castle Films Woody Woodpecker series (Woody Plays Santa Claus, The Hollywood Matador, and The Dizzy Acrobats); each was black and white, with sound, and lasted 7 min.

A second piece of apparatus was a white box, approximately one foot on a side, mounted on one of the tables such that $S$ could view cartoons and play with this "toy" at the same time. A bar projected from the front surface of the box. At the lower right side of the front surface was a slot from which peanuts could roll as a reinforcement for pressing the bar. Every bar press resulted in a mild buzz which lasted one second, but did not necessarily produce a peanut. A bar press could also result in a two-second interruption of any cartoon being viewed at the time, if the experimenter chose.

The third piece of apparatus was a commercial toy (Playskool) which was mounted on the other table. It consisted of a cage of sticks, inside of which a small ball could be made to jump up and down a devious route by flipping a small lever at the base of the toy. This toy was not within reach of $S$ as he sat viewing the cartoon.

## Procedure

$S$s were dealt with entirely by a young female adult, $A$. Before the experiment started, $A$ had been a constant member of the play group and was thoroughly familiar with the $S$s. Furthermore, she had told them that a trailer was coming and that all the $S$s would be allowed to enter and play games. This generated a great deal of enthusiasm.

Each $S$ was brought to the laboratory on five separate occasions by $A$. The first of these was to adapt the $S$ to the laboratory and acquaint him with the cartoons. $A$ would seat the $S$ in the correct place and retire to her corner. Then the cartoons would start, and all three would play without interruption. At the end of the third cartoon (i.e. after 21 min), the projector was stopped, and $A$ came out of her corner and took $S$ back to the play yard.

The second visit was to establish a learned response in each $S$. Prior to this visit, $A$ would ask $S$ if he would like to do something different that day. When $S$ entered the laboratory, $A$ then showed him the toy which could dispense peanuts, saying, "This is a peanut machine". The $S$ was seated by it (the same seat as visit 1), and $A$ retired to her corner. In very short order, $S$ would press the bar and receive a peanut. This started a series of bar presses, of which numbers 1, 2, 3, 5, 7, 10, 15, and 20 were reinforced with a peanut. Immediately after the twentieth response, as $S$ was eating the peanut, $A$ came out of her corner announcing, "That's all for today". They then left together before the child could respond further.

The third visit was to begin extinction of the learned response, punishing it as well in half of the $S$s. Prior to this visit, $A$ asked $S$ simply if he would like to come again. Inside the laboratory, $A$ seated $S$ in the same seat and retired to her corner. The cartoons were started immediately. $S$ was free to watch cartoons and to press the bar as he chose. For the five $S$s of the Punishment group, any bar press during this session would turn off the ongoing cartoons (picture and sound) for two seconds. For the five Control *S*s, the bar press had no such action. In either case, the bar press produced the usual buzz, but no peanuts at any time. At the end of the third cartoon the projector was turned off, but *A* remained in her corner for at least 2 min, saying nothing. This gave *S* an interval during which the bar might be pressed, and there were clearly no cartoons to be turned off. Almost every *S* requested to leave by two minutes after the end of the cartoons. In the case of early requests, *A* was instructed to delay until the 2 min had passed to give each child equal opportunity with the bar. Thus, the visit lasted 23 min.

The fourth visit was to allow *S* to show any spontaneous recovery of the learned response, without punishment. Prior to this visit, *A* asked the child if he would like to see the cartoons again. Inside the laboratory, *S* was seated in the usual seat, *A* retired to her corner, and the cartoon was started. *S* could press the bar if he chose, but on this occasion the bar press did not turn off the cartoon, nor did it result in any peanuts. It did produce a buzz as before. Because it was expected that spontaneous recovery would be slight in either group only one cartoon was shown. Again, *S* was kept for 2 min after the end of the cartoon. Thus, this visit lasted 9 min.

The fifth visit was to examine the strength of the learned response in a situation where punishment was impossible. Prior to this visit, *S* was asked simply if he wanted to come again. Inside, he was told that there would be no cartoons today, but that he could play with anything he wanted. *A* then retired, leaving *S* with only two objects capable of play: the peanut apparatus and the Playskool toy. The peanut machine buzzed but did nothing else when the bar was pressed. This session lasted 5 min, which is rather long for children thoroughly adapted to the laboratory, with only two simple toys to play with.

TABLE 1

*Sequence of experimental conditions for punishment and control subjects*

| Visit | Purpose | Number of cartoons | Consequence of bar press | |
|-------|---------|---------------------|-----------------|----------------|
|       |         |                     | Punishment group | Control group |
| 1 | Adaptation | 3 | bar not present | bar not present |
| 2 | Strengthen bar press | none | peanuts | peanuts |
| 3 | Extinction —session 1 | 3 | cartoon interruption | none |
| 4 | Extinction —session 2 | 1 | none | none |
| 5 | Extinction —session 3 | none | none | none |

In summary, then, $S$s were successively adapted to the laboratory and the cartoons, taught a bar pressing response, allowed to extinguish this response with or without punishment, and allowed to show any spontaneous recovery of this response, in situations where the means of punishment was present and absent. This sequence is summarized in Table 1. The interval between the first and second visits was seven days (plus or minus two).; between the second and third visit, three days (plus or minus one); between the third and fourth visit, five days (plus or minus one); and between the fourth and fifth visit, three days (plus or minus one). All experimentation was conducted during late afternoon hours.

## RESULTS

Recordings were made of the bar pressing response on a Gerbrands Harvard Cumulative recorder. Photographic facsimiles of these response curves are shown in Fig. 1. Session 1 in this figure refers to $S$'s third visit

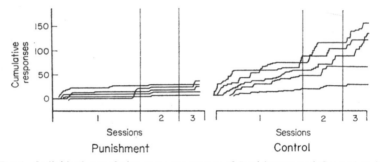

Fig. 1. Individual cumulative response curves of Punishment and Control $S$s during repeated sessions.

to the laboratory, during which the bar pressing response resulted in an interruption of the cartoon for Punishment $S$s and otherwise represents an extinction period for all $S$s. Session 2 refers to $S$'s fourth visit, during which one cartoon was seen without punishment. Session 3 refers to $S$'s last visit, during which he played freely with either the bar of the Playskool toy and no cartoons were shown.

It is apparent from Fig. 1 that the interruption of the cartoon serves to reduce sharply the number of extinction responses $S$s make to the bar. Furthermore, this reduction seems reasonably durable. During the last two minutes of session 1, Punishment $S$s show no particular tendency to increase responding, although there are no cartoons present, and hence they cannot be punished by their interruption. During session 2, where Control $S$s show considerable spontaneous recovery, Punishment $S$s make either one or two responses (which are unpunished) and then cease responding, nor do they respond during the 2 min after the cartoon ends. During session 3, Punishment $S$s direct their play to the Playskool toy rather to the bar far more than do Control $S$s.

These individual response curves are summarized in Fig. 2, which shows the mean number of bar presses made by each group during each session. Essentially the same picture emerges from a consideration of grouped data as from examination of individual curves.

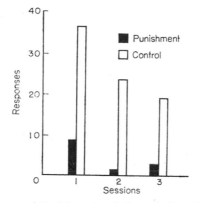

FIG. 2.  Mean responses of Punishment and Control Ss during repeated sessions.

The individual curves present a very clear case. However, there is one case of overlap between the two groups, and because of this an analysis of variance was performed on the data. The Punishment and Control Ss constitute two independent groups, and sessions 1, 2 and 3 represent repeated observations of these groups. Use of number of bar presses per session as a raw score is not justifiable because of the heterogeneity of variance between the two groups evident in Fig. 1. Consequently, a square root transformation was applied. The transformed data, subjected to Bartlett's test, yielded a $\chi^2$ of $5\cdot28\,(df = 5,\ 0\cdot30 < p < 0\cdot50)$. A summary of the analysis of variance of the transformed data is given in Table 2. Punishment and Control Ss are clearly distinct at the 0·01 level. The Sessions main effect is of no great

TABLE 2

*Summary of analysis of variance of responses during repeated sessions*

| Source | df | Mean Square | F | p |
|---|---|---|---|---|
| Subjects | 9 | | | |
|    Punishment | 1 | 71·10 | 11·83 | 0·01 |
|    Error | 8 | 6·01 | | |
| Within Subjects | 20 | | | |
|    Sessions | 2 | 11·00 | 10·78 | 0·01 |
|    Sessions × Punishment | 2 | 1·24 | | |
|    Error | 16 | 1·02 | | |
| Total | 29 | | | |

consequence, since response is bound to decrease during repeated extinction sessions, especially when the sessions are of successively shorter duration. The absence of any interaction between the Punishment groups and Sessions makes for a gratifyingly simple conclusion.

None of the Punishment Ss showed any obvious signs of emotionality during punishment. One S in this group, after making several (punished) responses during session 1, was seen to very carefully take hold of the bar, slowly press it down, and, as the cartoon went off, whip his hand away from the bar, saying, "Wow!" Apart from this, all Ss took the experiment with great equanimity.

## DISCUSSION

From the results obtained, it seems clear that the interruption of a cartoon which the child is viewing will serve very effectively as a punishing event: it will efficiently depress a recently strengthened response in the child's repertoire. The thesis that withdrawal of positive reinforcement is punishing is thereby strengthened, specifically for the case of the child. And it is tempting to wonder if the withdrawal of positive reinforcers may not possess punishing characteristics qualitatively different from the presentation of negative reinforcers.

An essential assumption here is that the cartoons are indeed positively reinforcing stimulation. Other research by the author with the same three cartoons indicated that they have a high and very uniform reinforcing value for children in this age range.[1] Testimony to this assumption is that almost any child will learn quickly to press a bar to turn the cartoons back on when they are turned off by the experimenter every few seconds.

It may be important to stress certain aspects of this experiment which could prove critical to its conclusions. One of these is the fact that the response weakened in this procedure is a weak one of short standing. Eight peanuts cannot be taken as a significant amount of reinforcement to a healthy child (who has had juice and cookies in school the same afternoon). These reinforcements, with the increasing ratio schedule on which they are delivered, are sufficient to set up a response strong enough to be studied and manipulated, clearly, but may not give the response much resemblance to other behavior of the child with more powerful and extensive histories of reinforcement.

Furthermore, in this study punishment has been effected in a very precise manner. Reinforcement was withdrawn immediately consequent to a response in a very consistent way. The fact that this procedure is effective may not guarantee that in a more typical situation, where punishment is offered to a child late, inconsistently, and perhaps incomprehensibly, the effect would be the same.

Finally, the effect of punishment in this study seems durable in terms of the duration of the study. But this is not a great deal of time. Possibly, given more time in the situation, Punishment $S$s would emit responses equal in number to those of Control $S$s. It seems more likely, though, that the $S$s would satiate with the entire situation before this would happen.

Apart from these qualifications to any widespread generalizations, the data give a clear picture of stimulus control in depressing a response in young children. The mechanism is best stated as the withdrawal of positive reinforcement. The technique used here would seem to be a fruitful one for further study of this problem in the laboratory.

## SUMMARY

Young children were taught to press a bar for peanuts. During later extinction of this response, five Punishment $S$s were punished by turning off a cartoon they were watching at the time for two seconds as a consequence of every response. This served to depress the response considerably, relative to five Control $S$s who were not punished for responding while watching the same cartoons. During later sessions, Control $S$s showed considerable spontaneous recovery of the response, and Punishment $S$s did not, even though no longer punished. It was concluded that the withdrawal of positive reinforcement is an effective technique of punishment, at least in situations like the experimental one.

## REFERENCES

1. BAER, D. M. (1960) Escape and avoidance response of preschool children to two schedules of reinforcement withdrawal, *J. Exp. anal. Behav.*, **3**, 155–159.
2. BIJOU, S. W. (1958) A child study laboratory on wheels, *Child Develpm.*, **29**, 425–427.
3. BRACKBILL, Y. and O'HARE, J. (1957) Discrimination learning in children as a function of reward and punishment. Paper read at Western Psychol. Ass., Eugene, Oregon.
4. ESTES, W. K. (1944) An experimental study of punishment, *Psychol. Monogr.*, **57**, 1–40.
5. FERSTER, C. B. (1958) Control of behavior in chimpanzees and pigeons by time out from positive reinforcement, *Psychol. Monogr.*, **72**, 1–38.
6. LEWIS, D. J. (1952) Partial reinforcement in a gambling situation, *J. Exp. Psychol.*, **43**, 447–450.
7. SEARS, R. R., MACCOBY, E. E. and LEVIN, H. (1957) *Patterns of child rearing*, Row, Peterson.
8. SKINNER, B. F. (1938) *The behavior of organisms*, Appleton-Century-Crofts.
9. SKINNER, B. F. (1953) *Science and human behavior*, Macmillan.

# Interaction Between Verbal and Nonverbal Behavior *†

O. IVAR LOVAAS §**

*University of Washington*

EXPERIMENTAL investigations on the relation between verbal and non-verbal behavior date back as far as Lehmann's study[5] on the effect of verbal labels upon discrimination. Since then, research has been oriented around discrimination learning, generalization, transfer, transposition, problem solving, etc. Thus, previous research on the relation between verbal and nonverbal behavior has been frequently tied in with traditional areas of psychological inquiry where most often the nonverbal behavior has been employed as an index of the effect of verbal behavior on a hypothesized basic process, such as discrimination. The conceptual formulations designed to cover the empirical findings have been primarily concerned with the cue properties (or discriminative stimulus properties) of the two kinds of behavior—the two behaviors have been thought to interact in so far as one provides discriminative stimuli for the other. Esper states this interaction in a broad formulation: "the stimuli associated with each type of response are among the conditioned elicitors of the other . . .".[2] A similar paradigm is employed by Kurtz and Hovland[4] to deal with the more specific problem of the effect of verbal behavior on discrimination; they apparently conceive of the effect as due to attending behavior elicited by the verbal response. Miller's[7] formulations on acquired equivalence and distinctiveness of cues similarly rely on the cue properties of the verbal behavior in effecting a change in nonverbal behavior. Indeed, all mediational hypotheses assume that it is the cue properties of the (hypothetical) verbal response that provide the "connecting link" to other behaviors.

In so far as one is concerned with the effect of verbal behavior on specific problems such as discrimination learning and concept formation, one can

\* This article is reprinted with the permission of the author and editor from *Child Develpm.* **32**, 329–336 (1961).

† This study was supported by grant M-2208 from the National Institute of Health, United States Public Health Service.

§ Gatzert Institute of Child Development, Department of Psychology, University of Washington, Seattle 5.

\*\* The author expresses his gratitude to Professors Donald M. Baer and Sidney W. Bijou for their assistance, particularly on the conceptual aspects in this study. He is also grateful for the cooperation of the staff of the Nursery School, Gatzert Institute of Child Development.

perhaps adequately conceptualize the relations observed by considering only the stimulus properties of the verbal behavior. It is apparent that in so doing one limits oneself to only one of several possible interactions between the two behaviors. It is, for example, conceivable that the two classes of behavior could interact on the basis of having common reinforcing stimuli, common emotional states which influence either behavior, etc. An analysis in these terms becomes more appropriate when one deals with broader classes of verbal and nonverbal behavior, for example, if one deals with social behavior, as in the study to be reported.

The purpose of the present study was to determine the effect of strengthening one class of verbal responses on a class of nonverbal responses. A bar-pressing response reinforced by aggressive doll action was observed immediately after a verbal conditioning session during which one group of children was reinforced for emitting aggressive verbal responses and the other group was reinforced for emitting nonaggressive verbal responses.

## METHOD

### Apparatus and Subjects

The research was conducted in the laboratory of the Gatzert Institute of Child Development. One room, the observation room, was equipped with one-way mirrors and sound equipment. The E (experimenter) could present the various experimental treatments from this room without being observed by S (subject). The other room, the "playroom", contained the apparatus or toys with which S would play and a partition behind which A (an adult assistant) could sit.

There were three pieces of apparatus in the playroom. Two of these, the doll apparatus and the ball-toy, have been described earlier.[6] Briefly, the doll apparatus, or "striking dolls", was arranged so that each depression of a lever in the box on which the dolls were placed would make one doll strike the other on the head with a stick. The ball-toy consisted of a ball within a cagelike structure; the ball could be flipped up and down inside the cage by depression of a lever at the base of the cage. Depression of these levers also activated electric counters. The two were placed on a table, enabling S to operate both simultaneously.

The third piece of apparatus was a "talk-box", a 15 by 12 by 12 inch wooden box, placed on a table at the opposite wall from the table containing the dolls and the ball-toy. A microphone, inside the talk-box, was wired into the observation room and enabled recording of S's verbalizations on a Gray Audograph recorder. Two dolls were fastened in a sitting position on top of the box. These dolls originally were similar in appearance, but one, "the bad doll," had been made very dirty; the other doll, "the good doll", was neat and clean. Reinforcement, in the form of small trinkets, could be delivered automatically to S through a chute emptying into a small tray on the side of the talk-box.

The Ss were children from the Institute's Nursery School. They were above average in intelligence.[1] Nineteen children, age 3–5 to 4–7, were randomly selected from this group (but Ss known to be uncooperative were not asked). Five Ss were eliminated during the experiment, two because they expressed definite desire to leave, two others because they failed to respond to the verbal conditioning procedure (one could not be differentially conditioned, the other did not respond verbally at all), the fifth one because he had an identical ball-toy at home. The remaining 14 Ss had experiences as Ss in other experiments, but had no previous contact with the apparatus employed in this study. The Ss were seen in the morning while they were engaged in free play.

### Procedure

A, a female adult who had visited the nursery prior to the experimental run and acquainted herself with the children, invited S to the playroom to "play some games". S was first made briefly acquainted with the playroom and then introduced to the striking dolls and the ball-toy. A pressed the lever on the dolls once and said, "When you press this bar (demonstrates) this (pointing) will happen. Now you do it (S is induced to press the lever five times). Now look here (pointing to ball-toy), when you press this lever (demonstrates) this (pointing) will happen. Now you do it (S is induced to press the lever five times). Now you play with the toys while I sit in my chair." S received a 3-min period of play, timed from the S's initial depression of either lever. This period constituted the pre-experimental or operant level of behavior for the striking dolls and the ball-toy.

A returned on signal by E and placed the dolls and the ball-toy out of S's view. She then seated him in front of the talk-box and said, "This is a talk-box; when you talk to this box, it will give you toys right here (points to reinforcement tray). Now see here are two dolls. This (pointing) is the good doll; this (pointing) is the bad doll. Say 'good doll' (if necessary coaches S to say, 'good doll'; this response is reinforced). See what you got; this is your toy; you can keep it. Now say, 'bad doll' (coaching if necessary; this response is also reinforced). See what the box gave you; this is your toy to keep. Now you sit here and tell the box all about the dolls; tell the box what is going to happen to the dolls." The dolls were included to give S discriminative stimuli for emitting aggressive or nonaggressive verbal responses. Additional instructions were needed for about one-fourth of the S equally distributed between the groups. If, after 2 min and again after 4 min, S had made no response that could be reinforced, A told him from behind her screen: "Say, 'good doll' (S is reinforced for saying this); now say, 'bad doll' (also reinforced); now talk about the dolls."

The $S$s were divided into two groups of seven each. One group was reinforced for aggressive verbal behavior (AV-group), the other for verbal behavior other than aggressive (NAV-group). The criterion used for deciding whether a verbal response was aggressive or not was whether it was derogatory to the dolls or denoted a wish on the part of the child to damage or hurt the dolls. In fact, the only responses the AV-group emitted that fulfilled this criterion were: "bad doll," "dirty doll," and "doll should be spanked."

The $S$s from the AV-group and the NAV-group were matched in pairs on sex, age, number of reinforcements, and length of the verbal conditioning period. The magnitudes of the last two variables were determined by the AV-member of each pair who invariably was run first.

The verbal conditioning procedure necessitated initially reinforcing both aggressive and nonaggressive verbal responses (e.g. "good doll" and "bad doll") for both the NAV- and AV-groups to produce a high rate of verbal responding. A high rate of responding was defined as at least 12 reinforceable verbal responses within any 2-min period. A reinforceable verbal response was any word, phrase, or sentence. The criterion of high rate was reached from 2 to 8 minutes after initiation of the verbal conditioning period. Once the high rate was reached, the AV-group became selectively reinforced for aggressive verbal responses while the NAV-group was reinforced for verbal responses other than aggressive ones. In the NAV-group, affectionate responses were reinforced as little as possible. If "good doll" reached a high rate, reinforcement was withheld in order to extinguish this response and produce other verbal responses. This condition was introduced to insure that any difference in subsequent play behavior between the two groups would not be a function of a contrast between "aggressive" and "friendly" verbal responding, but rather between aggressive and nonaggressive responding ("friendly" verbal responses could be incompatible with subsequent aggressive behavior, hence the data would be less clear than otherwise).

The length of the conditioning period was determined by $S$ in the AV-group. The period was terminated after 6 min once a high rate of aggressive verbal responses was established (not less than 20 reinforceable aggressive verbal responses in a 3-min period). Thus, the conditioning period lasted anywhere from 6 to 14 min.

When the conditioning period was terminated, $A$ told $S$ that the "talk-box" did not work any more, helped him put his trinkets in a paper bag, and told him: "I will keep these toys for you while you play some more with this (pointing to the striking dolls) and this (pointing to the ball-toy) for just a few minutes more." The child was then allowed to play with the striking dolls and ball-toy for a period of 4 min. At the end of the 4-min period, $A$ came out, gave $S$ a thank you and his trinkets, and accompanied him back to his nursery school group.

*A* interacted with *S* in a matter-of-fact manner. She remained behind her partition except when she introduced apparatus. She did not interact with him unless he came over to her chair, at which point she said: "I'll sit here and you be over there for a few minutes more."

## RESULTS AND DISCUSSION

Changes in the verbal behavior as a function of the verbal conditioning are presented in Fig. 1. Number of aggressive and nonaggressive verbal responses was summed and averaged over successive 2-min periods for the

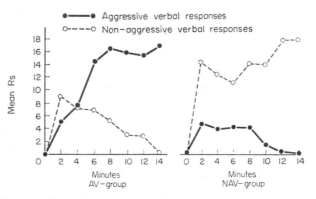

FIG. 1. Mean number of aggressive and nonaggressive verbal responses over successive 2-min periods in the verbal conditioning period. Aggressive verbal conditioning group presented separately from the nonaggressive verbal conditioning group.

various *S*s; the average aggressive and nonaggressive verbal responses for each group are presented in Fig. 1. Since some *S*s reached the criterion of adequate verbal conditioning after 6 min, the last 2 min intervals give the verbal responding of decreasing numbers of *S*s. Thus, Fig. 1 is only an approximate presentation of the changes in verbal behavior. The figure indicates that both objectives of the verbal conditioning were affected: first, there is an initial increase in rate of responding, and secondly, there is subsequent differentiation of aggressive and nonaggressive verbal responses. It should be noted that these *S*s emitted a very limited range of verbal responses. This was particularly true of the AV-group which in general was limited to "bad doll" or "dirty doll".

The effect of the verbal conditioning on the subsequent play behavior was calculated by taking the total number of responses for each *S* on the striking dolls and the ball-toy and converting this into the following score: 100 × total responses on the dolls/total responses on dolls and ball. This percentage gives the relative amount of aggressive play behavior and was calculated for each *S* both before and after the verbal conditioning procedure. The group means are presented in Table 1. As can be observed, the level of aggressive responding prior to the verbal conditioning is identical for the two groups. There is a significantly higher proportion of aggressive play behavior following the verbal conditioning period for the AV-group $S$s who were conditioned to make aggressive verbal responses ($t = 2.326$, $df = 12$, $p < 0.05$, two-tailed test). In other words, some control of nonverbal aggressive behavior was achieved by manipulating the children's verbal aggressive behavior.

TABLE 1

*Mean proportion of aggressive responding before and after verbal conditioning*

|  | Before verbal conditoning | After verbal conditioning |
|---|---|---|
| Aggressive conditioning | 55·2 | 78·4 |
| Nonaggressive conditioning | 55·4 | 59·4 |

NOTE.—Proportion = 100 × total Rs on doll / total Rs on doll + ball.

In evaluating these results, four possibilities should be considered. First of all, the aggressive verbal response, since it is reinforced and not punished, becomes a discriminative stimulus which marks the occasion when nonverbal aggressive behavior will be reinforced, or at least not punished. In popular terms, the aggressive verbal behavior provides a "green light" for subsequent aggressive nonverbal responding.

The second interpretation to be considered deals with the reinforcing stimuli held in common by the verbal aggressive and the nonverbal aggressive behavior. The common reinforcing stimuli may be primary (e.g. tension reduction) as well as secondary (e.g. other forms of self-stimulation). Frequently it appears that in everyday life verbal behavior achieves consequences similar to those of nonverbal behaviors (e.g. both may achieve the removal of some noxiously stimulating person); hence one would expect them also to have numerous secondary reinforcers in common. To the extent that the two response systems have reinforcing stimuli in common, it would be unlikely that an operation upon one system would not also change characteristics of responding in the other system. Both an increase and a decrease could be brought about in subsequent aggressive nonverbal behavior depending upon the operations on the verbal aggressive behavior. For example, one should be able to bring about a "sensitization" for aggressive reinforcers by presenting these briefly to the verbal mode of responding. This sensitization should bring about a subsequent increase in nonverbal responding for that reinforcer. This may well account for the effect observed in the present study. Insofar as the reinforcing stimuli are common between the two response systems, it also should be possible to "satiate" the organism on the reinforcer by presenting it amply for the one mode of responding, whereupon one would observe a subsequent decrease in responding for that reinforcer by the other mode of responding. The possibility of reducing nonverbal aggressive behavior by providing frequent and intensive verbal aggressive expression has been long recognized in clinical psychology, usually referred to by such terms as "cathartic expression". There is experimental evidence which supports this notion; for example, Feshbach[3] observed a decrease in aggressive behavior immediately following the writing of aggressive TAT stories.

The third manner in which verbal and nonverbal behavior may be seen to interact attributes to the verbal behavior a "directing" influence upon nonverbal behavior. This formulation presupposes that in the history of the person certain verbal and nonverbal behaviors have occurred together in such a manner that the verbal response becomes a discriminative stimulus for the nonverbal behavior.* This formulation may lead one to expect that one can vary the amount of generalization from verbal to nonverbal behavior by varying the degree to which the verbal behavior denotes the nonverbal behavior. For example, one would be led to expect more generalization than was observed in this study if the children in the AV-group had been reinforced for "doll should be spanked". This hypothesis is supported by observation of the behavior of some of the $S$s in the NAV-group. For example, one of these $S$s was reinforced for "what shall I say?" As this response increased in frequency with reinforcements, $S$ got up from his chair and walked toward $A$ to address his question to her.

Fourth and lastly, it is assumed that aggressive behavior has been associated with aversive stimuli in the past history of the child. It is conceivable that the occurrence of the verbal aggressive response allows for some extinction of the conditioned aversive stimuli associated with that response and that the effect of this extinction generalizes to the nonverbal response. If conditioned aversive stimuli suppress or inhibit aggressive responding, the effect to be expected would be an increase in subsequent nonverbal aggressive responding. In view of the resistance of aversive stimuli to extinction, this relationship is perhaps the least likely explanation of the present data.

## SUMMARY

The purpose of the present research was to determine the effect of strengthening one class of responses on another. A bar-pressing response reinforced by aggressive doll action was observed immediately after the children had undergone a verbal conditioning session during which one

---

* Informal observation on the $S$s while they were being verbally conditioned further confirms that such behavior was being emitted; many $S$s in the AV-group raised their voices and became quite loud, thrashed around, pounded the table, etc.

group of children was reinforced for emitting aggressive verbal responses; the other group was reinforced for nonaggressive verbal responses. The results of the study gave evidence for an increase in aggressive nonverbal behavior following reinforcement of aggressive verbal behavior. In other words, some control of nonverbal aggressive behavior was achieved by manipulating verbal aggressive behavior.

In evaluating these results, four possibilities should be considered: (a) the verbal aggressive behavior becomes a discriminative stimulus which marks the occasion when nonverbal aggressive behavior will be reinforced or at least not punished; (b) To the extent that the two response systems have reinforcing stimuli in common, operating upon one system might also change characteristics of responding for these stimuli by the other system (e.g. by sensitization of or satiation for the common reinforcer); (c) The verbal response has a "directing" influence on the nonverbal response since it functions as a discriminative stimulus for that response; (d) Occurrence of the verbal aggressive response allows for some extinction of the conditioned aversive stimuli associated with that response; the effect of this extinction generalizes to the nonverbal response and thereby reduces the amount of aversive stimuli inhibiting the nonverbal aggressive responding.

## REFERENCES

1. BIJOU, S. W. (1957) Patterns of reinforcement and resistance to extinction in young children, *Child Develpm.*, **28**, 47–54.
2. ESPER, E. A, (1935) Language. In C. MURCHISON (Ed.), *A handbook of social psychology*, Clark Univer. Press, Pp. 417–460.
3. FESHBACH, S. (1955) The drive-reducing function of fantasy behavior, *J. Abnorm. Soc. Psychol.*, **50**, 3–11.
4. KURTZ, K. H. and HOVLAND, C. I. (1953) The effect of verbalization during observation of stimulus objects upon accuracy of recognition and recall, *J. Exp. Psychol.*, **45**, 157–164.
5. LEHMANN, A. (1888) Über Wiedererkennen, *Phil. Stud.*, **5**, 96–156.
6. LOVAAS, O. I. (1961) Effect of exposure to symbolic aggression on aggressive behavior, *Child Develpm.*, **32**, 37–44.
7. MILLER, N. E. (1948) Theory and experiment relating psychoanalytic displacement to stimulus-response generalization, *J. Abnorm. Soc. Psychol.*, **43**, 173–176.

# Rapid Development of Multiple-schedule Performances with Retarded Children*

SIDNEY W. BIJOU and ROBERT ORLANDO

*University of Washington*

PROBLEMS encountered in the process of modifying simple operant behavior of a retarded *S* from what is observed at the beginning of a study to that required by a multiple schedule have two major implications. One bears on an experimental analysis of individual differences; the other, on the development of techniques for the efficient establishment of complex-schedule performances.

When a child enters an experimental situation, receives instructions, and sets about to perform the tasks, the behavior displayed is, of course, a function of the current situation and interactions with similar situations in the *S*'s history. The influences of such antecedents may be conceptualized as effects of independent variables (e.g. kinds of reinforcers received, typical schedules, and frequency of punishment contingencies), and of differences in behavioral processes (e.g. rate of change in operant conditioning) (Skinner, 1953). Such effects may be quantified by psychometric devices such as inventories of traits and abilities, or by experimental procedures. The latter, which involve observation of the successive changes in behavior required to perform an experimental task to criterion, may be approached in two ways. One consists of presenting the task and recording time (and "errors"). This procedure is often abortive. If the task is complex, even slightly so, learning may take an unreasonable length of time, or may not be achieved at all. The other approach involves presenting *S* with a series of graded tasks and reinforcing responses that approximate more and more the final performance required. The procedure is designed so that the *S* sets the pace; that is, each response class is strengthened to criterion before the next task is introduced.

This alternative has several advantages. Most important, it yields not only measures in terms of time, but also an account of the strengthening and

* This article is reprinted with the permission of the authors and the editor from *J. Exper. Anal. Behav.* **4**, 7–16 (1961).

This investigation was supported by a research grant (M-2232) from the National Institute of Mental Health, Public Health Service.

The authors are grateful to Russell M. Tyler and David A. Marshall, Research Assistants, for their fine work in conducting many of the individual sessions.

weaking operations necessary to arrive at final performance. Experimental studies of retarded children in which the second procedure is being used are currently in progress.

Studying initial behavior is especially pertinent from a technique point of view, particularly for investigations on human *S*s using individual base lines. At the current stage of our knowledge of operant procedures with humans, many *E*s spend considerable time and effort exploring ways of establishing a schedule or multiple-schedules. The objective of this paper is to describe and illustrate a method that has proven satisfactory for the rapid establishment of multiple-schedule performance in a single-response, free-operant, experimental situation with retarded subjects. A multiple-schedule has been described as one ". . . in which reinforcement is programmed by two or more schedules alternating, usually at random. Each schedule is accompanied by a different stimulus, which is present as long as the schedule is in force" (Ferster and Skinner, 1957, p. 7). The multiple-schedules discussed here have *two* components (one always involving extinction), with the accompanying discriminative stimuli presented in *regular* alternation.

Initial attempts in this laboratory to establish discriminated-operant base lines in children (Bijou, in press) started with principles outlined for infrahuman *S*s (Keller and Schoenfeld, 1950) and "hand-shaping" techniques popular as classroom demonstrations and developed most fully in animal training (Breland and Breland, 1951). Satisfactory two-component base-line performances were obtained, but only after an investment of seven or more weekly sessions. The technique reported here is the result of subsequent studies in which progressively refined procedures were explored in retarded children. Data to be presented are illustrations of the technique.

The steps in training to a multiple-schedule are described in detail, not because they are expected to be followed as given, but because this is a convenient way of giving an account of the technique. Investigators probably will find it necessary to modify the steps in accordance with the nature of their subjects, the type of multiple-schedules desired, and variations in the experimental situations.

## THE LABORATORY SITUATION

The experimental setting is a well-illuminated room, 10 by 8 ft, with a standard table and two chairs. A wooden box approximately 12 by 12 by 16 in. is on the table. A wooden chute with tray attached for presenting reinforcers is at the left of the box. The upper end of the chute extends through an opening in the wall separating the experimental and control rooms. On the front panel of the box are a red jewel light in the upper left-hand side, a blue jewel light in the upper right-hand side, and a sturdy metal lever (a handle grip for the squeezer of an O'Cedar sponge mop) protruding from a rectangular opening in the center. Pressing the lever down is always accompanied by a relay click and occasionally by a reinforcer dispensed by a Gerbands Universal Feeder in the control room. Reinforcers are: M & M's, Hersheyettes, candy corn, Payroll mint coins, and Sixlets. These candies were selected because they are readily consumed, easily dispensed, and are not sticky (Bijou and Sturges, 1959).

Control and recording equipment similar to devices used with infrahuman Ss (Ferster and Skinner, 1957; Skinner, 1957; Verhave, 1959) are located in the adjoining room. They consist of timers, tape-programmers, and relay circuits for scheduling stimulus events and reinforcements. Impulse counters and a Gerbands cumulative recorder are used to record responses on the lever. The cumulative recorder also indicates reinforcements and the type and duration of discriminative stimuli. "Blips" on the cumulative curve indicate reinforcements, while the event-pen base line under each curve records which of the two discriminative stimuli is present.

## SUBJECTS

The 46 subjects are residents at the Rainier School, Buckley, Washington. The 25 girls and 21 boys ranged in age from 9 to 21 with a median of 16 years, and in I.Q. from 23 to 64 with a median of 42. Length of residence was from 1 to 14 years with a median of 6 years. Their clinical diagnoses spread over most categories. Since all were ambulatory, they came on request to the reception room of the laboratory from their residence halls, classrooms, or work assignments.

## INSTRUCTIONS

Instructions are treated as drive operations, considered to be verbal and nonverbal procedures which may affect Ss' rates and patterns of responding. The instructions described here, deliberately simple and brief, were designed to get lever-pressing behavior emitted at a moderate rate. Uncomplicated instructions such as these may be applied without modification to a wide range of Ss (e.g. those with physical immaturities, sensory defects, and emotional disturbances, as well as normal children), and are less likely to contain discriminative and conditioned stimuli which may successfully compete with shaping the experimental operant (Azrin and Lindsley, 1956; Bijou and Sturges, 1959).

1. Instructions to a new S begin when E enters the reception room and says, "Hello, now it's your turn to get some of these". (He shows a handful of reinforcers.) "Come with me." (The E ushers S into the experimental room, closes the door, and points to the chair in front of the response box.) "Sit here."

2A. If S pulls his chair up to the table and works the lever up and down five times, a piece of candy comes down the chute. If S notices the candy and continues to respond, no instructions on performing the experimental task are given. Then $E$ says, "I'll be back when it is time for you to go", and leaves the room. He goes into the control room, where he observes $S$ through a one-way screen and monitors the controls for the next 60 sec in accordance with the next step in the procedure.

2B. If $S$ sits in the chair and waits for instructions, $E$ says, as he places his *own* hand on the lever, "Now watch me; I'll show you how to get candy." (Then $E$ responds at the rate of approximately two per second for five responses.) "Look. Here is some candy. It is yours. You may eat it if you wish. Now you do it. Go ahead and get some candy." If $S$ responds as instructed (a reinforcement is delivered after 5 responses), $E$ says, "I'll be back when the time is up for you to go", and leaves the room. As in 2A, $E$ enters the control room and observes $S$'s behavior for the next 60 sec. If $S$ stops responding during the 60-sec period, $E$ returns and repeats the instructions beginning with, "Now watch me". If $S$ repeatedly presses the lever in response to this repetition, but again stops during the 60-sec period following instructions, $E$ returns and terminates the session. (If $S$ is needed for the study, he is brought back on another day and given training to abolish this discriminative behavior.)

2C. Some $S$s do not respond to the lever after the first set of instructions. Under these circumstances, $E$ repeats the instructions beginning with "Now watch me." If $S$ does not work the lever after repetition, $E$ repeats the instrucion a third time. This time, however, he takes $S$'s hand and puts him through the motions of responding and handling the reinforcers. If $S$ does not work the lever with this assistance, the session is terminated. (He is eliminated if a substitute $S$ is available. If not, he is brought back another day, and an attempt is made to shape his behavior toward the lever response in gradual stages.)

3. When it is time to end the session, $E$ returns and says, "That's all for today. Go and sit in the waiting room." (If necessary, $E$ gives $S$ a waxed-paper sack for his candy.)

4. On subsequent sessions, $E$ goes to the reception room and tells $S$ it is his turn to go to the experimental room. After $S$ is seated, "Go ahead and get some candy. I'll be back when it is time for you to go." At the end of the session, $E$ terminates in the standard manner: "That's all for today. You may go and sit in the waiting room."

## PROCEDURE

The procedure has four phases: (1) rate evaluation and strengthening, (2) pause building, (3) rate-recovery evaluation, and (4) final multiple-schedule training. To simplify the description of the procedure, the *blue* light will be referred to as the discriminative stimulus for pause building and non-reinforcement, and the *red* light as the discriminative stimulus for reinforcement.

*Rate Evaluation and Strengthening*

The purpose of evaluating $S$'s inital rate of responding is to arrive at a workable rate for training $S$ to increase, for longer and longer periods, the intervals between responses in the presence of the blue light. If training on low rates of responding is undertaken when the initial rate is low or is weakened by the schedule in force, extinction may develop. Hence, this stage includes operations designed to strengthen rate when required. On the other hand, if pause training is attempted when the initial rate is very high, pausing may require an excessive amount of time to develop and stabilize. The second function of the evaluation procedure, therefore, is to detect high rates as early as possible to avoid dispensing any more reinforcers than necessary.

The $S$ begins (with the red light on) on a schedule in which he is reinforced every 15 sec (FI 15 sec). This continues for 1 min. If $S$ makes at least 20 responses and receives at least one reinforcement during this minute, the red light goes off, the blue comes on, and the next stage of training (pause building) begins. If $S$ makes fewer than 20 responses but shows an acceleration in rate during the latter part of the period, the red light remains on and the schedule remains in force for an additional minute. If 40 responses or more are made in the 2 min, the red light goes off, the blue comes on, and pause training begins.

If $S$ gives fewer than 20 responses in the first minute and does not show acceleration in rate, or does not make 40 responses in 2 min, the red light stays on but the schedule is changed from FI 15 sec to an "increasing ratio". In this schedule, the ratio is gradually increased from 1 : 1 to 1 : 5 by successively requiring more responses between reinforcements. The schedule used here reinforces response numbers 1, 2, 4, 6, 9, 12, 16, 20, 25 and 30. If the rate has increased by the end of this increasing-ratio regime, $S$ is again given the FI 15-sec schedule and re-evaluated, i.e. observed to determine whether he will make 20 responses in 1 min or 40 in 2. If he does not perform at the rate-level required, the session is terminated. Like those terminated in the other stages, $S$ is eliminated or requested to return for further training depending on the needs of the study.

*Pause Building*

The purpose of pause training is to strengthen response "withholding" for increasing periods while the blue light is present, and, at the same time, maintain prompt responding with the onset of the red light. To do this, pausing is differentially reinforced in gradually more demanding stages.

The procedure is:

1. After $S$ has demonstrated a rate of responding at or above the minimum required, the red light goes off and the blue light comes on.

2. When $S$ pauses for a predetermined number of seconds (IRT $x$ sec), the blue light goes off and the red comes on. The time unit ($x$) selected depends, in part, upon $S$'s performance during the rate-evaluation phase.

3. The first response (with red on) is reinforced, and the red light is replaced by the blue. The blue remains on until $S$ *again* pauses for $x$ sec.

4. This sequence is repeated until $S$ pauses for $x$ sec, $y$ times.

5. The length of the pause is then increased by an amount $z$, and the conditions alternated as previously described until $S$ pauses $x + z$ sec for $y'$ times.

6. The procedure in Step 5 is repeated with a further extension of time, and the whole process is continued until the duration of pausing with blue light on meets specifications.

The following is an example of pause building with three repetitions at 5, 10, 15, and 30 sec of pause ($x = 5$, $x + z = 10$, $x + 2z = 15$, etc.).

1. When rate evaluation is completed the red light is replaced by the blue.

2. The *first* time $S$ gives inter-response time of 5 sec, the blue light goes off and the red comes on. The first response is reinforced and the red light is replaced by the blue.

3. Immediately after the *second* 5-sec inter-response time, the red light replaces the blue. The first response is reinforced and the blue replaces the red light.

4. Immediately after the *third* 5-sec inter-response time, the red light replaces the blue. The first response is reinforced and the blue light replaces the red.

5. When $S$ delays responding for 10 sec, the blue light goes off, the red comes on, and the first response is reinforced.

6. The procedure in Step 5 is repeated twice more, and then a 15-sec pause is required.

7. After three successful 15-sec pauses on blue, a delay of 30 sec is is required.

8. After three successive 30-sec pauses on blue (and reinforcements on red), the next stage of training begins. This involves lengthening the time of the red light or of both the red and blue lights, and changing from a continuous to an intermittent schedule.

As is apparent, the objective of pause training is not only to increase the delays between responses in the presence of the blue light, but also to maintain prompt responding with the onset of the red light. There are two clear-cut indications if this stage is proceeding too rapidly: long periods of failure to pause, and/or increased latency to the red light. In both instances, completion of a sequence will be delayed and additional training may be required before pauses can be longer. The following procedure has been shown to be serviceable. When a given $y$ series has not been completed in 5 min, the entire series is repeated before training on a longer pause is begun. For example, if $S$ takes more than 5 min to make three successive 5-sec pauses, training is given in making three more 5-sec pauses (total of 6) prior to training on 10-sec pausing. Similarly, if more than 5 min is required to complete three 10-sec pauses, three more 10-sec pauses are programed before 15-sec pauses are begun.

*Rate-recovery Evaluation*

The objective in this phase is to assess the *S*'s reaction to lengthening the duration of the red light and to change from a continuous to an intermittent schedule. After the last pause in the final series under blue light, the red light comes on and *S* is given 1 min on a 15-sec, fixed-interval schedule. If he makes more than 20 responses, he is moved to the next (multiple-schedule) phase. If he makes fewer than 20 responses, the schedule is changed to increasing ratio (the one used for strengthening rate in phase one). This training continues until the rate reaches 20 responses for a 60-sec period.

*Final Phase: Multiple-schedule Training*

The *S*s who meet the criterion of rate in the previous stage are moved to the final multiple-schedule stage, provided the times of the discriminative stimuli are not over approximately 3 min each and the intermittency of reinforcement is not greater than a ratio of 50 or any interval of 1 min. If discriminative-stimuli duration or schedules are greater than these values, it is suggested that changes take place in graduated steps.

DATA AND DISCUSSION

The performances of eight *S*s in two experimental sessions each are presented as representative illustrations of the data. These *S*s show a variety of behavioral effects and demonstrate a range of schedules and procedures. The clinical diagnosis is included in the brief descriptions of each *S* for whatever value it might have. However, because this study was not concerned with the relationship between diagnoses and operant behavior, implications of such relationship from these data are not intended. To facilitate identification of the figures, each record is identified by *S* ( e.g. EMN), session number (e.g. S-1, S-2), and the schedule during the final phase (e.g. mult VR 25 ext).

The first four Ss shown in Fig. 1 illustrate the procedure, with particular emphasis on variations in development rather than in the final schedule. The last four *S*s, presented in Fig. 2, show some of the range of final schedules established with the procedure.

The top two records in Fig. 1 show the first and second sessions of EMN, a 16-year-old girl with an MA of 5 years 3 months and an I.Q. of 42. She has been living at the institution for 4 years and is diagnosed as undifferentiated. In these records, as well as in the others, the horizontal line under the cumulative-response curve indicates the discriminative stimulus in force. When the line is elevated, the blue light was on; and when depressed, the red light was on. The colored light serving as S$^D$ can be inferred from the reinforcement marks in the cumulative curve.

Since EMN's initial rate was high, rate strengthening was omitted. Pause building proceeded slowly and steadily. When shifted to mult VR 25 ext with fixed 1-min alternation of lights, she performed at a steady rate under VR 25 and showed some anticipatory responses during S$^\Delta$. The Session 2 (S-2) performance on mult VR 25 next with 2-min alternation is orderly, with some tendency to respond during S$^\Delta$.

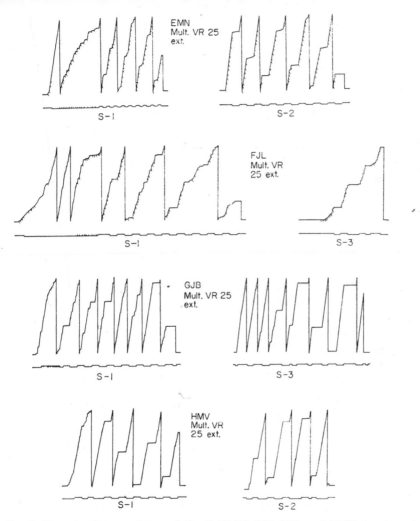

FIG. 1. Records of two sessions each for Ss EMN, GJB, FJL, and HMV showing the development of mult VR 25 ext.

The second S (FJL) is a 14-year-old mongoloid girl with an MA of 3 years 1 month and an I.Q. of 23. She has lived in the institution for 4 years. The initial reaction to pause building in Session 1 consisted of a rate increase. After pause building, a rate-recovery interval showed that rate strengthening was not necessary, and she was shifted immediately to mult VR 25 ext with fixed 2-min alternation of $S^D$ and $S^\Delta$. Evidence of a discrimination is shown during the middle part of the session. Performance is good, but rate drops toward the end. This extinction trend was continued during the second session, S-2 (not shown), in which only 2 responses were made. In the third session (S-3), the increasing-ratio schedule recovered the rate, and discriminative performance on mult VR 25 ext with variable 2-min alternation followed.

The third $S$ in Fig. 1 (GJB) is a 21-year-old mongoloid girl with an MA of 3 years 5 months and an I.Q. of 30. She has lived at the institution for 11 years. She began Session 1 with a high rate; and although pause building progressed well, she responded to the onset of $S^D$ with "runs" of responses. Rate recovery was good; and when shifted to mult VR 25 ext with fixed 2-min alternation, discrimination was only fair because of the large numbers of responses during $S^\Delta$ shown in the middle of the session.

Session 2 for GJB is not shown. The performance was almost continuous responding, very much as in the initial part of Session 3. In Session 3 the schedule was mult VR 25 ext, with variable 2-min alternation of the stimulus condition.

The final $S$ in Fig. 1 (HMV) is a 21-year-old mongoloid boy with an MA of 4 years 9 months and an I.Q. of 32. He has been institutionalized for only 3 years. His initial high rate and virtually continuous responding during pause building quite suddenly gave way to rapid learning to pause. The pause series was terminated at the end of five 10-sec pauses, and rate recovery showed no necessity for strengthening. Performance on mult VR 25 ext with fixed 2-min alternation was nearly perfect, and this high level of discrimination was continued in Session 2 on mult VR 25 ext with variable 2-min alternation.

The first $S$ in Fig. 2 is ADP, and 11-year-old boy with an MA of 3 years 2 months and an I.Q. of 46. He has been at the institution for 5 years and is classified as cerebral birth trauma. Subject ADP maintained a high steady rate for more than 2000 responses during pause building, then suddenly learned the discrimination. All of the series of 20-sec pauses were nearly perfect. Performance on mult FR 25 ext with fixed 2-min alternation shows good stimulus control, and regular postreinforcement pauses appear in Session 2.

Subject BRB is an 18-year-old boy with an MA of 6 years 6 months and an I.Q. of 43. He is diagnosed as familial, and has been in the institution for 12 years. Pause control was quickly established; and although no rate recovery was given, an adequate rate was immediately obtained and performance on mult FI 1 ext with fixed 2-min alternation was at a high level. This performance continued in Session 2, with some suggestions of FI scallops.

Subject CMW is a 17-year-old boy with an MA of 3 years 7 months and an I.Q. of 43. He has been institutionalized for 11 years and is diagnosed as cranial anomaly. His initial high rate in Session 1 was rapidly replaced by pause control. After pause building, both lights were turned off, and a buzzer was introduced as the cue in a mult CRF VI 0·5 schedule. Generalization is shown by continued low rate and few responses in the absence of the

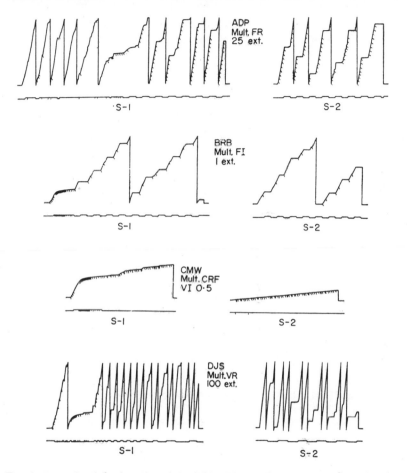

FIG. 2. Records of Sessions 1 and 2 of Ss ADP, BRB, CMW, and DJS showing the development of mult FR 25 ext, mult FI 1 ext, mult CRF VI 0·5, and mult VR 100 ext.

buzzer. Close-to-perfect performance is shown in Session 2, where he responded immediately to cue onset and refrained from responding in the absence of the cue.

Subject DJS is a 19-year-old girl with an MA of 4 years 8 months and an I.Q. of 36. She has been in the institution for 8 years and is classified as undifferentiated. Very rapid learning to pause followed a period of steady responding. She was shifted in gradual stages to a final schedule of mult VR 100 ext with fixed 3-min alternation of lights. Successively, the stages were 4 min on mult VR 25 ext (fixed 0·5 alternation), 10 min on mult VR 25 ext (fixed 1-min alternation), and 8 min on mult VR 50 ext (fixed 2-min alternation). This progression is shown by changes in segment lengths in the event line. Stimulus control is evident, but a strong tendency to make responses in the presence of the $S^\Delta$ persisted. During Session 2, discrimination increased gradually but did not reach a high level.

## SUMMARY

This paper deals with modifying simple operant behavior of institutionalized retarded children which is observed at the beginning of a study of the behavior required for a multiple-schedule. A study of such procedures has promise both for an experimental analysis of individual differences, and for the development of techniques for the rapid acquisition of discrimination relative to multiple-schedules. Concern here is with multiple-schedules. The technique, which is designed to allow $S$ to set the pace, is outlined in detail. All the multiple-schedules described consist of two components which alternate in some fashion. Sample data are presented on eight $S$s illustrating some of the phases and some of the final performances.

## REFERENCES

AZRIN, N. H. and LINDSLEY, O. R. (1956) The reinforcement of cooperation between children, J. Abnorm. Soc. Psychol., 52, 100–102.

BIJOU, S. W. and STURGES, PERSIS T. (1959) Positive reinforcers for experimental studies with children—consumables and manipulatables. Child Developm., 30, 151–170.

BIJOU, S. W. Discrimination performance as a baseline for individual analysis of young children. Child Developm. (in press).

BRELAND, K. and BRELAND, MARION (1951) A field of applied animal psychology, Amer. Psychol., 6, 202–204.

FERSTER, C. B. and SKINNER, B. F. (1957) Schedules of reinforcement. Appleton-Century-Crofts, New York.

KELLER, F. S. and SCHOENFELD, W. N. (1950) Principles of psychology. Appleton-Century-Crofts, New York.

SKINNER, B. F. (1953) Science and human behavior, MacMillan, New York.

SKINNER, B. F. (1957) The experimental analysis of behavior, Amer. Scientist, 45, 343–371.

VERHAVE, T. (1959) Recent developments in the experimental anaysis of behavior, Proceed. Eleventh Res. Conf., Amer. Meat Inst. Found. of the Univer. of Chicago.

# The Development of Performances in Autistic Children in an Automatically Controlled Environment*

C. B. FERSTER, PH.D., and MARIAN K. DeMYER, M.D.

*Indiana University Medical Center, Indianapolis*

THIS experiment reports data from a technique for producing behavior in autistic children[1] under an automatically controlled environment. The experiment is an attempt to develop techniques for enlarging the very narrow range of performances generally present in these children's repertoires. Performances were developed and maintained in order to determine some facts about these children's existing repertoires, and to discover what potentiality exists for extending them. We created each child's repertoire by arranging specific consequences to his performance (reinforcement) which increased the subsequent frequency of those performances. Early in the experiment, the reinforcements which were delivered were food, candy, and trinkets†; later, coins were delivered which could be cashed in for various other rewarding consequences.

The experiment involved pressing a key. This simple arbitrary act was chosen because: (1) The response took little time or effort to execute, and it left the child in a position to respond again. The frequency with which the child pressed the key could therefore vary over a wide range, from a few responses per hour to several thousand. Such a dependent variable is potentially sensitive to many independent variables, and gives a continuous measurement of their effects. (2) A performance such as pressing a key actuates an electrical contact and hence can be objectively and automatically recorded. It also permits the automatic programing of the entire experiment, so that all of the experimental procedures can be arranged precisely and without error. Extended training and long-term exposure to the conditions of the experiment which would be impossible manually become possible because the experiment is carried out by automatic devices. Over 50,000 coins were delivered and 400,000 responses recorded for Subject 1 alone. (3) The frequency of key pressing is intuitively analogous to the major problem in the

* This article is reprinted with the permission of the authors and editor from *J. Chronic Dis.* **13**, 312–345 (1961).

† Assortments of trinkets were purchased from the Penny King Co., 2538 Mission St., Pittsburgh, Pa., and Plastic Processes, Inc., 83 House Ave., Freeport, N.Y.

measurement of human behavior: measuring the child's disposition to behave; the probability of his acting. A simple recording of whether the child acted or not gives little information about his general tendency to behave. A single occurrence of an act may be caused by a strong or a weak repertoire. The child's disposition to act can vary from low to quite high, and the level of motivation is best determined by examining the frequency of key pressing; the child's disposition to engage in the experimental behavior is recorded as the frequency of occurrence of the key press. (4) The use of an arbitrary response, such as pressing a key, has been used extensively in animal experiments dealing with general problems in maintaining behavior of the organisms. Many of the processes discovered have proved to be phylogenetically general among a wide range of mammals, including man; and this information may be used to determine when we have established normal control over the child's behavior. Recording of the behavior as the effect of the animal's performance on an electrical switch makes possible the comparisons of the performance of a wide range of species.

These tendencies have already been used successfully in the study of the behavior of normal children.[2, 3] One of the problems in developing experimental techniques for creating new behaviors in these children and maintaining old ones is the development or discovery of reinforcers which are powerful enough to sustain large amounts of behavior. The problem of a reinforcer is especially acute with the autistic child because of his general deficit in positively maintained behavior. The frequency with which the child presses the key, particularly when it is reinforced only intermittently, provides a technique whereby new and more effective reinforcers can be discovered. By observing which experimental procedures increase and decrease the frequency with which the child presses the key, an experimental environment can be constructed which becomes increasingly effective in supporting strong behavior in the child. A major accomplishment of the research reported here is the development of procedures which can strongly maintain the behavior of a child under conditions where the form of the behavior occurs explicitly as a result of the experimental procedures.

A durable reinforcer is especially necessary for the development of complex behavior. While the child is being exposed to the development of new complex performances, nonreinforcement of inappropriate responses is inevitable. This nonreinforcement weakens the performance; and if the new behavior is to be developed, the child must continue to emit the performance first. After the child's performance can be sustained in the experimental environment, it should become possible to investigate many aspects of the autistic repertoire which have heretofore been inaccessible. The child's auditory and visual repertoires could be studied if various stimuli were presented to him while at the same time reinforcement was differentially given or withheld, depending upon which stimulus was present. The ability of the child to come under the control of the relevant stimuli would be shown by the differential performance in the presence of the various stimuli.

Complex forms of behavior could be developed after the child has begun performing by successively approximating more complex activities. Reinforcements can be shifted in the direction of the complex form of activity required. Once the child's performance conforms to the new condition of reinforcement, the contingency is again subtly shifted. Ultimately, studies of even such complex forms of behavior as speech may be carried out by reinforcing vocal sounds in the child's repertoire and gradually approximating more and more complex forms.

*Subject 1.*—The first subject is male, and was 8 years old and in good physical condition at the start of the experiment. Speech occurred at the later part of his first year, and proceeded to sentences of two or three words. Motor development and coordination were good. According to parental reports, the child's illness began when he was 18 months old. The father was under strong financial pressure, holding a job while maintaining a farm, and at the same time experiencing considerable ill health. The parents spent evenings "barking" at each other. During the period of development of the boy's illness, the mother was subject to severe depressions, usually stemming from arguments with her husband and sometimes lasting for several days. During these depressions, she was almost completely inactive, paying nearly no attention to the subject beyond minimal care. The subject began taking off clothing unpredictably, tearing down curtains, upsetting furniture, pounding his head against the wall, and wandering 2 or 3 miles from home. The father's ways of dealing with the boy's disturbances ranged variously from severe punishment to isolation; he built a fenced-in cage to control the subject's increasingly destructive behavior. Speech began to diminish at this time, and the child has been practically mute since the age of 4, when the parents sought medical care. At 7 years, the child was admitted to the LaRue D. Carter Memorial Hospital. During his stay there he remained nonverbal, except for rare occasions when he spoke one or two words. He characteristically tore his clothing and broke toys and articles belonging to other children. Severe tantrums that had no relationship to current events occurred frequently. He spent long periods of time simply standing idly, lying on the floor, or shuffling through the ward. His most frequent activities consisted of agilely climbing on objects and playing with water and clay. He also spent large amounts of time smearing and mouthing clay or candy. His performance during his stay at the hospital had changed little before the experiment described here.

*Subject 2.*—The second subject is a female who was $9\frac{1}{2}$ years old at the start of the experiment. The girl developed normally until she was about 3, when she began to lose speech, play destructively with toys, smear feces, and lose bladder and bowel control. She became phobic in regard to animals. Some speech remained, however. From the age of 19 months to 3 years, an adolescent high school girl was the subject's constant companion. The adolescent handled the subject completely permissively and with much "babying". The mother was passive and allowed the adolescent to take over all of her functions. The subject's behavioral difficulties began when the adolescent girl left and the mother became pregnant with a second child.

Neither subject showed any evidence of brain damage in standard neurological and EEG examinations at the time of admission or subsequently.

*Control Subjects.*—Control subjects were inpatients in the Children's Service who did not appear to have any intellectual deficits and were essentially normal except in respect to the general level of social control. The control subjects were approximately the same ages as Subjects 1 and 2.

*First Exposure to the Experiment*

When Subject 1 was first exposed to the experiment, only the single-column vendor was present (Fig. 1). During the first session, an attendant who knew the subject led him to the experimental room and gave him candy. During the second session, the subject found candy that had been previously placed in the trough of the vending machine. During the third session, the candy was delivered remotely by the solenoids on the vending machine; and during the fourth session, the key was installed, with every press of the key operating the vending machine. Several sessions later, the subject entered the room alone.

FIG. 1. Photograph of the experimental room. The eight-column vendor is at the extreme right, the single-column vendor on the left. The other devices on the wall, from left to lower right, are phonograph and color wheel. Above the color wheel is the coin dispenser with the coin key and the coin trough. The other two devices were installed subsequently to the experiment reported here. The pigeon is not shown.

With Subject 2 the eight-column vendor, the pigeon, phonograph, and pinball machine were present. The subject was brought to the room by an attendant whom she knew, and all of the devices were demonstrated. The session was completed with the attendant in the room. Starting with the second session, the subject was placed in the room alone, the door locked, and the normal procedure carried out.

Except at the beginning of the experiment, Subject 1's experimental duration was 60 min or 80 reinforcements, whichever occurred first. The duration was increased to 90 min on the seventieth session. Subject 2's experimental duration was 90 min throughout.

*Reinforcing Devices*

Food appeared to be the most effective reinforcer available. Nevertheless, an attempt was made to establish a more durable reinforcer by delivering a coin that in turn could be used in a wide variety of reinforcing devices. The experimental use of the coin parallels its use in the normal social environment.[4] It is an occasion which makes possible other behavior producing a variety of reinforcers. Such a conditioned generalized reinforcer has the advantage that it derives its reinforcing effect from other reinforcers which are effective under various kinds of deprivation. Should the level of deprivation in respect to several of the specific reinforcements used in the experiments be low, the generalized reinforcer would continue to maintain behavior through the remaining devices which might be relevant to current deprivations. If the number of reinforcing devices were large enough so that at least some of these would be reinforcing for each a subject, the same experimental room could be used for a number of subjects. There is also the possibility that the generalized reinforcer may have its effect by the sum of the specific reinforcers.

The children operated the reinforcing devices in the room either by pressing a key or depositing a coin. The key was a telephone-type lever switch, mounted in a translucent plastic panel which could be lighted from behind. A solenoid gave an audible click whenever the switch was sufficiently depressed. When the key was inoperative (before and after the experimental sessions and during time out) the clicker and light were disconnected. The coin slots resembled those ordinarily found on vending machines, except that small pilot lights next to them indicated when the slots were operative. Coins deposited when the coin light was off were recorded but did not operate the device. The coins were stainless-steel discs the size of a 1-cent piece. Reinforcing devices were added gradually during the early stages of the experiment. Tables 1 and 2 give the exact points of introduction of the reinforcing devices.

*Coin Dispenser:* The coin dispenser and key were mounted together in a wall unit. The coins were delivered to a tray just below the response key.

*Single-column Vendor*: The single-column vendor, a modified pastry-vending machine, was operated by solenoids which emptied the compartments of the six columns of the machine in sequence. When the vendor's 80 compartments were emptied, the light next to the coin slot went out.

*Pigeon:* A transparent plastic wall unit, 12 by 12 by 14 in., contained a hungry pigeon and associated devices so that the bird pecked at the disc only when the light was on. A coin deposited in the coin slot turned on the lights in the apparatus so that the child could observe the bird's performance for 30 sec.

*Phonograph:* An aluminium box, approximately 12 by 12 by 8 in., contained a speaker, a coin slot with an associated light, and a light that came on whenever the phonograph was operating. When a coin was deposited in the slot, the phonograph, which was located in the adjoining room, played through the speaker for 30 sec. A coin deposited in the coin slot while the phonograph was on reinstated the full 30-sec period. The records were generally lively marches or children's records. The material was varied from day to day, and was a rough attempt at presenting records of interest to the child.

*Pinball Machine:* The pinball machine simulated a baseball game with many moving parts, bells, flashing lights, etc. Depositing a coin in the coin slot of the pinball machine released two balls for play.

*Eight-column Vendor:* The eight-column vendor was adapted from a cigarette machine by installing solenoids, and an independent coin switch and coin light on each column. Part of the face of the machine was made of Plexiglas so that the subjects could inspect the kind of candy in each column. When a column became empty, its coin light went out. When the whole vending machine was inoperative, all of the coin lights were extinguished. The eight-column vendor was operated with coins only.

*Color Wheel:* The color wheel consisted of three discs, each red, blue, and yellow, rotating on a common shaft in respect to each other, and driven by a variable-speed motor. The result was a kaleidoscopic color change. The subject would vary the speed of the motor by turning a knob on the face of the panel, thus changing the kaleidoscopic color effects. A coin in the slot whenever the light was on provided operation of the color wheel for 30 sec.

*Organ:* A portable electric organ was modified by installing a rod which locked the keys until the solenoid was released. A coin in the coin slot freed the keys for 30 sec.

### Food, Candy, Toys, and Trinkets Delivered in the Vending Machines

In general, the kinds of candy, crackers, and foods delivered were varied during different phases of the experiment, and between subjects, depending upon their preferences. Candy and food delivered included candy corn, M & M's, peppermints, chocolate mints, Tootsie-Rolls, raisins, dried apricots, burnt-sugar-coated peanuts, marshmallows, various kinds of crackers and cookies, plain chocolate, and chocolate-covered raisins. The single-column vendor was used to deliver small trinkets, 1-ounce portions variously of fruit juice, water, and milk in covered plastic containers, candy, crackers, and some larger toys, such as Tinker toys, miniature cars and harmonicas, and blocks. The trinkets were selected from a large assortment and were changed daily.

## Schedules of Reinforcement

The schedule of reinforcement describes the program by which the experimentally recorded performance operates the reinforcing devices.[5]

## Fixed-ratio Schedule (FR)

Every nth response activates the reinforcer. This schedule normally produces a high, sustained rate of responding. When the number of responses required for reinforcement is increased, responding stops after reinforcement, followed by an abrupt shift to the high rate.

## Variable-interval Schedule (VI)

Passage of time determines when a response activates the reinforcer. The average interval between reinforcements is specified, but the actual intervals vary from reinforcement to reinforcement. This schedule normally produces a moderate, roughly constant rate of responding.

## Multiple Fixed-ratio, Variable-interval Schedule

The color behind the key changes between red and green after each reinforcement. When the color is red, the coin is delivered by the nth (e.g. fifteenth) response. When the color is green, the first response after a variable period of time produces a coin. The performance that normally emerges from each color is appropriate to the schedule of reinforcement in its presence.

## PLAN OF THE EXPERIMENT

Tables 1 and 2 contain a detailed summary of the experimental procedures for Subject 1 and Subject 2, respectively. These specific procedures were in effect for the session numbers indicated in the column. The second column refers to the schedule by which pressing of the key produced coins. The third column indicates the session at which the various reinforcing devices were introduced, and whether they were operated by a coin or by a lever mounted directly on the device. The fourth column, "Stimulus Control", indicates the presence or absence of stimuli correlated with conditions of reinforcement, e.g. the lamp which is on when the coin slot can be operated by a coin. Abbreviated procedures are explained in more detail in the paragraphs following the tables.

The experimental procedures are grouped into the following phases.

TABLE 1

*Summary of experimental procedures for subject 1*

| Sessions | Schedule of reinforcement (coins) | Reinforcing Devices* — Single-column vendor | 8-column vendor | Pigeon | Phonograph | Pinball | Color wheel | Organ | Stimulus control | Illustrations | General factors |
|---|---|---|---|---|---|---|---|---|---|---|---|
| 1–21 | VI** 7–30 (candy and coins) | Coins | | | | | | | | Fig. 2 | Sparine 50 mg t.i.d. |
| 22–30 | Multiple VI FR | Coins | | | | | | | | | |
| 31 | FR† 9 | Coins | | | | | | | | | |
| 32–37 | VI 30 | Coins | | Coins | | | | | | Fig. 3 | Sparine discontinued. Thorazine 50 mg t.i.d. |
| 38–39 | | Coins | | | Coins | | | | | | |
| 40–44 | | Coins | | | | | | | 10 sec time out after reinforcement | Fig. 4 | |
| 45 | FR 15 | Coins | | | | | | | 10 sec time out after reinforcement Multiple C.R.F. extinction 15–60 sec after regular session | | |
| 46–49 | | Coins | | | | | | | Multiple C.R.F. extinction 30–60 sec in coin slots | Figs. 5, 6 | |
| 50–56 | Key disconnected | Coins | | | | | | | | | |
| 57–70 | FR 13 | | | | | | | | Coin slot operative every 2nd–5th coin, 15–75 sec | Fig. 8 | |
| 71–78 | Mult VI 60″ | | | | | Coins | | | Coin slots operative continuously except when a column is emptied | | |
| 79–81 | FR 13 | | Coins | | | | | | | Figs. 9, 10 | |
| | FR—Mult·FR | | | | | | | | | | |

| Sessions | Key* | Coin schedule | Coins | Vending contingency | Fig. | Notes |
|---|---|---|---|---|---|---|
| 95–104 | | | | Coin slot operative every 2nd–3rd coin for 20 sec | | Tantrums and frequent atavisms |
| 105–128 | | Crf | Coins | Coin slots operative continuously except when a column is emptied | | |
| 129–137 | FR 2–5 | FR 2, Crf | Coins | | Fig. 13 | Pinworm infection. Tantrums and frequent atavism |
| 138–146 | FR 15 | FR 2, Crf | Coins | | | Experimental room remodeled. Pacatal 50 mg t.i.d. Tantrums and frequent atavism |
| 147–187 | FR 4–5 | FR 2, Crf†† | Coins | | | Electrical shock discovered and removed. Thorazine 25 mg t.i.d. Session 171. Pacatal 50 mg h.s. Compazine 10 mg t.i.d. Session 179 |
| 187–198 | | FR 2, Crf | Coins | Coin slots operative every 2nd or 3rd coin for 30 sec | Fig. 15 | |
| 199–204 | | | | Coin slots alternately operative and inoperative every 30–40 sec | | |
| 205–215 | | | | As above—coin in inoperative slot extends inoperative period | | |
| 229–235 | FR 8–15 | | | As above—coin in empty column makes entire vendor inoperative | | |
| 236–239 | FR 5 | | | | | |
| 240–244 | FR 15 | | | | | |
| 245–251 | FR 1–2 New Key | | | | | |
| 252–256 | FR 15–25 | | | | | |
| 257– | FR 2 New Key | | | | | |

\* Schedule of reinforcement by a key mounted directly on the device.   \*\* Variable interval.   † Fixed ratio.   †† Continuous reinforcement.

TABLE 2

*Summary of experimental procedures for subject 2*

| Sessions | Schedule of reinforcement (coins) | Reinforcing Devices* — Single-column vendor | 8-column vendor | Pigeon | Phonograph | Pinball | Color wheel | Organ | Stimulus control | Illustrations | General factors |
|---|---|---|---|---|---|---|---|---|---|---|---|
| 1-5 | | Coins | Coins | Coins | Coins | Coins | Coins | Coins | 10 sec time out after reinforcement | Fig. 7 | |
| 6-17 | FR 15 | | | | | | | | Coin slot operative every 2nd-5th coin | | |
| 18-37 | | FR 2-7 | | FR 2-4 | FR 2-4 | FR 2 | Crf | Crf | 10 sec time out after reinforcement | | |
| 38-45 | FR 2-5 | | | | | | | | | | Compazine 10 mg b.i.d. |
| 46-53 | FR 2-15 | | | | | | | | | | Pinworm infection discovered and treated. Piperazine for 2 weeks |
| 54-56 | | | | | | | | | | | Comp. discontinued. Thorazine† |
| 57-91 | FR 1-5 | Coins | | Coins | | | | | 8-column vendor coin slots operative every 2nd coin | Fig. 14 | Pharyngitis. Electric shock discovered and removed. Thorazine ††,** |
| 92-100 | | | | | | | | | | | |
| 101-103 | | | | | | | | | | | |
| 104-136 | FR 8-FR 15 | | | | | | | | 8-column vendor coin slots alternately operative 30 sec inoperative 30 sec | | 102°F. fever, Session 114§ |
| 137-143 | FR 5 | | | | | | | | | | |
| 144-149 | FR 15 | | | | | | | | | | 103·8°F. fever, tonsilitis, Session 149 |
| 150-155 | FR 2 Paper-drive | | | | | | | | | Figs. 16, 17, 18 | |
| 156-162 | FR 15-30 | | | | | | | | | | |

\* Schedule of reinforcement via a key mounted on the device.

† Thorazine 25 mg t.i.d. and h.s.; 3 days later, 40 mg t.i.d. and 60 mg h.s.;

\*\* 25 mg t.i.d. and 50 mg h.s.

†† Session 77, 25 mg t.i.d. and 50 mg h.s.

*Subject 1*

*Phase 1, Sessions 1 to 30:* During this period, the general technique was developed, reinforcers discovered, and the experimental procedures integrated with the ward routine. A stable key-pressing performance was developed on a variable-interval schedule of reinforcement.

*Phase 2, Sessions 31 to 70:* The schedule of reinforcement with coins was changed from variable-interval to fixed-ratio. Both subjects performed appropriately to the control normally produced by the fixed-ratio schedule.

Key pressing was brought under the control of the lights behind the key by periodically turning off the lights and discontinuing reinforcement. Both children stopped pressing the key when the light was off. Control by the coin lights was developed similarly. The coin light was only periodically lighted, and coins deposited when it was off were wasted. In another procedure, designed to make the subjects accumulate coins before using them, the coin light came on for a brief period with every *n*th coin delivered (e.g. 3). Coins deposited as soon as they were received (except for the *n*th coin) were wasted. During this period, the children's performances were weaker than those previously recorded. However, this was at least in part because both children had a pinworm infection and had received accidental electric shocks delivered by the experimental devices.

*Phase 3, Session 71 to 104:* Here, intermittent reinforcement of the behavior was emphasized, in order to determine the degree to which large amounts of behavior could be sustained with minimal reinforcement. The stimulus control by the coin light which had developed previously with the one-column vendor was lost when the eight-column vendor was introduced. There were many tantrums during this period, and the recorded performance became considerably weaker.

*Phase 4, Sessions 105 to 165:* Because of this weakened performance, the schedules of reinforcement were made optimal by delivering coins on small fixed-ratios and operating all of the reinforcing devices except the eight-column vendor directly by one two presses of the key mounted directly upon the device. At Session 138, all of the reinforcing devices, except the electric organ, had been installed.

*Phase 5, Sessions 166 to 186:* During this period, the pinworm infection was cured and the electric shock was eliminated, the schedules of reinforcement remained optimal, and strong performances were recovered.

*Phase 6, Sessions 187 to 235:* The control by the coin lights was re-established by additional coin-saving procedures.

*Phase 7, Sessions 236 to 239:* The reinforcing devices were operated only by coins, with the direct levers removed. The size of the fixed-ratio was reduced to facilitate the transition.

*Phase 8, Sessions 240 to 261:* During this period, the number of wasted coins approached zero, and a performance was maintained with the use of the coin as a generalized reinforcer at larger fixed-ratios.

### Subject 2

Experimentation on Subject 2 began some months after that on Subject 1, so that nearly all of the reinforcing devices had been already installed at her first experimental session. Fewer procedural apparatus changes were required for Subject 2 because of her generally more advanced behavioral repertoire, and because some of the experimental problems had been solved with the first subject.

*Phase 1, Sessions 1 to 37:* The first development of a performance occurred in these sessions. Stimulus control was developed by the lights associated with the coin switches and keys.

This subject came under the control of these contingencies very rapidly; and, in general, the procedures developed with the first subject were sufficient to generate the required performance during the early sessions.

*Phase 2, Sessions 38 to 104:* A severe pinworm infection was discovered and treated at the start of this period, and at Session 53, a high-voltage shock between the floor and the reinforcing devices was discovered. By Session 91, the effects of the shock disappeared. During this phase, all of the reinforcing devices were operated by direct levers except for the eight-column vendor, which still was operated by means of coins.

*Phase 3, Sessions 105 to 162:* All of the reinforcing devices were operated through coins produced by pressing the key, and the schedule of reinforcement by coins was increased first to 15, then to 25. Stimulus-control procedures remained in force during part of this period.

### RESULTS

*First Development of a Performance*

*Subject 1:* Figure 2 shows the continuous development from a weak performance at the start of the experiment to a well-sustained performance by the twelfth session. Only the single-column vendor with the key mounted on it was present. Compartments of the vending machine were loaded with either candy, food or a coin. When a coin was delivered, it could be deposited in the coin slot, thereby operating the next compartment.

The child's responses are graphed against time, and the marks oblique to the record indicate the occurrence of a reinforcement. The scale of the record is given by the grid at the right of the figure. Coins are delivered on a variable-interval schedule whose mean interval of reinforcement was increased progressively during the first session. Each segment is a record of the entire daily session. The amount of responding increased progressively over the sessions, reaching an overall rate of approximately 15 responses per minute.

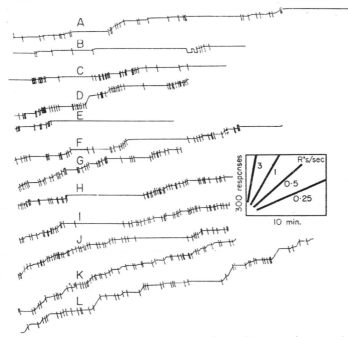

FIG. 2. Cumulative records of the first 12 sessions of the experiment under variable-interval reinforcement. Records A–E, VI (variable-interval) 7 (sec); Records F–H, VI 10; Records I–K, VI 25; Records K–L, VI 30.

Figure 3, Records A through E, continues the next sessions on VI 30, and shows a fall in the overall level of responses until the performance reaches a low, constant rate just sufficient to produce reinforcements roughly on schedule. Part of the fall in the overall rate of responding was produced by "ritualistic" climbing over the top of the machines which occurred between presses of the lever.

Beginning with the fourth session (Record D), a coin dispenser was installed inside the vending machine and the lever delivered only coins. These coins in turn operated the vending machine through its coin slot. Records F through L continue the twenty-second to the twenty-eighth session of the experiment when the schedule of reinforcement had been changed to multiple FR 5 blue, VI 30 red. There was no evidence that any differential performance emerged during the red and blue colors corresponding to the different schedules of reinforcement. However, the performance was sustained over the 60-min experimental session with a steady emission of behavior, and no pauses longer than a minute or two occurred. Much of the pausing involved time spent eating the candy. Approximately 200 to 400 responses were emitted per session. Key presses were frequently followed by the ritualistic climbing behavior, as in the early parts of the record. By the end of this period, this subject ate the candy as he received it, without the previous smearing, licking, and other kinds of handling.

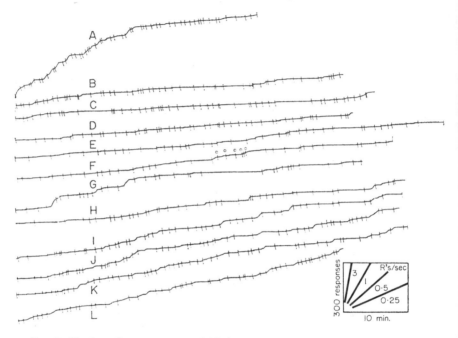

Fig. 3. Final performance on variable-interval 30 reinforcement and transition to multiple FR 5 VI 30 reinforcement.

*Transition to Fixed-ratio and Development of Stimulus Control by Time out after Reinforcement*

*Subject 1:* Figure 4 describes the development of the fixed-ratio performance on the thirty-eighth session after the previous reinforcement on this variable-interval schedule. The fixed-ratio reinforcement soon altered the performance, producing its characteristic pattern of responding: sustained responding at small fixed-ratios; pausing, when it occurs, after reinforcement; and an abrupt shift from pausing to the high fixed-ratio rate. The ritualistic climbing which occurred on the variable-interval schedule disappeared almost immediately on the fixed-ratio schedule. This sudden loss of the climbing occurs because it no longer accidentally reinforces as in the variable-interval schedule, where the probability of reinforcement increases after time spent climbing. The order of the records in the figure is inverted for more compact presentation. The fixed-ratio schedule of reinforcement was in force beginning with the fifth reinforcement of Record A. Records A and B, the first two sessions under FR 9, showed a very rapid development of the fixed-ratio pattern. By Record B, most of the responding occurred in sustained bursts; and in frequent instances, responding began immediately after the delivery of a coin. Any pauses tended to occur just after reinforce-

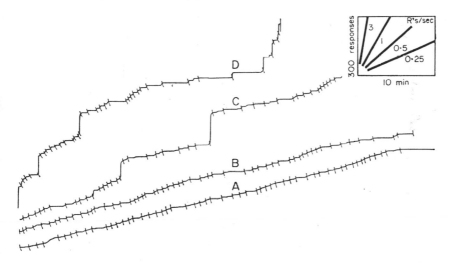

FIG. 4. The development of the characteristic performance under FR 9, and the effect of a time out following reinforcement.

ment. Beginning with Record C, a 10-sec time out (lights out, keys inoperative) occurred after each coin delivery. Any response occurring during the time out extended the time out its full duration to facilitate the development of the discrimination. The frequency of pressing the key when the light was out first increased as the new fixed-ratio program increased the overall responding and then gradually declined (Fig. 5) as the light behind the key came to control the child's performance. The graphic recorder did not run during the time out, so that the nonreinforced responding is evident in the vertical segments of the records. The amount of nonreinforced responding reached a peak of approximately 1800 responses. Five sessions later (Record F), no responses occurred during the 10-sec time out following each reinforcement. In addition to the nearly perfect control by the stimulus behind the key, the child performed almost continuously during the 60-min experimental session.

During the one hundred and nineteenth session, an extinction curve after reinforcement on FR 15 was recorded, where the coin dispenser jammed so that no further coins were delivered but the solenoid continued to operate normally. This extinction curve, shown in Fig. 6, indicates another aspect

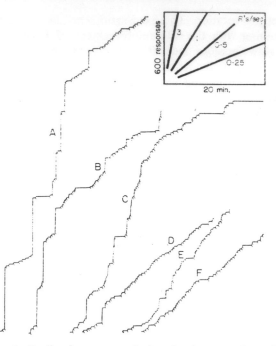

FIG. 5. Subject 1. Decline in response during the time out after reinforcement.

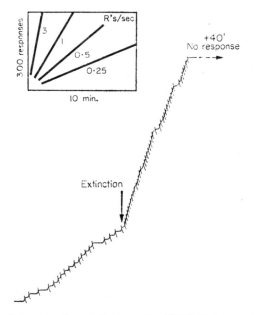

FIG. 6. Subject 1. Extinction after reinforcement on FR15. At the arrow, coins are no longer being delivered, although the coin dispenser makes its characteristic sounds.

of normal control by the fixed-ratio schedule of reinforcement. The pauses after reinforcement disappeared, representing the time that would ordinarily be spent in using the coins; and a high rate of responding was sustained for over 600 responses, followed by no further responding for the remaining 40 min of the experimental sessions.

*Subject 2:* This subject began using all of the devices in the room almost immediately, and quickly performed appropriately to the fixed-ratio schedule of reinforcement. Figure 7 shows records of the first four sessions after continuous reinforcement. The overall level of responding is high and

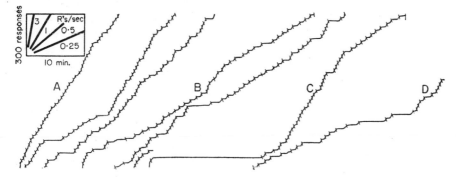

FIG. 7. Subject 2. The first four sessions of the experiment. The schedule of reinforcement is FR 15.

sustained in the first session, but falls progressively thereafter. The pigeon could be operated directly by a key mounted on the pigeon box. The subject operated the pigeon apparatus once in Record B and 26 times in the session represented in Record D. The lower rate of responding is partly attributable to interference from activity around the trained pigeon. Only the eight-column vendor was present at this time, and it was almost immediately controlled by the coin lights associated with the eight coin slots. A 10-sec time out occurred after each coin delivery. (The recorder did not run during the time out.) This subjects showed no tendency to press the key during the 10-sec time out after reinforcement.

Beginning with the sixth session, the coin-saving procedure was put into effect. Every second coin delivered lighted the coin-slot lights for 30 sec. Coins deposited when the lights were out were wasted. The procedure is the same as the one used previously by Kelleher[6] in the study of conditioned reinforcement in chimpanzees. Subject 2 soon stopped placing coins in the inoperative coin slots when the coin lights were off. During the eighth to the twelfth sessions, the numbers of coins deposited in inoperative coin slots of the vending machines were 2, 4, 2, 14, and 4, respectively.

*Development of Stimulus Control by the Coin Light*

*Subject 1:* In an attempt to bring the behavior of depositing coins in the coin slot under the control of the coin light, Subject 1 was given, variously, 200 to 250 free coins at the end of the regular experimental session beginning with Record D of Figure 5, and for four sessions thereafter. In the presence of the coin light, appearing every 15 sec (later 30, and then 60 sec), a coin deposited in the slot produced candy. Coins deposited in the vending machine when the coin light was out postponed the inoperative interval, and did not produce candy. The subject continued to place coins in the inoperative slot, and there was no evidence of any control of behavior by the light. For the next eight sessions, the regular experimental procedure was discontinued. After seven sessions, a small degree of control by the coin light began to emerge. Of the 110 coins deposited in the various devices, 56 produced reinforcement, 54 were deposited while the light was out, 6 were used in the pigeon device, 15 were used in the phonograph, and the remainder went in the single-column candy-vending machine.

The development of the control by the coin light was continued by reconnecting the key and arranging the coin-saving procedure described above for Subject 1. The coin-slot lights were made to appear for 15 sec after every second coin that was delivered. The coin-saving procedure was continued for 14 sessions, during which the coin-slot lights were made to come on after 3, 4, and 5 coins, progressively. The successful development of this technique makes it possible to record the key pressing uncontaminated by the intervening behavior with the reinforcement (e.g. eating). Pauses are difficult to interpret because they may be caused by either a disinclination to respond or time spent consuming the reinforcement.

During the first eight sessions of the coin-saving procedure, the subject inserted coins in the coin slots as soon as they were received, whether or not the coin light was on. Thereafter, the coin-light control began to emerge in the 6 sessions represented in Figure 8. The performance is sustained throughout the session and the child is performing continuously, either pressing the key and receiving coins, or using coins in the various devices. In Record A, the coin light appears after every second coin; 39 of the 77 coins received during the session were deposited while the coin light was on and 38 when it was off. This performance is typical of the previous sessions on the same procedure. Beginning with Record B, however, the subject saved coins delivered when the coin light was off, and deposited them later when it came on again. Of the 113 coins received during this session, 34 were deposited with the coin light off. In Record C, every third coin produced the lighted coin slot for 45 sec, and only 9 of 89 coins received were deposited when the coin slot was inoperative. In the following session, in Record D, only 7 coins were wasted. A 23-min pause occurred at the arrow. In Record E, all 84 coins received were deposited while the coin slot was operative.

A 14-min pause occurred at the arrow. In Record F, every fourth coin produced the coin light correlated with the operative coin slot, and eight coins were deposited in the inoperative coin slots.

The pinball machine was present for the first time and demonstrated to the subject in Record F, but it was not used. On the following session, however, with the pinball machine continuously operative, he played without interruption for 52 min.

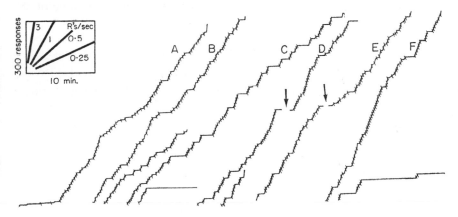

FIG. 8. Subject 1. Performances recorded under FR 15 when the light above the coin slot began to control the subject's performances.

In the following session, when the pinball machine could be operated only by a coin in the coin slot, 52 coins, of a total of 90, were deposited in the pinball machine. Much smiling and vocalizing of the form "Da-da-da", "Ba-ba-ba" occurred. The movement of the balls produced considerable excitement, and the subject frequently sat on the machine, following its action and the course of the balls. The detailed attention to the operation of the pinball machine disappeared progressively during the ensuing months.

*Subject 2:* The second subject's performance on the coin-saving procedure showed almost perfect control by the coin lights of the vending machine from the very start of the procedure.

### Performance Under Multiple VI 60 Sec FR 13 (Subject 1)

In his first exposure to the multiple schedule, the subject responded appropriately to the fixed-ratio in the variable-interval color, and hence emitted many more responses for reinforcement than usual. The normal control by this schedule—fixed-ratio performance in the one color and a variable-interval performance in the second color—never developed. Probably as a result of the decrease in the frequency of reinforcement, the overall rate of responding fell, reaching the values seen in Figure 9, containing

the sixth to the ninth sessions on the multiple schedules. By the eighth and
ninth sessions, Records E and F, the overall performance levels were
among the lowest recorded in the experiment. The fall in the level of
responding was also caused by the introduction of the eight-column vendor.
When the subject emptied a column of the vendor, he continued to deposit
coins in the same column even though the coin light went out when the last
compartment of the column was emptied. The previously developed control
by the coin lights did not transfer to the eight lights and coin slots of the
eight-column vendor.

*Transition Between Fixed-ratio and Multiple Fixed Interval, Fixed-ratio*

The effect of the multiple schedule of reinforcement in weakening the
subject's performance was explored briefly by alternating between blocks
of the simple fixed-ratio schedule and the multiple schedule. In general,

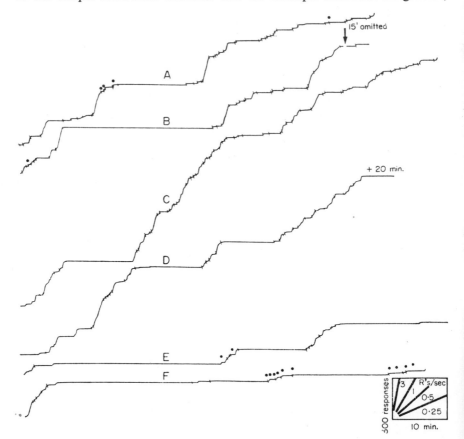

Fig. 9. Sessions 6 through 9 on the multiple schedule. The dots above the curves
indicate when coins were used in the pinball machine.

the subject's performance was well-sustained under the fixed-ratio schedule and weak under the multiple schedule. Record A of Figure 10 begins with only the fixed-ratio schedule; at the arrow, the schedule was changed to the multiple schedule. A high rate of responding occurs under the fixed-ratio schedule, and carries over in the multiple schedule for approximately the next 10 min, after which it falls sharply to nearly zero by the middle of the session. In the next session, shown in Record B, responding is sustained, as typical with the start of a session; but when the schedule is switched to fixed-ratio, the severe decline in rate that usually occurs toward the end of the session is eliminated. In the third session (Record C), beginning on the fixed-ratio schedule, responding is sustained with little pausing and high rates. When the schedule is changed back to the multiple schedule at the arrow, responding ceases for the remaining 50 min of the session except for two brief periods. During these sessions, the subject continued to place coins in the empty (unlighted) columns of the vending machine, even though this kind of control had developed earlier in the experiment with the single-column vendor.

*Extended Reinforcement on FR 15 and an Attempt to Increase Low Performances by Optimal Conditions of Reinforcement*

*Subject 1:* Figure 11 shows the number of coins delivered to Subject 1 from the eighty-sixth through one hundred and twenty-eighth sessions and some of the details of their use. The first part of the figure to Session 104 represents

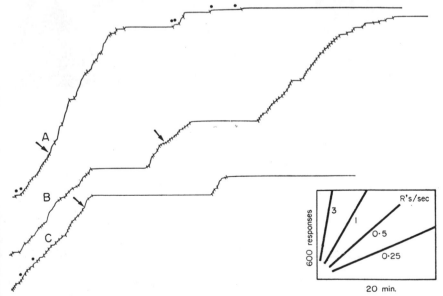

Fig. 10. Subject 1. Transitions between the fixed-ratio and multiple schedules. The dots above the curves indicate when coins were used in the pinball machine.

performances when responding is weakened because large numbers of coins are wasted in inoperative coin slots. The remaining sessions represent an attempt to strengthen the performances in the experimental room by providing optimal conditions of reinforcement.

The procedures used between Sessions 86 and 104 reflect the large number of coins wasted in inoperative (unlighted) coin slots. From the ninety-fourth through ninety-ninth sessions, 35 to 175 coins are wasted per session.

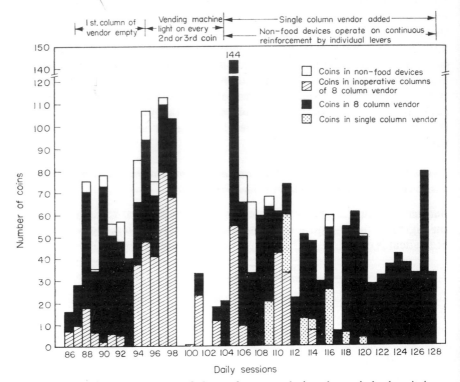

Fig. 11. Subject 1. Summary of the performance during the period when it is weakened by large numbers of coins wasted in an inoperative coin slot.

The performance becomes weak between the ninety-ninth and one hundred and fourth sessions, when the largest number of coins delivered was 30 (Session 101); and no coins were delivered during two sessions. Most of the coins in the non-food devices were used in the pinball machine. The non-food devices were, in general, not used.

The period of the experiment represented in Figure 15 was characterized by atavistic behavior, tantrums, and frequent disruption of the performances normally generated by these experimental procedures. During Sessions 99 to 103, the subject used the sharp edge of the coin to scrape slivers from the Plexiglas surface of the pinball machine and spent whole sessions marring the surface of these two devices. The child stopped scraping the Plexiglas only when the edges of the coins were smoothed.

When the performance deteriorated at about Session 100, keys were mounted on the face of each non-food device. A single press of the key operated the device. The single-column vendor (also operated by a key) was reintroduced, delivering trinkets, fruit juice, crackers, and toys. Under these more favorable reinforcement schedules, the number of coins increased to values comparable with those in the eighty-sixth to ninety-ninth sessions; but large numbers of coins were still wasted when a column of the eight-column vendor became empty. Toward the end of the period shown in the figure, the subject began to vary the column in which he deposited coins. No columns were emptied; hence, very few coins were wasted. During this period, the non-food devices, including the single-column vendor, were hardly used, even though the subject had to press a key only once to operate any of them. After periodic previous demonstrations, the phonograph was demonstrated again during the one hundred twenty-sixth session, and the subject began pressing the key mounted on the phonograph device. At Session 129, the severe pinworm infection was discovered and treatment was begun. It is not known for how long the infection had been present, but the period is presumed to have been at least 2 to 3 weeks.

Figure 12 gives details of the performances represented in Fig. 11, ranging from the well-sustained performance in the one hundred fifth session, where the subject is continuously performing during the entire session, to the one hundred seventeenth session, when only 7 coins were received. Toward the end of the one hundred fifth session, a column failed to deliver candy because of an equipment failure even though the coin light was on. After wasting many coins in the inoperative but lighted coin slot, the subject finally ceased responding and returned to scratching the Plexiglas on the pinball machine. A severe tantrum occurred during the last part of the session (*a* to *b* on the record), even though the vending machine was operating at this time. The subject went through the normal performance in the midst of shouting, screaming, and head banging. The subject was in the midst of a severe tatrum when he was taken from the ward to the experimental room at the start of Session 117. During a pause in the tantrum, the subject noticed the experimenter and went along quietly to the experimental room. He spent most of the session lying on the floor and on top of the pinball machine. Except for the few coins received, there was little activity of any kind except a brief period, of about 15 min, of looking at the pigeon, smiling and saying "A-a-a-a" in drawn-out syllables.

During the third session, the subject began putting coins in a slit in one wall of the experimental room during a tantrum that increased in intensity with each of the 10 or 12 coins that were deposited. He then hammered on the door with increasing intensity during the 20-min pause in the middle of the session. After a short period of quietly sitting on the floor by the door, he resumed the sustained activity recorded at the end of the session.

Figure 13 summarizes the main facts of the experiment from Sessions 129 to 166. These performances show the effects of the electric shock, the recovery from the pinworm infection, and the continued lack of development

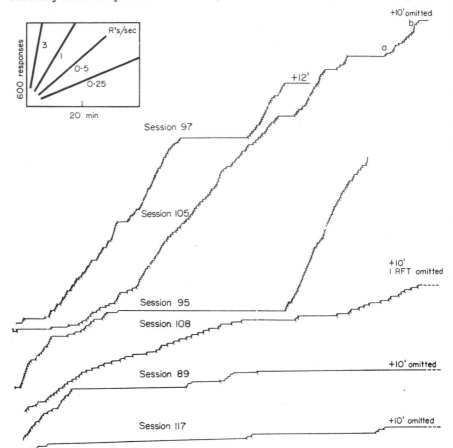

FIG. 12. Subject 1. Cumulative curves of representative daily experimental sessions taken from the period of the experiment shown in Fig. 11.

of the stimulus control by the coin-slot lights. The overall performance varies markedly from day to day, but is, in general, sustained. Responding occurs about equally among the eight-column vendor, the non-food devices, and the single-column vendor. The pinworm infection discovered on the one hundred and twenty-eighth session was treated, and was probably gone by the one hundred and thirty-eighth session. The exposed voltages were discovered on the one hundred and forty-fifth session and were removed, and the effects of the shock were probably gone by the one hundred and sixtieth session. Except for the one hundred and thirty-eighth to one hundred and forty-sixth sessions, the schedule of coin reinforcement was kept very optimal in order to sustain the subject's performance. All of the non-food reinforcing devices, as well as the single-column vendor, continued to be operated by keys mounted directly on them. Figure 13 records the total number of reinforcements received rather than responses or coins. In general, the non-food reinforcing devices are scarcely used; and most of the activity

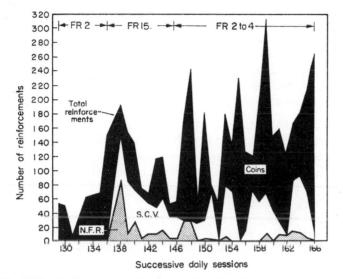

Fig. 13. Subject 1. Summary of performances from the period when they are being affected by electric shock, pinworm infection, and continued lack of development of control by the coin-slot lights. S.C.V., Single-column vendor; N-F.R., Non-food reinforcements.

produces candy from the eight-column vendor by coins, or trinkets and candy from the single-column vendor through the key mounted on the face of the unit. On the one hundred and forty-fourth session, the subject withdrew his hand from the trough of the coin dispenser as if he were getting a shock, and then began using his shirt tail to take the coins from the trough. He also began to deposit coins in the green vendor by holding them in his shirt tail to insulate himself from the eight-column vending machine. During this period, this child responded in bursts, so that coins accumulated in the coin trough, occasionally falling to the floor. Many of the coins delivered during this period were not used. Even though the electric shock had been eliminated by the one hundred and forty-sixth session, the subject continued to accumulate coins rapidly until the one hundred and sixtieth session, taking only those falling on the floor and using his shirt tail to deposit them in the eight-column vendor. The apparatus was probably delivering shocks between the one hundred and thirty-fifth and one hundred and forty-sixth sessions.

Frequent tantrums and generally large amounts of atavistic performances occurred: for example, urinating over the various devices; head banging; screaming; smearing candy into the various orifices of the room; and reversion to the older pattern of eating candy by rolling it into a ball and licking it from the hands, floor, etc., rather than placing discrete pieces in the mouth and chewing them. Most of the non-food reinforcements occurred about equally among the pigeon, color wheel, pinball machine, and phonograph. The subject used a variety of compartments from the eight-column vendor; but during those sessions when the larger number of coins was deposited, he wasted many coins in empty columns. Numbers of coins wasted in various sessions occurred as follows: Session 159, 45 coins; Session 161, 24; Session 162, 36; Session 163, 16; Session 164, 23; Session 165, 55; and Session 166, 144.

*Subject 2:* Figure 14 contains an overall summary of Subject 2's performance from the sixty-fourth to ninety-eighth sessions. The graph gives the number of reinforcements occurring among the various devices. These performances occurred when all of the reinforcing devices were present and were operated via direct keys, and after the pinworm infection and the effects of the electric shock had been eliminated.

Subject 2's behavior, controlled more by the non-food devices than that of Subject 1, was distributed about equally among the phonograph, color wheel, and pigeon. The pinball machine was not used. Consistent with the higher level of the non-food devices, this subject used the single-column vendor (delivering trinkets) more than the first subject. The large number of reinforcements in Sessions 96 to 98 occurred largely on direct keys on the color wheel and phonograph.

### Final Development of a Performance

*Subject 1:* Figure 15 summarizes redevelopment of control by the lights above the coin switches and the final development of a performance for the remaining 85 sessions of the experiment. The curve at the top of the black area gives the number of coins wasted in empty columns (C. E. C.) or when the vendor is off (V. O.). The curve over the stippled area gives the number of coins wasted when the whole vending machine is off. The number of coins deposited in inoperative slots falls slowly, reaching near zero around the two hundred and fiftieth session. Control by the coin lights when the whole vendor is off develops before the stimulus control by a single empty column. Before the end of the period, all of the devices operate by coins rather than by direct keys (Session 236); and the performance in the experimental room continues to be maintained under the conditions of a generalized reinforcer, although the overall level of activity

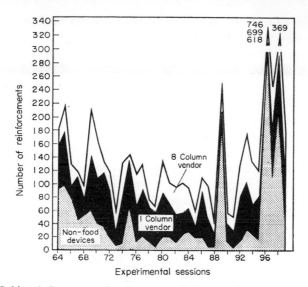

FIG. 14. Subject 2. Summary of performances during a period when all of the reinforcing devices were operated by direct keys.

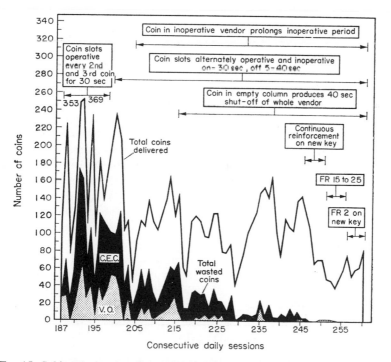

FIG. 15. Subject 1. An overall summary of the use of coins showing the development of stimulus control by the coin-slot lights.

is lower. The procedures by which Subject 1 learned to deposit coins only when the lights were on were as follows:

1. Sessions 188 to 197: The coin light came on for 30 sec at every second, then at every third coin that was delivered. Coins deposited when the lights were off were wasted. The subject continued to deposit coins when all of the vending lights were on. The coin lights flashed on and off at 1 c/s.

2. Session 198: The coin lights were lighted on a time basis rather than after a fixed number of coins as before. Coins deposited when the coin light was out delayed their coming on again. This procedure immediately reduced the number of coins deposited when the whole vendor was off, but did not change the number of coins deposited in empty columns.

3. Session 214: Coins deposited in empty columns shut off the whole vendor for 40 sec, a mild punishment. Further coins deposited when the vendor was off extended the inoperative period its full duration as before. The number of coins deposited in the inoperative coin slots then began to fall, reaching zero by the two hundred and fifty-fourth session. The number of coins wasted is roughly proportional to the total number of coins being deposited.

The schedule of reinforcement and the manner in which the coins were received varied from time to time during this period of this figure. Until the two hundred and twenty-ninth session, all of the reinforcing devices (except the eight-column vendor) operated by direct keys rather than coins. Beginning with Session 229, all of the keys were made inoperative and the reinforcing devices operated only by depositing coins. The schedule of reinforcement was reduced to FR 5 at the same time, in order to ease the transition to the generalized reinforcer; but it was increased to 15 with Session 240, when it was apparent that the performance could be sustained with the generalized (conditioned) reinforcer. From the two hundred and forty-fifth to the two hundred and fifty-first sessions, coins were delivered by new keys designed to explore the child's perceptual repertoire. These data are presented here only in respect to the continued development of the stimulus control on the vending machine. From the two hundred and fifty-second to two hundred and fifty-sixth sessions, the schedule of reinforcement was increased progressively to 15, the original key was restored, and the performance was examined under the slightly larger ratios.

The new key and the shift to the coin as a generalized reinforcer have produced a general decline in the total number of coins received. During the last 10 sessions reported in the figure, for example, the overall level of activity is considerably lower than it was previously, especially when we consider that earlier parts of the graph do not show performances on the devices operated directly through levers.

*Subject 2.*—Figure 16 contains the comparable performance for Subject 2 from Sessions 100 to 162. The number of coins received and their distribution in the various reinforcing devices is recorded. All of the devices operated through coins instead of by direct key as with the first subject. For the first part of this period, most of the coins were used in the non-food devices: the pigeon, phonograph, and color wheel. Table 3 gives the median and interquartile range for these devices. Approximately ⅛ of the coins were used for candy from the eight-column vendor, and only a small number in

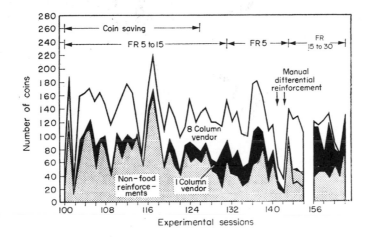

FIG. 16. Subject 2. Summary of the use of coins and overall level of performance during the final phase of the experiment.

TABLE 3

*Distribution of performances on the non-food devices during sessions 100–162 (Subject 2)*

|  | Phonograph | Pigeon | Color wheel |
|---|---|---|---|
| $Q_1$ | 36 | 1 | 1 |
| *Median* | 51 | 2 | 3 |
| $Q_3$ | 75 | 9 | 12 |

the single-column vendor. During the end of the period from the one hundred and fifty-sixth to one hundred and sixty-second sessions, the performance shifted more heavily in the direction of the single-column vendor, with a corresponding reduction in the number of coins in the eight-column vendor. The break in the curve after Session 143 indicates a period when a new key, not relevant to the material of this report, was used. In general, the performance is sustained at the small as well as at the large fixed-ratios, although the rate of responding is slightly lower on the latter ratios. This subject's performance was controlled almost perfectly by the coin lights. Figure 17 contains four consecutive performances at the end of this period

(Sessions 143 through 146), showing in more detail the continuous manner in which the performance is sustained in this subject. The performance is fairly continuous during the 90-min session, except for occasional long pauses, as, for example, at the end of the second and fourth sessions shown on the figure.

This subject sustained even the higher fixed-ratios in a similar manner. Figure 18 shows the three consecutive sessions (158 through 160) when the fixed-ratio was 25, and the performance remains characteristic of the ratio schedule.

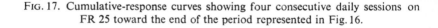

FIG. 17. Cumulative-response curves showing four consecutive daily sessions on FR 25 toward the end of the period represented in Fig. 16.

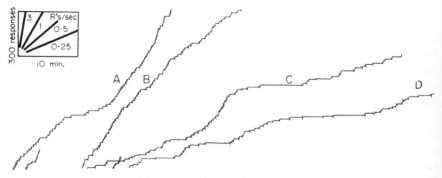

FIG. 18. Subject 2. Final performance on FR 30.

*Control subjects.*—Each of three control subjects received a 5-min explanation of the manner of operation of all the devices. The door was then closed, and the session continued as with Subjects 1 and 2. All of the devices were operated by coins. Records A and B of Figure 19 contain performances on FR 30 for 2 of the subjects, a girl and boy, approximately the same ages as Subjects 1 and 2. The performance conforms to the typical fixed-

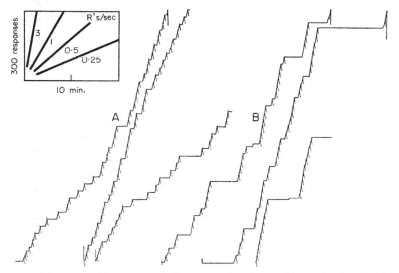

Fig. 19. Control subjects. Cumulative curves for three subjects showing the first performances in the experimental room with all of the reinforcing devices operated by coins (FR 30).

ratio pattern, with pauses after some reinforcements and an abrupt shift to the prevailing rate. Responding continues throughout the session, and the performance is sustained better than the best record of the experimental subjects. The coins received were used in all of the vending devices. At this time, the devices present were as follows: phonograph, single-column vendor, pigeon, pinball machine, color wheel, electric organ, television set, train, and eight-column vendor.

Table 4 shows the distribution of the total number of coins used by each of the three subjects among the various devices during the entire session. The records in Figure 19 show only the first 45 min of each experimental session. For the remaining 45 min, the subjects operated another type of key relevant to an experiment to be reported elsewhere.

## DISCUSSION

The major result of the experiment is a technique for sustaining and objectively recording performances of autistic children. During many phases of the experiment, performances were sustained continuously up to 90 min,

TABLE 4

*Number of reinforcements delivered and their distribution among the various devices (control subjects)*

| Subject | 1 | 2 | 3 |
|---|---|---|---|
| Single-column vendor | 77 | 42 | 82 |
| Eight-column vendor | 47 | 28 | 10 |
| Pigeon | 5 | 11 | 8 |
| Pinball | 18 | 50 | 35 |
| Color wheel | 3 | 3 | 3 |
| Organ | 5 | 2 | 2 |
| Television | 5 | 32 | 5 |
| Train | 17 | 5 | 13 |
| Total | 177 | 173 | 158 |

with no indication that this was a limit. These performances were under the control of reinforcers and other stimuli programed by the various devices in the experimental room. Altering the reinforcement program produced corresponding changes in the children's performance, similar to the efforts of those procedures in animals and normal subjects.[2, 7]

The results of these experiments confirm the observation that these children have small and narrow behavioral repertoires. The performance in the experimental room developed slowly during the experiment and in contrast to that of control subjects, who responded quickly and appropriately to all the devices in the experimental room.

Both autistic children's performances showed that their behavior could be brought under control of stimuli by the following basic processes:

1. Reinforcement: The frequency with which the subjects reponded was increased by using reinforcers such as food, music, candy, etc.

2. Schedule of reinforcement: Both the fixed-ratio and variable-interval schedules of reinforcement produced their normal and characteristic effects on the child's performance. The accidental reinforcement of responses during the periods of interval reinforcement and the loss of this "superstitious behavior" under fixed-ratio reinforcement demonstrated another aspect of normal control.[8]

3. Stimulus control: New stimuli, if present when a response would produce reinforcement and absent when it went unreinforced, came to control whether or not the child performed. Subject 2 came under the control of the relevant stimuli very rapidly. Subject 1 showed a slow development of stimulus control comparable, at least in form, with performances recorded with animals.

4. Conditioned and generalized reinforcer: The delivery of a coin was a conditioned reinforcer in maintaining the performances recorded, and the

coin was also used to actuate a wide variety of reinforcers in the manner of a generalized reinforcer.

The control of the subject's performance by the coin-switch light and the light behind the key is of technical importance. For example, the reinforcing value of the coin could be manipulated by turning out the relevant lights, thus restricting the use of various reinforcing devices. Also, the child's performance could be conveniently interrupted by turning off the lights behind the key. When reinforcing devices with limited capacity became empty, the particular device could be discontinued simply by turning off the coin light while letting the rest of the experiment continue. Furthermore, some performances could be punished by the turning out of the key light.

Both subjects emitted more of the experimentally developed behavior with continual exposure to the automatic environment. Conversely, they spent less time in tantrums or inactivity while in the experimental room. The final level of performances on the non-food devices may not have been possible without the gradual accumulation of experience in the experimental room.

The use of the coin as a generalized reinforcer was a second major technique developed here. By the end of the experiment, the experimental performances could be sustained in both subjects by the delivery of coins.

The 2 autistic subjects showed large differences in their experimental performances. Subject 2, who has more speech and a wider behavioral repertiore than Subject 1, quickly came under control of nearly all of the experimental procedures. The fixed-ratio schedule of reinforcement generated the typical fixed-ratio performance rapidly. This subject very quickly came to respond appropriately to the lights which signaled changes in procedure, as, for example, the lights above the coin slots and the lights behind the key. In contrast, Subject 1 came under the control of the coin lights only after one hundred or more experimental sessions. The 2 subjects differed also in the extent to which they used non-food devices in the room. The performance of Subject 1 was largely maintained by the delivery of food and candy, while that of Subject 2 was maintained by the non-food reinforcers, particularly the phonograph. The differences between the 2 children are closely related to the amount of speech present, probably because the verbal repertoire, by itself, represents a large potential of control by the environment.

Subject 1's slow development of stimulus control suggests that his perceptual repertoire is minimal. Both the time out after reinforcement and the coin lights came to control the subject's performance slowly, as compared with a normal subject, or even an animal. Even after the coin lights controlled the subject's behavior during the first part of the experiment, the repertoire was so minimal that similar lights on the eight-column vendor had no effect until after one hundred or more hours of training. The differences between the two machines were sufficient to completely break down stimulus control which had developed with the single-column vendor. The general complexity of the eight-column vendor was probably responsible for the large amount of training required to develop the stimulus control, compared with the relative ease with which the same type of control had developed earlier with the single-column vendor. A more appropriate procedure with such a debilitated subject would have been to introduce gradually small differences in the size, shape, color, and location of the coin light and coin slot while keeping the general function and pattern constant. Such a procedure would abstract the common features of coin slots and coin lights and make it possible for the child to respond appropriately to similar devices. The failure of the multiple fixed-ratio, variable-interval schedule to develop the normal performances characteristic of these schedules in the two stimuli also illustrates the child's minimal perceptual repertoire. Such failures of stimulus control are sometimes encountered in animals,[5] and may be corrected by special procedures such as reinforcement on the separate components of the schedule. No such corrective procedure was carried out. Furthermore, we do not know whether it would have been possible to develop the control by such corrective procedures or by trying again later in the experiment, after the subject had acquired other discriminative repertoires.

It cannot be assumed that performances developed in the experimental room will have general effects elsewhere. The performances of these children, as with most organisms, come under the control of the particular situations in which they are reinforced. The performances in the experimental room probably are under very close control of the room itself and are unavailable to the child elsewhere. Even if the behavioral repertoire developed in the experiment had general effects on the child elsewhere, we could not expect the development of normal social behavior unless some kind of social repertoire which could be strengthened were already present. If such social behavior is altogether lacking, there is no chance for any inductive strengthening of it. It still may be possible, however, to develop social behavior outside of the experimental room. Social reinforcers would be used instead of candy, and social responses reinforced instead of key presses. The general plan in developing social behavior would be to manipulate social reinforcers (consequences of the child's performances supplied by other individuals), with the use of the same general principles applied in the artificial environment.

In general, tantrums and atavistic responses appeared less frequently during the latter parts of the experiment, suggesting that these tantrums, at least in part, are socially maintained. Programs of reinforcements were not changed too swiftly because of the possibility of anxiety attacks, temper tantrums, or breakdown of newly formed patterns of behavior following too abrupt procedual changes. The procedure of keeping social influences out of the experimental room may have weakened the tantrums by nonreinforcement. The development of a strong repertoire in the experimental room may have been another possible factor in the reduction in atavistic behavior. The large disposition to operate the devices in the experimental room may have simply displaced the tantrums by prepotency, as with Lindsley's psychotic adults who showed no psychotic performances while under the control of the fixed-ratio schedule of reinforcement.

Much of the schizophrenic's behavior exemplifies very weak performances which appear strong simply because most of the normally maintained behavior is weak. Lindsley's showed that during fixed-ratio reinforcement, the bizarre behavior of chronic schizophrenic adults appeared only during the pauses after reinforcement. Once the patient began responding appropriately to the schedule of reinforcement, the relatively strong behavior maintained by the candy and cigarette reinforcements was prepotent over bizarre performances and other psychosis-like behavior. An example in the present experiment is Subject 1's scraping of the Plexiglas. This possibly occurred after he had deposited most of the coins in inoperative coin slots because his experimental performance became weak after the frequency of reinforcement became very low. If this analysis is correct, then the actual form of the behavior observed in psychotic patients is much less important than the absolute amount of behavior and, particularly, the levels of activity controlled by an effect on a social or socially derived environment. An analogous situation occurs frequently in normal individuals when they are placed in situations in which few of their currently available performances are relevant. Some examples are: experiments on sensory deprivation; waiting for someone to keep an appointment in a relatively isolated place; attending a formal meeting where the speaker's activity is not sufficiently important to the listener, but where at the same time, no behavior other than listening is appropriate. Under these circumstances, many individuals emit performances that are very similar to those of psychotic persons, such as rubbing the table constantly, scratching a particular part of the body, doodling, or some kind of oral activity. All of these activities have the common feature of not being supported by the external environment, particularly the social environment.

This experimental program is not viewed as an attempt at carrying out psychotherapy, but rather as an attempt to demonstrate what kinds of performances could be brought under the control of a specifiable environment with known behavioral processes. To the extent that variables manipulated in the experiment control the child's performances through normal behavioral processes, the child has advanced somewhat toward rehabilitation. Actual rehabilitation, however, would have to be carried out through the manipulation of social contingencies and the development of performances with which the child would interact with other individuals.

The results of these experiments show that the behavioral processes which have been studied are intact in both children, except for the multiple-schedule performance, which did not develop. This low over-all level of the performance, compared with the normal, is reminiscent of some kinds of brain damage which do not affect a performance except in its frequency of occurrence. The behavioral and physiologic histories are confounded in the present experiment, however. The facts are consistent with the hypothesis that these children underwent experiences that produced a very large deficit in behavior. Their repertoires actually may be inadequate because of deficits in performance rather than temporary suppressions by some debilitating mechanism, either physiologic or functional. These children may represent individuals in whom normal performances have never developed because the normal development of their repertoires was temporarily arrested at some time. Such a deficit might occur because the repertoire of the child is weakened through the normal behavioral processes by which behavior can be suppressed or eliminated. All of the basic processes by which new performances are generated, strengthened, maintained, eliminated, punished, suppressed, or controlled by special aspects of the environment are relevant to an analysis of how a particular history could produce a weak, positively maintained repertoire. Some of these conditions have been tentatively outlined.[4, 9] When conditions exist that severely weaken the existing repertoire of a child for any period of time, the performance becomes progressively more difficult to reinstate. The reason for this is that the environment of the now older child will not support the level of behavior of which he is capable, although this environment would support his level if the child were younger.

## SUMMARY

Performances of two autistic children were recorded in an experimental environment consisting of vending machines delivering food and candy, a trained pigeon, a phonograph, a color kaleidoscope, and a pinball machine. These devices were operated either by keys mounted on them or by coins. Coins were delivered on various schedules when the children operated another key. Performances could be sustained on the coin key for 90-min experimental sessions to demonstrate the normal effect of two schedules of reinforcement, to develop the coin as a generalized reinforcer, and to control the children's performances by the presence or absence of stimuli correlated with reinforcement or nonreinforcement.

## ACKNOWLEDGEMENTS

We thank Drs. John I. Nurnberger and Donald F. Moore for their advice and encouragement, and their assistance in obtaining the facilities required to carry out the experiment. We are also indebted to Mr. Robert C. Hudson for his invaluable assistance in the actual conduct of the experiment. Generous financial support for the project was provided by Smith Kline and French Laboratories and the National Association of Mental Health.

## REFERENCES

1. KANNER, L. (1944) Early Infantile Autism, *J. Pediat.* **25**, 211.
2. LONG, E. R., HAMMACK, J. T., MAY, F. and CAMPBELL, B. J. (1958) Intermittent Reinforcement of Operant Behavior in Children, *J. Exper. Anal. Behav.* **4**, 315.
3. BIJOU, S. W. (1957) Methodology for an Experimental Analysis of Child Behavior, *Psychol. Rep.* **3**, 243.
4. SKINNER, B. F. (1953) *Science and Human Behavior*, The Macmillan Company, New York.
5. FERSTER, C. B. and SKINNER, B. F. (1957) *Schedules of Reinforcement*, Appleton-Century-Crofts, New York.
6. KELLEHER, R. T. (1958) Fixed-Ratio Schedules of Conditioned Reinforcement with Chimpanzees, *J. Exper. Anal. Behav.* **1**, 281.
7. LINDSLEY, O. R. (1956) Operant Conditioning Methods Applied to Research in Chronic-Schizophrenia, *Psychiat. Res. Rep.* **6**, 118.
8. SKINNER, B. F. (1948) "Superstition" in the Pigeon, *J. Exper. Psychol.* **38**, 158.
9. FERSTER, C. B. (1958) Reinforcement and Punishment in the Control of Human Behavior by Social Agencies, *Psychiat. Res. Rep.* **12**, 101.

# Author Index

# Subject Index

Abdomen  25
Acrophobia  88
Adaptation studies  274
ACTH  408
Agoraphobia  37, 38
Aggressive behavior  476, 495
Alcohol  11, 183
Alcoholism
  treatment by aversion therapy  6, 10, 13, 176, 182
Amylobarbitone  398
Anorexia nervosa  10
Anxiety  21, 22, 23, 35, 42, 48, 62, 99, 139, 277, 341, 347, 403, 405, 430
Anxiety hierarchy  see Hierarchy
Anxiety hysteria
  use of auto-hypnosis in  433
Apomorphine
  in treatment of alcoholism  11
  in treatment of homosexuality  160
Apomorphine hydrochloride  164
Approach–avoidance conflict  373, 376
Assertion  23
Asthma
  as a suppressed cry  344
  conceived as a learned response  338, 343
  fixed interval treatment schedule in  426
  treatment by antispasmodics and antibiotics  408
  treatment by auto-hypnosis  426
  treatment by hypno-suggestion  407, 416, 420
Asthma-like behaviour  341, 346
Atavistic response  542
Audiometer  279
Autistic children  447, 509, 540
Auto-hypnosis  426, 432
Autonomic Nervous System  1, 287
Aversion therapy
  effectiveness of  180, 182
  follow-up  6
  treatment of alcoholism  6, 167
  treatment of homosexuality  159

Aversive control  202
Avoidance conditioning  12, 267, 268

Behavioral Adjustment Scale  329
Behaviour manipulation  9
Behaviour therapy  xi, 2
  administration of drugs in  9
  definition of  1
  in treatment of cat phobia  52
  in treatment of enuresis nocturna  12, 13
  in treatment of dysphemia  401
  in treatment of enuresis  176
  in treatment of transvestism  163, 172, 173
*Behaviour Therapy and the Neuroses*  6
Bell-and-Blanket Method  5, 7
Bethlem Royal Hospital  52
Biceps  24
Blocking  374
  secondary  402
Brain-washing  1
B.M.A., Council of, 1955  159

Castration  166
Catatonic schizophrenia  207
Cathartic response  91
Central Nervous System  1
Chlorpromazine  387
Chemotherapy  166
Claustrophobia  88
Clinician-variables  453
Closed cycle control system  366
  feedback signals  366
Color wheel  512
Communication  329
Comparator  see closed cycle system
Complex  153
Compulsion  147
Conditionability  183
Conditioned autonomic drive  117
Conditioned avoidance  see Avoidance conditioning
Conditioned inhibition  153
  maximal  382, 387, 391, 392, 398